BUILDING IN RESEARCH AND EVALUATION

Human inquiry
for living systems

About the author

Yoland Wadsworth is a research and evaluation practitioner, methodology theorist and author who has worked for government and community organisations in the health, community and human services sector over the past 38 years. She began life as a researcher with her first survey at sixteen years, and by eighteen was hand-calculating chi squares in the Mathematics Department at Monash University. She went on to pioneer in Australia the use of critical collaborative community research in the 1970s; consumer–staff participation in dialogic evaluation in the 1980s, and 'whole systems' culture change and quality improvement using multi-stakeholder participatory inquiry in the 1990s. She has managed three action research resource centres over twenty five years; held senior government roles in research and policy, including the Victorian Department of Premier and Cabinet; co-founded the Health Issues Centre and the Australian Women's Health Network and has been a recipient of multiple national evaluation awards. She is a 1995 Churchill Fellow, a Fellow of the Australasian Evaluation Society, a life member of the international Action Learning Action Research Association, and Distinguished Fellow of the Action Research Center, University of Cincinnati.

Being taken to see a lake infested with duckweed by her biology teacher at age fifteen marked the beginnings of her thinking about the conditions for living systems.

YOLAND WADSWORTH

BUILDING IN RESEARCH AND EVALUATION

Human inquiry for living systems

Routledge
Taylor & Francis Group

LONDON AND NEW YORK

First published 2010 by Allen & Unwin

Published 2020 by Routledge
2 Park Square, Milton Park, Abingdon, Oxon OX14 4RN
605 Third Avenue, New York, NY 10017

Routledge is an imprint of the Taylor & Francis Group, an informa business

This first edition published in 2010 by Action Research Press, a wholly owned imprint of the Action Research Issues Association Incorporated, 2 Minona Street, Hawthorn, Victoria 3122 Australia www.actionresearch.net.au

Cataloguing-in-Publication details are available
from the National Library of Australia
www.librariesaustralia.nla.gov.au

Set in 10.5/12.5pt Times Roman

Cartoonists/illustrators:
Simon Kneebone +61 (08) 8370 9152, simknee@bigpond.net.au
Merinda Epstein +61 (03) 9687 0011, www.takver.com/epstein/index.htm
Concept diagrams: Matt Smith

Cover teapot image: Courtesy the Estate of the late Cate Kyne
Cover architectural drawings: Andrew Inglis (mob) 0419 890772, www.ideasgroupaustralia.com.au

Book layout: Mal Oram, lazye2@bigpond.com

This book is the final volume in the methodology trilogy by Yoland Wadsworth:
Do It Yourself Social Research, 1st edn 1984; 2nd edn 1997; 3rd edn 2011; Allen & Unwin, Sydney
Everyday Evaluation on the Run, 1st edn 1991; 2nd edn 1997; 3rd edn 2011; Allen & Unwin, Sydney
Building In Research and Evaluation: Human inquiry for living systems, 1st edn 2010, Action Research Press, Hawthorn, and Allen & Unwin, Sydney

ISBN-13: 9781742375403 (pbk)

Foreword

An international audience may ask who is Yoland Wadsworth and why should we read her book? In fact Yoland is one of Australia's best known applied sociologists and has written that country's two lead bestselling texts on social research and evaluation. (If the sales figures of her first two books were replicated proportional to population in the USA she would never need to work again!)

In this the third and final text in her life's work trilogy she displays an extraordinary capacity to integrate many different perspectives, theories, constructs and approaches within an overarching accessible framework. She puts those perspectives and approaches in dialogue with each other, and provides the reader with a way to navigate the labyrinth created by the intersection of inquiry and practice.

Her own depth of experience and accomplished capacity for reflection as both a practitioner and inquirer make her insights important and innovative. Her style of writing, presenting and engaging the reader is uniquely her own—and therefore quite original. For example, Yoland pays a lot of attention to words. She delights in examining the Latin origins of words and considering the meaning of those words in light of their origins and contemporary use. I mention this because nowhere does Yoland *argue* that she is presenting an argument. Indeed, my sense is that she doesn't much like arguments. She prefers dialogue, interaction, mutual engagement, shared understandings, and most of all, shared inquiry. In short, my reading is that the connotation of the word 'argument' is at odds with Yoland's *living human systems* framework. So let me reframe this and observe that the *living human systems* framework is sound and persuasive and it is also insightful, important and inviting.

The book is an invitation for readers themselves to give the framework further attention in their own inquiry, practice, and application. Indeed the inviting nature of the book is one of its strengths. Yoland's writing and presentation is also characterised by multiple presentation formats that provide multiple points of entry into the material.

Having read the previous two books in this trilogy and used them in my own writing and work, I anticipate she will have a ready and eager audience. More generally, the book is interdisciplinary in orientation and will be of interest to people who are interested in the intersection between theory and practice. Wherever people are engaged in trying to make the world a better place and open to undertaking inquiry as a part of that process, this book will be a welcome addition to their journey. That means the book is especially relevant to any of the helping professions: social work, community development, mental health, human services of all kinds and extension workers—but also to government, philanthropy and the not-for-profit/non-governmental sector; and to academia, to applied sociology, practice-oriented psychology, social work, applied economics, political science, management studies and evaluation research.

The book draws on a lifetime of experience and insight. That itself makes it worth diving deeply into. How often does one get the opportunity to engage with a savvy scholar-practitioner's *magnum opus*? This is such an opportunity. Enjoy the feast of wisdom.

MICHAEL QUINN PATTON
St Paul, Minnesota
Author of *Developmental Evaluation:*
Applying Complexity Concepts to Enhance Innovation and Use (2010)

Preface

It is now nearly twenty-five years since Yoland Wadsworth's popular guide *Do It Yourself Social Research* was first published, followed by *Everyday Evaluation on the Run* seven years later. While they have proved popular (having together sold well over 50 000 copies to the present day), on their own they did not tell the full story of what was needed to 'build in' these processes to routinely collect data about important aspects of life; understand it; develop resonant insights and genuine breakthrough new knowledge; and then test it in new real-life experimental practice.

The key question this book addresses then is: How can we truly build in and embed regular cycles of curious, observant, sensitive, thoughtful and responsive small-scale practice-based research and evaluation processes by large numbers of individuals and their organisations.

In working to crack this puzzle, Yoland has developed a much deeper theory of *living systems* research and evaluation practice—a theory of life itself—in which purposeful inquiry or continuous evaluative action research may be thought of as life's fundamental driving dynamic process.

We think Yoland—in coming to this 'big idea' may have identified a key to the human species opening to an alternative to its hitherto tendency towards extremes in one direction or another—whether towards excessive repeated rigidity, rushing into short-term solutions or contemplating matters without action. In each instance of imbalance the threat to life may be occurring as a result of a lack of effective inquiry—or as Yoland would put it, not 'going full cycle'.

We think this book, which 'inquires into how we can inquire', was worth waiting the fifteen years it has taken although, like both the previous volumes on which it builds, it remains always and necessarily a work-in-progress, with feedback welcomed for its next iteration.

We hope it may serve as a useful link in the self-organising chain of human emergence towards a next era of deeper human individual, group and species self-insight and wise action. And we hope that the new age's subsequent inevitable decay may not be as catastrophically premature and unnecessary as the current one appears bent on being. May the question mark be with you.

ACTION RESEARCH ISSUES ASSOCIATION
Copublisher

DEDICATION

This book has been guided by a vision of all those
who are constantly building and re-building
more truly living human service systems
in which they are both happy to assist and resource
and from which they would be happy to seek assistance and resourcing

It is dedicated to the memory of
John Byrne, Cate Kyne, Christopher Newell, Wendy Weeks and Tony Peterson
who died in active service to this vision

And to all others who love life
in all its living processes and all its living forms

Contents

List of tables and figures

Acknowledgements

A lot has happened during the very much more than a decade that has gone into making this book. There have been countless contributing experiences, observations, questions, lulls, snags, growth spurts, people, projects, groups, networks and organisations with which and with whom I have engaged, talked, noticed, listened, questioned, responded, discussed, reacted, developed, been stretched, tested, thought more deeply about, incubated, been validated, challenged and changed. All of which has in the end given rise to the birth of a rather big idea about how evaluation and research—or inquiry per se—may be thought of as comprising the dynamic method by which living systems live. Ironically but predictably, it's taken a whole living system to achieve this idea!

Yet it is difficult to acknowledge all who comprise entire living systems!

Nevertheless the following have been some of my most important 'communities of science' or personal networks of 'communities of inquiry practice'. I thank all for the myriad ways in which I have been influenced and shaped, as well as encouraged to keep going when the task seemed insurmountable. While I have listed people in groupings it has most often been the moving *between* many diverse experiences of researching, evaluating, facilitating, using and providing a multitude of forms of human service—between all their standpoints, perspectives, roles and identities—that has meant the really creative insights emerged. In a systemic sense I acknowledge the following as something like my 'external mind'.

You have contributed, perhaps in ways you may never have realised (or wanted to!) My special thanks to:

1988–1996 The Victorian Mental Illness Awareness Council and Royal Park Hospital and its successors throughout the duration of the 'Understanding, Anytime' and 'Understanding & Involvement' (U&I) projects and subsequently—in particular, Merinda Epstein, Ross Findlay, Moira Somerville, David Meyer, Carol Andrew, Margaret Fogarty, Sharyn Clarke, Sara Clarke, Elizabeth Crowther, the late Marina Gloster, Bee Horwood, Norman James, Jon Kroschel, Jackie Kwok, Andrew McKenzie, Terry Melbourne, Heather Moore, Pru Pearson, Allan Pinches, Daniel Rechter, Joan Robertson, Catherine Roper, Rod Salvage, Julie Shaw, Ria Strong, Leonie Walsh, Rose Wodetski, Stephen Ziguras, Maggie McGuiness, Lyndal Grimshaw, Isabell Collins, Patrick McGorry, Graeme Meadows and Barbara Mouy of VicHealth.

1997–2000 At Victoria University of Technology, in particular John Alder, Paul Clark, Adrian Fisher, Delwyn Goodrick, Robyn Mills, Dot Bruck, Lesley Hoatson and Rhonda Hallett; the Lakewaters Hospital, in particular Vicki Geytenbeek, Julie O'Brien and Rozelle Williams; Glastonbury Child and Family Services, in particular Jenny Duffield and the late Vic Coull; the Royal Melbourne Hospital Community Participation project, in particular Denise Ruth; the Department of Human Services PHACS Quality Assurance committee; the Brotherhood of St Laurence Social Action and Research Department; Bear In Mind; Coonara Community House Action Research Taskforce, in particular Leanne Fitzgerald; and the ANU National Centre for Epidemiology and Population Health, in particular Bronnie Veale and Jane Dixon.

From 1986 Members of the Action Research Issues Association, Friends of Participatory Action Research and its successors, the VicARnet e-group and the statewide network Systemic•Participatory• Inquiry•Research•Action•Learning (SPIRAL); in particular 'thinking partners' Lucinda Aberdeen, Jacques Boulet, Elizabeth Branigan, Marie Brennan, Lynton Brown, Sally Cowden, Merinda Epstein, Anne Garrow, David Green, Robbie Guevara, Linette Hawkins, Kelley Johnson, the late Cate Kyne, Helen Lee, David Legge, Kath McKay, Jose Ramos, Jill Sanguinetti, the late Wendy Weeks and Jane Wexler.

Members of the local, national and international research and evaluation communities, particularly the participatory and action research, sociological and psychological type communities (including ALARPM, ALARA, ARLIST, ARMNET, ACTLIST, ARJOUR, SPARj, Aus APT, AES, EVALSYS and TASA), in particular Glen Barnes, Penny Barrett, Danny Burns, Robert Chambers, Raewyn Connell, Dick Couto, Jess Dart, Bob Dick, Peter Geyer, Pip Bruce Ferguson, Bob Flood, John Gaventa, Susie Goff, Delwyn Goodrick, Davydd Greenwood, Elwin Hall, Ros Hurworth, Jean King, Judith McMorland, Mark Oliver, Michael Quinn Patton, Roger Pearman, Fran Peavey, Patricia Rogers, Peter Tufts-Richardson, Sue White, Bob Williams and Jerome Winston.

Other 1995 Churchill Fellowship international study tour interviewees—especially (USA) Greg Owen, David Scheie, Paul Williams, Vanessa McKendall, Dick Kreuger, Jeanne Campbell, Jan Fritz, Orlando Fals Borda; staff of the Highlander Research and Education Centre: Candie Carawan, Ron Davis and Ekem Amonoo Lartson; staff and committee members of the Tennessee University Community Partnerships Centre: Cynthia Rocha, Kathleen Demarais, Juliet Merrifield; and, for additional assistance, the University of Tennessee Australian Studies Centre; staff at Cornell University: Ann W. Martin, the late William Foote Whyte and Morten Levin (and other staff of the Programs for Employment and Workplace Systems in the New York State School of Industrial and Labor Relations), John Forester, the Cornell Participatory Action Research Network, staff of the Mario Einaudi Centre for International Studies, David Deshler and Jennifer Greene; and in Boston: Bill Torbert and the late Donald Schon; in Delaware: Peter Park and in New York: Mimi Abramovitch; in the UK, staff of the Open University: Jan Walmsley, Dorothy Atkinson and Carol Komaromy, including in the Systems Studies Department: David McClintock, Ray Ison and Paul Maiteny; in Cambridge: Tony Giddens, Richard Winter, Maire Maisch, Caroline Currer, Carol Munn-Giddings and Bridget Somekh; in London: Peter Beresford, Suzy Croft and David Glennister, Jim Read, Jan Wallcraft, John Rowan, Maryanne Egan and Sue Wright; at Bath University, Centre for Action Research in Professional Practice: Peter Reason, Judi Marshall, Jack Whitehead, Peter Garrett, Alaric Newcombe, Michael Moran and Laurence Wiggens, and in the School of Management: Stephen Fineman and Paul Bate; at Bristol: Russ Vince; and independent consumer consultant Vivien Lindow.

Additionally during 2001 and 2006 overseas discussion tours: at NYU: Sonya Ospina and Bethany Goodsoe; at Cornell: Susan Boser and colleagues; at the 'Bridging the Gap' feminism and PAR meeting at Boston College: Patricia Maguire, Mary Brydon-Miller, Alice McIntyre, Bud Hall and others; in London, Virginia Berkholz, Hannah Sharp, Peter May, Su Glazier, and Sheree Parfoot, and at the Tavistock Institute: Elliot Stern and staff; at SOLAR: Susan Weill, Carlis Douglas and Janet Ferguson; at Bath University: Mark Baldwin and Alon Serper; at Salford University and the Reg Revans Centre: Steve Young, Mike Pedler, Rhetta Moran and colleagues; at the Hull Systems Centre: staff and (including later when at the New Zealand Environmental Science Research Institute): Gerald Midgley and Wendy Gregory; and in Sweden at the Skaraborgs Institute: Beth Maina-Ahlberg and Solveig Freudenthal; and Sylvia Maata and Christer Fallman of the Da Capo project, Skovde and Garden of the Senses, Stockholm.

Many other individuals, friends and work colleagues have contributed in significant and inspiring ways over many years: including the late Christine Amor Robertson, Rosalie Aroni, the late Ruth Crow, Joan Byrne, Inez Dussuyer, Pam Forsyth, Denise Fry, Rhonda Galbally, Maria Grigg, Anne Harry, Mary Harris, Susan Mera, Christina Metz, the late Marjorie Oke, Mike Pelling, Vicki Ponsford, Barbara Potter, Patricia M. Price, Christean Raptopoulos, Vivien Routley, Claire Runciman, Sarah Russell, Matt Smith, Veronica Spillane and Paul Whyte; from the Knox Project: the late Nancy Bastow, John Bottomley, Nan Ferguson and Nerida Melville Smith, and countless others from the early days of the women's movement and from children's services; from Scope: Erin Wilson and Michael Bink; from Grampians Community Health Centre: Jill Miller and staff; and from Melbourne Citymission: Anne Pate, David Carlos and other members of the reflective practice network.

I also want to thank those who responded with enthusiasm to the first tellings of the transdisciplinary living systems inquiry theory of this book—in September 2004 at the national conference of the Australasian Psychological Type Association, Ballarat, Victoria; the September 2005 Bob White Memorial lecture to the national conference of the Australian Sociological Association, University of Tasmania; the Victoria University of Technology in 2005; and an August 2006 keynote paper to the World Congress of Action Learning, Action Research and Process

Management, University of Groningen, the Netherlands—and to the first published accounts for audiences in the four key disciplinary areas which the theory draws together (Wadsworth 2006, 2008a, 2008b, 2008c).

I want to acknowledge the contribution of media coverage of wider local, national and international issues, debates and cultural context: ABC public radio, and *The Age* newspaper—their coverage of science, religion, ecology, health, law, media, sport, news and current affairs:, in particular ABC Radio National's Phillip Adams for his *Late Night Live*, Stephen Crittenden and Paul Collins for the *Religion Report*, Florence Spurling's *Encounter*, Julie McGrossin's *Life Matters*, Alan Saunders for *The Comfort Zone* (now *By Design*), Claudia Taranto's *Street Stories*, Rachel Kohn's *The Ark* and *The Spirit of Things*, and Fran Kelly for the *Breakfast* program. I also thank the US military for the invention of the Internet which allowed me to have significant exchanges of ideas, thoughts and feelings with people around the globe. Along with Wikipedia, it operates as one of the unexpected technologies of the post-modern era to aid autopoesis. I thank but will not name (as they have their own stories to tell) the small number of individuals and organisations whose negative impacts have, over the years, regularly stretched me to my limits and provided me with an invaluable constant stream of material on which to reflect regarding the conditions for life-damaging versus life-giving systems at every scale. A living system has life and death in right relationship. But individual and social systems that overly concentrate power and are 'in the grip' of their shadow selves can casually squander or suppress others' life energies and potential, bringing numerous promising life-giving starts to premature ends, whether through force, neglect, exclusion, diminishment, discrimination, self-defined necessity, unwitting unexamined presumption or unconscious conflict. The battered nature of the author's cerebral neural network is in evidence in this final book and I apologise for that. However it may have been the price paid to crack the puzzles needed to complete this book, so I am grateful instead that you are reading a finished book at all.

Books don't easily get written without funding assistance—especially unusual books (including ones that translate complex theory into cartoon form!) It is difficult to find a government department, charitable trust or foundation that will fund the writing of any book, and especially in this day and age of all-too-tight controls over copyright on intellectual property.[1] In this case it proved impossible and, after fruitless years of trying to find less restrictive venture funds or time to write at the same time as other paid work, I took several years without funding to complete it.[2]

I remain enormously grateful to the following three sources of funds that ensured I could carry out key empirical studies that have contributed greatly to testing the ideas, as well as to my reading more widely as I began to come to my conclusions.

Firstly, I thank the Winston Churchill Memorial Trust for awarding me a **1995** Churchill Fellowship for the purpose of a three-month overseas study tour to 'gain insights and information to enhance Australia's capacity to assist community services, organisations and groups to build in self-research and evaluation'.

Secondly, I thank the Victoria University of Technology for providing a three-year research fellowship **1997–2000** for a program of research for similar purposes, during which time I carried out three collaborative organisational action research studies: one in health, one in welfare and one in education. I specially thank the Department of Psychology for hosting me (during which time I received invaluable accreditation as an MBTI® practitioner), and the Department of Social Inquiry and Community Studies for further hosting in **2000–2001**.

Thirdly, I thank the Australian National University's National Centre for Epidemiology and Population Health, and particularly its then Director Tony McMichael, and Gabriele Bammer, for the timely provision of a six-month visiting writing residency in **2003–2004** and their important collaboration on complex systems thinking, including with Richard Eckersley, Colin Butler, and Peter Deane of the Integrative and Implementation Sciences Network, without which this transdisciplinary theory may not ever have come together so satisfyingly.

I am grateful also to John Wiseman and the McCaughey VicHealth Centre at the University of Melbourne, and to Chris Chamberlain and the Centre for Applied Social Research at RMIT University for giving the last stages of this intellectual project a convivial home.

For illustrations and particular theoretical and co-writing contributions—I thank Simon Kneebone for his ever more skilfully crafted realisations of my wholly unrefined cartooning style and his companionship on the publishing road for so long. Merinda Epstein for her friendship and wonderful cartoon realisations of our theorisation during the U&I and subsequent projects. Thanks too to Fran Peavey for her support and encouragement to 'run with it' as I explicated in ever greater detail our separate work on the sequence of strategic action research questions in Chapter 3. And Peter Tufts Richardson for his equally supportive encouragement for me to build on his work of a circular MBTI® arrangement. Andrew Inglis for his architect's drawings of the house used as the metaphoric 'building'. Matt Smith for patiently creating the technical diagrams regarding individual living systems inquiry preferences in Appendix 3. I thank all those who collaborated in co-writing or painstakingly checking the details of the exemplars in Chapter 5 (your names appear as agreed in those accounts), and I want to express my appreciation also to the four distinguished reviewers who read the initial manuscript for Allen & Unwin and gave their valuable feedback.

I thank copyright owners for their kind permission to reprint additional cartoons, poems and other extracts. Efforts have been made to contact every copyright owner of works included in this book. If we have been unable to reach you, we would appreciate it if you could contact the publisher, the Action Research Press (ARIA Inc.). I thank:

Michael Leunig and Penguin Books for the first four frames of 'It could be Live Human syndrome' from *The Stick*, Viking/Penguin Books, Camberwell, Australia, 2002 (Prologue), and 'Ahoy there' from *The Penguin Leunig*, Penguin Books, Ringwood, Australia, 1974 p. 47 (Ch 5)

Cath Jackson for 'Have you tried the Alexander technique?' in *Visibly Vera*, The Women's Press, UK, 1987 (Prologue)

Mark Dapin and Fairfax Publishing for quotes from 'The son also rises', *The Age Good Weekend*, 4 August 2007, pp. 31-33 (Ch 2)

Sting, Neil McCormick and Fairfax Publishing for quote from 'What's wrong with being pretentious?' *The Age Good Weekend* 8 November 2003, p.30 (Ch2)

Bill Mollison and Tagari Publications for the account of the tree from 'Deep Ecology', New Dimensions, ABD Radio National, 6 January 1999 (Ch 2)

Tohby Riddle by arrangement with the Licensor, c/o

Curtis Brown (Aust) Pty Ltd for 'Emotional Ecosystem' *The Age Good Weekend*, 25 March 1997, and for an idea from the 'Past now future' burning match cartoon *The Age Good Weekend*, 11 November 1997 (Ch 2)

Scott Adams and Auspac Media Pty Ltd/United Feature Syndicate, for the Dilbert cartoon 'This is my tiny realm' (Ch 2) and for an idea from the Dilbert cartoon 'Bad news about replacements' from *Casual Day Has Gone Too Far*, The Ink Group, Sydney, Australia, 1999, p.40 (Ch 4)

Katharine Betts, David Hayward and Simon Kneebone for Simon's cartoon 'What's the multivariate approach?' from Betts et al, *Quantitative Analysis in the Social Sciences: An Introduction*, Tertiary Press, Eastern House, Croydon, 2001, p.60 (Ch 3)

Bruce Petty courtesy of *The Age* for 'The sooner people are data the better', Animal Spirits, *Age* Business, Melbourne 1 April 2000, p.2 (Ch 3)

Russell Deal, Di O'Neill and St Lukes Innovative Resources for images from 'The Scaling Kit', Catalogue 2010 (Ch 3)

Raewyn Connell for *Margaret's kitchen* (Ch 3)

Simon Kneebone and the Health Issues Centre for 'Health system communication stepping stones', from the cover, *Health Issues* journal 2002 No. 71 Copyright © Health Issues Centre (Ch 3)

Jim Ife and Pearson Australia for 'Competing discourses of human services' from *Rethinking Social Work*, 1997 p. 47 (Ch 4)

Phil Somerville for an idea from the cartoon 'The problem with people is assumptions', The sum of us, *The Age Sunday Life* 10 February 2002

John Spooner and *The Age* for 'Chicken of dialogue offered to dragon' cartoon (Ch 4)

John Gaventa and Robert Chambers and the Institute for Development Studies, University of Sussex for Sudhir Dar's 'Of course they can participate' cartoon (Ch 4)

Liz Mackie for 'Why can't I cope like the others do', in Jo Nesbitt et al. 2e, *Sour Cream*, Sheba Feminist Publishers, London, 1980 p.47 (Ch 4)

The unknown artist of the 'What the experts proposed...' building of a swing cartoon from the 1970s, in this instance sourced from 'One World Week', *Journal of South–North Network Cultures and Development*, 1995, 27–28(3):48. (Ch 4)

Judy Horacek, courtesy of Jenny Darling & Associates for © Copyright Judy Horacek www. horacek.com.au,

'Postmodern cowboys' (Ch 4) and 'Are you getting up', both from *Woman with Altitude*, Hyland House, South Melbourne, 1997 (Ch 6)

Attorney-General's Department, Phil Crane and Danyelle Bodaghi for Danyelle's account 'A day in the life of Reconnect', in Phil Crane and Leanne Richardson's *Action Research Guide*, © Commonwealth of Australia, 2000 pp. 5.7-5.10 incl. 3.17 (Ch 5)

Kim Kruger for collaboration regarding the Shiny Shiny Blak Bling exhibition catalogue, graphics by Kye McGuire, Lisa Bellear photography, and Donna Brown for photography and design (Ch 5)

Theo Psathas for 'Poem for U&I', from the cover, *The Essential U&I* (Wadsworth with Epstein 2001) (Ch 5)

Merinda Epstein and the Victorian Mental Illness Awareness Council for their ongoing permission to publish cartoons, and reproduce previously published accounts of and from the 'Understanding, Anytime' and 'Understanding and Involvement (U&I) research, in particular Merinda's cartoons 'Reflection pool', 'Coming to the table', 'One day in a back room' (Ch 3) 'Speak of others' and 'Staff development/Consumer program' (Ch 4), and all our share-authored publications listed in the References section

Susan Lilley of Nova Scotia, Canada for 'How to Deliver Negative Evaluation Results Constructively: Ten Tips for Evaluators', online (Appendix 1)

CPP Asia-Pacific for their advice and direction regarding trademark usage (Appendix 3)

My thanks go finally to those who had sufficient faith in this book to want to see it published—to Elizabeth Weiss and Patrick Gallagher of Allen & Unwin Australia for their twenty-five years of collaboration; the members of the Action Research Issues Association Incorporated and Action Research Press Projects Sub Committee; and those who saw it as more than just a job to produce it—John Hinkson of Arena Printing, Alison Caddick and Criss Fawcett of Sans Serif for editing assistance; Mal Oram for layout, and Jacques Boulet and Borderlands at the Augustine Centre for housing the Action Research Press.

None of any of the above are liable for what I have made of it all, and I remain open to the next iteration of application, discussion, observation, discussion, critical reflection and further theory and practice. Like all human knowledge this book is always contextual, contingent and emergent, partial, particular, and only ever a 'best fit' for its time, however long that time turns out to be.

A note on use of the literature

It is important to say that, while I have attempted to acknowledge references to some of the relevant international literature, it cannot be assumed that any term or idea I have used has stemmed from any particular theorist. For most of the past fifteen years I have been submerged more in practice than in academic theory. Like many other research practitioners, I frequently find that the concepts and ideas we generate in our fieldwork are later to be found in some comparable shape or form somewhere in the international literature or popular media. Given a systemic perspective this is unsurprising. However I note this in order to say that I have found it most helpful when the literature is a resource to, and guided by the hard test of actual practice, rather than practice being framed, led and determined by the literature, given the inevitability of that literature being systemically formed 'elsewhere'. Practice-based researchers know the dilemmas of trying to introduce exciting but unfamiliar concepts and thinking from the literature back into the 'local' living systemicities in which we work!—not so early as to distort the grounded emergent understandings, concepts and theory, but not so late as to fail to usefully resource and inform them.

The bodies of knowledge which I have found both helpful and interesting have been too voluminous to cite in more than the already extensive bibliographical detail in this book, and I partly rely on my previous publications for this. However as a general note, it was from my reading of the sociology of knowledge and epistemological debates for my PhD in the 1970s and early 1980s that I made sense firstly of many of the rigidified social forms I was observing and working (and living) within, and secondly of the ways social change efforts seemed so often to 'revert to (prior) type' despite the apparent availability of the best research and evaluation possible. From my reading of the organisational psychology literature in the 1990s I made sense of the ways in which social change was generated from and within the individual and personal as well as the social and interpersonal. And my reading in systems thinking (the new physics, soft systems engineering, deep ecology and more) during the 2000s has renewed my thirty years of sociological thinking about systems to see a new way of thinking about them as *living* systems–integrating their appearances of stable unchanging replicating forms and the dynamics of change in such forms.

Yet the systemic contextualisation of the literature is the same for all the other sources and resources from which everyone constantly builds their working theories of the world—all are a product of particular 'systemicities' as the inquirer seeks inputs that address their own questions and observations from wherever they can be found, including all ordinary conversations, things overheard, seen, experienced or presented, from all the gatherings of friends and family, meetings, travels, events, workshops, formal and informal education, seminars, conferences, leisure activities, social gatherings, poetry, music, art, film, television, the internet, other communications media, works of fact and fiction, religious and spiritual practice. All play their part in people continuously building and rebuilding their working theories and practices in the world.

In the end then, it is the hard test of trying ideas out in practice, firstly in small ways and then building evidence and confidence, which remains the 'scientific' warrant of a theory.[3] Indeed it is people's ability to make thoughtful sense of *their own* situations in the *now* that may really count if inquiry is to be built in rather than relying only on external sources for authorisations about 'how things really are' (or how to think about things, or what actions to take), particularly those distant from people's lifeworlds. This seems to me to be also the critical warrant offered by participative, emergent and action-grounded living systems research against an 'elsewhere expertocracy' seriously 'getting things wrong', and those errors remaining untested and unable to be revised or rejected, particularly because of the defences that the desire for certainty and rightness generates for a system's self-protection.

It is also how those who provide leadership know that they are getting it right—by deriving their articulation from the results of 'whole cycle' participation of all people in 'whole systems' of knowledge generation, and not being too distant from local knowledge, or out of touch with experiential consequences, or prematurely imposing pragmatic decisions when none would be needed if inquiry could have proceeded in a more comprehensive, emergent and integrated way in the first place. That is, change and improvement and indeed life itself cannot wait until only a small group of people research, evaluate and decide, or until enough people have read all the literature. Indeed evaluation and research cannot await 'The' researchers and evaluators!

All people must be able to research and evaluate 'from where they are', striving to expand their contexts and frames of reference to actively include alternative perspectives and the inquiring of others elsewhere, including in specialist areas that we may not hope to be able to master individually.

At the same time, those of us who work as researchers and evaluators work to expand our context and frames of reference back to actively include all those with whom and for whom we research and evaluate.

In these ways, the taking of small and incremental, thoughtful self-determined steps to inquire, and to 'scale up' to a thoroughgoing participatory or deliberative democracy (Greek *demos* people, *kratos* strength), strengthens self-protectively *the whole system's* 'distributed intelligence' against any potential directions that risk not enhancing such a self-organising self-inquiring 'fabric' of individual and collective human social life. The results of the alternative 'imposed unchosen' can at best be lucky, and at worst subjugating and confining, risking reactivity; endangering equality as a form of systemic balancing; decaying or rigidifying otherwise perfectly useful 'containers' and 'channels' of the human spirit and its life-seeking inquiry.

The final warrant of the value and use of this book is not because it is weighed down with empirical evidence and authoritative endnotes and bibliographic details that reference its truths elsewhere (though you will find a good deal of this)—but rather because *you* the reader find within it important elements that resonate with and resource your own experience and 'living inquiring systemicity'.

Thus the faults of this book have arisen entirely from my own autopoetic embodiment in co-relation with a complex, often overly challenging larger field. I thank this larger turbulent life field for its teachings and all those who have helped me endure it to tell the story, albeit so imperfectly, of what I have learned.

My deepest thanks go to you for building in some time to give this book your inquiring attention. I hope you can find in it something of what I have come to see and hoped to offer.

Then let's continue to talk...[4]

Prologue

The paradox of 'We want change—and we don't want change'

This has truly been a hard book to write. Over fifteen long years and eight frustrating drafts.

It had all seemed so straightforward—do it yourself social research and everyday evaluation on the run were necessary and valuable activities. But insufficient to achieve their deeper purposes.

There was in fact a surprisingly extensive upsurge in their popularity. There are now lots and lots of tremendous examples of people successfully doing their own really effective and path-breaking small-scale research and evaluation, including by and with those to benefit from it. There has also been a detectable take up of the assumptions in mainstream social research and evaluation (Wadsworth 2005: 277–278), not to mention in large numbers of other fields of human endeavour, ranging from business and management to family therapy and deliberative justice, just to name a few of the hundreds drawing on these new epistemological assumptions. Research and evaluation 'capacity building' to achieve 'cultures of research and evaluation' have become major themes in the work of the health and human services professions, in the community and in the literature. Consumer participation, while still not thoroughly realised as a form of evaluative research, is nevertheless becoming *de rigueur* and mainstreamed. And the language of stakeholders has transformed action research from the sidelines to centre stage wherever valued change is sought as a result of collaborative inquiry processes. Even Kofi Annan, then United Nations Secretary-General, expressed thanks for the contribution of an action research strategy—appreciative inquiry—to the work of the United Nations (personal letter to David Cooperrider 2004).

And there are now also impressive examples of the small-scale having built up to large-scale and even 'whole systems' inquiry as larger organisations have developed increasingly effective, widespread and even entirely routine cultures of research and evaluation

that are starting to see a steady, valuable 'pay off'. Some of them feature in the 'Exemplars' section of this book and in a new wave of literature (see for example the work of Danny Burns 2008). A wide range of inquiry processes and techniques have now become routine. 'Asking others' about their experiences, particularly those who are to benefit from our actions and interventions, has seemingly become a given. Nine-year-old school children can confidently list the criteria of their monthly evaluation activities, now part of their regular school timetable. And the national media invites watchers and listeners to go to their live websites to 'discuss this further', while the social media centre on such mutual inquiry activity, including the heart of economic activity, such as seen in sociologist Fiona Stewart's notgoodenough.org. As a major electronics company franchisee and social media manager put it: 'Microblogging has given consumers a powerful new voice retailers couldn't ignore' (Wheelhouse 2010).

Even this week as I write I see my toothpaste comes with a 'whitening scale' for me to measure before-and-after impact for myself! A major telecommunication company is extolling their gathering of customer input in a TV advertisement featuring little furry animals with microphones saying earnestly, 'We're listening to you'. A letter writer to the editor of a major newspaper corrects a politician for believing he could know what the nation thinks about something, calling him to account on the basis of his *particular* situated socioeconomic experience. A university student reports experiencing 'pair buzzes' as part of his tutorials. Prison officers seek opinions and suggestions from offenders by using 'active listening'. Even law courts are trying dialogue rather than adversarialism to wind back escalating levels of violence.

There is a new culture of confidence around expecting us to inquire for ourselves and in turn have our own views heard and considered by others even if they conflict, or conflict with those of 'experts'. Indeed the experts—even the national Census—now have to explain their purposes and even their evidence in ways people can understand, and may now expect informed critical feedback rather than automatically obedient and dutiful acquiescence. We have a growing sense of the safe-guarding nature of this stream of participation and feedback, even as we still work to get right its extent and nature.

Yet, if we are honest, many of these efforts to engage widespread public and private processes of inquiry and feedback are still often quite routinely faced with quite incomprehensible countervailing opposition, defensiveness, pressure and difficulties.

Some efforts falter or end quickly after promising starts. Many don't get this far. And some don't manage to begin as intended, or even provoke the first glimmer of recognition of a need that they should. Other inquiry efforts that are becoming routinised may also become domesticated, 'safe' and comfortable—often losing the critical edge of truth-telling with which they began. Some data-collection efforts have become over-whelming in size in response to anxieties about risks, including fear of blame or litigation by a public who have not been part of a collective process of assessing and deciding about risk.

Especially and most paradoxically, the voices of those I have called the critical reference group (the ultimate 'For who?' of any evaluation inquiry): the end-beneficiaries, seem perpetually vulnerable to systematic 'slippage' and bit by bit exclusion and displacement by those deemed better resourced or who see themselves as better able or qualified to speak. Or alternative voices are excluded by commercial logic, or narrowed and restricted by electronic communications reductionism. Or somehow the talk of 'partnerships' between professionals and clients has slipped into becoming a focus on partnerships between professionals and their different service agencies.

Sometimes even after being initially accepted and even warmly welcomed, new end-beneficiary stakeholders enter the scene for a while only to again be subtly lost to the process, further down the track. Even organisations that may have invested considerably in reflective practice or participatory or action research, even purposefully including their clients, pull back at the moment of creating permanent inquiry facilitation positions or ensuring continuing research into and development of new practice and policy, employing statisticians instead who yet again merely describe the problem—the extent of poverty,

the numbers excluded or disadvantaged or the correlates of unequal income—for policy papers that yet again recommend action, that yet again seems unable to be taken, due to what is yet again seen as a 'lack of political will' or 'impracticalities'.

Perhaps a particularly common manifestation of this is the quiet decay of so may genuine efforts by professions, academics and managers to 'come to the table' (and stay there) with clients, customers, consumers, patients, students, residents or other local communities of interest—that is, to stay in conversation with all those who comprise the recipients of human service systems of any kind. Even as I finalise this book, I have just received copies of new management books for community services that start the gover-nance process with planning rather than the necessary prior observation, research into people's needs, reflection, and developmental evaluation with client or community stakeholders that will ground and give confidence to planning. Indeed there is actually no mention at all of the active presence of clients, communities or other end-beneficiaries or critical reference groups in the management and planning process. Instead there is a default reliance on disembodied statistics and lengthy chains of inferential presumption and high-risk second guessing. In the mail recently also was an invitation to a prominent human services policy conference on inclusion, which on the one hand succeeded in listing consumer participation at the top of its list of forums, and then on the other hand entirely failed to list a single keynote speaker who was a service user among all the numerous otherwise expert and academic speakers. Professors, directors and people from overseas often have important and interesting things to say. Their knowledge has usually been hard won. And sometimes it seems impractical for everyone to hear from more than one, two or a handful of people among hundreds attending.[5] But in a truly rounded living human system, for most of the time and in most of the places in which we meet and talk, the essential local knowledges, insights and standpoints of the critical reference group must have 'forms and processes' not only so they may represent themselves, but also so they can be a permanent part of a direct dialogue that traverses all the way from observation through reflection to planning and into practice, and of which outcomes, in the end, they are the final and most critical arbiters.

Recently there has even been evidence of insistent demands to demonstrate that people's participation has led to 'measurable benefit' for services. Apart from the prematurity of this demand, it appears to imply that it is an optional extra *for the services* rather than the central point of human service engagement *for their clients*. Why would anyone question the value of involving the people who are to benefit in giving feedback about the efforts which are assumed will benefit them? Would anyone seriously want to return to the separation, passivity and dependency on 'expert others' that was identified as part of the problem in the first place? Would we want to? And wouldn't that yet again result in the 'expert others' carrying unacceptable levels of both risk and the exhausting responsibility of having to get it 100 per cent right all the time? Wouldn't that result in passive and dependent folk yet again becoming helpless and hopeless? Depressed? Angry? Disempowered? And, as we have come to know from the new public health studies, the links between disempowerment, stress and ill health are now very well-understood and evidenced

(e.g. the Whitehall organisationally based studies of Marmot et al. 1991; Marmot and Wilkinson 1999; and the Californian community-based work of Len Syme et al. 1997a, 1997b, 2004).

So why *would* efforts to involve people in giving feedback about *their* experiences, observations, deep needs and desires be subject to anything but permanent 'built in' energetic encouragement and research and development to 'get it right'? Why would those of us who are providers not want to hear back from those who are in the situations for which our assistance is being sought in the first place?

If we providers were the assistance seekers, wouldn't we want to be acting as assertively for our own health or wellbeing as possible? And when we need others to do things 'for us' when we are unable, wouldn't we want it to be done as if we were still fully our own person? Why would we not want service users to be 'in on it' from the outset so helpers didn't get it wrong in the first place? So they might be able to adapt and correct 'in flight', before error accrues?

In these strangely paradoxical responses of: 'We *want* to do research and evaluation. We *want* change for the better. We *want* to hear from the critical stakeholders—And we *don't* want to', something deeper seems to be in play. Something about the part that inquiry—research and evaluation—plays in all our lives. Or not. The 'paradigm wars' still simmer, even as the new orthodoxy of 'quantitative-*and*-qualitative' *appears* to prevail, yet still there seem to be numerous disconnects between practice and its evaluation or research, and between these and policy plans and new practice that brings real change. Perhaps it is something as large and unfathomable as the broader social contexts in which research and evaluation take place—*the system*—as we call it, shaking our heads at its power over us, even as we seem to have few choices but to keep repeating its patterns. Or perhaps it is something as intimately familiar as what we are like and how we differ, and what we know and how we go about knowing it, and how we think or are thought about by each other. Or not. In the culture of professional human services there is often a deep anxiety about getting too 'up close and personal', and a perceived need to keep 'professional distance'. Do we fear we may not have a truly sustainable way of 'helping others'. Or fear things may be even worse than they seem? But wouldn't this be exactly the impetus to inquire? What *would* be a truly sustainable way of 'helping' people? Or getting to know them well enough to know how?

Time regularly emerges as a key factor when people think about why they don't stop and inquire, reflect, research and evaluate more and more regularly. But wait a minute. What are we saying here? That there is 'no time' to stop and think about what we're doing? Doesn't that strike us as a bit of a conundrum?! Why would we tolerate not taking the time to ask the key questions at the heart of the endeavour: 'For whom and for what' am I acting? And 'How do I know what they seek, want and need?' Why would we tolerate not taking the time to get close enough *together* to truly understand? And then to step far enough back together in order to get new perspective, insights and ideas? And then to try them out together in practice? Yet why do so many people seem to act on the assumption that they *already* have the answers? And why do they not seem able to see things going wrong—or act on their sneaking suspicions, or instead feel the compulsion to defend to the contrary? And why *are* some happy only to complain, or just describe over and over again 'how things are' without ever feeling driven to take the next step to research and evaluate 'how things could be' instead? And even when some good new idea bubbles up from a well-grounded process, why *is* there so often such 'slippage' in the swampy ground of expediency, and the all-too-soon loss of those well-grounded-in-evidence ideas for actions, often on the basis of 'pragmatic' judgement or utilitarian logic?

The 'silos conundrum' and repeated efforts to 'join up' 'seamlessly' the boxes of research-to-policy-to-practice remains so often 'on the whiteboard' as hopeful arrows going in a line from one box to the next. But how *did* they become so separated in the first place? And why have we more and more experts on every possible topic who are increasingly far removed from living the lives of those about whom they are 'expert'?

Particularly ironic—perhaps significantly so—is how we do not always seem able to practise what we preach in our own most personal and intimate settings: in our homes, families, workplaces and communities. How is it that the normal procedures for everyday do it yourself social research and evaluation are not extended into more effectively taking the time to inquire *ourselves*, to resolve *our own* difficulties and misunderstandings, so we may do what we all came to do in the first place—*help each other* achieve wellbeing, learning, meaningful work, re-creation and our other desired ends?

Indeed how could so many people be facing such stresses[6] in human services per se: health, education, community and welfare services, of all places? How could people, reacting so often to unsettling, stifling and sometimes even more-or-less unwittingly hurtful, even destructive and crisis-creating organisations, hope to provide stable, inspiring sources of supportive resourcing and service that could help others not be like this themselves? And harder still, how could they do this without increasingly distancing and cocooning *themselves* from the sources of stress and conflict? From individuals all the way up to entire nations? And how on earth did there get to be all this stress and conflicting and unmet goals for so many in the first place? How did we each, personally and 'individually', suddenly *all* come to be suffering collective epidemics of depression, anxiety, anger, or deficits of attention, 'resilience', 'optimism' or whatever is deemed the latest medical disorder or 'dysfunctional' condition?

Doctor I've got a feeling.

You poor thing, tell me all about it.

It's a little pang of lonely sorrow. Do you think it's a personality disorder? Can it be painlessly removed?

It could be LHS; Live Human Syndrome.

What is going on here—with ourselves and 'the system' that we ourselves 'people'?

At the same time all around us and related to these pressures, wholesale changes proceed apace, after two decades of restraints on public services that nevertheless continue to repeatedly 'restructure' and proceduralise ever more tightly, mostly with little apparent measurable benefit, and at the same time, unending competitive pressures to perform, achieve and look good. People's private troubles seem to be multiplying even behind increasingly impressive facades. In exquisite correspondence it seems that the more people's private troubles begin to come to public attention, the more the responsibility of a public response is privatised as personal 'disorder', 'dysfunction' or lack of 'resilience'.*

In response to all this, sometimes people take refuge in the belief it all couldn't possibly be that bad ('no use getting overly emotional', 'just need to get out and have a bit more fun', 'here we go again', 'it'll blow over', 'I'm pretty OK actually'), or that our pessimistic thinking could perhaps better be 'reframed' (maybe as a wonderful 'opportunity' or 'personal challenge'); or that it would be 'practical, realistic and sensible' to not

---

* Here, I'll put the worst of the mind-numbing litany of 'privatised troubles' and public issues down here in a footnote to keep it contained and bearable. We're talking about the number of people services turn away or can't help; the people who no one has got enough time to listen to (or listen to properly) about often complex and long-standing difficulties, sufferings, survival troubles and lacks that everyone faces to some extent at different times—with organisations, neighbours, bureaucracies, partners, parents, families, friends, schools or workplaces—the demands, the expectations, the inequities and injustices, the misunderstandings, the casual sharp even cruel words, hurtful judgements, short tempers, the bullying and harshness, the seemingly increasing violence. The sadness, the regrets, the guilt and the shame, the sense of failure, the overwork and long hours, the overloads, the bombardment of demands and messages via proliferating electronic techno-devices, the burgeoning electronic surveillance, the health worries, the unhonoured values or betrayed principles and unmet goals, the pressures, the not breathing, the work insecurity, the lack of autonomy, the relationship troubles and disappointments, the irritation, rage, and coercion, unemployment, underemployment, the too-low incomes, the astoundingly excessive incomes, credit card debt, the sheer lack of basic resources needed for life, the petty and not so petty injustices and inequities, the costly courts and legal processes, mortgage burden, sub-standard or no housing, the extent of homelessness, extent of hopelessness and helplessness, stigma, poverty of spirit, the unmet hungers and addictions, the drugs, the deaths, the still too much smoking, the way too much alcohol, too much gambling, too much spending, too little ability to purchase, too much eating, too little eating, too many suicide attempts (and 'successes'), the aching lack of self-regard and self-confidence, the casual disregard of others and seeing them as inferior, as 'rubbish', as 'losers', 'dumb', 'unevolved', the crushing misuse of authority and institutional power, the despair, the belief that nothing can change, the exhaustion, the inability to get up in the morning and get going, the inability to get enough sleep, the worries, anxieties and fears—of losing jobs, incomes, partners, homes—the rabbit-caught-in-the-headlights confusion, fatigue, aloneness, the preventable illnesses, disabilities, the industrial accidents. And industrial deaths. Too many problems. Too many people with too few resources. Too few known neighbours, close friends and loving supportive family. Too weak a social fabric. Too much mobility. Too few community resources. The one in two diagnosed as having a mental disorder. Too little public funding. Too few funding programs. Too tightly prescribed funding programs. Too much paperwork. Too much wealth in the hands of too few. Weak rights. Weak rights legislation, or its absence. Too all-powerful legislation. The sinister changes we don't know about. The too-sinister changes we don't want to know about…

Then we realise that all these 'private issues' are writ large on a national and global scale which mirrors it all: as institutionalised disregard and unconcern; unethical, unjust, unequal, unstable and unsustainable economies; hatred, conflicts, suppressed culture, repressed peoples, political unrest, terrorism, wars, catastrophes and poverty, or a fast-depleting, over-heating, poisoned and denatured environment. We glimpse our unbearable implication in all of this. And then we are told that we need to think positively and optimistically as all our privatised troubles are costing 'the economy' billions in lost revenue…But wait. The economy? The ways we exchange goods and services? *We* are a problem for *it*? But wasn't the economy or business and the 'free' market meant to be in aid of *our* human life in the first place?

'dwell' on things or be 'too pure' about them. That, hey, this is now life as we know it ('Hello. What did you expect?' 'A bit of realism per-leese'), and that, well, if all else fails, 'tough'. 'Get used to it'. People respond differently to privatised overload, pressure, powerlessness and not getting what they want or need. Many run on empty, get burned out, despair, over work, become anxiety ridden, lose sleep, self-medicate. Some find ways of objectifying, distancing themselves, getting comfortably further out of touch with the troubling detail of other people's daily realities. Some continue to have 'never had it so good'. Things are 'cool'. We become cool. Less moved. Cold. Play dehumanising computer games. Subject others to control. Subject the self to control. Discipline the sexual self. Others see themselves as doing the best they can under the circumstances. Hoping, believing things aren't too far 'off track'. Or that others really ought to just manage better. Pull themselves together. Some keep applying themselves to ever newer 'big picture' visions of a better future, moving boxes and arrows around on whiteboards to 'fix it all', endlessly reorganising the organisational structure. Or the furniture. Or spin out in an overdose of sensory input or imagination. Or paranoia. Or shopping. Or just keep their heads down, soldiering on; hoping 'someone' will eventually get it right somewhere, some time, while enduring the twenty years to retirement. Some 'surf' from a bad situation into a new one, and if that's no good, 'duck and weave' off to another. While yet others turn to confront it, combative, vigilant, seeing the dangers if the situation is left to persist, alert to the need to protect all that's necessary or worthwhile. Or seems so. Their 'canary in the mine' pleas, or their adversarialism may get ever more insistent, strident, even as it is ever more hotly denied, combated. Sprayed with hot pepper gas. Some might kill, thinking it necessary. As the public commentator Phillip Adams has asked memorably, what other species spent last century killing one hundred and forty million members of its own? Fight. Fright. Flight. And all of it so deeply embodied—whether in ourselves or in the 'body politic' of our organisations and institutions. Our hearts fail, our blood is pressured. Our muscles hurt and rigidify. Our immune systems break down. The body and 'body politic' become cancerous with uncontained growth. Our souls, spirits and minds register alienation, conflicted confusion, anxiety, flights of thought or imagination into alternative 'realities', or as a search for spiritual meaning. Churches or religions that offer new spirit begin to experience record attendances. And the search for health services and healing remedies escalates.

Yet, at the same time the economy seemed to be hurting us we were being reassured it had provided us with unprecedented wealth and material conditions of comfort for decades. We saw money and luxury being splashed around us. And by us. Some of us. Inequalities skyrocketed. Fences went up and elaborate gates were locked on some of the biggest most energy-consuming houses in the Western world. Expensive security systems were installed–whether in organisations, houses, businesses or shops, formalising boundaries everywhere... Border control has become a popular preoccupation.

© Cath Jackson 1987

But the good news might be that if we worked out how to 'build' such a deeply paradoxical system that 'delivers' for many (or some) but excludes all too many others (or most), we ought also to be able to work out how to build a more integral and life-giving one *for all*. Fortunately it appears that all the ingredients are known and even to hand, as we will see…

Meanwhile, over the past couple of decades, researchers, evaluators and organisational improvement consultants working to address all these urgent, pressing and monumental issues have been trying to do so in a kind of a high performance culture where everyone had constantly to be 'looking good' and performing 'to the max'. Yet in contrast, research and evaluation are most typically characterised quite differently.

Indeed everyone in 'the system' is having to try and make sense of their worlds in these ways the best they can—even if the stopping is momentary, the questions are pondered while rushing between activities, the 'data collected' comes from just one other person in

TABLE 1. PROBLEMS WITH CONTEMPORARY PERFORMATIVITY

Continuous performativity	Research, evaluation and continuous quality improvement
1. At top speed	1. Stopping and taking time and making space to ask questions, raise doubts and retrace steps
2. 'Taking leadership'	2. Being guided by hearing from all relevant stakeholders (*really* hearing from *all* relevant stakeholders, including about things not going so well, as well as the things going well)
3. With clarity and confidence, knowing the answers	3. Revisiting previous conclusions, concepts and theories, including raising questions about both treasured new as well as long-held ones
4. Producing 'world's best practice', 'delivering the goods', being 'up to it'	4. Producing 'better practice' (quite often), as well as finding new errors needing correcting, while 'generating good insights' that enable further sustainability, and sometimes failing to achieve any of this
5. Problem solving quickly and efficiently and with great certainty	5. Problem posing, sometimes with difficulty and requiring time to reflect more deeply; waiting patiently for perspective and new creative understandings to emerge, and better ways of doing and being to eventually be discerned out of a place of uncertainty
6. On the basis of gold-standard scientific cause–effect evidence	6. On the basis of a rich mixture of ever-changing observations and experiences, trial and error, all woven together to bring clarity to an overall contextual narrative of rhythmic cyclic movement back and forth between order and chaos, complexity and elegant simplicity
7. Meeting goals, achieving clear measurable outcomes, getting the rewards, ticking things off	7. Continuing to explore and experiment with potentially better, but untried and rather obscure ways forward, monitoring and revisiting the full cycle of inquiry over and again until clarity emerges
8. And quickly 'going forward' and 'moving on' to the next 'challenge'	8. Experiencing life as a work-in-progress, sometimes slow, sometimes rapid, sometimes timely, sometimes timeless, sometimes episodic, sometimes more like 'flow', all with a past, present and a future
9. All the while 'looking good', being competent and enjoying life 'to the max'	9. All the while sometimes looking clear and content, sometimes looking puzzled or pained, but able to appreciatively celebrate or accurately mourn, and know that both are inevitable
10. To go on doing more of the same	10. To learn in order to know what to do differently next

the kitchen while snatching a cup of coffee, and a conclusion is drawn in the middle of a sleepless night or in the split second before heading into a meeting to implement the next action. And even if monitoring comprises masses of statistical collections that end up rating little more than a glance…so far.

Caught between glimpses of the evidence that all is well and all is not well, and a resulting sense of confidence and impotence, yet with few opportunities to resolve these splits, many of us are both overloaded and flat out (with our metaphoric foot hard down on the accelerator) *and* paralysed, even mute at a deeper level (with our metaphoric brakes on). At the same time. Or we just keep trying to manage, to 'get through it all', perhaps having enough of a good time, or perhaps until the proverbial last straw of an organisation stuck on endless-production-of-outputs breaks our very tired camel's back. And something goes awfully wrong. Maybe someone gets hurt. Or sick. Or dies. Or many do.

Then we stand around a little bewildered. 'How did things get so bad?', we ask each other. 'Why didn't anyone *say* something?' 'How did we not see that coming?' 'Why didn't we *do* something sooner?'

The plaintive cry 'But we haven't got time' (to think about what we are doing?—maybe we haven't got time *not* to!), or the heartfelt question 'Why didn't they *say* something?' (Why didn't we?—or you, or I? What held us back?) demands our attention as to why sufficient essential feedback does *not* get into a system soon enough. Why is there not *enough* feedback? And

from the right people? Were the questions even asked? Why was the feedback inaudible, instead of in a form that could best be heard? Why, even with routine customer feedback and complaints mechanisms, do messages still not get sent, heard and responded to? Why do they sometimes, even quite often, get actively rejected, denied or minimised? Why did we stop giving out feedback forms? Why do we implement numerous 'quick fixes' instead of getting to the underlying problems? Or why, when major new breakthroughs *do* take place, is it seemingly so difficult to have them accepted and adopted? Why are there so many sacrificial lambs, dead 'canaries in the mine' and 'messengers shot' before valuable truths can be accepted? And when they finally do get acted on, why does their initial authentic purpose seem to get lost so quickly in the slippage to utilitarian pragmatism and the vagaries of goal displacement?

For decades three stories have been endlessly repeated: one about the stream of ambulances at the bottom of the cliff instead of the effort going into building fences at the top; one about the numerous dead bodies coming down the river but all we do is build more impressive services for fishing them out rather then going upstream to find out why they are dying; and one about giving the man a fish versus the value of teaching him how to fish for himself. All these stories are attempts to move us from our repeated tendency to *only* go for the short-term quick fix, and to strengthen our respect for deeper reflection on our experience and observation of evidence that might offer to *transform* the situation with a new and more deeply systemic solution.

Why does every new generation have to keep telling these stories of more complex 'bigger picture' causation, with different consequences for action? Are we 'getting it' yet?

Perhaps our current ways of researching and evaluating are not entirely ensuring we are getting to hear about and address issues so well after all. The frequent resort to expert top-down decision making may not be working in practice when so many seem unprepared to implement or act even on this well-credentialled advice. Somehow our systems seem too often unwieldy, short-sighted, rigid and reactive, clogged, and paradoxically all too quick to abandon effort for another ready solution in the face of impending chaos, forgetting what is already known. Or needlessly 'rediscovering the wheel'. Or brought to an awful halt, overwhelmed with a sense of helplessness. Till needed change just seems 'too hard'. Again. And professionals take refuge in more and more attractive high-security compounds for themselves.

A deeply new approach seems overdue.

A different kind of book

Amidst all this, why would anyone want to write a book about the joys of doing *more* research and evaluation? And 'building it in' ever more deeply and regularly to make a better world?! Who would want to read it?! ('Don't give me another thing to have to do', 'What's the problem?', 'We've moved on from all of that', 'We're managing OK'). And who would have *time* to read another book anyway? Especially when reading's not enough like work, *at* work. But *too* much like work, at home!

Yet research and evaluation, for better and worse, remain the major ways by which we expect to get reliable and comprehensive feedback about the nature of our world and work out what is going on and what to do differently (or better).

Without changing our patterns of thought we will not be able to solve the problems we created with our current pattern of thought
ALBERT EINSTEIN
(Quoted in Ackoff 2004)

In this book I want to propose a new way of thinking about research and evaluation, beyond our current frames of thinking—and especially extending more deeply to include small 'r' research, small 'e' evaluation, and continuous learning and adapting from feedback—as *the* way our species learns about itself (in relation to its environment), generates knowledge and works out what to do next. Especially when things are troubling us. Or we do not agree. Or we just do not know. But also when we are attracted to something else, or to something that is going well, or that is different and interests us. I will try and convey how this may be seen as a process of inquiry that reverberates back and forth between the very small and the very large, continuously. Not just in timescales of capital 'R' and 'E' research and evaluation in more depth or elaboration over timescales of months or years. Or medium 'r' and 'e' inquiry in more detail over weeks or months. But also in weeks, days and hours, and minutes and even in split seconds.

That is, these processes we grace with the names 'research' or 'evaluation' can be seen as following the same logic and sequence that they do when they are 'writ large' as when they are 'writ small' in the minutiae of our everyday lives. Indeed, perhaps rather ironically, unless someone, somewhere, actually *does* stop 'doing action', and *notices* something, raises a question and then goes in search of an answer, nothing much changes by purposeful intention, whether consciously or not.

To illuminate this, I cross some disciplinary boundaries to bring together four key domains:[7]
• living systems (ecology)
• research as inquiry (epistemology)
• by individuals (psychology), and
• by organised human collectivities (sociology).

To illuminate the integration of each of these domains, throughout the book I use the language and visual references of 'cycles' and 'corresponding sequences' of questions as a way of thinking about the *dynamic processes* of inquiry, and the metaphor of the house and its components as a way of thinking about the *'structuring'* or *building in* of a range of corresponding inquiry methods and methodologies. Sometimes these two aspects may be sketched more clearly than they actually are in practice to make them visible, however they remain conceptual, complex, fluid and not essentially determinate.

I use the term 'systemicity' to try and capture—in much the same way as Anthony Giddens (1976) used the term 'structuration' in an earlier era—to join these two aspects into a whole, a 'living integrality'. I particularly look at the diversity of individual and collective actor-participants' inquiry preferences, propensities and capabilities that assist, at whatever systemic scale or moment of the cycle, self-organising for life.

This integrated 'mental architecture' is the key to what I hope to offer in this book in order to understand better how we do or do not achieve the conditions for living systems. As such, it is a way—a device—for thinking about the sequence of life-becoming-itself. It is a 'best invention' for how I now think about being able to 'map, model, mirror, and detect a directional compass' (2001) in relation to the greater fields of systemicity (physical, social, political and economic) in which we find ourselves locally and globally.

In this way the mental architecture or theory of integral living systemicities as seeking–inquiring in a cyclic fashion, may be seen in its own terms, simultaneously, as:
• *A descriptive mapping* (based on observation)—while remembering 'the map is not the territory', and no observation comes without interpretation

- *A working model* (for planning)—while realising the model-maker (the observer) is the inventor and theorist of the model of the observed
- *An explanatory metaphor* (from reflection)—while remembering we know and understand the meaning of the worlds we map and model by the metaphors and other linking devices we select or create, and
- *A guide to life* (for action)—while noting that our maps, models and metaphors are always constructed from perspectives, and these derive from social, cultural and embodied value-driven hopes, purposes or intentions.

In its own terms therefore, what is on offer here is a way of thinking, a conceptual and theoretical resource that is necessarily now and always remains a continuing work-in-progress. Its use will always depend on the lens used: whether by 'individual' observer, theorist, planner or practitioner, or a collectivity of people in groups or organisations who together observe, reflect, plan and act in the various phases of their own complex individual and jointly lived lives. There are temptations to forget this is a construction of my (and our collective) mind—especially when it seems to most compellingly describe 'a real world out there'. I hope to use various devices to remind us that it is a creation of a particular time-space-place-situated human mind or 'cognitive neural network' (as is this way of describing it!) And that it is this 'situated systemicity' that gives it its relative use, truth, value and meaning, even if this appears stable over a long period of time in many different field environments.

What gives life?

Why can't we create a world which is more on the side of routinely 'giving life'?

But what would a more life-giving system look like?

After considering how we got to this paradoxical spot after more than thirty years of research and evaluation effort (Chapter 1—Some introductory foundations for building on), it seems a very good place to start would be by stopping, stepping back and getting a bit of perspective on what kind of 'system' might indeed be more life-giving than the one we have now (Chapter 2—Living systems). In an uncannily timely manner, a

whole new way of thinking about the world and the properties of living systems appears to be emerging or 'called forth' from many different directions. Although still dimly perceived by many, some of it, ironically, reflects some very ancient wisdom, now converging with some breath-taking new knowledge from physics, biology, mathematics, engineering, psychology and sociology in a transdisciplinary picture that may promise to give not just hitherto elites but all of us a whole new way of thinking about 'how we can be with each other' and our worlds.

A way of being-and-doing that is more perennially alive, lively and *life-giving*—more full of promise, more reliable and more satisfying than our current ways. Indeed having the characteristics of 'life' itself. What a good idea!

And what would a more life-enhancing system of research and evaluation look like?

By taking a magnifying glass to 'the system', we begin to detect a vast web of energised micro-interactions *between us* (and everything else): including all the daily familiar highly interpersonal and environmental inquiry interactions—what we notice, pick up on, see and hear and say to each other, all our inner and outer conversations to make sense of it all, how we feel, what we conclude from our experiences, what we remember, what we think and don't think, what we know, believe, value, expect and not expect, what we speak up about, and what we remain silent about, how we draw conclusions and reach new ones, and then calculate, decide, plan and try out the new implications: what we actually do next, and where we go, who with and why.

It is in *these* busy buzzing micro-inquiry actions that may be seen slowly, over time, to build up to comprise more (or less) viable exchanges and patterns for achieving our various desires or purposes—or not. Indeed 'the system' appears to turn out, in important ways, to comprise what seems like the highly 'individual and personal' in the here and now—but which gets *writ larger* and constituted as the patterns of social activities of groups, organisations and 'the collective'. And these in turn get *writ larger still* as communities, institutions, societies, international 'globalities', epochs, the cosmos and history.[8] Gazing from a distance at the staggering bee-swarms of earthly humanity, we can consider the prospects for us getting enough insight into ourselves and others to 'build'—within the micro-relations of the human bee-swarm—sufficient critical mass for more systemic mutual 'intelligence', wisdom and better directions. Or not.

I then look at research and evaluation, its methodologies, designs and techniques (Chapter 3—Inquiry cycles of research, evaluation and improvement) in this new way, using the metaphor of the house as a way of looking at how they might better be built in to contribute to and reflect a more comprehensive life-giving system. I note particularly how we all have all the capacities necessary for life-giving inquiry—in regard to how we take in information, process it and act on it—but that most of us show preferences for some rather than others of these capabilities, particularly where the systemic scale is larger. Overall, the human species seems to have the potential to cover the 'whole territory' in order to remain in less turbulent dynamic balance. But why don't we always practise all capabilities in a more integrated and balanced way, as we could?

What is at the heart of really human services, and really human research and evaluation?

The question now moves (Chapter 4—More truly living human services) from how we inquire to why—and the 'For who or for what?' that drives, or is intended to drive, all this inquiry—and why things could ever go wrong. And what a living systems approach might have to say about how research and evaluation can assist these human service purposes, in this instance, of responding or caring. How is a living human system responsive? How does it 'take care'? And why then would it ever do harm? How do we lose our way? How do we end up displacing our goals from care to not-care? How do we move from responding in order to preserve and nurture life, to damaging and denying life? And how do we reverse or counter this unwanted systemic tendency? How might we more routinely resource the life of each, each other and all?

What do organisations that have 'built in' research and evaluation look like?

Finally I describe ten examples of people and organisations who have worked to build in cultures of more or less effective everyday research and evaluation in order that they might become more truly living systems, able to respond with life-enhancing purposes (Chapter 5—Exemplars of 'building in' inquiry for living human service systems). I draw out from these ten exemplars and more than twenty years of their experience, the conditions that seem to have maintained more 'hale and hearty' human individual, group and organisational systems, ones which can recover more quickly from When Things Go Wrong.

I end with some concluding words (Chapter 6) and an Annotated bibliography of concepts and methods related to living systems research and evaluation and related concepts that might throw further light on the various ideas in this book. (These are available on a website from 2011.)

Finally, the thinking in this book claims a much wider sphere of relevance than just the world of human services' research, evaluation and continuous quality improvement. Its concerns and ideas go beyond those of services such as health, housing, education, community, recreation and welfare to how to contribute to a more life-giving world in general. These wider domains include all other service industries and areas of human endeavour—productive and sustainable economies, collective decision-making politics, hospitality, entertainment, the arts, architecture, information technology, engineering, law, business, design, management, agriculture, developing countries and the natural, grown or built environments. In doing so it also goes beyond the narrow professional areas of research and evaluation and continuous organisational improvement to *all* effective human inquiry and feedback systems as such.

All these comprise a much wider view of humankind's ability, potentially, to build in better inquiry and feedback processes throughout its large living human systemicities, with a vision of doing so in aid of more viable 'being, doing and becoming', including by all living beings. I think the need is now urgent if we, in sufficient critical mass, are to crack the puzzle of our paradoxical species, and for the contemporary iteration, not take our place as yet another collapsed civilisation, ecosphere or worse.

YOLAND WADSWORTH
Melbourne
Written between 1 January 2000 and 28 May 2010

ENDNOTES

1 For example originally this was to be a quadrella not a trilogy. The planned third of the four books: *Getting It Right—Doing Community Needs Assessments* was to be for communities of interest trying to build arrangements to meet needs from their own grounded autoethnographies. It was aborted after weary years of trying to get funds (see Wadsworth 1992 for some of the early thinking for this book). At the time, 'demand management' insisted not on critically referencing 'people's needs', but on provider-referenced 'service outcomes'. Ironically 'community capacity building' subsequently became popular as eyes turned again to the critical reference communities, and grants flowed for a time. Unfortunately the highly prescriptive funding guidelines did not prioritise books to help communities to research and evaluate how to build their own capacity! In a dry irony, the post-implementation evaluation of the Federal Government's flagship community building program found that it would have been enhanced if it had used participatory action research from the outset (Szirom 2005).

2 I would however like to acknowledge Rhonda Galbally, Teresa Zolnierkiewicz of the ANZ Charitable Trust, and Marlene McFarlane of Perpetual Trustees for their support and foresight about the need to establish an Action Research Program in a university setting.

3 Here also lies some explanation for my uncharacteristically liberal use of dictionary definitions. I am making use of them as common and accessible definitions in a way that recognises that their congealed meanings have been constructed and replicated over extremely long periods of time, thus mitigating, to some extent, their origins in the work of only particular groups of elite thinkers. Wikipedia now offers an even faster and more widely autopoetic approach (self-management that has been timed at seven minutes for average correction of errors) to the task, using relatively widely democratised input and feedback from a greater range of people, and simultaneously offering a valuable and healthy challenge to intellectuals to engage, explicate, defend and account for their offerings.

4 Contact: living.systems.research@gmail.com

5 Although there are now many new and exciting methods enabling this kind of inquiry to take place (for example, Open Space Technology, Cafes of Possibilities, Deliberative Polling).

6 Here I am using a definition of stress as: a state of mind ('mind' as embodied whole being) experienced as a result of 'systemic relationality' that exerts excessive pressure or crisis (such as conflicting demands, events, activities, situations, conditions or expectations) that block, prevent or frustrate the achievement of the human or other living organisms' desired, intended, needed or wanted ways of doing-and-being, expressed as embodied values, hopes, purposes, envisioned ends, mission, goals, aims, objectives, or tasks.

7 Four key summary papers have been published in advance of this book for each of these four disciplinary domains: *systems*, 'Systemic human relations in dynamic equilibrium' (Wadsworth 2008a); *epistemology* 'Researching for Living Systems' (Wadsworth 2008c); *psychology*, 'What's a Nice Sociologist like Me Doing Using a Psychological Instrument?—Integrating the MBTI®'s 16 Energy Systems with Cyclic Models of Action Research' (Wadsworth 2006a); and *sociology*, 'Is it Safe to Talk about Systems Again Yet? (Wadsworth 2005, 2008b)

8 This book was initially drafted prior to the attacks on the World Trade Centre in New York and military defence buildings in Washington in the United States on 11 September 2001. In the wake of these events and the violence that both preceded them and the escalating violence that followed, this discussion of the social fabric and people's capacity to observe, explain, understand and better act to create the conditions for life is ever more pointed.

Is everything now going so much better

Some introductory foundations for building on

The world seems awash with books and journals on research, evaluation and continuous quality improvement![1]

We are now so much more familiar with inquiry methods from the numerous specialised books on interviews, focus groups, surveys, case studies, randomised controlled experimental trials, in-depth qualitative cultural studies, feedback sheets, ethnographies and the burgeoning swag of newer constructivist methods such as appreciative inquiry, narrative, autoethnography and experiential dialogue. There seems now to be extensive and (mostly) meticulous presentation of research, monitoring and evaluation findings in numerous reports, books and journal articles. Streams of industrious activity seem to flow into a veritable torrent, funded by unprecedented numbers of research grants, evaluation and government reviews and consultancies costing millions of dollars every year: the most extensive budgets ever lavished on legions of highly qualified and credentialled specialist research and evaluation practitioners and academics—with the results consumed (or not) by the ever-burgeoning numbers of human services industry professionals, all seeking the latest evidence for effective practice. The demands seem only to be for more, then more again.

This veritable sea of commissioned and academic research, evaluation and continuous monitoring has flooded through bureaucracies everywhere until not only research and evaluation professionals but also large numbers of ordinary members of services and programs—social workers, teachers, police officers, farmers, IT personnel and managers—seem to be caught up in record-keeping and data collection, sometimes on an all too regular basis. Children are doing it in schools, young people are doing it online, and in one study even babies were described as participants! Even the prime minister of Australia had his cabinet doing participant observation in schools, homeless shelters and Aboriginal communities and consultative dialogue at Community Cabinet meetings within weeks of being elected—and in his inaugural address the new president of the United States referred not only to the value of science, indicators, data and statistics, but also to the less measurable but profound feelings of a nation, and the question of 'what works' for the common good.

So, can we ask, is everything now going so much better? Is all this work being read, discussed, absorbed, understood and used? Is everyone feeling

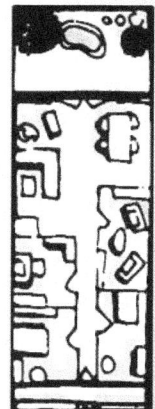

better informed and new practice wisdom the result? Have all the participating stakeholders and 'subjects' felt really heard and understood? Do they all now see the right and obvious conclusions to draw and thing to do? Are they going ahead in effective implementation? Has our understanding of the impact of our actions on ourselves and others changed as a result, and are we now effortlessly responding on the basis of our accurate new insights? Have vicious cycles become virtuous cycles as all the good research and evaluation smoothly becomes good policy, which smoothly becomes good practice? Are people cheering as their lives measurably change for the good as a result? Is there a closing of the gap between rich and poor? Real inclusion of the excluded? Have there ceased being such glaring human service issues, gaps and unmet needs? Hmm! Yes and no? Not quite? Depends? We like to think so, but maybe a bit patchy? Maybe quite patchy? Perhaps not changed at all?

And did anyone notice how we just spent the 1970s and 1980s researching and developing a whole new range of essential human services in response to meticulously identified new needs only to see them get thoroughly defunded and dismantled in the 1980s and 1990s? And are we now spending further decades painstakingly researching and evaluating permanently constrained service practice, where small portions of 'service' are allocated to highly selected population segments who must meet ever more restrictive criteria to qualify for help? Will we have to wait years more for the evaluations before we respond to the damaged generation of the decades of lost services? But truly, with all that original costly research and development, how *did* we end up with hospitals all over the advanced wealthy Western world with floors that did not get cleaned often enough and staff who use gloved fingers in open surgery because costly single-use instruments have been locked away to keep budgets down? How *did* young people get to go through twenty-seven foster care placements—now to reappear in new research studies as part of the homeless, drug dependent and mentally ill? Why do elderly people ever, anywhere, sit sedated and distressed in understaffed nursing homes? And why might so many staff be steeling themselves today under the strain of too much to do in too little time with too few resources for just too many troubled clients, patients, students, young people, older people or local community residents—who themselves are

caught in varying vortices of 'the system'? Systems not of their own choosing, and which seem inexorably to default to 'type', all too often, yet again, leaving out the human element or eliminating the discretion to respond with kindness to people's situations, rather than requiring them always to fit in with 'the rules'?

And how *could* all this have taken place at the peak of the eras of research, evaluation and total quality management?

Do we just need lots more specialised professional research and evaluation projects, and to gather lots more data, statistics, evidence, observations and measurement? And write lots more policies, protocols, procedures and performance improvement schedules, and more researchers and evaluators competing for more grants to produce more findings for more books and journals? Or, like the fat man at the pie-eating contest, are we risking feeding more of the same to a 'body politic' that is really suffering from something else altogether missing? Are we becoming something of a Tower of Babel with all the existing efforts clamouring without altering the patterns of injustice, exclusion, short-sighted reactivity and lack of compassion? Again the thought comes to mind that without changing our patterns of thinking we will not be able to solve the problems we created with our existing pattern of thinking in the first place (Einstein in Ackoff 2004).

Might it be worth asking then whether there could be a new and different way altogether of going about things? An approach that isn't quite so heavily dependent on such a strict division of labour in which most people are busy in action but only a very few get to observe, reflect and plan new actions that then seem so difficult to implement in new practice. Might it be that relying only on the very special skilled professional research and evaluation efforts by a scarce few—while leaving everyone else to go on repeating existing practice unquestioningly—supplies a clue to why there is such a lack of social and political will for change? Or that while waiting for careful, detailed, new evidence-based best practice from overseas, things have changed in the here and now, or things work for some but don't offer specific guidance as to whether *this* person in front of me this morning is one of the percentage for which it was found to be best practice, or not. Or that programs that have 'never been evaluated' might in practice have been closely observed by their staff and consumers since their inception...

Could more be made of what everyone has been seeing—rather than missing out on building in their insights? Perhaps new communities have migrated into an area and a local Mother and Child Health Nurse has been the first to notice; she has already developed some insightful hunches about what might be needed from her numerous conversations with them (long before the census picks up the change)—but how can she be resourced to take it further? Or there is the art gallery attendant who knows from years of overheard conversations which paintings attract the most attention and why, but the Gallery Board awaits the findings of a market research company who random-digit dials householders with questions that don't ever get to this level of detailed knowledge? Or a new CEO starts a visioning exercise for the next three years without finding out firstly people's experience of what has gone before. A new manager starts a restructure based on her experience in a previous organisation only to come up against an organisational culture that is different from that prior experience. Or staff meet to discuss what consumers need without consumers present. Or consumers want to give feedback and new ideas but have no routine way of getting it into 'the system' without offending hard-working professional staff. Or when their input is sought it is to 'add value' to staff's work—rather than staff's work being seen as arising out of and responding to consumers" input.

Of course new approaches do not arise perfectly like a lotus from the muddy waters. Mostly they have been quietly forming over a long period of time under the surface, fed by rich detritus that has been drawn from previous activity. So let's take a moment from our busy doing and reflect on the last thirty years of historically contextualised research and evaluation activity to see if we can detect the shape of new foundations for a possible better future.

> *Muddy water, let stand, become clear.*
> LAO TZU, 4TH CENTURY[2]

Sometimes it is only by getting some distance from a situation that it begins to be possible to really 'see' it—or see something new, or a new shape in it. For example, we'd lived on earth for millennia, looking up and out until, for the first time, we saw photos *of* the earth from space. We saw it from a radically different perspective that situated us not just as an 'us' but as an 'us looking back at us'. This book is reaching for just such a new way of seeing—a new 'mental architecture' to 'scaffold' us to a different view of ourselves and each other.

Three eras of human inquiry: from research to evaluation to continuous quality improvement

With hindsight I think it is possible to look back over the past three decades and perhaps helpfully distinguish three different eras: an era of research; then one of evaluation; then one of organisational quality improvement. At the time, they rather overlapped or merged into each other as we hurried to keep up with the rapid changes in language, purposes and priorities reflecting the changes in the wider economic and social 'body politic'. But now, stepping back to get a wider perspective, they might be seen as a *succession* of attempts to grapple with the really big themes in modern life in the last 100 years: the growing concentrations of large numbers of people in urban and suburban settings (in turn a response to change from agricultural–rural to machine–industrial to service–electronic information economies increasingly remote from the natural environments on which they nevertheless remain entirely dependent) and the challenges of human organisation to meet the diverse needs of such a complex 'body corporate'.

A 1970s–1980s 'spring' of research

After the post-war period, in a way the 1970s were a kind of a 'new spring' era of research devoted to examining the changing contexts arising in major industrialising and post-colonial Western societies. Detailed and relatively lengthy social science studies documented new conditions applying across city, suburbanising and rural settings (changes to demographics, parameters, contributing factors, the nature of impacts etc. etc.)[3]

It soon became clear it wasn't enough to only research 'objectively' by means of distanced questionnaire surveys and abstracted statistical analyses. The pressing need was for more 'up close and personal' in-depth qualitative and community-based research to gain new insight from contextualised 'rich, thick description' (Geertz 1973, Denzin 2002, Denzin and Lincoln 2003) and grounded interpretations about how people *actually* worked and lived their lives, and what new services were required to help them meet their new needs and purposes.

A 1980s–1990s 'summer' of evaluation

Yet by the 1980s it wasn't enough for research to only describe the new situations, or what people needed, or even what the new kind of services could look like. Now, as the nascent services funded by unprecedented amounts of government money 'hit the ground', the push was on to address questions of value and priorities—traditionally off limits for social science researchers, who rapidly morphed into (or were joined by) a new creature—'the evaluator'. Firstly, questions were being asked by those already on the ground about how best to shape practical, detailed implementation of the new services to achieve often still emerging purposes; and secondly, by those more remote from local practice, who were wanting to observe what was working and what wasn't (and to see if they'd 'got it right'). While *evaluation* drew initially on the same traditional methods as research,[4] it was taking the next step beyond describing social contexts to assist in the making of value judgements and decisions about 'issues' and 'problems' that in turn required active engagement with 'stakeholders' (rather than merely observing or questioning 'subjects')—integrating 'empirical evidence with standards and values to reach evaluative conclusions' and opening the way to embracing novel methods, including empowerment (Weiss 2005). Evaluation quickly moved to dominance, asking during program or service formation what was wanted (prospectively valued), and afterwards whether any of all this new effort was indeed (retrospectively) of 'value, merit, worth or significance'[5] to the critical stakeholders.

Services meanwhile were growing in number and kind until it seemed to 'those at the top' that the need for them was insatiable[6] and worried economic masters reached for the razor. In the context of a late 1980s economic recession, evaluation, secondly (and simultaneously), began to straddle somewhat painfully both the objectives of top-down audit review (sometimes aiding harsh or premature pruning, or justifying holding professional gains) and those of bottom-up developmental inquiry (still trying to encourage and nurture the tender new green shoots of responsive innovations).

A 1990s–2000s 'endless autumn' of continuous quality improvement policies

By the 1990s the new messages were registering throughout 'the system' that after-the-event evaluation was often too late. It wasn't enough for the pioneer short-term project-based approaches to be proved 'rationally' either worthy of continuing or superfluous to requirements and 'for the chop' (sometimes regardless of an otherwise favourable evaluation). The pain and carnage of uprooting or cutting new supports that had begun to be offered to clients and communities, or facing the defensive reactions of newly established large service programs, were proving insurmountable—not to mention the technical problems of evaluation trying to find out 'the truth' under such circumstances, or risk the disruption and demoralisation of 'the evaluated' who felt under the microscopes and magnifying glasses of others. People swiftly became adept at adjusting their goals to be reachable rather than desirable or necessary. The idea began to grow that it might be preferable instead to organise the development of more *self-correcting* responses to ensure quality *as you went along*, instead of waiting till 'the end' of a funded time period. Continuous refining until 'optimal 100 per cent world's best practice' could then be achieved permanently was the new promise. Although 'more for less' was perhaps the in-reality slogan.

So 'spring' moved into the heat of full 'summer' production, and seemingly endless 'autumn' harvest. No wonder everyone began to get a little tired! On the model of mechanised commercial industry, the demand became incessant for more 'outputs and outcomes' with fewer inputs, and of more tightly prescribed and controlled resources, time and people; and, most importantly, with less grounded developmental research to 'get it right' before 'rolling it out'. Suddenly it seemed easier for central authorities and funders to shift the risk and outsource services altogether, retaining only the task of producing policies, guidelines, frameworks, models, manuals and contracts to oversee someone else trying to do all that 'more for less'. In one fell swoop the body corporate had split and distanced itself into three parts, making new insulated boundaries and creating a new division of labour. Now there were new kinds of professionals: planners, project managers and policy officers centrally; directors, co-ordinators and administrators of programs regionally; and directly delivered services with their professional practitioners and service users locally. Plus there was a legion of research and evaluation consultants (and increasingly academic ones) to give much-needed certainty through the legitimising force of science. Now the plans and policies themselves became the 'products and services', and the hitherto 'projects' became externally contracted services 'out there' in 'the regions' or 'NGO (non-government organisation) land', with the researchers and evaluators elsewhere again certifying it all as evidence based with scientific certainty. Now there was a new challenge for research and evaluation—to try and bridge these growing gaps, communicate across the new boundaries and disconnects, and bring news of services and the community into the central policy bureaucracy.

In a way research and evaluation and continuous quality studies had themselves become like 'products' too. Indeed, like the fat man's pies, they were often being purchased and consumed without ever really being properly digested. With more time it might have been possible to extract more nutritional value from them. After all, detailed and elaborate research and evaluation reports take such a lot of time and effort for researchers and evaluators to produce—but who had the time for that? Some of course were received with eager anticipation and systematically enacted. But it was the fate of many to be read properly by only a handful of people. Then sometimes one reader might object to several paragraphs. Two think it OK. Then it

© S. Kneebone & Y. Wadsworth 2010

might never see the light of day again. Or an executive summary was glanced at, and yes, it conveyed what was already thought, or confirmed 'the message' that was wanted. Or, even if it didn't, it may have 'done its job' anyway and soon sunk from view and out of corporate memory. Chances are that some of that handful of readers would move on to other jobs soon anyway, resulting in even more loss of effort. And that's of course if the commercial-in-confidence clauses didn't prevent the research or evaluation being circulated to the relevant interested stakeholders in the first place! More recently the issues resulting from systemic distancing have proliferated.[7]

A closer look at the last three decades of human services research and evaluation

The accompanying Table 2 summarises my way of thinking about the past three decades. In each there was a distinctive *favouring* of a particular approach—in turn reflecting that decade's wider social, economic and political contexts. Each also exhibited a distinctive way of assisting the processes of giving 'service to humans' at the same time as experiencing all the corresponding pressures against this.

It is important to notice that each of these decades or eras did not *replace* the previously favoured approach but often 'consumed' or 'digested' it, assimilating it more or less into the next. Thus evaluation did not supplant or supersede research but continued to draw on its methods and logic. Research and evaluation weren't superseded by learning organisations and continuous quality improvement, rather critical lessons, concepts and techniques were absorbed from them. Indeed, all three continue to co-

exist now, as they have throughout more than three decades, and all three will continue to co-exist in any comprehensive inquiring system—just as the fourth era on which this book focuses—that of whole or intermeshed 'living systems' of inquiry—also incorporates elements from all previous approaches while in important ways also offering to unite and integrate them, not in a merely additive fashion but through a new understanding of the parts played by *all* for the purposes of building and sustaining living human systems.

Each new focus has thus attempted to address matters unresolved in the previous era. For example while *research* was still arguing over whether listening to people's words, stories and meanings was sufficiently value-free for them to be treated unproblematically as objective facts and figures (the great quantitative versus qualitative 'paradigm wars'), it was *evaluation* that quickly saw the necessity and possibility of value-driven purposeful and intersubjective inquiry. With a clearer practical mandate to pursue values-based improvement, evaluation was also able to forge ahead more effortlessly from routinely 'just looking at problems' or 'studying down'[8] while ignoring the questions 'For whom? For what?' It also was able to move beyond post-modern academic debates about the relativism of people's perceptions and experiences to embrace diverse perspectives as a way of considering what abductive strategies might best achieve valued purposes. Of course this situated value-driven approach had always been present in social science (particularly in critical theory), but evaluation as a mainstream practice was more compelled, even required (and also more free) to focus on questions of

Trust us, we're evaluators!

value in a way that most conventional social science, including its post-modern forms, were largely unable to. This of course did not mean evaluation escaped any of the complex politics involved in questions of value held by various stakeholders! Some of its most characteristic methods involve negotiating these power differences in complex emergent evaluation designs and has led to increasing interest in action-oriented, participatory, collaborative and dialogic methods.

Indeed an important discussion in 2002 (on the international evaluation listserv) resulted in a summary of 'How to deliver negative evaluation results constructively', which uncannily resembled a constructivist or action research approach to many of the issues, typical also of thinking systemically. With its advice to constantly engage in a participatory approach with clients from the outset and for knowledge to emerge in dialogue with stakeholders, it has become a popularly downloaded document. (It is included in full in Appendix 1.)

Yet in a way, just as *research* had got stuck in its inability to move to inquire into the conditions for *better* practice or *improvement* in people's lives because of its claims to be 'unbiased', 'objective' and 'merely descriptive-explanatory' (which ironically ensured things did *not* change for the better but kept being replicated in the old forms—a rather value-laden and conserving position to choose if you think about it!), *evaluation* also never overcame the twin problems inherent in the idea that firstly, one party or group of parties observes and decides the value of another party's work and secondly, that this kind of evaluation primarily occurs *after* the action has been taken and has often become well instituted and enculturated, and thus may be well defended. In any case evaluation, in providing descriptive data about the existing situation, gives few leads on what might work better regarding the things identified as needing change unless recommendations have arisen from discussion among the stakeholding system members.

It took more recent changes in *organisational development* and *quality improvement* to leap-frog over the negativities of evaluation's potential for causing anxiety and single loops of 'shame and blame', as well as to address the problem of evaluative judgement coming too late after the event, and everyone being stuck with (or stuck with defending) existing situations.

As Jeffrey Pfeffer, Professor of Organisational Behaviour in the Stanford University Graduate School of Business, notes:

> If we have learned anything from the quality movement, it is that the cost of finding and fixing mistakes is greater than the cost of preventing them (2007:1).

In shifting the focus back to how services (and products) get designed, shaped and formed in the first place, with evaluative activity accompanying formation and implementation from the outset (even from when they are still just 'good ideas'), the business and management discourse had shifted rapidly towards the assumptions of continuous improvement, total quality management and various versions of action research designs such as the business feedback cycle (e.g. PDCA—Plan, Do, Check, Act[9]).

The organisational development (OD) movement's use of the positive concept of 'learning' within a 'culture of inquiry' meant an immediate freedom to consider people's emergent actions as situated in networks of energetic exchange, information flow and feedback.[10] 'Systemic puzzles', errors and blockages are, in this approach, more enthusiastically sought out, examined and replaced much earlier by more smooth-flowing adaptation or deeper generative solution seeking. Instead of seeing one thing, person, event or activity as 'the cause' of another problem, all 'causes' are seen as simultaneously interdependent effects, and all 'effects' also 'causes' *in a larger frame of reference*. In complex 'fabrics' or fields of 'causing–effecting' it only really makes sense to chart the specific complex strands from deeply engaged participant-observation and then navigate a path into the next, just as complex territory, also being closely observed.

In business the reasons are urgent and compelling ones of bottom lines and survival:

> Organisations must scan and analyse environmental turbulence, formulate appropriate strategic plans and implement these through a change management process. In short, the organisation must routinely learn and relearn about its environment...' (Henderson 1997: 99)

These messages have been slower coming to human services perhaps because of the persistence of more linear or single factor cause–effect thinking,[11] although the Victorian Auditor General's office spelled out as early as 2004 to a meeting of professional evaluators how complex causation is implicated in program evaluations (VicHealth 2004), and some areas of health service management are beginning to receive the messages in in-service training about 'complex systems thinking'.

In addition, even the continuous improvement approach was largely silent about where things didn't actually need change or improvement. In response to so much repeated denial of *any* need for change, practitioners of the approach found themselves stressing the need for *constant* change. And while this is technically true (every new action is a new action, even if the nanosecond spent on reflection indicates it should copy as precisely as possible exactly what was done before), it did give *carte blanche* to a legion of new 'onwards and upwards' growth-oriented managers to set aside everything that had been done before their arrival and replace it with 'all new bigger and better' whatevers. Defences may or may not be the same as blind defensiveness. Perhaps rather than 'continuous improvement', what is needed is regular evaluative inquiry to ask whether there are any issues arising, or whether something actually doesn't need 'improvement', possibly even for a long time.

Finally, thus a *living systems* approach may be a way of moving to resolve two persistent sticking points.

Firstly: the 'systems' tendency to block or defend against raising *any* regular questions about 'how things are', and to continue, often rather automatically, to risk an unexamined 'tyranny of performativity', or making only trivial or superficial adjustments rather than tackling deeper issues implicated in a 'bigger picture' (e.g. ever more refining of the precise costs and times that should be taken for particular medical procedures, but not ever asking, 'Should we still have hospitals?')

And secondly: the systemic tendency to block or gatekeep against trialling innovative ideas in new practice—even when well-grounded in empirical evidence and human experience—whether in the name of conserving a hard-won status quo ('we've always done it like this before', 'it's worked up till now', 'the powers that be won't agree') or in the name of sceptical science ('we will need more research', 'we can't be sure this intervention will have the effect expected', 'there is risk associated with the new').

To these traditional gate-keeping defences, a living systems approach can not only make important quick adaptive 'single loop' 'fixes' but also reach for deeper 'double loop' or 'triple loop' understanding and solutions (Argyris 1993) at the same time as effectively dissolving 'systems defences' by extending 'an invitation to inquire', to seek new understanding, insight and desired innovation in areas that the people *themselves* have been free to identify as worthy of attention, free of penalty.

Additionally it can offer the evidence of ideas having arisen from the contextual field in a kind of 'pre-trial', a field in which they can now be more formally trialled or on a larger scale. In turn this can demonstrate that the ideas are 'working so far' and that some of the problems have already been ironed out while still small-scale ('small actions, small errors'). Already the 'powers that be' are involved and enthusiastic because they've seen it work in early 'try out' practice. Finally, the stakeholders themselves are prepared to assume the risk of trialling what they themselves have come up with, and have researched and developed it to their own satisfaction.

There are of course many sticking points in getting new ideas into actual procedural practice, or cracking the puzzles and coming up with better ideas to try in the first place. But these two liminal moments of, firstly, noticing there is a problem in current practice and, secondly, gaining agreement to try out even a well-grounded new solution, seem particularly demanding for all of us, often requiring a deal of facilitation and 'midwifery' (to use Ron LaBonte's term, 1997: 27).

Thus more regular use of processes of small-scale inductive–deductive trial-and-error (and trial-and-success) builds theory abductively (Pierce after Aristotle 1903, Blaikie 2007, Wadsworth 2008a, Barton et al. 2009) for a more viable living system rather than focusing exclusively on after-the-event performance measurement, fault finding or error measurement, with its risks of leaving problems ignored or denied until they are too big or beyond actors' proximal control. Indeed a more 'built-in' early inquiry system has freed some from the need to look at negative discrepancies at all, with the appreciative inquiry and strengths-based approaches having taken off as people have realised that looking at positive discrepancies and building *on* them ('carrots'/desire), often provides a more energetic fast track than looking only at negative aspects and trying to build *away* from them ('sticks'/fear). Such values-, attraction- or desire-driven inquiry has the advantage of more immediately beginning work on building the new life-giving system, while rejection and fear can often lead to protective walls being built, and defensive or coercive reaction regarding the problematic status quo (that nevertheless will eventually require clarity of observation in order to ground the 'next new') that quickly shuts down truth sharing and honesty—a position much harder to 'come back from' given its own self-replicating, self-fulfilling tendencies.

The time is ripe for a new era of sustainability—an era in which *all* the earlier approaches: research, evaluation, organisational development and continuous quality improvement, can find their proper places in more integrated and ongoing cycles of emerging life inquiry practised not just by the few but by the many throughout whole 'intelligent living systems'.

Towards a fourth era: living systems

Perhaps, in seasonal terms, after the 'spring' of the 1970s and 'hot summer' of the 1980s (including a cost-cutting summer storm and 'downfall' in 1987), we had a rather exhausting depleting 'endless harvest' in the 1990s, producing ever greater quantities of outputs and outcomes with barely so much as a tea break. Maybe we feel a bit 'touched by the sun', perhaps a little burnt out, 'losing our cool' more easily. Running on empty. Urged ever onwards by visions of greater productivity, more and better outcomes, and the unending exciting promise of the 'the new'. Called to produce ever more detailed documentation, policies, procedures and communications, with torrents of email, social media, spam, SMS and mobile phone calls, all now receivable anytime anywhere; and the shops ever so 'helpfully' open 24 hours a day, seven days a week, 52 weeks a year, year after year without end. Are we perhaps feeling a little tired out, hardened and leathery? Longing for a cool 'sea change'…and to 'see change'? There does seem to be an alarming message of some sort in the phrase 'work–life balance'—as if work is now no longer actually part of life, and 'life' exists only in snatched moments around the non-life activity of work!

And just when we thought the cool finger of a 2000s 'autumn' would never come to relieve us, we hear that a 'climate change' is threatening ever higher temperatures. After the triumph of the economic 'dries' we now seem to have widespread drought.

At a global scale, and at *every* scale, it definitely seems time to pause and take a break and—rather than rushing into more 'quick fixes' and solutions, using the logic that got us into this, short-circuiting yet again full-cycle inquiry—we might take enough time out to have a much deeper think. Rake up the fallen leaves of tasks never done, turn them into compost and prepare the soils for some much needed new insight. And all the more timely if we harbour even the slightest inklings that perhaps all our busy daily labours may not be *entirely* world's best practice, with truly impressive outcomes absolutely 100 per cent all of the time...much less just part of a happy balanced active living–working human system in which all stakeholders feel satisfied and proud.

What, we wonder, has gone missing in the general maelstrom of franticness that has gradually overtaken us during recent years? Is this as good as it gets? As good as life can be?

Persisting issues
What we can see at the end of the three eras—of 1970s research, 1980s evaluation and the 1990s move to

More haste, less heed

continuous cycles of feedback and learning for quality improvement—is that *research* can still be rejected, misused, unused or irrelevant, damaging, ignored or just plain 'wide of the mark'. *Evaluation* can still be too judgemental or too uncritical, and stakeholders and participants may be in mute agreement or disagreement about its assumptions and conclusions, but have no

comeback. *Corporate learning* can still become sloganeering or 'groupthink', and management's decision making based on too distanced or too abstracted 'helicopter' information and analysis. The results may still not be widely circulated and discussed, the insights not well-enough grounded in the on-the-ground issues and realities of the people

---

TABLE 2. THREE ERAS OF HUMAN SERVICES INQUIRY

An Era of Research

Early 1970s to early 1980s
Questions, fieldwork, data, analysis, conclusions, findings, recommendations, models, designs, plans
Social indicators
Community development
Issues of power

What was happening in human services?

- End of long post-war economic boom
- Expansion, decentralisation
- New suburbs, new services, more services
- New community needs, more community needs
- Social Welfare to Community Welfare to Community Services[12]
- Universal services, input/needs-based funding—'more for more'
- A sense of 'us' vs. 'them', professionals vs. 'the people'
- Community development and feminist politics

An Era of Evaluation

Early 1980s to early 1990s
Mission, purposes, goals, aims, objectives, formative, summative, open inquiry, audit review
Performance indicators
Stakeholder inclusion
Issues of interests

- Recession, government cutbacks, 'Razor Gang', budgets in the red, economic rationalism, program budgeting
- Regionalisation, de-centralising managerialism
- Rearguard action at local level: defensive justification *and* extend development
- Containing demand, central departmental standardised data sets, quality assurance, service agreements
- Community Services and Health Services combined into Human Services
- Efficiency/effectiveness outputs-based funding—'more for less', 'user pays'
- Some of 'them' had become 'us', and some of 'us' had become 'them'
- Politics of identity, difference/distance and discourse

An Era of Continuous Quality Improvement

Early 1990s to early 2000s
Culture, principles, feedback sheets, organisational learning/development, process, QA/QI, dialogue, critical mass
Outcome indicators
Capacity building
Issues of discourse, difference and representation

- Budgets back in the black, but with continued cuts and strict monetary control
- Anticipation of increased cost blow-outs, corporate contractualism (purchaser–provider split), commercialisation, competitive tendering, privatisation, outsourcing, amalgamation, devolution, business-philanthropy-community 'Third Way', risk-management strategies
- 'Customer' focus, quality improvement, concentrating leadership
- Stakeholder requirements, pre-set outcomes, project control and deliverables
- Human services 'joined up' seamlessly with each other and with business and communities
- Outcomes measurement—'better for less' (or 'more and more, better and better, faster and faster—worser and worser!'), capture learnings from implementation reviews
- The 'us' and 'them' were now to be a collaborating 'we'
- Community-building partnerships

they are ostensibly for and about. Indeed the right people may have not been involved in framing the questions in the first place, and the outcomes may all too often be invisible, goal-displacing or never followed up.

We can still see many research, evaluation and improvement efforts that do not get very far. 'Numbers people' and 'words people' can still be working without knowing and appreciating each other's contributions sufficiently for active collaboration, or get 'sticky-taped together' in newly mandated 'mixed methods' approaches rather than truly integrated at an early stage of establishing the *purposes* of inquiry. We still know that the great riches of people's life-practice

What were researchers, evaluators and consultants doing?	What methods and techniques were being used?
• Being *messengers*—sent out to study and survey 'subjects', communities and services, to bring back 'the truth' in published reports. Moving from being 'independent objective scientific experts' to being community-based field researchers • Working with a lot of 'us 'and 'them' (haves vs. have-nots, old-style service providers vs. 'new class' professionals, community vs. department, researchers vs. researched etc.)	• Community needs and attitudinal questionnaire surveys, individual and group interviews • Critique of 'quantitative' *by* 'qualitative' • Service/program illuminative and formative evaluation, search conferences, brainstorming, Delphi technique, participant observation • In-house and field-based government researchers
• Being *go betweens*—going back and forth between different 'respondents', stakeholders, cross-fertilising material in more collaborative inquiries; attempting to ground indicators and objectives using qualitative and participatory processes, at the same time encouraging reflexivity for service improvement and objectivity for funders • Working with the growing realisation that among the 'they' were now some of 'us', and vice versa at the same time	• Data collection about service delivery, Management Information Systems, PIs, feedback sheets, QA, CIPP, cost-benefit analysis, FMIP, MBO, Goal Attainment Scaling • Trend to 'quantitative' *and* 'qualitative' (mixed methods) • Objectives-based summative evaluation and reporting • Individual private consultants
• Being *dinner party arrangers*—facilitating dialogue across difference/distance between 'participants', joint studies of current situations, strategic studies of alternative desired situations, mainstreaming of action research and action learning, process management; learning organisations, organisational development, continuous improvement, 5th generation evaluation; consumer research and evaluation, collaborative inquiry • Accommodating the even deeper realisation that 'we' are all multiples of 'us' *and* of our changing standpoints	• QI, TQM, CCT, customer satisfaction surveys, focus groups, empowerment and 4th generation (multi-stakeholder) evaluation, 360 degree reviews, action research and participatory research (e.g. PDCA in business), values audits, program logic • Management program reviews (commercial-in-confidence, unpublished), performance management • Quantitative *or/and* qualitative (paradigm wars declared over)—provided it was 'evidence-based' • Large commercial accountancy company consultancy and academic/industry 'partnerships' for evidence-based risk-managed implementation 'packages' that are 'rolled out' as standardised 'one size fits all'

Research without legs

© S. Kneebone & Y. Wadsworth 2010

knowledge and their situated perspectives that the system greatly needs are underused because conventional techniques don't detect them, and we have not yet built in the new kinds of times and spaces needed to address this. While weaker and less heard voices are increasingly being listened to, we know that stronger voices can still all too easily go on feeling compelled to assert their views and second guess others: especially when speaking for and about 'them' in professionally guarded places where 'they' are not yet admitted. And leaders are pressed to take on ever greater responsibilities on behalf of others in a vicious cycle whereby people lose confidence in their own thinking, leading to ever greater assumption of powers by more certain others, leading 'followers' to feel even less confident, and so on… Leadership becomes ever more about 'already knowing' what's best for everything and everyone, without seeking more input that would assist more collaboratively supported decision making. This creates another vicious cycle of increasing leaders' stress and vulnerability that may only be bolstered by appearing even more knowledgeable and 'in charge', leading to ever greater chances of not hearing vital input and misrepresenting the wisdom of the collectivity and losing its support. Meanwhile 'the led' go on being rendered ever more dependent and possibly hopeless/helpless, unable to get their vital messages through increasingly over-managed forms of organisation.

What would it take?
What would it take for 'whole systems' to be more actively integrated, distributed 'intelligent systems'? Not just a 'head' doing the thinking out of touch with the rest of the 'body corporate'—but for all to inquire more in concert, drawing on all 'organs', as a whole? For research that truly would 'have legs' (and body, mind, hands, heart and soul)…

What if there was more smoothly flowing feedback *throughout* a system—not just one-way but *two-way* (indeed *all* ways between all relevant parties); with more observant, grounded, pulse-feeling inquiry by all parties; who were asking the right questions at the right time and in the right places, and then getting the answers into circulation in an organised and iterative dialogue about evidence and its meanings; moving from everyone understanding more accurately 'what is' and retrospectively 'has been', to researching and prospectively evaluating more deeply 'what could be' as well? And what if, when these hard-won new formulations emerged, they were already beginning to be embraced and trialled because they had come from the whole intelligent system, and were enabled to go on being tried out, corrected, discarded, refined and extended in continued, closely observed, engaged, complex real-life practice? And what if these processes and cycles were repeated? Not just as one-offs, but regularly planned for? Built in.

The 2000s—a winter reflection on hybridisation

By the 2000s we seemed to be facing a further paradox. On the one hand with ever greater attention to 'risk management' and legalistic requirements for ever more detailed specification, proceduralisation and recording, there has been the attraction of returning to the safety and apparent certainty of statistical evidence-based one-size-fits-all packages of log-framed, best practice, 'scientific' commercially patented knowledge. However the evidence-based randomised control trial agenda is driven by large complex pieces of research which clients are finding may rarely be delivered on time, and come with limitations and conditions from academics who are both working at a distance from real-life utility and unable to take enough time to increase the level of certainty being requested (often to a standard that would stand up to challenge in court). Meanwhile service and program teams are wanting to know if they are 'making a difference' but feel they must await the security of such large academic studies. Yet both they and managers need to make decisions in the here and now—fuelling a simultaneous search for more pragmatic and grounded methods such as 'performance stories' and DIY program logic. The engagement with academe regarding this kind of risk-management evidence-based practice has, perhaps, most recently been somewhat supplanted by a return to the big accountancy consultancy companies or favoured sole or small group operators who have the resources (and academic connections) to do more pragmatic meta-analyses of the literature. At the same time there is now more widespread understanding that diversity and change always mean the need for

Research with legs　　　　　© S. Kneebone & Y. Wadsworth 2010

constant feedback and flexible responses to ensure required changes can take place more quickly and easily. This has seen an upsurge of interest in complexity, systems thinking and action science with its stress on managing within uncertainty (Flood 1999) rather than the unattainable holy grail of watertight scientific predictability.

Perhaps the current pincer movement of 'multiple methods' on the one hand, and the 'morphing' or 'hybridising' of mainstream social science and evaluation towards more collaborative designs on the other hand, is beginning to mean a system that works more constantly on discovering new truths *at the same time* as working to implement the implications. Systems that act *at the same time* as monitoring, reflecting and improving on their actions.

Can systems do both—the building and retention of knowledge about 'best ways to do things round here' *and* remain open to those ways changing and improving when systems encounter new conditions and need to respond? Can a system of complex human relations avoid insulating itself from new inputs and truths that it needs to receive back about itself while meanwhile continuing its institutionalising of 'the way we do things so far'? Can we *act*, more or less at the same time, as *thinking about that acting?* And can a system—and the people who comprise it—regularly build in working with each other at all these necessary tasks of action, routinisation, observation and reflection, new insight generation, planning and taking new action?

Such an approach would certainly offer new hope for bridging the gulf between the old objectivist and newer subjectivist paradigms by understanding that any well-grounded knowledge is always experimental 'working knowledge', even while being replicated on a daily basis. It is always doing so *for the moment*, while needing to remain open not only to further 'testing' and refining, but also to further problem-atisation by new needs and desires, which in turn call for new understanding, new meaning, new theory and emerging practice. Chapters 2, 3 and 4 set out to chart the nature of living human inquiry and care systems to achieve these capabilities.

A living systems meta-epistemology

In the current upsurge of interest in systems thinking we can perhaps perceive therefore the outlines of a fourth era that might grow out of this hybridising and morphing of mainstream social science. I propose a radically wholistic approach that includes *all* moments of an epistemological[13] cycle of inductively observing and reflecting, abductively 'discovering' or creatively generating new insights and theory, and deductively planning new consequences for trialling in and of action. In particular this dynamic of inquiry moves across two key thresholds or 'phase changes': firstly, from *observing to reflecting*: to register where all is not well (or could go better) with current action, culture and practice, and beginning the search for new insight; and secondly, from *planning to acting*: to move to 'take up' and implement or trial the new 'discovery' in improved action and bedding it down as new culture and practice.

The meta-epistemology or 'mental architecture' proposed in this book is therefore a theory that *encompasses* all current methodologies (including quantitative, objectivist, subjectivist-interpretivist, participatory, qualitative and so on) in a new synthesis of how they might work *together* to better create and sustain life. Chapter 5 details this approach in ten concrete examples of practice, the first of which—the U&I studies—I will draw on at the close of each of the preceding chapters to illuminate that chapter's contents and provide a link to the next. I choose this particular example because of its comprehensive nature, rich quality and illustrative capacity, practical impact and widely published availability.

But first let's explore these ideas about living systems by taking a little journey out into this new way of thinking about research and evaluation. In exploring the 'properties' and processes of continuous cyclic inquiry that characterise whole living systems, we are moving into living systems territory per se. Better equipped, we will return to the more familiar territory of research and evaluation in Chapter 3.

So sit back and relax and spend some time becoming familiar with a way of thinking about ourselves and the worlds we inhabit as inquiring living systems. A way of thinking I hope might turn out to feel rather familiar…

A story of my own coming to see research, evaluation and improvement as systemic[14]

Over nearly a decade (between 1987 and 1996) I was design consultant and co-facilitator of a sequence of studies known popularly as the U&I project. 'U&I' stood for 'Understanding and Involvement' but also played on the aural sound of 'you and I'—a reference to the critical importance of the interpersonal relationships that underpinned the success of the project and the dialogic methodology that was developed. The other critically important element of the project was that it was both consumer driven and staff collaborative— and in a particularly fraught area of human service: acute psychiatric hospital admission. This approach marked a break from the adversarial stand-offs that had accompanied earlier campaigns against psychiatric injustice when consumers were still needing to problematise their experiences sufficiently for 'the system' to even acknowledge the urgent need for change.

The research set out to build in consumers' evaluation of their acute psychiatric hospital experience in normal hospital practices. We drew on a wide range of traditional 1970s–1980s era research methods, added some 1980s–1990s dialogic and participatory action evaluation approaches, and developed a 1990s–2000s era multi-stakeholder, quality improvement, organisational learning system. The resulting

model of building in the all-important processes of feedback to hospital staff and dialogue *about* that feedback between consumers and staff—and employing consumers as staff to facilitate the dialogue and feedback processes between consumers and staff —was subsequently 'scaled up' and adapted for use in every mental health area service in the state. The work also contributed to the creation of state government policy on consumer participation and its funding. However none of this work was without challenges or difficulties, sometimes of an extreme kind, yet its successes rested largely on our adopting a new approach to taking 'to scale' 'whole systems' change that started as a small discrete project on a single hospital ward.

The great U&I octopus of a project[14]

The project—which began with a conversation between a consumer and a hospital social worker and led to an invitation to the statewide consumer organisation to research consumers' evaluative views— could have started and finished with a planned one-off exit questionnaire. However by raising questions about what consumers wanted from the survey, it became clear that they did not want 'yet another survey', with 'yet another

exposé' of disgruntled views, yet more defensiveness and yet more inaction. They concluded that what was really needed was collaboration with staff to understand why things were as they were, and to see what else could be achieved instead.

As people got to know each other the staff–consumer research collaborative committee began morphing into an active inquiry group which realised over time that for change to take place in a single inpatient's experience not only would practices in the microcosm of that one ward need to change, but so too every other area of the hospital's procedures (including budgets, ward policies, management and administration practices, people's conditions of employment, job descriptions, training and so on).

It seemed that every microcosm of the hospital contained the same underlying 'operating logic' or presumptions as every other part and so also for the whole—and change to one microcosm needed to see matching change in each and every other and in the whole, or else the system and its parts would inevitably 'revert to type'. But since the 'type' was held by each person, so it changed only as each person's co-inquiry *with each other* changed the purposes and logic from that which *they* held both individually and together.

To achieve any of this, consumers and staff found they needed to get to know each other *more deeply*—to reach down into their most fundamental under-standings that were contributing to unwanted hurtful practices. Ironically one of the ways to achieve this was for consumers and staff to become friends or 'like friends'. Such friendships emerged initially from sharing feelings about the negative impacts of 'the system' and then exploring together why this was so and how could it might be otherwise, or from sharing experiences of positive practices, and asking what had made these possible and how they might be replicated. (In one notable exchange at the first meeting, a consumer researcher and a staff person involved in the research found that they had been patient and nurse together during an admission some years prior.)

The U&I inquiry group was then able to take these fresh ideas from incubation into research and development as 'prefigurative forms' of evaluative feedback and dialogue—firstly in the project's 'home' ward, then in all other wards, and then in all other parts of the hospital; then radiating 'up and out' to the larger government departmental regional area service office, to central state and then to federal government level, and eventually even into an international conversation. Changes then needed to be echoed in ever wider contexts, in professional conferences and university courses, as to what was presented, how it was presented and by whom. The researching

spread to include service users' friends and families and even general members of the public, the media, unions and other larger scale institutions—even religious and political—but in each and every case resting on the building of friendly relationships, with the friendliness emerging from getting to know each other and each other's purposes and intentions. Only when this basic mutual knowing existed could trust become a basis for effective shared action. It wasn't that trust led to action. It was speaking and hearing that led to understanding that resulted in trust that underpinned unified action, and this was the 'fabric' on which everything else rested.

Everything seemed to hold everything else in place in these great intertwined webs of shared searching, sharing, feeling, reflecting, thinking and practice. Over several years more than 300 people became involved in thirty-five micro-studies, bit by bit becoming, in varying ways, part of a snowballing 'community of inquiry'.

The core active inquiry group drew organisational charts and planned timelines and produced stakeholder diagrams on sheets of butchers paper and put them on the walls of the research office so everyone could 'hold the story'—yet it felt less like 'driving' lots of separate research and evaluation projects by different people in different units, areas, regions, and bureaucracies and much more

like 'going with the flow' to work, albeit highly purposefully, with or even *within* some kind of great living organism, like a large and many-armed octopus: a moving, seething, reacting, writhing, breathing, mostly warm-blooded (sometimes cold-blooded), fluids-and-capillaries 'living being'.

While the ways this organisation moved seemed in some ways mysterious, even rather unknowable and unpredictable, it simultaneously seemed quite highly organised, even orderly, if one could come to know its patterns and logic well enough. Things done in one part would have both expected and unexpected impacts on other parts, a single small 'no' could turn the whole in a different direction. Numerous small acts of 'yes' could add up to a wave of possibility that became unstoppable. Going with the flow here might lead to unexpected outcomes there. And ceasing pressure on this 'organ' could relieve pent-up frustration and gain the release of an energetic pulse sufficient to fuel something else.

Rather than 'conducting research' or 'carrying out an evaluation' it seemed more like something one 'got the hang of'—or 'got the hang of with'—more like a 'dance with' than looking 'down a microscope at', with the aim being to keep enough active feedback loops, enough questions to ensure the feedback, enough weaving and knitting together with all the other dancers, and enough removal of blockages to ensure the research and evaluation kept learning how to effectively 'scaffold' the living dancing creature to keep going in the direction of doing the good it intended to do in the first place, and how to avoid the baffling constant tendency to veer away from this to hurtfulness and defence. It was more like 'inquiring to be a living system'.

Unlike the citizens of Lilliput pinning down their great giant to the ground, it seemed more like we were little busy-bee builders clambering all over and inside the giant octopus or taciturn dancing bear, erecting footings, frameworks and trainer wheels, hollowing out clogged capillaries, splinting broken bones, and constantly working out how to help the living organism go more in the direction of being a 'health, healing and recovery system'.

Interestingly 'organism' comes from the French, meaning a living cell or group of interdependent parts sharing life processes, and the giving of an orderly material structure to these processes; and 'organise' means make organic, into a whole, living being. I turn to the importance of these ideas in the next chapter.

ENDNOTES

1 To the maximum extent possible this book will not repeat material already much available elsewhere, including the contents of its own two precursor volumes, *Do It Yourself Social Research* and *Everyday Evaluation on the Run*.

2 I am attributing this unsourced Taoist quotation to Lao Tzu, the Chinese sage intellectual, on the basis of the 1963 Penguin Classic translation by D.C. Lau of the *Tao Te Ching*, No. 15, p. 19.

3 This era followed a post-Second World War era when the range of 'tried-and-true' services was no longer keeping up with rapidly expanding new needs and new communities of interest. In the context of a boom economy, a major human services commentator from the United States, Martin Rein, described the 'vision of the social workers' for personal helping services in the 1950s–1960s for 'problem families' and individuals, being superseded by the boom-time 'vision of the economists' for universal services and a guaranteed minimum income (Melbourne Public Lecture, Ormond College, 1980). Services from the post-war era had become highly standardised and based on rigidifying assumptions that were crumbling (e.g. the idea that the home, in which only 'the Queen's English' was spoken, where the head was a male breadwinner and a woman's place was as a mother–housewife; where obedient hierarchies were the 'natural order' everywhere, and universities were overwhelmingly for the gifted sons of the deserving wealthy etc.) At the end of the 1960s a primary schools inspector could look at his (and it was his) watch at any time of the day and know exactly what children were doing at any state primary school. It was the same for infant welfare centres and hospitals and mostly every other institution. Advanced states of regulation meant anyone could know the exact height of the baby change table and the exact time spent boiling surgical instruments. Everything ran like clockwork, including the workers in factories. It was truly the age of the machine. But the machine was beginning to sway and crack. Immigrant groups were on the move to new cities bringing new situations; women born in the post-war baby boom period were enrolling at unprecedented levels for tertiary education and on the move out of suburban isolation and into the paid workforce. The old system had reached its zenith of structure and order, and change was afoot as the rigidified 'one best way' began to strain at its seams. There were movements for change as people broke free from restrictions and old institutions: as Indigenous, disability, environmental, health and whole food activist movements were 'going with the flow', counter to the old culture (Wadsworth 2005).

4 Evaluation was of course not new in the 1980s, just as research was not new in the 1970s. They were merely new to such intensified and widespread usage. See for example Guba and Lincoln (1989) for a description of 'four generations' of evaluation spanning the century.

5 The now iconic definition was originally Michael Scriven's (1991: vii); 'significance' was added later (untraced source).

6 As those with the needs mostly had no knowledge of the amount of funds available (others were in control of budgets). The irony here is that often the closer to the ground and more local and small the scale of self-management of the administration of funds—e.g. by community groups—the more careful and modest the spending and the more resourceful and creative the thinking to stretch it to meet deeper valued goals.

7　A presentation by the Manager of the Department of Human Services Evaluation Support Unit (Metropolitan Health and Aged Care Services Division), Dr Darren Harris, to an Australasian Evaluation Society seminar (2007) reflected on persistent issues of 'the disconnects' between public sector evaluations and departmental purchasers and their stakeholders. This was a distance initially encouraged by the legal 'arm's length' requirements needed as a result of central governments' commitment to national Competition Commission procedure applicability to all government business, including health, education and human services. This mandated distancing amplified the existing distance between government policy and funding contract holders, the non-government service deliverers, service users and arms length consultancy and academic researchers and evaluators.

8　'Studying down' is the anthropologist Laura Nader's term (1972) for the tendency of researchers to study the less powerful, disadvantaged, impoverished, colonised and excluded rather than turning the research lens 'up'.

9　Although it is worth pointing out that the PDCA starts with 'planning' and 'doing' and then only pauses to 'check' before short-circuiting in a single loop back to replicating 'action' (rather than observing and reflecting more deeply in double or triple loop thinking before re-planning and new acting, as accomplished in the action research cycle).

10　Although the term 'learning' may still be tricky for those steeped in the student–child, adult–teacher roles in conventional education systems, where a need to learn is often indelibly associated with being ignorant, and a learner is seen as a beginner—rather than learning being seen as an inquiry pathway to knowledge and wisdom by an active, lifelong, self-organising seeker.

11　As well as being a 'sheltered market' not essentially created directly by the 'purchasers', i.e. professional providers are the primary purchasers.

12　The changing titles of the (now) Department of Human Services, which is currently separate from but connected to the Department of Victorian Communities.

13　There is still no easy word for 'epistemology', sorry! It means the way we understand how it is that we go about knowing what we know (such as through research or evaluation). 'Epistemologies' are various theories of 'how we know'. Examples are positivism, interpretivism, feminism, empiricism, critical realism and critical constructivism. Chapter 3 sets out to make sense of all of these in the larger integrating cyclic and 'building' framework of this book and proposes a way of understanding the old so-called paradigm wars between epistemologies as clashes of inquiry preferences 'writ small' in individuals and 'writ large' in social organisations and institutions.

14　This account (as well as those at the end of each other chapter) is modified from a keynote presentation to the World Congress of Action Learning, Action Research and Process Management, Groningen, the Netherlands (Wadsworth 2005). Part of it appears in Burns 2007: 59–60. An account of the U&I facilitation is in Wadsworth 2001; its findings are in Wadsworth and Epstein 1998; and there is a compendium of all five monographs in Wadsworth (ed.) 2001.

15　A full list of the published references for the U&I project appears in *Exemplar 1* in Chapter 5. This account was first presented at the World Congress of Action Learning, Action Research & Process Management in Groningen 2005 and published in Wadsworth 2008c with parts of it revised for Burns 2007.

Living systems

It might seem strange to think of research and evaluation processes as the processes of inquiring within living systems. Or even to think of living systems *as* research and evaluation systems! Isn't research and evaluation just about questionnaires, statistics, focus groups and data analysis?! Hmm. Well yes—and no.

Let's look more closely at an example of a living acting-and-inquiring system. Picture someone who has just learned to ride a bicycle…

> Wobble, wobble. Fall off. Go a bit further. Wobble. Getting the hang of it. Staying on
>
> Going faster, easier, better. Keep going. Up this hill. Down the other side. Balancing OK
>
> Through a rather swampy bit. Oops! Slow down…
>
> Watching, watching carefully where the rubber hits the road. Noticing, swerving to the right, oops, not too far, swerve to the left a little, slow down again over these pebbles and some rocky bits.
>
> Keeping upright. Balancing…
>
> Keep leaning forwards. Dynamic…
>
> Speeding up now the terrain is smoother and more predictable.
>
> Same, same, different, same, same, same…
>
> Glancing up every now and then to check: yes, still on the right road. Taking a longer moment now and then to check the more distant horizons for bearings and progress…yes, still in the right landscape! Oops. No. Need to steer further that-a-way. Lean a bit more in that direction. But stay steady. Check the bigger picture again... yes, aligned again with destination. Still propelled by that need or desire (or does that other mountain look more tempting…? Hmm…May need to think about that; now what might be good about that?)…
>
> Keep glancing back at the road beneath…observing, observing. Constantly processing a flow of incoming information. Constantly updating it. Constantly responding to it. Constantly receiving more feedback. Constantly forming hunches. Constantly reacting, adapting, or generating a new approach. A human dynamo!
>
> Regularly needing to stop and make some internal riding-system transformations—some running repairs, a new tyre, a new set of brakes; a meal, a toilet break, a sleep…
>
> Other resources may be needed—a map, a compass, a rear vision mirror, GPS or an up close and personal chat with a local.
>
> Sometimes needing to detour to make some external riding-system transformations—a road peters out or reaches a fork; the mountain range gives way to the sea, something interesting appears in the distance seemingly off our track, or a desired town is reached…

Presto! We have a more-or-less successful bike rider.

So what makes this bike rider a more or less successful little acting-and-researching living system?

Inquiry in living systems

Well. Let's see. Our bike rider is more or less:

Constantly closely observing complex aspects of self in relation to a complex environment

Constantly making sense of and responding to what is observed in multiple simultaneous and interacting ways—slowing down when there is uncertainty, speeding up when it's familiar and predictable and the same course of action seems to be working

Experimenting with new tricks just for the joy and novelty of it when all seems to be going well!

Keeping a grip on reality and everything staying connected and purposeful

Enjoying the satisfaction of numerous small achievements, the pleasure of successful skill and anticipated environments, celebrating desired destinations reached, and unexpected happenings yielding unexpected benefits and surprises.

Challenges met. Obstacles overcome. Mourning those that couldn't be. Learning from the experience.

Repeating what works. Searching for the new where it's not…then interpreting, evaluating, analysing and forming conclusions about new valued states to add to or revise the old ones

Continuing to stay in balance

Continuing to keep moving forward.

Staying balanced by keeping moving forward

Keeping moving forward by staying balanced.

Looking every now and then to audit progress against intentions, plans and expectations

Pausing every now and then to take in inputs of fuel and resources (and deposit outputs :-)

Energies expended, outputs and outcomes identifiable

Bike and rider and environment in subtle communication: each subtly constructing and being constructed by the other

In more or less productive micro-sequences of doing and being.

In short, an organised bike-riding 'processual system': achieving dynamic stability (or dynamically balancing) in constantly reassessed relationship to regularly changing contexts, propelled by intentional purposes, sufficiently fuelled, energised and resourced.

Actually we have in this apparently simple tangible example a surprisingly good representation of pretty much all the definitive properties of all living systems. *To summarise:*

- An interconnected physically embodied stabilising-structure-in-dynamic-process
- A complex sensing, perceiving, feeling, thinking input, feedback and information-processing system
- Open outwards to input and bounded inwards to contain and perform its own functions
- A purposeful judging self-organising system
- A responsive adaptive and generative flexible system
- Sometimes certain, sometimes uncertain—moving between the two
- A pattern-forming pattern-following pattern-changing system
- Nested and recursive within a greater environmental network of related self-organising systems
- Independent within *and* interdependent with the outer

Let's see these characteristics more clearly in action by looking at some other key living systems—and some that are not—and what they have in common, and where they part company.

See for example how our bike rider can get off the bike and leave it lying on the ground. Rider moves. Bike stays motionless. Bike needs rider's energies to 'work'. Rider doesn't need bike to 'work'. *Dynamic equilibrium* is a defining characteristic of life here—'Life is like riding a bicycle. You don't fall off unless you stop pedalling'.[1] Not just 'balance' but also oscillation back and forth between states of equilibrium. But it's not enough on its own—and this means noticing that living systems come 'whole', not in 'bits' or components. We are talking multiple co-existing properties here. And what about the rider's ability to achieve that movement? Here we can see a kind of *self-organising ability*—to *intentionally* (from the Latin *intentio* meaning 'stretching, purpose') seek and

consume fuel energy, to 'get on their bike' and keep converting that energy into action to remain in motion towards their valued purposes or desires, possibly articulated as goals and tasks, but experienced within a generalised 'mind'. There's an unfamiliar word for this which is *autopoiesis*, from the Latin *auto* meaning 'self', and *poema* meaning 'make'.[2]

Let's look more closely at the bike rider as a self-organising living system.

Like the bike, we can distinguish bounded 'parts' of the rider—and like the bike, we see they can be 'put

together'. But to make them 'go', all the parts need to be organised, *connected* and 'fired up': driven by *energetic purposes* of some kind. The rider can do this but the bike on its own can't. But how did the rider get to be able to 'put together' their own embodying of these energies-for-purposes?

OK. Let's track that back. Where did the bike rider come from?!

What are we seeing here? Aha! Multiple 'nested' patterns of self-organising energetic matter.[3] Attraction, connection and exchange; bounded but permeable;

fertile-enough environments and matter propelled to 'be itself'—by wanting/desiring, 'asking for' and 'receiving' what it needs—to firstly survive in simple form, and secondly to organ-ise, 'complexify', thrive and grow. Sperm seeks, 'wants', and seeks engagement with egg to become what it can. Egg seeks, 'wants', 'invites' and receives the sperm to become what it can. Fluid and nutrients nurture the connection. Cells multiply. Becoming together. Emerging. Foetus repeats the process in the womb. Self-organ-ising. Baby pushes, is propelled and attracted in an exquisite exchange, a 'dance' between its self and its environment; now growing and self-organising with environmental resourcing exchanges, enough for relative independence and separation. More matter compelled and propelled to be itself! A lusty 'ask' for first breath, 'taken' sucked in, taking–receiving what the new environment has given–provided. We say the baby 'emerges' and *emergence* is a nice systems' concept to describe how living things become other living forms because of their own properties in relation to all else. For example the egg is a form that has shape-shifted into a foetus under new conditions, even while it continues to 'hold its form'.[4]

A brief aside here, on another matter of language usage. I'm also going to use the slightly clumsy but illuminative way of hyphenating the word 'organise' as 'organ-ise' quite often throughout this book to keep providing a small reminder that we are referring to both a *systems property* and a *systemic process* of actively making boundaries around a coherent pattern of repetition or 'dense energy' devoted to a particular purpose (while remaining connected to other relevant 'organs' of the same larger body or field). It is a verb indicating *doing*, even while we usually treat an organ as if it is a noun being some *thing*. The sociologist Anthony Giddens has used the term 'structuration' to try and bring together the ideas of 'structure' and 'process' in a single term, but I will use the verb 'organ-ise' to represent the way in which 'structure' (drawing on the new physics) is dense energy of repeated action. What you do repeatedly is who you are. The $E=MC^2$ of human social systemicity.

Note that the word 'systemicity'[5] is also trying to escape the reification of the word 'system', but, like structuration, is still a noun! Albeit both having, hopefully, a greater sense of dynamic movement.

So the baby continues to self-organ-ise in relation to its larger carer-system (just as that carer-system is self-organising in relation to the baby!) And in turn, in relation to and *with* their ever larger systemicities: families or household members, neighbours, commu-

nities, local and not so local economies, workplaces, markets, nation-states and globally. The baby is actively processing information learning-adapting, and responding constantly to feedback from surrounding 'systems' (like frowning or smiling face systems!), sensing discrepant states (hunger, discomfort, warmth, gentle resonant or harsh voices), learning to valorise inputs as negative and positive, then invoking the same with *its* environment using its own distinctive response signals, sometimes in no uncertain terms! 'Can't talk' certainly doesn't mean can't receive or send communication![6]

Over the next three years or so the baby's research, evaluation and continuous improvement skills are honed until they are exploring program logic and incessantly asking 'why, why, why…?'! In this way the toddler has acquired a new way of communicating that extends the sense data, reflexes and 'I want' sounds and reactions that can be 'read' by the sensing–interpreting surrounding bigger person-systems in their orbit. Now they can *ask* using word-sounds, the determination of the meaning of which will now become a lifelong hobby :-). Open inquiry questions: What is that? Why can't I go out? Why do I have to go to bed? Why do I have to eat my vegetables? What are those people doing? Why is that bird doing that to the snail? Why is the sky blue? Why does he look different from me? And then—in response to the received knowledge from those who've been at the 'organ-ising living systems caper' longer—audit review questions: Is this a beetle? Is that because…? Am I…? Are they…? Do I have to…? New experimental processes are hungrily pursued and replicated, and results even resisted in time-honoured fashion, until unavoidable evidence refutes or findings implicate action.

A facilitator-father's field notes (Dapin 2007: 31–33) read:

> I adored him when he first learned to point to what he wanted and before that, when he had to shift his weight in my arms to show me where he hoped to go…[He] closely watches everything I do, laughs, then attempts to do the same. Initially, he gets it wrong. This was especially true in the field of telephony…He long held out hope to find mobile-phone reception on the TV remote control. Later, when he believed he had a call coming through, he would often take it on his shoe…or a plastic

fish…After phones came trains—large and small, real and imagined—but his current field of study is the construction industry. Whenever we pass a building site, he demands, 'More digger! More!'…

A co-operative action inquiry is under way as the father is drawn in further as a co-researcher!:

> My son desperately wants to be useful, in any small way. He is a door opener, a drawer closer, a key turner, a shoe fetcher, a sock tugger…He is happy to help me on the computer for half an hour, provided I then aid him in various, urgent Play-Doh-centred tasks.

Even new language is created to conceptualise findings from the shared action experiments:

> 'Gaga, oh no!' means, 'Father, throw yourself on top of me as if you were a falling building.'

Fast forward ten years!

Our little constantly researching-and-acting budding sub-system has moved on from the strategy of incessantly interviewing the big two-legged macro-systems (and possible sibling sub-systems) in the household with 'want, want, want' needs study indicators, or later 'why, why, why?' observational inductive questions, and then 'is it…? are they…?' program-logic deductive questions, and has turned instead to books, the internet, friends and others for sub-teens answers to life's more pressing strategic questions! Now, if the surviving has proceeded well enough, thriving–growing may see our little sub-system beginning to experiment with constructing a 'womb of their own'—that perennial prototype of their larger self (or home of the future): the cubbyhouse![7] The necessities for a more-or-less living support system are industriously assembled in a corner of the adult super-system's homeland territory 'field': walls, roof, door and windows, tools, toys, décor, precious found items and tea sets. A new system is being built on the pattern of the old, but experimenting with innovative features. An early experience of both systemic replication *and* change agency being constructed from whatever resources are available; and of learning—for all children who are allowed to 'build their own'—which includes basic aesthetics, physics, chemistry, social systems, materials engineering and nature appreciation (Louv 2008).

The house is the larger self.
CARL JUNG

An experiment is being conducted in making a separate bounded space. An independent sub-system, an organ-ised container of life. With places to enter and leave; a safe place from which to observe, reflect, plan and play-act life: entertain friends, collect things, make, share and swap things, cook, eat and sleep. A tiny nascent household economy.

There is inner systems work: a place to lick wounds, ponder and dream desired futures. A place for secrets. A place to establish one's self. But also a place for the outer work with others. From this home base the child turns their energies to encountering, engaging and co-operating (and under stress or threat competing) with others and wider-world systems. There may be some joint venture primary industry (scavenging for cubby building materials), or trade—swap cards, marbles and the occasional biological specimen. Diplomatic missions may be extended or accepted, tea sets or joint projects put to work in the interests of strategic or generative dialogue; or there may be unbefriended next-door invaders bent on destruction. Internal and external defence systems may be erected and tested, both physical and moral, as learning takes place (or doesn't) about both push/force and yield/

attract and how to create, dissolve or destroy forcefield stand-offs using each of these energies or powers.

Intentions connect the inner and the outer, the one relying on the other, resourcing and being resourced, influencing and being influenced, affecting and being affected by. Each connected to and helping make (or sometimes break) the other. Nested. Interdependent. Sometimes not in alignment, not resonating, not in harmony. Sometimes damaging and hurting, or being damaged or hurt in return. Possibly leading to full-scale feudal wars. Then learning to work to restore more life-giving resonance and co-operation to move forward again with each other or without; to be more hale (from the Old English *hal*, meaning 'whole') and hearty (from the Old Germanic *heorte*, related to *heorth*, meaning 'fireplace' or 'heart of the home'). Interestingly 'hale and hearty' remains a common way of thinking about health—both an allusion to the organ of the body that moves the 'lifeblood', carrying the air bearing the oxygen needed throughout the 'body corporate', and also meaning 'central and innermost part of something' with connections to 'hearth', seat of fire and the energy source in a home. 'Wholehearted' also remains a common way of describing someone who can get things done (but not in a 'heart-less' way). We think of 'half-hearted' as a recipe for not-achieving something. Not being sufficiently energised.

So our small bike-riding cubby-builder is learning to move from old sources of life to new more life-giving ones, as wider frames of reference yield new possibilities beyond cubby wars with life-depleting neighbourhood bullies (themselves formed by and replicating their own depleted and depleting life fields).

More organ-ised systemicities and sub-systemicities for the child to engage and connect with! Hierarchies or holarchies of scale. Each 'level' or network node involving a new scale of intention and purpose, 'questions' and pursuit of 'answers', re-sources and challenges from which to build and adapt and shape form.

Human ecologies in ever-increasing self-organising dynamic balance. Sometimes specialising by 'sub-contracting' tasks to greater super-systems (such as parents!) And at other times mastering the tasks for generalist relative independence.

In this world may many worlds more be.
MARGARET CAVENDISH,
ENGLISH SYSTEMS THINKER 1653

Parents become ever more skilled research facilitators and helping resources, encouraging children in their observing and inquiring: 'What's happening now?', 'What can you see?', 'How are things going?'; in their evaluating: 'Is everything ok? 'What are your feelings telling you?'; and in their reflecting: 'What are you thinking about this so far?', 'Why do you think it happened?', 'Tell me something you would like to do about that?' 'Where could you look for what you want?'; and in their planning experimental actions: 'What would it take to fix that?', 'Is there any way you can see to do it?', 'Here are some ideas; are any of those useful to you?', 'If you did that, what do you think would happen?, 'Can you say why?'; and then in their enacting: 'Would you like to try that out?', 'What will you do first—and then next?; and to observe again: 'So how did it go?'

All the while contributing their own listening and responding, their questions and ideas from which the little ten-year-old living system is building their own self-organising inquiry capacity.

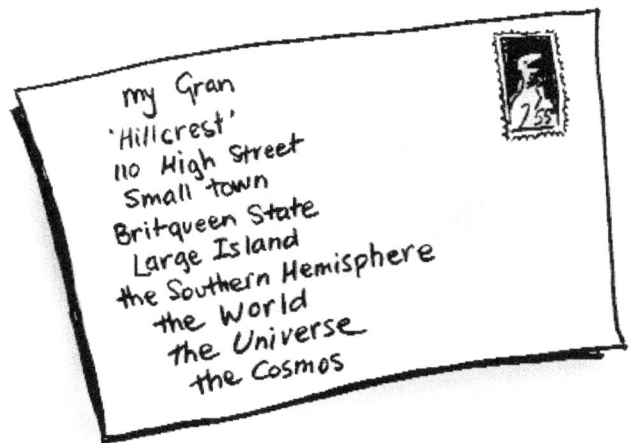

Evidence of acquired situated nested systemicity

When the cubby-building bike-riding child is effectively inquiring and asking these questions of themselves (and others), we call them 'self-starting', 'independent' and a co-operative 'initiative-taker'. Later still we will say his or her sub-system has 'come of age', is resourceful and able to deal with knock-backs and challenges, and has all the makings of a 'system' of their own that can make their way in relation to the wider world of other 'person-systems making their way' in relation to them—even without the initial co-research facilitators-cum-parents' constant presence! The capacity for recursive self-facilitation takes over, which we also call resilience. Unless overly buffeting or hostile or too poorly resourcing environments create crises that send him or her 'back on their own resources'; or home to families for help and support; or, as they get older, to friends and others for mutual 'tribal' or community support and resourcing, until they are back to whole-strength and able to offer to contribute in mutual exchange with others again. An extended and intricate mesh of mutual supports and life-giving exchanges, stabilising while remaining dynamic, over time.

The cubby house is in a tree. In a way the tree is a 'house' too—and certainly an economic living system of exchange, intimately connected with our own. The 'tree of life' is also an ancient symbol for humanity.

Let's see this display of systemicity close up through Permaculture founder Bill Mollison's spectacularly evocative verbal description of it,[8] in order to learn more of the wider mirroring systemicity of our bike rider's environment. The tree no doubt has 'met' the bike rider even if the bike rider does not yet 'see' the tree that submits its living branches to the nails of the cubby builder while breathing out the oxygen the bike rider needs and breathing in the carbon dioxide that is surplus to requirements...

With our 'normal eye' we can distinguish a trunk and leaves, but with a 'system's eye' we may see the vast cascading network of bounded energetic interrelated movement, 'building' and exchanging, processing and growing, just like human living systems:

> The tree is a big translator. It stands between earth and the air. It takes the light and makes sugar and 'seduces' the bacteria and the fungi with the sugar—sends it out of its roots—to bring minerals into the tree so it lets its hydrogen ions go, and minerals stream into the tree roots. There's this huge trade going on up and down the tree—sugars down, minerals up and fungi working for the tree for sugar; and the bacteria the same, they're fixing nitrogen for the tree. There's this incredible business going on...you can't believe all the things that are happening. And then the tree drops its leaves—several tons of leaves—boompff—boomp. Only for three weeks, but that's enough; they're gone—in four days. So it makes this big present of food to the earth. Which eats it. And it turns into black soil. And then out it comes again in leaf, because the earth is also 'bribing' it to keep going, and they're all sort of talking to one another. One tree's damaged—and a beetle comes along and lays eggs, and it sends out a chemical scent. They're all living in relation to each other. [The tree] affects the wind. Interacts with rain—intercepts light rain, collects phosphate and zinc, and funnels it down in precise ways, funnels it down the bark fissures—all the little plants are growing in [this] 'nutrient soup'. It's a very rich environment. It condenses as rain. Cut the trees down and you've finished with the rain. ...Trees make the rain. No trees. No rain...The trees look after us. We don't understand them. They're talking to each other all the time. Thousands of species live with them...(Mollison 1999)

And the same forest can be made out of fish!—as David Suzuki pointed out in his television documentary 'The Nature of Things—Sacred Balance' (2004) when bears hunt salmon and leave their carcasses to rot in the woods, and the nitrogen ingested from the ocean by the fish nourishes the trees. In the same documentary he noted that the complexity of the human heart generates ever so slightly randomised beats (dynamic and thus slightly oscillating equilibrium) that sound more musical than the monotone of an ailing heart. A landscape also has a 'soundscape' or biophony to which the human organism is attuned. Clear-felled forest or farmed remnants have sounds that are more cacophonic, while virgin forest has been found to sound more harmonic to the human ear, in the manner of a musical symphony (*Listening Earth* 2005).

> *The trees are singing my music. Or have I sung theirs?*
>
> EDWARD ELGAR, COMPOSER

The tree like the forest is also dynamically 'self-organising' to ever greater complexity within its co-inquiring forest (just like our growing bike rider within his social ecology), working perpetually towards and then away from homeostatic balance both internally and externally; branches and roots growing in relation to size and in response to context—soil, wind, moisture and temperature—and all in turn in communication with the clouds and air and weather and all other systems: all the way down into the earth, and all the way up into the atmosphere and beyond to the stars.

Like the child, the tree and the forest, all living systems started small, then the greater the growth, the more molecules there are to catalyse reactions in others, the more diversity can generate even greater numbers of 'growing points'. As Brian Swimme has memorably observed, 'You take hydrogen gas, and you leave it alone [for 13 billion years] and it turns into rosebushes, giraffes, and humans...Everybody comes out of the stars...The first step is just paying attention...[and] to participate' (2003). This principle (also called 'autocatalytic set theory') has been understood as one whereby development takes place 'at the edge of chaos', resulting in 'phase changes' between chaos and new forms or patterns of ordered activity. In Chapter 3 questions will be identified that can lead human inquiry to and from these critical points for both creativity and organ-ising.

For an astounding experience of complexity in forty mutually constituting 'systems hierarchies' or holarchies of scale—from the very very large 10 million light years away in the Milky Way galaxy, to the very very smallest quarks viewed at 100 attometers—see the website: http://micro.magnet.fsu.edu/primer/java/scienceopticsu/powersof10/index.

If you haven't seen this before, be prepared for it to forge new neural networks just by watching it![9] The medium makes for a rather static 'snapshot', so you will need to *imagine* 'the conversations' taking place between the unimaginable numbers of molecules and quarks involved! Think 'frequencies on a giant radio set' that every molecule is 'hearing', 'understanding' and responding to! Especially see if you can imagine these images, at all these different scales of systemicity, busily dynamically living and breathing *alive* as well!

Once you open the website, to maximise the moment for reflection I recommend sliding the manual delay meter with your cursor to the right to slow this speedy delivery. Drum roll as you prepare to meet your (and our) shared systemic cosmos!

You may like to repeat that a couple of times to let its significance sink in.

Whew!

'Built systems' as embodied living processes

Ecology, oikos, household, economy, self, workplace, human service

Now when we experience the tree in all its 'nested' interconnectedness—with all its 'speaking with', and 'responding to', it's daily and seasonal and biospheric 'breathing in' and 'breathing out' with all other living beings, the other trees, the cubby house, the bike rider, the suburbs, factories, farms, earth, sea and sky, atmosphere, climate and cosmos beyond, and all the ways in which these communicate their exchanges of 'queries', responses and 'data', and these get 'writ large' as a 'mega-system'—we have a name for it.

We call it *ecology*—that branch of biology dealing with the relations of organisms to one another: both *internal* relations (such as the exchanges between the xylem and phloem and fluids within a tree) and *external* relations (such as between the tree, the air, passing migrating birds and the atmosphere).

Now here's an interesting thing. The word *ecology* comes from the Greek *oikos*. And perhaps surprisingly it means 'house' or 'household'—stemming from a time when the household was the primary living

system of exchange. It comprises half the meaning of the word 'economy' from *oikos* and half from *nemo* meaning 'give what is due'. So systems thinking is both a very ancient wisdom as well as a very contemporary one too.

Even the word *oikos* itself could perhaps be returned to contemporary usage as a way of bringing together the worlds of home and work, currently commonly experienced as very separate. That is, it could stand for integrating the currently perceived unsustainable exchange economy as a more ecologically sustainable and human life-sustaining economy in which people co-inquired for self-organisation.[10] Throughout this book I will use the word *oikos* to indicate a more fully living economic system. This may be helpful later in order to think about human services, co-created inevitably with/within the larger economy—and how to achieve contextualised inquiring living human service systems that are more inclusive, life-giving and integral for all.

Indeed it may become important to re-conceptualise the ways in which all the experienced and perceived splits between 'culture and economy', 'economy and society' or 'work versus life' are, in more fully living systems, integral. The word 'culture' interestingly derives from cultiva, meaning '*cult*, collect, and till *terra* land'. In a contemporary sense, 'cultivate' may be seen as quite a wholistic ecological metaphor for how 'society' (from the Greek *socius*, 'companions', meaning 'break bread together') might, together around the table, co-inquire for the 'just exchange' of resources within the local-and-global household *oikos*, a sustainable living 'home' for all at any scale.

But can we think of a house 'on its own' as a living system? Well yes and no. Like the bike, when a living rider discards it, it appears to just lie 'lifeless', and interestingly, it soon starts cracking and decaying. But when inhabited, we can think of it as an aid or extension of our life—as an embodiment of our 'greater self'. This embodiment-as-a-house has been depicted explicitly by many world cultures:

> Throughout human history different cultures have seen the house as a living embodiment of the self, embodying the social structure of the society which uses it. For example in Savu houses have a head, tail, neck, cheeks, a place through which to breathe, a chest and ribs. Those in Timor have backbones, legs,

heads, faces and eyes—and a new-born baby is taken out through the door [symbolising birth] to be received by family members. In ancient China the ridgepole of the house is seen as the backbone and the front door faces east to greet the rising sun [the birth of the new day]. (Saunders 1999)

In western 'houses of God', the characteristic four-square cross shape symbolises the living body of the deity figure as the 'home' for a church community—with a head (an altar place for symbolic intake of nurturing food of wine and bread), and eyes (great windows traditionally facing east to the light of the new morning creation), transept 'arms' outstretched in action and protection of the 'body' or backbone of the church (where the communicant members of the congregation sit together at its centre), and lungs (choir stalls) for both solemn awe and joyous appreciative celebration of the work of the whole/holy, set within a churchyard and garden for burial of the dead, and external cloistered reflection and thought for deeper contemplation and inspiration for new life. A little *oikos* of its own (and historically full economies of their own in the middle ages). Traditionally the exit was through the great west door of the setting sun.

In Australian north-eastern Arnhem Land Aboriginal language, the landscape is also equated with the human body. For example the word for beach is 'sun on the side of the face' (Adams 2005).

Another 'scaled-up' kind of 'house' for people is a parliament house (from the Old French *parlement*, meaning 'speaking'), here described memorably as a co-constructing systemicity by an English Prime Minister during its rebuilding ('build' from the Germanic *bold*, meaning 'dwelling') after wartime destruction (Archer, 1999):

We shape our houses, and after that they shape us.
WINSTON CHURCHILL

Anthony Giddens alluded to this kind of shaping (with something of the contemporary sense of co-evolution) when he said: 'social systems are like buildings that are at every moment constantly being reconstructed by the very bricks that compose them' (1986: 12). Recent brain science conceptualises this for the individual as 'the brain that changes itself' (Doidge 2007) by analysing inputs and responding to construct different neural connections that can in turn do different things.

In feng sui, the same Chinese cultural conditions

for achieving the health of the human body are understood to apply also to other scales of embodiment: a house, public building, garden or landscape, to form the same safe, nurturing, harmonious but dynamic environment for action and growth as well as decline, contemplation and change. Chinese medicine saw the processes of growth and decay (input, processing and output) as achieved within the human body by its dynamic organ systems as in turn mapped onto the larger world. Scaling between the microscopic and the cosmic, this ancient Chinese culture—an amalgam of a Taoist earth spirituality informing Buddhist knowledge of change and its Confucian ordering/organ-ising—has for thousands of years drawn on a circular symbol to represent a two-phase 'way' (the *tao*) in which all of life produces, yields (yin) and 'breathes out' to breakdown and decay, and then, contextualised in a rich soup of diversity, elemental detritus and chaotic complexity, regenerates in new form, sparked by chi energy and inspired to 'breathe in', growing to the next liminal turning or (yang) outbreath as strong energy for viable embodied form or action, only to repeat the cycle of life and death again. In some cultures the integral body is considered literally to be a temple for the sacred (from the Latin *holos* 'holy', meaning 'whole').

A house is a machine for living in.
LE CORBUSIER, ARCHITECT 1923[11]

But wait. It is not so much a machine per se, because even the house is in a way an entropic live machine—albeit a Very Slow one. More like the 'house' growing on the back of a snail, or our fingernails…Part of a purposeful, energised self-ignited being, rather than an entirely non-living 'vacant entity'. But how so?

Think about how houses and buildings vacated by their human inhabitants may quite soon start to look 'down at mouth'. Under a microscope we can see that actually all the house materials are, in a funny kind of way, still 'living' or rather 'dying' (still a property of a living system). The wood is the remains of a tree, with its cellular construction ever so imperceptibly breaking down or even visibly rotting at the same time as 'persevering' in structured 'action'. More so, if without a hearth for fire and warmth and internal dryness to slow the decay. Even the bricks are getting ever so imperceptibly more fragile, and over immense

PAST   NOW   FUTURE

From an idea by Tohby Riddle with permisssion

time will crack and crumble and return to dust. 'Entropy' is the word that has been given to this characteristic of all living things. The process by which everything that grows and expands is also beginning to 'die', sometimes slowly, sometimes more quickly (think of a match burning), as its inner capacities to transform matter into dense patterns of energy deplete. So in a funny kind of way even apparently 'inanimate objects' may be seen as living (or dying) in their own way too. A structure that is still 'on the move', through its active cracking and decaying, increasingly limited in its capacity for autopoiesis, but still its whole-at-this-time self.

Self-sustaining buildings are even being designed with membranes that perform the same functions of breathing, moisturising role of skin, filtering of water and recycling human waste into bio-gas for heating and cooking. (Walters 2008: 24).

Little wonder the house has been seen by analytic depth psychologists as 'the larger self' or 'the inner state made manifest' (Mary Oliver)—and hence 'all really inhabited space bears the essence of the notion of home' (Gaston Bachelard[12])—reflecting our priorities, our preoccupations, our personalities and our responses to our outer environment. In systemic terms the individual or the house may be seen as the larger social collective system 'writ small', just as the larger system is in a sense our selves or our homes 'writ large': a kind of nested or holarchic *oikos* of bounded and connected, dynamic and stabilising living exchanges.

Scaled-up systemicity

Now think of feudal European and Chinese family villa-compounds. Large sprawling buildings, growing organically (from the Greek *organon*, meaning 'characterised by or designating continuous or natural development'), over time to house extended kith and kin, with huge kitchens and mighty hearths in which enormous amounts of food preparation took place; perhaps a hall for eating, entertainment and rituals; and sleeping places, housing also the farm animals in winter. All the same basic functions as an amoeba or an egg—but 'writ large' and more complex.

Or take the Middle Ages where, instead of all being housed within one building complex, the European mediaeval village replicated all the cultural institutional 'organs' deemed necessary for human life—a central nucleus 'heart': a village market square meeting place with its tavern public house for food and rest for travellers, a church and its school room and hospital(ity) for the sick and poor, with a manor house at a distance overlooking from the hill, taking control of governance, security and charity (until these functions began to migrate down to the municipal hall on the town square); and lanes bringing 'lifeblood' traffic in and out of the village, to and from farms and barns; and in the far distance another nodal village on the same pattern.

Think some hundreds of years previously to the Roman Empire, another time of colonisation, trade, exchange and production that called forth whole city states and large towns. From one end of Europe to the other, every main town or city replicating the same 'cookie cutter' pattern: highways and aqueducts, boundary walls around, and within: all the small industries and commerce for food, clothing, goods and services; public baths for health and leisure and political negotiation; an amphitheatre for entertainment; games for recreation; a temple for the Gods for devotion, duty, power, meaning and mystery; and a noisy marketplace and piazza at the heart of things for public gatherings and music resonant with the times.

Now fast forward to the scaled-up modern city of contemporary globalising American Empire, and all the 'system components' are reproduced again, but now even more highly specialised: as factories, cafes, battery farms, shops and housing estate dormitory suburbs. Freeway tangles above ground, sewers below, fenced and gated communities within, multi-storey 'stacks' of offices and apartments; 'chain' name-label-logo businesses, take-away fast food, franchised health facilities; 'super' markets; shopping malls, gyms for health and leisure; theatres and stadiums for entertainment; football games for recreation; churches, mosques and temples for the many faces of the sacred; a global electronic networked marketplace, outsourced industries; and parliaments on hills overlooking cities. We have even had to invent the term 'community-of-interest' now that hitherto close geographic communities have become so disparate and the people anonymous to each other. In some cases the post-modern apartment ('apart-ment' from the Latin 'to separate') does not even have a kitchen! Why eat 'in'—inside the sub-system—when eating 'out' (in the larger system) might work better for the younger fast-moving tribe-seeking café organisms?

Colonising from one end of the planet to the other—every city and town replicating the same new mass 'cookie cutter' pattern. Whole societies of people who no longer grow their own food or know how to cook it, no longer collect their own water or know where it comes from, don't generate their own energy resources, or build their own dwellings, or know how to. Just as the process of specialisation increases with complexity, so too does the process of complex inter-dependency, bringing with it both the focused power of the mass machine and the vulnerability of the tiny fragile cog.

Into this picture of Western societies comes another co-generated specialised sub-systemicity—that of 'human services' or 'welfare' ('well', meaning 'right way' from the Germanic *wyllan*, meaning 'will', related to the Latin *volo* 'wish'; and 'fare' from the Germanic *faran*, meaning 'journey')—itself a modern invention for what once was accomplished within and between families in smaller close-knit communities, clans or tribes. In a way human 'services' may be seen as a systemic reflection of the greater 'body corporate'—just as the individual human service 'user' is a creation of the human service system within the larger body corporate, and shaped by its character. Perhaps future 'human services' (relations of

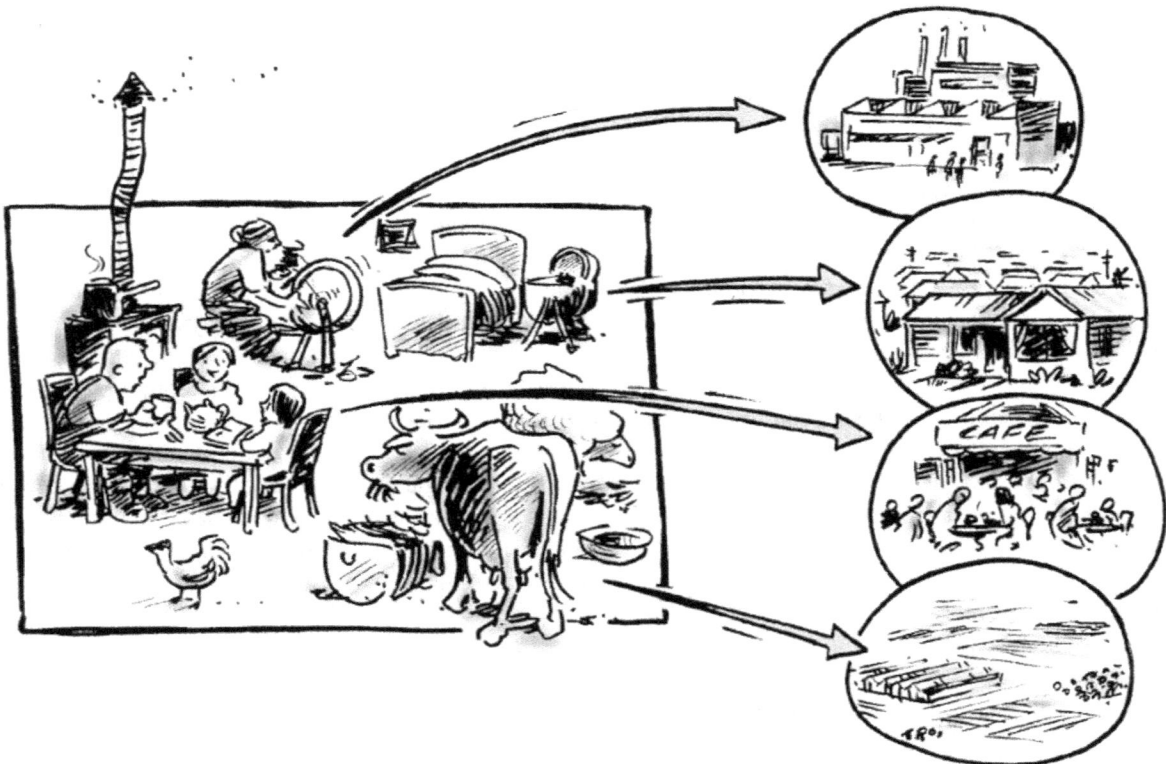

Emergent systemicity in one form of human settlement organ-ising[13] © SK & YW 2010

corporately organ-ised response to human need) are becoming globally dispersed, e.g. as 'health tourists' go overseas for cheaper hospital operations, or students travel to or from overseas for a Western education.

Or maybe the driving forces in these systems are already beginning to overreach themselves and their environments, having to ever tighten the grip of surveillance and command and control as centres become more distanced from their peripheries, making the whole systemicity ever more vulnerable to the perturbance and turbulence that comes from too great centralisation combined with too great size and complexity—until relocalisation emerges to restore organ-isation more appropriate to the scale of an autopoetic living system.

As each individual sub-system loses the capacity to carry within itself all the 'DNA' or intelligence it needs for self-survival—becoming ever more dependent and vulnerable as a result—it moves towards critical mass for both individuals, groups and whole systems to break down under the excess weight of their objectives, exceeding the balance of available resources.

What do we know of all previous human systems that have become this huge, this full-blown, far-flung or compulsively machine-like and 'monocultural' in their replication? That's it: they're about to die! They've simply begun to get too big, the parts too out of touch with each other, too complex, too pyramidal, trying to be too quick, and paradoxically too slowed down, too exhausting, too risky, overly-controlled, over-managed, over-led and overly empowering for the few, and too disempowering for the many. The systems logic excludes too many important living systems properties; in short it has become unsustainable.

What do we need to counter the risks associated with this systemic logic towards scenarios of unsustainability and collapse? Can we build more balanced and dynamic systems that respond to unwanted logics *sooner*? Can we move to operate on more healthy living systems logics, sooner and more easily?

Scaled-down systemicity

Since we can find the process-components of a household system (an integrated *oikos* or living economy) in individuals' lives, homes, families, friendship groups, workplace and human service systems, let's see what it might be able to tell us about the idea of building in the conditions for more truly living systems in the daily micro-actions that replicate and scale up to be the 'strong structures': strongly repeated cultures of our lives, communities and institutions. (Even though the analogy cannot be pressed to completion perhaps unless the home is our workplace or human service, or the workplace or human service is our home.)

Interestingly we *do* see some offices that are much more holistically like a living 'home' than others. Even more interestingly they are often the offices belonging to senior managers and directors, teachers, creative people and academics—those who have been able to act powerfully to retain their ability to self-organise in more nourishing and integrated environments. You know the ones: with a table and chairs for working in small groups; a little modular lounge area for relaxed discussion, entertaining of clients or restful thinking—with a lounge lamp, cushions, flowers, ornaments, Persian carpet and tasteful pictures on the walls; perhaps a small bar fridge and coffee-making kitchen-ette, and a large Madonna lily in a pot. Maybe even a small ensuite and shower. More recently some major corporates such as Ericsson, Boston Consulting Group, MedWeb, insurance companies and State and Commonwealth departments have included in their new buildings kitchens with breakfast bars and espresso coffeemakers, lounge chairs and TV and video areas with retro wallpaper, curved 'pods', 'play spaces' decorated like beaches or fish aquariums for 'think tanking'; 'Main Street'-style corridors for casual conversation, shower rooms with wardrobes full of towels and ironing boards, hot desking or 'hotel-ling' for flexibility and mobility; even a Nintendo arcade game! An architect from Bates Smart observed that 'organisations are realising that work[-based] collaboration occurs most effectively in informal spaces' (Bates Smart architects 2000: 18).

The need for contextual sovereign wholism may thus be voiced as a desire for more home-like workworlds, or homeworlds that include work-like spaces: dissolving overly strong distinctions between what is 'work' and what is 'life'. People who do not see themselves as ever 'retiring' from work to a life of leisure may have been fortunate to find ongoing work-in-the-world that is sustainably fulfilling and even

pleasurable. Of course the physical surroundings reflect only some of what is being made possible. Other less visible 'signs of life' might include regular times for work groups and teams to get to know each other and their broader contextual communities of interest and stakeholders; means to express values and principles in non-traditional ways; time for a range of life events; or a chance to work from home. Work with a soul. Life that is active, productive and contributing. Those without so much power over their environment may still create something of their own—an embroidered chair cushion, a family photo, bookshelf or a stem flower vase on their desk. Alternatively there may be hard-won and strict boundaries between 'work' and 'life'—with this 'choice' illuminating the loss of one from the other, invoking a determination to encapsulate and preserve at least something of an autopoetic life from the encroachment of work (non-life).

Home workers who increasingly take advantage of a mobile, electronically networked 'virtual office' operate from the other direction: from a 'home' that is more of a whole life environment within which they may then 'quarantine' a part, a compartment or subdivision (of time and space) to ensure and protect the 'work' activities. Work-related items may be allocated to a particular space to concentrate the systemic activity (phone, stationery, files, papers and books, laptop computer).

Thus one critical property of living systems involves gathering *into* an integrated (from the Latin *integrare*, meaning 'make whole') system what is needed for growth, maintenance and sustainability. An impetus to 'make whole' may come from a felt sense of the range of resources needed for a living system to indeed fully live. Consider the following gestalt or mental image with its wordless invitation to restore the missing piece within an 'implicate whole' (Bohm 2002)—in this case, the chance to give voice to feedback within a co-constructing field environment.

Whether services will morph to include more of what is missing, or workplaces will morph to include what is missing and be more like homes, or home (or virtual) offices morph to be more like workplace offices, or indeed whether towns will tend to create marketplaces or churches, or a bag of lemons will be brought to be shared in the corporate kitchen, or a statement of deep spiritual values will be carved in a hospital's stone forecourt—all will depend on whether the relevant organism is able to seek whatever components or properties it deems necessary and sufficient to comprise its being an autopoetically self-assembling living system in *toto*—and to the extent *there is the freedom for it to so do*.

Some workplaces or human services were once actually called homes, such as nursing homes or children's homes (not that the name necessarily did more than express good intentions). Some these days may be modelled on marketplaces with a shop or a café; some may have a garden or companion animals or other homelike or creative features (think of elderly people's residences with an art studio or a library, or the differences in colour and appearance between government department offices—say Treasury and Law compared to Arts and Education). Some workplaces, like a hospital, may include a chapel, or places where other deep-meaning rituals may take place. Those that have become monocultures may generate a search for ways to connect to other resources or activities to build rich complexity—again, only *if they are free to.*

From large complex networked systems that are richer in self-organising resources than those more strongly bounded 'siloed' or specialised ones, all the way down to a small centre, service or individual—the need for missing properties of living systems create discrepancies that register signals like sonar impulses or audio resonances, which are able to be picked up *if living systems are free to emit them, detect resonant responses and seek successfully to incorporate them.*

Eliminating any living system property creates risk as each property contributes to organic fulfilment of the organism's purposes—where an organism is commonly understood as 'a living individual [or] being, consisting of a single cell or a group of interdependent parts sharing the life processes' (Sykes 1976). Lopping off a box and a few arrows on a diagram might *look* logical on a whiteboard, but what was the actual organic reality—the now missing 'fine print' of real people in relation to each other, forming the corporate whole to achieve its life purposes—the fine social and psychological 'capillaries' that might bleed, the 'electric wires' that might short-circuit, the shared party walls that might be protecting interaction, or the ethical heart that beats for all?

As John Seed has observed (1999), it may not be such a good idea for the brain to decide it is the most important organ in the body and begin to mine the liver or downsize the heart as an inferior organ to the brain! Competing against a part of one's own system may seem to work in the short-term but in the longer term means systemically turning against one's larger self, like an immune response—or an autoimmune response. Distancing can thus be endangering, as the way to detect the value of the other is to be in proximal relation, to connect and receive data, observe, feel, 'question' and know it first hand. In this sense impermeable boundaries can also create distance that can eventually mean death for the organism as errors and misjudgements accrue and cross-purposes play out contradictory logics.

In a living system everything is connected, even though the parts may be separately organ-ised and not be obviously aware of each other's existence. The boundaries, while clear enough to contain and enact

specific actions, are also permeable enough so the totality is able to communicate to achieve coherence with its unifying purposes. Damage to one part may result in taking longer to adapt, thicken walls or grow new scar material. Removing the foundations may lead to collapse or time-consuming reconstruction. Draining out lifeblood funding might lead to heavy cracking of the walls: while not visible from the outside, in a few years the plaster might start 'inexplicably' making suicidal leaps from the walls. Or banishing half the household members to the lean-to on the back verandah may lead to other members of the household superficially feeling more comfortable but, in the forgetting of who the house was meant primarily to be *for* (including those who are now the verandah-dwellers), considerable unconscious energies may nevertheless be expended on maintaining defensive walls, boundaries and distances. As well, in their absence from a seat at the table, the house-dwellers may have to continuously try and guess at what the verandah-dwellers are like, what they are doing and what they might be needing. On the other hand, including and nurturing one part may assist the whole to access greater diversity of being. Inviting guests (or verandah-dwellers) inside may lead to valuable new shared experiences, unexpected new understanding, the bridging of system-endangering distance, and a whole new way of being with each other that is more resonant, unified and productive.

Case vignettes of systemicity

Some time back an experienced researcher was brought in to a major state government department to assist with some evaluative research thinking. Arriving at the appointed time, which was conventionally morning tea time, they were greeted by one person who instinctively offered hospitality, although there was no longer any kitchen. A boiling water unit had been installed on a wall, but there were no cups, no tea, no coffee, no milk and no biscuits. Nor a refrigerator. Instead, each individual had to have their own private supplies or leave the building to buy a drink from a nearby shop. The host drank jasmine tea. Which the visitor did not. Soon this 'lean and mean' approach to the needs of employees and human conviviality was reflected in the rest of the workplace culture. The meeting proceeded at speed, with no time spent on introductions or preliminaries about who was at the table and what they knew, nor any canvassing of what each had been thinking about the topic to date. The style was briskly confident, presuming and no question was framed that did not already have an answer worked out. The group *qua* group did not do any new generative work together. The meeting finished efficiently within an hour (as everyone had to rush to other meetings and tasks). Later, two of the participants produced their own output, did not seek feedback to it from the rest of the group, and there was no further follow-up. The new initiative decayed and dissipated within a few years.

An academic arrived at a research organisation to carry out a project. They were greeted by the relevant manager who invited them to sit down to discuss what they would need. Full advice was given of all the preparations that had been made for their arrival. The newcomer was invited to meet all the other staff at morning tea and was welcomed there. Forty staff attended every morning and afternoon tea in the organisation's busy, pleasant tearoom where a hospitality officer kept the large room in immaculate order and ran the staff club's generous tea and biscuit 'shop'. Most staff also used the tearoom's kitchen as 'their own' (given that most worked out of hours on projects about which they were passionate and which were of urgent global significance). Conversations about shared research projects and ideas ricocheted around the tearoom and people came to meet there often throughout the day. A strong sense of camaraderie was palpable and the staff's most recent publications were available in the room, not for show, but to be read and discussed. Annual photos of the full staff group for every year since the organisation's beginnings (more than 25 years earlier) lined the full length of the main hallway. This was an organisation that knew who and what it was, and where people knew and respected each other. There was high morale, administrative staff were treated with the same respect as researchers, and collective social events were attended by all staff. The director had a quietly ambitious vision which included the projects of all the staff, a vision which was regularly to be seen in practice at weekly seminars where all discussed and presented their work. Almost all staff attended these seminars, and the same applied to the packed monthly staff meetings. A steady stream of visitors was budgeted for, and these brought new ideas that were seized upon and argued about with enthusiasm. Regular clever, funny and interesting exchanges took place between all staff via the email system. There was in-house IT assistance and maintenance, and admin support was freely offered. The environment was dynamic, stable, collaborative and highly productive. That is, until the 'parent organisation' decided to amalgamate, upsize and eliminate financial 'fat'. The hospitality officer was the first to go...

Another organisation was suddenly being restructured from 'on high' with no official reason given. Entire sections were being amalgamated that had previously been self-organising. As separate entities some had prospered, although communications had broken down between them, breeding resentment. All the delicate but efficiently established routines and careful intrapersonal relationships, mutual understandings and long-lasting negotiated working agreements were suddenly severed. The rich 'local knowledge' held by each about the detail was suddenly also lost—the knowledge of this person's skills, that person's recent bereavement; the understanding of who needed advance warning of requests and who didn't; who it was who knew how the tricky photocopier was maintained; and who held the corporate history in their head about who had written which policies, who knew what had become of them (or not), and why. The three key people who remembered why they were really doing all the work were 'early-retired'. The managing director (MD), aloof in an upper floor office, announced that all the changes would be accomplished 'without cost' and that business would continue to be conducted entirely 'as usual'.

The impact was significant and costly. People left, taking with them years of experience and knowledge. Many of those remaining moved elsewhere, and of those who stayed, key figures no longer had such a high level of commitment as the new situation eliminated what they had had to offer in favour of the new 'tighter' vision. Despite many taking sick leave, holiday leave, leave without pay or early 'retirement' to recover from the stress, there were technically no casualties recorded because stress-related ill health due to organisational restructure was exempted from the workplace industrial agreement. The MD was thus able to claim an unblemished record of having achieved the restructure without staff loss. The staff satisfaction survey sampling method was changed to leave out the part-timers—a key group distressed by the situation that had led to the restructure in the first place. Reported staff satisfaction increased greatly. At the end of it all, the integration of the initially separated areas 'A' and 'B' (understood to be the unspoken rationale for the restructure) was not achieved, as group A exerted its power to go on with its own agenda as before, and group B went on being overly consumed by the work that it had always done, still unable to do more of the work monopolised by Group A.

A disaster took place in a street. Yet suddenly the scene was transformed as it 'acted as one'—as if everyone involved had been pre-briefed on how to

put the situation right. Two people immediately made eye contact and quickly worked out a plan. One–who had never taken a leadership role before in their life–sought help from a nearby shop-keeper and then offered explanations and suggestions to guide the crowd to the safety of the shop. The moment of shock passed and many people left the scene both for safety and to clear the space. Another stepped forward to advise of some details the two people who were taking the initiative regarding the overall picture had not noticed. Someone else went to the injured person to put a coat over them to keep them warm and provide comfort (*com-*, meaning 'with', *fort*, meaning strength). Another used a mobile phone to call an ambulance. Someone respectfully placed a blanket over the person who had died, and sat quietly with an arm around a shivering child. Others explained to newcomers to the scene what had happened and repeated the advice to clear the area and where to go to safety. Another group stood together at a distance and discussed what had happened, sharing their observations and making sense of it all to try to work out who would know the people who were hurt or died, and what next would need to be done…

On another street at another time in another country something similar took place. This time the scene was chaos. People started shouting conflicting orders, and no one listened. People were frightened, confused and darted in all directions. Nobody stopped to look closely enough to see what was really needed. No one rang an ambulance. The dismembered person who had died remained on full view as people stepped back and forth over 'it'. No one knew the person or anyone who would. No one could really say what had happened. The traffic remained blocked for hours, with the people in the cars —not knowing what had happened—getting angrier by the minute…

Danny Burns, a large-systems research facilitator in the UK, tells the story (Burns 2006) of working with the senior management teams of a city council and the local Primary Care Trust. They got to talking about care pathways for older people and were musing on a puzzle that they had observed. This was that there seemed to be a one-directional path from caring for yourself in the home, to homecare, to residential care, to nursing care and ultimately into acute hospital beds. If someone had a short-term medical problem and had to go to hospital they almost invariably ended up staying there longer than anticipated, and from there, instead of going home or back to residential care they ended up in nursing care. Some of them started to talk about the experiences of their own parents. One talked of the way in which older people who came onto the wards were routinely catheterised (a catheter is a flexible tube introduced into the urethra for emptying the bladder). This was because it took fifteen minutes to take each patient to the toilet and fifteen minutes to take them back again. There simply wasn't enough nurse time to do this. The effect of this was that virtually all of the older people who came onto the wards as independent individuals came out dependent. So they could no longer go back into their homes or into residential care. This meant that much greater pressure was put on available nursing care. Put this in the context of the national 'bed-blocking' crisis—

> A report on hospital bed management showed that two million bed days had been lost each year because of delays in discharging people who were fit to leave hospital. Two thirds of beds were occupied by people over the age of 65 and a key factor in their delayed discharge was the difficulty in finding them places in community facilities. (*The Guardian* 17 April 2002)

—and we can begin to see that the hospital service could find some answers to its bed-blocking crisis within its own ward practices. But it could not see this. It needed a systemic inquiry initiated from outside its own boundaries (within the social care sector) to see this…It was [also] clearly not obvious to those on the hospital wards that investing in taking people to the toilet could unlock a multi-million pound bed-blocking problem.

Entering a new systems thinking era

In illuminating the characteristics or properties of living systems in the bike-riding child, their surrounding physical and human 'person systems', the tree, the cubby house, parents and households, streets, hospitals, wider environments, economies and rural and urban service systems, I am summarising insights drawn from practice experience and thinking emerging from a wide range of disciplines over the past fifty years, as well as from various streams of more ancient thought and practice.

Use of these new theories of 'the systemic' have recently become widespread, with talk abounding of 'systems properties, global and meta systems, systemic process, whole or large systems, organic systems and complex living systems as emergent' and feedback-based in disciplines ranging from the new physics, biology, deep ecology, engineering, architecture, user-design, human organisational psychology and personal psychological 'type' theory, as well as in some areas of human science, evaluation, cultural studies, philosophy and social theory (Wadsworth 2005: 1).

Interestingly, in contrast to the older, more mechanically linear, objectivist, determinist or predictive, structural-functional models of systems thinking, the new focus is on models of change *and* stability, often addressing problematic situations, and particularly ecological sustainability, and recognising the connectedness in systemic fields of 'co-constructing relationality'. More confusing still for those accustomed to more mechanistic approaches to systems, this new and often transdisciplinary socio-bio systems-thinking (or *systemic* thinking, Flood 1999) explicitly integrates ideas of processual fluidity *and* organ-ised ordering.

Ilfryn Price, a British professor of resource management and initially a geologist, has traced its beginnings, in large part, back to the 'new science' or new physics studies of complex biological living systems (2004), and in particular the influential work of the Santa Fe Institute in New Mexico (e.g. Kauffman 1993, 1995, 2000). As the physicists, systems engineers and biologists found their way throughout the twentieth century to the human social world, they coined new terms like 'soft systems' engineering and 'social ecology'.

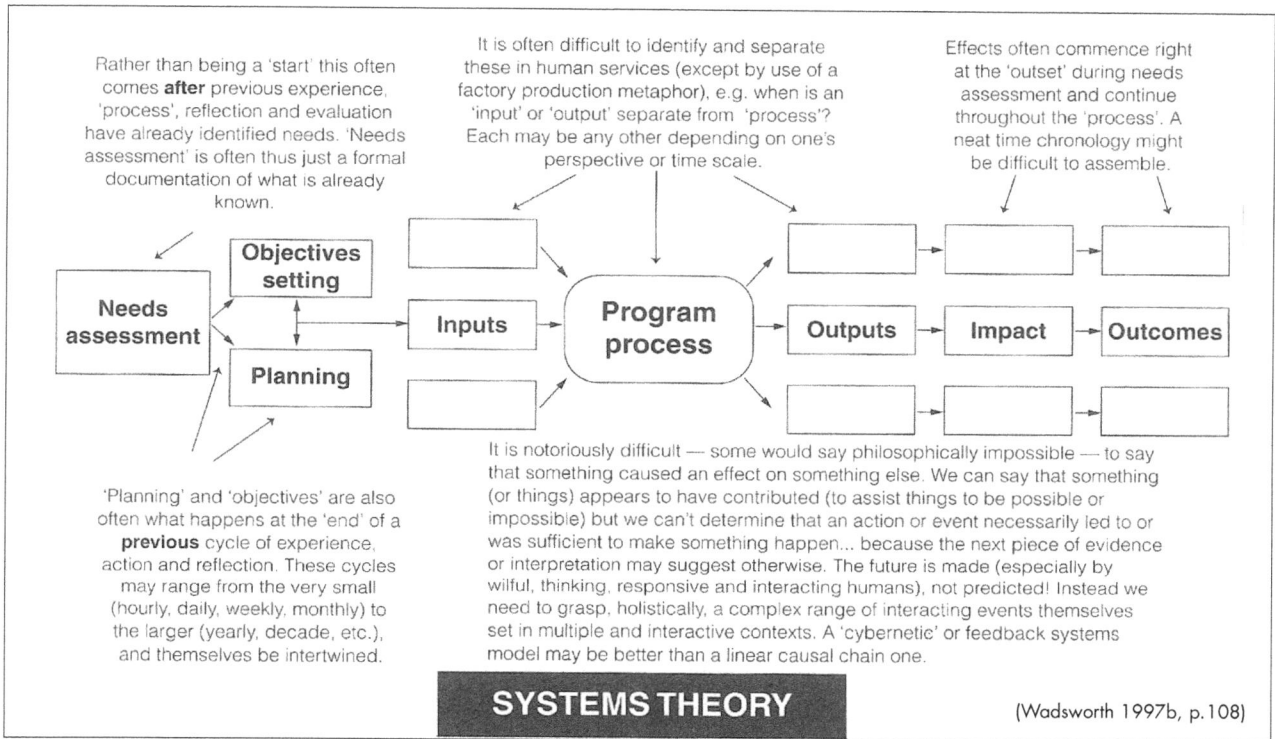

Rather than being a 'start' this often comes **after** previous experience, 'process', reflection and evaluation have already identified needs. 'Needs assessment' is often thus just a formal documentation of what is already known.

It is often difficult to identify and separate these in human services (except by use of a factory production metaphor), e.g. when is an 'input' or 'output' separate from 'process'? Each may be any other depending on one's perspective or time scale.

Effects often commence right at the 'outset' during needs assessment and continue throughout the 'process'. A neat time chronology might be difficult to assemble.

Objectives setting

Needs assessment

Planning

Inputs

Program process

Outputs → **Impact** → **Outcomes**

'Planning' and 'objectives' are also often what happens at the 'end' of a **previous** cycle of experience, action and reflection. These cycles may range from the very small (hourly, daily, weekly, monthly) to the larger (yearly, decade, etc.), and themselves be intertwined.

It is notoriously difficult — some would say philosophically impossible — to say that something caused an effect on something else. We can say that something (or things) appears to have contributed (to assist things to be possible or impossible) but we can't determine that an action or event necessarily led to or was sufficient to make something happen... because the next piece of evidence or interpretation may suggest otherwise. The future is made (especially by wilful, thinking, responsive and interacting humans), not predicted! Instead we need to grasp, holistically, a complex range of interacting events themselves set in multiple and interactive contexts. A 'cybernetic' or feedback systems model may be better than a linear causal chain one.

SYSTEMS THEORY

(Wadsworth 1997b, p.108)

Figure 1. A critique of systems theory

Speaking in 2003 at the World Congress of Action Learning, Action Research and Process Management in South Africa, the social ecologist Richard Bawden invoked Bertalanffy, whose original thinking in biology from the 1920s to the 1950s led to conceptualising organisations as open systems which diversified or 'co-existed' via a continuous flow of information and feedback between each other and their environment. Drawing on this theory, Richard offered a critique of the dominant idea in business of strategic planning (with its assumptions of controllability and a fixed field in which to predict outcomes and command specified action) and proposed the idea of *emergent* planning and the value of systems thinking in complex, unstable situations. A similar point was made by Allan Greenspan in his pre-retirement speech as Chairman of the US Federal Reserve Bank when he reflected rather painfully on what it meant to try 'to "manage" a complex and volatile "system" in the face of inherent uncertainties and the impossibility of knowing all the variables much less how to measure them' (Patton, 2005). The evaluation sociologist Michael Patton drew attention to Greenspan's struggle to explain 'why one can't monitor and manage a complex system with predetermined targets...[by picking] some small number of indicators and setting rules for how to interpret them'. Instead Greenspan found himself arguing for more 'moving and flexible interpretations' and basing action on 'watching how the system responds, not on pre-ordinate, mechanical rules and fixed targets'.

In this he was echoing Stafford Beer, an early cybernetic systems thinker, who charted the different levels of probability and predeterminism (Stephens and Haslett 2005: 398) from high, in simple, relatively static systems (think penny tossing), to middling, in complex systems (think multiple horses and riders moving down a field), to closer to nil in exceedingly dynamic, complex systems (think global ecosystems). Many areas of health and human services are realising the importance of shifting attention from over reliance on isolated top-down fixed planning of service delivery to resourcing whole organisational networks to build more closely engaged relationships with their clients and with clients' surrounding contexts. In this way they better encourage their collectively held cultures to change by supporting systemic responsiveness to feedback, including more distributed leadership, self-organising and initiative taking throughout such networks, all the way to individual clients and communities.

The influential business and management author and former professional engineer Robert Flood, has written of managers now facing 'managing within the unmanageable' and 'learning within the unknowable' (1999). In 1998 he renamed his respected, long-standing journal *Systems Practice* '*Systemic Practice and Action Research*' in recognition of the new understandings of complex dynamic relational feedback systems, as well as acknowledging the implications of this for a new critical constructivist science of action research. Stuart Kauffman, working at the intersection of physics and biology, speaks of 'organised being' as possessing 'formative power of a self-propagating kind which it communicates to its materials' in organising them' (Kaufman 2000: v).

The 1997 systems diagram in the 2nd edition of my book *Everyday Evaluation on the Run* (p. 108) (see Figure 1) raised questions about standard linear causal 'systems theory' models (one-way boxes and arrows: input, program, output, outcome etc.) It alluded to other forms of more cybernetic feedback and to complex, relational systems theory as ways of overcoming the twin problems of only seeing research as 'starting' with a theory or hypothesis (But where did it come from? Was it well grounded?), and 'ending' with a conclusion or recommendation (But did it work in the hard test of actual practice?)

That small reference in 1997 reflected my having found my way to a more cyclic, contextualised, feedback-based kind of systems thinking through three 'whole systems' research projects (or to be more accurate, large systems or *systemic* research projects).

The first, over a period of five years in the 1970s, nominally started with the top-down planning of a model for the provision of integrated early childhood services at a state policy level and then involved developmentally researching and evaluating the pilot project's actual 'live' implementation in a large local government area—a pilot which was subsequently scaled up (in no straightforward manner) state-wide (*the Knox project*, see Wadsworth 1976, 1979). The second, over a period of eight years in the late 1980s and 1990s, involved a sequence of four R&D

'grounded theory' or emergent action research studies in which several hundred service users and service providers in acute psychiatric services participated (*the U&I studies*, see Wadsworth 1998, Wadsworth and Epstein 1996a, 1996b, 1996c, 1998, 2001)—already alluded to in the previous chapter—and again subsequently scaled up statewide (again in no straightforward way, but beginning to benefit from socio-analytic systems thinking). While the third, over a period of ten years from the mid-1990s to now, comprised a sequence of ten studies that identified the conditions for building in small-scale research and evaluation processes throughout whole human services systems (*the 10 Exemplars* reported in Chapter 5).

In all of this work I began to grasp the problems of the traditional researcher or evaluator acting, in effect, as either a messenger or a go-between, and instead worked to knit closer co-researching relationships among all collaborating stakeholders or partners in the inquiry. In this way each research study came to feel less like 'doing' a discrete 'project' and more like 'navigating' within metaphoric 'giant living organisms'. Indeed as mentioned, we found ourselves referring to one of these projects as 'the ecosystem' or 'the great octopus of a project' (Wadsworth and Epstein 1996: 194, 198).

The work also called for far more complex, multi-component and emergent research designs as well as greater openness to what counted both as data and as research technique as we pursued our various practice-knowledge objectives within communities of large numbers of participants, and over many years.

Like the American action researcher Kurt Lewin (1946), we were finding that the best way to understand an organisation was to try and change it—or rather the best way to try and work out how to try to change it was to understand it and then change it, and test those learnings or theories.

None of this could be done (even conceptually) from outside that living system, so the challenge became how to be good observers, theoreticians and experimentalists *as part of it*, alongside and *with* those who were already there practising it and trying to understand and change it themselves too. This was not just a nice democratic idea or to be polite (though these turn out to be characteristic of sustainable living systems), it was essential to the science. That is, the observing researcher was not separate from the life being observed. The 'observed' were inevitably always an idea or experience in our minds, and in theirs and those of 'others'. But its objectivity was only *made sense of* in relation to definitions and interpretations of meaning that were essentially intersubjective and socially systemic in their construction and validation in subsequent practice.

The complexities of processing continuous sensing input by complex, individual person-systems each comprising 240 billion neurones and 100 trillion cells, in relationship with potentially unlimited numbers of other people (each with 240 billion processing neurones and 100 trillion cells of their own!) not to mention all other beings and elements, then all of this working individually and together to further process and make sense of this input over even the course of a day (or a minute!) much less a lifetime, renders the idea of 'research' being a special and separate activity only conducted by special and separate people for particular periods of time in particular places, limiting at best and dangerously misleading at worst!

Susan Greenfield the neuroscientist has made the point that the more observations we make and the more experiences of action we accrue, the more neural connections we make and the greater the complexity and the better the chances of making *new* connections, syntheses and insights (2001). In effect this may be seen as a physiological basis for experiential practice accrual and even as a case for collaborative human dialogue between bearers of this diversity of experience.

The level of complexity to which any living system has to 'attune' in order to achieve sufficient 'morphic field resonance' to achieve its life purposes, and in sufficient resonant harmony with others in their own 'fields of systemicity' so that all are able to work together to achieve their interconnected life purposes, is in startling contrast to some of our own often simplistic efforts to model such complexity.

It is a challenge to make time and space to:
- Be more aware of what we are observing
- Be more able to see other realities beyond first appearances
- Not presume only on the basis of past experience

- Match the complexity of our understandings and theories to what they represent
- Do so without doing too great or unhelpful 'reductionist violence' to their representation
- Find non-reductionist ways of representing our understandings
- Record or otherwise be able to retrieve what might be significant
- Inform deeper reflection on the situation's characteristics and complexity
- Make new and better connections between observations and experiences, and
- Generate better insights capable of bringing changes that are aligned with living purposes.

Elizabet Sahtouris has also noted that systems concepts like chaos theory, dynamics, complexity and fractals are currently proliferating, and sees the kind of 'living systems thinking' which I am describing here as drawing on 'new kinds of logic, and new ways of ordering human thought about a dynamically alive universe' (1999 online). While she identifies this firmly as an organic rather than a mechanical universe, I will try to show in Chapter 3 how I have re-understood 'the mechanical' within an epistemology that sees the psychological systemicity of the human mind in co-evolution with its environment. That is, 'the organic' may better be thought of as inclusive of *something* of what we call 'the mechanical'—but not to the point of being an overly ordered replicative form that eliminates other properties of life. I see this as a new unity of science, mathematics, physics, social science and ancient philosophy with the human social ecological. As Elizabet Sahtouris observes:

> Many of the new studies of self-organizing systems have been inspired by the work of Nobel Prize-winning chemist-physicist Ilya Prigogine, who revived the ancient concept of nature's creation of order from chaos, showing how self-maintaining systems even at a chemical level can re-create new order when they reach chaotic states. Prigogine's work extends the physics of equilibrium thermo-dynamics—which was invented to describe non-living systems—into non-equilibrium thermodynamics, which he used to model living systems (Sahtouris 1999 online)

The field is an exciting one, but also complex and full of debate. There are, for example, those who experience these understandings as referring to a 'real

Figure 2. Initially observed relationships between parties to the research

Strategic Group Model-Building Learning Sub-systems (SGMBLSS)

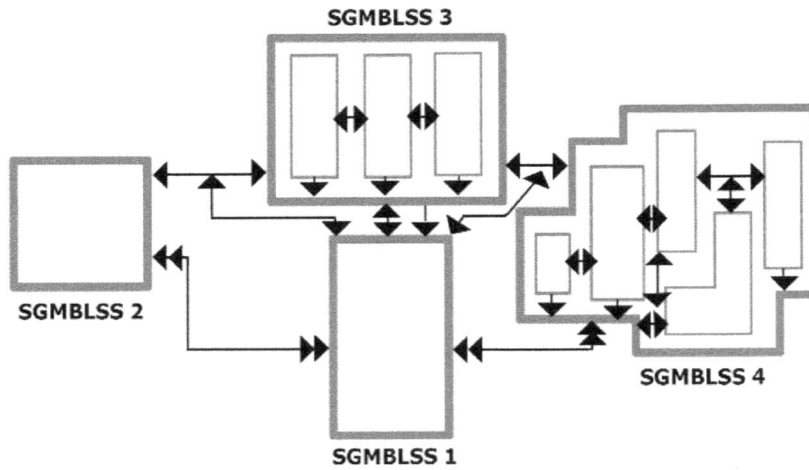

Figure 3. Mechanistically modelling the system

Figure 4. Organically what was possible!

world', those who experience it as referring heuristically to something we call a real world that we socially construct from input to our bodily systems (including our mind's sensing receptors and intuiting connectors), and those who consider it to be a matter of always going back and forth between an imagined/received 'sensing real' and a humanly 'socially constructed real' world, and thus inevitably always symbolic (even if we act recursively 'as if' it is real and 'out there', while trying to remain conscious of its always signified and metaphoric nature).

In Chapters 3 and 4 I conclude at a general systemic level that it may 'take all (these) types' of perspectives to assist in sustaining life at whatever scale. Furthermore, that it is a critical property of any living system that each autopoetic 'part' (each organism, 'sub-system', person, group, organisation or network) can 'hold' the 'DNA' knowledge (and has a viable way of always being able to seek out new and better knowledge) of the whole process for inquiring into, determining and acting on what both serves life and is life-depleting. However this may only come with better mutual understanding of how we can differently contribute to collective thinking in this way, at the same time as we all, given time and space, can and must (for life) 'get right round the cycle', experiencing each of these perspectives within ourselves.

Sequencing the properties and processes of living systems

Systems properties are conventionally presented as lists of characteristics,[14] but I have found it helpful also to sequence them to show the *dynamics* of their operation in 'living practice' as emergent systems-in-process (Wadsworth 2008a, 2008b)—creating and maintaining enough feedback loops (or process) and enough form (or structure) to ensure both stabilising *balance* and energetic *motion* for self-organising or autopoetic life. It is these two concepts—dynamic process *away from* and stabilising *towards* equilibrium—that paradoxically when combined with 'life-achieving purpose' deriving from detected discrepancy, or what Capra calls 'trajectory bifurcation' (1996: 171), comprise the key defining features of a living system. But don't take my word for it! Try it for yourself. Try and ride a bike without both! Try and live

a single day—or minute—of your life without both structure *and* purposeful process-in-response-to discrepancy. Try and raise a child without flexibility *and* meaningful rules. Try and work anywhere in any economy. Try and provide *or* receive a human service without stabilising forms *and* life-enhancing/changing purposes. Try and eat. Or breathe. Sometimes it may be more of one than the other, but sooner or later whichever is the lesser or missing will be needed, a discrepancy felt and energy expended to seek its restoration. And so it is with all the other related defining features. The whole is (indeed) greater than the sum of its parts since it is the integrated operation of all *together* that defines a being as alive or not.

These 'embodied processes' are depicted here in three ways—as a list of key properties (Table 1), as a sequenced narrative (Table 2), and as a diagrammatically cyclic process of forming, transforming and re-forming (Figure 5). All may be observed to operate at any scale, from the smallest cell or individual 'system' all the way up to and throughout the largest, most complex systemicities imaginable. Think of a single amoeba, or a 300-year-old Chinese dynasty, or a new human services program: all are embodied systems with fuel consumed to release energies for ongoing organ-ising, all take characteristic (while varying) forms, all have movement, purpose and change; all feature beginnings, active flourishings, eventual deterioration, dying away and transformation to new living forms. And all are situated within surrounding fields or larger environments of inter-dependent systems or sub-systems following the same logic in relation to each other.

And here's where the a simple conceptual cycle becomes so exponentially and infinitely rich and complex in practice as all living systems—all at different points in their and our living—are interacting with each other. What may have started out simply and predictably becomes complex and uncertain in the 'blooming buzzing confusion'. Yet even as living systems 'go to scale' we can identify the same fractal-like 'architecture' of new patterned forms as self-organising self-structuring for life, with the same inter-connection properties and exercising dynamic inquiring 'agency' or 'will' in relation to existing morphogenic (form-shaping) fields not of their own immediate making that generate the life-compelling comparative discrepancies.

TABLE 3. SUMMARY LIST OF THE STRUCTURAL PROPERTIES OF LIVING SYSTEMS[15]

Living – from the Germanic including meaning bodily capacity for action, growth; organic, functional activity; existing, continual, remaining, perennial, flowing
System – the 'embodying', from the Greek *sustema*, 'set up' of 'like things', *syn*, 'like' or 'with' and *histemi*, related to history (past learning)
- Organisms comprise boundaries, elements/cells/parts, openings/closings, thresholds, shape/structure
- Flows and patterns of energy as information (inputs, outputs, feedback) connect through fields, spaces and across boundaries, bridges and thresholds, being exchanged or blocked, merging, uniting or bifurcating in response to other energies (perturbance, turbulence)
- Information acts as feedback for processes of autopoiesis (taken here to mean self-organising): communication, action, selectivity, adjustment, adaptation and generativity in response to this 'intelligence'
- Organisms seek/receive/take in information, inputs, feedback, nutrients, sustenance, nourishment and resources by purpose[16]/intention[17] to concentrate energy to fuel form or identity, and to maintain actions, forms and connections with other parts of the organism and its life-sustaining field of holarchic systemicity
- Organisms (forms, patterns of dense energy) 'grow'/replicate/are conserved in relation to the resources available; adaptively in relation to the 'learnings' from input and feedback—positive feedback with amplifying (growth) loops that take the dynamic away from existing equilibrium; negative feedback with balancing (self-stabilising) loops that negate change or disturbance and return to 'centre' (small variations can have big effects)
- Organisms 'notice' and valorise what has been life-giving (attracted towards or repelled away), recursively replicating best forms, patterns and processes relative to what is available/'desired'/sought, or defending against, rejecting, eliminating, discarding or releasing those that don't, then recursively revising form
- Entropy of embodied energy as expiry/death, recycling and recovering energy-containing resources in new forms to feed new beginnings
- New beginnings incarnate when 'needs, wants, purposes, valued states or desires' 'require' and 'inquire' in response to felt discrepancy/bifurcation
- Increased diversity and complexity leads to increasingly complex co-evolution and the possibility of holarchic emergence (transformation–transgeneration).

To use the metaphor of seasons: in a well-resourced warming 'spring', a new organism—emerging from the dense complex matrix of prior resourcing and 'communication'—may germinate, sprout, put down roots and accomplish a growth spurt. In 'summer', the growth potential may be reached and, with small 'running repairs', continue to productively 'tick over' without either excessive growth or depletion. Then, when wear and tear and depleted energy (embodied resources) overtake the productive impulse and the materials available both within the organism and from outside, an 'autumnal' harvest of what has been produced may take place at the same time as a dying-off precedes a 'winter' of quiet mulching, turning things over and resource replenishment, until conditions are right for the new organism to emerge, or renew (re-novate or in-novate) and again experience a spring growth spurt (en-novate).

Not too structured, stabilised and ordered *or* too fluid, flexible and dynamic. Not too little or too much change, not too few connections or too many, or too much input or not enough—but always oscillating between these states.

This cannot be too greatly stressed: a system that becomes overly characterised by one or the other of any of these will not be able to continue to sustain full life over time. James Lovelock, the physicist, has used the metaphor of the Goldilocks story of the bears sampling the porridge and the beds, and settling for the ones that were not too big and not too small, 'but just right' (2002). The Protestant aphorism 'everything in moderation' is in similar territory if extremes of *any* elements are understood to take a living system too far from equilibrium. 'Too much of a good thing' may

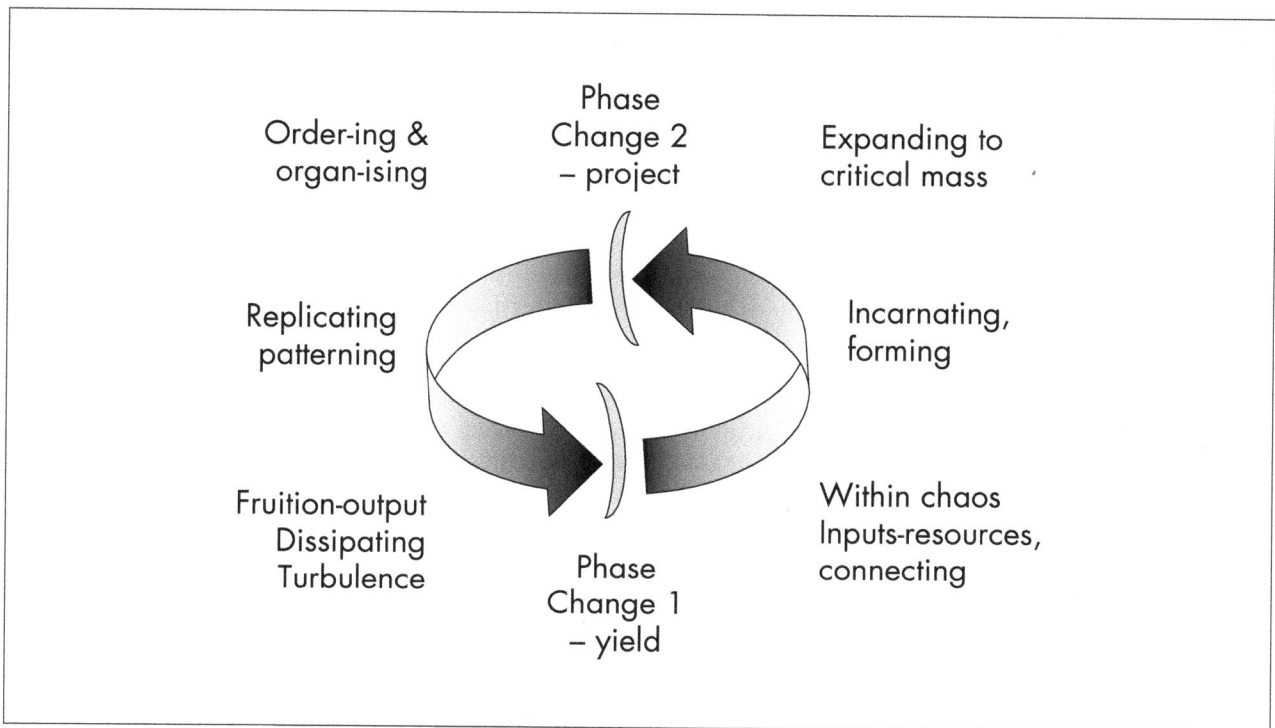

Figure 5. Cyclic representation of changing and forming in living systems

take its toll as much as 'too much of a bad thing'. Even too much moderation may be as life-diminishing as too much immoderation!

The critical matter is that each aspect remains constantly moving towards being, as Buddhist thinkers might put it, in 'right relation' to the others. Not to stay in static equilibrium or to stay completely out of it, but to 'oscillate', moving in and out of each state. A system which only copies or replicates existing forms and patterns without holding the 'DNA' that supplies 'the reason why', or without any room for fluidity and openness to new input, possibilities or feedback (contextual flexibility or discretion—from the Latin *discretio*, meaning discernment, being the ability to exercise a different judgement resulting from an alternative analysis or insight), will sooner or later accrue error because there is no way for the organism to recommence inquiry by noticing discrepancies and making changes to correct itself 'in flight'. It will also not be able to take independent initiative to know when *not* to reproduce a pattern or copy without also 'carrying information' (as knowledge) about the principle or initial value-driven purpose. At the same

time a 'system' or field without any order and closure (the ability to exercise a boundary judgement) cannot achieve its end purposes because it remains perpetually in a state of not yet organ-ised openness to possibility, fluid movement, and 'yet to decide'.

In this instance a system stays in perpetual change and chaos and is unable to create or hold a form by which to achieve purposes. To try over and over to begin growing (change to or expand a new form) only to be repeatedly deprived of the conditions for new life will eventually exhaust stored energies and the system will succumb, or be 'bonsai-ed', undergoing permanent change to its systemic logic or patterning. Or a system that tries only to produce and produce without rest or replenishment will also exhaust its reserves. Equally, a system that only consumes will eventually be unable to take productive action.

Peter Senge describes human social organisation or culture as systemic when it comprises ways of thinking which result in 'invisible fabrics of interrelated actions' (1990: 7) in which: 'we just find ourselves feeling compelled to act in certain ways' (44).

Chris Argyris calls these replicated social patterns

TABLE 4. SEQUENCING THE DYNAMIC PROCESSES OF LIVING SYSTEMS

'*Dynamic*' – from the Greek dunamikos 'power'
'*Process*' – from the Latin pro 'forward' and cede 'go'

Dissipation
The existing is dissipating...
A new 'beginning' is coming out of the fruition, decaying, ebbing, contracting, breakdown and entropic transformation of energies of an existing being which is becoming something else in response to prior conditions which are problematising (perturbance, turbulence), moving far from equilibrium, and being detected as 'discrepancy', valorised negatively in relation to its-self and its-environment
The existing is being defended at the same time as the new is being sought...
The existing form moves to adaptively fix, repair and correct, or continue to defend and replicate, copy, mimic, reproduce or 'roll out' consistent with the logic of its prior form; or yields to new possibilities in the morphic field to become something else (and not any other thing); until, reaching critical mass, it moves across a threshold or phase change when the systemic logic of its prior form transforms (e.g. from life to death)

Phase change 1
A new form is being generated...
A new living-being begins to 'come together', connect, co-operate, resonate in a receptive liminal void, chaos or time-space morphogenic (form-shaping) field, a 'rich thick soup' of possibility, diversity, or pherological[18] information that becomes/transforms resources by consumption/conversion into inputs,[19] sustenance and nourishment,[20] for 'purposeful' resonance and self-organising (or autopoiesis)

Within chaos—input, resources, connections
This amorphous beginning life moves 'intentionally' (compelled by purpose, need or desire) to incorporate or embody these life-giving conditions or 'inputs' into a new generative synthesis—and move away from (be repelled by) life-denying inputs (excluding, distancing or disembodying such aspects of the environment from its emergent self)

Incarnating, forming
The new being is organ-ising to become 'the way the organism can be to do things round here'...
As it 'builds' or 'grows' it creates networked or connected 'packets' or cells, divisions, sub-systems of bounded stabilising structure, incarnating, each in relation to the other, expanding in order and complexity

Expansion to critical mass
By further channelling of energies to connect, exchange and contain further input-resources as energies for purposes, it reaches viability

---

of practice 'routines' because they 'occur continually and independent of individual actors' personalities' and they are 'immediate', 'automatic', 'unconscious' and 'highly skilled' (1993: 20). Laboratory scientists have identified 'mirror neurones' they think brains activate to copy or mimic at an embodied 'felt' level by watching an action without need for articulation or analysis (Rizzolati and Craighero 2004).

Plausibly useful for absorption of existing knowledge as well as in a crisis, none of this proves problematic unless it means a system is prevented from making *needed* change, such as where 'how

things are' is so rigidly replicated and taken for granted that it remains impervious to realising that a changing systems' external environment means things are deteriorating (or could be better). Argyris and others have called such routines or thinking (in human systems) under these conditions 'circular', 'closed loop', 'self-sealing' and 'self-fulfilling'.

The systemic capabilities needed for self-navigation by individual and collective *human* systemicities have been described by sociologists as the '*the social*'—as social structure and social process; as culture, or any of many other specialised terms such

Phase change 2
The new life 'takes its first breath' and signals its identity (integral form for purpose), navigating across a liminal space/threshold and, competing to survive (retain viability and integrity) this second challenging phase change, it 'finds its place' within its field and then expands, protecting itself with further stabilising and connected organ-isation, replication and balancing or homeostatic and institutionalising complexity

Within ordering—organ-ising
Replication of patterns
It reproduces and renews the structures that reflect the logic of the system 'design' into ever stronger recursively replicating, patterning (proceduralising) systems and sub-systems, absorbing new energies while withstanding attacks

Fruition, output
The new becomes old
Eventually these slow down, 'mature' (use all the available energy resources incorporated in the available structure), reach fruition and, despite patching of defences, maintenance and restoration, energy conservation, compensatory moves, correction, substitution, 'quick fixes' and 'running repairs', the embodied forms destabilise or bifurcate (overgrow, expire, outgrow, rigidify, atrophy, weaken, age and decay); energies ebb and are expended; and the organism's systemicity ceases growing, yields and breaks down into outputs, fragments or its constitutive elements. These then go 'back into the soup', becoming the preconditions or environment of feedback, resources or inputs (nutrition and 'helpers' or toxins and 'detractors') detected, evaluated or sought by something else that is beginning to connect and combine with new information/inputs to become a new identity...
At any point the sequence or living system cycle can be assisted, facilitated and resourced to go full cycle 'naturally', or be 'prematurely' diminished, thwarted, deprived, depleted, coerced, attacked, raided, parasitically leached, overly pruned, prematurely harvested ,'short-circuited', over-hastened, overwhelmed, delayed, blocked, suppressed, rendered unproductive or destroyed, 'unnaturally'—with 'natural' or 'unnatural' being defined by the conditions of the 'participating' systems or holarchy of sub-systems or super-systems (embodied repeated energies in these are formed 'structures')—and knowable (or not) by communication and feedback e.g. identified and valorised as 'resource' or as 'toxin'.

And the cycle of life repeats itself...

as Pierre Bourdieu's field and habitus (1984);[21] or described by psychologists as *'the personal'*—as personality capabilities or personal 'type'.[22]

These social and psychological capabilities may be thought of as exercised around the conceptual living system cycle by all people-system 'organisms', whether at the scale of 'the individual', the group, the organisation, the network, state or community. The various research and evaluation capabilities are explained in Chapter 3, and their relationships with differing human service care capabilities are explained in Chapter 4, including when they become overly

disconnected or boundaries are established and defended that compromise the organism's need for new inputs and meaningful insights, displacing their own life-giving purposes. (Appendix 3 cautions against simplistic interpretation of these inquiry preference systemicities as tightly bounded identity 'boxes'.)

All living systems will protect their existing forms and even 'immunise' themselves against change in fear of an unknown and worse situation. But if the change is necessary to survival (particularly survival for its underlying life purposes) or for greater life, these defences may operate more like 'auto-immune responses' whereby the organism acts unconsciously *against itself* to prevent its own necessary or valuable (life-sustaining or life-restoring) development. It does this if it is unable to carry out more effective new observation or exercise responsiveness to that input. On the other hand there is the possibility of such endless fluidity and rapid movement such that nothing can ever be achieved for very long before everything has changed again. Here a world of indecision, fear or inability to make any kind of proactive intervention, or alternatively a relativist 'trying anything and everything' or nihilist 'try nothing', may protect against an unwanted situation that is no better than the old situation. However it may also prevent the desirable possibility of finding a clear way to go forward out of a 'stuck' situation to a new and potentially better 'form'.

'Enough running repairs' and re-sourcing to sustain long life and continuing productivity is an ancient dream and desire of many of our own species. But perpetual motion is 'the dream of the machine'[23]—with its deadly downsides of the illusion of achieving perfection, and the 24/7 'endless summer production' and 'endless autumn harvest', just as it has its out-of-balance counterparts around the cycle of the 'dream of eternal youth', or the 'dream of being absolutely anything you want to be', or 'the dream of world domination'—and all the other moments when living systems can get out of kilter and overdo (or underdo) some aspect or another of their properties or cycles.

But how can we recognise when both a system's stabilising organ-isation *and* dynamic change are in 'right relationship' with each other? How can we know when we are shaping living systems and correcting ones that are not? How can we know when to move forward and when to keep reproducing past structures? What does it take to be able to tell the difference?

And how can we build systems that turn away sooner from cycling too long in one part or too little in another? From overgrowth or depletion? How can we 'build systems' that carry out life-giving purposes drawing on *all* human capabilities that are, like Goldilocks' porridge and beds, 'just right' in size, complexity, feedback and so on?

In the next chapter I identify processes of inquiry as following the same dynamic that results in all living systems, and set out to illuminate the concrete connections between living systems properties and processes and social research, evaluation and continuous improvement.

A cartoon of fifteen years ago has perhaps proved uncannily premonitory!

...EVER GET THE FEELING LIFE IS A PERPETUAL ACTION RESEARCH PROCESS ?!!

Whole systems research to engage with complex living systems

In the U&I work I experienced the dawning realisation of the need for a far more complex and dynamic way of thinking about the evaluative research we were trying to carry out to improve the effectiveness of organisational and institutional life for its critical beneficiary group.

We needed to become fully engaged as 'whole (individual) beings' with other 'whole (individual) beings'—all the way till we were working with 'a whole (social organisational) being'. The deeper we were involved, the better we understood it, and the better we understood ourselves, the better we were able to step into the turbulence, the chaos, the conflict and rigid structures, and the silences and defences large and small. Everything was data. Every thought and response of our own or others' told us something more about the giant living system we were part of and working with.

Sometimes it felt like building Edgar Schein's 'parallel processes' (1987, 1988), or cycling alongside practitioners and consumers miming new actions. Sometimes it felt like building Vygotsky's 'scaffolding' to allow new ideas to be sketched as a kind of 'near-fit' blueprint or 'zone of proximal development' (1996: 138) and then built in as new practice. Sometimes it felt like Michael White's narrative therapy (2007) as we nursed the 'wounded care bear' to recover its good intents and revise some of the iatrogenic language of the existing story; sometimes it felt like we were getting out the ruler and measuring just how far the changes had come, how different the new practice was on the graph from the old practice.

Yes, we used questionnaires, surveys, interviews, case studies, narratives and focus groups. But day in day out, over weeks and months we were also weaving and ducking, knitting and intervening, observing and responding to the surging, retreating, moving, swirling living forms; stepping back to reflect and then going in deeper, like a deep tissue remedial masseur, seducing painful muscles to give up their load; finding the spaces to draw breath, finding the hooks on which to hang activities, clearing away the logjams and oiling the rusty patches; sometimes working alone, more often in pairs or small groups and sometimes all together; small cycles within larger cycles within very big cycles; shaping old things into new things, new ideas, conclusions, new concepts and plans and skilfully grafting them onto old strong practices—new procedures, new job descriptions, new kinds of ways of doing and being; then carefully watching those—did they 'take' and become part of the human ecology of 'the way we do things round here'? Or did they default and decay, and need to be re-examined and reworked?

But all the time we kept following (and were largely permitted to pursue) a logic of inquiry that saw us constantly able to follow our questions, share our experiences and observations with other participants, think them through together, leave them aside until later when things made more sense, or until new insights could emerge and there was clarity about what to try next. Then we could interrogate the outcomes— did it work? Were things better as a result? What was the concrete evidence? And was something more or different needed instead?

We questioned our way to our outcomes. We were inquiring to detect life and to form more of it.

ENDNOTES

1 Greeting card caption by Claude Pepper, Lonely Planet Images Collection 2005.

2 'Autopoiesis' was a word I first heard in conversation with Colombian sociologist Orlando Fals Borda, but it may be more generally known from its origins in the 1973 work of the Chilean biologists Umberto Maturana and Francisco Varela (1980) and its later articulation by Fritjof Capra (1996). It has been taken in this book to refer to one of the definitional properties of living systems and a key concept of this book. It has not been without controversy (including by Maturana and Varela), mainly because it can sound overly autonomous and self-referential—when instead it rests on the idea of holarchic connection or 'structural coupling' with other self-organising systemicities. As living systems scale up, the 'unit of autopoiesis' (to use Anisur Rahman's term, personal communication 2005) may also be seen as enlarging. In this way the larger social organism may be seen to be similarly inquiring collaboratively 'around the life cycle': observing, analysing, theorising, planning and acting in order to achieve collective life.

3 Elisabet Sahtouris (2005a, 2005b) the evolutionary biologist calls this a 'holarchy' (after Arthur Koestler) to distinguish it from a 'hierarchy' and thus alert us to the way in which a living system is a feedback network rather than a one-way top-to-bottom command system (which may not have the capacity for life-giving feedback if the 'commanded' cannot contribute to what is 'commanded'). Michael Quinn Patton has used the term 'panarchy' to get at these matters of cross-scale interaction in both time and space (2006) after Gunderson and Holling (2002).

4 Brian Swimme the mathematical cosmologist notes (Swimme and Berry 1994) that life on earth generated 6.5 billion years ago in co-creation with the sun as photosynthesis by the chlorophyll molecule. It then went on holarchically to self-organise/evolve out of repeated uncertain chaos into new and more complex levels of regularity. His interpretation is of a cosmos, or oikos in the sense of 'a home' for 'mutual relationality', even though 'getting it right' in its own experimental terms (with hindsight) i.e. generating life, took millions of years.

5 I will also use another unfamiliar word 'systemicity' as a generic term sometimes rather than the more familiar 'system', for all the different scales of living systems—cell, organ, organism, group, organisation, community, society, and inter-national system (Miller 1978). This is to to try to convey its living nature, even though this is still a noun of the word 'systemic' rather than a verb-like 'process'. While I will still use the more common term system, when we use the noun (indeed any nouns) it is difficult to remember that it is not a static wholly bounded 'thing' we are talking about but a mass of continuous energetic patterning continually being replicated (or not), forming (or dissipating), taking (a) shape (and losing or morphing from it), and all the while in relationship with other systemicities (whether bounded or open), all doing the same. Yet these are only 'things' to our perceiving eye (even while shaped by our desires, intentions and prior knowings and constantly re-shaped by these, since unavoidably we can 'only' perceive the world through our own pre-structured embodiment, no matter how independent, separate and objective we may feel ourselves to be!) 'Things' (material or cultural) may more deeply be understood as repeated energy patterns to form densities that we *call* and *experience* as 'real' or as a 'fact' (remembering that the derivation of the word 'fact' is from the Latin *factum* from *facere*, a 'datum of doing', *datum*, singular of *data* from the Latin *dativus*, 'a given'. That is, it is we who, by doing, give things—and arguably 'need' to give things—their facticity by so perceiving them in order to avoid having to rediscover every bit of our worlds every day. The colossal amount we learn as infants and children doesn't have to all be repeated throughout life. Instead it accrues as so much 'practice wisdom'—that we constantly revise both consciously and not. The trick of 'things' seeming real, solid, reliable and immutable is therefore a kind of labour-saving device! An anxiety-reducing illusion that enables us to avoid endlessly re-living *Groundhog Day* (an American movie in which each day was repeated until the lead character learned something significant about himself) and instead we are able to get on with living more of life as *if* it is all still going to be there, more or less the same, tomorrow.

6 For example close aural observation has recently led an Australian woman (who had been a concert violinist and operatic mezzo soprano) to speculate that there may be five distinctive 'baby language' sounds. These would appear to be systemic in the sense that the five sounds may be embodying the particular body sensations and feelings related to the five different referents they are expressing (e.g. the sound 'neh' for 'I'm hungry, please feed me' is physically like a sucking tongue-in-mouth reflex, or 'owh', 'I'm tired', like a yawn). Accessed 27 October 2009: http://en.wikipedia. org/wiki/Dunstan_Baby_Language Language development appears to follow similar properties of all living systems in that sounds may begin by being rather chaotic and random and then through selectivity begin to form shape, pattern and regularity.

As well, in a Yale university experiment, babies as young as six months were observed to demonstrate the rudiments of 'evaluative rational feeling' by selecting puppets that had been 'helpful' and rejecting puppets that had been either a 'hindrance' or neutral to another puppet trying to climb a hill. They noted (Hamlin et al. 2007), 'Our findings indicate that humans engage in social evaluation far earlier in development than previously thought'.

7   I thank Alan Saunders and the former ABC Radio National program *The Comfort Zone* for this timely exemplar on cubbies (2004).

8   In a conversation with Michael Toms and John Seed about what an ecological perspective means, 'Deep Ecology', *New Dimensions*, ABC Radio National, 6 January, 1999

9   Many thanks to Michael W. Davidson and the Florida State University for this remarkable public domain 'powers of 10' Molecular Expressions™ Science, Optics & You Interactive Java Tutorials website.

10 Interestingly the word 'ecumenism' stems also from *oikos* (the Greek *oikoumenikos*) meaning the wider 'unity of the inhabited earth' (at an historical time to encompass differences in doctrine among the religious communities of Christians).

11 Between 1947 and 1951 Le Corbusier designed La Cité Radieuse (radiant city), a block of apartments in Marseille that integrated the meeting of inhabitants' living needs within a single 'self-contained' (partially self-organising) building designed like a ship; with flexibly designed living spaces, an indoor 'street' with a grocery, a hotel for residents' visitors and family members, a nursery school, gymnasium, picture theatre, terrace roof area for recreation with a children's paddling pool, play areas and a stage for open air shows.

12 The words of Mary Oliver and Gaston Bachelard appeared unsourced on the catalogue at an art exhibition entitled 'House' at Boston College, Boston, United States, 2001. The references have not been able to be traced definitely but the words of Oliver may be from a work of ecological poetry from 2002, and the words of Bachelard may be from the French translated as *The Formation of the Scientific Mind*, Clinamen, Bolton, 1938.

13 Of course other, especially non-Western societies, have generated entirely differing shapes and forms. In contrast to the grids and square shapes of the Western machine age, many African villages consist of clusters or networks of round huts; or Australian Aboriginal traditional habitats had very 'light footprints', using natural materials and forms that were flexible to suit living while moving across the land. Mongolian traditional life generated portable round forms for a nomadic lifestyle, and so on. Different eras and even decades have done the same (e.g. 'little boxes' in the 1950s, organic and rounded earth forms in the 1970s, soaring towers in the 1980s and 1990s, and so on).

14 For example the biologist Fritjof Capra's table of the key criteria of a living system lists: pattern of organisation (the configuration of relationships determining essential systemic characteristics), structure (embodiment of the pattern of organisation), and life process (the activity involved in continual embodiment of the pattern of organisation) (1996: 161). The evaluator Bob Williams has developed a three point summarisation of: inter-relationships, perspectives and boundaries (2008).

15 A comparable list by the biologist Elisabet Sahtouris (applied to business) may be accessed at: http://www.via-visioninaction.org/via-li/articles/ Sahtouris_BiologyOf Business-full_version.pdf.
    In a further glimpse of the transdisciplinarity of this thinking, the architect Christopher Alexander (2004) has arrived at fifteen principles of life for a 'healed architecture' that correlate highly with other lists of living systems properties, viz, levels of scale, strong centres, boundaries, alternating repetition, positive space, 'good' shape/simple form, local symmetries, (field-looping) deep interlock and ambiguity, contrast, gradients (harmonious dynamic sequences), roughness (paying attention to what matters most), echoes (relatedness), void (the morphogenic field that draws the centre's energy to itself), simplicity/inner calm, not-separateness/connected/ complementary/wholeness (integral unity). Recently the idea of a 'healing architecture' has been applied directly to human services (Jencks and Heathcote 2010).
    A third cross-disciplinary thinker who writes accessibly about living systems, Maggie Moore, has combined a language of sensation with the familiar cyclic model in a short paper on change in organisations, see: http://www.sustainabilityleaders.org/pdfs/moore_rhythms.pdf.

16 'Purpose', from the Latin *proponere*, meaning 'propound'; 'offer for consideration', from the Latin *pro* 'for', 'on behalf of', and *ponere posit*, 'place'. This captures the moment of pinpointing experience of what is of critical underlying value or worth, 'readying' the energy of intention.

17 'Intention' from the Latin *intentio*, meaning 'stretching, purpose, tend, conception', related to 'intent, intense, intensity, intension, intensive', meaning 'increase the opacity, magnetic field, force, brightness', 'strong/deep feeling, emotion', 'highly concentrated', 'the internal content of a concept', 'directed to a single point', 'resolve'.

18 From the Greek, *phero*, meaning 'convey' and logos as 'signifier'; like a 'life-line'. I thank Colin Butler and Adrian Sleigh of the National Centre for Epidemiology and Population Health, Canberra for these respective conceptualisations (personal communications 13 July 2004).

19 I thank Wendy Gregory of the Environmental Science and Research Institute, New Zealand, for this distinction in conceptualisation that illuminates the consumption/conversion/value-adding taking place.

20 I thank Richard Eckersley of the National Centre for Epidemiology and Population Health, Canberra for his conceptualisation of 'resource' as 'sustenance and nourishment' as a way of alerting us to their greater resonance with the idea of living systems per se (personal communication 13 July 2004).

21 Pierre Bourdieu's concepts of field (as a structure of relationships in which people manoeuvre and struggle in pursuit of desirable resources), and habitus (as a system of

internalised dispositions or acquired patterns of thought, behaviour and taste responding to conditions) attempt to bridge between positions of 'objectivity' and 'subjectivity' (1984).

22 In Chapters 3 and 4 I am particularly going to draw on the implications of what Jungian Myers Briggs theorists have observed regarding what I will call human 'inquiry preferences'. The connections with systems thinking will be more fully explained there, for example human 'mental functions' as systemic capabilities to take in information, process it and act on it; to create order and closure (organisation), replicate recognised 'system logic' and knowledge patterns, and be open to possibilities to respond to new information in order to make creative connections to bring about adaptive or generative new knowledge and (processual) change. These capabilities may be thought of as operating both in relation to the inner system (as introversion, personal experience, personal constructs and constructionist identity and concepts) and in relation to outer systems (as extroversion, the interrelations between people and groups and the socially constructed). Systems' detection capabilities operate regarding the detail of separately organ-ised field-based elements, aspects, facts/appearances or entities (received concretely or literally through sensing), and in relation to larger contexts containing these elements or appearances (understood through intuitive 'leaps' connecting them). Finally, human psychological systems have capabilities to detect and evaluatively judge discrepancies between different states both by non-verbal rational inductive comparative feeling and explication of rational deductive comparative logic (as moral principles or community ethos).

23 Interestingly the word 'robot'—meaning a machine that has the appearance of a human but works mechanically and efficiently without sensitivity or emotion—comes from the Czech robota, meaning 'forced labour' (i.e. not self-organising).

Cycles of research, evaluation and inquiry for life

If living 'organisms' (single cells, bike-riding young people, trees, forests, groups of people, organisations, communities, cities, services, programs) are 'living their systemicity' by constantly 'seeking' to 'make their way in the world' and creating new forms and stabilising them until change is needed again—what does it mean for how we research and evaluate?

Certainly the inquiry[1] processes and forms that enable such continual seeking, acquire more far-reaching significance than perhaps hitherto realised.

One key implication would be that it is the *seeking*—the questioning from a position of *not knowing*—that marks off an epistemology of a living system, rather than the *knowing* of *answers* (and risking stopping there), since knowing will always to some greater or lesser extent necessarily be contingent, uncertain and relative. Indeed the iterative and recursive processes of seeking to continuously renew, re-organise, adapt, adopt and generate change in knowledge and practice are literally critical. Thus while 'knowing the right answers' (or rather, having arrived at the most 'right-for-this-time-and-place answers') will always be an important and desirable moment of any particular cycle of inquiring—it is the continual and sustained opportunity and desire to question, to seek to better understand and to become familiar (*en famille*, meaning kith and kin) with the unknown, and for the new to be emergent—that will be a key indicator of a living system.

Robert Way sees poetically and metaphorically the lover of *scientia*—the one who desires to know—as like a suitor with the soft power (Nye 2005) or necessary yin strength to yield to the attractor of co-inquiring in deep relation to the systemic field:

> Thereupon the stranger, for his soul greatly longed for the love of the Beloved, gladly paid the whole fee and stripped off the rich robes he was wearing which men call Knowledge and Pride and assumed the coarse gardener's habit, Humility...[He] threw away the jewelled rapier which he was carrying which men call Learning, and took in its place a gardener's spade, the name of which is Seeking. (Way 1986: 3)

Another key implication would be that the 'beginning' and 'end' of such seeking may more usefully (heuristically) be thought of less as linear from one question to one answer, and more as 'joined up' to make a cycle or spiral[2] of

emergent beginnings and ends. In this sense, we are all searching or inquiring our way 'round the cycle'[3] individually[4] and collectively all the time and at all scales of being and seeking, in order to live in constant co-construction/co-evolution with other 'systemicities' in the always-stabilising-always-changing fields in which we find themselves.

But how do we keep these processes of life-forming self-organising inquiry continuing both in our own lives and in our lives together? How do we use inquiry to keep moving forward, checking all the while where we have come from, what the current situation holds, and looking forward to an emerging future, and at the same time staying sufficiently balanced, with parts coherent and connected enough with all other parts? Not going ahead too quickly, nor waiting too long. Or going so fast as to hit a wall. Nor getting too stuck. Not missing seeing things going wrong. Detecting them early. Not letting errors or 'perturbations' build up until there is too great turbulence in the system. Not all being exact replicas[5] so that there are no differences to spark new possibilities. Nor being dangerously or painfully divided without connection. Not prematurely decaying or falling apart. Not too rigidified. Not too all over the place. Not hopelessly buffeted *or* becalmed. Not helplessly alone or adrift. How do we get organised when we need to, can or should; and 'sit with' not being so when we aren't, can't or shouldn't? How do we keep moving full cycle to wholeness?

And how do we ensure these properties of living systems characterise all our individual and collective lifeworlds, great and small?

How do we build in robust 'intelligent systems' of research, evaluation and continuous improvement that can help us individually and collectively to get from any 'here' of 'how things are', to any 'there' of 'how things could be'? How can we learn to traverse the same sequences of processes, habitually throughout our lives?

Questioning to assist traversing the cycles of inquiry
If answers are where we stop, then questions provide the key to movement—with each new beginning coming out of past endings, and each ending having once had a new beginning. Thus questions can be asked backwards in time (retrospectively) to observe current action or practice in the world, think through the logic of where it came from or what led to its current framing—and explicate what has been noticed, making more explicit the puzzle or discrepancy that has attracted attention to these observations (inductively). Prospective questions can be asked forwards in time (abductively) about the implications of what is observed in terms of new answers or better theories or new implications for future action or practice—and then what 'experiments' in real life could be tried to trial, refine or test this emerging theory and practice (deductively): Has it happened? Has it worked? And was replication possible?

The cycles of questioning may be small and rapid or large and slow; or with more time spent in one part and a speeding through of others. There may be short-circuiting, repetitions, 'steps' skipped or returned to later—all depending on complex circumstances in relation to the inquiring organism's own autopoetic capabilities. Yet with a kind of reconstructed logic, we see that reflection needs to be informed by observation, and that planning of new action comes out of those reflections on observed action, and so on.

But how and where does living systemic inquiry typically begin—and how does it keep going 'all the way around the cycle'?

The anatomy of inquiry
In a way we can see that all inquiry in practice begins in the midst of everyday life as there is no 'elsewhere' or 'outside' from which to start or even to go to—only, at best perhaps, a sense of getting perspective and distance on one part of everyday life from another. Another standpoint, still from within a field of action, from which to try and begin to observe life more consciously.

Critical to commencing observation and reflection is *noticing*—something pulls us up, is noticeable, remark-able. Discrepant between something and something else. A comparison bursts through into our consciousness and turns a current action into a current-action-noticed. The current action noticed may become a current-action-with-a-question-mark—about what is being observed or what it means. We might rest with making sense of the situation and conclude there. It's a such and such. Or a such and such is the case. And it is because of such-and-such. That may be enough. But if we are left with a feeling that 'all is still not well', we may move on to ask ourselves what it is that is still troubling us about leaving the situation at that.

Perhaps we can't rest with our observations because we are moved to evaluate it. It's somehow not quite right or good enough—or maybe it is spectacularly so—and the pressing questions become: 'How did it get to be like this?' and 'How can we do even more? (or less, or not like this at all…) Now we are seeking to make a new discovery: to understand the situation well enough to change it. Are we really prepared for that? How much do we want change, or to make improvements, or to restore or magnify something already working well, or whatever it is that we want? Now we search our deepest values and purposes for what it is that will form the heart of a new form—a trans-formed situation—and organ-ised activity, service, practice or other way of being or doing.

So we may not rest with observation and explanation, but push on for further reflection, understanding and new insights to assist the change or improvement. We want to go further with our questioning, all the way till we have possibly new answers. But will 'the answers' be enough to rest there? We could. But then we might want to ask questions about how it could happen in practice, and then we might want to question whether it did, and whether it had the intended or hoped for effects or outcomes…and then we might either refine further by going round the sequence of inquiring some more (iteratively, emergently)—or, if all seems well, we take a rest from questioning, unless of course something changes or we notice something else, in which case we might need to question again…

Interestingly we don't usually start with talking about methods or techniques. Or even by going and reading the literature about what others have done or thought. We start in the middle of everyday life by noticing something, stopping, and 'experiencing' a question (one that might not yet even be consciously articulated). A kind of question mark appears over the discrepancy like a genie coming out of the friction of rubbing a lamp. And the cycle of questioning may begin. Then we might think about how to inquire further or go and look at similar experiences. But first we start in our experience.

It is interesting that the word 'experience' comes from the same derivation as the word 'experiment' and 'expert'—from the Latin *experiri*, meaning 'try'.

Experience is, in this sense, the everyday 'results and findings' of previous naturalistic life-based experimentation[6]—something similar to the life processes in all other living systemicities.

Table 5 compares the sequencing of living systems explored in Chapter 2 with the sequencing of inquiry explored in detail in this Chapter 3. Figure 6 depicts this inquiry sequence as a cycle.

How well are we doing this kind of living systems inquiry?

So are our systems of research, evaluation and continuous improvement working well as full cycle inquiry processes?

Interestingly in a way, the three eras of research, evaluation and continuous improvement described in Chapter 1 can be thought of as 'mapping around' much of the living systems cycle—each taking up an area of inquiry that was missing or more silent in the discourse of the previous one. Starting with *research* and its observation and description of existing action and practice; then *evaluation* moves to ask about the value, merit, worth or significance of what was being observed, measured and described, and *continuous quality improvement* takes this into small-scale cycles of new ideas and feedback-based adaptation.

The great leap forward by the quality improvement movement resulted from its seeing the need to 'join up' the ends of the more linear retrospective quality assurance (QA) approach to measuring the achievement of goals, by then reflecting on those results and moving forward into a new quality improvement (QI) cycle. To achieve this it was soon realised that a 'culture shift' would be needed in human and organisational learning and development, and an exciting era opened up of seeking consumer feedback, creatively designing new services or products, and implementing them. Yet disconnects began to short-circuit even such full TQM (Total Quality Management) cycles when managerial planning (and applied research) proved reluctant to take the time to remain in continued reflection and dialogue with the up-close-and-personal business of people's perspectives about what was problematic, and what *they* thought might be of greater value, merit, worth or significance, especially the critical reference group and *their* end-beneficiary perspective. Short-

TABLE 5. COMPARISON OF CORRESPONDING LIVING SYSTEMS AND INQUIRY PROCESSES

Living systems

The existing is flourishing and dissipating and being defended at the same time as resources for the new are being sought…

Phase change 1

A new form is being generated…

Out of morphogenic chaos—with inputs and diverse resources

Communications form connections

The new being is incarnating, taking root, being nourished

Expanding to critical mass to mature to viability

Organ-ising to become 'the way the organism can be to do things round here'

Inquiry processes

Observing existing action…

The existing forms of knowing are defended at the same time as new ways are being pursued…

The inquirer monitors, measures, identifies, audits and confirms or disconfirms (on the basis of 'data', empirical and experiential evidence, analysis and synthesis) the previously established logic (reasoned theory)—adjusting experimental action to better honour/test this theory (including by single loop thinking and restoring replication)

But if discrepancies between an 'is' and an 'ought' remain…

Discrepancy observed

The existing ways of knowing, being and doing are problematising…

Incoming information is noticed, compared, felt, judged to be discrepant (appreciated or not), as adaptation or/and open inquiry evaluation and values/needs re-assessment are taking place simultaneously.

A new inductive process is emerging out of the current ('experimental') testing of previous conclusions in action, as the inquirer (individual or collective) retrospectively…

Reflects…

Phase change 1

Reflection on observations, inductive theory building

New understanding is being sought…

By observing and reflecting more widely and deeply (listening, hearing, seeing etc.), and expressing non-verbally as well as beginning to articulate, share, describe, interpret and analyse their own and others' states of 'what is' in rich, resonant, empathic, comparative detail, including reviewing current driving purposes, practices, experiences, concrete realities, interpretations, intuited contextual connections, paradoxes, conflicts and contradictions, sense is being made…

Within the diversity of 'data' and experience—

In the grounded contextual field, inquirers are beginning to make more strategic experiential connections on the basis of their new (or revised) values and desires about what would be better…

More creatively noticing and questioning on the basis of feelings, values, critical feedback and new (intuitive) reasoning (and double loop thinking or 'thinking about thinking')…

From the dialogue, inquirers begin to make inspired abductive syntheses, and a new narrative emerges

Out of the grounded theory are generated deeper, more insightful interpretations, new conclusions are drawn, and a more resonant value-driven formulation 'brings it together'…

Until the new story adequately understands and explains their and relevant others' situations and felt discrepancies in the observed realities…

And can image or envision desired alternatives, which begin to get momentum to viability

Now the inquiry is looking forward prospectively and…

Plans…

Hypothesising and deducing the possible implications and logical consequences (based on earlier observed strengths, weaknesses, opportunities and threats), confidence builds to select new courses of action that are envisioned, designed, proposed and communicated…

Within a specified field, a new iteration is negotiated to test and refine 'the new' in real-world actual practice conditions

Phase change 2
Within ordering—organ-ising
now for flourishing
Replication of productive
energetic patterns
Fruition, output 'celebrated'
The new becomes old as the
organism expires
As old boundaries break back
down into another rich chaos of
'compost' out of which the
cycle of life repeats itself…

Phase change 2
Acts…
The new naturalistic 'experimental' action is trialled and conducted to test its
hypotheses deductively, with goals being implemented and checked for
anticipated signs/outcomes of achievement…
The inquirers use the new knowledge about 'what to' and 'how to' to serve
their value-driven purposes repeatedly, observing, monitoring/auditing,
measuring and adjusting for success or correcting error in the 'experimental
action' to better honour the knowledge/test the theory (including single loop
thinking to make 'quick fixes' without altering the deeper logic)—but if
discrepancies remain or newly emerge, the cycle of inquiry repeats itself…
Action is again observed
The inquirer starts again wherever 'the field', a person/people are 'at' (in
practice or by inquiry preference), and again moving 'forwards' or 'back' or
'across' to any points round the cycle, reviews, re-assesses, revises, fills in
missed steps, or pursues further change—rather than persisting with error or
defence of error…
And deeper reflection commences again
New knowledge has been superseded by changing conditions
The inquirer assesses and evaluates (appreciative inquiry and critical inquiry)
and moves to deeper 'double loop' (thinking about thinking) or 'triple loop'
(thinking about the conditions for thinking) analyses not just to work with or
reconstruct existing knowledge forms but to create and construct radically new
forms of knowledge…
At any point the inquiry cycle sequence can be assisted, facilitated and
resourced to 'go full cycle' or be blocked, contained and deprived, depending
on the field that it is both part of and which it is in turn co-creating.
And the cycles of inquiry continue…

Define logical
consequences

Design, PLAN,
implement…

…administer'
experimental'
ACTION

Monitor, audit
Notice positive/
negative
discrepancy

Witness,
critically
OBSERVE
value

New formulation
& implications

REFLECT,
interpret
meaning, new
insights/theory

Resource dialogue
in wider contexts,
across diverse
experiences

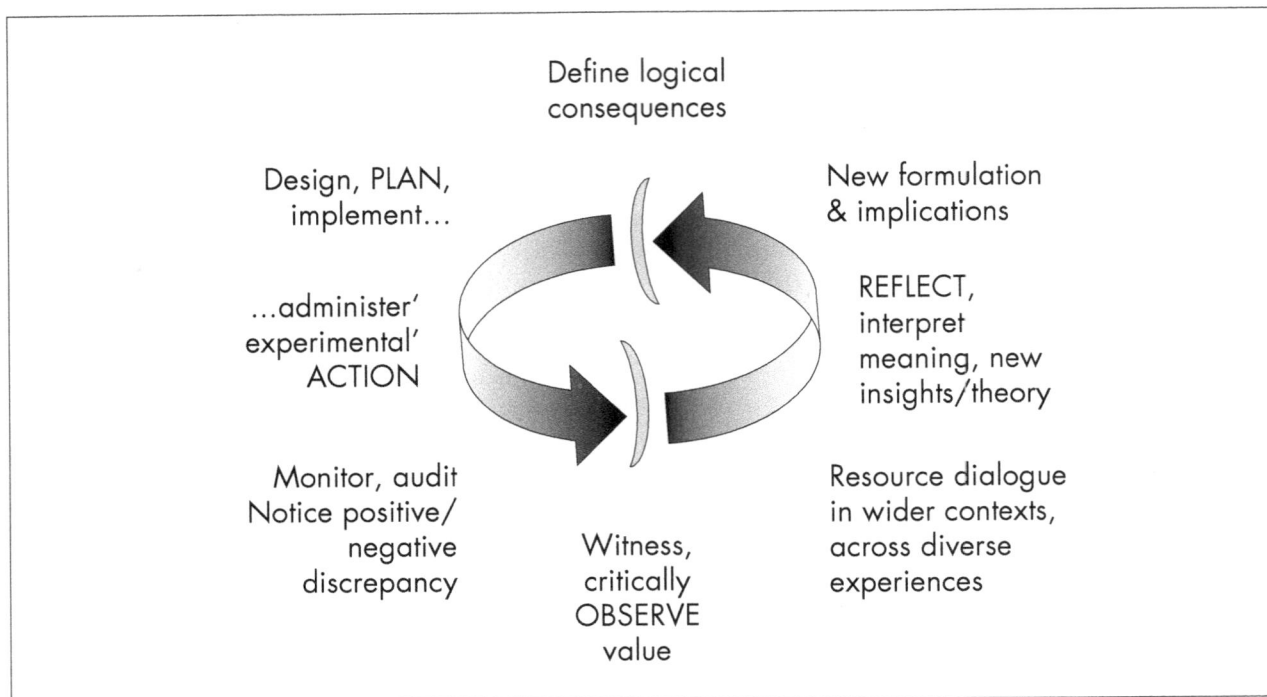

Figure 6. Cyclic representation of inquiry in living systems

circuiting this process into pragmatic replication of modified versions of existing 'solutions' proved frustrating, expensive and time-wasting, and worse, as the new solutions had not been developed sufficiently out of the field with its stakeholders and stakeowners, managers' uncertainty was 'risk-managed' by a dismaying trend towards more and more documentation, measurement and the disembodying of people's experiences in abstracted outcome indicators (rendering them merely providers of one-way feedback) and statistics, to try and provide reassurance that managers had indeed 'got it right' and hopefully would not have to face unhappy constituencies.

In effect the cycle was being short-circuited from quantitative observation of action straight back to re-planning—leapfrogging deeper qualitative and experiential reflection that might have better grasped meaning and generated more insightful ideas for abductive theory of change and innovation to address people's complex lifeworld discrepancies, needs, visions, hopes and goals.

Soon this systemic reluctance to engage more closely with people in in-depth front-end iterations of engaged, field-based, participatory inquiry meant the

TQM process was requiring voluminous after-the-event records and documentation as a hoped for way of knowing what had happened and whether it had been of value, often in the absence of having invested in more. Yet after-the-event statistics often told little about the *meaning* of observed comparative data, and even less about what to *do* about it.

OK. So how might the gaps around cycles of inquiry be bridged—including the gaps between the efforts of specialised researchers and evaluators and the efforts of more everyday inquirers? How can we 'build in' more robust systemic inquiring?

Matters of scale and complexity: building between the small and everyday and the larger and more specialising

'Building down' from specialised efforts into everyday field relations

Firstly, the attempt to increase systemic capacity to fully search around the inquiry cycle may be enhanced by building down or better 'grounding' specialist or outsourced professional, consultant and academic research or evaluation projects back into the lifeworlds of otherwise disconnected or distanced 'subjects', grafting inquiry efforts back into the fabric of daily and institutional activity, contextualising and deepening the observation and understanding, the feedback between participating parties, and strengthening the quality of their generativity by being more connected to the life-enhancing intentions and purposes of the field's critical inquirers.

Much capital 'R' research and evaluation by professional research and evaluation consultants and social theorists is informative and illuminating and can make a terrific contribution to both larger and smaller conversations, particularly by contributing meaningful comparative insights. Indeed so much store has been placed on this kind of expertise that, in a way, it is as if the everyday inquiry capabilities of most people have been 'outsourced' to capital 'R' researchers and evaluators and organisational development folk who do their observing, reflecting and thinking for them. It is an immense privilege, most researchers feel, to be able to go and ask a lot of people a lot of interesting questions and collect all kinds of insights, and then for we the researchers to think things through and come up with our recommendations. But of course we are

vulnerable precisely to the same extent that we are doing this separately from the field and our work may or may not go back into that living system into which we have dipped.

Thus a key drawback of thorough, detailed, lengthy, large-scale professional capital 'R' research and 'E' evaluation is that it is often under pressure to be conducted at too great a distance from the everyday lifeworlds of all parties, rendering it too out of touch, too after-the-event, with too fixed-in-time data, and people compelled to spend too long collecting overly detailed data, drawing conclusions that end up being of limited value to those in the real-world settings and possibly read only by a very special few (and perhaps under-used even by them).

Although rapid everyday assessments can for the most part be adequate—indeed essential to accomplishing much of everyday life—and slow detailed specialist research and evaluation can yield detailed and valuable time-series analysis, what we can also see is a tendency to diminishing returns, both from the everyday if it is too superficial and fast *and* from the intensive and specialised if it is too ponderously big and slow.

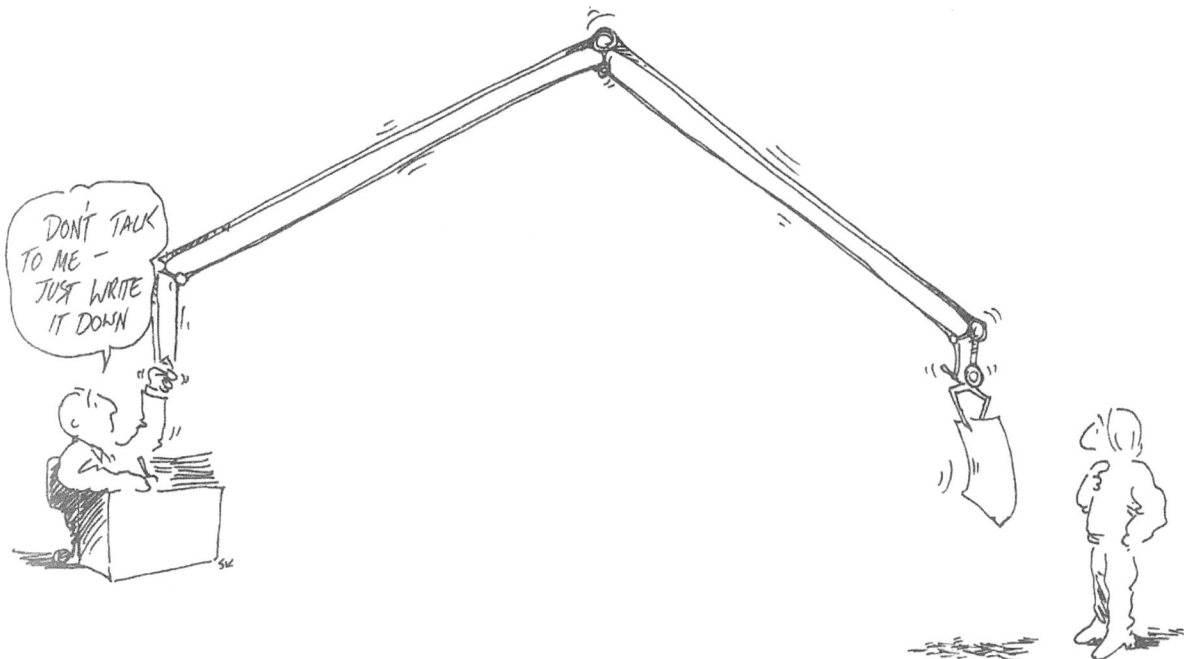

© SK & YW (Wadsworth 1977a, p. 45)

© Bruce Petty. Courtesy of *The Age*

Interestingly this is such a common experience we often hear the former referred to as 'quick and dirty' and the latter as 'only academic'. Perhaps the time has come to build the capacity of individuals and groups to accomplish slower and more thorough 'full cycle' everyday inquiry, and consultants and academics to accomplish more 'plugged in', dynamic, responsive, flexible and field-embedded inquiry.

'Building up' the quality and capacity of small-scale everyday inquiry

Thus the attempt to increase 'whole systems' capacity to fully search 'around the inquiry cycle' might be enhanced also by *building up* and strengthening everyday and in-house inquiry by individuals and groups: creating the spaces and places for *everyone* to be able to regularly stop and reflect, think and theorise, envision and plan, and try things out.

People's ordinary individual inquiry efforts (their 'everyday evaluative research' efforts) are skilled and competent enough to more-or-less effortlessly accomplish their lives. Yet people have become skilled inquirers to the extent their lifetime of interaction in their personal and societal fields of relationships have nurtured these capabilities. Where these have been lacking or where their attention has not been focused on any particular area of inquiry capability, there may be a need for special facilitation skills to accompany people not only right round the cycle, but also to bridge from familiar parts of the cycle to less familiar parts, for example from observing and feeling to thinking through the implications; or from planning implementation to retroductively checking the quality of the theory and its origins in the values and purposes that govern the planned action; or from taken-for-granted action to beginning to observe and question whether that action is working or not. One of the key and pressing drawbacks of people's existing everyday inquiry is that it is often forced to be too superficial in overly busy daily practice—with people compelled to make too hasty decisions on the basis of inadequate data, little time for thought and next to no time for reflection alone or together. Hence a need to consider how to build in methods to enhance this 'going full cycle' (see the later discussion of human services in Chapter 4, and the Exemplars of organisational practice in Chapter 5. See also Wadsworth 2001 on facilitation).

Both of these phenomena, the 'too quick and dirty' and the 'only academic', can result in a deskilled everyday populace becoming ever more disempowered and reliant on others *and* an overly skilled professional group dealing with ever more lengthy and esoteric processes of sourcing research funds and developing designs and field processes that distance them further from field realities, paradoxically often seen as preserving forms of defensible 'objective truth'.

But what would be the conditions for each to morph more in the direction of the other? To enrich overall 'systems intelligence' by avoiding the diminishing returns from both of these extremes. That is, if everyday folk came to see how they were already using evaluative research in small-scale ways all the time[7] and began to scale up, 'thickening' and enriching their

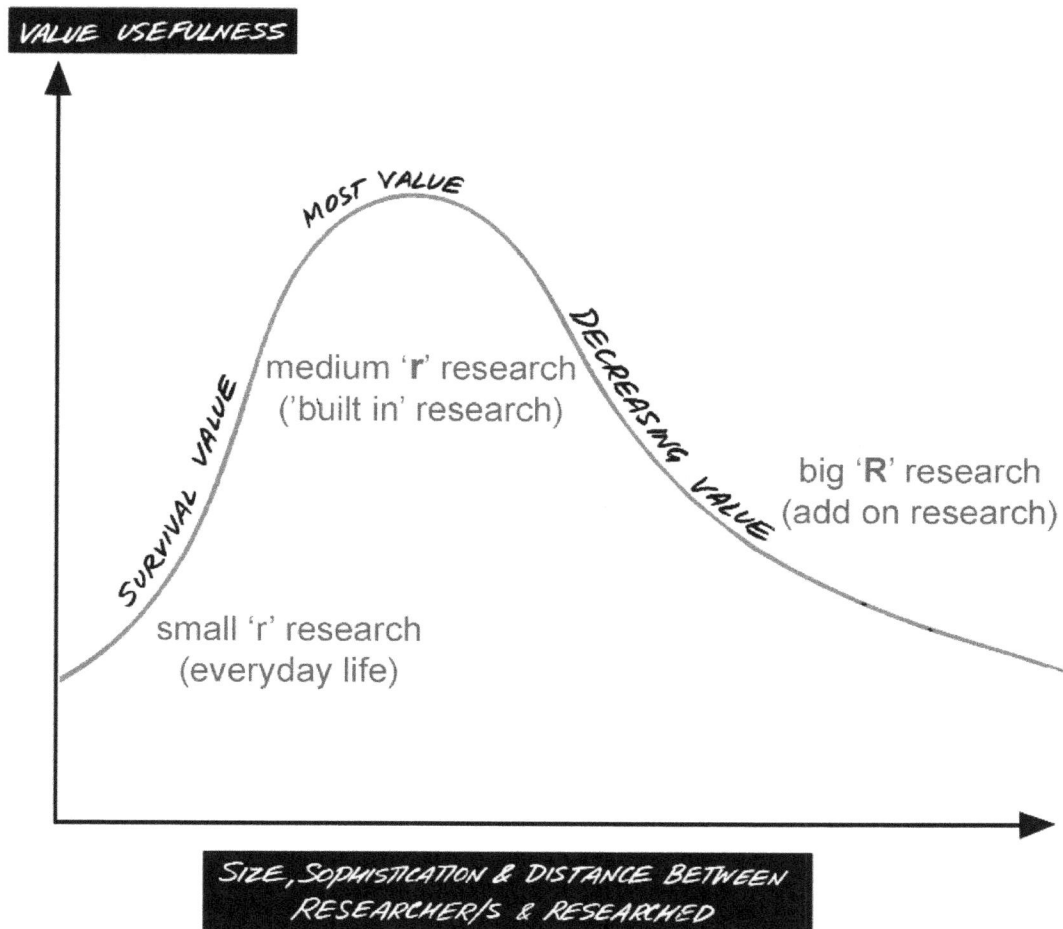

Figure 7. Wadsworth's speculative graph of the general tendency to paradoxical diminishing returns

efforts; and if professional evaluators and researchers realised how their efforts are in practice an extension of all normal human practice (like a kind of an 'external mind') and began to scale down to align their work more with the living environments in which they practice, then a more deeply embedded systemic approach could emerge.

Yet interestingly most of the time we don't find the 'times, spaces and places' in which to closely or consciously monitor, observe and record for reflection what we are doing, nor easily raise new questions and discuss them with relevant others. For most of the time we seem to be more-or-less on automatic pilot, more-or-less 'following the program'. We may have identified what works well (or others have) and we are 'acting' on it: enacting it. Repeating it. And repeating it again, perhaps with just small modifications. We don't often go 'right around the cycle', perhaps because nothing much is being noticed that strikes us as needing more than the existing solutions, or if it does strike us as needing attention we find it's all too much to contemplate, or 'there's no time for anything like that anyway'.

We work far more with implementing and replicating answers than asking new questions. And life would be chaotic indeed if it were otherwise. But it can mean we get 'stuck' at the point of repeating current action—especially where it may seem right and good, but all the more so when it is expected, easy, rewarded, familiar, comfortable or required. Or too uncomfortable to do otherwise. We may go on sticking with the tried and true, becoming literally impermeable to needed change the more we settle with 'how things are'.

Most ironically of all, the bigger and better any existing theory, the more hard-won it was originally and the more it 'worked' in daily experimentation, the stronger will be our presumptions when we encounter the next instance, and paradoxically the less likely we will be to revisit or even receive feedback about the situation.

'Spaces and places' for building in inquiry processes

However if daily activity allows us to ask at least one other person their view about something in the kitchen while snatching a cup of tea, then it may also extend to allow asking half a dozen relevant people, or practitioners and each of their next three clients, or enable the scheduling of an open roundtable dialogue about the meaning of a survey's results, or a follow-up session after time for reflection to enable deeper insight and a new idea worth trying.

Rather than at this point typically outsourcing to a researcher or formal evaluation (or planning to do this next year or 'some day'), thus risking severing the vital threads to daily practice at the point of readiness and interest in the local context of 'felt discrepancy' by those most involved—if instead a person or organisation has access to built in places and spaces for regular stopping and reflecting and raising of questions and searching for small-scale answers, they will be far more likely to expand their repertoire of personal and collective experience for their own local evidence-based action (Schön 1983).

Building an ever deeper pool of experience means an ever greater capacity for understanding and being more able to hear and respond better to the next person or situation. Going on to raise the question or issue at a meeting of others, and then present it to a larger group will mean even further expansion of repertoire. Continuing to re-raise it for months and even a year will mean the chance of even deeper understandings. The Lebanese philosopher Kahlil Gibran alludes to this kind of insight (being increasingly echoed in neuroscience) in his metaphoric observation that like a clay bowl, 'the deeper that sorrow carves into your being, the more joy it can contain' (1972: 36). That is, the more you have heard people speak about different forms of experience, the more forms of experience you now know of. The more you know the value of what comes after a silence following a question, the more you will be able to sit with silence. The more that deep witness to discrepancy has taken place in resonant dialogue, the more its meanings are likely to be knowable and the more possible it will then be to 'crack its puzzle'. Single loop responses (short-term knee-jerk ones) can often be an effective 'stitch in time'. But extending to deepen into double and triple loop ones (where the bigger web of context can be grasped to lead to more profound understanding of the conditions for action and much more effective and targeted response) can save a situation going on becoming ever more problematic.

Interestingly some of we specialist researchers found our own way to the knowledge, often almost incidentally, that we weren't the only ones researching and evaluating and acquiring all this practice knowledge (Schön 1987)—but that everyone we were talking to was! We may for example have experienced first hand the impoverishment of our 'data raids' to collect the facts and make our measurements. Or become aware we weren't really grasping their meanings in the lived lives of 'our subjects', or seen the risks inherent in our ventriloquism on behalf of research subjects, or of our trying to 'feel Braille through a doona' to know what was really going on, and our sleights of hand when it came to slipping in recommendations that were ours, not those of people from the field. Rather than trying to erect formal barriers between *our* 'scientific and objective' research-ing and evaluating, and *their* 'biased, impressionistic, subjective lay people's' inquiry, we began the journey to connect our inquiry and learning with *their* inquiry and learning, and have a conversation about where we saw things differently. The journeying from ivory tower down into the alligator swamp[8] and from the swamp up to lookout towers for reflective distance had commenced (Wadsworth 1985). It was a beginning to the task of improving the value of the former (ivory tower inquiry) and the quality of the latter (alligator swamp inquiry)—slowly building towards a more comprehensively distributed intelligent system.

In finding our way through the eras of research, evaluation and continuous improvement to the realisation that it took all—deep interpersonal engaged immersion, access to numerical description, reflective distance to achieve agreed but realistic 'achieved objectivity' and grounded theories, and creative new ideas to try further—we came to glimpse the full potential of the inquiry cycle for the life of the organisations and communities in which we were working. Some of these lessons emerged in experiences we thought of as 'irrelevant' or 'extraneous' to our research, only to see them be better addressed in the later eras of evaluation and organisational development.

A short story about an apparent 'epiphenomenon' in the era of research

In the 1970s social researchers were attached to some of the newest kinds of human service programs that were proliferating in response to the rapid explosion in new community needs for health, early childhood, housing, immigrant and education services. Such research generally commenced life in the style of the academic work in which it had been schooled: with researchers entering 'the field', sometimes for a number of years, with their clipboards and metaphoric white coats to carry out independent, objective, scientific social research on the populations and services. Mostly we researchers drew up our questionnaire surveys, and perhaps added a 10 per cent interview sample, but we also began combining these methods with some participant-observation from the tradition of urban community studies (which in turn were drawing on older anthropological methods).

Yet as researchers were sent out to carry out these kinds of detailed traditional community needs studies and then found themselves working with the new or changing services regarding 'the results', a very interesting thing began to happen.

Researchers became engaged.

Many quickly realised—despite our training to remain coolly aloof—that up-close-and-personal engagement was necessary if, firstly, we were to find out what was actually going on (and be accepted and trusted enough to enable this to emerge) and, secondly, if the work was to make any difference at all on a daily basis to the situations being developmentally researched and evaluated, for example to those who 'peopled' those situations, they themselves would need to learn from the same inquiry processes into how and why new and different actions could or should be taken as a result. Struggling with the critique that this meant the work would be, in the memorable words of the then permanent head of the Health Department, 'subjective, impressionistic, biased rubbish', some nevertheless got involved in the R&D of the new programs in order to assist people clarify their philosophy and purposes (what was to be of value, merit, worth or significance), and even took on small roles to become trusted parts of the organism (such as editing a newsletter to increase the levels of information feedback, or carrying out some small service element in an anti-poverty program). Almost all found themselves de-emphasising survey questionnaires (or did them more for the sake of those who wanted them), and instead worked more and more through direct personal and engaged methods, including 'naturalistic conversations' out and about in the communities or services, individual and group discussions of people's experiences in local people's homes, churches, playgrounds or women's centres and participant-observation became observant-participation for everyone. Much of it would these days be called auto-ethnography, and it worked: deeper, richer understandings ensued, and over time, clarity emerged about what should be done as a result.

When the job was seen to have been done, 'truths discovered', written up, reports written and submitted and the researchers 'no longer needed' (or the money ran out) we then had to move on to a new job elsewhere.

But then an even more interesting thing happened.

In many cases within only weeks or months, the projects—many of which had hitherto been exciting places of deep and challenging dialogue going on around meeting tables and in people's kitchens—withdrew from their creativity and settled down to business as usual. In some notable cases they even lost ground and reverted to the business as usual *prior* to the research and new reforms. They may often have gone on growing in size, but from then on it was mostly 'more of the same', without new insights or improvements taking place very often. This frustrated many who had expected the creativity and new thinking to

continue, and some felt they had failed to adequately convey their findings and recommendations; or that the old top-down professional service planning, central administration and decision making and exclusion of the local community from their own services was just too overpowering for the nascent efforts. Mothers may no longer have been locked out at the kindergarten gate, but the twelve-person parents' community advisory committee for the early childhood program soon began to recede in perceived importance; becoming more distanced from professional decision making, people began to lose interest, and it folded.

While some services were no doubt happy to breathe a sigh of relief and settle into a standardised routine phase or even 'revert to previous type', it was also the case that many of the original problems had only begun to be addressed and eventually returned later, still needing attention.[9]

Mostly, at the time, the problem was at best seen as one of poor 'uptake' of research or evaluation results, or of interrupted 'knowledge transfer'. This view stemmed from traditional science's seeing the scientists as the 'discoverers of truth' in the privacy of their social laboratory, taking the findings from the field, and reporting them in a journal article where it was hoped they would be read and then implemented by any who wanted to, or by those in charge.

Yet here were the beginnings of the 'disconnects' between research and policy, and all the more so when the people in the field communities were, in practice, the local knowledge holder's and co-creators of the 'truths' *and* the practices, but slowly being lost to (or disconnected from) those centrally deciding about their practice.

Accidental living systems inquiry
It is only now on reflection and with the hindsight of a living systems approach that it becomes clearer that the innovative services, projects or programs were more 'alive' and creative, not so much because of what the researchers came up with at 'the end' of their endeavours, nor even necessarily because they were

especially skilled facilitators (though they did often get quite good at this as they went along), but more because of the multiple and interacting effects of how they came to the 'findings' during the sometimes years that they spent working with these complex and semi-fluid projects, programs, services and communities:
• How deeply involved they let themselves become

(in shared space and place), and how well they got to know and be known by all the others in the field settings

- How much they made themselves responsive to what they were hearing and seeing, and thus how much mutual trust and respect formed with all the people in the field settings, leading to hearing more, especially the history and the hitherto 'unspokens'
- How energetic they were in questioning (or encouraging self-questioning) by the people, and in raising observations (and breaking silences) about the discrepancies between people's hopes and lives
- How much the 'subjects' participated in the processes of framing questions, discussion of how to best get the answers, evidence collection, experience sharing and knowledge formation *together* (again in amenable 'spaces and places')
- How much the material (survey results, interviews, observations, what was said at public meetings and in small groups, and so on), was exchanged further and further out through organisations and networks, thus becoming the shared 'intelligence' for the individuals, groups and larger 'systemicities'
- Whether people taking part then talked further to each other about the issues raised, and could get access to more and other ideas and thinking in comparable settings, as well as argue and debate sceptically with each other over the issues, beliefs, ideas, evidence and conclusions
- Whether there were ways they could be inventive and try out the implications of the new understandings and knowledge in their daily practice, and then be able to talk more about them and refine them as they saw what happened, and
- *Who* got to be involved in all of this; particularly whether those with the most to gain were involved (such as service users or the community), as well as all those farther afield; and their involvement supported, nurtured, fertilised, seen as worthy and legitimate, and not overlooked, ridiculed, edited out, cut short, blocked or prematurely discontinued
- *How long* people could know and trust that others were there for (particularly if people knew everyone was in it for 'the long haul').

We saw all of this at the time as 'epiphenomena' or unintended side-effects, but these were in practice the contexts, conditions and processes that *really* underpinned the success of the research.

We had unintentionally created what might now be recognised as the conditions for successful 'learning organisations'. Or built in living systems of inquiry. And living they were! As mentioned, these developing services and their staff and service user communities were often energetic, intense, enthusiastic, turbulent, inspirational and often quite profound experiments in both egalitarian collaboration and the wise servant-leadership that articulates such discerned agreement. Things were not easy. But communities of staff and service users frequently came to understand and care about each other deeply as the inquiry processes unfolded and new exciting services grew to meet the new needs.

But what happened when the official researcher-as-inquiry-facilitator left the field was that the questioning stopped. Things became more taken for granted, business-as-usual—replicating primarily whatever had been learned previously and passing this on to newcomers as 'the received wisdom'. Questions were now considering more how to refine and detail the procedures, with whatever logic and meaning lay behind them becoming rather set in concrete. Duty and procedure took the place of experimentation, and people began to lose touch with being able to explain exactly why they were doing what they were doing. Inspiration often diminished as it was now 'just the way things are done round here'…

Facilitation of 'intelligent systems'

Facilitating inquiry-in-action around living systems cycles

Some of these community-based researchers (whether consciously or not) had been playing roles a little like gardeners: watering seeds of ideas, cultivating and feeding the sprouts and seedlings, helping saplings put down their roots, fertilising them with the hummus from previous systems. But more: they also found themselves assisting the research 'subjects' (including those in related organisations and service provision) to become *their own* researchers or co-researchers together, traversing full cycles of observe–reflect–plan–act.

For example, researchers found themselves holding up 'magnifying glasses' to assist service systems get high-quality, detailed and more comprehensive feedback about itself—and 'mirrors' by which they could then reflect on this feedback. Or helping find new names to best express shared new ways of thinking about things, from which new theory and practice could be *mapped*. In the process, system members came to understand themselves and the systemic nature of the worlds around them, including its and their own 'compass'[10] values and purposes: and how to intervene to correct what it considered mistakes, smooth out bits that weren't working, analyse and understand what was blocking their intentions, and chart their desired new directions. In a sense we researchers were having to create communities of small 's' scientists.

What might then have been referred to as 'bias and contamination' or the unwanted 'Hawthorne effect',[11] is now partly what organisational development courses are teaching in management studies! That is, in aligning inquiries with their value-driven purposes, 'bias and contamination' transform instead into 'focused intention and purposeful shaping' by feedback into living systems' inquiring (while nevertheless continuing to make realistic empirical assessments of 'how things were before' in comparison to a proposed or actual 'after'—but now *relevant* in terms of those value-driven inquiry purposes, and always subject to autopoetic correction).

'System members' were found to be able competently to advise and give feedback when inquiry questions and methods were inappropriate, not working or used at the wrong time or place. Moreover they were able to take part in fieldwork as informants, *and* advise effectively about the meanings of the 'data'. And finally, they were able to then carry out their own comparative 'field experiments' with the new ideas, and observe and report back on the validation or refutation of these theories in practice.[12]

It was this focal field (including relevant extensions to regional and 'central' government at the state level) that comprised the living 'laboratory', providing detailed and accurate conditions for naturalistic 'experimentation'. Indeed some of we nominal researchers realised that we were somewhat 'parasitical' if we only saw ourselves as being there for 'others elsewhere' rather than for the whole field in order to further the self-understanding, practices and lifeworlds of the valued and critical reference group. The weak response to this was for some researchers to want to 'give something back to the researched' (such as an enjoyable time being interviewed, or a summary of 'the findings', or a movie ticket). The stronger response was to want to more actively contribute also to the processes of information feedback, knowledge development and larger life of the whole group, community or service—especially where that was the avowed purpose of our research in the first place!

Connecting up the 'virtuous cycle': Research—to policy—to practice—to evaluation

We had realised that the 'system' of feedback loops (and who should be 'in the loop') in the 'inquiry community' went right from, for example, the children and parents in the kindergarten of child health centre, or the person in the wheelchair or hospital bed, or the child care centre committee, all the way to professional service providers, researchers and evaluators to include all levels of human service organisation: local, state and federal government policy makers and departmental administrators. This was not just a nice democratic idea or even just to pay our accountability dues. It was necessary so that all might be 'joined up' in a co-researching learning community in which all their observations, analyses, conclusions and evidence were received and responded to, and subsequent futures envisioned and designed *to contribute effectively to the life of those to benefit and thus to the life of all*. This in effect joined up the processes of practice, research, policy, new practice and evaluation into a whole that 'got it right' *by joining up all the people* who were doing the inquiring: observing action, reflecting, planning and implementing new actions, together.

In this way we had together become more like whole systems co-researchers[13]—with new implications for our practice. In many ways we researchers were moving from being 'messengers' being sent out into 'the community' to collect data and report back to policy makers, funders and service providers to being 'go-betweens' representing the different views back and forth *between* the parties to inquiry, and finally becoming 'dinner party hosts' or caterers facilitating and resourcing more direct dialogic communication flows between all stakeholders—with the ultimate checks of validity lying in the hard test of practice, rather than risking remaining in the realm of plausibility, second guessing, deduced probability or too-early, non-resonant recommendations and policy.[14]

Yet while the desire to eliminate 'the disconnects' were there, there also remained a constant tension where differently 'siloed' purposes persisted[15] between internal quality improvement and external service reporting and accountability to funders and policy makers. However many services and their users persevered with genuine collaboration efforts beyond mere appearances and image making, and ironically it was from the commercial world that came the imperative that if business 'gets it wrong' and is unable to respond rapidly and flexibly to changing customer wishes, hopes and needs, then it will fail in the marketplace. Nevertheless human services operate something of a 'perverted marketplace', with professional service mangers for the most part deciding what to purchase *for* consumers, using funds acquired compulsorarily from the tax-paying 'commonwealth' in whose name they act. In the absence of a genuine market shopping logic being possible (e.g. how to 'shop' for and buy supportive community? or 'shop around' for friendship for a suicidal child) there has been a new impetus to ask about 'satisfaction' and 'evidence of benefit'. The compelling logic for including consumers in the loops of evaluative inquiry lie in the observation that it is *they* for whom the system is intended—for it to revolve round, align with, and centre its focus on resourcing the inquiry-and-action efforts of them, its end-beneficiary users. This raised the question of how human services could inquire in ways that would better yield quality in those services themselves. How could inquiry in a sense 'give life'?

What does life-giving inquiry feel like?

When we encounter research and evaluation that doesn't connect with us, we can often feel our metaphoric 'screens' freeze! This can be a common experience of both those who provide and those who use services. The wrong questions, unwanted, inappropriate or weak questions, rigid research or evaluation designs that should be able to change and

© S.Kneebone in Betts et al. 2001

respond to feedback from the field, overly changing and unsettled ones where some format (e.g. comparative analysis) needs to be better 'held', unwieldy techniques, research that is too rushed or too long term and drawn out, interpretations and analyses we haven't had a say in, results we can't see the evidence for, wrong recommendations that are acted on (possibly having to be imposed), or right recommendations that are not tried out or inexplicably discredited—all these might make a person's own personal living system rather sluggish, reactive, or even bring it down!

On the other hand, people's energies are attracted and further generated by 'spot on' questions stemming from the real-life concerns of we the service users and service providers, or by questions we are relieved are being asked, or ones we *want* to answer (or about which we can't wait to see what other people say), or clever designs that we can see will ask all the right people in the right ways and give us the answers we are desperately searching for (note this is not the same as the ones we are looking for, i.e. wanting to find!), easily used techniques, well-worded and well-evidenced analyses and conclusions, well-told stories with clear implications, ideas for 'what next' that jump out as obviously great things to be tried, and people clamouring to experiment with them (or who may have already gone off and begun to give them a go), plus the freedom to then monitor and alter where need be. In short—questions and methods that get us 'right round the cycles of inquiry' doing justice to each stage result in a flow of 'lifeblood' insights, ideas, beliefs, values, practices, responses, data, information, energetic impulses and nurturing resources that move through all the channels and capillaries of any big living system or ecosystem, that is constantly growing, flourishing, repairing itself and transforming.

This may throw some light on the drawbacks of so much conventional research and evaluation that starts in one part of the cycle and either does not search forward 'all the way around', or does not retroductively re-search 'back' around the cycle to substantiate its starting point or standpoint, or misses key moments around the cycle, that:

- Has not had clarity about its purposes and subsequently proves to be 'uninteresting' or unable to discover anything new or valuable
- Is built on assumptions attributed from other settings and contexts (e.g. published theory, hypotheses, tests or questions developed) but not resonant with the current field setting
- Is expected, *prior* to beginning fieldwork, to know how it will be carried out in detail (e.g. design, timelines, methods, theory, what questions will be asked, of whom etc.)
- Is not oriented to resourcing and building the field's own understanding
- Reduces the complex field situation to generalisations that are too abstract or irrelevant
- Is judged by distal or non-relevant others (e.g. published in international journals or revealed to distant managers without their participation) rather than fed back into and tested within the field from which it was generated and with those for whom it was intended
- Is experienced as intrusive, circuitous, controlled or inappropriately secretive/or 'revelatory' because lacking organic development within the relevant field and among stakeowning parties
- Lacks transparency to those who should be participating, or enables intervention by those who are not sufficiently accountable
- Uses inappropriate methods for the issue or field situation or gets the scale of the effort wrong (e.g. opts for sophisticated data collection, analysis etc. but is unused/or unusable, or too rapid and superficial to advance beyond quick fix solutions)
- Tries to establish 'laboratory' or controlled experimental settings rather than observing the details of interactions within the complex naturalistic situation
- Suffers discontinuity from a separate 'project-by-project' basis, resulting in disconnects around the cycle, often due to sequential tendering without those tendering being able to enter into relationships with all relevant parties over time, resulting in non-cumulative, disconnected or lost local knowledge, or projects that operate as add-ons or extras to 'the real business' of services rather than being integrated with (as part of) their core business
- A kind of division of labour emerges between researchers, policy makers, planners, implementers, practitioners and evaluators, with messages being passed around the cycle like a rather risky game of Chinese whispers
- Researchers go on researching, policy makers go

on producing polices, planners keep on planning, actors act and evaluators keep reporting after the event

- In the interests of 'objectivity', uses methods and techniques and forms of writing that reduce, obscure or abstract people's experiences, including their suffering or other subjective feeling, capabilities, intentions and purposes
- The researcher adds in their own reasoning to answer a question post hoc rather than feeding this question into the research field during the inquiry itself (e.g. recommendations)
- 'Findings' or 'results' are not returned to the field site for checking by the actors or parties for accuracy, interpreting or trying them out in practice
- Participants are left without having learned skills in evaluation, research or facilitation/resourcing, and instead wait for the next rare and expensive research and evaluation study as their source of guidance
- Academic researchers are left without being able to say anything with certainty about the implications and consequences of what they have found, often calling instead for 'more research'
- Non-academic applied social researchers and evaluators most often have their contracts end without being able to take the recommendations forward into actual 'live' practice—either to test if it can take place as designed or to see if it then has the intended desired impacts and outcomes for end-beneficiaries.

What if we could pay attention to the living processes, 'structures' and 'systems' for research, evaluation and continuous organisational improvement so that they more effortlessly furthered the life of human systems, rather than them suffering all these disconnects and wasted efforts?

What we know of life is only where we have decided to rest with our questioning
FRAN PEAVEY, 1994 p.86

A living systems inquiry methodology can take up this challenge of continuing to research with all the relevant stakeholders the desired changes from initial observation of discrepancy right through to observing new action. Additionally it treats the 'answers' or ideas for new action that have been generated as worthy of testing—moving to trial them in the hard test of complex 'live' practice, in a form of naturalistic experimentation.

By being clear about its starting purposes of wanting change or improvement to some situation, practice, service or program of activity (that was the point of embarking on the inquiry in the first place), and allowing recommendations and changes to emerge and be tested iteratively in the field during the research, living systems inquiry is able to move through a full sequence of questions that get it from an 'is' of 'how things are' to an 'ought' of 'how things could be', and from the 'ought' to a new 'is'.

Instead of a risky division of labour, it offers a way to join up, in an integrated continuous process pursued by a co-operative critical inquiry group comprising all the people with the relevant interests and inquiry capabilities; to work through the hitherto separate boxes-and-arrows linear progression of research–planning–policy–implementation–outputs–impacts–change outcomes—to monitoring, review and evaluation research again.

While this may seem more possible at a small scale, we now have interesting examples of it taking place 'at scale' (e.g. whole 'national conversations' pursued by both contemporary Australian Prime Ministers and the US President in their respective Commonwealth and Federation, and even globally by 'whole of earth' organs such as characterise international, multinational and united nations' responses to climate change).

Some 'mental architecture': properties and dynamic sequencing of built in research and evaluation processes

The simple two-word description 'action research' gives a clue to the sequence and critical 'phase changes' that take place between *action* and observing and reflecting on that action—and then planning on the basis of that *research* new action to try. A sequence of questions—each relevant to a particular stage or phase—can assist us through such an inquiry all the way from 'how things are' to 'what could be', and from 'what could be' to 'how they (now newly) are'.

In the later grey-shaded section of this chapter this full cycle sequence of questions is explicated in detail—whether it might be used in a small-scale everyday inquiry *or* in specialist professional research, evaluation and continuous improvement. I will avoid repeating material covered in the previous two volumes (*Do It Yourself Social Research* and *Everyday Evaluation on the Run*) regarding the detail of particular methods and techniques. I also do not reiterate the extensive writings about descriptive surveys, interviews and observational and formal experimental methods available elsewhere. More than anything else, the value of this chapter is about seeing how *all* of these take their place around a coherent and integrated cycle of inquiry, and that when this 'whole cycle' operates in dynamic balance, no methods become overly magnified or 'ethnocentrically dominant', nor so detailed, technical, exoteric or arcane that they can no longer be understood by the members of that inquiring human systemicity at whatever scale is necessary to sustain life.

The sequence of questions thus provides a conceptual framework, or mental architecture, that I hope might provide a shared methodological language to assist knowing where we are, where we have been, where we want to be, and what we have to do to get there.

To call this a form of mental architecture is to allude also to its being something that can 'scaffold' (Vygotsky in Jaramillo 1996) our moving through often complex and confusing territory, to keep finding or generating our way. This 'structural metaphor' of architecture also alludes to the seeming solidity of the shapes and forms we make, even though it is our own persistence with purposefully repeating in energetic effort the 'holding' of these initially imaginal shapes, identities or forms that makes them seem so. In a sequence of activity (noticing, questioning, listening, receiving input, processing it and acting on it)—this is how we make the forms of our world and then they make us. When we repeat the inquiry process, but differently, we re-make our world differently and then it makes us differently. The world and we—through our seeking—are emergent together.

In using the metaphor of a house, whether for an individual, a family, a group, organisation or whole community—like the idea of the larger *oikos* (as an integrated 'household' for the self, the group, whole regions, states, countries and worlds)—I want to suggest 'places to visit' on the journey of inquiry within the house-as-a-living-organism, as well as the inquirer 'putting in place' the differing parts and

processes of their inner self-making as well as the processes of the outer 'parts-making' of their greater 'social self'.

For the remainder of Chapter 3 I elaborate this mental architecture for thinking about the dynamic processes of the 'inquiry life cycle' as built in 'spaces and places' or 'moments and standpoints' using the structural metaphor of the house and its parts, as a living system/systemicity.[16]

From action to research-in-action.

From research-in-action to new action-that-is-researched.

Other integral and transformative theories
This dual (dynamic-cyclic and structural-house) representation provides a nice reminder that such mental architecture is human-made for heuristic assistance for the particular purposes of the human organism (including references to it as the 'DNA of the human/social organism' or being traced to genetic or biological characteristics).[17] Sometimes it is difficult to maintain these different ways of knowing as the product of the human systemicity itself.

Indeed there are many other ways of thinking even just about the integral nature of change, organisation and life that are in the same territory of endeavour as this book's (see Appendix 5). In Appendix 5 I also try and indicate how these various theories may be understood in terms of this book's integral theory.

This integral and transformative theory
While what I present may be seen as having much in common with many of these other integral 'theories of everything', here I am setting out to create a yet larger mental architecture that is able to accommodate them (and map areas omitted if the theorist has focused through the particular lens of their own characteristic inquiry preferences) because the critical project we share in this instance is that of achieving integrality per se, that is, systemic integrity of the 'structures' and processes for fullest life.

My approach stresses that all humans have *all* these inquiry capabilities (to greater and lesser extents). And to the extent we are (and are to be) fully and sustainably living beings ourselves and with each other, then we exercise them more-or-less regularly and successfully ourselves and with each other to 'get right round the cycles' of our inquiring for personal-social life.

And, just as we are the 'knowing subjects' (Schutz

1976) of our own autopoetic inquiries, making our way in relation to ourselves and others—so also are we part of greater 'knowing socialities' making autopoetic human collective life possible as well.[18] Indeed just as individuals show preferences that make us all the distinctively and identifiably characteristic kinds of inquirers we are, so also as we engage with each other and co-organise social groupings do we construct distinctively and identifiably characteristic kinds of inquiring organisations, communities and institutions. But more of these later.

Let me depict graphically the mental architecture of the sequence of living systemic inquiry in Figure 8 its simplest form (action–research), then elaborating slightly in Figure 9 (action–observe–reflect–plan), and then more so in Figure 10 (old-action–observe–values –reflect–theorise–conclude–implement-plan–new action) in the accompanying three illustrations.

Fran Peavey has used the term 'strategic question families' for the sequence of ten questions that she identified as helpful for those working to bring about change (1994, 2008). They are a particularly systematic and comprehensive compendium of questions that corresponded to the sequencing of the participatory action research cycle that many of us had been using around the world for many decades in education, health and human services, business and organisations, community and development work.[19] Over the years I have added to them and made some changes[20] (for which Fran does not bear responsibility!) and have continued to trial their use in a wide range of research and evaluation projects over the past fifteen years (see Exemplars in Chapter 5).

Full cycles of questions at any scale

This experience has shown that it is in the asking of *all* these questions—whether or not in this order or with the 'reconstructed logic' of hindsight—that enables human systems to make more fully life-sustaining changes and retain more fully life-sustaining forms.

Figure 8. Two moments: Action–Research

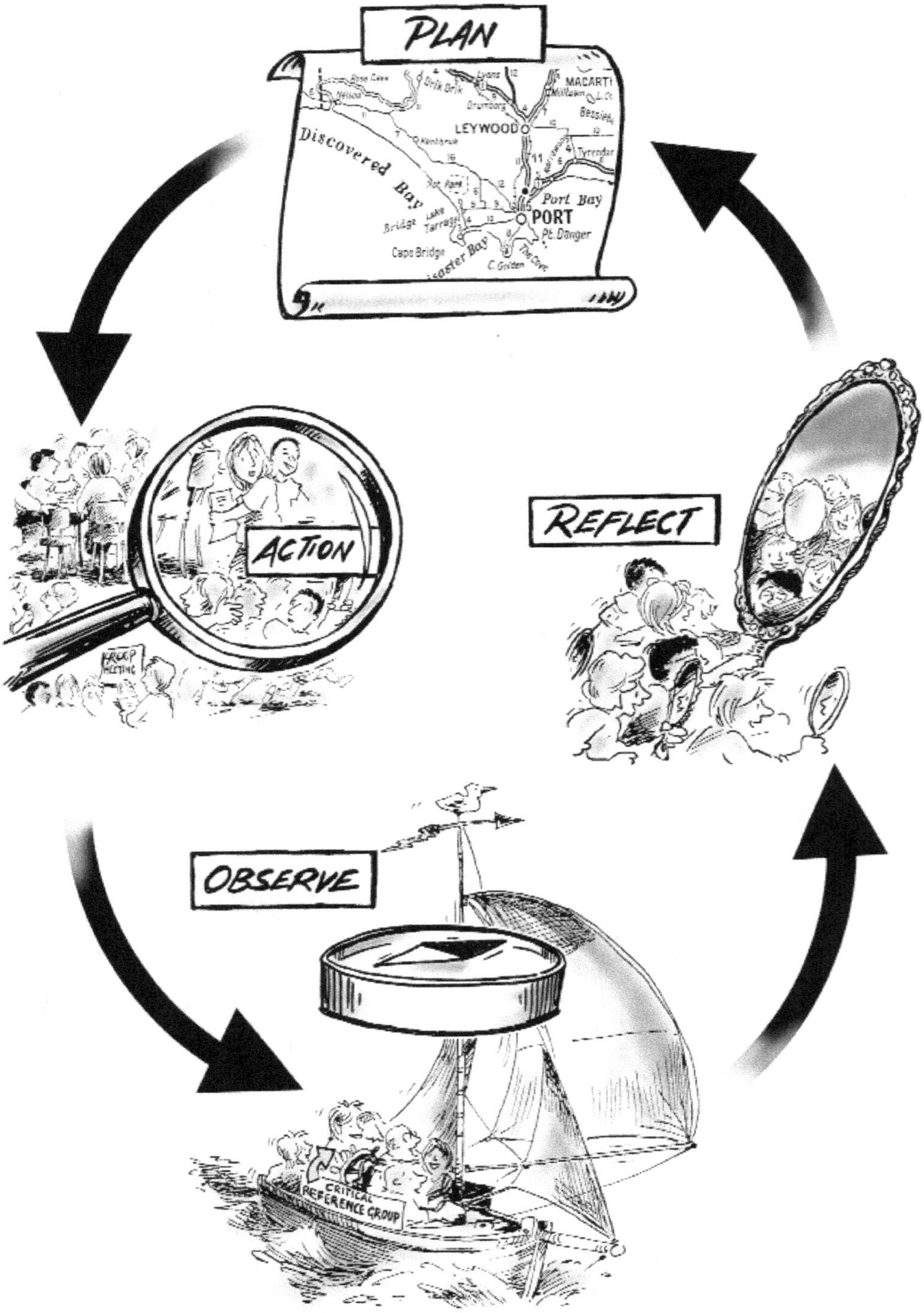

Figure 9. Four moments: Act–Observe–Reflect–Plan

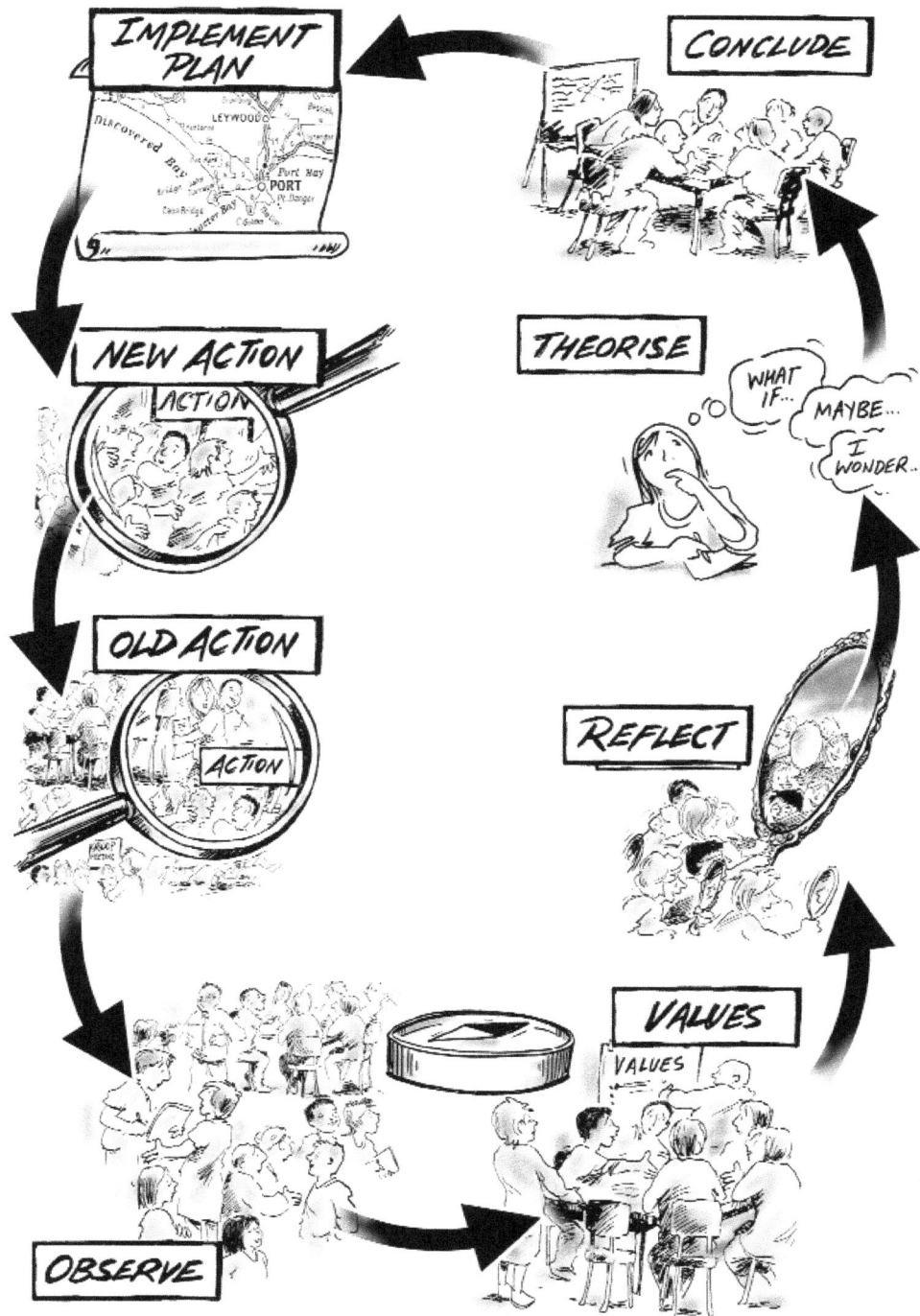

Figure 10. Eight moments: Action–Observe–Values–Reflect–Theorise–Conclude–Implement Plan–New Action

As previously discussed, the full sequence of questions may be used at any 'unit of autopoiesis' (Anisur Rahman's term, personal communication, 2005), that is, at any size or scale of the self-organising 'system' or 'organism'—whether as an individual, group, community, organisation, whole institution, country, planet or cosmos. To this end, the questions can be asked *by* or *of* any participants in a living system, that is: of oneself ('I'), or of individual participants or 'subjects'; or of any collectivity or combination of collectivities: groups, stakeholders, communities, organisations, societies, and larger systemicities ('you')—and by a 'me' or a 'you', or any 'us'. The individual self ('I') can ask these questions of themselves in an inner dialogue, or of and with another or others ('you') in an outer dialogue. In this way they guide the co-inquiry of whole complex webs of living 'relationality', no longer constrained by conventions of one-way questioning and one-way answering by 'the other'. Questioning and answering becomes two-way and multi-way feedback.

Critical mass at key phase changes
I have also added 'liminal' or threshold questions at two points of 'phase change' between differing states of action (answers) and research (questions). Firstly, a *Phase change 1* (between Fran's Levels 1 and 2) concerning whether hoped for change is indeed really wanted (enough to sustain the inquiry) or not. Many people 'go home' at this point, preferring (or being compelled) to stick with the familiar 'tried and true', even if it means having to live with feelings of unease that perhaps things are not quite as they should be (or are wholly so). Or perhaps are complying with existing actions and practices, forms and patterns and ways and means, because of a range of threats, fears or anxieties.[21] Many 'canaries in the mine' also die at this threshold before enough heed is taken of their heartfelt early warning observation and the 'caravan of inquiry' is able to move further forward around the cycle past the range of defences we erect to protect the existing.

And secondly a *Phase change 2* (between Fran's Level 2 and the new Level 1) concerning whether implementation of the planned for change is really wanted in actual practice (enough to sustain the experiment as designed) or not. Many bearers of good new ideas may baulk at the point of 'giving it a go'— perhaps deciding to carry out 'more research' or

pragmatically adapt/alter the idea, calculating that it won't 'take' in the existing environment or given the current climate of power ('This is new', 'Where's the evidence that it's been done to our benefit before?', 'How could it possibly be better?') Many 'messengers may be shot' at this threshold before the eagle-eyed gatekeepers realise it is in the long-term interests of the organism to let through the life-giving experimentation to see if it can take root and be observed to flourish.[22]

No expectations except for those the co-researchers set themselves
A further feature of these critical threshold questions is their effective assistance of the inquirer, inquiry group or learning organisation to see if there really is a 'critical mass' of those who *do* want change both in theory and in practice, and in doing so, they can also assist revisiting any neglected questions that might help revise just what kind of change *does* attract energy and 'give legs' to sustain inquiry all the way into trialling new practice in real life.

In this way, this question sequence facilitates sustainable self-organising and can ensure that no one is encouraged to express their needs and then sit and wait passively for others to 'do something'. Nothing moves forwards, nothing is decided, and nothing is done, except for what the inquiring group or person want to try out themselves. Nor does it encourage others to feel they have to take all the running on the action in the absence of the collectivity—or worse, having done so, to have to 'sell' it so that others will 'buy in' or 'own' something that didn't come from their inquiry efforts in the first place (managers glimpse freedom from having to lead in the sense of its original meaning '*loder*', of having to 'pull along behind you'!) Instead, all parties journey more-or-less *together* through all the moments of inquiry, *all* have been posing the questions and considering the responses and drawing the conclusions and talking through the implications *themselves*. Not unlike the original small-scale Greek *democratos* (albeit with all its still exclusionary drawbacks at that time e.g. regarding class and gender) that took place in the *agora* or meeting or market place—an equivalent to the spaces and places that this book proposes be built in organisationally.

This points to the way in which ethics are addressed

in a living systems/systemic inquiry approach. Resting on a participatory ethos, the inquiring collectivity moves forward through cycles of self-chosen inclusive dialogue and reflection about observations and their meaning and implications. One of the hallmarks of success of this kind of ethical living systems inquiry is that self-organising action begins when the participating individuals, groups, organisations or communities have the evidence and understanding sufficient to see what should be done. Effortless change that is supported by all does not need coercion by anyone. Change that is not supported 'goes back to the drawing board' for further revisiting of earlier questions to achieve more understanding of any aspect that is not well enough researched, understood or agreed about.

Plan–act–observe–reflect? or
Observe–reflect–plan–act?
The inquiry cycle casts light on another common problem in research, evaluation and improvement activities. Much conventional social science appears to get stuck in observing and analysing without easily moving on to planning and action—or alternatively may get stuck in experimental action without easily incorporating the relevant field-based generation of that theory. Additionally much conventional planning and action may get stuck in powerful patterns of 'business as usual' that is not stopping to observe more deeply, and reflect on and think about what is being observed.

The addition of *Phase 2*-type 'reflection' and 'planning' questions can overcome the drawback of being stuck at standard *Phase 1* observing action—and proper attention to *Phase 1* questions can overcome the drawbacks of trying to begin in *Phase 2* 'plan' and 'act' without strong grounding both in observation of 'the facts', and also in value-driven reflection on their meaning and implications for new action. Indeed, when asked as continuous cycles of all questions, the problems of starting or finishing at any or only one point can potentially be more easily overcome.

However if most new inquiry starts in practice with a felt discrepancy that provokes the raising of a new question, then most often cycles of inquiry may tend to 'begin' in observe and 'end' in new *action*, rather than beginning with planning. That is, those working as planners are really needing to begin in longer periods

of field observing and reflecting (and listening to and dialoguing with others in those fields about their observations and reflections). Perhaps it's time to integrate the roles of planning with those of action, observation and reflection, just as in the past observing-reflecting researchers were cut off from planning and trialling as part of their research practices.

Non-linear sequencing
Of course inquiring is not plain sequential sailing! Often we will find ourselves 'jumping about a bit' in the cycle, or having to retrace our steps to revisit earlier points (or leapfrog between earlier and later ones). Indeed there may need to be considerable fluidity between 'where we are at' in order to fast forward or revisit or move on and then return to wherever we 'were up to'—but now better informed and better able to incorporate critical missing aspects into the emerging picture. In this way the cycle may be better seen as reconstructed logic, although at times it may also serve well as logic-in-use (Kaplan 1964).

Some will 'cross the cycle', zigzag, or do 'snakes or ladders'—'snakes' where a critical step has been missed, going 'back down to earth' to observe or feel, even at the point of being about to implement a plan in action (perhaps pragmatic slippage has been too great)—or 'ladders' to quickly 'scale the heights' to an aerial 'big picture' overview in readiness to implement (perhaps because all the groundwork evidence and new theorising has already been done, and people are ready, eager and able to try it out).

Theorising may find itself without enough data. Planning may have skipped over some crucial expressions of feeling or not sought them out. Action may have 'lost the plot' on its original value-driven purposes. Post-action evaluation (observation) may not know what is (or was) valued and why. Indeed values may need to be revised altogether after action has been implemented—sending the whole inquiry 'back to the beginning'. Observation may not have a 'big enough' context to shed light on what else is going on—or what is *really* going on relative to values, intentions or purposes. The first solution suggested may have been run with—only to find it hasn't been well enough thought through (or felt through) and was the wrong one in the first place. Or it becomes so when tried out in practice. Research and evaluation in complex living systems can indeed be complex and uncertain, although not always entirely chaotic (although in this kind of mental architecture there *is* a clear and certain 'moment' when chaos and uncertainty are not only to be expected but necessary!) Indeed questioning in complex living human systems will most often be iterative and emergent (holarchic, inter-nesting, networked or complexly cybernetic) rather than linear and straightforwardly causal (apart from brief times of this being both possible and viable).

However in the end it is in 'doing justice to all the questions' that ensures a balancing/stabilising and dynamic/fluid living system is able to be achieved, incorporating all the necessary aspects of humanness without ending up overly favouring any in particular or neglecting, suppressing or denying others.

Different questions, different methods
It might also be noted that research and evaluation 'mixed methods' designs are increasingly combining various forms or techniques in order to try and grasp the complex nature of social worlds. Converting this to a *sequence* of differing methods and techniques may better show a logical path for emergence towards better and deeper insights and conclusions—that is, different methods at particular times for the different purposes (Crotty 1998). Holding an overall picture of the full cycle also militates against overly separating them out (with technical sounding names and overly detailed instructions about their usage). On the 'up' side we can see their difference and variety—which gives the possibility of more creative and accurate responses to any particular situation. For example, if a particular group needs to achieve new ways of understanding their experience of a painful topic, they might use Frigga Haug's 'memory work' technique rather than a questionnaire (Haug 1987). Or if a group needs to expand its range of ideas about something it might go for a brainstorm rather than an interview. If there is conflict or different perceptions, we might use a dialogic methodology. As well, by naming and 'having' a defined-in-time-and-space inquiry effort (with a technical sounding title), people may be able to more easily show they have been 'doing something'—say a 'focus group' rather than only being able to say they 'had a bit of a yarn around the table'. On the 'down' side, people may feel compelled to pick a technique that may be more elaborate and specialised than

necessary, and it all end up being too big an effort, not finishing collecting data for a very long time (or ever!)

Preferences for some kinds of questions
People often start where they are most familiar, comfortable and able (if free to)—more 'at home'—or are culturally encouraged to start in a particular 'spot' depending on context. For example academic research often starts by considering the abstract theoretical possibilities of various already published 'answers' to questions about a topic, and then generates questions in the form of hypotheses from one of these theories. Field-based research might typically begin by observing, describing and perhaps measuring practice in the light of observed frequencies or interpretations. And policy research might typically start with planning an intervention then measuring to see if it meets its goals. While action, critical and collaborative research typically starts with noticing something discrepant (whether problematic or appreciated) that propels a new cycle of inquiry. You yourself might feel more drawn to action, or to observation, or to refection or planning, or to a couple or a few of these.

You may have a sense when you read through the second half of Chapter 3 that questions associated with one or more parts of the cycle are more familiar, attractive or easy for you. You may even notice that, on the *opposite* side of the cycle from your most favoured kinds of questions in the inquiry cycle, are those you might least favour asking, or are more under-used by you. You may even be inclined to dismiss them as 'not so important', 'unnecessary', or even 'dangerous', 'wrong' and to be avoided.

Yet we all traverse the 'thin ice' of the unfamiliar, or least favoured parts of the cycle, when we need to 'go full cycle' whenever we need to bring about a wanted or necessary change or a new way of doing or being. It helps if there is self-awareness of this natural consequence of specialising in our particular inquiry preferences, and we either actively seek out what is less available to us in our inquiry (or inquiry style), or choose other ways to compensate for their absence, including accessing it using our favoured style, or perhaps by finding people whose capabilities are strong in that area and seeking their close collaboration, co-inquiry, input and advice (even though you will still achieve that unfamiliar part in your own characteristic way, not theirs).

However it is also common for 'like' to choose 'like' (especially if there is pressure to exercise or not exercise particular inquiry preferences). Hegemonic communities of research practice may then form around those particular preferences (or communities of solidarity around the devalued ones). On the upside is an ability to go 'further faster' with familiar and shared assumptions, but at the risk of systemically excluding or even suppressing the alternatives. In these instances, a larger social grouping, organisation, community or social 'system' will run the risk of losing vital aspects of its full living human systemicity. A lot like any monoculture, it can be a pathway to difficulties, disease or systemic death. I will revisit this train of thought at the end of the chapter.

Systemic reactions and defences
Thus questions 'open up' when observing, listening and reflecting, and answers 'close down' for planning and acting.

We seem to be very much an answers-seeking species—valuing the clarity, certainty, safety and security of knowing what to do, and how, when, where, with whom and why in order to survive. Good heavens! We've tried hunger and cold and we prefer plenty and warmth! (And we have pursued those relentlessly through the current economic mode. As John Kenneth Galbraith reminded us, 'When a person is in a supermarket, they are in touch with their deepest needs'.) Though if we have become single-minded about this we may be risking replicating in overdrive not knowing when enough is enough for our supporting environment to provide if we never look outside the supermarket and at the earth that is doing the providing. That is, our 'plenty and warmth' may have been achieved without proper benefit of observation and reflection and seeing the bigger picture of complex causation and consequences. We might even, if we are not careful, find ourselves bewildered in a global overheating climate emergency.

Conversely, while needing questions to elicit answers, for the time we are asking questions we have the freedom of 'not knowing' the answers to, but we also have confusion, uncertainty and anxiety! How hard is *that* to tolerate!? How hard is it to say, 'I don't know what is going on', 'I don't understand', 'I don't know what to do' or 'I don't know why I am doing this'.

The rewards to stick with known logics and 'the tried and true' are powerful (not just familiarity, efficiency and so on, but material means for survival)—and thus single loop thinking, or short-circuiting across the cycle to patch, fix or otherwise re-align with the received model to 'make it fit the way it was meant to be', may be tempting and common but effectively avoid deeper observation and more thoughtful reflection to work out how to change the faulty systems logic per se.

Sometimes there is a powerful forcefield to be overcome just to pose a question and for people to sit with it long enough for an answer to emerge. When the answer is 'I don't know', the dissonance both helpfully but also uncomfortably escalates.

Indeed all too often to be an adult is To Know. So question-askers can be seen (and treated at times!) like disconcerting children: we hope they will grow out of it as soon as possible. So also to be a professional is To Know. And sometimes the stakes are high—especially where people have been offered and have accepted the chance or risk of being highly reliant on others' knowing. Or where they are highly paid (and highly insured) for it as a sign of this dependency relationship.

Yet, as soon as we say 'I know', we have stopped our inquiry and our chance to think something new, learn something different, improve something, and change our minds and practices.

So while asking questions can create unease, it is the dissonance that can help drive the movement towards answers—even while that dissonance can feel queasy, like vertigo, and for some unhealthy, even life-denying, if there is not able to be movement to resolution. Given 'freedom' (a systemic field that enables), people will generally move to clarify things, or have the curiosity to 'find out', or will not always take a quick or easy answer to be the best answer.

He who asks a question is a fool for five minutes
He who does not ask a question remains
a fool forever.
CHINESE PROVERB

So here's a challenge for all human systemicities, including all human services systems—how to know *and* to 'not know'? How to have (always provisional) answers *and* always be open to questions?

Or, as we will see, *how to know how to move*

between these two points, oscillating more-or-less all the time, between feeling good about questioning in order to be able to feel good about having (albeit always evaluable) answers? How to feel confident enough in those current answers to be able to ask more questions? Or how to feel confident enough that we will always be able to find our way back again from uncertainty to new certainty?

> ...problems do not arise by themselves. It is precisely this that marks out a problem as being of the true scientific spirit: all knowledge is in response to a question. If there were no question, there would be no scientific knowledge. Nothing proceeds from itself. Nothing is given. All is constructed. (Bachelard 1938)

When to listen—questioning without words
Yet the point of questioning is to listen carefully for the answering. And just as questioning can be repeated until meaning emerges or clarity about situations is achieved, so also listening does the same. It may not always be a matter of 'forging onwards' with new questions but a matter of 'resting with' them—particularly at the point of trying to achieve deeper understanding or new insight. People specially need to be able to speak freely and for the questioning process to be responsive and allow for emergence. Short-circuiting this can store up unresolved difficulties (irresolvable even to the point of fatal conflict) for later.

So while all inquiry rests on questions, not all questions need be asked out loud. For many participant-observers, we may not even be aware of the questions that are nevertheless framing our filtered 'receipt' of information or input and shaping out decisions in response to it. Sometimes it may be just as helpful to ask, 'What am I hearing?', 'Why did I think what I just heard was significant?' or 'What is the question for which my noticing this action, practice, belief or value was the answer? or 'What have I learned?' Sometimes all of these articulated thoughts may be preceded (or surrounded) by nothing but listening, even in silence.

Timothy Radcliffe, a Dominican and Oxford scholar, quotes Simone Weil as saying we do not always need to 'go in search' but that 'this way of looking is, in the first place, *attentive*' (my emphasis), emptying itself of its own contents in order to receive the truth of the human being who is face to face (2004: 4). This has more recently been called 'presencing' or 'hearing from the heart' (Senge et al. 2004)—the *empathetic placing of oneself* imaginally in the *other's critical field of experience*. David Carline, an Indigenous Kooma man from Queensland, drawing on a stable cultural tradition that had sustained itself for more than 40 000 years, observed that 'in country' it is 'rude to ask questions', and that learning was about waiting, being shown, saying 'I don't understand that', and keeping the peace of the group (2005: 9). This attentiveness can ensure that 'a person is listened to respectfully and fully', and that there are 'spaces between the words' for thought, reflection and new insights.

In a deep sense then, while the act of inquiring and the act of questioning is to go forwards, the act of listening and receipt of answering is to yield in receptivity. In a day and age of always 'going forwards', 'pushing the envelope', 'showing leadership', talking with a certain and conclusive voice and of being goal-focused, all change ironically involves a time of not doing any of these. The Chinese sage intellectual observed at this point what has been translated to mean the 'small dark light':

> *What is of all things most yielding can overcome that which is most hard.*
> *The yielding conquers the resistant, and the soft conquers the hard.*
> Lao-Tzu[23]

Each of the key phase changes may particularly involve silence, whether in yielding from action into what physicists and cosmologists have called variously the 'universe of implicate order' (Bohm 2002), or 'ground of being', or 'all nourishing abyss' of morphogenic formlessness (Swimme and Berry 1994); or in *pressing* forwards with a new unified form or action that has come out of reflection. It is interesting that each of these phase changes is frequently characterised by wordless, musical, artistic or poetic expression (think Michael Leunig the Australian cartoonist's direction-finding duck and 'duck-whistle politics', or 'the blues' music at *Phase change 1*; or Bob Dylan's 'answers blowing in the wind' or Pete Seeger's prophetic 'hammer of justice and bell of freedom' at *Phase change 2*). This, it will be seen, has implications for the research methods and techniques we use to express experience at these critical moments.

A final introductory word about questioning
Questions in living systems are perhaps best thought of as invitations we offer rather than demands that we issue if we really want to hear or 'read' what people are able to tell us. (Orders or demands may actually bring the act of inquiry to an abrupt end.) What seems like a straightforward question to the asker may be anything but that to the answerer. Our questionnaires suffer from this to the extent people want to answer by saying 'Well it depends…' Questions may need to be put, the responses heard, and then the questions revised to better reflect what both parties intended or meant. This iterative nature of more accurate and useful questioning emerges in the co-forming of the inquiry *in relation with and between* the questioned and the questioner: in a space into which the questions and answers are placed. Questions may need—especially if they are very significant or have not been asked before—to be placed in this way into a receptive field for a while before seeing what or if any answers are possible.

Take the time needed. Let the questions change if need be, to better 'gel', or resonate more widely, gathering a greater range of responses and ideas, broadening the scope or field, and expanding the possibilities from which to draw conclusions. The more important the question, the longer it may take to do it justice, and the more it may need to be revisited (even when it *seems* that 'we've dealt with that and shouldn't go backwards'). Often it can be helpful to sit with silence after a question—even if it feels a little queasy to do so, like sitting at the edge of a gaping uncertainty. But picture our minds that are hearing the question as the great and complex computers that they are, chugging through numerous programs until something precious is located, offering an important insight. Then be open to that insight. Don't be too quick to think 'I already knew that' or 'That's not important' or 'I think that's wrong'. Some people routinely need to take a question back into their burrow to gnaw on it, turn it over and look at it from all sides. Others need to bat it around with others to hear responses to see how they 'fit' with relative field realities.

…and about listening
Allow plenty of space for the initial answer to be 'I don't know', 'It's not clear to me yet' or 'I don't think

I've got much to contribute'. Feel free to say: 'We can come back to that later'; 'Let's revisit this next time…' or 'Well that's what we think so far. Let's see what (else) we think when we next meet'. Even when certainty emerges around an answer, you can still say 'Well we'll go with that for now shall we, but we can revisit it further down the track if need be'. Faced with uncertainty—offer a safe form to 'hold' it. Faced with certainty—offer some open exit doors.

As Fran Peavey emphasises in *Strategic Questioning* (1994), listening is as important as asking. Her detailed and valuable advice about listening is available at: http://www.thechangeagency.org/_dbase_upl/strat_questioning_man.pdf.

Remember this is not a simple matter of listening to a message sent. The 'message' that is 'sent' is a complex matter of language with multiple meanings situated both in the historical and cultural context of the 'sender-in-relation-to-that-context' *and* of the receiver in relation to theirs—and which may be changing for both even as it is being sent! Indeed sometimes before the words are barely out we are already reaching to re-word things, whether because we are re-aligning our own thoughts differently, or in rapid response to incoming facial, verbal or body language or spoken responses, or messages from the background context. Action science *can* be fast on its feet! Though check that such rapid responses remain subject to reflection too.

Summary of sequence of research cycle questions

First phase—moving from 'what is'
('what has been up until now')

OBSERVE-ACTION 79

Field-of-interest focus questions

e.g. What are you looking at? What is noticeable, or an issue or concern or of interest here?

1 **Observation, description and retrospective evaluation questions** 79

e.g. What is happening? Who is doing what, when, where and how? What do you see, observe, hear, know, believe, value, think etc.?

2 **Analysis (and synthesis) questions** 82

e.g. Why are things as they are? What was meant to be going on here? What is *really* going on? How else can things be interpreted or explained using the existing logic or theory?

What is the story so far?

3 **Feeling questions** 90

e.g. Does it seem like things are going well or 'being done right'?—or not? How are you feeling about it/this? Easy? Or uneasy? Celebrating or mourning? Can you say why?

Phase change 1— moving to 'what could be'
Liminal (threshold) questions
e.g. Do you want change from the current situation? Enough to keep going?

REFLECT 96

4 **Envisioning (the ideal), prospective evaluation questions** 96

e.g. What would be better than now? How could things be as you would wish/prefer them to be? What are your deeper hopes, values, purposes and intentions? What could realise them?

5 **Change the theory story (new synthesis) questions** 100

e.g. What would it take to bring the current situation towards your deeply valued ideals? To be something better? What would need to change? Is there a new insight of use here? How can you think differently about this? Why would that be better?

What is the new story?

PLAN 103

6 **Alternatives-seeking questions** 103

e.g. How might this change/changes come about? Name as many ways as possible.

7 **Consequences-considering questions** 104

e.g. What would follow (from each suggestion)? What are their SWOTs?

Phase change 2—moving to (the new) 'what is'
Liminal/threshold questions

e.g. Are you really committed to making the desired change? Enough to keep going? Have all the possible difficulties and challenges of trying out the new practice been considered enough? Do you think the new proposed action/situation/practice will 'take'?

8 **Action design questions** 108

e.g. What would you like to do? How could you contribute? Who else is in a position to want to do something? Who could you work with? Who could work with you?
What are your priorities, goals, aims or agenda? (To do what, when, where, how and why?)

ACT 111

9 **Support and resourcing questions** 111

e.g. What would it take for you to be able to do what you/we want to do?/make this contribution? What support, assistance, information, people, etc. do you need to take intentions into practice? Are there other ideas that could be helpful from elsewhere? Are there any precedents?

10 **Implementation and monitoring questions** 114

e.g. How do you actually do this new action? And how will you know if it's been done? What would the signs be? What would be good indicators and targets for those?

Coming full circle 115

OK—you've taken an action, tried it out, put it into practice: What has changed? Was that good? Or not? Is it making the intended difference? What do you observe?…

Yes! it's back to 'the start', back to observing action…!

A comprehensive sequence of research questions[24]

...to navigate around cycles of living systems inquiry

First phase: moving from 'what is' (and has been) to considering 'what could be'

Beginning
...by stopping

It seems ironic that—no matter how fleeting or for how long—inquiry starts with *stopping* in order to *observe* what is going on, to *notice* something that is happening, to watch and *see*, listen and *hear*.

The starting place is where you and others and the field situation are 'at'—trying to step out of the taken-for-granted familiarity and security of everyday action based on the certainties of previous conclusions, to look at that already existing action in order to make better sense of something. You are starting in everyday experience, in the field of action that is being inquired into, because that is where you are. It is *this* field of relations that is to be closely understood, not in the first place so much through the eyes of others at a distance from that field, but from *within it*. In this sense research starts with its own capacity for awareness (and self-awareness of the observer's own connectedness within this field) to begin to understand anew what is going on.

Let us use inquiry—our magnifying glasses, compasses, mirrors and maps—to build a 'house for our self' and for our greater self, our 'body corporate'. Here is a way of thinking about building in inquiring to all the 'rooms of our house', as we move through them, exploring and traversing the inquiry cycles of action–observation–reflection–planning...

OBSERVE[25]-ACTION[26]
Retroductive-inductive phase

Field-of-interest focus questions

Identifying the field or domain of inquiry

Firstly, say briefly, just in a few words, what is it that you are observing—or think you might be wanting to look into...
Q. What is the area, issue, activity, program, service, interest, claim, concern, practice or problem that you have been noticing or want to inquire into?

1 Observation, description and retrospective evaluation questions

About 'how things are' or have been/should have been until now

It is a time for beginning to move 'outside the square' of everyday action and practice and all the governing assumptions and theories, logics and prior objectives that have hitherto constructed its knowledge. A new journey of inquiry and evaluation is beginning (albeit one understood in the first place in terms of what came before)...

DOORS AND WINDOWS
Doors and windows allow—both in and out—the needed exchanges of information enabling both permeability and structure (to meet purposes). New inputs and perceptions supply a stream of intelligence about the environment, preventing the risk of becoming internally besieged, rigidifying or toxifying becalmment. Windows are the 'eyes'

allowing observation outwards, and energies and information inwards. Observation helps the organism make different and more creative responses to meet its deeper purposes. When closed or shuttered they may protect from the elements but also keep out the 'winds of change'. Rooms sealed off from each other may mean house-dwellers dissociate from what they enable—so hallways inside are also needed. Doors allow more full-bodied passage in and out across thresholds and invitations to conversation on doorsteps. Open plan designs provide even greater exchange at the same time as separate purposes can co-exist, perhaps only needing symbolic dividers: a carpet square marking a piece of floor, a reading lamp signifying purpose, or a planter providing a wall.

Through the front door things can be 'taken in' and through the back door whatever is no longer needed can pass away. Hermes, frenetic and energetic messenger of the Gods, was guardian of the threshold. But hermetic sealing can lead to losing the ability to breathe in life-giving oxygen.

THE HOUSE'S MONITORING AND MAINTENANCE SYSTEM

The ways by which the organism keeps watch on itself—both its interior's workings and its exterior's protection from the 'outside' world—'keeping a watchful eye' or 'an ear out' for what is going on and what should be taken in, given out or exchanged. When fearing attack on a weak interior that is thought to be defenceless under assault, hyper-surveillance, security, defence and 'Big Brother' control may be resorted to. Fixing and adjusting, tending to all the ways needed to keep itself in good working order. At the point of its boundaries with its outer world it employs all of its senses to notice itself and others in its community and what is passing between, using magnifying glasses or binoculars—like a bodily immune system: detecting, neutralising, repelling, overwhelming, securing or encouraging, inviting and bonding.

THE SEWING ROOM

A stitch observed in time saves nine! Single loop embroidery. Many perfectly workable items can be patched, mended or reinforced. Although if there is not enough time it may get popped in the too hard basket until a less busy 'rainy day' for more considered reflection.

AND THE SHED/GARAGE

See what is broken. Take it out to the shed to have a look at it. See if it can be quickly fixed. And if it's too big or too hard, pop it in the corner or lean it up against the back wall, until that quiet rainy day.

These are places of maintenance assisting the organism 'hold its form' as intended and designed. Places of inventive industry and playful opportunities, for use of leftovers and cast-offs, the broken and the worn, bits and pieces of things and raw materials; where the precious and useful can be mended, reformed, restored, recycled, re-used, or new things invented to 'fit in' with existing system logics wherever possible.

> *People, even more than things,*
> *have to be restored, renewed,*
> *revived, reclaimed and redeemed.*
> *Never throw out anyone.*
> AUDREY HEPBURN

How do human systems ensure both the desired organised bounding and ordering and open permeability of their systems so they are able to exchange important information and experiences, retain what is needed and be open to the process of inquiring further? How can everyday research and evaluation and continuous improvement processes aid in resourcing this, both by monitoring and adjusting action to be more like it was previously intended, to perform much needed 'quick fixes' and find effective 'single loop' solutions (Argyris and Schon 1978) to small problems arising in implementation—*and* be able to open up new lines of deeper inquiry that might lead to revised intentions, logics and new and better actions where need be?

Questions to help traverse this 'observing current action' monitoring-and-auditing part of the cycle

Open inquiry (goal-free)

If the domain of inquiry (identified above) is something new (or new to you—then you may want to start your observation here
Q. How would you describe what's going on? What are you seeing?—or doing?—or has been done?
What is happening?—or has happened? And what has occurred as a result so far?
What has caught your attention? What is of interest?

Recapitulate any observations already made

What do you and others see, observe, hear, know, conclude, believe, think and currently value, want or desire?

Audit review (goal-driven, retroductive)

If the domain of inquiry is something that is already established according to plans, beliefs, theories and objectives—then you may be starting your observation here...

Q. How would you describe what you (or others) are doing in terms of what you were originally setting out to do? What was the original vision and the (larger) goals, and (smaller) aims and objectives that were meant to contribute to achieving this vision?

What was the logic or theory lying behind each of the intended actions?

Recapitulate any formal plans or policies on which they were based

Where did the vision come from? What were the values and principles that underpinned these? *Here you are tracing backwards even further round the previous inquiry cycle to what came before...*

What were the conclusions from needs studies or evaluations that led to the plans, policies and goals you have been implementing?

Can you say why you (or they) set out to do things in this way?

What was it that was hoped would be achieved?

What were you doing before this?

What were people's situations that gave rise to these hopes and plans?

When you (or they) embarked on what was originally to be done, were there any signs or indicators identified that it was thought would show if what was intended was being achieved? Can you describe them? Was what 'good results' might look like worked out? How have you identified (or did you intend to identify) or measure your achievements, or what you've learned along the way? Were these set as hoped for 'targets'?

Recapitulate any a priori indicators and targets

Did you do what you set out to do?

What did you actually do? (Who did what, when, where, how and how often?)

Work through all elements of the action/s, service/s, program/s with these questions

Methods and techniques to help traverse this 'observe–action' part of the cycle

- Diaries/notes and journals
- Learning logs, online blogs
- 'To do' lists
- Comparative data, baseline data
- Counting, measurements, scales
- Time series and other statistics
- 1st, 2nd, 3rd generation evaluation
- St Luke's[27] 'Scales' pads
- Records, memoranda, minutes or notes of meetings
- Management Information Systems and routinely collected statistics
- Surveys, questionnaires
- Recording, monitoring, transcripts
- Reception/foyer/image/first impressions
- Open house/Open door policy/Open day
- Noticeboards
- Feedback sheets
- Written reports, annual reports

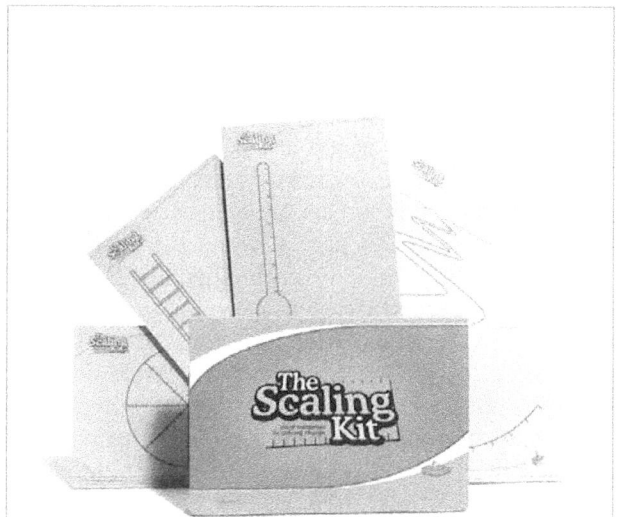

The *Scaling Kit* is a set of 10 scaling pads, each printed with a different, simple line drawing which can be marked or written on to measure change. The ten visual metaphors in this kit are: Balance – Circle – Ladder – Pathway – Pendulum – Rating Wheel – Sun Up/Sun Down – Thermometer – Ups and Downs – Water Tank.

2 Analysis (and synthesis) questions

THE VERANDAH AND THE GUEST ROOM

Verandahs, doorsteps and window ledges are all liminal (threshold, borderland, frontier, boundary, lookout and forcefield) spaces. They are where we may encounter visitors and guests, and welcome what they have to offer. (Or not.) The verandah was originally an external corridor between rooms, a place of communication and exchange (that later moved indoors to become hallways). Overcrowding and exclusion saw some consigned to a verandah 'sleep-out', or were later brought inside to a guest room.

A guest sees more in an hour than the host in a year.
POLISH PROVERB

LOUNGE, (WITH) DRAWING ROOM AND DINING ROOM

It's getting late in the day. Getting too cold and dark to stay out on the verandah. Time to go within. People gather to sit, relax, take time out, talk about what they've done and seen and heard, and learn more from each other; celebrate the day's achievements and pleasures, and ponder difficulties, losses, worries or puzzles. Places to share experiences of the wider world in audio, visual, musical or poetic form, pursue interests, make conversation, 'chew things over', and find a way to mention any white horses on the table, and see new synergies released...

How can human services providers and users come together with each other to make sense of what is going on, to ponder unanswered questions, unresolved issues or problems as well as to celebrate the good things, enjoy the fruits of people's labour and what has 'worked'? To sit back comfortably, open up, appreciate each others' strengths and whole being and expand each other's minds. How can providers and users and other stakeholders come *alongside* each other, not staying in negatively charged 'face-offs'; how can they 're-pair their ions' so the 'forcefields' can release their power and energy? And how can everyday research and evaluation processes 'build in' such 'time out' to ponder the situation and analyse where it came from, and start to make better sense of what has been happening?

Questions to help traverse this 'analyse observation' part of the cycle may include

Can you go more deeply into what you've seen or done, or what has been happening so far? How can you analyse *how* things have been happening, theorise *why* they might have been happening like this, and begin to synthesise *the implications* of past practice to date?
In both general and specific situations—You have looked at what was done, how, when, where, with whom, and why.
Now ask: Is this the case? *Really* the case (from your perspective)? Correct, right, accurate or true for us? How else can things be interpreted?
*In the wider situation—*What else is going on? Begin to reflect a little more deeply...

Teachers' capabilities need to be measured, but let's not do it with half a ruler. Yes, let's measure their skills, how they obtained them and especially who trained them, but also measure all the other factors that help to make a good teacher. Measure their workload, the work they take home, their timetable, their preparation time and the extra work they are asked to do. Measure their resources or lack thereof, the age and suitability of the equipment they use and the training they have had in using this equipment. Measure the number of students they have and the size and condition of their classroom(s). Above all, measure the pressure and stress teachers are under, and then maybe we can have some measurable understanding of what makes a good teacher (Letter to *The Age*, Vic Camilleri, Keilor East, 13 January 2007).

What are our lives like? And those of others with whom we work and live? How does the world work for us at the moment—or not? How has it worked in the past? How do we think 'the world works' per se? How do people see things are organised or structured? What are the governing rules or logic they identify? What are the effects? Who do people think benefit, do well (and who doesn't)? Who do people think should benefit or not? What are the principles and ethics people see as currently operating? What are you allowed to do—or not? Say—or not say? And under what circumstances, and with what consequences? Who relates to whom, and in what ways and with what consequences? Why do others think people are doing what they are doing?

Draw out the intentions or purposes, and the logic that seems to be operating

What would you say is the meaning of all this (these actions, words etc.) at the moment? To you/others/the people themselves? How is the world experienced as real and 'fact like' to you/them? Or as fluid and able to change? What is the evidence for seeing things in these ways? How certain are the understandings? How clear in their implications? Where do you or other people think you/they are headed?

What would you say follows next into the future from the logic of 'how things are' now? What looks like it would happen on current projections?

Here is where qualitative and quantitative descriptive observations are most relevant. You are seeking all the ways of understanding 'how things are' for people—both empirically and experientially. And different groups' different perspectives on 'what is'. More than at any other time, you are wanting to capture what Stafford Beer memorably called POSIWID—the Purpose Of a System Is What It Does:

> According to the cybernetician the purpose of a system is what it does. This is a basic dictum. It stands for bald fact, which makes a better starting point in seeking understanding than…sheer ignorance of circumstances (Beer 2002: 209–219).

Methods and techniques that may help traverse this analytic part of the cycle

- The 'discover' part of the appreciative inquiry cycle
- Two-column comparisons: LH-what is said; RH-what is really thought
- Analysis of written documentation
- Action sheets/plans
- Matrix spreadsheets
- Statistics, statistical analysis of variance
- Inference, tests of significance, confidence intervals
- Audits, Quality Assurance measuring/calibrating
- Standards reviews
- Risk assessments
- Fact-finding expeditions, 'diplomatic missions' to neighbouring systems
- Conversational analysis
- Conferences, seminars, workshops, teleconferences
- Visitors', guests' and students' (on placement) observations
- Consumer groups, community/citizen representatives who 'enter the picture'
- Critical incident analysis, sentinel events
- Satire/cringe comedy, mokumentaries
- Networking, community forums, public meetings, consultations
- Interviews, questionnaires
- Case studies, narratives (e.g. use St Luke's cards 'Views from the Verandah')
- Open space technology (first stages)
- Published 'findings'

Noticing discrepancy

You may notice that you are observing something compared to something else. Whether in terms of pre-articulated expectations or not, this is the critical element of human inquiry that means the inquiry 'life force' is at work. And it is these comparisons that generate the discrepancies which, if detected, generate movement from 'a this to a that', from 'a here to a somewhere else', from a past to a future—whether in the direction of expanding or contracting the discrepancy; they are the dynamic out of an otherwise unwanted state.

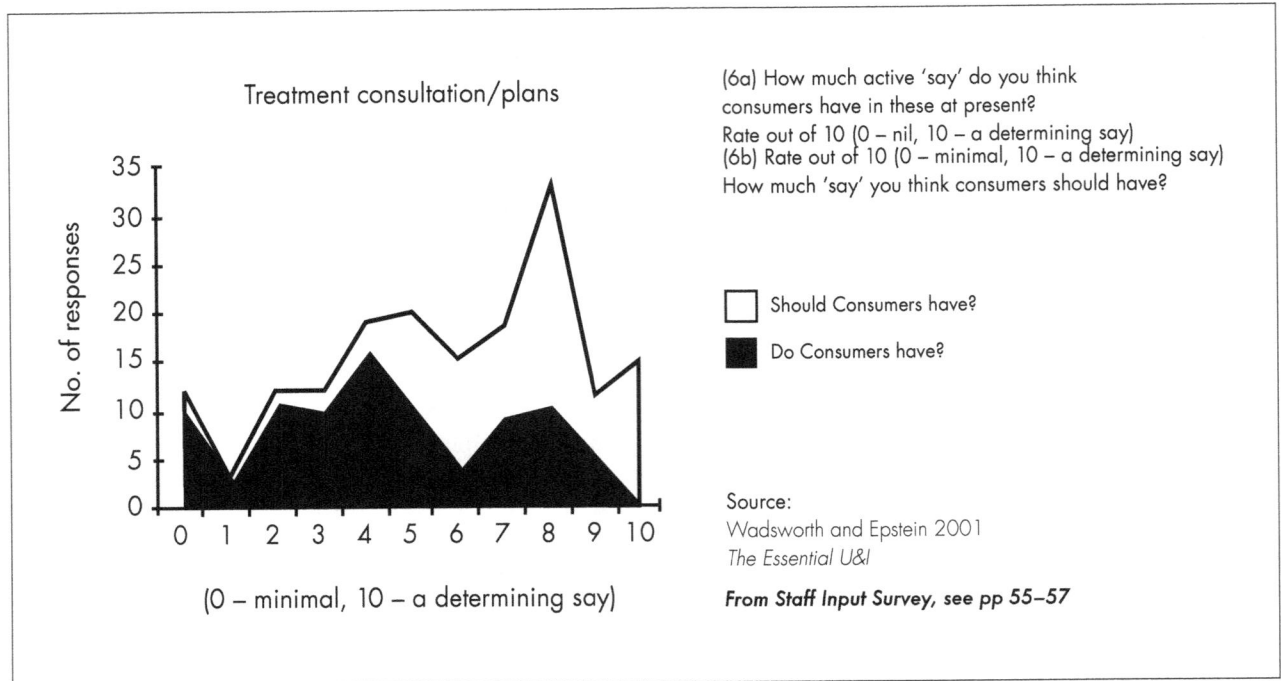

Treatment consultation/plans

(6a) How much active 'say' do you think consumers have in these at present?
Rate out of 10 (0 – nil, 10 – a determining say)
(6b) Rate out of 10 (0 – minimal, 10 – a determining say)
How much 'say' you think consumers should have?

□ Should Consumers have?

■ Do Consumers have?

(0 – minimal, 10 – a determining say)

Source:
Wadsworth and Epstein 2001
The Essential U&I

From Staff Input Survey, see pp 55–57

Figure 11. Noticing discrepency

'Discrepancy' means 'discordant' from the Latin discrepare, dis—'intensification of', crepare—'creak', harsh scraping sound. And 'discordant' means 'at variance, not harmonious', from discordare, where dis means 'absence of' or 'separation from' and cord means 'heart'. Note that cord has the same derivation as cords, strings, ribs, ribbons, and the antonym of discordant, 'resonant', comes from the Latin, meaning 'echo' from re, 'again', sonus, 'sounds, vibrations'.

The dynamic towards life rests in the valorisation of the discrepancy—is it a good discrepancy or not for the organism? Does the 'more' or 'less' mean the organism is receiving life-giving relationality or resourcing (or whatever the discrepancy indicates) or not. Values are embodied as stored memories or images of what has meant what. Quickly we calculate the meaning of the perceived discrepancy on the basis of these past stores of valorised experiences, experiments, learnings and logical conclusions. Here is the source of all our pre-judgings, the store of

practice wisdom necessary to equip us for whatever might next loom onto our radars. Sabre toothed tigers or a new kind of leadership—looking at whatever confronts us in the task or action with which we are preoccupied, we note its congruence with 'how things were meant to be' or its discordance with these or some unstated other values. When our current actions or purposes have not been v   alorised (or ever even encountered before the new incident or phenomenon), then we dig deeper into a more ancient capability for largely non-verbal, even non-conscious, albeit rational detection of value—something we call 'a feel for it', a 'gut feeling', or a feeling we identify as 'from the heart'. The relational exchange of energies the Buddhists call suffering, which in Sanskrit means 'unsatisfactoriness'.

Thus catalysed, we can go deeper with evaluative questions, accessing feeling stored in the body to ground our evaluations in answers to the questions, 'What is desirable—what is of value, merit, worth or significance?' We can ask, 'What will nurture life?' And what will not? What will resource, aid and assist? And what will not? What is hurting and causing suffering, and what will not?

It was a matter of personal and professional annoyance to a health statistician that a research institute was claiming 40 per cent of the population was suffering from 'mental illness'. He was particularly able to articulate this observation as a definitional anomaly in comparison to a statistically 'normal' figure of 8 per cent suffering 'physical illness'. Moving quickly from observe to plan to act, he speculated about the financial burden that might result from requiring funding equity, yet he did not see fairness or logic in curtailing funds for physical illness either. Under the prevailing circumstances there appeared to be no sufficiently strong rationale to proceed to try and gain the interest of policy makers and service planners in being interviewed. Another health researcher in the same inquiry group took up the issue by noticing what felt discrepant to her about potentially being defined iatrogenically as a 'mentally ill' person when her observations of her own work experience indicated to her that her not sleeping (and other signs at risk of being defined as individual internal pathology) were more related to systemic stress resulting from the performance pressures on her job (health emergency work), combined with feeling disempowered by ever more tightly measured and circumscribed organisational work practices imposed by management in the interests of 'financial efficiency'. It was this personally felt discrepancy that offered to drive an interest in continuing to inquire 'around the cycle' into deeper reflection on 'what was wrong' and what might be 'more right' without there yet being a solution in sight. Indeed such energies would need to be strong enough to pursue the issue in the face of heavy existing social-cultural norms of shaming about 'revealing' signs already strongly culturally defined by a professional medical specialty as 'mental illness', as well as established scientific norms rejecting the expression of such personal embodied feeling as irrelevant or even biasing. At a later point in the cycle there would be a need for careful checking of any new idea against further empirical 'realities' as well as broader principles and values to test the logic of trying a different course of action. However firstly deeper reflection would be needed in order to generate such a new and more compelling theory about how and why change was needed and from which a more viable course of action might flow. The inquiry perhaps therefore stood a better chance of getting going and continuing full cycle into such new theorising and better practice if it was driven by the 'heat of friction' that came from people's felt compromise to their own life conditions. Far from biasing the effort, such feelings might even be a valuable warrant against settling for anything less than an outcome that truly worked.

Epistemology is always and invariably personal. The point of the probe is always in the heart of the explorer...
GREGORY BATESON, 1979 P.87

Thin skin is the only kind humans have
SUSAN GREENFIELD, 'THE SCIENCE SHOW', RADIO NATIONAL, AUSTRALIAN BROADCASTING COMMISSION, 2008

Questions to traverse this evaluative observation part of the cycle

Audit review observation

Regarding any objectives, targets, values etc. identified previously
Would you say things are going as you intended or expected or hoped?
If yes—is that still good?
If not—is that bad?

Here you are looking for unintended outcomes, that is, false positives or false negatives
What new questions are arising for you from your observation of how things are to date?
Whether there are pre-articulated objectives and goals or not, values may be accessed by asking open questions

Open inquiry observation

How is it going? Is it going well (or not)? Has it worked (or not)? In what ways—or/and to what extent? Can you say why you think it's going well or not?
Hear any description that refers to hitherto non-explicit values/valued states
Can you draw out whether there is something unexpected, wrong or problematic for you about this—or something really good or successful? Can you say why? What is 'making a difference'?—is that what was intended?

What evidence are you seeing of good, promising or better practice?

What are you celebrating? What are you particularly appreciating? What is making you feel good and joyous? Can you draw out what are the values or principles that are being successfully honoured in this discrepancy you are observing?

What evidence are you seeing of weak, poor or problematic practice?

What are you mourning? What is particularly grieving or troubling you? What is making you feel unhappy? Is it as yet a 'problem with no name'? What would you say it's about at this stage?

Can you draw out what are the values or principles that are being violated in this discrepancy you are observing? What have you noticed has resulted (or not resulted) from the discrepant situation?

What has changed (or not changed) significantly? Most significantly? Does it matter? In what way/s? To whom? What leads you to draw these conclusions? What was the evidence and why has it been particularly noticeable?

*Draw out in detail what it is about these states that is (or is not) of value, merit, worth or significance…*Is there some kind of repeating pattern that you don't like or want? Or a pattern you do want, and want to amplify?

'I think I've only written one song. It's about feeling trapped and gaining release. It's something I find in the very structure of the standard song form: verse-chorus, verse-chorus, bridge, key change, coda. You're making a statement, making it again and then, with a key change of a middle eight, you get some kind of change of viewpoint, so suddenly you're in a different space…It takes you out of a loop you might be in…'
(Sting 2003: 30)

Methods and techniques to traverse this evaluative part of the cycle
· Any observational methods that illustrate evaluated comparisons
· Two-column comparisons: LH-what is said or done; RH-what is felt
· Discourse analysis
· Analysis of goal displacement
· Stories/narrative/digital narrative (multi-media)
· Journalling, memoirs, reflections and souvenirs

· St Luke's 'Shadows' picture cards; 'Inside Out' (journalling kit),
· St Luke's 'What works?' (strengths kit) http://issuu. com/innovativeresources/docs/what_works_website _booklet/1
· Catholic Education Office's Photolanguage™
· 'Message' plays, theatre, photos, paintings, audio, music, lyrics, poetry
· Theatre feedback, puppets
· Cartooning, drawings
· Video and musical production workshops
· Reflexive/evaluative Photography/photo essays
· Model-making, 3D play, synchronicity in non-goal-directed play
· St Luke's 'Scales: Tools for Change' pads (as a basis for experiential progress evaluation)
· Natural social situations in which people continue to get to know each other better, celebrate, commiserate, nurture and learn from and with each other
· Focus groups, group interviews
· Café of the Oppressed
· 4th-generation evaluation

Beginning the deeper conversation
Abductive phase

The inquiring process has shown it is time to come to even more of a stop. This time the stopping is more like *yielding* to the deepest realities of the situation, and, having breathed out, there is an imperceptible pause before *beginning* to breathe in again.[28] Sometimes it's a very big yielding—a huge catastrophe stops us all in our tracks. More often it is a little yielding, especially if there is a routine culture of inquiry built in and discrepancies are able to attract attention sooner.

So for the sake of the living system it is time to look into things more deeply. All the possible adjustments, adaptations, endlessly repeated 'single loop' actions and skilled quick fixes have not been able to address the deeper underlying factors. It is time to stop putting things in the too hard basket. The white horse or the elephant or the entire cast of worn-out or troubled people standing quietly on the table at last demand attention.

Time to sit down and ponder the far deeper reasons why we would like things to change, as this takes us to a threshold between the known and familiar and that-which-is-yet-to-be…

But before we can do that, we need to identify *who* is inquiring and wanting to stop and look more deeply in order to address these discrepancies for a more life-giving way forward. Who are our travel companions for this journey? Who wants to inquire? And who does not?

Who is observing current action taking place in the world and beginning to raise value questions?
Who is doing all this observing? And of whom? Is it you—because of your own interests? Or is it with or for or about others as well? Are all the relevant people beginning to talk about what they are seeing together? Could they be? Can you begin to invite them into even this early conversation? Even if informally and in a low key way at this stage? After all it's just some niggling thoughts and 'noticing' at the moment. But helpful if you can raise with others your own beginning observations *now* rather than getting way down the track with your conclusions and missing out on *their* early responses, their input…especially if they are seeing the same things as you are, or have a different take on them; and even more importantly if it is really *their* issue you are observing!

Later you may need to keep inviting even more people into the inquiry as it unfolds, especially as its emergence reveals new people who are relevant or who become implicated by a new line of inquiry. But certainly at the earliest possible stage, see if you can float the questions to see who is interested and what they have to say. If you are able to do this transparently, out loud and openly, more may join you because they know of your interest, and others will not feel excluded by boundaries they might view negatively.
Be as clear as you can about the nature of your concern and let it be an energetic attractor.

Some may feel unable to inquire—perhaps the current situation seems OK. Or OK enough…Or maybe they are a little anxious or believe 'disturbing sleeping dogs' might only lead to 'trouble' or unearth irresolvable problems. Or perhaps they are still prepared to trust the existing situation as authorised by previous experience. If people haven't been part of inquiring processes before, they may not know and trust what they can achieve.

Perhaps if you stay in touch they may join later if they see a connection with their own situation emerge. Perhaps the circulation of some interesting articles or a newspaper cut-out, or some puzzling comparative statistics, or some stories of people's experiences will nurture a line of inquiry. Perhaps the holding of a small informal meeting will attract.

Forming an inquiry group …and a wider network

It's not that there may not have been an inquirer or inquiry group prior to this moment, but that whoever the inquirer or group or team has been up to now has been able to continue making adaptations in the light of existing logics and narrative. These may have been relatively easy 'goings around the cycle' without needing to go very far or very deeply into the unknown. Indeed they may really have been able to miss having to observe very much at all, and barely pause for reflection before quickly re-planning or re-charting the previous course. It's more like now, the destination has entirely disappeared off the radar. Or that the existing destination is beginning to look like the wrong one.

The 'tried and true' is not working, and those who see this first are the 'canaries in the mine'—those who just 'get a feeling' something is really wrong. They begin to sing more and more insistently but their songs are ignored (since they do not make it into the published literature for a while yet).

Pausing at a threshold: considering the need for change
At this moment of as yet unarticulated sensed and felt discrepancy there may just be a nagging feeling that all is not well; that there is something going on to which we shouldn't be turning a blind eye; something needing to be understood better. Or a sense of yearning need or desire for 'something else'. So far it may seem like 'just anecdotes', or a sea of data, a mass of observations, or lots of statistics not yet analysed through the lens of interpretive experience, not yet voiced for what else they might represent or mean. Looked at, but patterns not really seen. Or, if it is more obvious than that, people may be feeling unsettled by something 'too big to handle', or wanting to deny the need to look at something that is so far 'a problem that has no name'.[29]

Ironically, at the moment when people may most want to return to 'business as usual' they least should. Instead what is most needed is for all relevant stakeholders to come together to share their observations so far, ask the still tentative questions, and avoid the escalation of 'the drama' that can take place at this phase change, which risks sweeping things back under the carpet...

'What do you mean there's a problem?'

'Well I don't want to say it's a *problem*, but I do think we might be seeing a bit of X happening.'

'What X? I haven't seen X. Has anyone actually seen X? How much X are you saying there is?'

'Well we don't really know *for sure* there's a *lot* of X, it's just a bit of a trend...'

'So there's no real evidence yet then?'

'Well not a great deal of data, but if we go on without changing course we may get into trouble if X *is* starting to happen.'

'Well I'm not going off on some expensive whim, Y has been working well, I haven't seen any signs of X myself, and I don't see why there should be any trouble developing.'

'Well actually we have seen some trouble...'

'What trouble?'

'Well we've seen signs of X at A.'

'Ha! That's not trouble.'

'Well if it's at A then it *could* develop at B, C, D and E.'

'Oh rubbish. That is just scare-mongering speculation. I don't want to hear any more about this until the data's in—and you, you come and see me in my office right now.'

This is not a culture of inquiry! (It is also an organisation most probably riding for a fall.)

But how to build in the times and places to encourage these kinds of early exchanges?

Amongst the Exemplars described in Chapter 5, one universal feature associated with success in establishing a culture of inquiry is the way in which communities of reflective practice—groups of interested people who choose to meet and look into things together—are not only allowed to meet but required to do so. In these could be shared the graphs and tables showing differences from 'the norm', or differences between experience and the yearned for and desired; the questions could be asked, 'Is this what it seems?', 'What is going on?', and 'What could be done about it'?

This can feel like the beginning of difficult and uncertain territory. A foray into chaos—what I've always myself called the 'swamp phase' of research.

Before the new connections are made and new shapes and forms emerge to be foregrounded.

The inquiry group's journey together around the cycle has begun!

They begin to explore the data and layers of direct practice experience and close observation, insider local knowledge of what has been done and said, the perceptions and feelings attached, and the outcomes or results seen so far. They choose the questions raised, and design how to get answers to address them. They know what are the values and the concrete images on which they draw. Together they develop new meanings and theories, look at the knowledge of experience elsewhere, remember which ideas have been considered and discarded and why, and assess the arguments, hypotheses and claims until they settle on and rehearse the best ones, both in theory and then in practice. Then the participating co-inquirers again share their observations of their new actions.

To slough off or otherwise leave behind any of the critical players associated with each of these steps and stages is to risk losing the continuing contributions of that vital source of perspective, evidence and experience. The worst case scenario becomes a form of 'pass the parcel' or Chinese whispers, with progressive reduction in what is passed on until increasingly abstracted versions of the original rich realities lose their meaning altogether. On the other hand, when free to continue to inquire together iteratively and emergently over time, the individuals within that group or network gradually knit together a coherent body of relevant new complex knowledge and a robust new story, each contributing their particular ways of knowing (and knowledges), which take them all the way into new practice. None of this may prove easy, especially to begin with. But as mutual knowledge builds, each comes to see what the other knows and is able to contribute, and builds trust from which to want to seek repeatedly each other's input and perspective.

Questions to assist forming an inquiry group and emergent network

Who is interested in this particular topic, issue, discrepancy, concern, problem, desire, claim or question? What interests do we have in this issue or phenomenon? Are they shared enough between us to be viable? Are they different enough to aid our inquiring?

Who are we who have come together so far? Is anyone missing? Are we the 'right people'? Enough of the right people?

Are we who it's all for? That is, are we the critical reference/inquiry group? Are some of us? Any of us? If so, are there others we want to invite to join us? If not, who are we in relation to the critical reference group? How will we know the will and judgement of the critical reference group? Can we invite them to join us—or can we ask to join with them?

Who else might want to join in? Who else *should* join in? Who else might need to be invited?

Or should we be joining others elsewhere?

Methods and techniques that may be helpful for groups or/and networks that together can inquire 'full cycle'

· Communities of Practice (Wenger 1998)
· Critical reference groups/critical inquiry groups (Wadsworth 1997b)
· Action learning sets (Revans 1980)
· Learning circles
· Working groups
· Taskforces
· Study groups, syndicates
· Research and evaluation teams, committees
· Workplace teams, partnerships, collaborations (if free to question)
· Staff, interdepartmental, disciplinary or interdisciplinary meetings
· Meetings with other systems/levels of systems
· Stakeholders' groups
· Nodes in networks, networks, networking
· Networks of networks, networks of communities
· 5th generation evaluation, in-house and participatory groups (Guba and Lincoln 1989)
· Co-operative inquiry and Collaborative inquiry (Reason and Rowan 1981, Heron 1996)
· Participatory or Deliberative democracy

Summing up: what is the story so far?

OK, so by now you have a pretty comprehensive and detailed description and understanding of how and why 'things are as they are' (so far). So this might be a good time to draw it together…What would you say you've learned from everything you've observed, described, thought and felt to this point? If you were to tell someone the story so far, what would it be?

Questions to summarise the journey round the cycle so far

Now you've thought about it more together, summarise in just a few sentences…
What has happened—or been done—or resulted so far? What is good that's going well and needs to be kept—or repeated—or extended? What are the things that currently give life to the situation?

What is a puzzle or problem or still lacking, an unfulfilled desire, draining the life of the people? What would you say is the *real* issue? What is really of concern? What is of most interest, or significance here? *Now summarise who is 'here at the table'.* And your relationships to the situation, problem, claim, issue, concern or interest—and to each other. And if you think there are others who might want to join and add to this developing story.

This brief shared story should sustain the life of your group in its retelling by anyone in the group, and whenever a new person joins. Changing and adapting as each new iteration or recursion is traversed.

Now it's time to move on, as to stay here is to keep asking for more research that will only keep describing more observations about 'how things are'. To be able to move on with the inquiry is to be able to say we now know enough about 'the story so far'—about what is happening and what has been of value or not—and are ready to cross the threshold from looking back at how things have been, to looking forward to researching how alternatively they could (or should) be for you or/and the critical inquiry group. The old dwelling is beginning to crack and groan. But, as Leonard Cohen sings in Anthem, 'that's how the light gets in'. Time to look at what is (and would be) more deeply valued. Time to go to the heart of the matter.

While still integrally connected to the world of action, you have stepped a little way 'outside the square' of the existing boundaries and forms and begun more deeply feeling a way into a rich chaos of elements, wavy lines and fragments in which to seek new, more life-giving possibilities and forms

3 Feeling questions

The last rays of the sunset have flared and dazzled, and now there's just a rosy glow remaining—witnessing to the received: the beauty and the pleasure appreciated and the celebrated harvest of outcomes achieved (the source of continuing sustenance for the lean times); and witness also to entropy, difficulties, suffering and the 'dying into darkness' of what has been.

It's time for supper and a late night cup of tea.

Time to step back and away from everyday busy life and the routines of work and return to the source of all things of real value[31]—with some reliable questions and the warmth and light of the hearth to get us through the long night of the inquiring soul.

KITCHEN HEARTH

The central source of 'energy', at the heart of the organism—where nourishing resources, fuel, and nutrients are gathered and the spark arising from discrepancy becomes a warming that will keep up the circulation of the life-blood of interest, desire and purpose, re-oxygenating to achieve that which is most valued. The 'heartland', the soul of what is left after the summer sun has burnt away all extraneous matter; the centrally important element of a living system; the source of deepest comfort—'comfort' from the Latin confortare, meaning 'strengthen' from com, 'with' and fortis, 'strong'—and the turning point for nurturing the healing-back-to-wholeness process. Where the most heart-felt can be expressed. Hestia the Greek goddess of the home looks inwards, focusing on the hearth.[32]

Margaret's kitchen

This room she planned herself. It flowed
Into the breakfast room,
Which was also the sewing room,
And the room for writing letters,
Paying bills, giving cups of tea,
And keeping the toys for children on a visit.
This was the destination of the house.
It smelt of bread, detergent, roasting lamb.
It made me think of a vicarage
In a country town: things centred here.
But here, too, she kept a Russian carving,
A Chinese sketch, a Danish paper heart.
This kitchen connected to the world

RAEWYN CONNELL, 2008

What is at the heart of human systems and human services?

What are the deep values—the valued states and images[33] of what is of merit, worth or significance; of heartfelt desire, truly wanted or humanly needed? The deepest, truest purposes of life?

Your ethics or the 'ethos of the people' which form the basis for intentions and later abstraction as 'principles' to guide action; held here at 'the heart of the enterprise' (Beer 1979).

How can everyday research and evaluation processes aid in strengthening this? Fortunately the process has already started in all our previous observation, in the noticing—the looking, listening, smelling, touching, tasting—which has provided the 'data' for the now *deeper* 'seeing', insight, hearing and feeling…

Empathically—both within our selves and in relation to and with others—*feel* the alignment or lack of it, *feel the lack of resonance* of inner states discordant with outer states and outer states discordant with inner states. This is to begin to approach the realm of the transpersonal—what some traditions call the sacred, a word which simply means 'wholly' and 'all'. A state where all is admissible, where brokenness may be repaired, a place of deep inclusion. The more that can be included, the more that the next creation might find the resources to be resonant with need and desire. Mystery enters the picture of chaos and uncertainty as a new pattern is yet to take shape from 'nothing'— from nothing more than what is coming in and out of flow—what the physicist David Bohm has called a 'field of implicate order' (2002).

In a way, in the realm of feeling, our own bodies are like the 'Geiger detectors', sonar pulse detectors, 'instruments' able to calibrate when things are 'out of kilter' with the vibration. Or 'out of focus'. Here we seek questions that will address fears and anxieties and enable confrontation and conflict to be replaced by 'alongsideness', collaboration, calibration, co-operation and dialogue, and eventually a new form of harmony and unity. There is something of a 'chicken and an egg' here. To come into enough resonance to begin the task of deeper understanding that will bridge across distance and difference requires enough understanding, enough of a glimpse of a possibility to believe this is even possible. Yet to achieve even that glimpse, when things are very fractured and divided, when judgement is hardened rock-solid, requires at least some minimum prescience to want to even try.

Since we can store discrepancies between an 'is' and an 'ought' (or ought not) in our bodies, then surfacing states of feeling as emotion can be a pathway to understanding the discrepancies. In beginning to name and honour rather than suppress or deny the presence of a valued or appreciated state, or its violation and the presence of an unvalued, unwanted one—we commence the process of seeding the possible life-giving new. We may feel unwell or energised. We may be excited or uncomfortable. We might sit uncomfortably or start jiggling in our chair in anticipation. The classic states of activated feeling—illuminated through emotion—are an entire database in themselves! A set of indicators awaiting interpretation. Indeed the word 'emotion'— coming from the Latin *movere*, meaning 'move' (agitation, stir, progress, disturbance, change position)—gives a fast-track immediacy to realising when there is a life-depleting (or life-affirming) difference present between an 'is' and an 'ought'.[34]

Here is a 'technical illustration' of what may be encountered in inquiring, researching, evaluating and improving human systems and services (Figure 12).

We are still in the realm of observation—of seeing and experiencing feelings for what they are and what they can tell us about the deeper values that are 'seeking' the new forms to carry them. Next comes the effort to articulate what the feelings *mean*. To ask about the wider contexts that have shaped these feelings. But for now we are seeking *deeper* listening, to really hear the messages of feeling and emotion that life is compromised. Sitting with silences, hearing what hasn't been heard—or possibly even said. Surfacing the 'undiscussibles', the suppressed, the repressed, the hidden, the hurt, the broken, the damaged and difficult. Along with whatever else hasn't had a chance of expression—the delight, the happiness, the triumphs, the confidence, the freely spoken and the open: the signs of life, glimmers of light, energies unbidden, the creative.

The heart has its reasons
that reason doesn't know at all:
a thousand things declare it
BLAISE PASCAL, PENSÉES, 1670

In a way this is the most deeply embodied moment of rational 'mindfulness': in the 'mind' as whole body and (beyond body) as socially embodied, and far from being 'mindless' even if not articulated verbally. It can take longer (especially when oceanic) for feeling to find and become words, but time and space and a receptive 'open field' of listening and a range of aids for expression—such as non-verbal methods and techniques from which to construct images, rich pictures, narratives, metaphors, newly coined and creative use of words—can enable rational feeling to

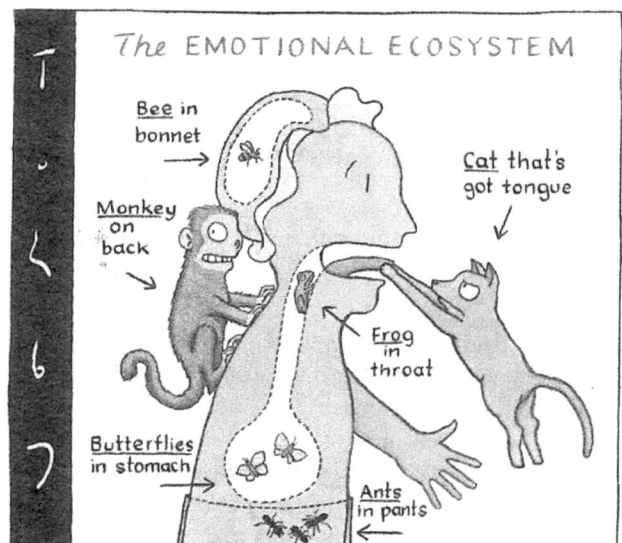

Figure 12. The emotional ecosystem

articulate accurately what has been observed and registered as discrepant in value terms.

In the process a transformation takes place. The old words and received discourse are now able to be seen differently, a little like in a figure/ground gestalt picture where suddenly something can be distinguished 'for what else it is' in contrast to 'what it is now not'. At this edge—at the boundaries, the borderlands of sensing, feeling and intuiting in pursuit of something better and more valued—lies the transformative, chaotic (in the sense of yet to be organised) space in which the new sparks of life ignite fresh inspiration, new words, a new way of speaking, a new way of being and doing. A new *logos*. The story can begin to change…

Questions to traverse this part of the cycle

How do you feel? Is all well? Is all well with you? This other person? With the world?

What emotions are you feeling? Consulting your bodily feelings—how would you describe them?

Can you locate in your body where you have these feelings? What kind of feelings are they? What are they 'telling' you?

What is it that feels bad or wrong? Can you talk about the 'down sides'—the things most troubling you, or troubling you about things?

What is it that feels good or right? Can you talk about the 'up sides'—the things most making you happy, or happy about things?

How do you feel about this situation as it is or has been to date? Is it ok—or not? Can you say whether your 'feeling judgement' is that things are good, bad, right, wrong, positive or negative? A good thing or not a good thing?

Methods and techniques to help traverse this feeling part of the cycle

- Focus Groups
- Values-clarification exercises
- Memory work
- Experiences exchanges
- Check-ins, check-outs
- St Luke's 'Bears' cards (talking about feelings), 'Koala Company' cards (talking about moods and feelings), 'Stones have feelings too' cards, 'Shadows' cards (meanings of pain and suffering) and 'Strengths' cards

- Testimonio
- Co-counselling, re-evaluation counselling
- Active listening to others or your own 'voices', 'scripts', feelings, conscience
- Drawing, artwork, music, drama, narrative, story-telling
- Left column (appearances/what is said/or done) / Right column (feelings about them)
- 'Kitchen table talk', 'deep and meaningfuls'
- Conversational/naturalistic methods
- Appreciative inquiry
- Café of Possibilities (Theatre of the Oppressed), café table groups
- Affinity groups
- Consumer groups
- Deep dialogue groups
- Needs identification exercises
- 4th and 5th generation evaluation (Guba and Lincoln 1989)
- Annual story-telling days

Moving to change: from 'what is now' to 'what could be'

Phase change 1

Liminal/threshold questions

You are well onto the threshold now, in a liminal space: Janus-faced you are looking back and looking forward. It is a time for deciding to act on feelings (or not). A time for testing the strength of the energies sparked by the felt discrepancy. A time for deciding and testing resolve. Do you want to go on with the inquiry?

You might like to check for sure by asking: Do you want things to change? Really want things to change? How much do you want things to change from the current situation?

A lot? Not so much? Only a little?

Now is the time to be really honest about this. It is often much clearer by this point round the cycle when people have communicated fully about 'how things are' and how they feel about them, and the sources of those feelings. Because if there is not enough energy behind the issue or question then it can be dropped—indeed it will be best to let it drop. Let it go. Walk away from it. Say 'OK, there doesn't really seem to be enough going for this issue or question'.

Or you could try asking whether there is something holding you or your group back—a blockage that could be removed—and perhaps find that you've been asking the wrong question, or pursuing the wrong issue, or people are too afraid and then you could retrace your steps to observe and analyse the real issue, or what is needed to overcome the fears.

If it is not a driving, burning question or issue, and people are not ready, willing and able, then going on with it now will be a recipe for the inquiry becoming an increasingly dead weight. One day you will look up from trying to push something very big and heavy uphill (perhaps while ploughing through 300 questionnaires) and wonder why no one is there beside you!

This is the joy and practical benefit of autopoetic inquiry—if you (or others) don't want it, it doesn't happen. If it's not your or their burning question—it doesn't proceed.

No one will be coming up with a great theory that is not grounded in real evidence, desire and experience but remains frustratingly 'only academic'.

No one will be asking others what they want and then leaving them waiting expectantly—only to find they are going to be unable to provide it 'for them', and disappointing the people who had become reliant on you.

No one is going to be deciding actions to take and then finding no one wants to take them, and that they are breeding resentment and resistance.

No one is going to have to talk people into 'owning it' when it hasn't been theirs from the beginning, or it's got too far down the track without them.

So this is definitely the place, right now at the start, to test—and test hard—by asking…

Questions to help traverse this liminal part of the cycle

Do you want things to change? For the better (to be not like they've been)? Or change to be more like (or more of) the things that have been great?

Do you want change *enough* to keep going with the inquiry? All the way into trying new action? How interested, keen, enthusiastic, compelled, determined, annoyed, desperate, courageous or hopeful do you feel about pursuing this? How energised (or not)? How moved are you, by the (discrepant) situation?

How much do you really want to change (on this) at this point?

Would you say it's reached (or you have achieved) a 'critical mass' of interest?

Or does it need more talk? More clarification? Other more interested parties to take it up?

Do you have 'lift off'?!—Or not?

Here you are making a leap of faith.

Crossing the threshold from the known to the unknown is a relief to the inquirer compelled by unanswered questions, but perhaps not quite so to the one holding tight to current answers, or unable to imagine anything else. Because without at least a glimpse of something better to inspire leaving behind the known, this can feel a lot like a self-sealing forcefield—held between moving on and staying put.

> *One does not discover new lands without consenting to lose sight of the shore for a very long time.*
> ANDRE GIDE, LES FAUX-MONNAYEURS, 1925

You may well be frozen on shore with one foot in the boat and the other on *terra firma*. Perhaps caught in self-sealing defensive routines—*'What do you mean there's something wrong?'* *'What do you mean there could be something better?'* *'Better the devil we know'*. It can feel like a face-to-face confrontation, whether it's groups facing off, or just within one's own conflicted self.

Now here's a trick to disengaging an unwanted forcefield.

Physics advises that for particles to break their 'face-to-face' stand-off—that is, to dissolve the power of a 'can't-come-closer-but-can't-move-away' forcefield—they need to move 'alongside'. (See the threefold forcefield Figure 19 at the end of Chapter 4.)

A critical question can sometimes achieve this—such as 'How do we see things?' or 'What were the conditions for seeing it like this, and so what would be conditions for seeing it differently?' Or 'what do we most appreciate about each other's action so far?'

Or a further appreciative question that moves from a self-sealing argument about 'what is' (or is not) the case, to an envisioning question about 'what do we think is or could be better' that identifies new shared ground, a common field of being.

Or observation questions that ask each of the 'sides' of the forcefield how and why they see things as they do, possibly enabling a shift from presumed but misunderstood (or not known) realities.

In dialogue it can be possible to move from energetic clashes and conflicts between potential parties to inquiry, to a snowballing co-inquiry group that is in shoulder-to-shoulder dialogue *together*: continuing to clarify the meanings of 'what is' and the observations underpinning past conclusions, and continuing to consider 'what could be better' instead...

But first, the ability to yield.

Yielding: the 'yin' moment of release

Before being able to move to the new, before being able to take up the possibility of new ideas and picturing the ideal—first the feelings associated with the old must be fully experienced, witnessed, honoured, articulated and understood. They have carried their load faithfully, possibly for a long time, awaiting addressing and healing—the work of making whole, of rejoining what was split, resolving what was bifurcated and conflictful, harmonising old dissonance and addressing discrepancies—making a pathway for the transformative, the releasing of new energies and the enthusiastic taking up of new ideas, at last sloughing off the old pains and hurts signifying old forms that weren't working; like old outgrown skins, or scarred ones now worn with dignity and acceptance.

There is a leaving behind. But not because it has been enforced, required, demanded or even encouraged. Not because someone said 'best to move on' in imperious tones or 'you've got to let things go', but more because the opening of new empty space, the ceding, the unfreezing and melting takes place when either all the necessary stories have been told and understood, and that new understanding releases the energy to create something better, or because the space becomes an attractor, aching to be filled by more joyous possibilities.

As Jung has said, 'All the greatest and most important problems of life are fundamentally insoluble...They can only be outgrown'. Rather than being solved logically, they fade 'when confronted with a new and stronger life urge' (1967).

The more-or-less effortless releasing of 'the old' not-so-life-giving comes about in the nanosecond it takes to glimpse a new way that won't repeat the pain, mistakes or unwanted patterns of the past, or offers the resonant happiness and satisfaction of new life.

Skipping this expression of feeling skips learning its precise evaluative lessons.

The process of fully understanding what was done is complete only when what was being protected by healthy 'stubborn grief' is seen for what it is—as the bearer of life-giving value, the compass to guide and steer by. There is energy in 'cursing the darkness' (and knowing the details of that darkness and how things were damaged, disadvantaged, hurt, failed or lost)—and that energy and knowledge now begins to fuel 'the lighting of candles' in a return from that nadir. Clarity about values means the compass is retrieved and built back in to a new form of the living organism to go on pointing in the direction of what is most right, good, of value, merit, worth or significance—what is most life-giving.

The muddy waters are cleared of confusion.

THE LAUNDRY

A place to deal with the dirty linen, the errors, stains, mistakes, perpetrations, the things needing washing away, refreshing and renewing—in which we can think instead about the contexts and 'situatedness' of all the webs of complex causation of unwanted actions and incidents. Releasing the stubborn spots of guilt and blaming–shaming not only through analysis, explanation, understanding and moving to examine what to do instead, but by firstly achieving clarity and focus about what is valued, right, good and desired. By cleansing intentions and purposes.

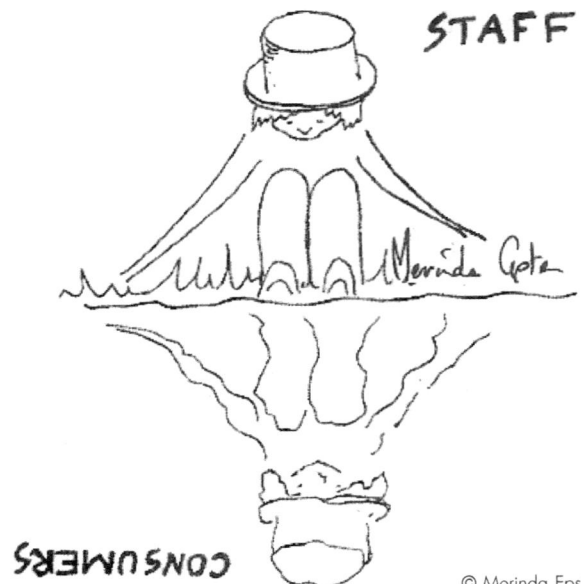

© Merinda Epstein

THE BATHROOM

Like its original forms—the well, the stream and the pool—conveniently located near the garden, the shed, the laundry and the compost heap; here is a space for relaxing, and closer examination and contemplation; a place and time to cleanse the old, a time for 'eureka' moments of insight, for healing rituals, a relaxing bath and the occasional spot of full-throated shower singing at the end of a hard day's action. A time to be alone with one's thoughts and feelings...

A time for some joy, and perhaps a yellow direction-finding rubber ducky for company.

As well, a handy device—historically called the 'necessarium' (Archer 1998: 127)—that any good Taoist knows can turn excreta into marvellous organic compost matter suitable for growth in the garden of philosophy!—philo, meaning 'lover of', sophos, 'wisdom'. A small amount of reading matter may resource concentrated thought processes, while stuck positions are eased.

Pools of water aid reflection and contribute to reverie.

It is preparation for being present for what can emerge in the time to come...

A threshold beckons...

How can human services users and providers get the regular time and space they need to speak frankly, heal the hurts, share their differing understandings, acknowledge loss and grief, and make apologies and restitution before things get set in concrete? To be able to 'come home to themselves and each other'? Letting the events of busy action pass through them, leaving behind what is not wanted, and continuing the process of returning to full life together. And how can everyday research and evaluation processes assist this?

Methods and techniques to help traverse this liminal part of the cycle

- Peer support/listening partnerships
- Mirroring exercises
- Presencing (Senge et al. 2004)
- Self-awareness exercises
- Personal inquiry processes preference-identification (e.g. MBTI®)
- Self-help group sharing
- Silence, retreats
- Drama, story
- St Luke's 'Signposts' cards (transitions, meanings), and 'Sometimes magic' ('happens if I...') transition/learning cards
- Fishbowl technique
- Witnessing, testimonio
- Complaints mechanisms
- Debriefing adverse/critical incidents
- Reconciliation rituals
- Non-verbal methods—music, poetry, dance, movement, metaphor, visual (painting, drawing, photography, collage, other artwork), kinaesthetic (clay etc.)

After the yielding comes the time to be able to receive—all the new input, diverse ideas, insights, a wide range of resources, 'fuel for thought'. All the essential matter from which the new will be built.

REFLECT[35] [36]

4 Envisioning (the ideal) with prospective evaluation questions to clarify what is wanted instead

© Merinda Epstein

KITCHEN TABLE AND CHAIRS

In friendly safe comfortable places of the house, people come together for sustenance, to let down their guard and 'be themselves'; a place where their experiences, resources, ideas and energies can go 'in the pot' and something can be 'cooked up' on the expansive hearth, 'chewed over' and nourish the making better sense of things. Where we can 'put things on the table' that are precious, or uncertain, or have remained hidden, perhaps unspoken, unspeakable, unsayable and undiscussible—or all too obviously needing contemplation. The kitchen table can be a tiny Switzerland in a warring world.

How can human services providers and users come together in the busy press of daily practice to think more deeply in dialogue together about 'human service'? And how can everyday research and evaluation processes facilitate this kind of 'coming to the table'? (Wadsworth 1998)

> *Come to the table, they said*
> *We're sorry but we haven't got time*
> *Come to the table they said*
> *Actually we're anxious about what you'll say*
> *Come to the table they said*
> *And they did*
> *And together they flew*

ADAPTED FROM A POEM BY
GUILLAUME APOLLINAIRE, 1880–1918

The imperceptible moment of breathing out has 'turned', and the process of breathing in the new has begun. After having touched base with what is most deeply valued, a field of possibilities now exists—not yet priorities or goals for action—more like a field of morphic resonance that places a diverse range of ideas and experiences and observations and reflections in 'the realm of the possible', opening to intuitive connections and synchronicity more aligned with deep values, as you seek 'the growing points', the new, the different and the creative…

The *dialogue* between people now assumes central importance. Like the people in the apocryphal story whose spoons were too long for them to ladle their own soup and who began to starve, compared to those who saw they were at a table *together* and who instead began feeding each other with their long-handled spoons—and thrived. As with those who fed each other, now emerge the fruits of listening, clarifying and connecting.

You may actually be surprised to find that moving forward among all the possibilities and unknowns is easier now than you expected. Having done the detailed work of examining, analysing and understanding the details of how things are to date, and determining what is and is not more life-giving, it becomes clearer what is now needed instead.

Chance favours the prepared mind.

LOUIS PASTEUR, 1854

'Realistic idealism' and more accurate selection of visions can flow, and sometimes the most obvious insight immediately springs to mind. But it is worth spending proper time and attention at this stage too, in case there are more hidden possibilities that would be much better. What we are trying to do when we are identifying valued possibilities as individuals, as groups, as organisations or as whole 'social systemicities', is to get in touch with this deeper intuitively felt rationality. In we humans this can often get drowned out by the impatient articulations that move all too quickly to what is 'practical', 'expected' or 'feasible' to our logical consequentialist thinking. Sometimes this propels us too far too quickly round the cycle and right up the garden path—possibly into a house not of our own building!

This is a delicate point. It is terribly easy for our voice of the practical–empirical to come in too soon and judge any imaginary (and unfamiliar) idea as 'unrealistic', 'too idealistic', 'just dreaming', 'romantic', 'magical thinking' or 'way out'. Particularly if it is from another discourse (e.g. a consumer's 'untutored' thinking compared to a professionally educated discourse). For example, when carefully heard, a service user of acute psychiatric facilities who worked in the hospitality industry brought the refreshing analogy of 'hotel standard' to a discussion of what would constitute a more respectful and healing-inducing environment than the drab 'hospital green' room appearance, battered lone telephone and penitentiary-style beds.

'Ideals', idealism and being idealistic have all come to be perversely discredited (perhaps by those for whom current reality is their most accessed part of the cycle) given that an 'ideal' simply means 'highest conception, embodying an idea, dependent on the mind', from the Greek *idea*, 'form, pattern', with a stem *id*, 'see'. So in practice this part of the inquiry cycle embodies the critical moment of 'seeing' a new form or pattern that has not yet been created in 'actuality'—bridging from past 'realities' to future 'realities'—but now with new life-giving shape and form resulting from a successful process of change. In fact for the critical moment of seeing things as they have not been seen before, one literally has to in a way take 'leave from one's senses' to occupy the imaginal! Soon to return, of course, but nevertheless a necessary moment of forging new neural connections apparently out of 'nothing', although in practice from intentional energy operating within something like a well-resourced 'field of morphic resonance' (Maturana and Varela 1973) or implicate order (Bohm 2002).

We appreciate creative originality, authenticity, the unique and the first, more than we do the later copies, imitations and replicas because when something is created at this point in the cycle it is integrating past realities with values and needs and future forms. It takes its time to do this and then it captures something we call the 'wholistic'. We are accustomed to this creating something rare, valuable and costly because it is 'inefficient'—yet when all are participating at this

moment and imbued with the properties, content and process, the 'good design'[37] can be retained all the way into the later actions and practices without resort to loss of integrality, proportionality etc. Benchmarking and talk of 'best practice' are trying to ensure this, but 'being there' is the best warrant for 'getting it'. And understanding the new logic not just in theory and not just in formulaic practice, but in felt theory–practice.

Yet this, in one sense, is exactly what the work of inquiry is doing here—being a 'way out' from the here and now, purposively not real(istic), entering into the realm of the ideal, and 'the impossible dream' (indeed dreams may be used as a very useful research method at this point, as some scientists have described how their discoveries came to them). So this is a time for 'way out' ideas—as in 'a way out' (or a way forward) rather than staying way out as in outer space.

> *If at first the idea is not absurd*
> *there is no hope for it.*
> ALBERT EINSTEIN

> *All great truths begin as blasphemies.*
> BERNARD SHAW

> *A man with a new idea is a crank*
> *until he succeeds.*
> MARK TWAIN

> *Where there is no vision,*
> *the people perish.*
> PROVERBS 29:18

and, we might add to the latter—where there are no people proposing and accompanying the vision (the same people who have grounded it in the observational evidence, created it through their reflections, and generated it through their seeking—it will perish.[38]

Every cell of every living organism judges what it needs for life. As our social organisms complexify, that judgement scales up as we resource each other back to health and wellbeing—but only if this is not blocked, stressed or distorted from so doing.

All relevant parties (or parts of our self) are now 'at the table' in thoughtful dialogue between felt values and the 'facts' and evidence of observation and experience. In the light of how things are and why, the questions turn to, 'What more life-giving patterns of action can we try?' Now is the time to ask, 'What would be ideal?'

Questions to traverse this part of the cycle

Describe your concrete image/s or scenario/s of what you would prefer...

How could things be as you would prefer? Or really wish? What have you seen or thought that could be better than now? What have you not yet thought of that could be better? What do you really want?

Sit with silence on this if need be—listen carefully for what has not yet been said. Remember that this is a moment for imagining what has not yet been. What is yet to come to mind...

What are your dreams or desires? For a better situation? For a better future? What do I want to be, do, achieve...?

You may need to play a little to free up the ideas. Fantasies or daydreams might point in a surprising and fruitful direction when explored further. Let imagination run free. Later questions will shape action to be do-able. But right now you are trying to get as close to your 'heart's desire' as possible.

Try questions like: What would you do if you won the lottery? How would you spend it? On whom? For what purposes? And most importantly, Why? (Or what would you do if you lost your house and all your money—what would be your first priority?)

You may find yourself ricocheting back and forth between desired concrete situations (e.g. 'I will need a new...')—in which case, ask: 'Why? What are the value/s I'm trying to achieve with this?'

Or more abstract values (e.g. 'I want freedom')—in which case ask: 'What would that look like in concrete practice?'

What *else* can you imagine that would be better instead of what there is now (or what you've thought of so far)? What new thing, or practice, situation, method or activity would be better? What would fill me with the most energy, excitement and *joie de vivre*? What *would* be good? Better? Best of all?

What is most life-giving? For me? For you? For us? For all others? What is most important? Most of value? What is *really* most important and why?

Try questions like: What is one thing that would most help make this a great year?

Or look at scenarios: What if we...?

Or ask questions that anchor future desired states in already glimpsed ones:

What have you most appreciated in existing practice?

And why? And why again (until you get to the deepest core value state).

Or ask, what needs to be kept? (Or needs to stop? Or start?)

Or how do you think you could have done things differently? Better? What have you learned? What do you already intend to do, or do differently or try for the first time? Is there anything like what you are seeking that you've already seen?

Stop and check: Are there enough different answers and ideas being suggested here?

Are there enough different relevant people suggesting them? Seek out more if need be.

Do not give up too quickly on this search.

Again it may be worth returning to, just prior to finally settling on a course of action.

Now draw out in further detail if possible what it is about these preferred states that is of value, merit, worth or significance...

Describe as fully as you can:

Why *these* images and visions rather than any others? Why is *this* important? Why is that *not* important? What is of value here?

What is it that you *most* value?

What for you is of the deepest meaning?

Keep pursuing this iterative form of questioning until it 'hits bottom' and becomes tautological.

Another way to access values (or valued states) is to ask:

Can you turn your values into an image, a picture or metaphor? What happens to it/them under stress? For example, when you are having difficulty keeping hold of them, and they feel like they are getting more and more d*istant from what you are having to do? And what would bring them back to life?*

A further surprising way to access your values is to look at the last time you were defensive. Defensiveness can stem from someone having made assumptions about a person's values that are not what the person experiences their own values to be (Wadsworth and O'Brien 2002). The effort to listen to a defensive explanation (one's own or another's) and then clarify the discrepancies between valued states and experienced realities can facilitate clarity about what is really valued. We often call explanations 'rationalisations' (i.e. specious) but they are only this where the questioning process is prematurely ended. If they are instead offered (and sought out), they take the form of observation—in effect a review of data, the theory or logic derived from that evidence, and the consequentialist reasoning ('I did... because I thought that... on the basis of...'). In this form they lead you back to being able to ask: 'Was the action the best one aligned with the desired values?' Sometimes it is enough to just ask 'What would you have preferred to have done?' to capture the image or vision of more valued practice. Or 'What would you now do differently?' And then ask 'Why?' to identify the changed logic for a new story...

Can you sum up in a few words now what you might call your values, hopes and visions for the future?

Methods and techniques to help traverse this hopes and dreams part of the cycle

· The 'dream' part of the appreciative inquiry cycle
· Individual reflective practice
· Meditation
· Values-clarification, positive psychology and strengths-based work
· e.g. St Luke's 'Reflexions' cards (feelings, values, identity); and 'Strengths' cards, 'Scrapbook of strengths', and ABCD (asset-based community development)

· Narratives of imaging (art, visual, poetic etc.) and other values-visioning methods
· Dreaming-the-future (theatre, drama)
· Brainstorming
· Deep dialogue
· One to ones (not one on ones—one to and with ones!)
· Individual and service plans
· Roundtables, stakeholder exchanges
· Collective reflective practice
· Vision workshops
· Socio-morphogenesis technique
· 4th and 5th generation evaluation
· Collective peer support (staff and consumers)

This is a time when the wavy lines and fragments in the rich chaos are beginning to come together into new patterns, harmonious resonances and forms. Sitting in circles of understanding, it is a time for selectivity and encapsulating the changes in a new 'naming', a new discursive, semantic and symbolic identity.

5 Change (the theory/story) questions

Abductive phase

GARDEN, THE CAVE AND THE WELL

Places of deep contemplation and revival, in fertile resonant living systems in which to seed new possibilities. Old elements have been composted, mulched and dug in; and the ashes of the burnt-out now make fertiliser for the new. Verdant surrounds provide oxygen, beauty and food for the phoenix soul. Jung's temenos was a sanctuary in which to meet one's soul. And the garden pathways of a labyrinth signify a 'whole' which is in full view, offering an intuitive and creative 'bigger picture' experience grounded in the small-scale twists and turns of life on the archetypal journey to 'the centre', always different while contained within the stability of the 'going in' and 'coming out' journey pathway.[40] *Or the going into a cave or forest—a safe space in the wild, 'away', in aid of the imaginal. Or a well, or water pool for reflection and immersion ('When in deep water, become a diver!'), or running spring water to learn about change. It is interesting that in the original Persian the word for a park or garden was paradeisos— the basis for the later Greek from which the English word 'paradise' is derived, and which came to mean 'heaven' or an ideal state of harmony, free from dissension, until the alienation from the garden of Eden (Hebrew for 'delight'). Plato's garden (akademos) was a place for philosophical thought away from the immediacy of decision making and action. In Australia the outdoor toilet (interestingly named the 'outhouse') has traditionally been a place of contemplative thought aided by a view of garden and the stars.*

How do human services providers and users become 'gardeners' of a living 'home for the life of the mind' (as Raimond Gaita has put it, 'Philosophers Zone', Australian Broadcasting Corporation, Radio National 2008), in which to think collaboratively the as-yet-unthought-of and create the new ways forward? Places for coming to see things differently, and find the breakthrough inspirations…

In the outer reaches and the borderlands of the house… How can everyday research and evaluation processes facilitate this?

BEDROOM

A place to rest, free associate, review the day's activities, ponder on unresolved puzzles, sleep, and dream visionary dreams, awaking with new answers. A place for the deepest contemplative moments, to reach into the unconscious, the subconscious, the non-conscious, the transpersonal—the realm of the imagination, of 'soul giving rise to spirit', messages, archetypes, symbols and images. Where the newly detected important features appear foregrounded, where the less important drops away. Where clarity about the meaning of things and their consequences sharpens and resolves.

How can human services providers and users make the times and places in which they can come together, to bring forth in the shared space new insights and valuable ideas that can better explain the previous situation and offer the new leads to a better future for all parties? How to grasp the whole—seeing the *integrality* of seemingly hitherto separate but in practice linked elements—and incarnate a vital new way of seeing, a new theory and a new story?

The trick at this point in the cycle is to extend *from* the existing, via touching base with what is most deeply valued, to bridge to the valued ideal. This is a kind of embroidering, weaving and knitting *from* the current pattern, situation, environment or field-systemicity to becoming something new. Not to replicate 'more of the same', but to make a change which alters, diverges from, creates, generates and incorporates a new pattern. A new systemicity.

There is a transformative moment here which scientists like to call 'discovery' as if it was there waiting already formed somehow in the implicate order, but in practice it is more like the creation or construction of a new *idea*—from the Greek meaning 'form, pattern', from id, 'sees'. That is, it is *we* who 'see' the pattern and in this sense create or generate it within our own neural networks, driven by the energy of purposeful intention.[41] Nevertheless it feels like a eureka moment of 'finding' something as the 'aha moment' of conception of a deeper truth joins up a pattern that calibrates with a more valued pattern already charted and embodied by our intentionality. Some have called this kind of co-generative gestation and birth 'alchemical' or 'shamanistic', as if it were the conjuring of a mage or an act of wizardry.[42] Yet there isn't anything particularly supernatural about this abductive 'magic'—except that it may seem rather by chance, synchronistic, synergistic, even 'spooky', or more-or-less unplanned 'unbidden knowledge' if one doesn't take into account the broader frame in which it is taking place—the complex multi-causal field of rich and diversely resourced relationality in which 'the possible' is autopoetically made explicable. This *systemic* explanation may not, however, be so easily accessed by an empirical observer 'on the other side of the cycle', preoccupied for the moment with the up-close-and-tangible.

The critical inquiry capability at work in this new creation is an ability to intuit connections in a 'bigger picture' within which the change in the pattern or a different structure makes new sense. That is, *within a larger whole*, a new framework or conceptualisation *connects* both with the old and the valued in a new way, doing justice both to how 'the old' was previously generated and how the new could now emerge.

To achieve this, try different ways of seeing and thinking about the situation, analysing and synthesising, theorising, imagining and concluding. You are after a breakthrough. A new insight. Since the old pattern or form is not working, you are looking for a new pattern or form that will more resonantly make sense of things and align with your deepest values. You have cycled round to the same conceptual place in the cycle where you or others were before—but want to find a new substantive shape you will then plan to trial in practice in place of the old.

You are trying to draw a different or bigger picture that will give new meaning to the existing situation. It is a place of morphing…of half one thing, half another, of the centaur. Where one moment it is a particle and the next it is a wavy line. Where an empirical 'packet' becomes part of a kind of 'ley line' or pattern with a different meaning. Where things can be both things at once, where boundaries overlap or subsume each other. But where in the 'bothness' there can also be the possibility of a new 'anotherness'. A form emerges.

When we stand back far enough to see how everything relevant has contributed, yet we are still informed about the fates of individuals in each of those transactions, what we do next is more likely to be morphogenically consistent with such complex causation. We cease seeing individual actions as 'to blame', and nor do we feel powerless about a reified 'whole system'. Instead we 'get it' that what is to be done is to provide the new resourcing or counteracting inputs that our grounded abductive theory indicates we can make, and then observe again, repeating the cycles of inquiry and complex patterning of feedback until the shape and form is 'bringing life'.

There is an irony here, too, as the only way we can ever understand anything better is by comparing the things we don't yet understand with other things we do—things that are familiar to us, which help us 'scaffold' or 'bridge' or overlay/overlap the (unwanted) known with the (wanted) unknown (or the wanted known with the unwanted unknown). We say 'it is like…' and use metaphors or analogies to try and convey meanings that weren't there or as clear before. We are 'the brain that is changing itself'™ (Doidge 2007) just as are our 'corporate minds' of co-inquiring groups, communities and organisations too.

Somewhere deep in our neural networks our embodied minds and our brains are literally trying to 'build themselves'—self-generate new 'knits, networks' and connections. 'Jumping the wires' and forging new struts. We are indeed inevitably needing to 'jump to conclusions' to answer our questions!—but now from a strong base of well-grounded, well-evidenced, well-shared and well-discussed observations and reflections.

This is in part the transpersonal and in part the detective part of the story. All the apparent facts are in. But the current story doesn't explain well enough why things can't be better. Your theory about 'why things are as they are' determines what you will do about them. A new theory generates a different form or identity with a different logic leading to a different course of action.

The activities of life can be changed in no other way than [by] changing the current ideas upon which [they are] conducted.
JANE ADDAMS, 1925

Questions to traverse this transformative part of the cycle

Now you are turning over in your mind's eye all that has been observed, said and experienced.

What does it all mean? What does it *really* mean (in your context?) What *else* could it mean, given that there are still unanswered questions stemming from the observed discrepancies? How else can you think about this? What new connections can you see between everything that's been said and observed so far? Can you see commonalties between things? Possible links? New ways of relating things?

Step back from the proximal and examine the distal

What is a new way of seeing things so they might make better sense? What different theory of change would better help explain why and how you could achieve your new purpose, or reach your new goal? Or help make your desired situation necessary and possible? What is your deeper thinking about this?

You may need to return to ask: 'What else do you think is going on in the current situation? What is really going on here—relevant to your interests? What else is going on here? Why else do you think things are as they are? What do you think it all could mean other than the apparent meanings at present? What is the still remaining unsolved puzzle?

Or try finishing this kind of sentence: 'It's not so much that it's because of…(the current explanation for why things are as they are), it's more like it is (or they are— or are not)…' (the possible new explanation—with implications for what to do differently, creating new potential or possible realities).

Who or what are you now wanting to be (and do) in the future?

Explain why: 'Because…' (our new way of naming it and reason for this)

If you've imagined (imaged) a 'desirable new action or practice', try asking: Why would you like it to be like this?

Can you think of metaphors to help describe what it's like—and what you are reaching for?

How could I and my story change? How could we and our story change? Has it already begun to change?

You have reached for the new form, 'shape-shifting' has altered the existing 'program logic' for your next actions-in-the-world.

Something more satisfying—perhaps more valuable— even truly life-giving has emerged…

It is the 'oh now I see' moment!

It is a moment that will sustain you into new action…

Methods and techniques to help traverse this transformative part of the cycle

- Metaphors chosen or developed by the inquiry group
- Analogues
- Allegories
- Symbolism
- 'It is like…' comparisons
- Lateral thinking
- 'What if…?' finish-the-sentence exercises
- Concept generation, concept mapping
- Program theory
- Language generation, juxtaposition
- Dictionaries, word-smithing
- Annual reflective retreats
- Residential retreats
- Labyrinth walking
- Sleep, silence
- Double loop/triple loop thinking (Argyris 1993)
- New language, new juxtapositions, new forms, shapes, designs…
- Futurology
- Scenarios
- Search conferences (Emery and Purser 1996)
- Insight generation, transpersonal and gestalt methods
- Foresight (Ramos 2002)

Michael Patton the evaluator reported he had emptied the contents of his kitchen utensil drawer into a bag and taken them to a community organisation and asked questions like—'can you choose a utensil which represents to you the nature of your service as it is and talk about it—or one you would most want it to be like and tell the story of this?' Michael also asked members of human services organisations to play differing Myers-Briggs capabilities in response to an issue to see how things might alternatively be taken forward.

PERSONAL COMMUNICATION,
ST PAUL, MINNESOTA, 1995

6 Alternatives-seeking questions

The 'aha' moment has taken place and there is something new 'on the table'. It has come from the 'local' or relevant field situation and seems most relevant and appropriate. You are keen to talk about your plans for the 'new day', for putting it into live real-world practice. But before forging on, it might help not to stay with the first idea you thought of. Take it as your starting point—it has been carefully generated from the actualities of the specific field. But see if you can hear from others or take an even wider lens on similar situations further afield—that may provide a range of comparative or related ideas to usefully extend or nuance what has come out of your own field.

So, while the idea you first thought of may still end up being the best (so don't discount it), take the time now to check what other alternatives there may be, or that may not have even been thought of yet.

NEIGHBOUR'S BACKYARDS

Others further afield are doing similar things—or perhaps not. What are their gardens and homes and streets like? Are they doing things differently? Do they have good ideas that might help your situation? They are growing all kinds of different things. You could ask them about all the things you've seen. Would that be good in your backyard...

Questions to help traverse this part of the cycle

Just before going on to think about enacting it, pause and ask...

Who has another idea? What else could we be? Or do? What else could we try instead? What has been the experience of others wider afield? What other ideas can we generate? Do we have any other options?

Name as many ways as possible—brainstorm firstly without comment

Now think of some more...

What else? How else might these changes come about?

Let all the different possibilities 'come onto the table'. Play a bit. Don't be afraid to leave things on the table till another time, as it may be literally useful to 'sleep on it' again.

These are further moments of deep creativity. You are trying to imagine what else has not yet been imagined that might still be useful. Indeed it may take many ideas before there is the very best resonance. You may need to revisit your previous expressions of what was of value...Or cycle forward to 'try them out' in a mental experiment (try the next questions at number 7). Maybe something else is altogether better than you first would have thought—with much greater resonance...

A better solution, beyond even an acceptable 'quick fix', something that will truly 'take' and last a very long time...

Now ask: Do the new ideas improve on what we've come up with so far?

Talk through why each of these alternatives might be better or adds something worthwhile. Draw out the 'Why?' (theory) that lies behind suggesting each of them, and decide on any new directions or formulations in the light of these deliberations.

Think about what further challenges might lie ahead that could be prepared for.

Is there a way of integrating your inquiry with other research and evaluation? Can an even larger number of ideas, worldviews, methods or perspectives be understood by (or incorporated, 'swept into') your new theory without losing what you are valuing most about it?

Methods and techniques to help traverse this alternatives-considering part of the cycle

· Brainstorming
· Search conferences
· Visioning exercises
· Open Space Technology (Owen 2008)
· St Luke's 'Name the Frame' (principles and values) and 'Views from the Verandah' cards
· Priorities and goals-setting exercises
· Program theories
· Individual service plans
· Service/program planning
· Peer support for consumers
· Professional supervision for staff
· Reference group meetings

Morning has dawned—and you are feeling spruce after the long night of the inquiring contemplative soul. Clear and full of energy, you sally forth with the best new way to go forward. It is a power-full moment!

It is a time when harmonious circles have become centred and that centre 'takes off' skywards—soaring to pyramidal heights of optimistic confidence in the new insight. The certainty of knowing powers strong energy to want to get on with planning to try the new action in practice.

You are approaching a second critical phase change—a time of testing, a threshold that will determine whether the new way forward will founder and prove unviable or 'take' and start to become the new 'way we do things round here'...

PLAN[43]

7 Consequences-considering questions (logical inference)

While optimism has built from what has been learned from inquiring, yet enacting the new always involves a degree of risk. So before trying things out in actual practice, it can be worth putting the ideas through a 'thought experiment'—and thinking through all the implications in as sceptical a way as possible to strengthen certainty that all possibilities have indeed been assessed and addressed. In preparation to cross the threshold to viability, the idea/s can be tested by playing 'devil's advocate' to think whether and how it might be operational in the real world conditions from which they have come and are now to be tried out further.

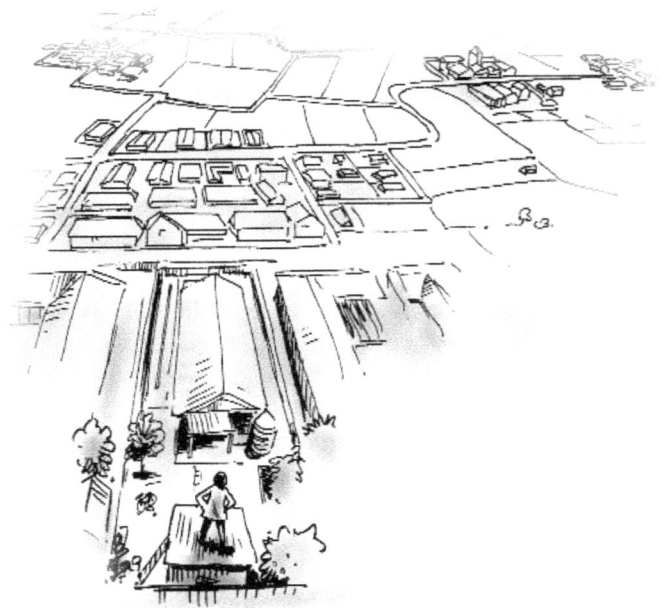

So try and take a bit of an aerial view and scan the horizon to see how the idea, theory or proposal (or each of them if there are several options on the table) might work. Think through all the consequences, assessing what will work in the current environment, challenging yourself, and imagining the soon to be 'in practice' experiment, picturing its acceptability and feasibility for implementation. Think through the practical planning steps—who will need to give permissions, what 'permits' will the works require, have all sensitivities been considered, what other logics or sets of rules exist that need to be considered?

Of course it will do best if it has to 'work' in the real conditions of life rather than at too great a distance, or under too special conditions, too sheltered and artificial. So don't spend too long at a distance from the realities of practice. (Chemicals or metals may not be able to tell the difference between real life and a laboratory but humans usually can :-). But if you have already started small and been round the cycle a number of times before 'scaling up' at this point, then the uncertainty will be all the more reduced by people having participated in this 'research-and-development' trialling, and already anticipated and advised about the context.

So you may not need to spend too much time on this, but, for what it's worth, try and think things through further to see if you can see any snags ahead, or can move to better conditions and opportunities for things 'taking'. This is a time for some critical realism, some clarity around definitions and 'word-smithing' them—holding carefully the hard-won, real lifeworld-grounded knowledge in which the ideal new idea has germinated and is beginning to take root in people's imaginations—and looking forward to see what the seedling might encounter in terms of challenges (and assistance).

If all stakeholding and particularly the stakeowning parties to the inquiry have stayed 'at the table' together this far then their thinking will already have changed and this stage will pass more seamlessly into trying out the agreed action with little compromise or need for pragmatic utilitarianism. If there are new parties joining at this point, the story may need to be re-told (and possibly revisited and the evidence shared for the rationale).

LIBRARY OR STUDY

The stored collected resources of what others have learned from their situations and real-life experiments can be explored as learnings and teachings to inform, stimulate and question new activities and practice. Contextual information, 'corporate memories' of past actions and events, other people's concepts, definitions, ideas and forms of 'identity' may be helpful in this study of other 'bodies of knowledge', other 'embodied knowing'—for what they can offer your situation. Some of this will have already been done in considering the alternatives prior to thinking through all the consequences in practice. It's nearly time for the gatekeepers to fling the doors open and let the new begin!

THE FRONT GATE
...AND THE BACK VERANDAH

Verandahs, doorsteps and window ledges are all liminal and public thresholds, borderlands, frontiers and transformational spaces for the movement of proposals from practice-based theory to further-theorised practice. As a special place of gate-keeping and forcefields—where we can welcome back those returning from hunting forays 'outside' or we can shoot messengers. Back verandahs may be handy places to do delicate business, gently negotiate encouragement of access and take up through the back door, and talk through in advance the implementation of possible scenarios and their rationales.

How do human services providers and users review, widen their scope, situate and compare their ideas with other models or experiences from elsewhere without losing what has been carefully grounded in the local field? And how can they talk through how things can be introduced? How can everyday research and evaluation processes facilitate these?

As you think through the consequences of the course of action (or courses if there are several options or different pathways) try and resist only judging the new ideas in terms of the old ones—instead consider the deeper purposes that have led to their revision or 'invention'. How will they go? Here you are thinking through systematically what you might be 'up against' as well as what you might find will help.

Here logical consequentialist reason steps forward—the capability to sceptically question, including questioning about unpalatable possibilities without flinching. In playing devil's advocate to try and argue against the proposition/s in order to test it or them, you are bringing to the surface any unexamined assumptions. To not (too soon) give unqualified approval, but instead to carefully and kindly use 'unappreciative inquiry' to blow cold winds and pour a little cold water on the seedling to see what strength it has. You may not know the full value of your own conclusions until you get these chances to challenge yourself. It may be that in the flash of initial inspired intuition you have entirely 'got it' for which is the best way to go and why—but it never hurts to check you haven't missed anything in the ideas that are now building such a head of steam. We call it 'casting a cool eye' over the plan, or trying to spot a logical error in our evaluative reasoning. It is being our own best sceptic.

We sometimes call this the perspective of a 'critical friend'—someone who we know shares our deepest values about improving the situation or achieving the conditions for life. Think of someone you would choose to 'tell you the truth' about a choice you've made. You need to be able to trust that they want the best for you, *and* that they know your values and purposes and that they are prepared to give you 'frank and fearless' *realpolitik* feedback about what they think or see in the wider scheme of things that you may have overlooked or not realised, no matter how distasteful that 'intelligence' is.

If you can, consider also asking those who have an openly hostile view or who don't know you or your group at all to comment. You will need to know in what ways their deeper values diverge from yours to be able to fully judge what they say, but they too can often give good intelligence in advance of unanticipated sources of opposition (and clues as to the deeper differences that may need to be re-explored or understood). Best to know now the basis on which you are proceeding—and are able to argue—so your thinking can compete and survive to cross this threshold to viability. Ideally these people should have been 'at the table' as early in the process as possible. So if proposals need to go into too heavy combat now, consider stopping and revisiting early phases, especially the matter of gathering an inquiry group and wider network to share in the information gathering, reflection and concluding for themselves. Remember that whatever is imposed at this point is either going to have a hard time without a critical mass in support, or it will require force to implement (and thus potentially be the end of inquiry and risk contradicting valued intentions to improve life for the whole). On the other hand if the fabric of relationships is strong enough, the reluctant may be persuaded to try (or not actively to oppose) introduction of something new on a test basis, and then also be able to contribute their feedback as soon as they want to give it, and have that feedback count in the continued dialogue.

Questions to traverse this prospective evaluation part of the cycle

Firstly, ask: Is our preferred plan in touch with people's concrete realities? Or has it become overly remote and out of touch? Or was it not properly formed in the first place?

Now look at all the other options or ideas to see if they would work in your particular setting, environment and conditions. Ask: Would this idea work better? Be more useful? Contribute in any way to our thinking? Are any other ideas or conclusions from other people's practices, research or evaluation of relevance and use to you?

Now ask regarding your favoured pathway and each of the different possible paths of action:
What will be the effects of going down this track? What might we encounter...? What might happen? What would happen if we did X? Y? Z...? What if you found ourselves encountering...(x? y? z? ...?) (If this —then what? If this—then what?...etc...)
Think what might be the impacts in each different situation or scenario? What might be *other* effects? What might be the outcomes? What else might happen?
What is the likelihood of each option being successful? What might it encounter? Might anyone object? Who might support it? Who needs to know and understand more? Who has the power to help make it happen?—or not?
Try asking: How would I, you or we *feel* about taking each of these different courses of action (or the preferred one) ourselves? What might be the responses by all the various stakeholders to each one?
What are all the strengths? Weaknesses? Opportunities? Threats? Barriers? Obstacles? Enablers? Supporters? —associated with or facing the preferred option (or options)?
You may find it useful to retrace your steps and ask: Why did the idea seem to be so good in the first place? After taking action you might ask 'why did we do it?' (*retroductive*—looking back at the governing logic), but here, *before* action, when you are clarifying your logic, you are being *retroevaluative*—looking back at the values you were holding in relation to the existing experience and evidence ('what was meant to be of value?') and then *prospectively* evaluative—'What *will* be of most value?'
Don't discard the idea just because the going may look (or be!) tough. This part of the cycle isn't associated with the idea of 'a mission' for nothing! For example all the research literature may be counter your findings—but your situation may be different. This is what you now need to work out.
There'll be plenty of realists who'll be quick to say, 'That can't be done here—it's never been done before—the powers that be don't do it/don't want to do it/say it can't be done—it's just not practical—the research evidence isn't there to support it', and so on. You may just need to think through carefully what you want to do and why; 'rehearsing' how to respond can be a useful technique here.

Don't forget that life-affirming change is necessary for living systems to go on living!

Either way it is helpful to think through how hard it will be, or if there is a 'water' way instead of a 'rock' way (that does not compromise the idea to be trialled). *This may be a time for really good 'systems intelligence' and negotiation if it hasn't happened sufficiently in wider spheres till now, so that in the business of talking the ideas through to implementation it becomes clearer what others are thinking, so you can rework the messages to maximise their meaning.* This is not about spin. This is about carefully understanding the other to be able to present, communicate and calibrate the truths resulting from the inductive-abductive inquiry *so they can be understood* by the next relevant audience. It may involve taking the people back around the narrative of the cycle to see what you have done, learned, generated and concluded (especially if they are new parties to the inquiry) and then if need be, taking a step back to you hearing what *they* have done, learned, seen, generated and concluded in their situations. Hence the greater the need for additional sources of 'intelligence' about what is taking place beyond your situation or field, and alternative communication channels opened up to take messages across the threshold from 'good idea' to 'idea in practice'.

Which course of action do you now think would be best and possible—and why? Check it is still what the *critical* primary intended beneficiary stakeholder needs, wants and prefers. This is no time for slippage, or you will have to repeat the whole cycle of inquiry again, but this time with the wrong practices in place to have to re-make! It is not necessarily better to do whatever is do-able (something, anything) rather than what *should* be done. Remember how hard it is to change something that wasn't right, but which you 'compromised' on to overcome dissonance and keep the peace. There is a profound and critical difference between *dialogue* and revisions (that are either an actual improvement or at least nothing fundamental lost) and *compromise* where the outcome ceases being resonant with fundamental values and purposes. If there has been slippage, there may be a need to retrace your steps for further participation and dialogue rather than impose trialling a solution that could be problematic later.

Recall how very much more difficult it is to respond to a negative evaluation of something once it's fully in place, than it is to slowly, emergently and iteratively 'get it right' now in the first place. Lest we forget!

And once we've reached our general conclusions, and look to apply them to a new situation which may inevitably differ from the situation in which it was created, always remember that 'All generalisations are dangerous, even this one' (attributed to Alexandre Dumas fils).

Fortunately with a living systems cyclic approach to inquiry we will also build in reviewing and revising!

We should always remember that the future is not somewhere we are going, it is something we are creating
PROFESSOR IAN LOWE, 2009

Methods and techniques to help traverse this consequences-considering part of the cycle

· Critiques, reviews, assumption testing
· Forcefield analysis
· SWOT analysis (Strengths, Weaknesses, Opportunities, Threats)
· Cost-benefit analyses
· Modelling, simulations, blueprint checking
· Forecasting, regression analysis
· Scenarios, hypotheticals, satire
· Science fiction/science 'faction'
· The existing research literature
· Library collections, journals, books
· The internet (e.g. Wikipedia)
· The 'grey literature'
· Other programs' theories/logic
· Other organisations' procedures, benchmarking, reports, annual reports
· Corporate memory work
· Individual and service/program planning

8 Action design questions

BLUEPRINT, DRAWING BOARD AND FOUNDATIONS

This particular inquiry journey is coming to an 'end' as we at last 'settle' into designing the details of the 'building' that has been firstly envisioned and now envisaged in more detail, then methodically planned for its operationalisation…

The initial meaning of 'plan'—from the Italian *pianta*, meaning 'an intention or proposed proceeding; a design or scheme'—is now about to be *realised* in more concrete form as 'a floor plan of a building', 'a drawing, diagram or map'; and 'a formulated and detailed method by which a thing is to be done'.

The new idea or theory is beginning to come all the way back down to the ground in concrete details—so now is the time to see what will be needed in practice to get from the 'here' to the now agreed 'there'. Energies and certainty have peaked and definitional boundaries now need to be built that will align the identified ideal blueprint forms with their construction in material reality so they can be the intended carriers, channels and spaces for the organism's valued purposes and intentions.

You do not begin a house by first building the roof but by laying well-grounded foundations.

However the greater any external threat (e.g. rejection or competition by parties who have not been part of the inquiry collaboration to date), the more likely the boundaries will need to be clearer, thicker and stronger to withstand the storms—but remember this will risk immovability and the containing the still needed flows of energy. So it may be better to return to dialogue and a new exchange of views, or trace your steps forwards round the cycle to examine the 'lay of the land' as it is now at the point of implementation. It is a time for practical foresight.

The more co-operative, trustworthy and secure the environment, the more likely the boundaries can be lighter and more permeable—even though they must be clear in purpose—and thus able to retain the more tentative voice of experiment, and the flexibility to adapt and change, even at this 'late' stage.

How do human services design the secure well-grounded foundations, for the safe, orderly, organ-ised but permeable and flexible 'containers' needed to assist them?

How to build in the need for refinement and revision, and even eventual exchange of this dwelling for an-other (especially if it becomes too rigidly set in its ways)? How does this change take place so new prac-tice honours, modifies, replaces or supersedes the old?

And with an eye on current realities—how does 'the preferred new' avoid being swamped, subsumed and overlaid by the old superseded pattern and logic? How to minimise reaction and rejection and slippage back to unwanted prior patterns? How to avoid the slippage of principles when they began by being well-grounded in observation, experience, values, purposes, reflection, findings and conclusions:

You don't like these principles?
Here, I have others.
ATTRIBUTED TO A PRIVATE CONSULTANT
WORKING FOR GOVERNMENT

How to avoid too-early pragmatism and giving up on the new ideal forms that have resulted from such careful work? How to avoid defaulting to a false utilitar-ian efficiency such as 'one size fits all' when the inquiry processes had shown how something much more accurate, satisfactory and acceptable to all partic-ipants could be achieved? How to reorient and dissolve forcefields of existing power and reward structures so that the new arrangements that offer greater life can take their place? How to find your way through para-doxical peak certainty and confidence in the new form at the same time as that new form, being new, is essen-tially uncertain to a greater or lesser extent regarding its future outcomes? All the modelling and scenarios in the world only manage that risk, not eliminate it.

How can everyday research and evaluation processes aid in strengthening this part of the cycle?

How can inquiry offer a way to start small and continue learning and evolving, rather than risk a large and costly set-up and roll-out with no real margin for error?

Questions to help traverse this implementation design part of the action cycle

What would it take for things to actually happen as desired? What would need to happen? What would need to change?

What are the ways that might achieve this? What could be done? What would it look like? How would it feel? What are we doing and how are we going to do it?—both in principle and in practice?

To see if there are new clues as to what is needed now, try asking: Why hasn't it happened so far?

Think about the nature of the new interrelationships you are now wanting to see.

What are the boundaries and connections needed to achieve what you are trying to achieve? Who can help institute the new action, to trial it in real-life? Who has the ability, strong energy, skills and commitment?

Do the goals follow from the purposes? Do the purposes have a basis in people's realities?

Check each link within the whole sequence of logic:

Is there a flaw anywhere in the reasoning? Do the actions follow from the goals? Is it specified (or generalised) enough? Are the desired changes achievable? Identifiable? Measurable? Realistic? Do they retain their deep purposes? Ideals? Principles? Values? Are they time-bound enough? Open-ended enough?

Methods and techniques to help traverse planning action to remain in line with the inquiry conclusions (that were aligned with deepest values and intentions)

- The 'design' part of the appreciative inquiry cycle
- Whiteboards, drawing boards
- Philosophies, principles, policies
- Mission statements
- Goals- and objectives-setting exercises
- Service agreements
- St Luke's 'Optimism Booster' narrative cards (goals, possibilities, strategies)
- Other narratives that hold the story e.g. high quality Executive summaries

- Maps, 'road maps', blueprints, plans, agenda
- River and tree diagrams
- Program logic, logic models
- GANTT charts and Critical pathways
- Policies-to-practice matrices, logframes (logic frameworks)
- Evaluation targets and indicators
- Contingency plans
- Nominal groups, planning meetings, summits
- Individual and service/program plans
- Diplomacy, negotiation

Moving from 'what could be': to enculturating the (new) 'way we do things round here'

Phase change 2

Liminal/threshold questions

You are well and truly stepping over a second threshold now, occupying liminal space: you have a plan for something better than what was, and you are looking forward to its implementation with anticipation. It is a time for acting on conclusions (or not). A time for testing things out in new practice. A time for testing everyone's resolve to do so.

You might like to check for sure by asking—Do you really want to try out what you've decided? *Really* give it a go? *How much* do you want to put it into practice? A lot? Not so much? Only a little?

Now is the time to feel confident about this. It should be easier by this point in the cycle when people have collaborated fully on analysing 'how things are' and how they feel about the current consequences, and have accompanied the process into deciding on the best possible actions from among the alternatives. If there has not been enough observation, participation and reflection among all relevant stakeholders long before this point, then all the planning and diplomacy to entice the plans into action across this phase change now may well be half-hearted or futile.

If there is not already enough energy, enough of a 'head of steam' behind the proposed new action, then it will not make it. It may already be 'dead in the water' and you will not be able to take it further. You may need to either retrace your steps to gather together around something more agreed, or start again with a new process or new participants.

Any who are involved at this point without having traversed the previous stages themselves may consider it all just so much 'academic theory' or 'harebrained idealistic pie-in-the-sky' and call for 'more proof' rather than risk supporting its trialling. Or they may want to try it out in a safe laboratory somewhere at a distance—rather tricky when it's human systems we are talking about! Or if—because of their considerable interests in and familiarity with the existing situations that mean they may not be able to see something better in the new, and they have not been part of a dialogue to understand the compelling need for it—the autoimmune defences may spring into action.

On the other hand, if confident change champions take it up at this point, and it is not accompanied by enough people who did go through the long recursive period of building through smaller cycles and can translate and explain, then it might have to be 'sold' to people who have not participated in its making. This too may risk reaction, including the sceptical, suspicious and the subversive. It *is* possible to use power over people to entice or coerce take up—but at that point the science stops and the first casualty of implementation may be people's willingness to speak up and give the necessary feedback (and the role of court jester is a bruising one). And all the more so if things cannot be changed by feedback because it is too late, and perhaps a particularly concrete form of building is already at 'lock up' stage.

If those to enact it are not part of the inquiry conversation that created it, it may not easily happen. Or, if it does, it may become distorted, prove too difficult or decay early, only to be continued by the expenditure of awfully hard effort in the face of subtle (or not so subtle) opposition or disinterest. It may even become 'the way we do things round here', but there may be a certain lack of life surrounding it; more a matter of grim duty and 'soldiering on'. And at the first opportunity to change it, there may be shouts of relief and joy…

Thus continues the practical benefit of autopoetic inquiry! No one is going to have to talk people into 'owning it' because it hasn't been theirs from the beginning. No one is having to police implementation for fear of 'non-compliance'. No one is constantly having to stand over people checking their work. No one is standing around 'awaiting orders' because they don't know what is to be done and why. And no one is

going to find, way down the track, that there is either deeply rooted resentment and resistance or widespread apathy and goal displacement.

Questions to help traverse this liminal part of the cycle

So this is definitely the place, right now at the start, to check there is unity around moving into action by asking…

Have all the options given way to clarity about what is judged the best way forward?

Are we sure we have the evidence and the logical reasoning for our choice/s?

Can we tell the new story strongly enough? Clearly enough? Is it compelling and inspiring?

Do you feel up to this task? Confident, resolute, enthusiastic? Have you the courage? The heart? ('Courage' from the Latin cour, 'heart', ag, 'strength', meaning strong energy derived from the heart.)

Are you committed enough to taking this change forward so it gets tried out in new action?

How much do you really want change?

Have the barking dogs at the gate been satisfied?! Are the gatekeepers with you?! Or at least prepared to step aside and hold the gate open, rather than committed to blocking your way.

Can you say enough about what you expect to see as a result, to know when it is being achieved or not?

Sometimes it happens that a daring step
into the unknown gives us
great gifts for the future.
JØRN UTZON, ARCHITECT, 2002

Now that you are heading back to earth from the pyramidal heights of visionary planning, you are starting to roll up your sleeves to get to work 'inside the—(albeit hopefully now more flexible)—square'.

9 Supporting and resourcing questions

The world is awash with good intentions that don't always get into action!
Even the ones that are turned into practical steps may still not be taken forward into actual practice. A month later— have we done it?—well, er...no!...Are we surprised?! No we're not!

SCAFFOLDING, LADDERS, TOOLS, SUPPLIES
To get this building in place we need to draw on whatever resources are needed to help get things functioning, create the extensions, the renovations or restorations. It's back out into the garage, the garden tool shed, the office, pantry or workroom to find whatever is needed.

Questions to help the practical implementation part of the cycle

Now it becomes important to ask...

What would it take for you *actually* to be able to do it—all the way to completion? To make this contribution you want to?

What support, assistance, resourcing, tools, information, people or contacts do you still need? (What have you already got? What are you thinking so far about what you still need?)

Now what might *still* hold you back? What would you need to help with *that*? Do you need to rehearse what you will say or do? Need other practical support...?

Can you still tell the full story (to yourself and to others) of what you want to do and why? And locate its basis in the evidence of what was wrong or what would be better?

You may need to revisit whether anything about the story needs to change or be revised.

Might another kind of action be better than this particular one?

Can you describe a 'Day in the life of...' what is to be done? What people will actually say and do? Can you model it?

What will increase our strength, purposes and energies to act effectively?

What scaffolding is needed to bridge safely from what could be to what now is?

Methods and techniques to help traverse this actual implementation part of the cycle

- The 'do' part of the appreciative inquiry cycle
- Inventories
- Checklists, 'to do' lists
- Indicators, exemplars, templates
- Lists of resources
- Role plays, rehearsals
- Test runs
- Mentors
- Inquiry group or wider network
- St Luke's 'Angels with attitude' (team building)
- Supporters
- Consultants who are 'hands on'
- Critical friends
- Critical reference group's own self-help group
- Professional development, networks
- Conferences, seminars, staff meetings

ACT–OBSERVE[44]

10 Implementation questions: from good intentions to good practice

Work is love made visible.
KAHLIL GIBRAN, 1972

FOOTINGS, FLOORS, WALLS, ROOMS, CORRIDORS, ROOF AND UTILITIES (ELECTRICITY, GAS, WATER AND VALUES) 'FUEL SYSTEMS' ARE ALL CONNECTED...

The scaffolding is now in place, and the self-organising begins to make visible the work of forming, bounding, shaping, channelling and structuring for this experiment in meeting the identified purposes of the emergent living human organism. Boundaries create and safeguard the organism's identity and its further organ-ising for its diverse purposes—and remember the value of open plan designs with their symbolic boundaries where strong inner core relationships make these possible. Strong but flexible floors are built on foundational footings well-grounded in previous inquiry. .

Passageways ensure movement and permeability, enabling access and communication. These are the house's arteries, veins and capillaries through which lifeblood 'information' and people can flow easily, travelling around all parts of the system. The sustainable utilities provide the resources, energies and flow of elements needed to feed and nurture the new forms. What is it that we wanted to see take place in these spaces? Open spaces enable gatherings and mixing. Quiet private spaces enable thinking things through. There are warm hearty places for nurturance and resource-sharing, cool garden oases for contemplation, and all the other spaces necessary for a fully living system. But wait, some in the house seem to be confined or excluded...Take care to build the pathways and meeting places so no one becomes too cut off (or has to cut themself off just to survive). No dissociation disorders should be created here. Strengthen one, strengthen all. United in diversity, as one interacting body of many parts under one roof. Protected from weather and external turbulence, so that all within can proceed safely...

While at the next scale this dwelling is but one organ in an even larger house, connected still by networks of communication channels so it can be part of the inquiring at this larger scale too...

In some cultures the roof is designed like an upturned ship's hull—like a Noah's Ark come to rest on terra firma. In other cultures whole dwellings and villages are floating on stretches of water. In yet others they are mobile.

THE HOME OFFICE SPACE

Set up some systems, some files or spaces that put 'like with like' so things can be together and found when needed—but let there be a few quirky spaces in the togetherness, and a bit of overlap for the safeguard of systemic redundancy. Set up the production, supplies and support systems and the recording, monitoring, reporting and feedback systems. Perhaps a nerve centre or HQ to and from which people can come and go, somewhere where the foundation stories can be kept, where the present is processed, and plans for the future are made.

But remember, this is a living system you are creating—not a machine!—so go easy on the perfect order, expect mistakes and adaptations and ensure regular little micro cycles of change, adjustment, refinement and 'tweaking'. Allow even for the need to return to earlier stages (or fast forward to new stages) of questioning to trace steps more accurately to the 'right' (revised) design and action. Don't let things get too set in concrete even when they are working well enough to be instituted for the long term. Take care not to hermetically seal or too rigidly delineate. Keep the windows open a little, and doors and corridors plentiful. Every human living system needs breathing space and room to move. Include some wavy lines, and some circles, triangles and dots. Remember, even the square—'the box'—the rooms, walls and hallways are living things too...

Just as you regularly sought some structure and form as you moved into desirable change—let there now be movement in the stabilising 'structures' and procedures you are building so you can always keep inquiring to realign with your deepest life-giving values...

Now down from the zenith of energetic and confident hopes and presumptions—you are getting to work! With some determination and humility you've rolled up the sleeves. It's time to 'make it happen', time to leap into action, time to 'just do it'. The rubber hits the road and in a critical sense 'the future is [now being] made not predicted' (Applebaum 1977).

Time for action!

Time to research how we actually *do* this new action if the details haven't been worked through.

Time to not be too certain and presumptuous...

Remember that even the most decisive action is still *and always* in a literally critically important way, experimental, subject to trial and error.

How do human services providers and users ensure their own good foundations are well laid and then are built to grow with healthy boundaries and permeable circulation maintained among all the parts of the system—united around strong value-driven purposes and expressed in codified principles and resonant practice?

How can everyday research and evaluation processes facilitate this? And how can implementation evaluation continually align the original value-purposes with actual actions—keeping open the possibility of new value-purposes forming that will need flexibility and change even in the middle of trying to bed down new actions...

Firstly, we might start some recording systems to be able to show ourselves and others what has been done by whom, where, when etc... and with what effects in practice.

Then we might need to write down some of the 'how we worked out how to do it'. Some written manuals of 'how to'. Maybe some standards documents, some procedures, instructions, methods, protocols and techniques—unless things can safely be left 'in your head', to memory, collectivities and embodied skill.

Then we start to watch and monitor, making some measurements to identify changes, collecting some feedback, stories, anecdotes—and then more routinely, so we can compare and detect any changes.

But not too complicated and detailed.

Yet already the time and context in which the new actions are being taken may vary subtly from that in which the ideas formed. The royal road to getting it wrong is to be blind to this living reality, unable to make adjustments, unable to continue to adapt and respond to the now current environment. But also unable to take time out to foresee future needs and plant the oak plantation now so as to be able to replace the building in 600 years time.

Much of what we enact—especially if it has been through a full and participatory developmental process over a substantial period—will last for long periods of time. But sometimes even with elaborate preparation, conditions beyond our foresight intervene to cut things short. (And sometimes things last a very long time that everyone knows should have been nipped in the bud at the outset!) And other times things are only fleeting that are still needed and should have been very lasting.

So, always build in space for encouraging questions, even at the moment of most certain action. Ensure a capacity for discretion and flexible response, even from the outset. Any system without discretionary powers is on dangerous ground as it is precluding new inquiry and the admission of new interpretive data.

Some of this needed uncertainty is in the way we speak—for example the principles of living systems are served well by retaining the 'uncertain voice' of the scientific experiment. We might say: 'It may be that', 'We think it could...', 'We expect it should', 'Would you like to...?' 'It is best to...?'—rather than, 'It is...', 'This will be...', 'You must...', 'This will result in...', 'You will learn...'

Overly certain language, no matter how intensely attractive, also rests on dangerous ground, precluding more alternative realities being the case whether in the past, present or future.

However it is also important to carry out the living 'experiment' as much as possible as it was designed and not be *too* quick to change it, nor try to evaluate its impacts or effects, much less outcomes and results, *too* soon (when these may not yet have had a chance to get going).

Remember that, under non-crisis conditions, 'invitationality' and non-coercion means a minimum of unnecessary perturbance (and potential turbulence) for living systems' ability to exercise their self-organising capacity and minimise unnecessary helplessness and dependence on others to do all the organising (questioning, thinking, planning and acting) for them. Crisis conditions that invoke top-down, one-way authoritative direction and coercion put on hold the ability to receive bottom-up and sideways-in, two-way and multi-way feedback from the organism, commencing the risk of making uncorrected errors.

Time to turn great ideas into actionable realistic identifiable steps...

Questions to help traverse this implementation part of the cycle

Who would do what, when, where, how and with whom? What steps can we take? First step? Second? Third? Etc...

When—Is it timely? Is it the right time? Is there a better time?

By or with whom—Who are the best people to do it? Are there others?

And why—You may need to keep asking: Why are we doing this? What are our guiding values and purposes? (so goals are not displaced)

Always keep checking each step is consistent with your intentions and vision—all the way back to your original deepest most valued purposes, needs, desires and interests.

Where—Is this the right location? Have we chosen well? Who benefits?

How—What are the ways our actions or activities will achieve our purposes or desires?

How will we know when we are carrying out the new action/s? Implementing them correctly? Effectively? Efficiently as possible without sacrificing effectiveness? What will things look like? How will we know we have reached our goals? Or achieved our purposes? What will be the signs and indicators? (Consistent with your original values and purposes, expressed in your goals and objectives, based in your line of reasoning or program logic.)

What are the ultimate outcomes we are working towards? Do we need to begin making observations and regularly evaluating from now on, so that in future we will know if we've reached them?

Next you can ask: What can be done to introduce all this—to make it work?

Make this real and practical (so that people are empowered to act) by asking: What would you personally (or the group as a whole) like to do? Or would most enjoy contributing to 'making it happen'? What are you most interested in? Or able to offer at this point in time?

What would we like to do about it? Or can contribute to this together?

Now ask: What might keep you from doing it? And what might assist?

Remember slippage comes when we do what is do-able!

Rather than doing what is do-able that should be done.

Methods and techniques to help traverse this implementation part of the cycle

- The 'deliver' part of the appreciative inquiry cycle
- Action learning
- The 'deliver' part of the appreciative inquiry cycle
- Process evaluation
- Learning organisations/organisational development
- Workgroups, teams (if they have been the inquiry group)
- Administrative systems to track and record action in meaningful ways
- Action plans, goals/aims/objectives matrixes/log frames
- Manuals, codes of conduct, codes of practice
- Advance care directives
- Charters of practice and rights
- Procedural rulebooks
- Standards, standardisation
- Performance/practice management systems
- Management by walking around
- Surveys (comparative baseline/before and after data)
- SurveyMonkey®, SurveyBob®
- Newsletters, bulletins, websites, blogs
- Report-ins, early feedback, satire

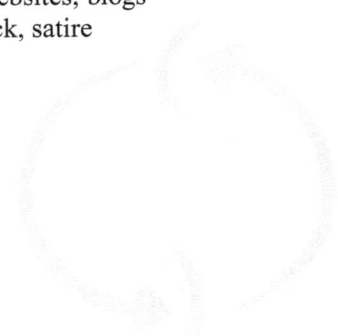

What is the story now?

It is a good time to be able to check that everyone can 'tell the story' at this point in time. And for all to be able to 'hold' that shared story. What would it be?
This last set of questions should help with being able to outline to someone the full narrative structure of:
What happened previously and what was planned to address it? (and why)
What then was put in place? What has been done and how and by whom, where, when?
What has been observed to have resulted so far? (and if there is anything that has worked or is still a puzzle, and if anything is suspected to be still not right at a deeper level: what is already being done or considered as a response?)

Acting[45] without questions

OK—so now it's happening, you're taking the action, trying it out, putting it into practice.
Things are 'in place'. Systems have been created. Programs and services are running. Everything is 'on the go'. Soon things may be starting to work smoothly, and small 'quick fixes' are enough to refine and adapt the processes until they become 'second nature'. People may be starting to relax—watching 'the system' starting to be productive, 'all systems go'—producing, producing, producing…well enough managed, well enough maintained, protected and well oiled.

We start to work a bit by rote. We begin following the procedures without thinking so much about what we are doing or why we are doing it. It gets more like orienteering between known points; like following already mapped territory. Like being guided by our own previously programmed GPS devices! New people do what others are doing by 'following the leader', 'getting with the program', maybe only learning later the rationale for what is being done (or maybe not). Subtly we are less self-organising and more robotic.

As our store of practice wisdom grows, we find our learning curves beginning to flatten out. We expect to be able to 'follow the rules': 'if this, then that', 'do this, then do that'. Do what we have been told. Now we inquire less and less often, and only when we strike a small new puzzle, problem or query or an instance we haven't come across before—although usually not before we try and make it fit a previously stored

instance! It starts to feel very comfortable to be so confident, certain and knowledgeable. For things to be 'taken for granted'. We 'get it right' and it feels great. Like hitting a little bar and receiving a pellet. We keep hitting the same bar. It worked last time…We are on 'automatic pilot'…
Replicate, replicate, replicate!

The 'living experiment' is successfully reproducing itself—like the 'new' axe that has had many new handles and heads and is still the 'same' axe. The 'checking and monitoring' data on effects (results, outputs, changes, impacts, outcomes) are becoming available and observable (*if* they are observed….and don't just become assumed to be predictable or pour into a large database, never to be retrieved and examined!)

At first sight all may seem well—especially if the inquiry work has been thoroughly conducted through all the preceding moments around the cycle, or through many cycles. The statistics are starting to look like it's pretty reliably good. People are saying it's going well. Things seem to be working. People are pleased with early anecdotal feedback. It looks like it might be a 'go-er'—even for the long term.

It may even feel uncomfortable to express uncertainty or to be asking 'why' or 'whether'. *What's your problem?*—we challenge the asker. It's working fine for us.

Coming full cycle…
Observing-in-action

Monitoring and auditing questions

Now we are back to the 'start'—well into action— and things are really speeding up. We are busy, busy, busy. Things still seem to be working…
But wait, on second thoughts, what was *that*…?
Hmm…
But our vigilance has weakened. We have been lulled from early sharpness about establishing and implementing the practice as planned into such a sense of all being well that we can't bring ourselves to raise little queries 'so soon'. We have shifted to 'taking care of business' mode, and the routines have become familiar—we are letting the experiment 'tick over', rather than observing what is resulting. We are getting ever faster, and the new soon becomes the old, and

eventually will be the 'same old, same old'. We have ironed out every last wrinkle and bump till, as we say—'it's all running like clockwork'.

Welcome to our machine!

Now you may find there's *no time* to stop, and others may be reluctant to disturb something that seems to be going OK too. And anyway, now the carrots and sticks are urging us to ever greater 'productivity', to become faster and faster with ever more outputs, and it does feel rather exhilarating to be doing so much so quickly.

So with no time to evaluate (and anyway, last time the feedback was ok) we rocket on, relying ever more on someone, somewhere collecting the statistics according to the indicators and formal targets we set, to confirm that it is all really worthwhile...

Wait a minute! What do you mean no time to stop and ask 'How is it going?' Is it still really of value?

No time for we the people who are best positioned to observe and audit what we are *actually* seeing, against what was expected or hoped for (or not)?—not to mention best positioned to say how we *feel* about what we are observing, and *reflect* on whether what we are doing is actually still worthwhile in terms of all the deeper values and intentions...? That's if we have long enough to stop and draw breath to remember what they were. Much less think whether there might be something different that would be even better.

So now a few little doubts are creeping in...

Someone circulates a funny email that's gone viral—'*101 things to do with a dead horse'. Ride it harder. Get two of them. Change the rider. Change from one dead horse to another*' We exchange grimaces and comrades-in-the-trenches stories in the kitchen before rushing back to 'get on with it'. But we still hope what we are doing is going to have some desired outcomes. Surely it will contribute *something*? Someone would say to stop, wouldn't they? Surely?

Ironically the better the idea seemed, the more compelling the logic, the more exciting the new action, service or program initiative was at the beginning, and the longer it goes with enough success, the more fiercely we may be likely to defend it. Everyone in research and evaluation knows how the North American Head Start early childhood services initiative was evaluated, prematurely as it turns out, and proclaimed a failure when its results weren't measurable for another twenty to thirty years. How can

things not be going well when we were so well prepared? So well-meaning, and it was so well-evidenced, so wanted and everyone saw it as excellent when we started. Didn't they? 'Oh really?—you never said anything at the time.' All the experts agreed it was what should be done, and they'd spent years researching it and seemed very well qualified to know...Wasn't this what we were meant to be doing? Surely we're doing it right...

This seems almost to be part of the human condition—to find ourselves caught between wanting the comfort and certainty of having already got the right answers and settled into the 'tried and true', versus tolerating the discomfort and uncertainty of new questions and re-entering the realm of the unknown on the journey to something better. If we have any power we may well use it, even harshly, to discourage new questions or circumvent an evaluation if our anxiety prevails. When someone says 'I've just got a feeling things have changed', we ask slightly tersely 'WHAT DO YOU MEAN "*THINGS HAVE CHANGED*"?!' And if we cannot imagine a better possibility, we may well not be propelled to inquire at all.

We can see how we may eventually get a bit stuck, or even in a very big rut we cannot see a way out of. One day we are shocked when someone drives a bulldozer through it. And if we get warning of the bulldozers we may paradoxically build ever stronger walls of commitment and defence. It is an irony that when the existing is suspected not to be 100 per cent world's best practice, that is exactly when we might erect the impregnable defences rather than remaining permeable to new input and feedback—a phenomenon that, even more paradoxically, we might be able to trace back to our deepest values (that we can't bear to realise are not being honoured) (See Wadsworth and O'Brien 2002 and Exemplar 3 'Caring to ask' in Chapter 5). On the other hand, if we have enough confidence and sense of empowerment and the time and space built in to routinely explore alternatives, we may much more happily take a little 'ride around the boundaries' to check the fences and ask how things are going. To see if the garden is still flourishing...

No time to stop?

No time NOT to stop and ask! And the earlier the better.

OK. So it's time to slow down. Time to take the time.[46] Time to make the time. Beyond putting the essential monitoring and feedback systems in place, but also to spend time reflecting, thinking and talking together, as well as planning to review more formally at the end of particular periods of time (or sooner). And being there to welcome hearing the early warnings from the human 'canaries in the mine'—as well as whatever signals the radars and sonars of statistical collection can pick up.

Key questions to recommence the questioning while in action

Checking our action and inputs: Am I (or are we) doing what I thought I should be doing? Am I getting it right? Are we on course? Can we see, identify or measure whether we are doing what we'd said we'd do? Have we done or supplied or provided what we planned to? The way we intended? Are we measuring and rewarding what we wanted to see repeated?

Checking our outputs: Is what is happening as a result, what we hoped?

Beginning to check our results: Can we see that our original value-driven purposes are still on course to be met by our outcomes? Are we thinking we should be doing something different...?

Beginning to check our outcomes: Is it working? Can we see that the complex causality from immediate to longer term is beginning to take place—or is it leading elsewhere? Are there unintended outcomes or consequences? (Are they good or not good?)...

Yes! It's back to 'the start'
Back to observing action!

At first it may be a bit difficult, a bit ad hoc and haphazard to again 'start by stopping', and 'start to begin' seeing, observing and recording anew. Maybe at first there are just some nagging anecdotes, or things that seem to have been going on in the statistics...

Or you might find it easier because you've been foresightful enough to have built it in!
You may have already created (or soon are able to move to) more systematic and regular ways of monitoring, collecting and sharing early observations, and of recording and feeding them back for others to discuss. You may also have become increasingly adept at working out how to 'tell the story' of being 'here', having come from a past 'there' and looking forward into the future...

Interestingly, it's when a new question offers something that is more engaging, meaningful, fulfilling, exciting, pleasurable or rewarding than an old answer that we are more likely to move *gladly* to question and potentially shed 'the old', even quite painlessly, like an old skin. Hence the current worldwide popularity of appreciative inquiry,[47] and strengths-based, capacity-detecting (capacity-building) methods—as they focus *directly* on what invokes life-giving images. And we are even more likely to feel like this when we get to have a say about what we think the answers might be by contributing *our* experiences and observations; and then getting to see everyone else's answers, experiences and observations too (and also get access to yet more ideas from further afield to stimulate our imaginations).

So now the feedback is flowing, and you are more systematically observing. It is...

Back to noticing the discrepancies: both positive and not

And moving into a new sequence of research questions to take you round the cycle of life-giving inquiry again.

Registering what is unexpected. Celebrating the good. Listening for the canary in the mine, gratefully rewarding (rather than shooting) the messengers. Mourning what's not right. Or unviable. Resolving to cross yet another threshold to find a better way...

Getting the hang of the full cycle questions sequence

Even the full compendium of questions above of course barely scratches the surface of all the possible questions that could be asked! There is truly an infinity of questions[48] and a matching infinity of listening.

Yet we may also whiz through the whole cycle in a very much shorter time, even in a micro- second in active engagement with others.

What is important is to sample at least from each moment or standpoint in order to get movement right round the cycle, not missing any critical steps, nor staying overly stuck at any one spot in particular.

You could ask a set of ten quick questions, one from each section:

1. What do you observe is happening? (regarding what you are interested in)
2. What do you think is going on here? (Really going on, more deeply or widely?)
3. How do you feel about it? Is it OK or do you want it to change?
4. What would be better? How could things be as you'd really wish or prefer them to be?
5. What would need to change? Is there a new way of understanding things that would be better here?
6. How might things change? Name as many ways as possible, and calculate which would be best.
7. What would you like to do towards realising this in practice?
8. What would it take for you to be able to take your intentions into actual practice?
9. What extra help do you need?
10. How will you know if its' working?

Or just four questions, one from each quadrant:

1. What is happening now? (observe)
2. What would you prefer? (reflect)
3. How could it become a new reality? (plan)
4. What needs to be done to implement it? (act)

Or if you are really pushed, you could ask just one from each of the two halves of the cycle:

1. How are things now? (observe and reflect)
2. What could you try instead? (plan and act)

Here are three quick examples of the use of the full sequence of questions reaching 'right round the cycle of inquiry' from past to new action.

Four quick examples

Example 1. *Questioning the creek*

Fran Peavey describes several small-scale uses of the question sequence in her Strategic Questioning. Here is one. She writes:

> Sue and Col Lennox came to one of my workshops on Strategic Questioning in Sydney, Australia. The following Monday morning they returned to the schools in Maleny where they teach. The students were in an uproar about a chemical spill in the creek behind their school. All the fish in the lagoon (which is fed by the creek) were dying. Sue thought, 'Here is a chance to practice strategic questioning'.
>
> She taught the children briefly how to do it by asking: 'What do you see?' 'What do you know?' 'How do you feel?'
> 'How could it be?' 'How should it be?'
> 'What needs to be changed?'
> 'What should we do?'
> 'What can you do?'
> 'What support do you need?'
>
> The students went out to use these strategic questions to question their neighbors, their fellow students and teachers. They also went to the creek and consulted the creek. In doing this they opened their hearts to the pain of the creek. They knew that they had to do something. They came back from their consultations with many perceptions and expressions of concern. From their questioning they had uncovered some good ideas of what to do and what others would be willing to do.
>
> The students had to determine which ideas fitted their own talents and time, and which seemed to be the best ideas. For the past three years they have been working on testing the water of that creek, talking to the local city council and community, finding the exact nature of the pollution of the creek, making video tapes and teaching other students all over Australia to do the same. All this was catalysed by the strategic questioning process. (1994: 109)

Example 2. *Questioning disability*

In an even more simple exercise, the sequence of questions was used to bring together in a single workshop on one day a large number of parents and workers with young people living with autism and related situations in New Zealand. Their energetic and lively discussions followed the strategic action research question string:

Focus on an area, concern, interest: How will we assist the learning of people with this disability?

Observations so far: What have we seen work so far? Or not work?

Analysis/synthesis (reflections/theory): Why do we think that's been so? (Speculate...) What has really been happening? What do we believe?

Feelings: How do we feel about what we've been doing so far? What feels good? Or not so good?

Visioning: What are our ideas about what would work better to help?

Alternatives: Are there other possible ideas or approaches?

Change: Which is best and what would it take to try this out in practice?

Implementation: Now who will do what, when, where and how!?

Example 3. *Questioning acute psychiatric hospital care*

In the initial U&I research in 1990 (Exemplar 1, Chapter 5), a dialogic interchange took place between staff and consumers over about two months, structured by two sets of questions—one to consumers and one to staff. The resulting two sets of answers were exchanged so consumer saw what staff were trying to do and staff saw what consumers' experiences were, and then the further responses exchanged again, and then again. Below are the two initial sets of starter questions (Wadsworth 2001: 14–15) that follow the same strategic action research questions sequence of: observe, reflect, and move to think through planning new action.

The first set of questions to consumers (observe)
These centred on the consumer inpatient experience:
What was your experience of coming (or being brought) to the hospital? Being there? And leaving? (detailed descriptive questions of what happened)

How would you have liked it to have been? (Can you think of any other ways?)

Do you think anything will be different for you because of your time here?

The first set of questions to staff
These centred on observing and reflecting on their consumer-responsive goals:
What do you do that works for consumers?

How do you know what you do works in the eyes of consumers?

What does not work, and how do you know?

Can you say a bit more about your intentions and purposes? Broad visions, day-to-day objectives?

Are you managing to achieve your visions and purposes?

What are you up against? (in trying to do so)

What conditions are needed for you to achieve what you want to achieve?

The second set of questions to consumers (reflect)
These responded to staff's answers to the first questions to them
What comments would you like to make? (notice)

What sense do you make of them? What does it tell you? How does it change your views?

What does it tell you about what can be changed/achieved?

What now do you think consumers should recommend that staff could do?

The second set of questions to staff (plan–act)
These responded to consumers' answers to their first questions
What does it tell you? Does it have any value for you? Does it change any of your ideas?

In the light of it, what improvements would you really like to make for consumers? (visions and hopes) What would be needed to make these happen? What on earth could you do?

Questions to the readers
We also realised that the readers of the book in which the research was written up (McGuiness and Wadsworth 1991) were participants in a wider inquiry network of a sort too.
The questions we posed readers were:
What sense do you make of this material? (*observe*)

How does it assist your understanding? (*reflect*)

What kind of changes would you want to make in the light of it? (*plan new action*)

Example 4. *For use in implementing integrated health promotion*

There is a longer example in Appendix 4 showing the sequence of questions used to help structure narrative annual reporting by health promotion workers to government funders. This was part of a project to build in narrative evaluative action research (the NEAR project—Exemplar 8 Chapter 5) to achieve integrated health promotion. The project's success was recognised by the Australasian Evaluation Society's 2007 National Evaluation Policy and Systems Award. A manual of guidelines and resources was produced for open access on the government website (see website cited in Appendix 4).

Concluding words: inquiry styles that reach around the cycle

We all do all

This chapter has looked at research and evaluation through the lens of *questioning* as the *dynamic* for *full cycle* inquiry, and the *metaphor* of the *house* has been used to illuminate ideas about the self-organised, *self-organising 'building in'* of such continuous inquiry to relevant field environments.

There has been particular emphasis on illuminating how we all have all the capabilities necessary for these cycles of life-giving inquiry—indeed all research and evaluation and continuous learning builds on these ordinary human inquiry processes: the ways we take in information, observe action, feel and process experience, intuit connections and meanings, and think things through into acting on it, both...

Individually

Individually within our own minds we all to greater or lesser extents experience the *internal* conversations that get us around our inquiry cycles, asking ourselves, 'What am I seeing?', 'What counts as good enough evidence for me?', 'What is of value to me?', 'What do things mean to me?' 'What are their consequences for me?'

And collectively

We go 'full cycle' together, with these same conversations *between us* as friends, partners, families, colleagues, groups, teams, organisations, institutions, networks, communities and wider state, national and global environments.

Overall therefore, both individually and together, the human species has the potential to cover the 'whole

Figure 13. Integrated inquiry

territory' in order to remain in dynamic balance. And indeed for the most part we are remarkably capable and competent in doing this, as we make our way through our lives together, and have done so for millennia.

Yet why *don't* we practice all capabilities in a more integrated way all the time, as we could? And why don't we routinely appreciate those using capabilities different from our own? How indeed have we come to see various capabilities as less important and some as more important, and based entire systems of reward or deprivation on this?

Then why don't we do better?

Why does it so often prove elusive to move to a picture of inquiry together 'around the table' of all the relevant parties on the human life journey and move away from a picture of separation and potential misunder-standing, distancing and disconnection (see the two cartoons of the different parties to the research in 'Entering a new systems thinking era' in Chapter 2).

Indeed in a kind of neo-Tower of Babel[49] we daily observe our speaking at cross purposes as each of our ways of seeing things and thinking about them does battle in assertion and counter-defence. A bit like the four kinds of inquiry perspectives riding the bike for a fall in the Prologue, we all too regularly seem to pull in different directions, unable to detect or understand the value of each other's different 'takes' on life, unable to inquire peacefully together as a whole, including through periods of friction or turbulence, seeming often almost to speak different languages at the different 'moments' around the cycle, with an unsurprising mismatch of end solutions or goals in regard to the problems or desires that were there at the beginning.[50]

Tohby Riddle has noted in a personal exchange that: 'The more rooms (and the greater complexity) we add to our houses the greater the challenge to be an integrated social being'. Indeed it gets even trickier if we remain exclusively in our favoured room, or worse,

Figure 14. Disintegrated inquiry

start closing the door to others (either because our room seems superior or seems enough, or else it is being seen as inferior and avoided by others). Before we know where we are the chances of integration and human equality have become ever lower.

So traversing full cycles of inquiry, whether on our own or together, is not always easy. This is something you may have already discovered for yourself!

But why is this so?

The concept of inquiry styles and inquiry preferences: 'gifts differing' around the cycle

While we all *can* get right round the cycles of inquiry—and indeed *must* in order to continuously inquire to 'achieve life', especially at smaller scales of life—it is also the case that, at any *particular* time and for any particular issue or situation, we will be *somewhere* around the cycle, and not any or everywhere else at the same time.

Yet precisely because we can't be in every part of the cycle at once, when we need to move, especially quickly, say in an emergency, there may be a delay as we extract our focus from one inquiry mode and shift it to another (e.g. from observing to planning; or from acting to reflecting).

At an individual level we need to take that time. Even in an emergency we'll still *need* to make or find that time. And it is the same for social groupings.

Yet if we are with someone else, or in a larger group, community or organisation, and a crisis takes place, the chances increase that *together* we can more quickly 'cover the bases' if we have a combination of people who can 'chip in' from different vantage points; for example if one person can focus on applying existing knowledge to a situation (*acting* based on current knowledge/*plan*) they can more quickly begin emergency treatment (using rules and procedures that have worked in the past). Meanwhile if another person is focused on the bigger picture and sees there is a different set of conditions applying (*reflect on observation*) they can bring this to the situation. While another, who is thinking through the new implications of the situation (*plan* on basis of *reflection*), and who can hear this analysis, can quickly identify a new strategy—and all can then be ready, willing and able to respond to the situation in a more integral way.

In a way each is acting as a kind of 'specialist consultant' to the group, as the group, *qua* group, moves together around the cycle. This may look like a division of (epistemological) labour, but it is in the field of *communication in relation to each other* (which may work better if people already know and trust each other over time) that group members are galvanised for a more rapid 'whole system' response to a 'whole system' situation.

However a down side can ensue if such a crisis/emergency situation persists and people become more skilled and familiar with one position around the cycle and stay with that, slowly losing the ability to exercise capability and competence at all other positions. Both the 'parts' and the whole become fragile and lack the potential for resilience if *each* and *all* cannot be allowed to retain the knowledge of how to observe *and* feel *and* reflect *and* intuit *and* plan *and* act. As well, if people are not working in close enough proximity to know and trust each other's differing inquiry preferences (and judge the basis for their being exercised), then the arrangements can also break down, and life again resemble a Babel tower of competing or mutually demonising voices.

Favoured questions and the concept of inquiry styles and inquiry preferences
It seems that, over time, and whether due to socialisation, biology, genetics or an interesting systemic combination of all these, people do grow to have what I am calling *inquiry preferences*. And further, if they become very adept at some of these rather than others, they may also consolidate them into what I am calling an *inquiry style*, which is replicated over time. For example some people may gravitate to *action*, with inquiry preferences in the *plan–action* or *observe–action* quadrants. While others may gravitate towards *reflection* on observations and thinking about their implications for planning new action. In this way some people seem to find their way 'naturally' to being more observing—descriptive quantitative or qualitative—or more philosophical or 'big picture' critical researchers, and so on.

If you were able to identify particular sets of questions earlier in Chapter 3 that you thought were 'more important' or more familiar (or favoured by) you, and others which you thought less so, then this might give you some insight into your own favoured inquiry preferences—with implications for a preferred methodology or 'inquiry style'.

In turn these preferences can shape the nature of a person's 'full cycle' inquiry style as well. For example individual people may be inclined to start from their preferred location in the cycle, and move to other parts of the cycle on either side of this (backwards or forwards) around the cycle as it travels towards action or change; or they may approach the unfavoured quadrants through the lens of their own favoured inquiry preferences. At the collective level these distinctive inquiry preferences may come to be expressed as the culture of a group, a community, and organisation or a whole institution.

If you thought about which of the sets of questions and typically associated methods have been the ones you'd be most likely to use, and which ones you'd be inclined to skip over, you may also be able to see when your favoured inquiry mode might have 'clicked', 'resonated', 'gelled' or connected well with someone else's (or not). This might not only be as co-researchers in a more formal sense (influencing job choices), but also whenever sharing observations, questions or reflections, or trying to make sense of changes informally in your lives with friends, family or colleagues in an informal sense. Or doing this as clients or professional staff of a health or human services, or as members of groups, teams or communities.

You might also be able to think about where you've been able to 'chip in' and assist others through the processes with which they were unfamiliar, or they've done that for and with you. Or where you've successfully right round the cycle together, or leapfrogged sections when you think you shouldn't have (or not leapfrogged them when you think they *should* have been skipped), or been at odds and got stuck.

Say you feel particularly comfortable observing and describing, or analysing and theorising about what you observe. But say the issue calls for change. It may be that you go on observing and describing, and analysing or theorising what you see—rather than risk moving into the unfamiliar territory of researching what to do instead. You may not want to make such a commitment, knowing change is constant and the next research study you read might show a better way; or

you may not be at all convinced there is even a need for change. You might prefer to call for 'more research'.

Or, say you feel comfortable with the up-close-and-personal expression of feeling and are working hard to assist people make personal changes but they cannot easily envision how things could be different—or see how to research a pathway between a 'here' and a 'there'. You may feel either comfortable or a little queasy asking about goals and what things might look like if they were achieved, depending on your own inquiry preferences.

Or, say you are most comfortable with developing new theories that do a stellar job of explaining not only how things are but also provide a rationale for an alternative different future—but you glaze over at the impossibility of supplying detailed facts that prove in advance of trialling the action that it *will* bring about the desired changes.

Or perhaps you are adept at turning plans into action, but new information that comes in from left field that suggests this was the wrong plan in the first place leaves you ready to explode at the thought of having to listen to people's problems all over again.

An epistemological game of Chinese whispers in a Tower of Babel?

But rather than resourcing each other's inquiries from our own preferences and building in all preferences to 'full cycle teams' or communities of inquiry practice, these differences may often become institutionalised as separate parts of 'the body politic', with some observing and measuring quantitative statistical differences and others hearing people's observations in in-depth qualitative interviews or through participation, and yet others working with group processes to create abductive theory for change, and yet others still articulating the logic in policies or implementation of the actions in practice.

Faced with misunderstanding, discomfort or frustration, people who are doing planning or managing may begin to meet more and more with others who think in terms of doing planning or managing. At this point in the cycle, abstracted data and assumptions may be at a distance from 'the personal' where people are being hurt and damaged by past decisions made 'for their own good'. There could be a risk of replicating the same kinds of decisions.

People who are reflecting on ideas and theories for change may tend to seek the company of others involved in cultural creativity to nurture their imaginations of the integral and share stories of deep meaning about what is or would be 'really of value', not at that moment considering ways of feeding this lifeblood back into 'the body corporate'.

Those who are in care roles and working to feel deeply and sympathetically may gravitate to the company of like-focused others to protect their perspective from unacceptable realities or the logic of the currently dominant program. This may limit their capacity to resource others with alternative experiences.

People who need to be observant and practically action-oriented may see what is happening and gather with like folk to express the hope there are others *somewhere* 'doing something about it', but be pessimistic that things will ever change, feeling fated to just keep doing more of the same.

As economic, political and socio-cultural organising has 'scaled up' to whole-of-population levels of consideration, research strategies and methodologies and their accompanying techniques have *also* become ever more specialised and increasingly disconnected from each other.

But if one part is divided from the other and no longer direct communicating, the possibility arises of an elaborate game of Chinese whispers or 'baton passing' developing as the messages and insights associated with each of the differing parts of the cycle are either missed or subtly reinterpreted by others 'further around' who do not have those inquiry preferences themselves. In the U&I project described in Exemplar 1 in Chapter 5, consumers had the experience of managers not understanding the importance of key elements needed to ensure consumers could effectively participate, for example, repeatedly 'rationalising' the carefully constructed teams of two or more part time consumer consultants (working together for safety and strength), into a single full time lone worker position. Or not seeing the importance of a discretionary small flexible fund to pay for casual consumer participation, or child care or travel costs.

Worse, if people are pressured to 'take up residence' in one part of the cycle, mixing only with 'like minds' in order to enhance the strengths and contribution of

that preference, they may even come to mistrust, dislike and conflict with those at other parts of the cycle, and particularly those most distant on the opposite side of the cycle (or alternatively to idolise them).

Indeed when any inquiry preference is isolated, dominated or suppressed, *their* systemicity may replicate in a way that is missing the logic of the lost or opposite quadrant.

Those acting can get stuck in action, unable to stop and observe, or take enough time to reflect on what it's all for.

Those observing can go on observing, painstakingly hearing, measuring and documenting what has already been noticed, heard and documented before.

Those reflecting can keep hatching ever more alternative visions, theories and models of what could be, but be confined to the periphery to await take up of their ideas.

Those planning keep on planning, even as they fear they may not be well enough informed or that it may already be unacceptable to people. They may opt for a 'crash through' approach as 'necessary' to convince 'the troops and underlings' to take up the new forms. Under this kind of stress, planners may find themselves calling for every closer measurement, documentation and reporting in the hope that will help their fears, until systems grind to a halt under the sheer weight of reporting and risk-management proceduralism!

Soon the new forms may become faithfully institutionalised and dismayingly reified, difficult to alter, re-form or liquefy in future when outcomes may prove variable, elusive, uncertain or insignificant.

Each person is seeing, hearing, diagnosing and responding to the original point of it all—of assisting people to full life—but separated from and at odds with each other, all risking regularly failing to go full cycle, or even to value the parts being played by all others.

Inquiry preferences and routine 'reach' around the cycle

For the most part the daily emphases in life are on *acting* and *observing*—after all, they are what we all do on automatic pilot pretty much all the time. We are all doing *something* (even if it is 'nothing'), and our empirical senses are 'switched on' and processing more-or-less constantly. Your head may be down with 'no time to stop and think', especially if 'time is money' and 'money is the measure of all things' or there's 'yet another crisis' ahead. It's perhaps not surprising that those who can 'think on their feet' step forward with plans and confident suggestions because they may quickly calculate how to refine the system to better achieve its logic. Furthermore the action-observers, who would otherwise need to take time to think things through (and feel things through), might acquiesce, especially being more familiar with the existing logic anyway. The fact that consequentialist thinking means others are quick also to calculate benefit (often firstly to themselves or their organisations or institutions), and with action-observers relieved there is someone doing their thinking for them, they may also find themselves acquiescing to endangering and growing levels of inequality (Wilkinson and Pickett 2009). Perhaps they wait, trusting 'them' to redistribute things more fairly according to elevated principles and virtues 'the system' claims to be conducted by, or step outside the laws and rules, or sink into hopeless or enraged helplessness.

Here might be the way in which living human system cycles of inquiry get routinely short-circuited into quick fix, single loop solutions, with these then triggering further crises and emergencies as more things go wrong when the unexamined wider contextual issues still don't get examined until the last moment. In turn, people increasingly act from their inquiry preferences and styles—unable and without time to appreciate the discounted parts in themselves, and either projecting these onto others to take up or rejecting them when they see them in others because they consider them of little value.

In a perpetual state of emergency and stress, no wonder we see this 'writ small' in individual 'sub-systems' where it can't be seen that things are not working till too late, and which either act with very fast with impulsive energy to immediately defend, or else do more and more of the same—or give up in the face of it all being 'too big'. Further, we may see it writ large in institutions and organisations (where culture is generated by 'person sub-systems' exercising lots of resistant defences or ever more of the most familiar ways of being and doing) either fast-acting and repeating the same mistakes, or losing the race and becoming moribund or going under.

Soon there is inefficient communication and corridors full of Chinese whispers, voices competing in different discourses in towers of Babel, and conflict at every scale, congealed into forcefields. While a degree of discrepancy, dissonance, 'disconnect' and conflict fuels or 'gingers' life-giving inquiry, excesses (or their complete lack) drain life away. From an era starting out with a degree of participation that is necessary in actually putting things right (think of a popular uprising) there eventually develop increasing concentrations of certainty/power and calculating/accruing of whatever the system values, which then call forth more conflict to attempt to re-balance out of kilter dynamics. Coming back from all of this once it is systemic is incredibly hard.

The alternative is to hold a culture that values the input of all—since all have characteristically strong contributions to make in one or more quadrants of the cycle—and build in the spaces and places to take the time for full cycle inquiry.

It 'takes all types' of inquiry preferences and inquiry styles to go full cycle

With the time and space for people to question their way right round the cycle—including venturing into their unfavoured quadrants (and having the time and space to manage their queasy feelings and defensive tendencies as they traverse that thin ice), and collaborating on the process with a range of people who together have the necessary 'reach' right round the cycle—all may instead end up together on the 'same page' of a shared meta-narrative.

But hey! *That* would involve stopping doing by those incessantly doing!
And considering the 'possible new' by those most adept at the tried and true
And starting 'feeling it through' by those most accustomed only to thinking it through
And sitting with silence and the unknown for those keen always to speak with certainty
And engaging in collaboration for those prone to only doing their own thing
And being alone with one's thoughts and feelings for those 'joined at the hip' with others
And dialoguing across differences involving conflict for those who feel it's easier to let sleeping dogs lie
And creating the new within the realm of existing

realities for those adept at imagining the ideal
And seeing beyond 'realist pragmatism' for those not easily able to envisage a better world for all.

Implications for human services

What do people in human service systems (end users and providers alike) face when they get on their bicycles and set out around their own inquiry cycles? How do they retain their valuably different inquiry preferences and favoured inquiry styles, yet exercise good enough 'reach' round the cycle *and* an ability to traverse their own 'thin ice' with grace and good-natured assistance from others, especially when they might fall through the cracks?

What are the implications of all this for human services if they are there to assist the 'humans served' to inquire *their* ways to greater life, out of their currently depleted, compromised or at risk states, drawing on their abilities, skills, capabilities and competences? How do both the 'human servers' and the 'humans served' inquire in *their* own ways to

achieving this? And how particularly do they achieve 'inquiry resonance' *together*?

Actively pursuing meaningful inquiry with a co-operative individual, partner or group to create a more healthy living system co-creates people individually and together as more healthy living systems. To be there 'with and for' each other, as we traverse our parallel and mutual journeys of inquiry to restore and keep restoring and furthering life in health and wholeness may even be thought of as the primary task of every living system.

Is this a real clue to (more truly) human service? To be 'alongside' and resource the other's practice-based and action-oriented inquiry? Assisting the other's autopoesis in relation to all their 'relevant others'? And to do this *with and for* each other's own self-organising? As both sovereign-bounded *and* integrally-related individuals and socially systemic groups, organisations and communities? Just as in any healthy living ecology?

My own story of developing an epistemology for living systems

Initially in the U&I staff–consumer research into acute psychiatric services, we found ourselves spending substantial time building an inquiry group. Yet the process of the group members getting to know each other turned out not to be a mere preliminary, but slowly emerged as the core methodology of the evaluative research process per se. Beyond being a means to an end, it was prefiguring the end of contextual understanding itself. Its longevity, commitment and insightful realisations all rested on the sharing of observations and reflections (initially appreciative and sympathetic, given the imbalance in that direction, but later critical and

more even-handed). Then, as trust built, consumers exposed staff to more and more of their history of deep hurts and traumas experienced during their admissions to acute psychiatric hospitals, and staff shared more of their fraught experiences and their successes and failures. The work deepened.

Importantly the expanding core group and active inquiry network did not proceed without the support of all key parties throughout 'the system'. This approach of 'so far and no further' unless there was a critical mass wanting to move forward (including senior managers) meant that the whole effort painstakingly only took

steps if doors were opened or 'OKs' signalled.

As we moved through the three-year U&I research project phase, the range of research methods we used to assist staff and consumers was extensive. They included both conventional data collection, and innovative techniques. We drew on many of the methods detailed in this chapter as we traversed our cycles of inquiring.

For example at one point we were stuck and needed to 'try a different tack'. When it seemed almost no staff were able to step forward to inquire into change, we sought a statistical 'reality check' on whether they really wanted to involve former inpatients in giving feedback at all. We used a standard survey and generated a graph which told

The involvement of former inpatients

(7a) How much value can you
see to yourself having access
to opinions of former inpatients?
Rate out of 10 (0 – nil, 10 – a great deal)

No. of responses

(0 – nil, 10 – a great deal)

Source:
Wadsworth and Epstein 2001
The Essential U&I

From Staff Input Survey, see pp 55–57

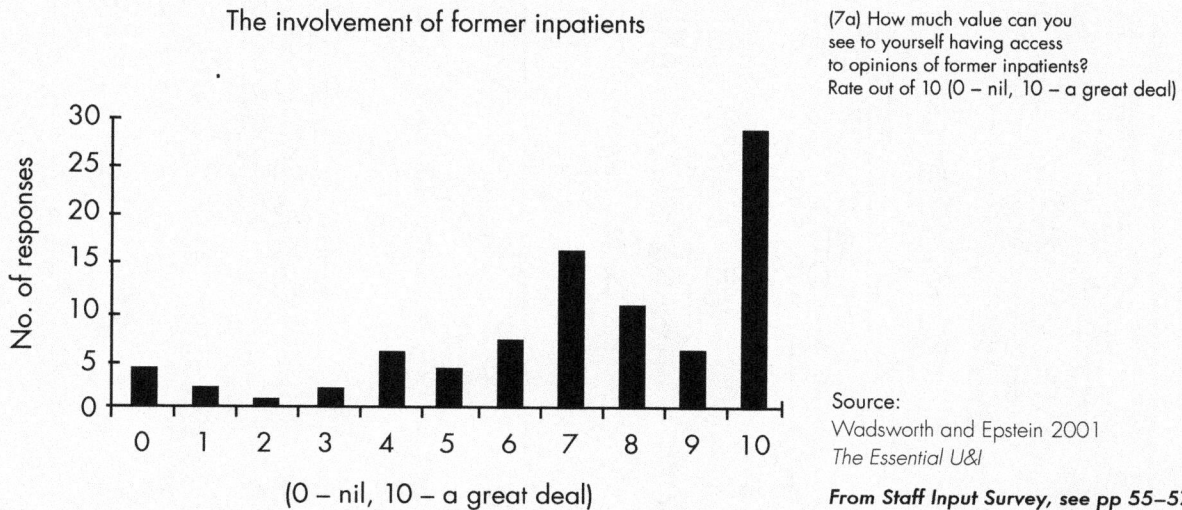

Figure 15. A method for asking the hard questions (survey)

us that yes there were many staff who couldn't see much value or even any need for this—but that there were unexpectedly substantial numbers of staff who did.

This standard confidential staff input survey did a good job of addressing the silence encountered on the wards. It not only engendered a high, 50 per cent response rate (107 of the total 209 staff working over a four-week roster period), but staff volunteered an astounding 1400 questions they wanted to ask of consumers (Wadsworth with Epstein 2001: 54–58).

Yet these methods only took us so far by seeking one-way feedback of observations (e.g. by end-of-stay reviews, suggestion boxes, complaints procedures and spot surveys using interviews, or even discussion groups). Such standard

consultation methods also often left staff anonymous and thus potentially unclear and left second-guessing consumers about what would be best or of priority for them to do. And it also left consumers having to wait for staff to 'do something'. There was no way for staff and consumers to exchange views about the feedback.

So we utilised more interactional methods that allowed two-way discussion and reflection on the meaning and implications of the feedback (e.g. rejuvenated community ward meetings, active involvement in treatment plans, more sensitive interpersonal conversational exchange and use of non-iatrogenic language). These took people together in dialogue further around the cycle all the way to trying out new

actions. More innovative methods and techniques that did this better job of 'getting at' new meanings of people's experiences and practices included: structured dialogue with transcribed conversations (that could be studied for better reflection); consumers as quality improvement consultants; narrative, poetry and cartoons. Here is one such 'research report' on a staff–consumer collaborative dialogue project to analyse, re-frame and re-interpret language at Figure 16.

Looking back on this three-year experience, we probably crossed *Phase change 1* early in the process when the Director of Nursing Services quietly called in her deputy as a witness to a meeting with us in which incidents of violence were frankly conceded, including

Figure 16. A method for tor reporting results (narrative illustration)

those directed by staff at inpatients. And we intuited we were crossing *Phase change 2* nearly three years later when the sixteen senior managers of the hospital and state government department all signed off on a letter of support for the pilot trial of the model of resourcing (which included the historic appointment of consumers as staff to aid communication between staff and consumers about consumers' evaluative input into quality improvement). We probably knew we'd crossed it to a point of no return when we were asked to draft the position description for staff–consumer consultants using the government department's pro forma.

Nevertheless this was challenging 'deep end' work, familiar to anyone working with highly hurt groups who are experiencing systemic exclusion, injustice and diminishment, and who are trying to build bridges to create spaces to bring change to the damaging practices. Indeed one sad day, after nearly a decade of 'the dance of co-inquiry', new grafts onto the mental health system organism appeared to grow hydra-headed and mistook its own staff–consumer collaborative research for 'the enemy', and chewed it off and spat it out. Fortunately not before the work had changed the greater health services creature to a significant extent—advanced an innovative dialogic approach to consumer engagement, created a whole new role in the mental health

system—that of staff–consumer consultant—to sustain this dialogue; empowered a legion of consumers and many professional staff to persevere with institution-alising participatory feedback processes; contributed to new government policy on consumer participation; won two national awards; and inspired many other human and community services to employ consumers or community members as facilitators of feedback from consumers and community members and of discussion between staff and consumers/ community about that precious feedback and what its implications might be. However we had also come to see defensive reasoning as the way the system created structures to contain its own fears and anxieties (Menzies 1970)—including, in the end, to seal itself off from the challenges offered by the U&I insights. The next chapter takes up this paradox.

Yet during the peak years of the U&I project's success, staff and consumers alike became more fully alive and hopeful. Even more interesting, we noticed that as we conducted our research in a psychiatric hospital in which service users were employed as competent and insightful research consultants, many of those same consumers were reporting going long periods without an acute admission themselves. And staff who were despairing of ever 'changing the system' were finding themselves drawn to the research's optimistic and

energetic research group meetings and office in which truths were welcome and new insights honoured.

In deeper engagement with each other, although with some significant exceptions, the confining boundaries began to dissolve that had created one category: of patients and consumers, as incompetent and unable—and thus restrained from showing strength or self-managing their own change and recovery—and another category: of staff, as wholly competent and able—and thus unable to experience inability or make errors from which they too could autopoetically recover.

What we had begun to realise was that the U&I project was in practice *prefiguring* what staff and consumers might do together in the real life of hospital practice—that is, 'come to the table' to inquire together, share their perceptions, experiences and evidence of what each had observed, and slowly come to deeper understandings and reach new insights with implications for better practice.

Interestingly our research and evaluation had itself begun to become more like a healthy healing 'human service' at the same time as staff members' 'service delivery' and consumers' 'service receiving' had also started to become more like co-inquiry.

ENDNOTES

1   I am using the word 'inquiry' to refer generically to all the many processes of living systems' 'research, evaluation and continuous improvement'—a word which, at its base, means 'to seek' ('inquiry' from the Latin in, meaning 'before', and *quarere*, 'to seek', with 'seek' from the Late Latin *circare* meaning 'go around' cf. re-search as 'go around again'). I am choosing *inquire* (rather than *enquire* with its less formal meaning of 'information seeking'), given my purpose of conceptually and practically bringing together both the informal and the more formal (e.g. small 'r' research and 'capital 'R' research) into a new unity of aware practice, research and theory (exemplified in Chapter 5). This is critical to what I mean by 'building in' more consciously integrated living systems of 'distributed intelligence' that are informed, forming, formalising *and* re-forming. That is, I don't think we are going to overcome some of the current distinctions and 'disconnects' that are diminishing global human life without integrating more strongly shared 'forms' to hold and maintain the participation of all, 'right around the cycle'. Fritjof Capra refers to what the mind does as 'inquiry' and as 'immanent in matter (1996: 172), and in this way goes beyond more narrow definitions of 'the brain' or 'cognition' as a centre of 'rational logic' alone, to include all forms of human intelligence or 'inquiry capability' for an integrated 'whole systems intelligence'. Peter Reason and Hilary Bradbury describe this elegantly in their introductory chapter 'Inquiry and Participation in Search of a World Worthy of Human Aspiration' (2001: 11–14).

2   A *circle* illustrates the similarity of the repeated epistemological processes, while a *spiral* shows how the 'ends' of one cycle differ in 'distance' and content from the 'beginnings' of the next (to an extent dependent on the degree of change achieved).

3   This is another way of thinking in search of new words to describe it! For the time being I have settled on 'seek' and 'search' from the same derivation as 'circum'—from the Late Latin *circare*, meaning 'go around'. 'Searching' ('looking for thoroughly') seems apt given that 'inquiry' comes from the Latin for 'seek'. I am using inquiry as 'looking for something' by 'searching around' a mental 'cycle' of moments or 'stations' (which is a usage in some ways not unlike 'the stations of the cross' of the Catholic religion except these traditionally traverse only half of the full cycle of inquiring from evaluative judgement to death, or the scriptural stations which describe from fruition to death, or Protestant reformist and recent Roman Catholic influences describe further round the cycle to resurrection to new form/life.

I considered 'circumverse' (from the Latin *circum*, 'round about' and *vers*, 'turn'), and 'circumcircle', 'circum-volution' and 'curcumsearch' (the latter of which would be

to 'go around' twice—which does capture something of the repeated cyclic nature of the circling–cycling). However I have stayed with the more familiar 'seek' or 'search', related to inquiry or inquiring, and in the diagrammatic form I rely also on the arrows to indicate the iterative dynamic of searching or 'inquiring around the cycle'.

4   It is worth clarifying that all references to human 'individuals' in this book are always understood to be about social beings, that is living organisms ongoingly shaped by (and shaping) social and all other relational contexts throughout life.

5   It is significant we refer to some kinds of replication as 'mindless' or robotic (like a machine), where the implication is that life is no longer being served. However when replication is mindful it can also be checking that the form remains life-serving. Life-serving forms may thus continue to be maintained for extraordinarily long times.

6   An 'expert' is someone who has 'tried things out' a lot—given them a go, and is thus deemed especially experienced. But anyone's experience has always and inevitably been both to some extent different and to some extent similar to anyone else's. We look to experience (and experts) when we lack it ourselves. But we always have it ourselves as well—in fact only we have it in our own actual lifefield: the real-life conditions of our own particular 'experimental conditions'. So we can be in a position to make judgements about others' expertise on the basis of our own. A 'laboratory' experiment (from the same derivation as 'labour' and 'laborious') is 'trying out' something in a special place away from (usually trying to reduce) the complexity of 'real life', to see if factors can be isolated as 'causative'. This can work well with simple situations, e.g. chemical compounds where adding one may not mean all the rest respond and organise their behaviour differently in unexpected ways as a result of feedback. Experimenting in real life systems (where complexity is a condition for the life of the whole) can however be difficult, as trying to separate out factors can alter or eliminate 'the whole' being observed. Indeed we may not want to eliminate that complexity for the sake of the experiment—as the 'cause', once restored to complex life conditions, may not act in the same way. The concept of complex causality becomes important where 'causes' not only can 'cause' other 'effects' but also can cause effects to the original causes and re-cause effects to themselves or other effects in unpredictable ways. Even if everything can be analysed separately—broken down into constituent parts—how exactly do they work together to be effectively alive? Rather than 'delivering a package' of a list of constituent elements, it may be more like learning to 'work with the growing points' in an existing 'relational systemicity' that is continuously 'putting itself together' in relation to other

organism-systems 'putting themselves together'. Our best warrant for knowing 'what caused what' becomes observing and understanding all the rich systemic relationalities 'up close and personal', rather than trying to see them in the first place from a more abstracting distance.

7   Observing discrepancies, questioning what is going on, working out what would be preferable, trying out new ideas in practice, checking, refining or revising them until the situation is right, and so on.

8   A popular saying at the time was, 'If you are up to your arse in alligators, it's hard to remember you came in to clear the swamp'.

9   For example, 'the community movements' (such as in health and welfare) were all trying to deal with the consequences of the absence of community and individual empowerment. After so many services had given up on these efforts and reverted to individual professional casework or treatment approaches, the problems (manifesting now as youth suicide, middle-age unemployment, child bullying and so on) remained. Later there was yet another upsurge of interest in what was originally called 'community develop-ment' but subsequently also termed 'community capacity building', and empowerment (now termed 'personal mastery', 'self-esteem' or 'resilience'), and social solidarity (now 'social capital', 'group identity' or 'connectedness').

10 The use of these four metaphors—'the mirror, the magnifying glass, the compass and the map'—are explicated in the chapter on facilitation in Peter Reason and Hilary Bradbury's *Handbook of Action Research* (Wadsworth 2001).

11 A researcher called Elton Mayo working in Chicago at the Western Electric company from 1927 to 1932 noticed that if research 'subjects' at the company's Hawthorne factory knew they were being researched they altered their ways of acting. For a long time it was incorrectly believed that this was due to the effects of being observed. The effect, however, was in practice due to the workers collaborating together to improve what they were doing (Kiviat 2007). Action researchers intentionally build their inquiry processes around this phenomenon which we now understand to be a cybernetic feedback phenomenon—a critical property of all living systems. Ironically Elton Mayo and all other traditional researchers eventually often intend the same (feedback of their findings into the system)—but circuitously (via other parties, managers or remotely available published literature), often resulting in something of an inefficient giant game of Chinese whispers. Action research is happy to hasten the feedback for the purposes of system members more quickly and directly achieving their shared purposes.

12 These kinds of insights later formed the basis for national guidelines for consumer participation in health research funded by the Australian National Health and Medical Research Council.

13 While some of these larger, more participative and applied action-oriented studies were early examples of what I would now call 'whole systems' research, one difference from those conducted nowadays would be that the older studies did not include as participating stakeholders the research commissioners, managers, funders and policy makers. Neither our nor their definitions of 'subjects' extended to include such an idea at that time, even though they were occupying contexts that were very much part of the research field. Thus most of the informal material about their views went unrecorded in fieldnotes and reports. In later work research designs became much more explicitly inclusive and dialogic in relation to all relevant participants, stakeholders and partners—terms that quickly superseded 'subjects' as the boundaries between researchers and researched were re-drawn to encompass the fuller field of inquiry, once the implications of not doing so were understood.

14 See Wadsworth (1998) for an account of moving from researcher as 'messenger' to 'go between' to 'dinner party hostess/caterer'.

15 For example, the dramatic increase in secrecy in recent years in the name of certain actions being 'commercial-in-confidence' has meant that, with few exceptions (such as the formal studies legally mandated to be published by the Victorian Auditor-General in Australia, and the release of some executive summaries), neither the participants/respondents are able now to be kept fully in the loop, nor does the public have much idea of what has been done or found out. Often even when a project is stipulated as 'action research', a quite contradictory 'independent' (that is, systemically not connected) externally conducted, pre-test post-test audit evaluation will be 'added on'; or strict conditions attached to the contract to prevent circulation or publication of findings to the participants/respondents in the name commercial in confidence—a policy meant to improve exchange (in a 'market') for consumers, not deplete it. These arrangements introduce a number of 'disconnects' that mean loss of much systemic intelligence.

16 The cycle I am using in this book differs in appearance, but not conceptual content or sequence, to that in the previous books in this series, *Do It Yourself Social Research* or *Everyday Evaluation on the Run*. (It is valuable to remain flexible about the forms of the cycle! This helps us remember that a theoretical device is created in *our* minds, and is a constructed compass and mirror, even as it seems to be a magnifying glass and map of our 'realities'.) In this book I rotate (reverse) the content of the cycle 180 degrees to illuminate how change may be thought of as 'moving forward' (psychologically from left to right) and, once implemented (from right to left), it is in a sense then 'being conserved' as a result of what is now 'previous' inquiry, taking its place in an 'already-past'. Implementation and reproduction rest on attending to integrating the new with

the existing and past forms and then to 'holding' that new 'form'—stabilising and conserving it as 'how we (or I) do things round here', now as convention, program, culture or tradition. Continual and continuous change, on the other hand, requires always having the spaces and places to 'break away' and 'go ahead' to attend to 'the possible new'. James Lovelock's Foreword in Sahtouris (1999) clarifies this point further.

17 Some would see human-made mental architecture as 'purely socially learned and entirely culturally relative and flexible'; while others would think of it as 'behaviourally transmitted in neuro-chemistry', or as 'biologically-structured experience visible on brain scans', or as 'prefigured in innate makeup to be found in determinist gene sequencing'; while others still may see culture as embodied through 'nurture switching on nature', with 'genes as the adaptive sensitive servants of experience' (Ridley 2003), or that social communication and what we call learning are 'creating larger neural networks' that enable the greater 'reach' of capabilities to inquire and conclude and re-inquire, with reflexivity being theorised as 'neuroplasticity'.

The 'mental architecture' I propose can be understood as capable of generating all these ways of seeing: literally, figuratively and metaphorically in their own diverse terms. That is, all these different 'ways of knowing' may be seen as our species' differing 'embodied epistemologies' for how we inquire to ensure life. I particularly see connections between these and the differing capabilities exercised around the inquiry cycle that I explicate in the remainder of this chapter, and in Chapter 4 and Appendix 3. The critical point to maintaining whole living systemicity for me now is that all kinds of inquiring need to remain in dialogue *together* to resource autopoetic life within the individual (in a kind of 'voice dialogue') and within and between all social systemicities (a kind of multilogue) at any scale.

I think of these differing inquiry preferences themselves as heuristic metaphor, somewhat like the 'hardware' and 'software' on a computer. Our biological hardware—whether genetic or socially acquired or both—can enable and constrain our overall activity. However what we create with that hardware once we lay down various kinds of 'software inquiry capabilities' and content is infinite in its differential response to input, as well as emergent. For example, a spreadsheet/grid matrix package enables the receipt and expression of characteristically different forms of input or experiences than does a dot point or graphics presentation software package, which will zzzcharacteristically differ again from what is possible with a concept mapping package. But what users of each of these programs *do* with their different software will be as rich and infinitely complexly different as all the expressions of human experience possible throughout history and the life of our species. If we use a full cycle sequence of questions as described in this chapter we will produce *systemically* something very different from what we will generate if we only ever ask *some* kinds of questions and not others, just as if we operate systemically from some questions or inquiry preferences and not others we will generate typically different systemic realities. Hofstede articulates this in the context of understanding cultures of organisational life in his *Cultures and Organisations: Software of the Mind* (1991).

18 And, just as we are 'knowing human systemicities' making our way in relation to ourselves and each other, so also we are part of the greater autopoetic 'ground of being' that includes all other 'knowing living being systemicities' that make all of life possible.

19 **IP statement**—this sequence of questions was originally structured by the content of ©Fran Peavey's 'Strategic Questioning' (1994: 93–98). See also: ©Fran Peavey (2010) Strategic Questioning: An Experiment in Communication of the 2nd kind, http://www.thechangeagency.org/_dbase_upl/strat_questioning_man.pdf.
This version is based on 'Questions for Living Systems', ©Yoland Wadsworth in association with Fran Peavey 2005. Note: I have retained the ten sets of questions although I have them slightly differently configured to relate to the eight-fold four-quadrant familiar characterisation of the action research *plan–act–observe–reflect* cycle. I overlap the 'beginning and end' in 'act' to absorb the ten.

20 The additions, changes and modifications I have made to Fran's schema make some connections to other bodies of practice/theory. For example, the SWOT (Strengths, Weaknesses, Opportunities and Threats) analysis from the business world can be situated in Fran's 'consequences-considering' moment. My retrospective open inquiry and audit review evaluation questions (Wadsworth 1997b) feature primarily during Action and Observation before *Phase change 1*, and my prospective questions belong to the Reflection and Planning before *Phase change 2*. I have altered Fran's more static hierarchy of 'levels' to a more dynamic 'joined up' cycle of 'phases' because, while more profound systemic change does feel 'bigger picture' (and it is tempting to see it as 'high up' and superior), I think in complex systems it is more a matter of achieving holarchic conceptual distance—that is, an ability to step back and see ever wider arcs of connectedness—but remaining integral within a continuously self organ-ising whole, interdependent with all sharing the experience of having successfully navigated through all other phases (to gather what all are offering). The DNA spiral might suggest a way that Fran's 'levels' could describe the cycle idea, although there is still a temptation to see it as spiralling up for success and down for failure! I think of it more like a bicycle wheel: rolling along, even though the anti-clockwise movement makes it roll 'backwards to the future'. Yet this seems to me to be exactly how it feels when

trying to move *forwards* to work on change against a backwards-pulling 'draft' or as Australians might know it from our beaches, a tidal 'rip'. It certainly feels tricky to try and move forward towards genuine change without succumbing either to the backward pull into the mainstream of 'what is'—or, having crossed Phase change 1, to an embodied experience more like being 'centrifuged to the borderlands' when one detects the need to be 'outside' the mainstream in order to generate and hold a new imagined 'what could be instead'. See for a moving graphic of the DNA double helix—a way of illustrating my choice about this—http://upload.wikimedia.org/wikipedia/commons/8/81/ADN_animation.gif.

I also identify rational 'feeling' questions as belonging to Fran's Level 2 in that they not only yield a form of Level 1 descriptive observation, but commence the process of evaluative judgement (between the past and a possible future). When the discrepancy between an 'is' and an 'ought' is stored in the body as rational feeling this may be accessed via questions which surface and articulate emotion (initially often non-verbally, calling for a range of research techniques and methods such as art, music, drama etc.) When discrepancies are stored cognitively, e.g. as logically violated principles, these may better be accessed by thinking-reasoning questions. In a way the rational 'thinking' questions may be thought of as belonging at my second phase change between imagined possible futures and an actualised (new) future that is being championed and implemented (trialled)—a move from Fran's Level 2 to a *new* Level 1. At this point we are thinking through the consequences of different courses of action with questions that surface and articulate logical consequences.

I have also added to Fran's formulation a section on 'implementation-monitoring' with its own evaluation questions to take the sequence 'full cycle' back to the starting point of 'scanning-observing' (the new) current action.

21 In the 1990s, in one of those global email epidemics that make theories of mimetic replication indeed seem viral, an apocryphal story, originating in a petroleum company that was using organisational learning processes, circulated about how chimpanzees could be culturally stopped from climbing a ladder to get a banana. The means had been to hose the first who tried with a jet of cold water, and then all the others acted to constrain any new attempt, even as each original direct witness of the cold hosing was replaced by one who had not actually ever seen what the source of the fear was. The punchline in answer to the question 'How could this all be sustained' was 'Because that's the way things are round here'. George Orwell's *1984* described a powerful version of maintaining 'how things are' by means of manufactured crises and anxiety, manufactured 'successes' over them and pleasurable relief, combined with the threat of unspeakably fearful perpetration if questions were asked or alternative realities imagined.

22 There are many other key 'phase change' moments of course—but these two are key to the organism firstly altering its form, and then that new form 'taking' as viable and holding its shape or pattern.

23 I have based this on an unsourced reading close to that of Ursula Le Guin's translation, with J.P. Seaton, of *Lao Tzu Tao Te Ching—A Book about the Way and the Power of the Way* (1997: 47).

24 The following ten sets of questions chart around the four quadrants of the living systems inquiry cycle. Each appears in a numbered section that includes some introductory text, several poetic house metaphors, and two lists, one of relevant questions and one of methods and techniques that roughly correspond to that process moment (or standpoint) around the cycle. Some methods may be used to traverse much or even all of the whole cycle, but a research or evaluation design may need to utilise a number of methods to address each part of the cycle, possibly (bit not necessarily) in logical sequence.

Indeed an understanding of the full retroductive–inductive–abductive–deductive cycle would lead to a different approach to many methods as currently practised. For example a standard survey that asks questions about 'how things are now' (*observe*) could also include questions about 'what would be preferred instead and why' (*reflect*), and even include a voluntary contact details page or tear-off invitation so the person could join an inquiry group if they wanted to collaborate on the inquiry themselves (*plan* and *act*). This cyclic formulation has the potential in this way to integrate the hitherto competing quantitative and qualitative methodologies that did battle in the 'great paradigm wars' of the 1970s (Wadsworth 2005).

A good way of integrating them is by use of a consistent 'full cycle' design articulated (possibly as narrative) and managed by the inquiry group.

It is beyond the scope of this book to analyse each method and technique in more detail for their contribution, but it will usually not work for them to be 'wheeled in and out' in isolation from the rest of the inquiry design and processes being used by the inquiry group or individual. Otherwise, for example, constructing a *scenario* at the *planning* stage without prior detailed 'up close and personal' knowledge from the *observation* stage, and having interpreted its meaning and identified a new theories, logics and narratives at the *reflection* stage, will render it potentially meaningless and at worse destructive if taken straight into new *action*.

25 'Observe' from the Latin *ob,* 'before', *servare*, 'keep' meaning 'watch' (perceive, note, become conscious of; watch carefully).

26 *Inquiry preferences* Note: questions 1 and 2 of a new cycle overlap with questions 9 and 10 from the previous cycle. This *observation-of-action* quadrant centres on the perceiving capabilities of empirical knowing or sensing. It reaches back round the cycle into rational thinking and

forward round the cycle into rational feeling, both of which are concluding-and-decision-making capabilities. This is not of course concept or theory-free sensing of reality (as we inevitably experience the world through the 'software' of all previous stored sense-making of experience, providing the preconceived beliefs, ideas, theories and values through which our minds receive new input, and the 'hardware' of our minds' complex 'mapping' apparatus that 'holds' or mirrors the systemic interactions we have with the world). When we experience the world through our senses of sight, hearing, touch, taste and smell, these critical human inquiry capabilities are either making sense through reference to this past stored 'material' (as knowledge) or registering something 'new' about this data of which sense is yet to be made. For about two-fifths of the population, this particular capability for receiving and processing information about the world is the most familiar part of the cycle. Yet while this approximately 38 per cent (all statistics from Myers et al. 1998) have this as their most primary and immediately used capability, the great majority has access to it (approximately 85 per cent) as a dominant, auxiliary or tertiary capability. Only approximately 15 per cent of the population has this as an unfavoured or under-used capability (freeing them characteristically or in an emergency to use their intuition to focus on the bigger picture and see the connections and patterns between things rather than the individual things themselves). Nevertheless to the extent we all have our senses more-or-less 'switched on' for most of our (particularly waking) hours, it is perhaps the most constantly accessed and accessible inquiry capability for virtually all people.

The quadrant traverses the cycle from sensing-thinking about 'the already-known-and-decided' to sensing-feeling and feeling-sensing, the initial judging of whether things are 'going well or not going well'. In terms of the focus of 'reach' described in Appendix 3, this quadrant reaches back to overlap with ISTP and ESTJ inquiry preferences for sensing-thinking-in-action, and traverses through ISTJ and ESTP acting-observing (dynamic energy constellations of primary reality sensing, existing-logic thinking, yielding to new feeling), to ISFJ and ESFP inquiry preferences for observing–doing–acting (dynamic energy constellations of primary reality sensing, new feeling, yielding from old thinking).

In terms of associated methodologies/epistemologies, this quadrant is most often characterised by use of: logical empiricism, realist objectivism, experiment (including randomised control trials), surveys, quantitative and descriptive statistics, participant observation, audit and retroductive evaluation, experiential-qualitative case studies and narrative.

In terms of other metaphors of integrality (e.g. temporal, seasonal, cardinal, elemental, colour), this quadrant traverses midday to evening, summer growth to autumn harvest (during which dynamic built structures grow to maturity, fruition and begin their decline); west to south, fire to metal and yellow to orange.

27 St Luke's Innovative Resources are an internationally known producer of creative strengths-based techniques for self- and self-in-group knowledge. They are widely used in child and family services, social work, family therapy and school education contexts. Access the resources online, http://www.innovativeresources.org/

28 Later after expiration, when we've 'filled our lungs' with new inspiration, conclusions, intentions, ideas and plans, we pause again as the subtle shift takes place from 'breathing in' the new, to beginning to push the breath out: breathing life into the new form, with the energetic certainty of new knowing and deciding, until later again, we become 'spent', and it's time to yield, pause, and receive breath in again.

29 As the second wave feminist Betty Friedan famously called post-Second World War women's experience of felt emptiness, diminishment and radical separation from the worlds of adults, men, education and paid work in *The Feminine Mystique* (1963: 11).

30 Ron LaBonte has a 'story dialogue' method (1997) that he developed in health development that asks *What?* (description), *Why?* (explanation), *So what?* (synthesis in relation to values) and *'Now what?'* (action)—the last of which fits in the visioning phase described further round the cycle below.

31 …or not (as the case may be). Fear of the dark and the unknown has sent many on the threshold of the journey of deeper reflection back to the light of the tried and true—or to keep looking under the lamp post for the lost key because that's where the light is best. Crossing this threshold is an easier task when the scale and reach is small (e.g. a social worker 'thinks outside the square' to come up with a more engaging activity for homeless men in poverty). A greater challenge comes when the scale and reach is large (e.g. a social worker asks why is there poverty and what could be done about it). Many who studied after the Second World War saw how authoritarian totalitarianism got such a grip on 'the square' of mechanically replicated action by prohibiting the raising of questions to inquire into the conditions for change—typically associated with systemic reaction, defensive controls and exclusion of those who imagined things being different (see, e.g. the political philosopher Hannah Arendt's 'conscious pariahs' or 'history's outsiders', in Ring 1991: 433). It can indeed be a solemn point on the cycle, but fortunately there are many for whom this is their strongest area of inquiry 'reach' (see Appendix 3). Indeed this is increasingly a time that is built in to organisations, which are becoming wise to their need for cycles of improvement and the inevitability and necessity of change, just as it is becoming routine for individuals to regularly ask 'What am I doing?' and 'Is it what I really most value?'

32 It is interesting that we turn to 'focus' groups for what the quantitative data cannot tell us, as the word 'focus' comes from the Latin for 'hearth'. Focus groups have traditionally been styled on the archetype of the free-flowing dinner table conversation. 'Coming to the table' is a powerful metaphor for what takes place in this quadrant where, in living systems terms, the task is to find, spark or generate the seed of a new form from finding a new set of relationships which bring new clarity and unity, and from which more healthy order and organ-ising can develop. At this stage dialogue at that table is a conversation 'with a centre, rather than sides' (Isaacs 1999).

33 Jacques Boulet was the first I heard articulate this insight: that values are most often *imaged* rather than initially described in words; that is, they are, in the first place, detailed, valorised, felt or as we might put it now, embodied experiences.

34 Key signs of dynamic life as emotion include anger, fear, sadness, happiness and disgust. Note how the absence of being able to feel or show these is often referred to as being robotic or having a mechanical appearance, i.e. one without much life. Later we'll see how 'having a cool head' is a point in the cycle where—having honoured emotion and its messages—we can think clearly about what is the rationally right or logical thing to do when considering options for new action. But at this point in the cycle it is the time for the rationality of feeling. The time to lay down a strong basis for *which* logic to choose.

35 'Reflect' from the Latin *re*, 'again' and *reflectere*, flex, 'bend', meaning 'meditate on, think about, consider, remind oneself'.

36 *Inquiry preferences* This observing part of the *reflection* quadrant centres on experiential *feeling* and reaches back around the cycle to empirical sensing *observation* and forward around the cycle to intuition. Our first reflections may take place wordlessly in an embodied and intensely personal way as we begin to register the observations of our 'realities' as experiences and start to articulate what we feel and why. When we begin to bring reflective judgement to bear on our perceptions and experiences we are comparing the apparent facts of observation and experience with valued states or valorised images we have stored. In doing so we are in touch with our metaphoric 'life-detecting compasses' for knowing what is good or bad or right or wrong for us. For just under one-third of the population (statistics here and following from Myers et al. 1998), this particular capability for using rational feeling to make judgements about the value of experience is the most familiar and immediately used part of the cycle. However the great majority of people do have access to this basis for judgement (approximately 81 per cent as a dominant, auxiliary or tertiary preference). Less than one-fifth of the population (approximately 19 per cent) has this as an under-used or unfavoured capability (freeing them up characteristically or in an emergency to use rational logical

thinking to calculate the consequences of one course of action rather than another).

The quadrant traverses the cycle from observing to feeling (the initial judging of things 'going well and not going well') to intuition. In terms of the focus of 'reach' explored in Appendix 3, it traverses from ISFP and ESFJ inquiry preferences for observing-feeling in action (dynamic energy constellations of primary rational feeling, sensing-observing intuitive reflection) to INFP and ENFJ inquiry preferences for feeling-based observation for intuitive reflection (dynamic energy constellations of primary rational feeling, and sensing intuition).

What I am identifying as *Phase change 1* takes place in the middle of this quadrant as a threshold is crossed when feeling judgement peaks (between sensing-feeling the discrepant nature of 'what is', and intuitive-feeling towards 'what could be' better). It also marks a shift in perception from the old to the 'possible new'—signalling a new phase of necessary radicalism (from the Latin *radicis*, going to 'the root') to uncover the sources of complex causation and alter this systemic patterning.

In terms of associated methodologies/epistemologies, this quadrant is often characterised by use of in-depth symbolic interactionism; qualitative, constructionist, subjectivist–relativist perspectives; cultural analysis; participatory research; critical appreciative inquiry; empowerment; and 4th generation evaluation

In terms of other metaphors of integrality (temporal, seasonal, cardinal, elemental, colour), this quadrant traverses evening to midnight; autumn harvest to winter rest (during which built structures have dissipated and the new is being composted and incarnated deep in the earth); south to east, metal to water, and red to purple.

37 I thank Alan Saunders' *By Design*, ABC Radio National, featuring a BBC program, 11 October 2008, for clarification of this insight. Ikea, the Swedish home furnishings retailer, is an example of a company that believes in the possibility of mass replication of good design without loss of aesthetic integrity, in part I think because the reach of its design inquiry traverses from intuitive thinking around into the sensing-felt natural world—a significant 'warmth' component of the success of Scandinavian design.

38 At the recent Australian parliament 2020 National Forum (at which a number of living systems methods were used, including World Café and Open Space Technology), the Australian prime minister said he 'just wanted good ideas and didn't care where the ideas came from'. In terms of living systems theory, however, it matters enormously where the ideas came from, and particularly from whom. If they are to have the best chance of 'taking', they need to have already been thought through and tested in practice and accompanied by an inquiry group that ideally has worked with a wider engaged network of all relevant

stakeholders, if the ideas are to have a chance of traversing *Phase change 2* into implementation in new practice. Indeed further round the cycle, when (and if) the people's vision derived from their prior collective inquiry is enacted in new practice, Proverbs 29:18 further notes that, 'he that keepeth the law, happy is he' (until evaluation indicates change is needed of course!)

39 *Inquiry preferences* This planning part of the reflection quadrant centres on intuition. When we experience the world through a 'sixth sense' we are moving from seeing the 'packets' of separate proximal sensing 'factual data' to seeing or grasping meaningful more distal connections between them, 'seeing' the bigger picture and the implications and consequences that come from realising or assigning and understanding meaning and 'getting' the 'identity' of things. We speak of 'flashes' of insight and intuition where things that appeared to be one thing turn out 'really' to be something else in terms of these connections that can be made. This critical human inquiry capability is building on past stored observations (tacit knowledge) and the evidence of the senses, how the facts appeared, but making crucial leaps of experiential realisation that alters the original apparent meaning/s. For about 15 per cent of the population (this and the following statistics from Myers et al. 1998), this is the most familiar and immediately used capability for receiving and understanding information about the world, but a majority of people are able to draw on this as a preference (approximately 62 per cent of people have primary, secondary or tertiary 'reach' to intuition). Just under two-fifths of the population (approximately 38 per cent) has this as an under-used or unfavoured capability (to free them up characteristically or in an emergency to use their sensing to focus on the details of the actual things—to see the dots rather than the lines of possible connections).

The quadrant traverses the cycle from intuitive-feeling reflection about the difference between what is and what should be, to intuitive-thinking reflection on what should be tried as the new 'what is'. In terms of the focus of 'reach' in Appendix 3, this quadrant traverses from ENFP-INFJ dynamic energy constellation inquiry preferences of feeling-intuition (dynamic energy constellations of primary intuition, incorporating feeling, new thinking) to INTJ-ENTP inquiry preferences for intuitive thinking (dynamic energy constellations of primary intuition, new thinking, incorporating feeling).

In terms of associated methodologies/epistemologies, this quadrant is often characterised by use of inductive and abductive theory building; interpretivism; Verstehen; critical theory; constructivism; relativism; communicative action; idealism; feminist, humanist, anti-colonialist and integral methodologies; and developmental, prospective and utilisation evaluation.

In terms of other metaphors of integrality (temporal, seasonal, cardinal, elemental, colour), this quadrant

traverses from midnight to early morning; winter to spring (during which time 'new forms' incarnate in the rain-softened earth and take root); east to north, water to wood, and blue to turquoise.

40 It is interesting to contrast a labyrinth in this *reflection* part of the inquiry cycle with a maze that belongs to the *plan–act* quadrant (with its pre-ordained right and wrong pathways, where dead-ends lead to confusion and anxiety). Logical rational analytical calculation aids finding the pre-ordained one best path through a maze, where the idea is to complete the action, while 'grasping the whole' and 'making the pathway by walking it' characterise the breakthroughs to new understandings and the confidence, questioning and risk-taking needed to traverse this labyrinth-like quadrant.

41 Contemporary laboratory-based imaging of this moment of innovative thought is quite evocative— showing electrical charges leaping chasms within the brain's neural network, visibly forging new pathways, synapses and 'structures'. Some community workers and organisational developers understand the metaphors of 'rich fields of diversity and relationality' as writ large in human interpersonal terms when 'things happen' to create new possibilities out of social fields of implicate intentional order. Some scientists (and human systems workers) find these transformative and generative moments hold mystery, even awe, invoking new naturalistic, secular or religious images of 'the hand (or mind) of God', the transpersonal, 'the divine' or, possibly even literally for physicists, of 'the light out of darkness'.

42 Some scientists dissociate themselves from the idea of shamanism in science altogether! (Robin Williams, 'Ockhams Razor', ABC Radio National, 18 January 2007). However the shamanic moment in the 'discovery' of DNA is described in detail by James Watson in *The Double Helix* (1968). He and Frances Crick's search was for a new form or pattern that would make better sense of the biochemical evidence for how 'life happens'. Seen initially as literal circles of dots by Rosalind Franklin (whose detailed x-ray photos provided the clue to an alternative pattern), the 'same facts' were then suddenly 'seen instead' as evidence of a three-dimensional *spiral* in an intuitive leap made by Crick, and validated by Watson's mathematical calculations. This was 'jumping to a conclusion' prior to the proofs and tests ('a structure this pretty just had to exist', Watson 1968: 161) and was inspired as much by thinking on the tennis courts and at the pub and between parties with 'pretty girls', sitting on buses, walking along the Cambridge backs, competing with another research laboratory, long uneventful periods, a particular constellation of people from a range of disciplines in the lab, and a capability for felt intuitive thinking, as it was grounded in the hard, disciplined work before and after of empirical observation and logical calculation in relation to the details of chemical structures, sequenced actions and known causation.

In practice all good science includes such moments of pure imaginative conjecture that arise from intentions and purposes plus observations but are essentially intuitive, ideational and constructed. In theorising about better human social life, these abductions are necessarily idealist. That is, at this point in knowledge construction the theorised relationships between ideas are constructed ideationally in the mind. Furthermore they are driven by purposes—whether of judgement stemming from feeling or calculation stemming from logical thinking. Systemically each will result in something different. To put the case bluntly, science without heartfelt imagination will systemically evolve mechanical knowledge. Or human scientists who proceed as if life is machine-like will systemically evolve machine-like worlds. This is arguably bad science if science (from the Latin *scientia*, 'to know') means being aware, informed and able to understand 'in order to'—since calculative knowledge on its own does not embody the answer to the question 'for whom or for what' regarding human value-driven intentions and purposes (a value freedom for which the dominant form of science has indeed itself long argued). A science without this might end up evolving a world that is good at calculating quantities and consequences but dying for want of ethical value-driven, life-enhancing purposeful action. The reverse holds true as well. A science that is full of heart, and intuitive and idealistic imagination will lead nowhere without carefully thought-through realistic plans and actions, even if the reference to these may seem as momentary as the reference to heartfelt principles may be in traditional laboratory science. We omit, or disdain, any step 'round the cycle' at risk to fully human inquiry for full living humanness.

43 *Inquiry preferences* This planning quadrant centres on rational logical *thinking* of the kind that can calculate 'if this, then that', and at a distance have a sense of observing the existing 'realities' ('structural realities' created by the repeated patterns of action and practice that have been understood 'up close and personal' in the earlier phases of inquiry). When we make judgements on the basis of thinking we may be setting aside for the moment what we think might be right and good (which we might nevertheless hold, particularly by now as 'touchstone', shorthand summaries of abstracted principles) and countenancing the logical possibilities given these 'realties'. We might then 'think through' and calculate the chances of valued and principled new ways of doing and being accepted and taking root for viability in future action. For about 20 per cent of the population (this and the following statistics is from Myers et al. 1998), this is the most familiar and immediately used capability for making judgements about the world, but nearly three-quarters of people (approximately 72 per cent) have this as a primary, secondary or tertiary capability. Less than one-third (approximately 28 per cent) have this as an under-used or

unfavoured capability, leaving them free or in an emergency to stay in touch with critical rational embodied feeling.
The quadrant traverses the cycle from thinking intuitively about what feels like 'a possible future' to thinking through a sense of 'how things will (or might) work or not'. In terms of the focus of 'reach' in Appendix 3, this quadrant traverses from INTP-ENTJ inquiry preferences for planning based on reflection (dynamic energy constellations of primary logical rational thinking, intuiting, and reality-sensing) to ISTP-ESTJ actions derived from planning (primary reality sensing, and acting pragmatically on big picture thinking).
What I am identifying as *Phase change 2* takes place in the middle of this quadrant as a threshold is crossed when thinking peaks (between intuitively-thinking 'what could be' and sensing-thinking about how to make it happen as the new 'what is'). It is also a change from the new to the 'new old'—signalling a new phase of 'being' and its conserving.
In terms of associated methodologies/epistemologies, this quadrant is often characterised by use of logical realism, historical materialism, philosophical positivism, critical realism, hypothetico-deductive and structuralist approaches, evaluation logframes and program theory.
In terms of other metaphors of integrality (temporal, seasonal, cardinal, elemental, colour), this quadrant traverses early morning to midday; spring new growth to summer peak production (during which 'new structures' are implemented, refined and repeated); north to west, wood to fire, and green to yellow.

44 *Inquiry preferences* Note: questions 9 and 10 of a new cycle overlap with questions 1 and 2 from the previous cycle. This put-plans-into-action quadrant centres on empirical knowing or sensing-thinking. It reaches back round the cycle into rational intuitive thinking and forward round the cycle to overlap with rational sensing-feeling. It focuses on acting on the basis of the knowledge previously generated by logical thinking and evidence, and overlaps the observe–act quadrant with which this questioning sequence began. When we are acting in the world according to the new logic and new sensing-observation we are generally head down and tail up, not paying so much attention to 'the bigger picture', and operating more on bigger picture, values-driven, policy-derived logical rules and procedures. For just under a third (approximately 30 per cent) of the population (Myers et al. 1998), this overlapping sensing-thinking constellation of action, stretching back to the new logical thinking and forward to observing action (where this question sequencing section began), is a primary capability for receiving new information about the world and acting on it. But to the extent we all have our senses more-or-less 'switched on' for most of our (particularly waking) hours, and when combined with thinking about things as 'we now usually do' as a primary or auxiliary capability, this characterises approximately 57.4 per cent of the population.

Here is the major source of replicative stability in life, while only 16.5 per cent are focusing on the 'opposite side of the cycle'—the intuitive–feeling dynamic change quadrant stretching between feeling and intuition, where intuition and feeling are primary capabilities (although the figure rises to 42.9 per cent when this includes these as a dominant or auxiliary capability of people). It perhaps seems clearer now why change is experienced as so difficult to achieve, and so well resisted and tested!—even to the detriment of our species' survival (e.g. when human-made environmental change is outstripping our adaptive responses and threatening to overwhelm us with unprecedented life-threatening change, while more immediate existing logics that seem to 'pay off' are much more effectively replicated, conserved and continued).

The quadrant traverses the cycle from thinking-sensing about 'the newly-known-and-decided' to sensing-thinking about the 'currently enacted-and-observed'. In terms of the concept of 'reach' in Appendix 3, it traverses from ISTP and ESTJ inquiry preferences for acting–observing (dynamic energy constellations of reality sensing, existing-logic thinking, moving from intuiting) and overlaps with ISTJ and ESTP inquiry preferences for sensing-thinking-in-action and observing-thinking-in-action (dynamic energy constellations of primary reality sensing, yielding from old thinking to new feeling).

In terms of associated methodologies/epistemologies, this quadrant is often characterised by use of logical empiricism, objectivist realism, randomised control trials, surveys, quantitative and descriptive statistical techniques, audit and retroductive evaluation.

In terms of other metaphors of integrality (temporal, seasonal, cardinal, elemental, colour), this quadrant traverses early morning to late afternoon, and early to late summer (during which 'built structures' grow to peak productivity and defended boundaries); from north-west to south-west, wood to metal, and lime-yellow to burnt orange.

45 'Act' from the Latin *agree*, 'do' (something done, a deed, an action; the process of doing something; to behave; perform actions or functions, operate; exert energy).

46 And, as it is stressed in Chapter 5, time for 'taking, making and building in' times, spaces and places for inquiry, just as this chapter has detailed the kinds of questions and methods that keep open the lines of life-giving inquiry in such times, spaces and places.

47 Appreciative Inquiry (AI) is a comparable inductive-abductive-deductive cyclic action research strategy that uses the same four-fold (four-dimensional or 4-D) questioning sequence: 1. What can you discover? (observe) 2. What can you dream? (reflect) 3. What can you design? (plan) 4. What can you deliver? (act) (Ludema et al. 2001).

48 The popular media has taken to asking people from different walks of life to respond to some stimulating and imaginative questions as a way to get unexpected insights, e.g. 'Who were you in a former life?', 'What was the best job you ever had?', 'When have you ever thought "I have never been happier?"', 'What keeps you awake at night?', 'Define creativity', 'Market or Mall (for shopping)?' etc. Although mostly these are questions about 'how things are' rather than about changes they might like to see or things they'd like to stay the same, they nevertheless indicate a more popular take up of 'the question' as a way of getting to know each other better. Popular lists of questions to ask one's doctor also sometimes traverse much of the cycle, e.g. 'What do you think I have got?' (identify the doctor's theory), 'What leads you to that conclusion?' (identify the doctor's 'program logic'), 'Why would I have it?' (seek the doctor's perception of the bigger picture), 'What can I do about it?' (test the doctor's change strategy), 'Are there any consequences of that course of action?', 'Are there alternatives?', 'What would be your recommendation?', 'How can I find out more?' Indeed the patient can then—having researched their adviser's knowledge base—ask the questions of themselves: 'What do I think I've got?', 'What led me to my conclusion?' etc. to identify any discrepancies with the doctor's narrative that either means a need to ask more questions or to enter into dialogue or to chart one's own way forward.

49 This is a biblical reference (Genesis 11:1–9) to the Israelite God's response to mankind setting out to build a tower to reach heaven and to make itself as God. The narrative of God's response recounts God's coming amongst the people to confuse their language, causing them to fall into greater confusion as they could no longer understand each other, and thwarting the arrogance of the project for humans to become God per se. (I thank the sociologist, researcher and Uniting Church minister John Bottomley for this explication.)

50 Indeed Isabel Myers and Katherine Briggs developed their indicator of personal preferences in the hope of helping people better know and understand themselves and others, as they observed that most human conflicts—including most significantly in the lead-up to world war—stemmed from misunderstandings of this nature.

More (truly) living human services

CHAPTER

4

In Chapter 2 it was concluded that the dynamic process by which all living organisms, individual and collective, self-organise involves them continuously seeking, finding, concluding and changing action. In this way they live adaptively and generatively through purposeful intentionality in response to the environmental discrepancies they detect between 'what is' and what could or should be.

In Chapter 3 it was concluded that these repeated cyclic sequences of inquiry by which we all do the seeking, finding, concluding and acting, are accomplished by the full range of ordinary human inquiry processes of noticing, observing, sense-making, feeling, reflecting, intuiting, envisioning, deciding, planning, thinking through and recursively taking new action to build and rebuild our practices, forms, patterns and 'structures' to achieve optimal life. I also noted how we have differing preferences from one another, and that this diversity can both enrich and sustain our collective inquiring particularly under conditions of crisis when we are not able to take the necessary time to be as autopoetic to scale as possible; but that that same stress can also lead to 'inquiry ethnocentrism' if we come to see our own inquiry preferences as superior.

What is at the heart of truly living human service systemicities?

In this chapter, I consider how health and human services[1] might also be thought of as organised processes and practices by which people arrange the resourcing of each other to inquire and co-inquire to achieve individual-within-mutual-systemic human life (social 'well fare'). In this way what is at the heart of any truly living human system may be thought of as the individual and collective 'resourcing of life'.

Everyone needs help from everyone.
BERTOLT BRECHT

In the larger systemic sense it has become clear from the previous chapters that this 'inquiry relationality' is how we 'go full cycle', and in practice, we are indeed *all* already doing this inquiring and co-inquiring for life—'clients' and 'professionals' alike—all of the time. Each critical inquirer is receiving and seeking inputs, information, 'nourishment' and 'fuel' through a range of resourcing relationships that are sought out to be as resonant and 'there for them' as possible in their lifetime of traversing a multitude of inquiring-

139

learning cycles. Peter Senge and his colleagues have, in recent years, called this 'presencing' (2004), and both Peter Reason (1994) and Kenneth Gergen (2009) have taken a systemic perspective beyond the individual and the group to an understanding of it as 'relationality' or 'co-operation' per se.

It is in the other's ability to listen, hear, co-observe, co-reflect and co-respond (from their own embodied store of images, observations, experiences, analyses, reflections, conclusions, knowledges and experiments in past practice, and various powers of material action) that lies potentially the capacity to resource the co-inquirer. It might be the contribution of a receptive ear, an unexpected idea from an unlikely source, a reframing, a different kind of response, example, pattern, evidence or experience, or a material contribution that helps the other grasp better the possibilities, nature, reality and new meaning of what they, the critical inquirer or inquiring group, are experiencing, and articulate an alternative plan and take a new action. Through understanding and other resourcing, a new way forward is forged within their own situation, puzzle, difficulties, dreams, desires or issues in relation to their context and those around them. The experience of 'inside' and the experience of 'outside' together create something new in a synergy that transforms or generates conditions for new life.

When we *do* encounter one another in this way, we do so from wherever we are 'at' with our own inquiry cycles, questions and answers. When we don't engage we might say, 'they weren't where I was at'. Or, rather, I wasn't where they were at. We were not 'connecting'. Or 'our interests lay elsewhere'. When we *do* connect—bringing one's group or self alongside, to 'dock' with, connect to, help, resource, or offer assistance to another's inquiry journey in terms of one's own—we might say 'I got a lot out of it'. 'There was electricity—a real buzz', 'good vibes', 'the chemistry was there'. We might say 'we were in sync'. Synchrony.[2] 'On the same page'. 'Attuned'. 'Displaying structural coupling in fields of morphic resonance', the new physics scientists might say! The exchanges call forth the new, limited only by 'where we last rested with our questioning' (Peavey 1994) or the point at which the organism is no longer in co-inquiring relationship with others.

Whether we are in the particular instance the helped or helpers, we bring to these exchanges all the 'accrued results' of a lifetime of our countless everyday micro 'research and evaluation studies', accomplished in an infinity of complex and changing circumstances; each within a field of resource and capability. The only difference between the parties on either side of any desk or table at any point in time will be the extent to which they each have or have not been able to acquire (or have not been systemically blocked or excluded from acquiring) enough of the conditions for life—that is, *the lifeblood relationships to others* that ensure the information and resources needed to give freedom without loss of stability to self-organise effective responses to the conditions in which they find themselves.

In meeting, the co-inquiry begins. Inquiry that may primarily in the instance be *for* one party. In a critical sense it is *that party's* inquiry cycle that is the organising focus of the encounter, and thus as 'stake-owner' they become both compass and ultimate judge of the directions to best take. Meanwhile the other party is engaging as a resource, enabler, supporter, partner or 'everyday research and evaluation facilitator' of the critical inquirer's endeavours—to the extent the critical inquirer may seek such assistance, and to the extent the helpers are currently able to offer this from their own inquiring being.[3]

Twenty-five years after coining the term 'critical reference group'[4] to try and describe the answer to the question 'For whom and for what?', we might add 'critical inquirer' or 'critical inquiry group' to make explicit the active way in which the critical reference person or group seeks to self-organise, including 'with' any who might assist, resource, support, serve, care-give, care for/nurture, care about, care with/inspire, enable, contribute to, provide/help and so on, *with and for* this critical inquirer.

In the moment of turning to attend to fellow life-travellers' inquiries, we are re-focusing our inquiry *on and with* that of the other, bringing our own inquiry journeys *alongside* theirs in seeking to connect and achieve resonance, as we listen, watch, notice and feel for the right questions to understand them and their situation, issues and lifeworld (just as they are doing this with us).

- What are they observing and experiencing?
- What is going on for *them*?
- What sense are they making of how things are for them?
- What are they already assuming (and have concluded from their previous inquiry)?
- What are they thinking and feeling about it all at the moment?
- What are they seeing as the discrepancies between their own 'is' and 'ought'?
- What are they most deeply valuing or wanting?
- Do they have thoughts, ideas, plans, goals or objectives they are thinking would get them from a 'here' to a desired 'there'?
- What actions are they thinking they could or would like to take?
- How would they know if they've achieved their purposes? What would count for them as the signs of that?
- And how would they work out if they'd prefer to be aiming to be doing something else? (and why…)

And why am I here with this interest, asking all these questions? What is driving *me*? What do I think *I'm* doing? And what do I hope to bring to the encounter? What do I want and value most deeply…?

And who are we together? What is driving us? What do we think we are doing? What do we each bring to our encounters with others? Here is the deeper life-giving rationale for Aboriginal educator and social worker Lilla Watson's frequently quoted assertion[5]:

> If you've come to help me, you're wasting your time.
> But if you've come because your liberation is bound up with mine,
> Then let us work together.
> (Quoted with permission, Wadsworth 1991: 17)

Here Lilla isn't saying 'we can work together'—as that is yet hypothetical—but 'let us work together': an invitation to 'stand with', in recognition of the possibilities of 'alongsideness' (Pound 2000) with the

other on a joint journey (for the time being). Together expanding the possibilities of generating something new and better by, for and with the critical inquirer. 'Better together', as the Victorian Health Promotion Foundation's slogan has it.

> *Don't walk in front of me, I may not follow.*
> *Don't walk behind me, I may not lead.*
> *Just walk beside me and be my friend.*
> ALBERT CAMUS

Being very human: people resourcing and facilitating each other's inquiry and co-inquiry to create living human systems

Whether the critical inquirer is you, or me, or someone else; or a group, or a community of interest, they and we are all attempting to be small self-organising living systems within larger autopoetic systems—a kind of nested autopoesis or holarchy of systemicities—where each gains their own living integrity in relation to that of others. We are finding our way in webs of relationships that furnish feedback in the search for nourishing 'resources' of all kinds. In a dance of mutuality, living beings and the elements that make up the webs of life,[6] within the field,[7] matrix[8] or shared surrounding environment[9] are doing the same. Curiosity and noticing is sparked by need or desire, leading to observing closely, interpreting signs, theorising meaning, making connections in dialogue to respond with intention to further what is necessary to the life of the connected 'wholes'; then acting given the circumstances[10]—the existing systemic capacities (and restraints) to assist being and becoming more fully living systemicities. A kind of 'Do unto others what you would have them do *with* you' prevails (or 'Do not do unto others what you would not have them do unto you' plus its deeper corollary, 'Do not automatically do unto others what you would want them to do unto you'). This is not just a 'golden rule' found in all major world human religions (FWCC 2007), it is also 'living systems thinking' in its description of the absence of unnecessary harm or unwanted service *if* organisms are to be able to live (and inquire effectively) for themselves *relationally* (Gergen 2009) for their shared life.

'Organisms needing assistance' may range from everyone requiring a myriad of tiny inputs on a daily basis to help nourish, create, 'hold their form' or restore it, through to major systems breakdown and crisis where the entire form may need change or even replacement, calling forth new sources of input and creativity where perturbation or turbulence prevail under unprecedented conditions.

What does this mean for how we think about what we are doing in the human service interaction in which we are resourcing or being resourced for new life by life-giving inquiry?–and in this way able to free the dynamic energies for our own life-giving action, or have this intended for and with us? What does it mean for the kinds of communication needed to achieve this? The kind of languages used? The ways things are said or conveyed? And the way things are subsequently organised, at differing 'levels' of systemic scale?

This chapter contemplates the proposal: what if in *every* human services system encounter—whether between clients, workers, managers, staff, board members, government policy makers, funders or the wider public—we were all actively co-inquiring into the conditions for the fullest life of each and all of us together? Speaking our truths about how things are now? Being determined to get to the bottom of issues? Grieving together about hurts? Celebrating signs of life? Moving to resolve discrepancies to achieve greater life through new insights and new human value-driven actions? Thinking things through? Celebrating new wellbeing wherever it occurs, and inquiring for its ongoing continuance and regeneration? And then noticing where it is absent and inquiring again?

Social work and health have experienced lively discourses over the last few decades in attempting to factor back into their work such full cycle inquiry about systemically situated and generated 'problems'. The distinction between individual, group and community work dimensions in social work, or the distinction between treatment and prevention in medicine versus health development, were all attempts to broaden the systemic inquiry frame from the personal (and more narrowly proximal and simple) to the public (and more broadly distal and complex). Systemic thinking offers a way of seeing all of these as nested holarchy—that is, not as oppositional/between but as fractals/within. So what is done regarding the individual 'scales up' to the very largest scale. Tiny inquiry cycles within every individual and one-to-one encounter are scaled up using the same life-giving whole inquiry cycles by groups, organisations, communities, nations, internationally and globally.

On a smaller scale
A common story is of young people gathering in shopping centres and leaving behind them syringes, graffiti, damage and a string of petty crimes. When inquiry processes only draw on existing 'partial cycle' knowledge about what has been done before (e.g. to defend the existing patterns and forms of shopping centre life), it can result systemically in *more* security guards, more lighting, fences and increased costs to the tenant shops, in turn escalating the loss of mutual trust and potential resort to coercion when the young people find themselves drawn inexorably into a stand-off with the security guards. Alternatively, if full cycle inquiry processes can be used by youth peer workers to listen to and get to the bottom of young people's life experiences and then assist the communication and dialogue with all other stakeholders, this can result instead in 'reconnecting' young people, reducing stand-offs and the need for stronger boundaries, and potentially result in joining together, for example to organise a band concert, or even to being offered paid employment in a shopping centre.

On a larger scale
For wider levels of the organisation of human services, and their intersections with systemicities at a scale beyond those bounded as 'human services', Jim Ife has usefully theorised four competing discourses by which—reflecting those wider systemicities—human services professionals (reflect and plan), managers (plan and act), market players (act and observe) and community organisers (observe and reflect more deeply) are each producing different ways of inquiring into and understanding the nature of human services (Ife 1997: 46–49, Fig.2.1, reproduced below).

This conceptualisation describes the ways in which the systemic separation of 'professional human services' from 'the managed marketplace of business and industry' and from 'the community' (that is more local to people's lived lives) have thus evolved separate discourses, losing a sense of an interconnected whole, instead becoming 'specialised' around particular inquiry preference clusters.

By remaining separated and oppositional, bearers of each of the four discourses can go on speaking at cross purposes 'across the cycle' at each other, held at

Resourcing people's inquiring self-organising in preference to doing 'to', 'at' or 'for'

*If we plant a seed in a desert and it fails to grow, do we ask 'What is wrong with the seed?'...
[or do we] look at the environment around the seed and ask
'What must change in this environment such that the seed can grow?'
...stop saying what's wrong with people and start asking 'how do we create hope filled, humanised
environments and relationships in which people can grow?'* [my emphasis]
PATRICIA DEEGAN, 'RECOVERY AND THE CONSPIRACY OF HOPE', IN MERTON AND BATEMAN 2008

There is a Zulu word, ubuntu, *which literally means 'humanness'...[it is] a social and spiritual
philosophy, the essential meaning of which is 'a person is a person through other persons'.*
ROBERT RABBIN, 'HUMAN CARING FOR CUSTOMERS—BUSINESS WITH SPIRIT', 2001

Empowerment is all about being treated as self-determining peoples, not client communities.
MURIEL BAMBLETT, 'SELF-DETERMINATION NOT INVASION', 2008

*[O]ur hope is that people will be 'met' rather than 'worked on'—treated [as] 'real' people rather than
'cases' or 'clients' or 'patients'. I resist most of the collective nouns that they use of the people we
serve...because deep down I believe that when people become real, most of our distinctions ...are
blown away and irrelevant...[it's] a two way deal...We are all healing together or we are all
shrivelling up together. This is why I leave Wayside most days, more alive than when I arrived.*
GRAHAM LONG, WAYSIDE CHAPEL, KINGS CROSS, 2008

*One sign of a nation moving toward progress is that in such a nation
every person's insignificance is disappearing.*
RABINDRANATH TAGORE, 'BATAYANIKER PATRO', KALANTAR 1919

*I don't use the term 'carer'. I support people. I don't care for them—there's a really big difference.
Being a 'carer' has connotations of 'I will decide for you'. Being a support worker, the (client)
drives the bus and you're there to make sure the wheels stay on—not to decide where it stops,
when it starts, where it goes.*
PETER COOKSON, DISABILITY SECTOR DOCTORAL STUDIES, *THE AGE*, 2008

*Ours is a support role and, at the end of the day, family relationships are the relationships that are
going to continue for their whole life – not us as support workers. I think sometimes the helping
professions can get caught up with that and feel like they are the key person in a client's life,
whereas our job is to make sure that it's those other relationships that are fostered, that they
learn about themselves and do some reflection and that we're able to do that too.*
ERIN ASHMORE, YOUTH SERVICES, MELBOURNE CITYMISSION, *THE AGE*, 2007

*[After the bushfires] Our approach to the temporary villages was to enable the empowerment of
residents to manage their own recovery...to walk alongside the community...We don't see our role
as a 'manager', there to enforce rules and regulations. Everyone is at a different point [we]
proactively respond to the residents' needs rather than try and predict what [we] think they need.*
ANDREW MCGUCKIAN, UNITINGCARE, APPEAL UPDATE, 2010

TABLE 6 COMPETING DISCOURSES OF HUMAN SERVICES

HIERARCHIC
(top-down)

MANAGERIAL   **PROFESSIONAL**

POSITIVIST ———————————— **HUMANIST**

MARKET   **COMMUNITY**

ANARCHIST
(bottom-up)

Competing discourses of human services

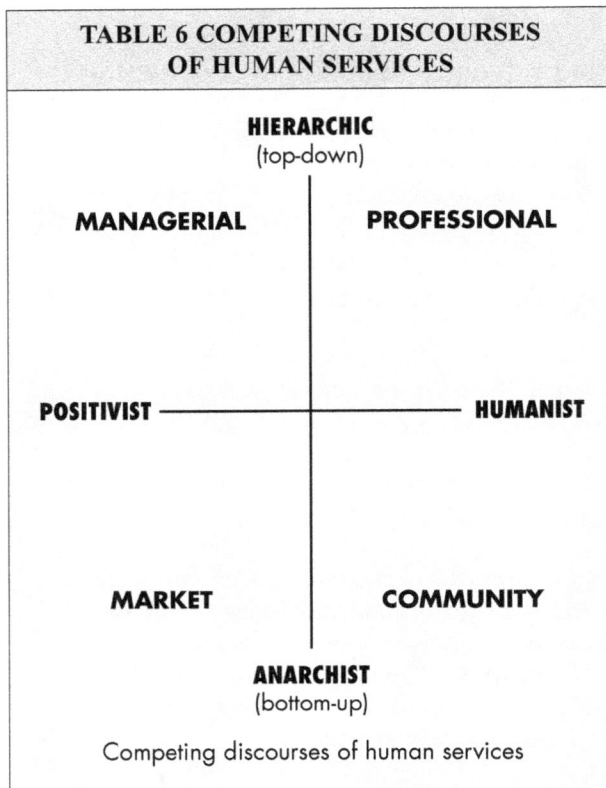

Reproduced with permission from Ife J. © 1997 Pearson Australia p47.

arm's length by a set of dissonant forcefields. The *managerial* discourse thus may go on losing depth and meaning while resorting to empirical measures that fail to get at the real meanings of people's deeply lived experience—while reproducing the dominant forms of exchange. Yet the *community* discourse also wants to achieve practical implementation of the kinds of desired co-operative, humanly nourishing relationships in people's lives too, and would like to know the signs of so doing, even across large groups of people. However it faces a marketised discourse that primarily renders human relationships in contractual terms in a mass society as exchanges of monetarised value. In this discourse, 'lean, efficient and fast' are seen as good, and 'messy, circuitous and slow' are seen as bad. But the *professionals* also see that this will factor out what makes good human services good, that is, time to talk deeply; enough diversity and complexity to provide the necessary range of resources and backup; and time to ensure things are stabilising and working well. Indeed without this, people become

vulnerable to trying to 'intervene' top-down, short-circuiting the uncertainty by having to make people become something that may not be what they would want to become (if they were better resourced within their community contexts to be inquirers-for-themselves).

One way to break these interlocking systemic impasses might be to see the four discourses—currently depicted in a double binary classificatory matrix—instead as representing the quadrants of the cyclic living systems epistemology of Chapters 2 and 3.

That is, we might reframe these four dimensions from categorical binaries on a two-by-two grid by instead thinking of each as occupying a 'place' or process moment around the inquiry cycle (picture arrows going anticlockwise on Jim Ife's Diagram 6 from bottom-up observation of community needs-expression, translation through a professional lens on planning and action, implementation by managers, and then becoming part of a 'market'-like exchange for providing-receiving service outcomes). In a typical scenario the separation of each from the next of the four round the cycle may result in a somewhat 'bumpy ride' as each attempts (think Chinese whispers) to feed into or influence the next, in the absence of the four groups of stakeholders being able to go full cycle *together*, ensuring their inquiry preferences remain actively in dialogue to assist and not be overridden/overwritten by the next. Thus each might be unable to move from only experiencing the typical range of problems described so clearly by Ife (1997: 47–57) in 'their own quadrant' as they try to make the world in the image of *their* particular discourse (e.g. more-or-less meaningful understandings generated within communities, then slippage to be overwritten by pragmatic and presumptive intervention by professionals, then people's individual differences being overly unified by managers in a top-down, utilitarian operationalisation of a standard service market model 'roll out', and so on).

Alternatively, if the relevant stakeowners and stakeholders move out of operating only within their preferences for differing parts of the cycle, and *together* inquire around the cycle, they might all experience 'starting on the ground' in the actual circumstances of people's lived lives in and with their 'communities of interest', and closely observing their responding to these situations, out of which reflection

© Copyright Judy Horacek www.horacek.com.au

together might generate ideas to produce a provisional working 'body of knowledge' that can then be trialled and 'managed' in practice. Indeed these full cycle processes of research, evaluation and continuous inquiry practised by individuals, teams and communities of practice could become the micro fractals of full cycle inquiring *oikos* in larger spheres of human exchange relationships.

Informed better by intensely detailed understandings (and self-understandings) of people and their communities' or fellow members' experiential journeys, people see what each other has 'been through', understand why things are as they are, and what they most want and need as new ways forward, strengthening their confidence about what to take into action. People assisting these processes are thus feeding the spirit of inquiry that might take all to greater life, at whatever scale. As the inquiry group uses its processes to pursue valued outcomes right round the cycle, they are also there to ensure that what is done finds its place in a viable living oikos of exchange relationships.

As Tim Costello has observed, 'community' becomes possible without people's lives being reduced to 'programs', 'hospitality' can avoid becoming condescending 'charity', and 'companions' can be a better metaphor than 'clients' or 'customers'(1998, chapter sub-headings, pages 100–108).

Given the co-systemic generation of health and human services *in response with* the mainstream

economic systemicity that is generating most of the ill health and less than fully human relationships in the first place (e.g. indicated by the extent to which 'business values' are in contrast with 'human values'), then the work of most health and human services is inexorably focused on restoring the brokenness and damage experienced by (and done to) individual, group and community sub-systemicities. The observation and analysis of 'how things are' has in the past therefore most often focused on the negative impacts on people, and the systemic impetus of helpers to right wrongs, correct injustices, and restore a higher degree of autopoetic dynamic stability for all. However systemically repeating *only* this problem-based focus of inquiry has tended systemically to result in more of the same—repeated observations of such negative states of affair—without necessarily finding a way across Phase change 1 to envisioning better alternatives.

In pursuing whole cycle inquiry, many health, human and community services practitioners—particularly those who have remained closest to their critical inquiry groups or are themselves part of self-help critical inquiry or mutual advocacy groups—have been moved to ask how things might be instead and what changes could be more life-giving.[11] This new focus of attention has resulted in a turn to the language of appreciation of what is going well and to identifying existing strengths, to observe effective survival skills and positive capabilities that have not easily been picked up on the measurement radar of problem-detection alone. This is especially the case if such observation is at too great a distance from people's actual lifeworld contexts. Under these circumstances observers have very often concluded that lack of agency must lie somehow within the individual suffering systemicity. Similarly, if people are replicating rapid responding 'case' by 'case', they may not have the time and space to reflect on such wider implications.

Systemically enacting the new logic of life-resourcing

The language of 'being the change you want to see' has picked up on this move, as have the proliferating examples of living systems and action research approaches to human services that may begin by observing negative discrepancies between 'is' and 'ought' but then move to 'what is better' or 'could be better' (see also the ten exemplars in Chapter 5).[12]

■ For example the *St Luke's* strengths-based approach uses appreciative inquiry (itself a full cycle action research strategy), choice theory, community capacity building and a range of 'seriously optimistic' resources that work as aids for inquiry and Helping Other Possibilities Emerge (e.g. journalling, visual scaling, images for use in narrative therapy, storyboarding, strengths cards, reflexions cards etc.). These support children's, parents', teachers', social workers', careers counsellors', prison educators', and other professionals' and community members' reflections and thinking in a wide range of human service, child and family welfare, education and community settings, now used worldwide: http://innovativeresources.org.

■ Or the *Eden Alternative building in life to older people's residential services* in which hospital-based sterile aesthetics and an industrial culture in nursing home 'facilities for the frail and aged' are superseded instead by light-filled 'habitats for health and wellbeing'. Here the growing of vegetable and flower gardens and a culture of a 'life worth living' without loneliness, helplessness and boredom is nourished through participation and opportunities to give and to care to increase residents' sense of control, and responsiveness, companionship, variety, spontaneity and cultural sensitivity by staff: http://www.edenalt.org/.

■ Or the *Active Participation Strategy in government disability services* that tries to build service around consumers' autopoesis, or the *Collaborative Recovery Model* in mental health rehabilitation that sets out to turn 'disability workers' into 'recovery support workers' who take their lead from service users' 'lived experiences/realities' and who can hold images of people's glimpsed 'possible selves', as well as other more strongly *Consumer Initiated Activities* which take seriously consumers' insistence that they chart the pathways they themselves actively want and choose: http://www.dhs.vic.gov.au/disability/improving_supports/self-directed-support http://media.uow.edu.au/news/2005/0916a/index.html www.health.vic.gov.au/mentalhealth/publications/cons-part.pdf http://www.ourconsumerplace.com.au/index

■ Or the *Appreciative Inquiry* movement, as explicated by its originators David Cooperrider and Suresh Srivastva (1987), Jim Ludema et al. (2001), and later collaborators such as Ken Gergen (2009) and Diana Whitney (Cooperrider and Whitney 1999) and the work of the Corporation for Positive Change (CPC) and the Taos Institute—now used worldwide by organisations from neighbourhood centres, hospitals, schools and large private businesses through to the United Nations. It uses a four-concept epistemology matching that of action research—*Discover* (observe)–*Dream*(reflect)–*Design*(plan)–*Deliver*(act) —it rests on the familiar living systems assumptions of recursive emergence and construction, and works as a fast track to the reframing of problems as 'already in the process of being changed for the better'. http://appreciativeinquiry.case.edu/ http://www.new-paradigm.co.uk/Appreciative.htm http://www.icvet.tafensw.edu.au/resources/appreciative_inquiry.htm

■ Or the worldwide community capacity-building *Assets Based Community Development* (ABCD) approach of John Kretzmann and John McKnight (1993) and the Asset Based Community Development Institute of Northwestern University, which swept through Western governments in an attempt to rebuild community infrastructure in the wake of the late 1980s wipe-out of public policy and funding for community development. Based on the same critique of the systemic 'slippery slide' offered by only seeing problems and deficiencies (leading to only seeing more problems and deficiencies), it observes the opposite systemic tendency—that if citizens are able to discover, map and mobilise their own skills, abilities, gifts and talents and the physical and economic assets of their diverse communities, associations and formal institutions, and envisage compelling positive futures as already being called forth, they themselves will autopoetically bring them into being through networking, inquiring together and the resulting creative synergies. http://www.abcdinstitute.org/ http://www.connectccp.org/resources/library.shtml

But what can keep a human services system wanting to stay in this more life-resourcing mode, sufficient to overcome the considerable pressures that present the great paradox (explored later) experienced by most health and human services, indeed all human systemicities, of not doing this?

In pursuit of this question on a Churchill overseas

study tour in 1995, one answer leapt to my attention in the very first minutes of travelling to North America in the in-flight magazine. The then Chief Executive of Qantas, James Strong, had written in his editorial:

> One of the most important aspects of any organisation is its internal atmosphere or 'culture' in terms of how things are done, how people are treated, standards [of practice], levels of confidence, trust and reputation...[and the creation of] a climate where people look forward to going to work every day because they enjoy what they are doing, get satisfaction from their personal contribution, and feel proud to be involved.

In such a 'vibrant and healthy organisation' he anticipated critically aware inquiry processes so that:

> no-one would ever contemplate or tolerate doing things which would in any way harm or negatively affect a customer or client, or indeed a colleague...[Instead t]hey would use personal initiative and awareness to observe what is happening, what needs to be done, and how the customer or client is being affected and treated...No-one would allow minor procedures or problems to impede their drive to finally present a more-than-satisfactory result for...the delighted customer or client.

The 'proud and satisfied' staff and 'delighted' service users of this organisation certainly sounded like reasons indeed to want to research and evaluate the creation of ever more life-giving systems of mutually encouraging individuals, groups, organisations and communities elsewhere.

Indeed in practice[13] nearly every one of us who has ever called on a human service has had that experience of being delighted—of getting exactly the assistance we needed, being welcomed and listened to attentively, of being considered in a really thoughtful way, of being asked for our input, ideas and experiences, of having our words, feelings and ideas truly heard and respected, and of the person from whom we have sought help 'getting it right', understanding us accurately, and responding in a truly helpful way. Someone who has been really 'like a friend' to us—who has not made us feel like a lesser 'other'—even though they were just 'doing their job' and earning an income from the exchange. We are happy for them to be paid, as they have acted more like 'our consultant',

as a valued source of information, observations and ideas that we might never have time in our lives to gather for ourselves. Furthermore they may have asked us the right questions so we could work out what the right answers might be for ourselves. We have emerged feeling less broken, ill, hopeless or stupid. We feel more confident, capable, self-determining and 'whole'.

We know what this feels like. We flourish and come alive, and become our best selves. We get back on track. Back 'in kilter'.[14] In this way we heal (from the Germanic *helan*, meaning 'whole') and recover, and become active and productive again—in whatever ways are possible and life-giving to and with those around us. We positively valorise and store every tiny incident of such life-giving interaction, searching and scanning for more in the next encounter; antennae extended for discouraging, 'toxic' or exclusionary messages.

Similarly, nearly everyone who has ever provided a service has also had an experience of contributing positively: of noticing someone's need for assistance, of listening, speaking carefully and asking the right questions (or amending them iteratively from feedback until they are right), of making someone feel at ease, of honouring their experience, feelings and thoughts, and then truly 'hearing' what they are saying, of asking that extra question and getting a new insight or understanding, of discovering a deeper truth, of responding well, perhaps even 'bending the rules' to take a 'bigger picture' perspective to avoid or address an injustice, of being in the right place at the right time, and being of true service to someone. Being 'like a friend', even while remaining focused on the larger issues and responding to the experiences of many others in the course of 'doing their job'.

We know what this feels like too. We feel as if we've contributed, 'made a difference', in a positive way to someone, or some group or organisation's or community's life. We too thrive and become our best selves. We stay on track, in kilter, feel whole, connected and remain productive. We too valorise the precious times we've been able to work like this; and we enter each new situation, job or service hopeful of an environment that enables this again.

And when we can both give *and* receive without feeling either overly relieved to be giving (because we have been given or taken too much) or overly uncomfortable about receiving (because we have not been able to take or been given too little), then all feels particularly right with the world. We think and feel that then we are in more truly and realistically shoulder-to-shoulder collaboration. Like a marriage (where there is no real partnership possible 'except between equals') in which neither party feels overly, always, or only up *or* down, but instead feels 'alongside'. Like an ally[15] in which each gains from the encounter, even as the 'direction' of the assistance may at that particular moment be towards one (or the critical) party. Both response-able *to* (Fisher 2006) and receiving responses *from* each other on each other's inquiry journeys, we come to realise ever more deeply that,

No one person is more of a human being than another.
JUSTICE MARCUS EINFELD,
'RIGHTS UNDER THREAT, OBLIGATIONS FORGOTTEN',
2001

A genuine energy comes from encounters and services that have centred in this way around an *alliance with and for* the critical reference group within a sense of mutual solidarity for a greater whole, dissolving the boundaries between the 'you' and the 'I' (Buber 1958), or drawing a larger boundary that includes both. As a consumer consultant researcher has said of professional–client relations for quality services in the aptly named *The Essential U&I* (Wadsworth and Epstein 2001):

For this is all about...the way we are with each other and within ourselves, and finally, what else is there?
CATH ROPER,
THE ESSENTIAL U&I 2001, P. 204

Under such conditions we come alive, service users and service providers alike and, now we know, so also is every other major adverse aspect of society mitigated by this sense of 'alongsided' fairness and equality in our relationships that both results from and contributes to our inquiring and acting together to rectify the threats to the life of our organisms—whether from ill health, lack of community, substance abuse, obesity, violence, power and economic imbalances, mental illness, overly long working hours, escalating prison populations or excesses of atmospheric carbon that threaten the life of all earth species (Wilkinson 2006, Wilkinson and Pickett 2009)

The paradox writ small at the heart of human services

At the same time as almost everyone knows what a more truly living system feels like, people *also* have an experience of being ignored or spoken to too coolly or too abruptly, being told rather than asked, being made to wait too long, being made to feel a nuisance, or embarrassed or ashamed or guilty to ask, of being 'condescended to', of not being listened to carefully, not believed, not respected, and not responded to accurately, or of being in anguish—and being held at arms' length or becoming entangled in depersonalising 'red tape' yet required to remain compliant with rules and regulations that prevent us getting what we desperately need; or of just not being understood, or replied to, or not even being asked in the first place.

And mostly every provider of a service also winces to remember ignoring or speaking too coolly or abruptly to someone, telling rather than asking, making someone wait too long, making someone feel like a nuisance or embarrassed, helpless, ashamed or guilty; of being condescending, of not listening carefully, or not believing in someone's potential, or dismissing something they said and subsequently finding they were right, of wielding red tape and 'the rules' against someone, of distancing themselves, or of just not responding or inquiring further. Our defensive routines can be legion, and sometimes we don't even know when we've hurt others, or when we just haven't understood them at all.

We know and feel what these experiences are like too— they give us pause for thought, and may mortify us, sap our energies, deplete and sicken us,[16] and we generally go to great lengths to avoid them, even as they persist and may become systemic. Signs go up in hitherto community centres: 'staff only' and life becomes ever more materially comfortable for professionals almost in inverse ratio to the increasing awfulness of the lives of those they are to help. Services devote more and more time and money to staff members' occupational health and wellbeing as their stress rises, compromising their abilities to help. Yet service providers may actually recoil from seeking help from their health and human service professional colleagues—as one social worker said to Stephen Fineman in the book *Emotions in Organisations* (1993: 22), 'I wouldn't want to be social-worked by

MANIPULATIVE VENTILLATING NON-COMPLIANT ACTING OUT! RESISTANT DEPENDENT FABRICATING LACKING INSIGHT

"SPEAK OF OTHERS AS YOU WOULD HAVE OTHERS SPEAK OF YOU?"

© Merinda Epstein

them'. Professionals accustomed to a modicum of power may find themselves subjected to an unfamiliar experience of humiliation from 'being assessed' in order to navigate the welfare system to receive a benefit —as were those who lost their homes to bushfire in the political capital of Australia some years back. Or as have the many 'wounded healers' who have ended up on the other side of the desk or bedside (Fisher 1994).

Yet counter-intuitively there are also times when service users have winced at how they have treated people or reacted out of their own powerlessness to service providers, and times when stressed service providers have been confused yet chuffed to receive comfort from sympathetic service users. These seem anomalous in a system that only codifies one group as 'only ever strong and resourceful helpers' and the

© S. Kneebone & Y. Wadsworth 2008

other as 'only ever with problems and needing assistance'. In a living human service system stressed and pressured staff would receive resourcing too (although not usually from the critical reference group primarily there to be assisted *at that moment*, although it would be life-affirming to acknowledge that possible temporality)—just as there would be times and places for the critical reference group to have a chance to heal system-induced damage done to (or by) them as well.

As Patricia Deegan has observed, 'no one comes into this work to do harm' (1996)—nor only to stay in 'safe mode', like a computer restrained from performing at its normal best, bound up by procedural algorithms derived from prior experience or at a distance, based on What Can Go Wrong and What to Say and What to Do So Nothing Goes Wrong. Despite the hopes of curtailing all risk and uncertainty, in practice this can be a self-defeating and even endangering game of chicken and egg, as *reliable* safety and sustainability lie less in rigidifying around any single certified theoretically evidence-based one best way, and more in being able to remain alive and open to flexibly revise actions and practices in the light of new cycles of inquiry.

So here is the paradox of human service providers

seeming so often to have a hard time honouring their deepest values and highest principles to stay close enough to their clients, beneficiaries, and primary stakeholders or stakeowners to genuinely engage, listen, question, get to know each other, think together, understand, celebrate and mourn together, in the inquiry journey for better actions to bring life.

The paradox writ large in the institutionalisation of human services

At the same time as we were observing this paradox at the heart of human services in the late 1990s (e.g. Wadsworth and Epstein 1998) we were witnessing dramatic cuts at the policy and funding level to services and funding. This raised a further question about the paradox, but this time at a more systems-wide scale, of why those responsible were so apparently unable to see the negative consequences for the very people the services were for—even as they wrote a burgeoning stream of ever more elaborate policies and procedures. Why *were* planners and managers so impervious to advice from those who could see what the painful results would be in terms of weakening and excluding key groups from even the most basic forms of social support? Why *was* there such a profound failure of 'systems intelligence'? At heart, a failure of 'whole cycle' inquiry. And in the end a failure of politics, a failure to include *all* the necessary players in a bigger 'community of science' that should have included clients, staff, managers and funders, and extended out to the broader public, the media and other major feedback and educational institutions.

Some decision makers even seemed resolutely to want to stay out of the loop that passed through the experiences of those so hurt, damaged and distanced. Some were proud to know nothing of human services or health and instead to know only about how 'to manage'. Tenders were sought for the provision of sensitive human relationships (e.g. for preventive mediation for child protection) in the Public Notices in newspapers alongside water mains construction, termite treatment of power poles, bus replacement services and tram track works. For most during this stressful period, the 'participation' of broader constituencies was ever more and more as recipients of 'good news stories', and referrals to increasingly distanced, tightly funded, but overloaded outsourced services. Yet even the information and referrals were becoming matters of image and appearance rather than actually offering real help, as the discrepancies between human service actuality and the human service imaginary widened.

As Tim Costello, a prominent activist clergyman speaking at the 1997 'Cutting Edge' Children's Welfare conference in Melbourne put it:

There are only two things I disagree with [the most senior executive of the Department of Human Services[17]] about, regarding human services. One is his definition of human. And the other is his definition of service.

Over the subsequent decade, as the evidence of damage began to come in, resources were pumped back into human services, although too late for many. Yet curiously the issues of 'disconnect' between central policies, practice, research and evaluation, and particularly the 'forcefields' holding professional service providers at a distance from service users, have been subtly maintained, and even extended until it is difficult to not see them as endemic, despite repeated explicit policy intentions to the contrary to have 'seamless' 'joined up' integrated service systems. Regular restructurings and regroupings of various services under differing organisational units, ministerial portfolios and departments seem to bring with them the same systemic issues they were intended to fix.

The paradoxes persisted of people collecting statistics that showed the problems—and then continuing to collect more statistical data as the problems persisted unabated. Or of others wanting to present the personal experiential evidence of impacts and outcomes on people's real lives, but finding they could not prioritise doing this as it would 'take too much time' away from meeting existing goals and targets, or feeling discouraged that 'the problems would be too big to do anything about anyway'. Or of wanting to involve service users, but finding it quicker, easier and 'more efficient' not to, or to tightly 'manage' their input, while continuing to make the key

1980s
WE ARE REPLACING SOME OF THE HEALTH PROFESSIONALS WITH A TRAINED AIDE CUT COSTS

1990s
WE'VE HAD TO END THE CONTRACT OF THE TRAINED AIDE BUT HAVE BOUGHT AN INFORMATION WEBSITE PACKAGE TO ENSURE BEST PRACTICE

2000s
WE'VE BEEN ASKED TO CREATE OFF-SET REVENUE FROM THE WEBSITE. PLEASE COME UP WITH A BUSINESS PLAN BY FRIDAY

2010s
RISK COMPLIANCE IS REQUIRING EVALUATION OF OUR SERVICE TO DEMONSTRATE MEASURABLE HEALTH OUTCOMES FOR OUR SERVICE-USER POPULATION

From an original idea by Scott Adams © Dilbert with permission

decisions behind closed doors. Or of wanting to assist people traverse their own inquiry cycles, but feeling compelled to quickly add or substitute professional conclusions instead. Or of putting money and energy into encouraging professional reflection and then having such efforts discontinued and a new fashion take hold, or the priority shifting to appointing more statistical researchers instead.

Even where organisations had made important headway in incorporating more regular reflective practice, participatory consultation, action research or other developmental utilisation-focused evaluation, the paradox often sharpened as it became *professional* reflective practice research, rather than involving clients, or action research was more between *service provider* 'partners' than with consumer partners. Or evaluation was focused on utilisation by *decision makers*, managers or funders, rather than on utilisation by end-beneficiaries, with the latter continuing to be seen as 'too time consuming' or 'left till later'. Or the research or evaluation reverting to relying on a survey or quasi-experimental methodology conducted at a distance from consumers' actual lifeworlds, unable to elicit better shared understandings of what was *really* going on or why and what to do about it.

In the absence of the needed resourcing and facilitation of dialogue or 'scaffolding' to assist collaborative inquiry efforts, neither human services party could move closer together for exchange and better mutual understanding; yet nor could either party leave the situation (although some senior managers and academics appear to be able to make successful efforts to so do!)

A forcefield is a good metaphor for the paradox many people experience when they want to move away from compromised service and deeply constrained care and towards the positive, desirable and nourishing, but instead find themselves inexorably drawn to replicate old ways and patterns, remaining suspended between the two poles of attract and repel.

Being only human: when things aren't right

Thus in any picture of illuminative and life-changing collaborative inquiry and dialogue, it can be easy to underestimate the risks associated with standing at the edge of distance, separation, difference, misunder-standing and uncertainty, hoping to bridge the gaps with nothing but questions and the desire for new understanding. It may rightly seem daunting to proceed without the hitherto certainty of 'already knowing', telling or being told, instructing or being instructed, directing or being directed, compelled, required, or even coerced on the basis of decisions resting on understandings held by authoritative others.

Indeed the mere raising of a question can bring discomfort, uncertainty, dismay, anger or joy, hope or clarity. Sometimes the more important the question, the more explosive the feeling stored away about the discrepancy it represents[18]—something which may apply to helper or helped.

If you want to ask us how we are repressed, listen carefully to what we are not allowed to say...
QUOTE ON WALL OF U&I PROJECT OFFICE
UNKNOWN SOURCE
(WADSWORTH 2001, P.168)

Thus, as noted in Chapter 3, the body is able to generate rational feeling (or the frank expression of emotion that can be traced to such a rationality), indicating how it has effectively and silently embodied an experienced discrepancy between an 'is' and an 'ought', that remains stored until such time as an inquiry process can tap and release it.[19]

It may simply seem altogether easier and safer to persist with the known—no matter how inadequate, ineffective or repressive—not venturing over the threshold of *Phase change 1* to see if there might be a better way, or else leaving it to braver souls to try and get to the threshold of *Phase change 2* with an offering that differs from the normatively powerful. 'It'll all end in tears', someone intones from the sidelines; 'Someone should *do* something', others grumpily assert, taking care to be out of earshot of the powers that be. 'Best to leave sleeping dogs lie', say those who go on waiting and waiting for change.

Social research and evaluation that might be able to 'surface the undiscussibles' (Argyris 1993) and clear the way to identify and achieve desired change and improvement is rarely for the faint-hearted. Whistleblowers of injustice may be silenced, qualitative canaries gassed in many mines, and messengers of the new may be resoundingly shot. Indeed the early warners, early observers, early innovators, the change agents and 'cultural creatives',

© Sudhir Dar. with permission Institute for Development Studies Sussex

all those who ever questioned How Things Are, may well experience being isolated, targeted, derided, demeaned or dismissed; and in direct proportion to the extent of power available to protect the existing familiar situation from which all the benefits and privileges of current certainties derive.

When I measured the hungry, they called me a social scientist and gave me a grant,
When I asked what it felt like to be hungry, they called me subjective and impressionistic and funds were more difficult to secure,

When I asked why people were hungry, they called me biased and unscientific
And when I asked what would it really take to eliminate hunger, they closed down my research program

FROM AN IDEA AFTER DOM HELDER CAMARA[20]

Who would ever embark on inquiry?
Who would be an asker of questions?!
Only small children—and determined researchers who want to research all their way around the full inductive-abductive-deductive cycle to assist the ongoing emergence of truly living human systems!

Sometimes it may even seem for all the world like offering 'sacrificial chickens' of questioning and dialogue into the fire-breathing dragon mouth of conflict, concentrated power, uncertainty, fear and confusion.

So what *would* attract people to want to inquire?

In 1995 I set out overseas on a study tour to look into the conditions for building in research and evaluation to user-responsive community services—somewhat overwhelmed by the central paradox encountered during more than twenty years of work with child and family services, community health,

Nothing to worry about, business as usual

welfare, hospitals, general practice, adult education, and a wide range of other local community, government and not-for-profit human services. At the time, our work on a large 'whole systems' participatory action research study of the complex conditions for consumers to be able to express evaluative feedback about their experiences of acute psychiatric hospital services, and for staff to be able to hear this, was leading us to doubt there was actually an answer to the overwhelming issues facing this particularly fragile and under-funded 'David' of human services, set as it seemed to be up against the might of the giant Goliath economic world that seemed intent on excluding increasing numbers of its human 'family members' if they couldn't survive in an often harsh, hurtful and competitively stressful and excluding environment, until they lost their minds in confused or unwanted realities.

We had coupled our efforts in the large hospital environment to the then nascent quality assurance area, as this appeared to be the one 'time-space-and-place' in which staff had a legitimate chance of being able to conduct small-scale consumer research projects. There we had identified the complex paradox whereby psychiatric services staff and consumers struggled in what seemed almost a fractal-like mirroring of the wider society's equally paradoxical and defensive daily response: with staff *wanting* the best for people's health, healing and recovery, yet *at the same time* regularly causing further suffering by responding out of their own stress and anxiety in hurtful, albeit mostly unintended, ways. We documented in detail the numerous defensive routines and distancing methods adopted to avoid any unpleasant feedback that kept blocking the commencement of consumer–staff collaborative inquiry processes (Wadsworth and Epstein 1998).

© John Spooner and *The Age*

This was not a new paradox. It was an impasse already described eloquently forty years earlier by Isabel Menzies in her classic study of nursing services in a London hospital: *The Structure of Social Systems as a Defence against Anxiety* (1970). It has also been easily observable, albeit similarly largely undiscussible, in almost every area of human services in which I had worked over thirty-five years. And of course this has been the experience of many others, not just me. You can probably easily summon examples of your own to mind. It was just that this area of acute psychiatry, as with Indigenous communities, the homeless, people with disabilities and other groups who are among the most harshly excluded, really brought the human services paradox into sharp focus.

We want to say and do the right thing. But we sometimes, even quite often don't.

We want to help. But may end up hurting, or just getting in the way.

We want to assist. But may end up distancing ourselves.

We want to lend a hand. But may end up helping ourselves instead.

Practitioners, in feeling often inexorably drawn to reproducing undesirable patterns of response which they *know* don't work or sense are deeply goal-displacing may also feel unable to resist being drawn into the repeated whirlpool of unwanted action. Mirroring a similar systemic vicious cycle, their clients may feel just as inexorably drawn to doing the same in their own lives. Defences become ever more elaborate as the real values and intentions of each may become ever more deeply buried, and each find themselves cursing 'the system'—the mass of repeated unwanted actions that seem to have come from elsewhere and are bigger than either of them, even as they are part of it. Both may think: 'If I just keep going a bit longer, or if I just make these few

© S. Kneebone & Y. Wadsworth 1997

more small compromises, if I can just hang in there…things will change, the bad situation will go away' (or the particular 'difficult person' will leave, or retire or…), or 'I will try and influence them to change...' Soon neither can sleep. Or a new tough-minded 'survival mode' emerges. And then one day a staff person is horrified to find they have become more sympathetic to their fellow professional colleagues than to their fellow consumers, clients, patients or community members. And the latter, detecting this immediately, take a step back. Both plummet down Sherry Arnstein's ladders of participation back to manipulation, cajoling and resort to behaviourist carrots and sticks approaches. Or to mild-to-extreme forms of distancing, perhaps in the name of occupational health and safety or risk management; or perhaps via a promotion to a Very Important Management position. Not to mention frank coercion or even the use of force. Soon clients,

consumers, patients and community members are amongst the excluded.

We ask bewildered, 'How did this happen? Why am I over this side of the fence and you are on the other side?' Deep down we sense that while 'the other' may feel and be excluded, in practice, we both are…from each other. Rather than mirror images of synergistic growth, we have become mirror images of separation and unwanted patterns of reaction on one side and spirit-breaking depression or rage on the other. Paradoxically *everyone* feels disempowered and may think that the other isn't. The consequences emerge as sickness, whether personal or systemic (Wilkinson 2006, 2009) and as needing yet more rationalisation of conflict with deeper values (e.g. 'inequality is good for economic growth').

But how does the power,[21] the 'push-energy' capacity and strength to 'be able', get so excessively taken and so excessively yielded?

And why would any self-respecting living system do this? Why would any one species split itself into differing 'camps' on the basis of devaluing, demonising or inferiorising its parts? And then, when one group acts powerfully at the expense of the devalued group, even render them increasingly incapable of life when the avowed purpose of their efforts is to nurture, care, strengthen, help and support? How could it get to this? How could we think we would be better off without the contributions and abilities of our whole species, especially once we understand the entirely unique contribution each makes to the cycles of living systems inquiry, large and small?

And most unspoken and perhaps undiscussible of all—why would this happen in human services of all places—the very system of social relations that has taken up the responsibility of all the care work not taken up throughout the rest of the social, economic and political systemicity? How, in an era of client-centred practice and consumer participation did it come to be that we are still an 'us' and a 'them'?

'People are not crucified for helping poor people. People are crucified for joining them'
SHANE CLAIBORNE, 2006, P. 129.

Perhaps it is worth taking a moment to examine these defences in more detail to see where they are coming from, what they are there for and what they are defending. Perhaps in identifying their underlying purposes a key can be found to being able to move in the more life-giving directions people are nevertheless and paradoxically pretty much always driven to wanting to seek. The human history of our species may seem daunting on this count, but if we *are* living systems, then our autopoetic property should equip us to evolve on the basis of feedback. So let's not stop at the first fence of despair! But let's not discount the difficulties either.

© Liz Mackie 1980

Defences or fences: what are they telling us about what they are protecting?

Never take down a fence without
first knowing why it was built.
ATTRIBUTED TO ROBERT FROST

A little way into a follow-up action learning project, this time looking at defensive routines with professional staff of a medium-sized general hospital (Wadsworth and O'Brien 2002; see Exemplar 3 Chapter 5), the above quote appeared on my date pad. The inquiry group had laboured long and hard on the nature, extent and logic of their own defensive reasoning that they saw prevented them taking the time to hear feedback from their patients or consumers or to just get to know them and inquire into how things were going for them. Indeed this was a follow-up study to the long period of collaboration by consumers and staff in acute psychiatric hospital settings, in which the research had identified the deeply paradoxical culture of *wanting* to hear from patients and not wanting to hear. This paradox, summarised in the earlier cartoon ('Of course we must listen to what our consumers are saying…but…'), was what attracted the participants to the general hospital action learning set discussions.

We transform space into containers
of our desires and fears.
CURATOR'S CATALOGUE INTRODUCTION TO
'HOUSE: CHARGED SPACE' EXHIBITION,
MCMULLEN MUSEUM, BOSTON COLLEGE, 2001

It is possible to read the lengthy lists of defensive routines generated by both these projects as socially systemic responses to contain fear and anxiety about uncertain or potentially unwanted change, as already noted (Menzies 1970). It also strikes me that these defences are not unlike the range of responses to death and dying described by Elisabeth Kubler-Ross (1969) of shock ('cannot'), denial ('is not'), isolation ('will not'), anger ('should not'), fear ('must not'), resistance ('will not'), until *Phase change 1* is reached in struggle ('could/couldn't') and bargaining ('might if'), then full yielding in depression ('have to'), and finally transformed and reintegrated into a new identity in reflective acceptance ('want to'). If every form or pattern of the living organism involves a boundary, and every boundary is itself a defence, then every question about that form or pattern and its

boundary is like a threat of a little death or ending—invoking a kind of an immune system response.

We concluded the staff's defences operated as actions, practices and institutionalised cultures (including defensive deflections against the defences even being surfaced and discussed for what they really meant to people) to manage structurally and routinely a wide range of feelings: of inadequacy, incompetence or failure, and dread at the real or glimpsed threat of loss of existing certainties, solutions and familiar ways of doing, speaking and meeting needs.

But most significantly, we came to see that defences act most powerfully as ways of protecting their bearers from the feared truth that they are *not* acting on their deepest values—the purposes of the form, pattern and organism in the first place (Wadsworth and O'Brien 2002). In fact ironically we found that the fierceness of those defences appeared to stem from *the strength* with which those values were held in the first place. Even what we call fear of 'losing face', or having 'a big ego', or the fear of appearing 'incompetent', 'in error' or 'a failure' could be traced back ultimately to fears of 'getting things wrong' and hurting or failing fellow humans. We realised that if someone *truly* didn't care, they wouldn't be accessing those values to defend in the first place, and their response might not even be a sharp retort like 'tough'. It would be real indifference.

An analogy: an immune system, or an autoimmune response?

Defences are the way we organise our response to crises or threats in order to safeguard our current ways of being and doing, whether as individual 'psychic structures' or as organisational collective 'social structures'. Whether we are defending current actions, our observations, our reflections or our plans, they also work, however, as defences against realising there may be a valuable question about our operating theory or 'program logic'—something that calls for a deeper or fuller inquiry process—to renew confidence that we are indeed meeting our expressed purposes, needs or goals.

We found it useful to think of these relational defences as analogous to the biophysical processes of the human immune system—there to protect the integrity of the organism's current form right from the moment of their creation. Problems arise only when the systemic protection either blocks useful resources, mistaking them as endangering, or it attacks itself, thinking parts of its own 'being' are hostile or endangering, when in fact they may be benign or actually necessary.

Paradoxes of goal displacement

This is familiar ground in which all too often the issues are quickly translated into risk management or training programs to 'manage' and further contain and constrain 'difficult customers' or 'challenging behaviours'.[22] Practitioners are taught to 'be

Paradoxes of systemicity

■ 'The unit manager was complaining about someone coming into the hospital today—and I said to her "But they're *meant* to come in here, they're *sick*, we're a hospital! They're *meant* to come here"; and we just had a big laugh [wince in tone of voice]'—*Senior social worker, general metropolitan hospital*

■ A government department trains its staff not to keep saying 'sorry', builds high-security buildings to separate staff from deeply distressed and impoverished clients, and enhances those compounds with art glass and attractively decorated themed meeting rooms. Staff morale is maintained, but the department becomes increasingly out of touch with its clientele, unable to question or notice or act on discrepancies with its deeper purposes. It ends up being reported in Parliament as having an exceedingly high rate of bureaucratic error and poor service.

■ It is nearly thirty years since the London Edinburgh Weekend Return Group (1980) described the government department that had to house the excessively disempowered and disadvantaged members of the body politic one day, evict them for non-payment of rent the next, and then having the statutory responsibility to rehouse them again the day after that.

■ Today, disadvantaged, angry, alienated or suicidal young people whose lives are in chaos may find it too difficult to get social security payments from a highly ordered, centrally controlled hierarchy with fixed procedures to which they are unable to conform *because* of their distressed lives. They then qualify for a 'marginalised youth inclusion program', and get back on a benefit with the help of a professional service provider, only to fail to 'comply' with the next compulsory interview appointment that is set as a qualifying test by the same original tightly prescribed organisation. A government-commissioned research report that details this contradictory situation and offers to provide valuable intelligence to the system is prevented from doing so by the strict limitation of its circulation.

■ A business project in a commercialising government communications utility removes easily vandalised and non-profit-making public phones from low income areas on the grounds of 'due diligence to business values'. A justice partnership project involving the police and housing departments gets the communications utility to reinstall the public telephones in low income areas as 'vital in emergencies and for addressing social isolation'.

■ An insurance system is set up to pay for treatment so workers can remain in the workforce. It routinely denies the same workers treatment in order to decrease its service costs. It does this for example by tightening the eligibility criteria to exclude treatment on the grounds that it 'palliates rather than cures', or that employers 'are responsible for providing ergonomic aids', despite the fact that it is palliative treatment that is keeping the worker in work— and that is meant to be the purpose of the insurance (rather than 'curing'

professional' and 'put aside' their emotions or defences as if they were able voluntarily to be left on the ground at will or on command. But if the defences are there to hold protective systemic forcefields in place, then each party to an encounter will go on unconsciously constructing new and even more elaborate defences against the uncertainty of opening up any questioning process and feeling vulnerable to hearing unwanted responses or incomprehensible or useless answers. In the absence of seeing how to go forward with ideas to theorise better, they may still see no ways to address, fix, heal, mend, prevent, create, generate or otherwise resolve the deeply unwanted discrepancies and undiscussibles. We may even recognise our own protective routines, yet seem

compelled to endure the risks of shutting down the inquiry process, over and over again.

You could test your own preferred defensive strategies by re-reading the 'long litany' footnote at the bottom of the page in the Preface.

What did you notice about the thoughts or feelings that came up in you? How do you typically defend your self from the overwhelming implications of all these signs of unwell and broken systems, large and small, struggling for life? What are your own typical and preferred defensive methods and routines?

Thus it is not that there is anything wrong with defences per se. They are there to provide certainty so as to be able to live, protect our efforts based on existing knowledge, keep going and survive,

permanent injuries), and being out of work due to injury means there is no employer to provide the aids. Analgesia is allowed, however, but the medical prescription service that is the condition for the analgesia being reimbursed is excluded.

■ At one moment a psychiatric nurse is chatting in a friendly fashion to a patient hovering on the edge of hope and mistrust in the doorway of the staff office— and the next moment they slam the door shut when the patient's fingers on the door jamb cross an invisible boundary mark in the staff person's anxious mind.

■ A mental health consumer is kept at arm's length to such an extent that she becomes deeply distressed. An intervention order is taken out against her by the community mental health service from which she was seeking help. After a period of distressed reaction, and the service telling a voluntary community group to take care of her, the woman sets fire to herself. After a period of time in semi-consciousness during which a final wish to see her child is denied by authorities, she dies from her burns.

■ A busy ward manager (who is trying hard to remain coolly logical), accuses a hospital social worker (who is trying hard to not become depersonalised) of getting 'too emotionally involved' in the deaths of babies on their unit. The social worker finds herself saying, 'Someone has to feel something'.

■ A person with severe depression is routinely given shock treatment, anti-depressants, heavy doses of tranquillisers, has their clothes take away and is

confined to a locked ward. A psychiatrist observes wryly that this is intended to make [them] feel better (Rosen 1994).

■ A parliamentarian, on the advice of the Attorney General's Protective Security Co-ordination Centre, locks down his local electoral offices against a 'security risk' that is coming from a small group of disabled children and their families wanting to speak to their elected representative about the lack of long-term accommodation for the young people. The young people's wheelchairs have created the security risk because they 'threaten' to block the doorway into the office.

■ A consumer with arthritis is placed as a representative on a committee to introduce a program of 'community friends' to visit women with arthritis in their homes. When she repeatedly requests that the 'targeted' women with arthritis be interviewed to see whether this is what they want or whether there might be something else they need, the staff person responsible for the program threatens to resign. The consumer representative is sacked instead.

■ An overly tired and busy nurse is annoyed at the wet bed of a patient, but hasn't time to reflect on how the man's brain tumour and fractured pelvis might be making his getting up to the toilet painfully difficult— or that the patient's pride as a former social worker himself may have made him unable to ask, or provoked his anger at the nurse's irritated reaction as a defence of his own, thus escalating the turbulence.

especially when we are in crisis or being attacked or otherwise stressed in achieving life goals. We try and solve the paradox by working out how we can respond to others' needs and demands without losing our 'selves' in the process. We construct safe containing walls and barriers, possibly literally, as well as comfortably satisfying zones of language.

But when we build zones of certainty, containment and privilege, we may be risking seeing parts of our 'body corporate' as 'outside', to be labelled, excluded or even attacked, unless we can build in ways to routinely re-open the inquiring process. We know the moments when we have happily jumped over our old fences, enthusiastically pushed holes in the constraining walls, or drawn a wider frame that includes instead of excluding. We have come to see our fears are groundless once we have better got to know the situation or that of another; and can see a way forward.

Perhaps it turns out the larger world is safer than it was thought. Instead of crouching behind walls, receptivity turns out to be the way out. Trust grows, not as a goal *but as a consequence* of having been open to new learning which in turn leads to drawing different conclusions and an ability to act differently as a result. We regain confidence and flourish.

Mirroring the growth of health development and positive wellbeing approaches for and by individuals,

From an idea by © Phil Somerville with permission

much of the 'healthy organisation' movement in the past ten years in human resources has been devoted to strengthening what we called in the U&I project 'the missing fourth site'—a site that mirrored a much needed consumer-only site with similar purposes: to be a place in which to resource tired and battered people, to offer understanding and peer support, and to attend to people's health growth and development needs.

In their most positive guise we might call all these 'defensive driving'[23] or self-care practices. Indeed we can see in them the clue not only to understanding when, where and how they are activated—but also why they are activated. In grasping the 'why' we can see their 'positive intention' or systemic value—and in doing so, see how a dynamic imbalance might be corrected before self-sealing defensive routines in fact become self-defeating.

The necessity of 'building in' boundaries, closure and safeguarding defences…and 'building in' openings, beginnings and co-operation

We know that any organism organ-ises. And in doing so creates essential boundaries to encapsulate, include and 'keep in' the focused, concentrated, repeated activities that are particular to the purposes of those 'organs', simultaneously excluding and 'keeping out' what is not needed or is unwanted (inputs, information or resources not conducive to aiding its functioning).

We also know that a truly living system must always also remain permeable so its boundaries enable the living organism to continue to receive *needed* environmental inputs, information and resources, so needed exchange and change can take place, including to those existing structures.

Thus at any point around the cycle of living inquiry we may *need* to defend, safeguard (or assert) the value of each of the different process moments[24] or 'stations'[25] of the journey—*and* be open to receiving (or yielding to) the messages incurring the defences and, if need be, to be able to see how to move forward.[26]

This may mean defending and appreciating hard-won 'received (propositional) knowledge' such as statements of rights or principles, facts and factors, *and also* critiquing them. Defending hard-won routines, actions and culture, *and also* questioning them. Defending hard-won observations, *and* being open to alternative observations. Defending bright new ideas, *and* sceptically checking them, and so on.

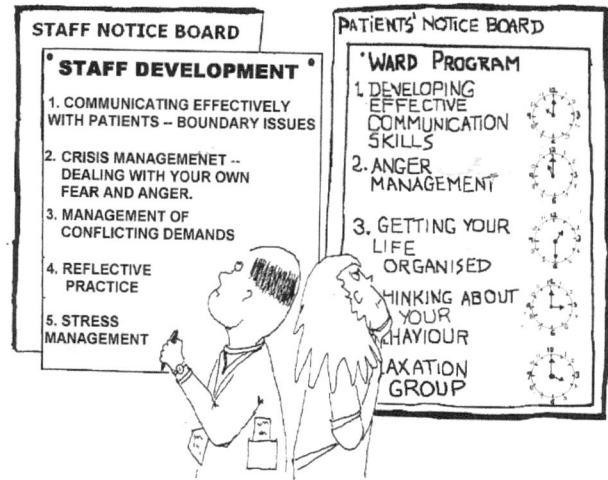

© Merinda Epstein

In this way we need times and places to be defending (explaining) and continuing what needs to be defended, explained and continued—*without fearing defensiveness, certainty, continuity and sameness per se*. And we may need to be open to and receiving what needs to be taken in—*without fearing receptivity, uncertainty and change per se either*.

For example, what of when we defend as a 'duty of care' the imposition of a service that is unasked for and unwanted, from a point in time where we are drawing on previous knowledge that is assumed (in the moment of imposition of planned action) to be of value?

What of when 'taking care of' people (without observation and reflection) disrupts their autopoesis? And when not taking care of people also disrupts their autopoesis?

There may be times (or even over time) when we may want action taken, even strong intervention, into our own or another's systemicity, especially at times of crisis. It may be a moment for minimal, compromised, 'outsourced' or interrupted autopoesis, and a more-than-usual division of inquiry labour. Operating on an unconscious patient, restraining someone from going back into a burning building for their child, enforcing hospitalisation against one's will after an accident, or other forms of rescue or treatment without consent are moments seen as 'an emergency' when some do things 'for our own good' without our agreement. Later we may thank them. Or we may not. But in those moments

Speaking across purposes (north-south)

we or our fellow humans are operating on faith on the basis of prior knowledge drawn from previous and assumed similar situations—the hoped-for strong 'evidence base' that will offer bridging reassurance to intervene so powerfully in others' self-management. We do not usually rescue people when they are floating in the sea. We may swim out and ask if all is well. But we also do not offer swimming lessons when someone is drowning. We usually assume they want to be rescued.

The saving grace of a living systems epistemology is, however, that these moments of coercion and presumption are *not where the inquiry cycle ends*. While those who only remain in the action moment may consider 'action needed–action taken' to be sufficient, in a living system it is not. An entirely linear sequence that is 'completed' is only ever so as a kind of partial device. We *do* think of ourselves as taking steps in a sequence to achieve certain ends, and they may seem to have a start and a finish, but only if we don't ask where the 'start' came from (e.g. the procedure or task being carried out) or what the effects were for (e.g. the impact, outcomes or further effects of taking such actions). Thus for every action (including life-saving and life-restoring action) in which 'power-over' type certainty is exercised in these ways, an equal amount of checking, observing and later reflection, including potentially restorative practice, will be necessary to properly review that always provisional action—not just in case the intervention might turn out to have been negative, and need to be fixed, repaired or healed, but also because

every one of our decisions *on* or *on behalf* of others (even the most thoughtful, helpful and healing) also means one less decision is resulting from *their* own purposeful inquiry, thus displacing their autopoesis and short-circuiting their self-organising processes, which may subsequently need even further effort to restore.

If inquiry does not recommence as soon as possible after action, and where insufficient attention is paid to hearing all relevant critical parties' and other stakeholders' views, observations and experiences, we move onto shaky ground. In such cases the concept of *epistemic insult* has emerged in the UK legal context to describe incidents of *testimonial injustice* (Fricker 2007), a concept which might be extended to all human encounters where not inquiring perpetuates or introduces new damage to people individually and collectively.

Indeed whenever there are mismatches in the inquiry cycles of helper and helped we can risk both 'getting it wrong' *and* diminishing the life-giving self-inquiry processes of others, even as we may act from our deepest sense of a 'duty of care'. It could even be that *not* being with the critical human service inquirer at *their* point in their inquiry cycle turns out to be a deeper dereliction of duty in the longer run.

Crucial to the success of collaborative inquiry, then, is the centrality of resourcing the critical inquirer's *own* capacity to question, observe, feel, reflect, think through and 're-build' their own 'life practice' narrative—a capacity that can be strengthened to also in turn collaborate with others.

It becomes clear what the risks are of any human

Speaking across purposes (east-west)

services or group of professionals (or researchers and evaluators) conducting their own separate inquiry or perhaps only with other professionals—observing, second guessing, theorising, concluding and then implementing actions independently of the critical inquirer.[27]

Even situations where it is thought there is 'no time' for communication (either for the critical inquirer to acquire the knowledge they need to make their own judgement or for the helper to ask and check and convey enough of what they are doing to receive informed consent), or where the critical inquirer is seen as 'incapable of communicating', inquiring processes may be more possible than seems. Over recent decades, babies, children, those without speech, and those seemingly so disabled or aged as to not be communicating, have been found to be ready, willing and able and actually emitting constant efforts to do so. Additionally, a bridging relationship of trust can be established to scaffold the gap, personal or contractual, by which the critical inquirer gives provisional consent in some way (e.g. by legal arrangement, allocating power of attorney, making an advance directive, resting on publicly transparent professional codes of conduct, or through elected or nominated representation, or other kinds of provisional consent procedures). And *after* the action a process of inquiry is added to review, debrief, re-analyse and either affirm what was done, or conciliate, arbitrate, heal and correct it if it proved to be damaging or in error.

In the final analysis the critical inquirer remains the ultimate judge.[28]

To stay in a perpetual world of crisis and reactive 'doing to, for or at' is to stay in a constantly short-circuiting 'single loop' between *plan* and *act* (or observe and *act*), eventually diminishing and depleting the capacity of all parties in the living system, and in particular both the capacity of helper and helped to step back, *observe* more deeply, *reflect*, rethink, replenish and rebuild more planfully their all-important autopoesis—risking remaining perpetually dependent on systemically increasingly and exhausted resourcing. Burnout awaits as everyone is systemically confined to 'overdoing their particular inquiry cycle preferences' at high speed without moving to look forward (or back at past experience) and fully achieve the full cycle. Matters of what is 'necessary autopoesis' will vary at differing levels of nested systemicity (for purposes), but the ability for each cell in a body, each body in a collective, and each collectivity in a the greater *oikos* to be both 'self-organising-in-itself' and 'self-organising-together' (without an excessive division of inquiry labour) rests on the scale at which resilience, surviving and thriving must be assured against too great systems' change or overly rigidified stability and collapse versus continuance possibilities. That is, the greater the need (or potential need) for responsiveness at whatever the scale of 'the organism', the greater the need for autopoesis at that scale.

We might usefully reconceptualise the 'ladder of participation' (Arnstein 1969) as steps around emergent iterative cycles (or emergent spirals) of initial dependency on others for actions done 'to, for and at' for survival during dependency and crisis (for received learning, resourcing or direct service), through to increasingly taking part in determining what is needed by critical inquirers themselves, through to collaboration to aid fuller self-organising of new actions, with 'control' at the 'top of the ladder' meaning maximum autopoetic or participatory control over the organism's own destiny (whether as an 'individual', group, organisation, community or other social collectivity), being capable of running one's own inquiry cycles to fruition and renewal; that is, live more fully autopoetic life within larger more fully autopoetic living systems. 'DIY' within 'doing it together'.[29] The 'individual' is in this way a microscopic reflection of the larger 'collectivity', in turn mirroring the life inquiry cycle processes of its smallest 'component'.

For human services practitioners (and those assisting their efforts) it is a way to 'accompany' critical inquirers compassionately through a time of yielding to the decay, ill health or loss of 'what is' or has been, celebratory appreciation of what is or has been life-giving, the making of new connections between old elements and new resources, generating new meanings and drawing new conclusions, creating new ways of being and doing, working out how to implement them, and moving from old to new more fruitful ways of being, that do observable justice to the critical inquirer's life and their inquiry efforts within and between scales of the living 'organism'.

Human systemicities do not lose their wisdom about the need to 'put things right' and how to do this, even if aspects of them—experiencing themselves as separate—think they will or want to. But 'the sleep of reason dreams of monsters', and every living organism retains more or less of the capacity to respond to discrepancy that drives their own life-giving inquiry away from the imbalanced or the stalled, the overly dynamic, or the overly perfectly balanced and to more sustainable, 'oscillating' dynamic equilibrium.

Being fully human: inquiring to set things right

To minimise the 'going wrong' and maximise the 'going right', how can we instead keep up the seeking and the being open to new questions and answers in order to keep our and each other's full cycle inquiring alive?

How to build in routine times, spaces and sacrosanct places for observing and speaking (especially at cross purposes), far far *sooner*—before too much damage is done, and before too many unwanted ways become 'the way we do things around here (or else)'? How to be able to 'power up' the strength of people's individual and joint questioning in the direction of more healthy life?

To protect the integrality of whole living systemicities, and receive the input and responses of all, we may most need to assert or defend the value of engaging in *all* of these moments and standpoints in collaborative interconnected[30] inquiry—both *within* an 'individual' organism[31] and also with and *between* 'the outer'[32] worlds of collective social relationships;[33] while also asserting or defending the value of moving between encapsulating and organ-ising the new (forming, order-ing, shaping and bounding), *and* being open to flux,[34] yielding and change (dissolving, fluidifying, receiving input and moving to re-form and re-shape in response).

Rather than 'putting aside' defences, a living systems process would *inquire* into their nature and purpose and the deeper values and observations driving them. Only by seeing how *this* action or practice (observation, reflection or plan) has been valued in its current most preferred 'vehicle' will there be a way for the organism to pursue its own evaluative criteria to assess whether an alternative vehicle would be better. The explanation of why what is being defended is of value is available from a deeper understanding of actions in relation to purposes within one's own *experienced systemic contex*t.[35] If and only if the new 'vehicle' (action, idea, image, vision, theory) appears to be better, offering a 'new and stronger life urge' (Jung 1967: 15) will it effortlessly *attract* the organism autopoetically to change.[36] In this sense 'change comes from within', but only through responding to a 'calling forth'-resonant environment. The 'resource' cannot know it is needed unless it is in close human 'ecological' relationship with the organism, and able to detect 'the request/invitation' for input into its being.

Take the example of routine geriatrics practice of removing people from their homes when they have been deemed a danger to themselves on the basis of a standardised cognitive functioning test. They may indeed be unable. And in such an instance it is resonant human service practice when the older person's own inquiring reaches the conclusion they would like a more convivial enabling environment and the professional can assist this change into fruition. But frequently professionals may reach this conclusion more quickly, and much pain, anger and wrenching feeling results from what may in practice be a mismatch in inquiring. However professionals' reflective inquiring practice has also led to some startling insights about the ways in which older people, even with Alzheimer's disease—when free to be their own 'researchers'—have designed and managed their living environment to be an effective enabling extension of themselves in ways largely invisible to people coming in and out of their home environment.

Andy Clark, an American cognitive scientist, has argued the mind extends beyond the brain into the world using the idea of the 'cyborg' (from the Greek *cybernentes*, steering and *borg*, through environment). He builds on the observations of Caroline Bowman and colleagues who realised that elderly people were structuring their home to support their functioning, for example, by leaving books with pictures of known people or other important items in open view instead of being hidden away in drawers. They noticed they might leave the doors open so they could see what the room was. He concluded that taking them out of that environment and putting them in a home where they don't have their things organised around them in this way would be tantamount to imposing a kind of cognitive damage on their neural networks, like the effect of a brain lesion (Clark 2003).

Usually, among a living system's cast of players someone eventually can or will stop and notice the discrepancies, whether positive or negative, and feel compelled enough to observe more closely and begin a conversation about what they are observing. Then they and others may be inspired or driven to commence and then continue a dialogue (and 'multilogue') about their observations among ever increasing numbers of people, until movement builds all the way to breakthrough thinking and a critical mass for new productive action. Voices of intention can thus promote the breaking of the impasses that allow a start to inquiring to solve problems and generate better worlds.

This brings us full cycle to the moment when people, groups, organisations or communities first make a move *towards* something or some state, towards some resource or input positively sought after, striven for, desired, needed or wanted to bring greater life—in contrast to withdrawing into 'safe mode' away from the negatively valorised. Here the point of questioning is to reconnect or touch base with deeper valued images and visions that 'feed' purpose and meaning to the seeking. Whether the search is for basic foodstuffs, dwellings or rituals, certainty, comfort or adventure—from babies' in-born capacity to distinguish nutritional input at birth, to adult human service providers' and users' ability to identify when they feel most 'alive' in relation to each other—the identification of 'what gives life' may be a 'royal road' to identifying the conditions for life.

Thus we would ask, 'What is it that people seek in their lives? What it is that brings human services workers into their jobs, professions and vocations in the first place? What is it that attracts critical reference groups to seek assistance and resources? How could things be better?

The mental architecture of living systems inquiry cycles provides a way of answering these kinds of questions—and shows why times and spaces in which people can engage together in such inquiry become so critical. So much can flow from these exchanges and from sustaining continued iterations of exchange over time. Inquiring is risk-taking for both sides. A legion of familiar defences will be there safeguarding and 'protecting' both parties from the inherent risks of unanswered questions—from avoiding them altogether to processing them within a narrow procedural repertoire overly derived from the already known and assumed, or tightly prescribed in a professional or job role, to financially insuring against such risks altogether (e.g. by very narrowly circumscribing legal responsibility).

But 'first do no harm' didn't attract anyone to a human services profession, nor does it offer enough to the person seeking the cessation of suffering and instead being more fully alive, and a 'duty of care' is as often a rationale for coercion. So the questioning journey begins—partly for 'the helper' to understand

Someone will reach out to communicate

better, but as a means to the end of 'the helped' on their own inquiry journey.

If asked how they would want to see their fellow human or community group currently before them by the end of their time together, they will answer—'back in kilter', 'back on their feet', back being 'together', 'good in themself', strong, energetic, confident, rowing their own boat, healthy, fit, glowing, active and feeling good. Not only might they co-inquire to discover how the person is already self-organising with 'growing points' for more, but also because this is pretty much what they would want for themselves. In this way the effective grounds for 'alongsided' solidarity form, as they do for co-inquiring with services, groups, organisations, programs, communities and larger social systemicities, all the way up to the greater oikos.

Human services workers as facilitators of inquiry
Facilitation of the inquiry process thus consists of holding the shape of the inquiry cycle process[37] described in Chapter 3—and accompanying, remembering, reminding, noticing any skipped stages and urging revisiting, or noticing where territory is already well-mapped and offering these observations; encouraging, supporting, resourcing, offering, pointing in the direction of further cybernetic[38] self-organising, scaffolding, enabling, and sometimes supplying what is needed. At the two crucial phase changes or liminal thresholds—firstly, from a known but unwanted past to wanting a possible better future and secondly, from a possible better future to a new living reality that is checked and potentially revised— the 'telling of the story' is sought, all the while sitting with (and holding open) the space in which resonance may take place, with the co-inquirer taking their lead from where the critical inquirer is 'at'.

When we are facilitating others' inquiry it will depend as much on our openness to questioning as it will to our ability to listen to the answers. We will do better the more we know ourselves and others, the more we can see the interconnections and identify the driving energies, purposes, intentions and experiences to date, the more we bring resourcing to bear, shape the inquiry, and accompany the transformative moments through the layers of protective defence that may have needed to be built (the density of 'structuring' relationships in which people are themselves held—constrained *or* enabled).

Inquiry scales up from smaller to larger systemicities
What may start as an internal co-inquiry (or within an 'inner inquirer') can quickly cross the boundaries when the connections are made and others join or are included. In turn these small groups may extend to include other people's situations and experiences, drawing those others from the relevant critical inquirer's lifeworld, included 'critical friends', or other like-minded individuals from the human services practitioner's work-world (whether practitioners or other clients), self-help, community-based groups or other kinds of human service people or material possibilities. As the co-inquiries expand, the methodological principles remain the same, but scaled up, repeating tiny cycles of observation and discussion of existing situations faced, needs and desires, and 'first thoughts' about possible actions, resulting in invitations being extended to the next relevant stakeholders,[39] the reflections deepening into new plans and actions, and the cycles repeating until the size and scale may warrant the language of small 'r' becoming that of larger 'R' research (or evaluation).

In a deep sense co-inquiry becomes dialogue and then 'multilogue', across differences and distances in understanding, emerging through many iterations and 'morphings'—bringing to bear on the puzzle or desire whatever bodies of evidence and observation, perception and experience participants can muster. In a sense the real work of understanding begins in the exchanges about the meaning of what has been observed and the implications for changed or new action in relation to what is most deeply valued. In this way,

Much of what research and evaluation involves is coming to see the other person's perspective.
MICHAEL PATTON, ST PAUL, MINNESOTA, 1995

The design of the inquiry process becomes the way a living system as a kind of 'community of scientists' comes to know itself:

Action research is the way groups of people can organise the conditions under which they can learn from their experiences.
ROBIN MCTAGGART, 1991

Think of the two strands of the DNA molecule with little scaffolding bridges built between the two: as dialogic communication provides a feedback system. (See Figure 20 Cross-over 'snakes' dialogic research design in Chapter 5 exemplar 1 in the acute psychiatric services area. For a more dynamic image see: http://upload.wikimedia.org/wikipedia/commons/8/81/ADN_animation.gif.)

It now perhaps becomes clearer why the human services enterprise may be unable to afford not to make dynamic change at least as welcome as it makes stabilising organisation welcome.

Human inquiry styles and preferences around living systems cycles at any scale

The following Table 7 analyses living human systems—whether individual, group, community, organisational and 'service systems'—both at their best and characteristic as they move through the processes of inquiring to change, take new action, stabilise, and respond and adapt again; and also at their most stressed (when their inquiry preferences are blocked, short-circuited, unbalanced or missed altogether).

There is here a strong argument for understanding one's own and each other's inquiry preferences so as not to think that others' preferences (if they differ from ours) are thereby mistaken or inferior (and 'mistake the other for the enemy')—and also to understand the ways in which inquiry proceeds (or can cease) under conditions of distress.

This may be the next great frontier for human exploration—understanding both how different we may be in our inquiry preferences and how we find our way round the cycles of inquiry in differing ways, at the same time as discovering how we are all nevertheless using the same kinds of human inquiry processes or underlying mental architecture, whether in our own minds or in a group mind 'around the table', or in a kind of 'greater mind' (at any scale).

In Table 7 there are two sets of possibilities articulated—one of the preferences exercised in resonant relationships of 'alongsided' inquiry, the other showing the preferences exercised in dissonant relationships of ' cross-purposes' co-inquiry.

The table depicts the distinctive patterns of human thought and action resulting from the corresponding patterns of preferred mental inquiry processes for observing, reflecting, planning and acting by taking in and processing information using perceiving (sensing knowing and intuitive knowing) and for organising,

concluding and deciding about it by two kinds of critical judging (rational thinking and rational feeling)[40]—'writ small' in the 'individual' inquiring organism or systemicity, and 'writ large' for inquiring social 'organisms' or systemicities, that is, embodied in living holarchic nested systemicities at any scale.

This not only offers a clearer picture of why people might develop characteristically different systemic responses to human need, but also why they might also show characteristic patterns under stress and be less able to exercise their usual inquiry preferences in those circumstances.

Because all can and do continually get 'right round the cycle' to accomplish life, any person or group can usually step forward and draw on their possibly unpreferred inquiry characteristics to respond to a situation if need be. The loss (or socialised removal) of this capacity for full cycle autopoesis may result in significant and endangering loss of resilience and flexible capacity for life by the organism at whatever scale.

A word about language in human services

Since language is critical to any modal or dominant narrative or discourse about the presence and impact of differing preferred responses as 'human service', as we saw in Chapter 3, it will also be a clue to transforming systemic responses. Words encapsulate meanings for those using or encountering them (including multiple and fluid meanings), and thus agreement around meanings and definitions is the work of shaping and deciding about the nature of the valued and desired 'built form' of human service practice.

At different times, professionals and other systems players have, for example, variously named and renamed the end-beneficiary[41] group in human services—as charitable[42] cases,[43] problem[44] families, dysfunctional[45] clients,[46] patients,[47] recipients, service-users, consumers,[48] customers,[49] purchasers,[50] service units, participants,[51] partners[52] and collaborators. The derivations and meanings of these tell part of the story that has come to be congealed in usage that stigmatised (much as the proximal 'aberrant cell' can be blamed for the larger organism's systemic but more distal impact). A matching nomenclature has developed for the 'helpers' class—of almoners,[53] service[54]-providers,[55] service-deliverers,[56] staff,[57] educated professional practitioners,[58] helpers,[59] care[60]-givers,[61] therapists[62] and consultants.[63] Each of these terms may be inquired into for the extent to which their meanings 'give life' or perpetuate systemicities that do not.

In a way all these terms have taken the ancient mutual care roles of families, friends and communities and created divisions of labour in which some are transformed into paid professional workforces in industrial and post-industrial societies, and others become the unpaid professionally helped. In doing so, the meanings of the descriptors often start out with life-giving intentions but end with stigmatising, punitive and life-diminishing meanings.

Perhaps in future we may want instead to name 'human services': 'human life resources', if rather than some being 'slaves to' or 'managers of' others (whether for duty, love, instrumental or material advantage), we might prefer to more willingly resource the autopoetic *life* in each other and in all of our collective social 'organisms' (for meaningful duty *and* thoughtful love *and* effective fair benefit).

In what follows then, the sequence of terminology flowing from and expressing a living systems epistemology identifies a time and place for differing responses as one inquires 'full cycle'—beginning in current 'action' based on previous assumptions and received knowledge with 'serve' (although newly interpreted), then moving to new 'observation' with '*care-give*' and '*care for*', and '*reflection*' with 'care about' and '*inspire*', then 'planning' with '*activate*' and '*enable*', returning full cycle to new 'action' with '*contribute*'.

The language chosen is a best attempt (see the detailed endnotes for the rationales for selection). However the most important thing is to observe the differing *forms* and *processes* of care that take place at the differing 'moments' or standpoints around the inquiry cycle. The debates between these may be able to give way to understanding when and under what conditions each is appropriate (not if).

Diagram 4 below represents the above table cyclically—'writ small' for the individual inquiring human systemicity and their preferred preferences for taking in, processing and acting on information to achieve life; and Diagram 5 represents the same processes 'writ large' for the inquiring social systemicity, showing the modal cultures that form at different moments around the cycle.

Being really human: building and rebuilding stable dynamic living human (service) systems

Some implications for practice

In a systemic sense then, 'overdoing' or 'underdoing' any inquiry preferences may generate a dominant culture that simultaneously suppresses or denies unpreferred opposites in the cycle. While a certain degree of this provides for the necessary oscillating flux (e.g. the cycling between dynamism and equilibrium) that generates enough life-giving discrepancy, perturbation, change and new organisation, it can also become more-or-less life-threatening when not within the limits that the organism can self-manage. Yet the warning signs may be all too easy to overlook when small oscillations that make us uneasy often remain unremarked, and large ones can quickly become undiscussible for reasons that the previous Table 7 made clearer. That is, to greater or lesser extents:

- In the moment of concentrating on *acting* based on an existing rationale it is hard to think about a new or alternative way of acting based on a different logic
- In the moment of deciding about observations on the basis of rational *feeling*, it may be difficult to decide on the basis of logical calculations about the consequences of a new theory
- In the moment of contemplative *reflection* as we are intuiting new connections, it may be difficult to be asked to absorb, provide or act on new detailed observational data
- In the moment of calculating possible logical consequences when *planning* a course of action, it may be difficult to respond to strong unresolved emotions expressed in response to past actions or these new conjectures.

If we are pressured, or blocked regularly in any of these ways, we may find ourselves 'in the grip' of asystemic reaction—a reaction that may be where it 'needs to be' if that is where the focus of inquiry is, but needing to be carefully examined for its origins if that isn't the case.

More conscious inquiry may then be needed to re-include the lost or excluded aspects.

The key ways to limit these difficulties are firstly, to do justice to the questions when traversing around

CONTINUED PAGE 181

TABLE 7. SYSTEMIC INQUIRY BY, WITH AND FOR CRITICAL INQUIRERS IN HUMAN SERVICE SYSTEMS

Inquiry cycle focus	At best (resonant)	At most stressed[68] (dissonant)
Number and description Matches the sequence of questions in Chapter 3	**Form of human assistance**[67] Description of characteristic form of inquiry (epistemology) at this moment of the cycle	**Characteristics when 'in the grip'**[69]
Associated most used inquiry preferences[65] *And opposite and least used inquiry preferences for the particular part of the cycle*[66]	*Characteristic grace* *Characteristic risk* *Questions to ask to inquire more deeply*	*Take time out to return to inquiry mode by…* *Signs of return from stressed state*
ACT		
1 [Overlapping with questions 9, 10 of previous cycle] **Implementing the planned action and beginning to observe, analyse, describe** *Most used inquiry preferences for this part of the cycle:* sensing sensing–thinking sensing–feeling	**Serve**[71] At this point in the cycle close and detailed attention is given to what has to be done to accomplish existing 'duty of care' goals; ordering and classifying assists systematising pattern formation/recognition (to align with 'the way it's supposed to be' from the prior cycle of inquiry), tracking, describing and measuring progress/achievement (or deviations from the program theory), with reliance on empirical evidence. Enables adapting and refining/perfecting within the (new) now existing system logic; with a value on identifying the best way/s to achieve the given ends; combined with attention to past and present accrued experience and the already known ('tried and true'). Focusing on current realities can mean an ability to move quickly to puzzle solving and improvement, or refinement within the existing agreed and prescribed parameters. *Characteristic graces:* Accuracy Safeguarding organisation Diligence	At this moment of specific practicalities, intuition about wider connections may be less relied on; thus there may be discomfort with 'winging it' or imagining or brainstorming outcomes other than those already identified that are being enacted. Insistence on focusing on concrete forms of observation and measurement may mean rejection of vital new or missing ideas, experiences, symbolism or metaphor, and result in not seeing (and even denying) the impact of the unseen as being 'unreal' or 'unrealistic'. As this is a time of 'making things happen' that are logical in terms of the theory behind them, there can be a risk of depersonalising what can become a rather mechanical replication of the planned form, and over resort to authoritative 'doing to, for or at' to achieve the intended goals. This is meant to enhance efficiency or control the risk and uncertainty of the unknown, but may be taken to the point of domination and loss of responsibility characteristic at this point in the cycle (thus systemically creating dependency or passive compliance). It may also mean moving too quickly to insisting on behavioural procedure or rules, or to quelling disorder and not taking into account hidden implications or deeper consequences;

Opposite and least used inquiry preferences for this part of the cycle:
reflection
intuition
intuitive–feeling

Characteristic risk:
Dutiful or efficient action can lose meaning or inspiration if lose sight of original deeper guiding values and purposes

Ask: Is this task, activity, action or practice (still) life-enhancing for the critical reference (inquiry) end-beneficiary group? Are the signs and indicators of effectiveness still meaningful for them, the clients, groups and communities to benefit?

or these may be explored too slowly if seen as untrustworthy. Meaning may be misread, and people seen as 'difficult' or 'a problem' and punished as 'deviant' —when in practice 'the dysfunctional' points to people who are systemically stressed or distressed, indicating the system or practice is not working.

Take time out to ask: what other meanings or implications might the apparent facts have through others' eyes or in other contexts?—particularly those who are meant to benefit. Notice what is good or not good by reference to the original values and purposes of the action

Sign of return from stressed state: accurate insights and the ability to act on them humanely

OBSERVE

2

Taking the implemented action and observing, describing, synthesising
Most used inquiry preferences for this part of the cycle:
sensing
sensing–feeling
sensing–thinking

Care-give[72]

Here there may be increased sensitivity to realities of human comfort, suffering or difficulties, and early picking up on things going wrong; an appreciation of the facts of what people are capable of, based on evidence of past experience and observation of people's responses in an emergency. Value on 'doing the right thing' by people as exercising a 'duty to care' using tried and true methods, and handbooks of procedures.

Characteristic grace:
Practical meeting of needs

Characteristic risk:
Replicating old ways and duties that are no longer effective rather than seeing the need to move to try new and better ones

Ask: How might seeing things differently help explain things better? What else is going on in the bigger picture? What steps could be taken in regard to that?

In addition to overlap with the above, an increasing sensitivity to uncertainty for people may result in confusion, fears of the worst and even the catastrophic; a loss of characteristic control over facts and details may provoke overly quick acting or rigidity to try and act to hold onto feeling values. A search for understanding may rest on proximal explanation that can come across as personalised blaming (who or whatever is systemically closest), or distal explanation may invoke fatalism or super natural forces when there isn't time to explore more meaningful connections for actions that can be taken.

Take time out to clarify what's most important in the longer term and what can be done in the short term that is consistent with deeper human values

Sign of return from stressed state: Broader perspective on the future which restores optimism about possibilities

Opposite and least used inquiry preferences for this part of the cycle:
reflection
intuition
intuitive–thinking

TABLE 7. SYSTEMIC INQUIRY BY, WITH AND FOR CRITICAL INQUIRERS IN HUMAN SERVICE SYSTEMS CONTINUED

3

Reflecting on action, ethical evaluation

Most used inquiry preferences for this part of the cycle:
feeling
sensing–feeling
sensing–intuition

Opposite and least used inquiry preferences for this part of the cycle:
reflection–planning
thinking
thinking–intuitively

Care for

Evaluative ability is exercised at this point to identify what is going well for people, and acute awareness of when it is not; and an openness and flexibility to enable people to come to new realisations for themselves or change their thinking to align with the deeper human values available in the system; trusting that information or understandings will emerge, comfortable with non-verbal communication, silences, optimistic about what can emerge from positive feedback and attuned relations between people, and that solutions people might select from a repertoire might offer rapid relief.

Characteristic grace:
Personal devotion to observant caring

Characteristic risk:
Not advocating for what is of most value in the face of conflicting views or complexity
Ask: What would it take to move to better actions or practices?

In addition to the above, conflict and disharmony may induce uncharacteristic criticism, all-or-nothing (black and white) judgements, inflexibility around changing existing approaches, and trying to 'make people do the right thing' rather than continuing to resource their autopoesis. If not able to take the time to think further round the cycle there may be a compulsive search for 'real' or absolute truth involving resort to convoluted logic or blind adherence to regimes that might be recommended by those who sound certain or speak from positions that have always seemed authoritative.

Take time out to touch base with deeper values to re-chart directions

Sign of return from stressed state: Ability to sit with unreconciled conflict

REFLECT

4

Reflecting on observation, empathetic imagining

Most used inquiry preferences for this part of the cycle:
feeling
feeling–intuition
feeling–sensing

Care about

Observational abilities hold up a subjective and personal mirror to how things are, or how they may be going well or not for people. Ability to accept wide diversity in ways of being or doing and trust in the potential of people and situations provides a poetic outlook. Tolerant of things that are not explainable (or not yet been explained), but highly interested in new ways of perceiving and understanding that might lead to real improvement in situations for people. Value on creating the connections that can be channels to resource human responsiveness, and a value on narrative as a whole/healing (integrating) method for understanding.

Characteristic grace:
Concern about others

Characteristic risk:
Not moving to look at how to implement what is of most value
Ask: What would it take for a more ideal course of action to be achieved in this situation?

If unable to respond adequately to others' feelings and particularly to overwhelming pain or suffering, may forcefully 'over care', or burn out or become critical if human values neglected, and even 'excessively' logical or categorical, cynical, distrustful or reactive. May act precipitously or resort to hyperbole in the search for certainty about promoting values or to subtle 'bossiness' or pressure experienced as manipulation to try to exercise uncharacteristic command and control.

Take time out to validate own feelings, values, competence and effectiveness

Sign of return from stressed state: Confidence in the transformative power of a well-resourced field of possibilities

Opposite and least used inquiry preferences for this part of the cycle:
planning–acting
thinking
thinking–sensing

TABLE 7. SYSTEMIC INQUIRY BY, WITH AND FOR CRITICAL INQUIRERS IN HUMAN SERVICE SYSTEMS CONTINUED

5

Reflecting on Observations and moving to Planning from new theory

Most used inquiry preferences for this part of the cycle:
intuition
intuitive–feeling
intuitive–thinking

Opposite and least used inquiry preferences for this part of the cycle:
action replication
sensing
sensing–thinking

Inspire[73]

At this point there is a need to rise above a sea of observational details and see new connections between the 'facts' within 'bigger picture' contexts that give them meaning in relation to people's wellbeing (or lack of it). There needs to be a persistent search to understand and explain why things are as they are and create new theory and concepts for life-giving change, particularly through conversation or dialogue between the differing ways of seeing. This can then generate innovative re-framing and a fresh perspective, particularly bridging between negative situations for people and envisioned positive alternatives. At this point what is valuable is the sensitive and harmonious integration of transformed meaning for the emerging form's identity and narrative.

Characteristic grace:
Insight

Characteristic risk:
Confusion
Ask: What is the most important thing to do next to further the implementation of these insights?

Because change in the light of valued and purposeful meaning is critical at this point in the cycle, then rules or procedures applied for their own sake without relevance to their value-driven purposes, or systemic violation of human-centred values can result in vigorous reaction. An overload of unrelated details or undigested facts can result in confusion and inaccurate insight, or the absence of facts and details prior to this moment can mean 'not having enough to go on'.

Take time out to reassess the factual/ experiential basis for what is most important, and specify the most desirable goals and outcomes to be pursued next

Sign of return from stressed state: Clarity

6

Planning on the basis of reflection on observed action, to envision alternatives

Most used inquiry preferences for this part of the cycle:
intuition
intuitive–thinking
intuitive–feeling

Opposite and least used inquiry preferences for this part of the cycle:
action routinisation
sensing
sensing–feeling

Activate[74]

As above, and, energised by thinking things through and able to abstract the consequences of conclusions, characteristic optimism at this point emerges about the impact of well-planned innovations and actions aimed at realising ideals and principles and overcoming difficulties. Aim at catalysing the wider world from 'what could be' to 'what will be' by exposing others to, or conveying to them new learnings, knowledge, logic and methods. A preparedness to take risks is needed to meet the associated challenges and move an expressed desirable or needed trend further in the direction of take up and adoption. Value autonomy to pursue an effective integrated approach.

Characteristic grace:
Sharp mind

Characteristic risk:
Over-extension

Ask: How could these plans be operationalised to maintain the valued principles that will further the situation of the critical inquiry/reference group?

As above, and, because the focus is on moving forward to 'make a difference', then inhibiting rules, repetitive activities, not being taken seriously, or too-close supervision can lead to redoubled exertion (but with less effectiveness) and to the generation of possibilities without being able to follow through, plus annoyed and impatient reaction, or urgency that results in unnecessary competition to implement ideas. If there has not been widespread participation to this point, may be spearheading an empty force, and an insistence on cognitive strategies will be premature.

Take time out to rest and reset priorities that will benefit people

Sign of return from stressed state: Optimistic energy

TABLE 7. SYSTEMIC INQUIRY BY, WITH AND FOR CRITICAL INQUIRERS IN HUMAN SERVICE SYSTEMS CONTINUED

PLAN

7

Planning new action and its protection, calculate consequences

Most used inquiry preferences for this part of the cycle:
thinking
intuitive–thinking
sensing–thinking

Opposite and least used inquiry preferences for this part of the cycle:
observation with feeling
intuitive–feeling

Enable[75]

At this point there is most focus on deducing the logical consequences of a range of ideas and ways of thinking about (or modelling) possible future actions in the light of existing realities. Capability for sceptical critique ('playing the devil's advocate') and remaining open to alternative ways of thinking is needed to bring clarity about the various emerging options for envisioned action or problem solving. Value competence by use of logic, and the mastery of ideas, definitions, models or plans, for proposing, enacting, strategising or advising about them for best effect. At this point in the cycle may approach the world with a poetic threshold-straddling sense of perspective or feel like an objective observer from a strategic distance, aerial 'helicopter' or big picture viewpoint.

Characteristic grace:
Principled agenda

Characteristic risk:
Swamped by the expression of felt emotion and unresolved issues

Ask: What would the people affected think and feel about this plan; what would they say will be the implications? Will it meet their needs as they themselves express them?

Because personal feeling may be in the background at this moment of generalised logical calculation, there may be discomfort with people's expressions of lived felt experience, and a resulting apparent detached coolness, or poor timing in describing what is theoretically logical (as opposed to humanly desirable); or even active expression of suspicion, mistrust or disdain for sentiment or personal compassion. There may be an unpreparedness to move decisively to action on the basis of the ideas (if drawn from overly distal contexts) for fear of 'getting it wrong', or a lack of transparency or resort to secretiveness for fear of losing control of the subsequent action. In order to take some (or any) action, the need to perform or succeed may mean too-quickly opting for engineering the pragmatically possible rather than championing the ethically desirable, or else succumbing to aligning with existing powerful realities ('structures'), thus appearing to relinquish the commitment to/or responsibility for acting on principles to further human wellbeing. Intuition and logic can give a sense of 'seeing and knowing it all' that can appear arrogant, dogmatic, prescriptive or lacking in humility about how events might turn out.

Take time out to observe and take into account one's own and others' feelings, and be prepared to retrace steps back to the values and evidence that are driving the principles and thinking in the first place

Sign of return from stressed state: Gracefulness

ACT [new]

8, 9, 10

Implementing the planned action design and its support and observation

Most used inquiry preferences for this part of the cycle:
thinking
sensing–thinking
thinking–intuition

Opposite and least used inquiry preferences for this part of the cycle:
reflection on observation
feeling
feeling–intuition

Contribute[76]

Clarity around implementation means a need at this point in the cycle to spot logical flaws in causality, especially regarding efficiency and effectiveness as defined. Attention to precision, clarity, agreed truth, accuracy and detailed measurement allows authoritative correction of errors so things can follow the new program logic and pattern. Instituting and faithfully following the schedule of tasks and activities to engineer the planned 'good works' may require articulating and following rules and standard operating procedures and fulfilling these duties in valued teams, programs and institutions that ensure reducing variance and getting things done 'the way they should be'. Actions are then ongoingly monitored, inspected or watched over by the organism (supervised).

Characteristic grace:
Want to do the best and right thing for others

Characteristic risk:
Loss of harmony with deeper human values and purposes

Ask: Who will be able to do what, when, where and how? How do people feel about this? Is there another way of seeing it? Listen carefully to new incoming input or feedback, particularly from the critical inquiry/reference group. Check that own conscience feels (truly) clear. Consider how a decision could be revised to take new information into account.

In order to focus on enacting the agreed presumptions in an orderly and organised way for maximum certainty, can react with denial, rigidity to expressions of deviance, dissent or unresolved felt emotion, with apparent loss of sensitivity to people's welfare, and even harshness. Tendency under these conditions to treat others (and self impersonally even as machine-like and perfectible. Such a reaction can transform characteristic 'servant leadership' at this point in the cycle into a 'dominating master', and result in active rejection of vital problematisation of still existing discrepancies needing further inquiry. This 'doing to, at or on behalf of' others is intended to achieve perfectionist implementation, but can be experienced as fear-inducing authoritarianism and lead to repression of input, feedback, hunches, insights and creativity; and treasured teamwork can become conformist groupthink.

Take time out to check actions are still aligned with achieving original guiding purpose, ethical values and principles to serve the critical inquiry/reference group.

Sign of return from stressed state: Ability to act responsibly with sensitivity

Change to
new way/s

Rational
Thinking

Intuitive
Thinking

Sensing
Thinking

Intuitive
feeling

Sensing
Feeling

Rational
Feeling

Change
from old
way/s

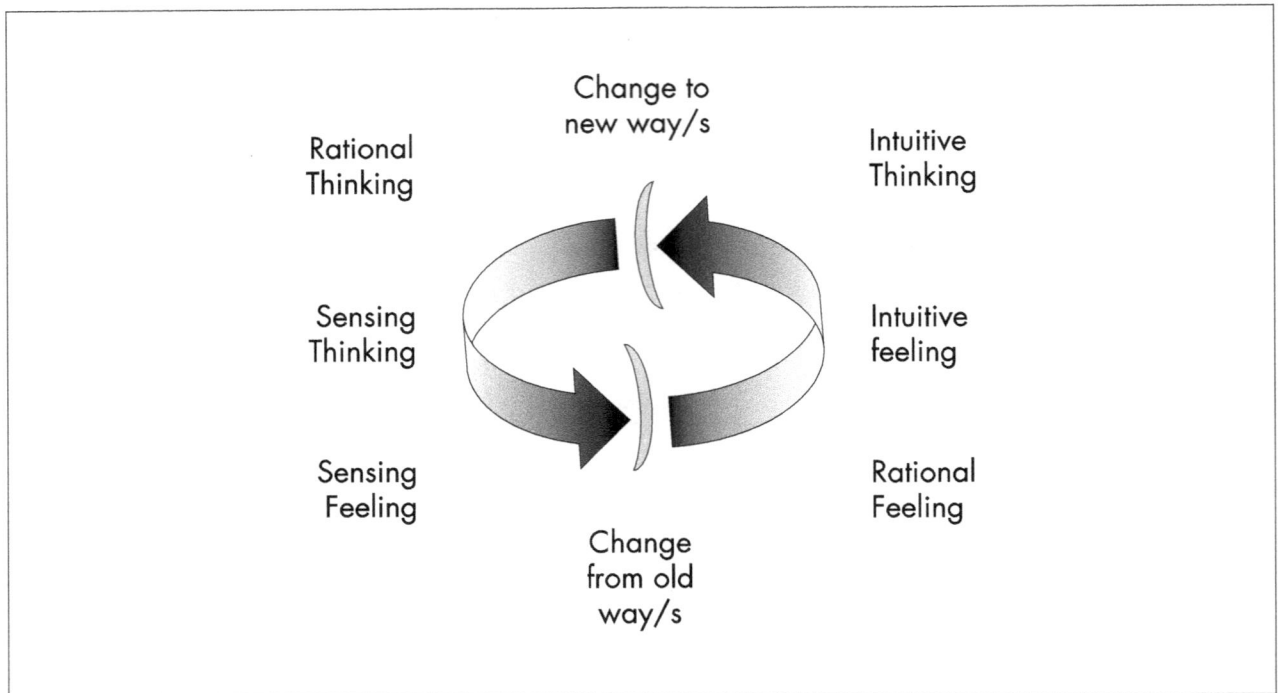

Figure 17. Cyclic representation of embodied individual inquiry processes

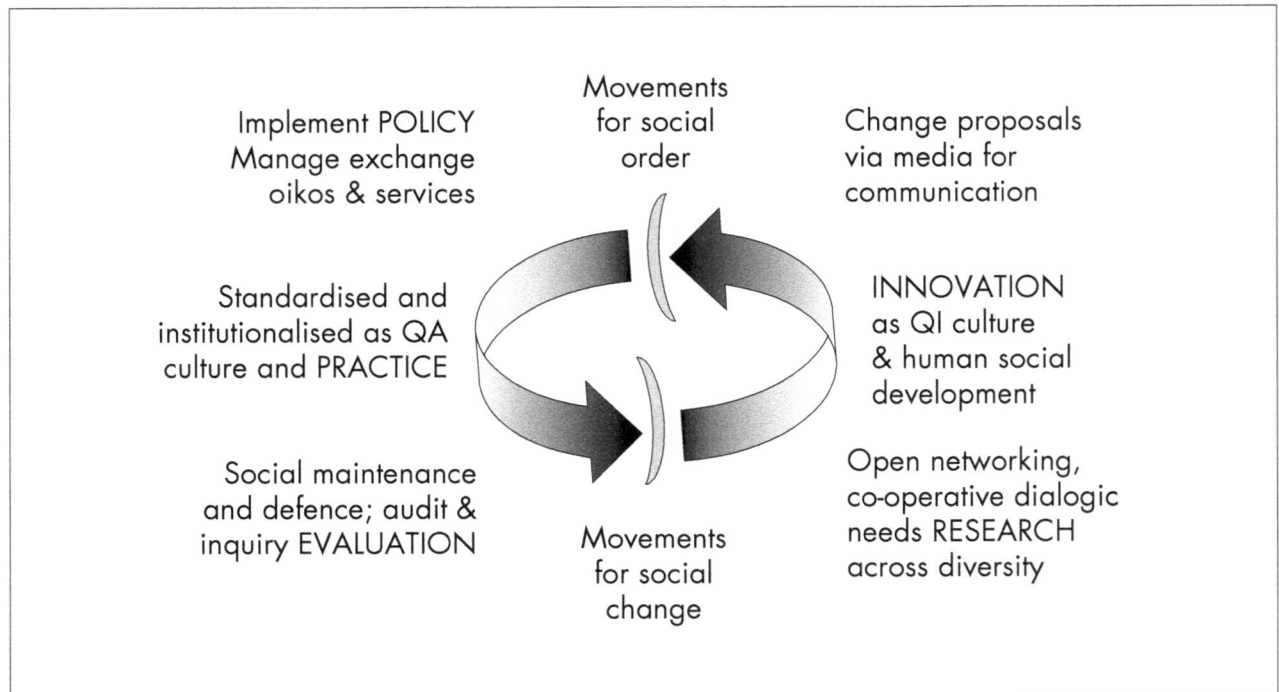

Movements
for social
order

Implement POLICY
Manage exchange
oikos & services

Change proposals
via media for
communication

Standardised and
institutionalised as QA
culture and PRACTICE

INNOVATION
as QI culture
& human social
development

Social maintenance
and defence; audit &
inquiry EVALUATION

Open networking,
co-operative dialogic
needs RESEARCH
across diversity

Movements
for social
change

Figure 18. Cyclic representation of embodied social forms in which inquiry in living human systems takes place

CONTINUED FROM PAGE 171

the cycle *at the time*, and secondly, to build in ways to return to inquiry mode no matter at what point difficulties arise. That is:

- To have *observed* (or return to observing) action until we are *really* clear and open-eyed about what our monitoring senses are telling us are the apparent facts (the visible, audible, literal and perceivable), as well as the facts of thought and feeling regarding all the relevant experienced action and practice.
- To have *reflected* (or be able to return to reflection) on those observations until we have properly clarified their meaning for *all* relevant parties, both apparent and immediate, as concrete signs, as well as more deeply embedded in wider field relationships, and connections, past, present and future that change their symbolising meaning in significant ways.
- To have *planned* (or be able to return to planning) until we can think through well-grounded new conclusions (but not before time) and then work out what the principles would be and consider their consequences, and calculate how they would work in relation to existing action and practice.
- To have *acted* on those plans (or returned to current action) in their forms, programs and procedures until well-institutionalised in cultures of practice with which relevant parties are truly satisfied.

Matters of scale and size

Here then is a reminder of the deeper rationale for inquiry groups, teams and communities of practice (Wenger 1998) that are at a scale and size to be autopoetic enough to be able to identify their issues, ask the questions and pursue the answers together right round the cycle—together deciding how long it should take, who should be involved, what methods should be used, and what sense to make of the observations, and what to try out in action next—all the while building carefully from the critical values driving the inquiry. The idea of nested systemicities in a holarchy is one way of trying to express this matter of the dynamic balance within each organism that makes up any larger 'organism' which in turn constitutes even larger organisms—all in 'right relationship', or at the relevant scale for sustaining the principles and practices of inquiring living systems.

Not to do so is to again risk 'overdoing' any of the moments or standpoints, for example staying too long and exclusively in any particular moment or 'station of the cycle'; or alternatively risking 'underdoing' any by moving too quickly through them. The signs of dynamic imbalance become visible whenever living systems make unnecessary or uncorrected errors, become too stressed or pressured, too fast or too slow, too out of kilter, overly rigid, forceful or inaccurately interventionist, or too flexible, fluid, laissez faire and yielding; in all cases unable to realise their most deeply valued and embodied life purposes.

Participation full cycle as the essential 'field' of human (service) assistance for autopoesis

The need for participation is obvious now, not just as a nice democratic idea or politeness or optional add-on 'if there is time', but as the essential relational vehicle for life-giving co-inquiry. Participation is thus not to be confused with 'being participated', a term that has arisen out of people's frustration at superficial or enforced inquiry consultations for appearances sake, and not otherwise aligned with the critical inquirer's process. Participation is the essential field of relationality that ensures the conditions for life.

This is why it is necessary to attract and keep all 'at the table' throughout the process, with none relevant rendered unimportant, and none too all-important. All understood to have critical intelligence, observations, thoughts, feelings, reflections and ideas to contribute—aided and assisted (but never replaced) by those who may be particularly good or quick at any of these 'stations of the cycle'—yet with time and place built in to give all a chance to contribute from their essential and differing perspectives and experiences. Some may step forward (or be sought out) at particular points to offer such inquiry preference 'consultancy' to the larger inquiry group, team or community of practice. However it is critical that any specialisation or division of labour that spins out from the central inquiry process 'comes back in' to the collective journey around the cycle—contributing their special or detailed data collected, bodies of evidence, judgements, advice or insights, to equip and inform the autopoetic collaborative decision making, and not to substitute for it.

The necessity of integrality and the risks of unconnected 'divisions of inquiry labour'

To do otherwise is as noted to seriously risk endangering imbalance or ending up having to resort to 'Chinese whispers' with the subsequent loss of critical messages as they are handed from one process moment to the next, being 'edited' or discounted by those 'further round the cycle' who did not adequately participate and now do not adequately grasp the full import of all the previous moments and standpoints—no matter how much they might *think* they do. Most important of all, to remove the inquiry from the hands of the critical (autopoetic) inquirers is to risk error as well as the helpless passivity of those excluded and their increasing reliance on those coming in later to the inquiry process. As the locus of control and thus the burden of responsibility shifts to those who may not fully know what they are doing or why (but *think* they do or think that they should because of a kind of 'inquiry preference ethnocentrism'), the life of all eventually becomes endangered.

We know how it feels to be surprised, unwilling or bewildered 'participants' in 'team meetings' or corporate fora where enthusiastic (or cynical) leaders or managers, who have already planned or been 'given the line' (or their orders), are asking people to 'take ownership' and 'be responsible' for the 'next new thing', whiteboard grand plan, design, program, product, restructure or policy change that has not ensued from prior collaborative inquiry processes.[77]

The grumbling but often good-natured 'troops and minions' are urged to share in a sense of commitment to it and, as the punchline usually involves carrots (achieve your dreams for our clients) or sticks (achieve your soon-to-be-measured performance to keep receiving your salary), everyone goes off to try and get a handle on how the new plans from 'above' are to be operationalised. The grumbling may remain mostly suppressed and undiscussible until, further down the track, things are not working. Or worse, if 'outcome data' is indeed 'after the event' and can be ignored to save face or trouble, service solutions may linger on for a very long time never being quite right, but now firmly entrenched as practice and culture. Or worse still if there are remnants of deeply entrenched 'divisions of inquiry preferences labour', based on gender,[78] or Taylorism's take on class that some are the thinkers and planners and some are the action doers.

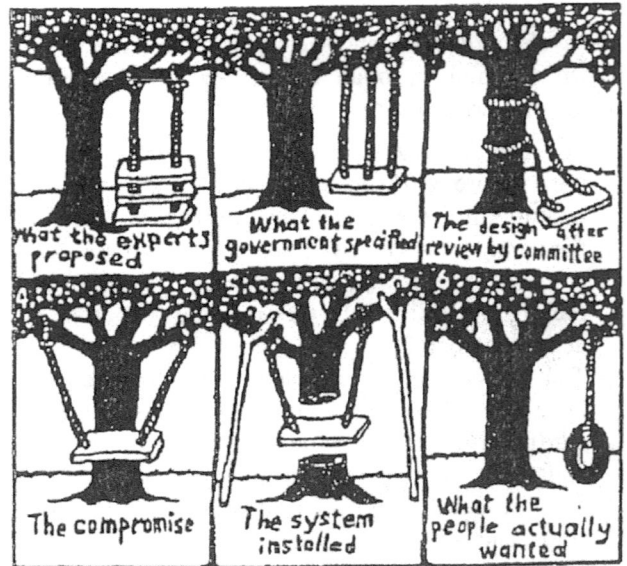

What the experts proposed
What the government specified
The design after review by committee
The compromise
The system installed
What the people actually wanted

Source: Journal of South–North Network Cultures and Development 1995

In this regard Alan Roberts quotes Frederick Winslow Taylor's starkly prejudiced (prejudging) and endangering presumptions guiding 'scientific management'. This was a movement that contributed to the creation of the now endemic modernist and mechanistic social, economic and political monoculture focused on narrow parts of the inquiry cycle, increasingly ensuring few grasp the whole and all are compromised by the humanly ecologically unsustainable outcomes:

> All possible brain work should be removed from the shop and centred in the planning or laying-out department...As the workmen frequently say when they first come under this system, 'Why, I am not allowed to think or move without someone interfering or doing it for me!' The same criticism and objection, however, can be raised against all other modern subdivisions of labour...The man who is physically able to handle pig-iron and is sufficiently phlegmatic and stupid to choose this for his occupation is rarely able to comprehend the science of handling pig-iron. (Taylor quoted in Roberts 1979: 128)

More starkly, when such systemic preferences can override the good sense of the 'intelligent whole', and action can be required without providing[79] time to stop and think,

*What good fortune for those in power
that people do not think.*
ADOLF HITLER

If instead all people in a setting are able to exercise together their abilities to act, observe, feel, reflect, think, plan and implement, then they will all already 'own' the outcomes, as they will have genuinely *been part of* the inquiry processes that have *generated* these outcomes in practice. Indeed they will already be moving into implementation, with any leadership acting to articulate the narrative of what is being done and why as a satisfying and comprehensive confirmation of what *together* has already been concluded.

The costs of not engaging in this 'epistemological democracy' include the time, money and energy spent:

- Trying to 'get people on board' with some course of action that has not arisen from their problems and seems unconnected with them
- Encouraging or requiring people to do things which are not life-giving and which they don't see the sense in
- Having to manage from 'top down', the recurrent bouts of perturbance and turbulence from defensiveness, anger, projection, helplessness, depression, reactivity, aggression and conflict
- Holding people and their actions in unwanted patterns when they continuously try to veer towards more preferred patterns
- Punishing those who deviate from enforced, unhealthy, unwanted or excluding patterns
- Having eventually to retrace the steps of incomplete, corrupted or distorted inquiry back to a point where all may be back 'in sync' before the critical inquiry group can go forward with assistance in more life-giving collaboration
- Having to 'break concrete' after the event of the new practices that 'everyone knew' should not have been implemented in the first place, incurring the risk of even more heavily defensive reactions as these structures now carry power and rigidity of their own
- Having to repair, apologise for and compensate the damage done that resulted from the incomplete or unbalanced cycles of inquiry that yielded the incorrect, poor or damaging results in the first place.

These are the practical costs of not operating 'distributed' self-organising 'intelligent systems'.

Indeed with enough poorly conducted inquiry processes we can get enough misunderstanding, lack of feedback and stress to result in any amount of conflict, exclusion, competition, inequality, destructiveness, hatred of self and others, bullying, cruelty, individual, organisational and societal breakdown, and even the death of whole ecological systems.

*Those who can make you believe absurdities
can make you commit atrosities.*
VOLTAIRE, AUTHOR AND PHILOSPHER, 1694–1718

Large-scale wars like all human conflicts have their roots in small-scale inquiring processes that accrue observations, reflections and planned actions from vicious cycles of mutual life-destroying distortion.

The first casualty in war is truth.
HIRAM JOHNSON, US SENATOR, 1918
ALSO TRACED TO GREEK WRITER/POET AESCHYLUS,
525–456 BC

Interestingly 'truce' comes from the same Germanic derivation as the word 'truth'—so to seek the truth of some matter (or seek a truce to conflict) is to begin to come back from potentially life-destroying conflict and use a search for life-seeking resolution. This is not to seek 'the' truth, or truth independent of context, but the truth or truths of *particular situated people* taking and observing action and making true observations, recounting true experiences, engaging in true reflections and exercising truth in planning—all truth/s *relative to their human relational purposes*, in actual context. And then these being brought into dialogue with others and their truths until processes of mutual inquiry and of checking each other's trains of rational thought and feeling can generate new insights and restart virtuous cycles of mutually enhancing life.

Here lies the wisdom in building in and rewarding the myriad of small 'right relations' in inquiry in response to the small 'wrong relations' that might start in the tiny actions of shutting down any aspect of the inquiry cycle. Of establishing enough systemic intelligence for everyone to hold the story of the way to proceed in relationship to each other. And to set in train life-giving replications rather than proceeding in a way that begins the replication of deterioration, unhealthy decay or distortion in human systemicities.

To take a familiar saying further ('Give a man a

fish and he eats for a day, teach a man to fish and he goes on being able to eat'), the implications of which are that a human service would involve all needed responses that result from engaging in full cycle inquiry:

> *We give people fish when they ask (because they are starving)*
> *We teach them to fish and how to pass on those skills to others (once they are no longer distracted by hunger)*
> *We work out together how to take down the walls that have been built around the fish pond (so that all can eat)*
> *Then together we work out how the pond is getting polluted (to protect everyone)*
> *And we invite the polluters for dinner (for which we will cook fish)*
>
> FROM AN IDEA AFTER SHANE CLAIBORNE, 2006

Research, evaluation and continuous inquiring for life

When conversations have been able to begin in small ways, initiated by those who first notice discrepancies between the expected and the not expected, and the desirable or not; *and* they are encouraged and resourced to build self-organising communities of inquiring practice, *and* those conversations can extend and spread to include all relevant parties, from all parts and levels of organisations; and together they are able to constantly revise the narrative of what has been observed and noticed, what are its perceived meanings and consequences, and what might be done differently in the next iterations of action and practice, then there are not only 'no surprises' but all are already beginning to take the new actions as the desirability and logic is created within each step of the integrated inquiry process (acquired directly by the inquirers within their participation) with less need for later special efforts to motivate, persuade or 'incentivate' with carrots or sticks.

We know what this kind of inquiry feels like—we feel like we 'have the plot', are part of creating it, are heard and listened to. We see others' responsiveness, as we also are responsive to them. We are in awe of what others see, hear, experience, think and are able to work out—and they similarly of our inquiry processes. Initial irritation gives way to deeper understanding. 'The normal' and expected expand in meaning and

variety. We go beyond teeth-gritted tolerance to frank appreciation. These kinds of inquiries result in ways of doing and being that we love to be in and around. Indeed it is in these kinds of communities of experience, communities of practice, or communities of in our homes, local and wider environments, services or workplaces, in which we have our best and most significant times, remember being our best person, and really feel we have contributed or that we are 'making a difference' that is positive and life-affirming in actual observed practice, and not just in theory or intention. We acquire lifelong friends when we have journeyed deeply together over long periods of time like this—whether we are 'clients' or 'service providers', the gaps and boundaries begin to become permeable, irrelevant or disappear.

There is an effortlessness or flow to this kind of effective 'distributed inquiry' as people:

- Are interested in 'how things are working out'
- Clear about 'where they are at' (even if it is smack in the middle of necessary periods of uncertainty, chaos, trouble or conflict!)
- Confident of being able to move forward (even if it means retracing steps to clarify missed or hidden information, observations or alternative ways of seeing things)
- Excited about pursuing and achieving break through insights
- Keen to experiment to test and check the value and truth of the new ideas
- Just as keen to seek new and better ideas if things are not working as well as hoped
- And proud of what they know and have achieved so far.

Because there have been many small flexible recursive iterations, a more accurate and relevant approach has been reflexively tried out to 'get it right' in the first place and to hold the story of the adjustments subsequently made. This minimises reliance on after-the-event evaluation, error detection and negative criticism. While these may still play an important part they will be more able to focus on refinement, and relevance in other settings (recursively 'going to scale').

It also becomes clear why those whose critical questions are driving their own inquiry are the least interested in getting it wrong. The critical inquiry group (collaborative community of practice, clients,

© S. Kneebone & Y. Wadsworth 2009

consumer groups etc.) will have the highest interest in 'getting it right' as it is they who will not be positively benefited (or suffer most) if they and their committed partners do not. Not that this—like any science—will always be self-protective against unexpected or unwanted sources of distortion, distraction or self-interest unaligned with that of the critical co-inquirers; nor lack of ideas, poor resources or any or all the other barriers to inquiry. But in the end the best results come from the 'multitude of counsellors'[80] offering all possible contributions to the critical inquirers' group, while all else risks goal displacement and a shift to serving the interests of unintended others. A university will not raise its staff's work satisfaction rate by eliminating casual staff from a satisfaction survey, or a government will not define as 'employed' for the purposes of its national employment statistics anyone who is 'working' as little as one hour a week, if the university's casual staff and the unemployed, respectively, become actively involved in assisting these institutions' inquiring remain better aligned with their deeper values and purposes.

The communications company that says 'we hear you' and offers a more generous market product, or the company that consults its employees about an office move, or the local council that encourages ratepayers affected by a particular issue to join a new residents' action group—all are opening themselves to the possibility of better feedback, even while they may still move to curtail this to 'protect' themselves from unwanted truths.

And for global life
Here is also a clue to recreating a more humanly productive *oikos*—Greek for the ancient and enduring greater human 'household' or 'economy' (*oikos*, meaning 'exchange', *nemo*, meaning 'manage') in which life-giving exchanges of all kinds may take place. An *oikos* which has morphed in the past through many different forms to one currently so large, specialised and goal-displaced (to producing privately owned money for a few and the loss of a common wealth for the many), that it is no longer producing what that money is *for*—the means for the sustainable meeting of human and related life needs into the future. Business values that do not stem from human values are not going to engage in full cycle inquiry processes, and eventually we see the impact in unnecessary or damaging products, growing in-equality in living incomes and conditions, and unending consumption of resources without consideration of the ecology of the whole.

There is a similar paradox in the phrase 'work-life balance' as if they could be two separate things. Yet where else would 'work' be if not as part of 'life'! And what kind of 'life' would not involve productive activity to achieve it? A 'new *oikos*' might integrate working along with resting, playing, nourishing and creating in an intelligent whole-of-life system that combines all inquiry preferences, all human capabilities, and through such diversity find its strength, resilience, generativity and sustainability.

An archetypal narrative of full cycle inquiry
Perhaps the startling popularity of the contemporary North American story of *The Wizard of Oz* speaks to its deep representation of the journey of human inquiry. Starting out on the yellow brick road from the world of daily action, it seems that when *action* is unexpected,

uncertain or lacking, the pathway leads all too quickly to the authority of the Emerald City and its throne of ruling knowledge occupied by the great wizard, answerer of all questions. Our heroes and heroines represent all the faces of the inquiry cycle: the innocent honest Dorothy, blown off her feet, off-balance and off-course by the winds of turbulence, who seeks such existing authoritative advice about how to find her familiar stabilising home, and similarly the answers to her fellow travellers' questions. Joining her on the yellow brick road to the answers-that-lie-elsewhere is the cowardly lion who lacks the courage of his convictions and seeks an ability to *reflect* on what it is that should drive him; the tin man who lacks a feeling heart for *observing* people's pain, and is seeking to bring life to his reliable and dutifully uncomplaining but machine-like doing of works; and the straw man who lacks a brain for how to think and make plans to complement his otherwise cheerful, practicably simple and flexible responding to the world. Eventually, after trickery and delay and finally finding their way (assisted by both good spirits and bad spirits 'in the grip'), they reach the anticipated source of omniscient and fearfully thundering wisdom and knowledge. But the 'wizard' turns out to be a small boy who fears being exposed and made vulnerable for the truth of his real abilities and instead 'puts on a show' to *look* strong. Yet in that revelation lies the chance to discover that the wizard's real gift has been to show that each of the answers to the travellers' questions are to be found *within themselves*, setting them free to be individually and together their own whole best autopoetic selves.

Finally the characters come 'full circle' back home to 'where the heart is', having helped each other on the journey of transformative inquiry: from being uprooted by an almighty discrepancy between an 'is' and an 'ought', to going with the flow, despatching the tyrannical, remaining aligned with their purposes, taking many trial and error actions along the way; making mistakes, arguing over evidence and its interpretation, questioning, sharing answers and supporting each others learnings, eventually harvesting the fruits of their inquiry in celebratory appreciative evaluation, and then going on to lead lives of action reflexively informed by their new insights.

Being all too human: understanding and responding to the challenges of human services that are working to be (truly) human

At the peak of our work with the mental health system in the U&I project (Exemplar 1, Chapter 5), we noted that it felt for all the world like working in and with a giant living organism, sometimes like a many-armed octopus, sometimes like a huge and ponderous hibernating bear— sometimes part 'care bear' driven by love and a desire to heal, and sometimes part 'scare bear' driven by fear and anxiety in response to the pent-up violence in people and systems. Facilitating inquiry under these circumstances often felt like partnering a rather Jekyll and Hyde character (Wadsworth 2001b).

Indeed at the time of launching the set of monographs resulting from the U&I work, we had come to think of the hospital system as having gone through its own 'acute psychiatric autoimmune' response' episode.[81]

The earlier cartoon told the story of the paradox-within-a-paradox whereby even those who said they wanted to hear were also often the most convinced that they *already knew* what consumers would or could (or should) say, while those who often reasoned the most defensively (and seemingly without end) also often harboured a deep desire to really know the truth of consumers' experiences.

It now becomes clear what the risks are of any human services professional or group of professionals conducting their own separate inquiry or perhaps

only with other professionals, observing, second guessing, theorising, concluding and then implementing actions independently of the critical inquirer's own life-seeking inquiry efforts, no matter how fragile or indecisive they may be.

Perhaps it could even be a first line of defence to speak of 'delivering human services' as if they are an external impersonal disembodied 'thing' that is delivered like a box of goods by a truck—a noun rather than a verb—when they are in practice much more a matter of *human relationships* in which closely calibrated inquiring works to 'serve' or resource the life of the other. So perhaps it should have been no surprise to discover—as we probed more deeply into the paradox beneath carefully constructed defences that distanced people from each other in self-protection forcefields but also unwittingly produced misunderstanding and unresponsive practice—that we began to hit painful nerves, sore patches and knee-jerk reactions. It was clearly not welcome news that the loving 'care bear' of a human service systemicity could show its teeth and turn on its own critical reference group, its suffering patients, sometimes with such ferocity as to explain precisely why it had become such a thoroughly undiscussible dark secret (Argyris 1993). Yet when we eased up gently to sit alongside the giant bear we found the hard shield had some cracks in it that, as Leonard Cohen sings, 'let the light get in'. Indeed its

cracks made it so fragile that, while maintaining its defences seemed often more important than responding to patients, in a safe place away from the workplace we knew that it often wept inconsolably.

This is what we might call the delicate problem —not so much of the wounded healer, since it is the awareness that stems from the wounding that humanises the carer—but the much feared problem of the too wounded healer, that is, a healer *too* wounded to go on assisting. The result seemed to be the 'protection' of ever more impenetrable defences by staff to ensure their invulnerability through increasing distancing and other forms of 'professionalism', and consumers having to be, to an equal degree, vulnerable and defined as 'unable'. In a kind of elaborate systemic no-win deal, staff in effect had to demonstrate 'I'm OK/You're not OK' and the consumer had to comply with 'You're OK/I'm not OK'. Yet this doesn't enable the consumer to recover and *become* OK—nor does it allow the staff person to be *not* OK and seek the supports *they* need. Instead many succumbed to appearances of retaining command and control over every last instance of practice, even deciding when to 'allow' a patient to 'recover' (such as by releasing them from an unnecessarily locked environment), rather than supporting their recovery of autopoesis. Under these circumstances it was often a lose-lose or Catch 22 situation.

In the deep dialogue sessions that were so critical to the success of the project we saw that we had created a more-or-less safe place for staff and consumers to meet across this seemingly unbridgeable divide. In these we came to realise that the dark secrets of the system were writ small not only in every human service practitioner who responded with anger or depersonalisation to the stress of trying to heal and take care of people whose minds raged or blew fuses, but that it was mirrored also within consumers themselves who were responding in the same way to the stress of a wider world that split, broke and alienated them by constantly blocking *their* capacity to live their lives.

More like deep tissue masseuses, the members of our staff–consumer team were in search of ways to maximise the organism's return to fuller life; sidling up gently alongside the great human bear, reaching out in ways of greeting, inquiring sympathetically through tentative care-full touch into the painful layers of tissue that had built up. As the inquiry proceeded more deeply into the sources of the protection, trust built through noticing, understanding and giving more accurate feedback and, when better understood, 'the system's' painful defences relaxed and sometimes released: giving up their load, freeing the lifeblood to bring oxygen and clear away the toxins. Life returned and the body corporate flourished...at least for the years we worked together.

However a puzzle remained.

While it was clear that the success of the U&I project had rested on it being a staff-collaborative project from the outset, it was just as clear that the driving 'engine power' had in practice been the large group of dedicated consumers it had attracted. The other half of the paradox was the driver of *staff members*' intentions to assist the health, healing and recovery of their patients. The unanswered question remained: what would it take for staff throughout a system to sustain *their* enthusiasm for actively inviting consumers to participate in services decision making, including about the nature of care itself?

The staff-focused Understanding Staff study

A follow-up study to U&I was then conducted in a medium-sized general hospital.[82] The Under-standing Staff (US) study commenced where the U&I study had left off with the paradox of staff *wanting* to involve consumers, and *not* wanting to involve them. As in the U&I project a group of keen very hands-on senior professional management staff took part (including the chief executive officer/director of nursing, the deputy, nurse unit managers, a senior doctor, the senior social worker and the medical practice manager). They met regularly as a quasi-action learning set over a period of some months, reflecting on their own reactions to the idea of patient feedback and consumer participation. Without consumers present they were very candid yet generated exactly the same lists as we had collected in the U&I project regarding why they wanted to hear from consumers, and exactly the same long lists of defensive routines as to why they couldn't. It seemed that the deeper we went into the defences and difficulties, into exploring the busy distancing and trained second guessing about patients' needs, the more self-sealing the thinking became.

At times the line of defensive reasoning against asking patients for their input or feedback seemed to default almost instantly to the worst possible scenario. There appeared to be an unbroken thread between glimpsing even so little as a pained expression on a patient's face and fear of the possibility of full-scale unresolvable complaint, litigation and professional shame. Yet on testing this logic it was clear that out of 15 000 admissions and 20 000 emergency department attendances each year, only a small handful of perhaps half a dozen issues ever proved irresolvable. This systemic defence—while protecting staff—

Figure 19. Unfreezing the forcefields

© S. Kneebone & Y. Wadsworth 2009

also left them largely unable to actively seek consumers' input. In fact the group never got to the point of inviting consumers to join in the discussion; although plans were sketched of some desirable formal methods to do so (see Exemplar 3 in Chapter 5).

But there *was* a breakthrough in the group's thinking, which came in the realisation that underpinning these fears was a deeper feeling of anxiety that what they were doing was in some way not felt by them to be fully worthy (this was a time of pressure on the hospital to do vastly more without funding for additional staffing to keep pace). This created a chicken and egg situation whereby they couldn't hear from consumers until they felt more confident they were doing a good job, yet they couldn't do a good job without consumers' input to suggest better ways of 'doing things differently' (better, and not necessarily more expensively). Systemically this created a closed loop, defaulting away from needed change.

Three more breakthroughs
A further significant breakthrough in thinking came when the staff group realised that their defensive routines were in practice, and somewhat ironically, indicating the existence not of a lack of care, but rather the presence of deeply held compassionate values on care-giving. We went in search of those values and found they were buried deeply in people's consciousnesses and surprisingly hard to articulate in words. They seemed to be quite literally embodied as feeling (people pointed 'here' or put their hand on their solar plexus, or just below their throat). Instead we asked people to think of visual metaphors that might represent their deepest values, and in this way were able to open up a rich conversation about how they were maintained or operated under stress and pressure. Yet

despite this seeming to remind, affirm and strengthen peoples' confidence that they were indeed 'good people doing their best', there were still no consumers being invited 'to the table'.

Another new and particularly fruitful insight emerged (and one which has helped to inform Table 7 in this chapter) when the staff group realised that the term 'care' was *itself* paradoxical in that 'caring *for*' patients meant *already knowing* what was best for the patient without having to ask—even though this risked not guessing correctly, missing messages, making incorrect attributions and errors, and rendering the patient passive rather than active in their own recovery. We concluded that *caring to ask* could become an alternative way to *care about* patients, and one which might give more choices in determining what was done, thereby both reducing the risks for staff and increasing the active part of the patient in their own inquiry journey back to health.

For some participants this realisation was enough to return to work determined to make changes to ensure they would seek out and listen to clients' feedback. For example, one reported that whenever a patient asked to say something to her and she felt a defence rising, she now thought, 'that's great, there's a sign of my good values again', and found herself more open to feedback. However the staff group remained stymied by its reluctance to envisage new or positive ways of actually doing this. We then tried a different tack altogether. Since people reported holding their values for a long time, we thought we could try *reviewing previous practice* to see whether there were instances of patient care they remembered when they had effectively sought and gained helpful consumer feedback. We thought if we could build from these memories of actual positive experiences it might make it less difficult to think about some kind of seemingly unfamiliar process like having consumers on the hospital board.

We then used a memory work exercise (Crawford et al. 1992) to create an appreciative inquiry (Cooperrider and Srivastva 1987) that produced a remarkable response.

We asked staff to recall and describe a memory that had all three of these characteristics:

- They had sought or gained direct feedback from a service user or group of service users
- From this they had got a new idea, which they then tried out
- And they had then received further feedback from service users that it had indeed 'worked' for them.

This marked a highpoint in staff's interest and energy and, if the developmental research process could have continued around the cycle for the longer term, consumers may indeed have eventually been sought out for their participation. However the exercise was interrupted by yet another crisis when the hospital fire alarm was set off by a radiator which, by a singular irony, had been brought in by a patient feeling the cold who had not wanted to trouble overly busy staff with his feedback and request.

Perhaps the key insights from both the U&I and US studies centred on these critical moments of resonance:

- Of *staff* moving from the despondency of the truth of 'how things were' (and the need to keep defending against hearing about them from consumers) to the release of energy that came from experiencing consumer input 'paying off' in terms of better, more accurate and resonant care *of and with* a more actively autopoetic consumer
- And of this being matched when *consumers* experienced energetic wellbeing when they were free to express their experiences, have them appreciated and affirmed, and were able to work shoulder to shoulder with sympathetic staff who wanted to improve things

with their highly valued input. Just as the names of the research projects: 'Understanding, Anytime', 'Understanding and Involvement', and 'Understanding Staff' proved resonant and attractive to both staff and consumers, it was the experience of being deeply listened to that resulted in the greatest mutual understanding and appreciation, and the pleasure and enjoyment that accompanied the subsequent finding of exciting, clever and creative new ways of responding to need that proved the real attractors and drivers of change for *all* feeling like they were involved in human services that made them feel more truly alive.

The 'stick' of fear *could* create services and coerce their use—but they would be ones characterised more by the need for defensive bunkers, barriers and restraints.

And the 'carrot' of achievement *could* create the motivation to care about health, healing and recovery—but possibly without translating into more deeply effective outcomes.

But in the end it was the return to affirming and strengthening the internal 'compass' core of deeply embodied human values, beliefs and desires that fuelled more autopoetic life-giving intentions, purposes and objectives that resonated between staff and consumers, and that proved the most essential to successful inquiry for (more truly) healthy living systems.

Building it in

The sequence of strategic questioning in Chapter 3 supplied a framework for 'intelligent systems' of people inquiring together to address issues, solve problems and 'bring life'. This Chapter 4 has looked at its implications and applications in human services.

Chapter 5 now takes up the ways in which such a life-giving culture of inquiry might be built in and sustain itself throughout whole social organisms or large-scale systemicities. It provides ten key exemplars of working to build this kind of integrated 'intelligent living system'[83] of regular inquiry practice in to a range of health, education, community, organisational and human service settings.

The challenges are considerable. For every realisation that there are discrepancies between life-giving and life-depleting facing us—and the impetus is there for us to step forward to inquire, question, critique, appreciate, bridge gaps in experience and understanding, replicate all that is good and mourn all that is not going well, all with the intention of making a more congenial[84] future—there is also the all-too-human retreat from the unknown and the unfamiliar and from 'things too awful', to the raising of defences of the already-existing, the digging of trenches, the drawing of boundary lines and the prevailing of competition and struggle.

How can we avoid repeatedly getting too far down the track from guiding human values, desires, needs, goals and intentions? How can we institutionalise not turning a blind eye—and instead respond more quickly to the early warnings of the life-detector 'canaries in the mines'? How can we normalise ways of 'welcoming the messenger' of the new and carefully considered? How can we indeed distribute whistles to all with the cheerful instruction they are to be blown whenever we stray from our felt sense of human ethics? And create rituals for seeking out and honouring those who can and do detect the discrepancies, and can and do help us respond to them?

How can we constantly nurture the conditions for more healthy growth of life?—accepting differences as necessary for life-resourcing diversity and knowing not only that we need the chances to observe, feel, reflect and think together, but also when and how we will be able to do these *because they are built in to the fabric of our culture*—whether at work, home or elsewhere. And thus continuously create, sustain and recreate forms, patterns and cultures that in turn create, sustain and recreate us. All of us.

ENDNOTES

1   I will use the generic term 'human services' to refer to all health, community, education, welfare and other kinds of human services, both government and non-government, commercial or not-for-profit organisational, community, business, home or (non-home) workplace. Beyond this formal meaning, however, the ideas may be extended to any setting in which people orient to other people in order to assist or resource their viability for sustainable and fully living co-systemicity (e.g. hospitality, customer service, urban and rural planning, architecture, media and communications, law etc.) This human ecological perspective, as described in Chapter 2, also includes all other beings or elements that constitute the living systems sustaining our species. While these have been called natural 'resources' and currently environmental 'services', where the focus has been on 'them' resourcing or serving humans, in practice, the mutual relationality of a living system described in Chapter 2, and explicated as collaborative or co-operative inquiring in Chapter 3, indicates the dangers of seeing 'serving' as only ever one-way rather than, in a bigger picture, as mutually resourcing (my term), mutually

nurturing or sustaining, as Richard Eckersley put it (personal communication, National Centre for Epidemiology and Population Health [NCEPH], ANU, 13 July 2004), mutually pherological, 'meaning-conveying' (Colin Butler, personal communication, NCEPH, ANU, 13 July 2004), mutual life-lines or synergies (Adrian Sleigh, personal communication, NCEPH, ANU, 13 July 2004) or mutually enhancing (Jacques Boulet, oases seminar, 1 May 2010). As Adrian Sleigh noted, 'it is a big ask' to seek a single generic term for 'such a big concept'. But if sufficiently needed, a living system may call it forth!

2   From the Late Latin *synchronus*, meaning simultaneous occurrence in time of significantly related events, with no discernible connection. There is a sense of this being fortuitously internally autopoetic rather than externally planned. Or achieved by the presence of (or contributing to) a field of dense resources and relationality in which such autopoesis can take place, rather than through an act of distanced ('socially engineered') co-ordination. Lilla Watson uses the word 'liberation' (see later)—in the sense of the freedom to choose which 'relationalities' and

'systemicities' give life and which do not. I use 'autopoesis' to capture the 'self-managing' nature of 'freedom'; that is, it is socially relational 'freedom in order to…(do life)' rather than freedom per se (e.g. to inflict meaningless hurt, avoidable damage or premature death). Holding a shared 'mental architecture' of full cycle inquiry in turn becomes a critical resource to these life-giving co-inquiry processes. Chapter 5 explores the conditions for 'building this in' to the culture and institutionalisation of human service organisations.

3   While secondarily the assisting co-inquirer/s (even while they may suspend the traversing of some of their own inquiry cycles) is bringing alongside whatever close-to-matching inquiry cycle they can. This may be brought explicitly into the encounter (e.g. as in the 'taking turns' in co-counselling or in self-help groups, or by a 'wounded healer' able to listen and speak from parallel experience), or implicitly (as the helping co-inquirer listens actively, searching to go beyond their own experience in order to grasp the unique meaning of the account of life they are hearing or seeing). If the listener's experiences being brought to bear are too narrow or too distant, and further questioning still cannot yield enough comprehension to result in accurate and resonant responses, then the primary inquirer may need others. The more complex the situation the more likely it is that any one helper (or helping agency) will not have the repertoire to do this. Hence the move to choice of practitioner, or group, or community-based work as an essential expansion of the human 'services' resourcing palette. The ideal that a full standard (same) service could be 'supplied' by any trained or qualified practitioner stems from a model of the recipient as also standard (the same) in their lifeworld. This might apply for simple transactions and reliable causal calculations but is likely to break down under conditions of complexity. Even use of the full cycle sequences of questions rests on 'starting where the critical inquirer (or inquiry group) is at', a matter that may present a challenge to someone who is preoccupied or more comfortable with other questions (or answers) around the cycle—requiring them to take time to be able to enter the resourcing relationship with more effectiveness. An antidote to this is an ability to hear and receive any account of experience with interest and, even if not understood, continue to assist the inquiring 'round the cycle', asking the speaker what sense they are making of it so far, and so on.

4   In 1984 in the first edition of *Do It Yourself Social Research* (see also in 2010) I generated the term to refer to all those for whom the research or evaluation was being conducted (e.g. end-beneficiaries in human services). In 1991 in the first edition of *Everyday Evaluation On The Run* (see also in 2010) I elaborated that this was an attempt to name something for which we did not have language and that a better replacement might hopefully be found, but that it meant at least that one did not have constantly to describe

who the human services or evaluation and research were ultimately to benefit. This critical stakeholder was 'critical' in the sense of the Greek origins of the word *kritikos*, meaning 'judge, decide' (not as fault-finding criticism per se, but all forms of discrepancy detection and judgements about these, whether positive or negative, and decisions about what to do as a result), and a 'reference group' in the sociological sense (Homans 1975) of providing an influential source for its members and from which others may take their lead, including forming benchmarks for evaluation.

5   Please note that Lilla Watson has recently been reported as 'not comfortable being credited for something that had been born of a collective process' (Our Consumer Place, 2010: 111).

6   'Web' from the Germanic, meaning weave or connect threads, membrane or nodes together (with possible Norse connection to 'weave' from *velfa*, meaning 'wave').

7   'Field' from the West Germanic, variously meaning a natural environment or open area, an area rich in resources, an area for designated purposes, an area where co-operation or competition can take place, a region where a force is effective, an area of operation or activity.

8   'Matrix' from the Latin, meaning womb, from *mater matris*, 'mother', meaning shaping mould or environment, mass or substance in which things are embedded; including grid-like array of rows of separate elements treated as an entity.

9   'Environment' from the Old French *en*, meaning 'in', viron, meaning 'circuit', from *virer*, 'turn, veer'

10   'Circumstances' from the Latin *circum*, 'round, about', and *stare*, 'stand', meaning the external conditions, facts, occurrences, conditions (time, place, manner, causes effecting, details etc.) or surroundings of an act, incident, event or occurrence.

11   A good example would be a health promotion impact analysis developed by the former executive officer of the Victorian Health Promotion Foundation and national disability activist Rhonda Galbally (1994: 19). This asked questions like: Does contact with the health care system strengthen or weaken people? Contribute to them trusting their own judgement and making informed choices (as opposed to giving informed consent)? Contribute to consumers having high self-esteem? Foster the resilience of those who come in contact with it? Contribute to a capacity for self-advocacy and so on?

12   This has much in common with the Success Case approach extended into human services by Bob Brinkerhoff from its widespread use in business (2003). Like appreciative inquiry, it also moves quickly to defining, in this case, what will be considered 'successful', then identifies actual success cases; interviews to learn how the success was achieved; and then communicates the messages throughout the organisation. Like all strengths-focused and appreciative approaches, it works particularly well where there are blockages at the two key Phase changes (whether defences, resistance, being discouraged or other forms of

'stuckness'). Most Significant Change (Davies and Dart 2005) is also an approach that may highlight positives or negatives as a basis for narrative to tell stories the story-teller is keen to tell (in this case to managers, via telling peers and other stakeholders).

13 And despite understandable cynicism resulting from dramatic funding cuts corresponding to this kind of idealism (which resulted in a popular office poster at the time: 'Another month ends—All Targets met—All systems working—All customers satisfied—All staff eager and enthusiastic——ALL PIGS FED AND READY TO FLY').

14 Both metaphors imply the states of being in or out of balance or equilibrium, characteristic of any living system (see Chapter 2). A certain degree of imbalance or discrepancy is necessary to any organism's dynamic movement, incurring a move by that organism to counter-support its part that leans out of balance, falls or is damaged or ill. Even long-term or permanent support will be forthcoming when the mutuality of relations is restored, or understood in a larger scheme of things, and 'supports for the supports' built in—still within the meaning of 'self-governing'.

15 'Ally, allied, alliance', meaning union, joined in pursuit of common interest, from the Latin al/ad, meaning 'towards', and ligare, from the same word as religion, meaning 'ties'

16 And as it turns out, quite literally sicken us, as has been documented by public health researchers in the United Kingdom and United States who have now closely measured and documented the relationships between physical illness and disempowerment and helplessness (resulting in further loss of autopoesis). See for example Marmot and Wilkinson (1999) for the Whitehall study's application to professional civil service staff, and Syme (1997a) and Townsend and Black (1988). Leonard Syme's Californian heart health study's application to service-users and communities (1997a) and Michael Wilkinson's subsequent national comparative studies on numerous indicators of the relationship between inequality and unhealthy states of being and how to reverse these (2006).

17 A senior executive who was most strongly (and with undisguised force) driving the policy agenda of competition between privatised human services simultaneously with a retreat to the most minimal provision required by law, ironically with a desire to disempower health and welfare professionals who were seen as overly controlling the lives of their clients and patients. Yet these were the same professionals mandated in the minimalist (residualist) increasingly controlling economic rationalist welfare state, but now without the essential community supports either for their efforts or those of their clients.

18 Understanding emotion as an individual person system's response to an external situation inevitably extends the framing of its causation not only beyond the internal 'merely psychological' to the social, but also beyond an immediate social context to reflect on greater patterns of

social systemic interactivity and reactivity over time and space. In this way a systemic perspective on emotion refocuses on the collective phenomena between individuals in a 'nested', networked, holarchic, mutually constructed and interdependent way (Wadsworth 2008b).

19 One example might be the current 'epidemic' among young women (and some young men) of cutting and self-harming. A common answer given when asked why is that it is a way to 'let out the awfulness'. That is, self-harm is operating systemically as an internally suppressed reaction ('intro-jection') to an external systemic force ('projection') which is then 'sealed in' by the suppression of inquiry processes (e.g. of autopoetic questioning, observing and reflection for new, more resonant insight). A little like pushing apples under water in a barrel, the suppressed 'data' about discrepancy awaits accurate narrative analysis and re-theorising—in a rather literal sense in this example: 'the truth must out'. The widespread experience of depression might similarly be 'read' systemically as an extreme of 'yielding/not knowing' (at the entropic point of uncertainty, powerlessness and as yet 'formless chaos', around what I have called Phase change 1) in reaction to extreme 'power/knowing' (at the point of presumptive certainty about the desired form/order/pattern, around my Phase change 2).

20 Originally: 'When I fed the hungry they called me a saint; when I asked why the poor were hungry, they called me a communist'—The late Catholic bishop Dom Helder Camara (Claiborne 2006: 129).

21 'Power' from the Latin posse, meaning 'be able', and the transitional French form poeir from which the words derive for both poetry (connecting imagination and expression to 'being able'—a feature of both Phase changes 1 and 2), and also of autopoesis (self-organising), as well as posse, possession and possible.

22 At the 2005 Australian Psychological Society national conference 'Informing Psychological Interventions', one paper was entitled 'Working with "Demanding, Manipulative, Attention-seeking, Challenging, Selfish, Cantankerous, Difficult, Time-consuming, Self-centred" Behaviour in Aged Care', locating the problem in 'difficult personalities' that were often understood as psychiatric mental illness. However the paper reported effective disappearance of such 'behaviour' if the social environment gave responses of comfort, inclusion and identity affirmation instead. Another paper at the same conference reported agitation and depression in people with dementia diminished significantly and talking to others increased if people could sit in a sensory garden.

23 I first heard this appreciative reframing from Stephen Campbell at an Australasian Evaluation Society monthly seminar discussion, Melbourne 2007.

24 'Moment' meaning 'short period of time', from the Latin momentum, meaning 'move'.

25 'Station', meaning 'a regular stopping place', for an

'habitual or definite purpose', from the Latin *station-onis, stare*, meaning 'stand'.

26 The Jungian Myers Briggs theory I am using to identify this systemic characteristic calls the order/closure aspect of a defence the 'judging' (J) aspect or attitude, and the diversity/openness aspect the 'perceiving' (P) aspect/ attitude. These map evenly around the cycle (see Appendix 3) and are available to all living systems, even though in individuals one may be reliably preferred over the other.

27 See Wadsworth 2006b for a case study published on open access online, detailing the difference between professionals conscientiously researching the needs of young women with arthritis but without consulting them, and then later researching *with* the women themselves— generating a radically different program logic with radically different outcomes in terms of meeting needs accurately and successfully as well as autopoetically, and with great numbers mutually served at unexpectedly modest cost.

28 For an extended practice-based research discussion of doing 'with and for', rather than 'to and at', see Wadsworth (2006b). See Reason (1988) for an influential account of these ideas. See also 'An Analogy', in Wadsworth in association with Epstein (2001: 173–174) for conceptualising how critical reference group-driven inquiry processes might best proceed following incidents of hospital iatrogenesis.

29 In a way this mirrors what happens in the course of a new human life—when a baby is firstly born into 'action' where survival needs are initially met on the basis of existing knowledge pre-held by mothers and others and then, as confidence grows, based on increasingly effective symmetrical relational responses learned in the first months between the new mother and baby. Then the toddler goes through a period of freedom to 'play' and make autopoetic connections between things in a kindergarten (German, meaning 'children's garden') of creativity and pattern formation until about the age of five. Having traversed this first stage of reflective learning and conclusion drawing about a more up-close-and-personal world, the child graduates to a more didactic form of received schooling about a larger, more distant world that structures current social and economic practices (learning the existing 'body of knowledge' and 'ways we do things round here'). Then, moving from a primary to a secondary form of this schooling (from about six years through to about seventeen), schooling 'ends' with opening out to an even 'bigger picture' of reflective learning about the nature and practices of global and transhistorical worlds, and increasing learning about how autopoetically to create new knowledge on a continuous basis for lifelong learning (such as in colleges, universities and life itself).

30 'Interconnection' from the Latin *inter*, meaning 'between', *co*, meaning 'with', and *nex*, meaning 'bind'.

31 In the Jungian Myers Briggs theory I am using, this is termed 'introversion' from the Latin *intra*, meaning 'into', and *vertere*, meaning 'turn'.

32 In the Jungian Myers Briggs theory I am using, this is termed 'extroversion' from the Latin *extro*, meaning 'outside', 'beyond' and *vertere*, meaning 'turn'. Both the inner and outer aspects map evenly around the cycle (see Appendix 3), with each available to all living systems, even as one may be routinely preferred over the other.

33 'Relationship' from the Latin *relatio*, meaning state or condition of being related—associated terms include narrate, recount, connect, ally, kin.

34 'Flux' meaning flow or continuous change, from the Latin *fluere* flux, meaning 'flow'—associated term: fluid, and the Latin word for river.

35 'Context' from Latin con, 'with', and *texere*, text 'weave', meaning the surrounding words or circumstances that give something its (relative) truth or meaning. The current usage of the term 'place-based' alludes to this.

36 When the internal–external relational conditions are right, 'buds flower' of their own accord, without external forcing. The desire to flower comes from within the bud, in relationship to the rest of the plant and outer environment that has been 'inquired into'. The desire is real-ised when the resourcing context is there to 'call it forth'. A change that is forced externally is not able to supply the evidence of it having been assessed prospectively as of 'value, merit, worth or significance' by and for the life of the critical living system. This is why a before-action 'participatory' process to achieve understanding of the existing and new insight into the 'desired possible' is more important as a warrant of 'getting it right' than an after-implementation control, audit or measurement as, by then, the new systemicity may have altered the 'organism' to its own (i.e. others') purposes, rather than the other way around. As Einstein is popularly quoted as saying 'Peace cannot be kept by force. It can only be kept by understanding' (unknown source). It is also why coerced change continues so often to require the excessive support and 'enslavement' of the (artificial) systemic conditions that brought it into being— and why it retains the power to exclude and continue to take away those conditions for life.

37 I have written in detail about the full gamut of living systems inquiry facilitation capabilities in 'The Mirror, the Magnifying Glass, the Compass and the Map', in Peter Reason and Hilary Bradbury's Sage *Handbook of Action Research* (Wadsworth 2001).

38 'Cybernetic' from the Greek kubernetes, meaning 'steersman', viz. someone using communication to receive (observe) feedback in order to keep re-charting their course (reflect, plan) to better move in the direction of what is valued, desired, required or needed (act).

39 Here too we could do with new language. 'Stakeholder' alludes to a representative role in a gamble, where one person holding the 'stakes' or bets is waging them on behalf

of *other* relevant parties or stakeowners. 'Co-inquirers, co-researchers, co-evaluators' are perhaps better terms, since it is the stakeowners whose direct input is most critically needed. Yet, as an inquiry scales up or spreads throughout relational networks, even these terms may seem restrictive in relation to the extent and complexity of intertwined questioning and learning processes that might be going on in 'whole' systemicities. At this point I settle for the overall idea of an 'intelligent system' to refer to this latter large, more complex, adaptive or generative 'living breathing' integral 'stakeowning' organism.

40 For those familiar with Carl Jung and the derived Myers-Briggs Type Inventory®, this focuses on the 'mental functions'. Behind these lie the 'attitudes' of where these energies are oriented (inner/introversion or outer/extroversion) and how they are sustained (whether with openness/perceiving or closure/judgement). See Appendix 3 for details of the value of these various characteristics to illuminate a living systems inquiry epistemology and for a critique of the sixteen MBTI® four-letter 'types' (viewed instead as living constellations or dynamic systemicities, with 'reach' around a living systems inquiry cycle).

41 From the Latin *bene*, meaning 'well' and *facere*, meaning 'do', from the same derivation as 'facilitation'—surprisingly meaningful in systemic terms, despite the additional meaning of 'needing a benefactor', which might imply loss of autopoesis.

42 'Charity' from the Latin *caritas*, meaning 'beloved',

43 'Case' from the Latin *cadere*, meaning 'befallen'; a person receiving professional guidance or treatment.

44 'Problem' from the Greek *proballo*, 'something thrown'

45 'Dysfunctional', meaning abnormal or impaired function

46 'Client', meaning person using the services of a professional, or customer; from the Latin 'hear, obey'; originally the historical Roman plebian under the protection of a member of the patrician class.

47 'Patient', meaning a person receiving medical treatment, from the Latin *patiens*, meaning suffer.

48 'Consumer' from the Latin *com* with *sumpt*, meaning take up, take into, use up.

49 'Customer' from Latin *consuetude*, meaning established and regular purchaser.

50 'Purchaser' from the Old French *pourchacier*, meaning pursuing, seeking to obtain, acquire, achieve.

51 'Participant' from Latin *particeps*, meaning one who takes a part in/of.

52 'Partner' from Middle English *parcener*, meaning one who shares parts in/with, or joint heir.

53 'Almoner' from the word for 'alms' or charitable gifts of money or food, from the Greek *eleemon*, meaning compassion (in the Latin, *com* with, and *passion* suffering).

54 'Service' from the Latin *servire* from *slavus*, meaning 'slave'.

55 'Provider' from the Latin *pro*, before, and *videre*, see, meaning 'foresight'.

56 'Deliver', meaning 'set free' from the Latin *de*, from, *liberare* liberate—associated meanings: deliberation, deliberate.

57 'Staff' from the Old English *staef*, from the Germanic, meaning 'staves', a person or thing that supports or sustains; or a stick or pole as a sign of authority.

58 'Practitioner' from the Greek *practiikos*, meaning 'do, act'.

59 'Helper', meaning provider of the means towards what is needed or sought; assistance, support, contribution, use.

60 'Care', meaning having concern or interest, paying attention, protection, provide for, look after, keep safe.

61 'Give', meaning transfer, hand over, confer, grant, accord, bestow, yield, commit, deliver, provide.

62 From the Greek *therapeuo*, meaning wait on, cure, heal.

63 'Consultant' from the Latin *consulere*, meaning a person providing information, advice or opinion based on learning or experience, usually for a fee.

64 Yet more difficult language for new ways of speaking about things! I could have subtitled it 'Responses to Personal/Individual/Group/Social (Holarchic) Systemicities that are In and Out of Dynamic Equilibrium' but that might have been worse! (Albeit more definitionally accurate from a systemic perspective). Alternatives are needed!

65 I have used shorthand terms derived from Jungian Myers Briggs theory in this table partly because this language now has the widest currency worldwide (due to its popularisation by the Myers-Briggs Type Indicator®) and is thus a familiar way for many to access the analogue inquiry processes that I use to describe traversing cycles of inquiry. And partly because it is a systemic (non-pathologising) theory for understanding the living human 'organism' as moving in and out of dynamic equilibrium (i.e. between change and order, process and structure). In Appendix 3 I address both the value and the dangers of this body of knowledge, particularly in relation to individual systemicities, and describe a new concept of inquiry preference 'reach' as a way of understanding how we may be more comfortably 'at home' with one, two or several 'quadrants' of the cycle, and less so with one or more others, while nevertheless retaining more-or-less of a capacity to traverse all preferences to get around the full cycle. This concept applies both at the level of the individual and also at other larger scales of systemicity in modal or dominant organisational and community culture.

66 'Most and least used' are descriptive terms for how it seems to be for most people when they are at any particular point in the cycle, i.e. most of us, when we are in the middle of action, would typically need to stop in order to reflect on action (even if only momentarily); or if feeling a critical emotion, would then need to move into another mental mode to think through the consequences (again even if only quite soon afterwards) etc. People appear to be drawing on separate mental functions for the differing moments around the cycle, even while the key point about a living systems

inquiry methodology is to be able to more-or-less master each (e.g. to be able to reflect on observations of what it's like from other people's perspectives, to intuit the key factors regarding which action to take, and then grasp the organic/systemic complexities that then emerge as a result). Recent neuroscience seems close to charting these differences within the hemispheres of the brain (though possibly not in exactly the way popular accounts have to date), but sociology and psychology have built enough observational studies of patterns of human action to aid us here for the time being.

67   I use the generic term 'human assistance' here in preference to 'human service' drawing on the Latin origins of 'assist' from *ad*, meaning 'with a sense of motion, directionality, change', and *sistere*, meaning 'take one's stand by'. This captures better the sense of resonant 'alongsideness' by one organism in relation to the autopoesis of another organism within their greater shared systemicity. Since all forms of human assistance are in this sense 'standing alongside' the person being assisted, this has the meaning of 'helping', in the sense of resonating in some way with a person's, group's or community's own agency for self-organising life, this term I think more effectively captures the generic meaning of *all* the differing forms of human service I describe in this Table 7. I might have preferred 'human resourcing' but 'human resources' have already become associated with seeing people or 'personnel' as an analogue to non-living industrial materials, mining, natural resources and fodder. I retain 'human service' for a more specific meaning within the following explication of the living human service systemicity's inquiry cycle.

68   I have used the term 'stress', but the alternative systemic term 'pressure' may be more accurate as it is not only an intra-systemic property but also a co-relational (inner–outer) one. That is, the pressure is a result of something acting on, against or co-varying with the organism, preventing it achieving its purposes or intentions (where purposes or intentions may themselves be socially constructed, co-interpreted and relational). It is instructive to know that the linguistic origins of 'stress' lie in the French, meaning 'narrowness, oppression', in turn from the Latin *strictus* and *stringere*, meaning 'tighten', 'precisely limited, defined, without exception or deviation, requiring complete compliance or exact performance enforced rigidly'—i.e. by definition, excluding critical properties of all living systems, viz sufficient flexibility, diversity, dynamism and openness.

69   The key reference on which I draw for this articulation is Naomi Quenk's book *In the Grip* (2000 1st edn). This uses the MBTI® (see Appendix 3) to achieve a comprehensive description of the range of characteristic human living systemicities (including the concepts of 'characteristic grace' and 'characteristic risk'), as well as those systemicities' characteristic responses to stress, far more

detailed than would otherwise be possible in this chapter. While the Quenk reference does this at the personal/interpersonal scale of systemicity, I have also drawn on William Bridges' book *The Character of Organisations*, 2000) to chart the social-political scale of *collective* systemicities possible around the inquiry cycle. However my own emphasis on the dynamic cycle means that even individual and social typifications of this nature are contextually autopoetic and thus not essentially reducible to any particular preference constellations in any particular instance, even while people may be able to self-identify their own relatively reliable inquiry preferences over time. I have made the selections as relevant as possible to their implications for people researching, evaluating and 'learning their way' around cycles of living systems inquiry in human services. See also Quenk *Was That Really Me* (2002, 2nd edn) and Pearman and Albritton, *I'm Not Crazy I'm Just Not You* (1997), as well as the MBTI® Step 2 for more comprehensive detail and explication of the Jungian Myers Briggs formulation. As a complex systemic non-pathologising theory for understanding a wide range of human individual and socio-political defences, reactivity and other responses to stress, this has been chosen over other psychological constructs that tend to positively valorise or pathologise (and even demonise) some human traits (e.g. psychology's 'big five'). (It may be that there is a relationship to the theorists' own dominant inquiry preferences and what is demonised may also be mirrored socio-politically institutionally). Similarly non-pathologising in the Jungian Myers Briggs schema is the understanding of stress as systemic perturbance or turbulence that takes the living system far from either oscillating pole of dynamism or equilibrium, thus incurring a counter-acting tendency. This counter-tendency stems from the ability of the nested systemicities to generate and receive feedback and thus inquire. Quenk's analysis also indicates what each 'type' or living systemicity is likely specifically to gain when emerging from a period of being out of balance or overly becalmed while 'in the grip', which also suggests a living systems characteristic, even of stress.

70   *Note*: This number 8 (as well as number 1) traverses what appeared in Chapter 3 as overlapping numbers 8, 9 and 10. This has significant implications for bedding down and routinising *new* actions (based on the prior cycle of inquiry and 'having answers') *at the same time* as people may be carrying out the *old* actions that are resulting in 'having questions'. This is again a strong argument for maximum participation of all parties in all the inquiry processes both for change, and from and to stabilising replication.

71   In this context, 'serve', from the Latin *servus*, 'slave', is used to mean that I, you or we are engaged in industriously providing the safety and resources that reliably secure the ability of the organism to meet its needs according to the current prevailing ethos and knowledge. This accepts the

'authority/authoring' of the governing community of knowers (body corporate at whatever scale). In order that 'serving' avoids the machine-like denial of autopoetic life implicit in unchosen 'servitude' or 'slavery', this standpoint in the inquiry cycle (and to successfully traverse this moment and go full cycle) rests on the fullest empowered/political participation of those serving and being served in the ongoing co-inquiry, and their own free choosing to want to so do ('because their liberation is bound up with' that of the critical inquiry group—and thus each other [Lilla Watson, in Wadsworth 1997b: 17]).

72 In this context, 'care-give', from the Germanic *karo*, is used to mean that I, you or we are engaged in 'freely giving over' what is needed in order to 'look after', protect and exercise concern, especially where there is cause for anxiety possibly not addressed by existing means. It involves a 'care-fulness' in responding that may require observational discretion or flexibility regarding application of the 'received wisdom' and 'the rules'.

73 In this context, 'inspire', from the Latin *inspirare*, meaning 'breath in/into', is used to mean that I, you or we are engaged in the moment of insightful new 'taking in' of a connection, a 'discovery', and a new explanation of what has been observed and reflected on, which can then be examined for its logical implications for new action.

74 In this context, 'activate', from the Latin *activus*, meaning 'bring into action', is used here to mean that I, you or we are engaged in the moment of maximum energy for going forward in taking a new idea into new action and more or less experimental practice.

75 In this context, 'enable', from the Germanic en, and Latin *habere*, meaning 'give the means or authority to do or hold onto something', 'make operational', is used here to mean that I, you or we are engaged in the moment of moving ahead together with trying out something that has emerged from the inquiry process as both ideal and practical as possible.

76 In this context, 'contribute', from the Latin com, meaning 'with' and *tribuere*, meaning 'bestow' or 'make a place for', is used to mean that I, you or we are engaged in the moment of using all the resources at our command to articulate and champion a well-researched and well-developed new idea for action into actual practice by those who have had a hand in its R&D. When well-accomplished, this characterises leadership as the articulate expression of the narrative that the inquiring person, group or larger collective of people have come to tell about what they want to do and why.

77 We can now also see the attraction but also the risks of relying on an 'executive summary'. On the one hand, it may helpfully summarise a narrative based on enough detail and extensive enough inquiry processes by a relevant group of stakeholders with and for the critical stakeowner/s, and end with recommended *Phase change 2* plans that are already beginning to be enacted by the critical co-inquiry group. On the other hand, it may be overly reductionist if the readers have not been involved in the R&D process, or misleading if it has been a Chinese whispers-style inquiry process chunked into lots of separate components with the messages lost in the 'the disconnects', or involve contested but truthful keywords that are so heavily disguised by a self-editing process (if second guessing an unconvinced audience or one with different intentions) as to be missed or, alternatively, 'dog whistle words' against the intent of the effort are included for the same reason, heard, seized upon and implemented instead of what was most wanted and needed.

78 The literature on these asserted (and denied) differences in men and women is too voluminous to do justice to here. For a single example on the range of inquiry preferences among women see *Women's Ways of Knowing* by Belenky et al. (1986); for an analogue regarding men, see Connell's *Masculinities* (2005) and Appendix 3 for a Jungian Myers Briggs analysis that reinterprets the gendered data to reach similarly nuanced and less rigidly bifurcated conclusions in the name of biology.

79 Interestingly 'provide' derives from the same origin of the word 'provident', with the meaning of having foresight to set aside in advance what is necessary for later.

80 Here 'counsellors' mean citizens, from the inscription literally built into the tiled floor of the foyer of the Australian state parliament of Victoria.

81 This was a time when the cutting of public funds from hospitals had resulted in inadequate and high turnover of staffing and a third of patients being cut from the files (using tight new definitions). This was combined with increasing pressure on people suffering disadvantage and economic and social disempowerment in the community and also from admission policies that meant people had to be dangerously ill before qualifying for admission. Staff were tried to their limits. At the peak of this time, all these factors combined when police were called to one of the wards and shot an involuntary patient for refusing to comply with staff orders.

82 Wadsworth and O'Brien, 'Caring to Ask?—Some Deeper Staff Reflections on Seeking Consumer Feedback in a Hospital Setting', Unpublished monograph, Victoria University of Technology and 'Lakewaters' Health and Aged Care.

83 'Integrated' from the Latin *integrare*, meaning make whole, integrity, soundness, honesty, uprightness; 'intelligent', from the Latin inter, meaning between, among; *legere*, meaning pick out (discrepancy), choose, gather (facts, data), read (feel, interpret); *intellectus*, meaning perception, understanding, reasoning

84 The word 'congenial' has been chosen carefully—it means 'together we beget/give life to'.

Examples of building in inquiry for living human service systems

We have learned to create the small exceptions
that change the lives of hundreds.
But we have not learned how to make the exceptions the rule
to change the lives of millions.
LISBETH SCHORR, 'SCALING SOCIAL IMPACT'
STANFORD SOCIAL INNOVATION REVIEW

It is now twenty years since *Everyday Evaluation on the Run* first put forward in 1991 the idea of building a culture of evaluation (Wadsworth 1997). This chapter will present case studies conducted since that time that have researched and developed this idea in long-term practice. In particular it reports on practice that has taken the idea 'to scale'—that is, taken the research and development up and out from the small scale to a whole-of-system scale. The integrating methodology offered in these exemplars is that described in previous chapters of people purposefully enacting such a systemic research and evaluation culture through repeated use of processes of whole cycle inquiry, assisted in this by a sequence of questions and other resourcing 'scaffolding structures'.

Despite the numerous challenges, there are now many health, human and community services that have embedded such inquiry processes in the fabric of their organisations, finding ways to incorporate creative innovation as well as retain 'the tried and true', maintaining stability without discouraging change and reorienting themselves to take their lead from critical inquirers. In some of these instances, policies, plans and practices are now developed from the initial and continuing participation of critical inquirers in collaboration with many relevant people from throughout the organisations and communities whose observations and reflections about current realities actively contribute to identifying desirable ways forward.

However while there are now many one-off, small scale or recent examples of the use of cycles of action learning and research in organisations, there are fewer examples of services working to 'build in' a culture of continuous living systems inquiry throughout whole large systems over extended periods of time of up to a decade or more.

The exemplars that follow have worked in this way to try also to 'join up' research, policy, implementation, practice, evaluation and ideas innovation

through inquiry-in-practice at all scales. In many of these exemplars an energetic culture of commitment, critique and appreciation has begun to build on large numbers of people's inquiry strengths. Some efforts have decayed, been routinised or standardised at the expense of remaining more 'alive', while others have seen that the real strength and resilience of organisations and communities lie instead in encouraging plenty of 'full cycle' inquiries in alignment with participants' deeper human values.

Ten exemplars are drawn from the key areas of health, human, education and community services. The chapter concludes by drawing out the underlying conditions that have helped these services build in more continuous cultures of inquiry through research and evaluation, where clients, practitioners, managers and relevant others have inquired and 'learned their way into their desired futures'.

A theory of change through systemic inquiry
The attractions of encouraging more wholly living intelligent systems lie not just in people achieving knowledge—though what is learned creates an essential resource—but more importantly, in people knowing *how to keep finding out*, pursuing inquiry 'outwards, upwards, downwards and forwards', encompassing more and more interested players until effective new knowledge is continually emerging and adapting in support of needed change to more resonantly and routinely 'get it right'.

> Interest in the topic of systems change... emerges from the growing recognition that the implementation of discrete programs aimed at delivering services to vulnerable populations is likely to fail or not be sustained in the long run if the surrounding context and supporting systems do not shift in order to support the goals of this effort. (Call for papers for special issue on systems change for *American Journal of Community Psychology* EVAL-SYS list-serv, 24 November 2004)

A more systemic approach to change means that people's immediate and more long-term relationships can absorb perturbance and de-escalate turbulence with fewer difficulties because the pace and direction of action is self-organised on a regular basis. It is thus potentially a more life-sustaining way of navigating transitions—including the bumps and unevenness—from any 'here' to a 'there' as well as stabilising the

new most life-giving forms. Unsettling (or appreciated) discrepancies can be explored and become understandable through recursive processes of inquiry as people become ready, willing and able to go forward. The familiar and reliable inquiry methodology assists them work towards their shared visions and implementing of the practices that have arisen from—and, most importantly, stay connected to—their own deeper purposes.

Often attempts to scale up innovations rely on the idea of 'rolling out' a model, replicating it on the basis of predicting that if a program or service worked in one place it will work elsewhere. This chapter draws on the orienting framework of the inquiring group's or organisation's self-organising, primarily taking a lead from their own context-specific observations, reflections, purposes, conditions and participation (while drawing on other people's efforts for ideas). It is this inquiry culture or methodological 'mental architecture' that is scaled up and replicated—a kind of underlying shared language of a living system—rather than any particular findings, conclusions or practices.

That is, we make an 'intelligent system' by knowing how to inquire—and frequently enough so that our inquiry practice builds life-giving density or 'structure' until it becomes a culture of 'the way we do things round here'. That culture comprises the strongly patterned shared meanings, definitions, expectations, ideas, beliefs, knowledge, norms, values, purposes and intentions that bound and shape (and are bounded and shaped by) the purposeful actions of members in ever-changing dynamic, permeable and stabilising recursive processes of interactive exchange.

A storehouse of ideas for building a culture of inquiry

This chapter is intended both as evidence and a source of ideas about how to assist 'scaffold' and build in to organisational, community and professional practices, regular thoughtful practice-based inquiry at different scales. The exemplars report the findings of more than twenty years of practice-based research and development that generated the book's 'big theory' of inquiry for (truly) living human systems, and the conclusions that appear at the end of this chapter. What follows are the experiences of a representative range of human services that set out systematically to build in research, evaluation and continuous quality improvement over relatively extended periods of time. They include health, education and welfare, non-government organisations, local, state and federal government, community groups and associations working with youth, homelessness, disability, community and mental health, health promotion, hospitals, schools, universities, child and family services, neighbourhood houses, the disadvantaged and excluded, agriculture, environment, Indigenous people and one commercial small business to indicate the broader reach of the ideas. They range from small to very large in scale—from the individual, group, community, organisational, city and suburban, to rural-regional, statewide and national.

While the exemplars focus on the innovative aspects of the approach taken in this book—particularly in weaving it more deeply into the fabric of organisations—they also integrate current, already well- established elements (such as quality assurance, accreditation, management information system databases and more traditional research and evaluation projects conducted in partnership with academic or consultancy organisations). On the basis of this range of experiences, the chapter ends with a summary and conclusions about the conditions needed for success in 'building it in'.

Some early precursors

The ten exemplars I will describe are ones with which I have worked closely. But there are a number of others I am aware of internationally (e.g. carried out by the Asian Development Bank, the World Bank and the UN Development Program), as well as nationally, regionally and locally that have also worked at a large scale. As there is already a literature concerning the international work available through those agencies I will briefly sketch some of these local, regional and national historical precursors with which I am familiar to indicate the reach of this approach into quite diverse fields such as those of schools improvement, land care, local government and agriculture.

Schools improvement[1]

In the 1980s a team of teachers and parents through the Victorian Education Department led a statewide

program of resourcing school teachers, parents and students to carry out their own participatory action research and group self-evaluation. Supported by Marie Brennan and Ruth Hoadley in the department, and Stephen Kemmis, Robin McTaggart and others in the School of Education at Deakin University, the School Improvement Program (SIP) achieved significant take up and change in participating schools, and created conditions under which other programs—such as the federally funded Participation And Equity Program (PEP)—could build in their work with schools. This conjuncture generated one of the earliest methodological literatures in education action research (e.g. Lynton Brown's *Action Research—The Teacher as Learner* (1981), Marie Brennan's and Ruth Hoadley's 'School Self-evaluation' (1984), Lynton Brown's *Group Self-Evaluation—Learning for Improvement* (1988), Susan Noffke's and Marie Brennan's 'Student Teachers Use Action Research' (1991) in Kenneth Zeichner and Robert Tabachnik's collection, *Issues and Practices in Inquiry-oriented Teacher Education*), and Stephen Kemmis and Robin McTaggart's *Action Research Planner* (1988) which has remained continuously in print to this day.

Land care

After 200 years of European colonisation and extensive land clearing, in 1983 a major soil salinity control project commenced under the aegis of the then Victorian Minister for Conservation, Joan Kirner. A senior public servant, Anne Morrow, who had had involvement with an action research association, saw the issue was one that crossed many boundaries and that it might work with the encouragement of self-organising community-based groups of farmers and others who could 'inquire their way' towards trying out local solutions, with multi-disciplinary resourcing and statewide collaboration. The Minister for Conservation created a partnership with the president of the Victorian Farmers' Federation, Heather Mitchell, and within seven years around seventy groups had formed across both rural and urban areas. Similar to the successes of the community-based AIDS initiatives in Australia that had gone on to be a model for the world, LandCare has to date resulted in not only around 800 LandCare groups in ninety networks, plus 500 urban conservation groups, and extended to 300 CoastCare associations as well, it also went international (in

Kenya, South Africa, Uganda, Canada, New Zealand, the Philippines, Fiji, Sri Lanka, Jamaica, the United States, Iceland and Great Britain).

The factors identified as relevant to the success of this large-scale, complex systemic action-inquiry work included the following (Youl et al. 2006).

Its local scale

- The strength of existing rural community networks and a culture of mutual assistance
- A determination that local knowledge was critically important; translating into an egalitarian, democratic, local decision-making, self-organising style, all consistent with Australian bush culture
- Local flexibility preserved without a move to national standardisation or rules
- An ability to respond quickly to new ideas and establish practical projects
- A learned and collective ability to sustain energies through experiments that fail as well as those that work, to take a long-term view, and a grace and tolerance that comes from resilient social structures
- Strong roles played by both men and women, and a junior program developed within schools

Its regional or network scale

- The existence of precursor organisations and agricultural advice (extension), at both the local and central levels, with a focus on soil and conservation
- Wide community support (local business, farms, schools, media, education institutions, service clubs)
- The ability to grow and organise as independent enterprises

Its state and national scale

- Personal, friendly working relationships between key organisation head visionaries who had become convinced of both the need and the evidence, became organisational partnerships sufficient to cross traditional boundaries (e.g. between farmers, conservation, technical support, culture and arts, philanthropic trusts and political organisations)
- Strong government support without imposition of control
- Funds to support paid full- or part-time local regional co-ordinators (as organisers, facilitators etc.)

- Tax incentives to undertake land degradation reversal works

Nearly thirty years later some of these conditions that helped take the work so effectively 'to scale' are beginning to decay (e.g. loss of the community consultative approach, an increase in government interventionism, a demand for documentation and accountability by central agencies in exchange for reduced funding, and a form of complex corporatisation that has brought more centralised management control). Yet as the activity remains essentially local and regional, many in the LandCare movement report remain forthright about continuing into the future given new and urgent demands to respond to the climate change emergency, permanent lack of water and the threat of desertification.

Local government

Many local governments took up a set of inquiry practices derived from business and management in the late 1980s and early 1990s, as did federal and state governments and numerous non-government organisations. Of particular relevance were those of total quality management (TQM) and to some extent organisational learning and development. Some of these local councils worked towards a more wholistic approach, wanting to engage genuinely with their ratepayers and other stakeholders, not just as a matter of prescription but from a desire to know how people were actually responding to and benefiting (or not) from programs.

The City of Maroondah in Australia was a good example of an early adopter. In 1998, key features of its approach included a focus on customer service, customer satisfaction approaches, building a 'culture of service' by 'continuous improvement', 'reflective practice' and 'citizen-focused service delivery'. As part of the wider movement, the state government was requiring Customer Service Charters of all its agencies as a counterpart to Service Standards Charters. But municipal councils like Maroondah were 'going a bit beyond this' (Mike Marasco, Maroondah CEO, personal interview, 24 September 1998) with a cluster of activities that included two-way communication mechanisms facilitated by:

- Appointment of customer services officers
- Local customer service outlets
- Workshops with staff to develop the new culture of

service standards, combined with positive reception to critical comments

- A training kit detailing the program messages for all staff
- a customer feedback program with a special ratings-and-suggestions form
- A customer action program (including three levels of 'request' regarding 'issue resolution'—avoiding the anxiety-creating word 'complaint') using Customer Link, an electronic request tracker with a service standard of a maximum ten-day turnaround
- Attractive brochures to let people know about the customer action program (including service-specific ones, e.g. for child care and meals-on-wheels) that made it clear citizens' feedback was wanted and needed
- A review group that met quarterly to solve problems around feedback
- Other forms of public consultation, including public meetings
- Community representatives on advisory committees
- Phone surveys of residents and other customer groups to check that services were indeed communicative, responsive and seen as doing an acceptable job.

There were critical voices raised against these reforms given that services were at that time being increasingly restricted (rationed) in the name of 'productivity savings' as part of corporatisation and its associated competitive tendering, with the new management becoming more remote from increasingly outsourced, on-the-ground practice.[2] And indeed many councils were asking only 'broad brush' questions in feedback sheets such that the data was unusable for improvement and only really being used to register a 'big tick' on a general customer satisfaction 'report card' (Caddick and Moore 1998). Some of these issues of collecting too much data, of the wrong kind or of unusable nature persist to the present day, with the increasing reification of 'risk management' procedures.

Nevertheless service systems did begin to enable service users to give feedback and make complaints, and it became more culturally normal, easy and acceptable to say 'may I have a feedback form please?' It was certainly a time when absent or old unused complaints systems were dusted off and reformed, and organisations began to see feedback and complaints in

a more positive light. Eventually a request for a feedback form did not inevitably mean a useless scramble under a counter for an always elusive form![3]

In some actively inquiring local councils (such as Nillumbik and Moreland) there were further efforts to learn how to hear from the 'hard to reach' by using more effective forms of consultation and engagement. For example while one-off public meetings, community forums and questionnaires were found to have some value, other more 'full inquiry cycle' approaches involving iterative and deliberative methods became increasingly popular:

- Firstly canvassing or sharing information about 'the problem'
- Then seeking input, including action suggestions
- Subsequently reporting back on the recommendations or actions taken
- Then seeking residents' responses to these based on their observations
- And so on for a number of iterations.

There was also more take up of standing consultative or participatory 'panels' (whether made up of convenient ongoing statistically representative 'database' population survey samples, or more face-to-face recursive 'focus group' type panels that work more like 'live' communities of practice, or both). The idea of resident consultants who run focus groups and who can peer interview has also since become popular and widespread as the practical outcomes have become observable.

Deeper inquiry by some of the more progressive councils also yielded more systemic insights, for example, that it was possibly as much a matter of services making *themselves* hard to reach through exclusionary practices (e.g. appointments-only systems within highly restricted hours or referral only to website information but not to actual human assistance) as it was residents' lifeworlds being distant from the work-worlds and assumptions of service providers (through language, discourse, disability or sheer busyness). Finally, there has been a small but growing appreciation that 'the usual faces' at consultations (the activists, trouble-makers and busy bodies) are in fact 'participation gold' given their characteristic inquiry capabilities. They are likely to be effective early warning 'canaries in the mine' noticing the discrepancies in local residents' lifeworlds and have quite polished capacities to come up with innovative ideas that are more likely to work in the realities of the actual local environments they live in and know intimately.

Slowly these efforts are 'joining up' into wider repertoires of autopoetic inquiry, with inquiry taking place at the neighbourhood and street level of local life feeding in and out of local council-level activity until the balance is beginning to shift from 'the centre' seeing itself as *using* the local people for its own top-down decision-making needs and purposes, to councils seeing themselves as *resourcing, co-ordinating, and assisting residents*' more bottom-up re-localising efforts as they inquire into addressing their own needs and purposes. This approach is becoming more significant as the world enters the crisis phase of the global climate change emergency.

Two-way agricultural extension work between the farmer and the science lab

Also in the light of climate change, another particularly well-developed effort to build in a systemic approach statewide throughout the activities of a whole government department—one drawing on a tradition of critical social and natural science research and developmental evaluation applied to science extension—has been that of government activity for primary industry. The following account tells the story of nearly a decade's worth of intensive effort to 'build in' evaluation by the Victorian Department of Primary Industry (DPI).[4]

In their award-winning article 'Teaching People to Fish?—Building the Evaluation Capability of Public Sector Organisations', Bron McDonald, Patricia Rogers and Bruce Kefford (2003) describe the strategies they used to develop the DPI's evaluation capability within primary industry research and extension teams. The question mark in the title is important (although most references to the article leave it out). While acknowledging the systemic distinction of needing to 'teach individuals to fish' (rather than continuing to hand out food, simultaneously and unintentionally rendering passive the recipients of such giving), their approach also questioned whether this was sufficient without addressing the whole fish marketing system—that is, the 'demand' end of evaluation.

Core components of the resourcing approach included:

- Securing and maintaining active senior management support
- A Departmental Evaluation Support Team (EST) responsible for ongoing development of internal evaluation capability, with support for them to undertake short courses and postgraduate studies in evaluation and attend evaluation conferences
- EST support of and participation in local practitioner teams
- EST provision of individual consultancy
- A secondment program whereby practitioners could come and work as part of the EST
- Engagement of local and international experts to provide training, review work, and undertake research
- A formal training program (three sessions run over six days) for nearly one in five of the staff of the Agriculture Division
- Use of Bennett's (1977) hierarchy as an action research methodology or inquiry program logic[5]
- An across government evaluation community of interest that grew to eventually include most government departments, holding well-attended meetings every four months. These meetings were used to: explore issues such as fit-for-purpose impact evaluation, skills development and evaluation theory.

The DPI's work identified four phases in building an evaluation capability. These correspond with four loops of the action research cycle itself—firstly, initial R&D; secondly, trialling with a wider group; thirdly, organising for all new projects to necessarily incorporate the approach; and fourthly, a consolidation phase to institutionalise the work.

From their first three years of experience, seven themes were drawn out in regard to building an evaluation capability:

1. Think big, but start small—stage, trial and grow evaluation
2. Address both supply (e.g. training staff) and demand (e.g. partnering with stakeholders)
3. Use a pincer movement, working top-down and bottom-up
4. Address fears and anxieties, don't just focus on technical skills
5. Use a common evaluation framework, language or program theory-of-action (e.g. Bennett's hierarchy)
6. Build R&D knowledge that is context-based and relevant

7. Walk the talk—systematically and visibly evaluate each stage.

From the very first experiment to the end of the fourth phase, the work was sustained for eight years. At the end of that time, and with a reorganisation of the department, the evaluation team was moved into 'cost recovery' mode. The team had to fully fund all its activities, including corporate contributions. It did this by charging internal projects for its services, seeking research funds outside the department, and offering services to external stakeholders.

There were several persisting consequences of this evaluation capability-building work. Those in charge of resource allocation continued to demand evaluative activity, and this provided the incentive for projects to continue to grow their evaluation effort. These managers also required projects to undergo internal six-monthly reviews of progress asking the questions: What worked? What didn't? What needs to be changed? And what were the key lessons? At the same time the demand for services from external clients grew, which ultimately tempted some members of the evaluation team to leave and set up in private practice. So, was the capability-building unit in place long enough, and in the right way, to ensure an evaluative culture with the right level of capability well into the future? The experiment continues and the longer term outcomes are yet to be observed.

References

C.F. Bennett, *Analysing Impacts of Extension Programs*, USDA Extension Service, Washington DC, 1977.

B. McDonald, P.J. Rogers and B. Kefford, 'Teaching People to Fish? Building the Evaluation Capability of Public Sector Organizations', *Evaluation*, 9 (1): 9–29.

C. Bennett and K. Rockwell, *A Hierarchy for Targeting Outcomes and Evaluating Their Achievement*, a synopsis introducing TOP (Targeting Outcomes of Programs). See the graphic at http://citnews.unl.edu/TOP/english/index.html.

Related organisational development activities and efforts

Many other organisations and sectors of human services besides those addressed by these four and the following ten more detailed exemplars have, since the 1980s, also instituted changes devoted to improving the research, evaluation and learning life of their organisations—particularly in relation to quality assurance, quality improvement and end users. There has, for example, been a renewed focus on professional development, partnerships with staff, and staff health and wellbeing programs to ensure staff come to the task of co-operative, committed, mutually supportive and creative responses to their clients and end-beneficiaries with energy and enthusiasm. In this way there has also been a slow realisation that more committed, collaborative, co-operative, supportive, informing, consultative and creative resourcing of and responsiveness to service users by co-inquiring staff is mirrored and sustained by committed, collaborative, co-operative, supportive, informing, consultative and creative resourcing of and responsiveness to staff by their co-inquiring organisations. Some of this has been framed by the concept of the 'healthy organisation'.

There has also been something of a return to in-house research support and evaluation capacity-building units. These are sometimes within strategic planning, policy and performance reporting areas with a quality improvement and consumer participation function—although others are within Human Resources or 'People and Culture' (personnel) areas with more of a risk management, quality assurance compliance and staff satisfaction outlook. (Ideally, using living systems theory, these would not be 'siloed'!) Nevertheless where central units operate, there is a slow growth of capacity to conduct inquiry at different levels, for example, more outsourced, specialised academic-style projects alongside a much greater number of smaller scale collaborative inquiries by practitioners, stakeholders and critical stakeowners supported by internal researchers (or experienced practitioners or client consultants) operating as facilitators and mentor–coaches—with insights from each scale of effort being fed into others.

Diagram 5, at the end of Chapter 4, illuminated the virtuous cycle sequence, including various managerial activities that take organisations 'full cycle' in the terms described in this book. Sequentially the cycle comprises the following—firstly summarised and then in more detail:

Summary of virtuous cycle: Needs studies → *QI* → *Policy* → *Planning* → *Procedures* → *Standards* → *QA* → *Practice* → *Services/Program Research* → *Evaluation* → *New needs studies again...*

Details of cycle: **Observe** • research into unresolved issues, needs, desires and purposes • **Reflect** • critical and empowerment evaluation • developmental evaluation • *Quality improvement* **(QI)** • generate new program theory • **Plan** • identify implementation program logic • define policy-principles-mission-goals-indicators-actions-procedures-standards-targets hierarchy for intended outcomes • formative evaluation • input evaluation • process evaluation • monitoring • *Quality assurance* **(QA)** • output evaluation • summative evaluation of existing policy and practice • realist evaluation • goal-free and impact evaluation • narrative evaluation • *repeat living systems inquiry cycle...*

Ten detailed exemplars of the conditions for building in systemic inquiry

The following health, welfare, education, community and human service organisations are highlighted as ones which set out deliberately to build in research and evaluation often over many years, and with which I worked closely enough to be sufficiently familiar to draw out the cluster of interconnected conditions under which they were able to achieve their purposes. Some of this material is published here for the first time to form a comprehensive evidence base for this book's key conclusions. The small business example with which this section concludes is included to show the use of the underlying ideas in a much wider context.

ONE

'The essential U&I': building in understanding and involvement in consumer evaluation of psychiatric services[6]

A sequence of collaborative evaluation research projects were conducted over a decade in the 1990s to build in consumer evaluation, and staff–consumer dialogue about that evaluative feedback, within a particularly 'tough end' of human services: that of acute psychiatric services.[7]

This exemplar has featured in earlier chapters,[8] but the focus here will be on the conditions achieved that allowed the inquiry processes to be successfully built in to the fabric of the services system.

Strong movement of end-beneficiary group to address discrepancy

It is important to note that many of the most powerful changes to human services have been initiated from the bottom up by those whose life conditions have been most compromised. Indigenous people and acute psychiatric service users are examples of those for whom the conditions of the greater *oikos* or lifeworld have been particularly unresponsive, hostile, excluding or otherwise insensitive. In the case of psychiatric services there have been strong challenges by 'csx' (consumers, survivors, ex-patients) in the last fifty years to practices that are iatrogenically stigmatising, damaging or coercive. There are contemporary complexities here, including the restriction of funding for quality interpersonal human support or a range of more wholistic therapies, and increasing reliance on an expensive private pharmaceutical drugs industry where a model of individualised bodily disease, disorder and illness has effectively factored out the complex social, economic and political pressures that contribute systemically to people's extreme states of anxiety, depression or loss of touch with reality.

Under such conditions psychiatric services staff are constantly torn between observing people's actual situations and defaulting to a regulated but constrained ability to address them. And, while 'the system', on the one hand, seeks to normalise, reassure and build confidence, on the other hand, the default response remains referenced to a model that sees people's mental lifeworlds as pathological and largely incomprehensible, responding by (more-or-less sympathetically) suppressing proximal behavioural and mental life until the baffling responses go away. People then return to the same distal systemic environments that helped co-produce the distressed mental life in the first place, only to repeat the same reactions and readmission. Alternatively, if there is change within the individual, it is towards adapting and aligning themselves 'better' to fit in with the problematic endemic environment, or the person may acquire more resonant assistance from particular staff (or other people) who can better resource patients' autopoetic inquiry, and in some instances, staff and consumers can even work to alter not just individuals but also their problematic environments at more 'structural' or wider systemic scales.

In attempting to resource the latter kinds of co-inquiry, a sequence of funded research projects commonly known collectively as the 'U&I project' unfolded between 1987 and 1997.[9] All were auspiced by the statewide peak consumer organisation, the Victorian Mental Illness Awareness Council, and were conducted in collaboration with an inner city regional area and its metropolitan hospital services.

Like the later youth homelessness 'Reconnect' exemplar, the beginnings of the U&I project were small and built from the 'witnessing of discrepancy' that, through a complex set of conditions and intentions, was able recursively to set in train ever-expanding connections and cycles of inquiry that were able to reach critical mass for long-term viability.

A small and personal beginning: 'the invitation', set within a favourable climate

Since all inquiry, evaluative research and learning cycles begin at some point with one person making an observation that raises a question and then feeling moved to share it with another or others who may have been making their own observations and raising questions—the first condition for survival is at the very least a favourable 'micro-climate' able to incubate and nurture that first question and reaching out.

The 'U&I' project 'Ahoy there' logo cartoon, provided with kind permission by the cartoonist Michael Leunig at the time, expressed this hopefulness about what might come of an offer of dialogue in the form of better mutual understanding from 'involvement anytime'.

In the case of the tiny beginnings of the U&I evaluation research, that first reaching out conversation took place between a thoughtful and

Michael Leunig's cartoon 'Ahoy there!' became a kind of 'logo' symbol for the project

© Michael Leunig and Penguin 1974

observant psychiatric hospital social worker and a social worker who shared enough of his misgivings to want to get on with taking an action. The latter social worker had retired from a life of public service and was active in the then new statewide organisation representing the concerns of mental health 'consumers'. Importantly, that new organisation was physically sharing offices within a lively and activist disability resource centre at the peak of the disability and deinstitutionalisation movements.

Early managerial support is secured

At that time the human service terrain was newly opening to the business world's preoccupation with customer satisfaction, and so the retired social worker and the manager of the consumer organisation proposed an 'exit survey' questionnaire for which they sought expert input. It all could have ended there with 'yet another questionnaire', but the new system logic of needing 'consumer input' was taken to a next critical step with an invitation being extended to a research evaluation design consultant with experience in involving critical reference group enquirers for key decisions on design 'right around the cycle'.[10]

Management supports strong consumer guidance of the evaluation research from the outset

Like other exemplars in this chapter, the success in aligning the inquiry with the critical interests of those most likely to benefit was what underpinned the value of all other subsequent successful outcomes. In this case the 'compass work' guided by the critical reference group perspective encouraged the research into a new phase of 'reflection-on-observation', rather than the refining of an instrumental procedure which turned out to be in this case premature.

Questionnaire surveys *did* emerge later in the U&I project but by then were not at risk of isolation from the fabric of practice and were instead rooted in an inquiry culture where professional staff were more engaged in closer personal relationships with actively involved consumers. This first critical moment involved the research consultant, who describes this significant decision point in the design:

> When asked to give comments on the proposed exit survey I could have done just that—made that conventional 'expert' intervention—and that could have been the end of the matter. Instead I arranged to meet with

the co-ordinator and other service-users involved with the organisation, and, rather than just going ahead quickly, we talked... (Wadsworth, 2001: 421)

Research as dialogue

This 'talk' also turned out to be not just peripheral 'establishing rapport' for instrumental purposes to move more efficiently to commence fieldwork. In the first place, such 'talk' is itself a deeply 're-searching' activity—as the word rapport indeed suggests[11]—of 'doing something reiteratively' before a relationship can carry through on its intentions. In this sense it is achieving what qualitative researchers would recognise as the beginnings of an essentially mutual co-inquiry—including into the apparent intentions themselves. When explicitly joined with its purposes—in this case, that 'users of acute psychiatric services' evaluation of the services' (or, as it unfolded that 'people experiencing suffering in relation to themselves and their world, might find the resources to assist them and their world heal')—the 'talk' came to be about the 'subjected participants' own observations and reflections.

And thus already the research had begun! 'Data' was 'live and happening' even in the very first interactions, and already subject to analysis and conclusions! The action research cycles had commenced.

Initially, after the external consultant's reconnaissance study had commenced a formal process (Otto 1990), the consumer organisation appointed a sympathetic non-consumer to conduct the *Understanding, Anytime* pilot (McGuiness and Wadsworth 1991). This took the process to a more fully fledged dialogue, which became the characteristic methodology for 'building it in' in all the ongoing work (see Figure 20 below).

Dialogue across distance

The early critical reference group compass work detected:

- The deeper values and purposes of consumers in changing acute ward culture
- The state of the existing desired (but alienated) living systems
- The strength of the driving energies for this inquiry.[13]

People talked of their experiences of questionnaire surveys as not really telling *their* stories, and also typically not being acted on. On probing it emerged that they wanted staff to *understand* their situation by putting themselves in the consumer's situation—so they would see the need for change, and then work out how to do this with the input and active *involvement* of consumers...Further probing revealed that consumers preferred to speak face to face about their experiences in their own words as a way of doing justice to the rich meanings of their 'whole' stories...[and the]... questionnaire survey for patients being discharged, transformed into an idea for some kind of participatory evaluation conducted in dialogue with staff...The consumer organisation then offered to conduct a series of informal interviews with a total population of all inpatients at one ward admitted during a one-week period...and match this with a series of consumer-perspective questions to staff. (Wadsworth, 2001: 422)

An emergent self-organising process continued in a balanced way: with escalating dynamic resonance

The consumer discussions heard people's experiences of coming to, being in and then leaving the ward, and the staff were asked consumer-perspective strategic questions about what they were trying to achieve for consumers, what they were up against, how they knew if they achieved useful things for consumers, and so on. The material from each of the two groups was then swapped and further discussions arranged to reflect on it. In this way people became the researchers of their own and each others' experiences. The results of these reflections were swapped once more before time and funds ran out and the process came to a temporary halt. (Wadsworth, 2001: 422)

Many people were extremely interested in *what* staff and consumers had to say. However the consumer organisation was concerned with *how* these kinds of reflective and illuminative conversational processes might *continue* in busy daily work to the point of innovating new practice—especially as they seemed to have ended just as they were really beginning. (See Wadsworth 2001: 14–15 for a detailed depiction of each of the segments of this process of dialogue.) To examine how to build in such talk and dialogue between staff and consumers as a permanent element of any mental health services, a further, four-year project (U&I) commenced. (Wadsworth, 2001: 422)

Full documentation showing details of the inquiry journey: including prefiguring intra-organisational and inter-system communication (e.g. by bulletins)

The work was exhaustively documented in monthly bulletins that circulated feedback about the research's thirty-five staff and consumer sub-projects to all within the hospital and increasingly outside, and were collected and published in annual monographs and eventually in the compendium *The Essential U&I* (Wadsworth 2001). This was not only because the research was providing new primary evidence of the value and processes by which the mental health system could move to a consumer-driven systemic logic (rather than just what hospitals *said* they would do), but also because it was cutting new and controversial ground in understandings about what consumers could contribute. 'Patient involvement' in this field setting shifted rapidly from the idea that a 'successful graduate' could come back and visit a ward to tell a grateful story of recovery and discharge, to the idea that former consumers might return and be employed as paid consultant staff to assist the system respond better to people during their admissions (including their sitting on management and staff appointment committees). While this has since become more mainstream, they were startling ideas for many at the time. Additionally the work faced all of the issues raised in Chapter 4 (and which continue today) whereby the system wanted to help its consumers towards health, healing and recovery *and* regularly defaulted instead to iatrogenic fear, control and coercion. The U&I research noted that these responses mirrored (even fractal-like) the individual responses of which we are all capable, which in turn reflects the macro socio-political larger systemic responses which from time to time escalate into conflict and frank authoritarianism.

Taking the time that is needed

To cut a very long story short (and it, like all other successful exemplars is a long story of often many years, probably a minimum of three and perhaps more usually around ten for human service-sized deep culture shifts) I summarise here the components of 'the model'.[14]

Trialling lessons learnt in new settings

The model, like all models, is not for precise replication, but comes as 'an offering' from one set of

THE STUDY DESIGN AND PROCESS

The basic design of the project allowed for the stages illustrated.

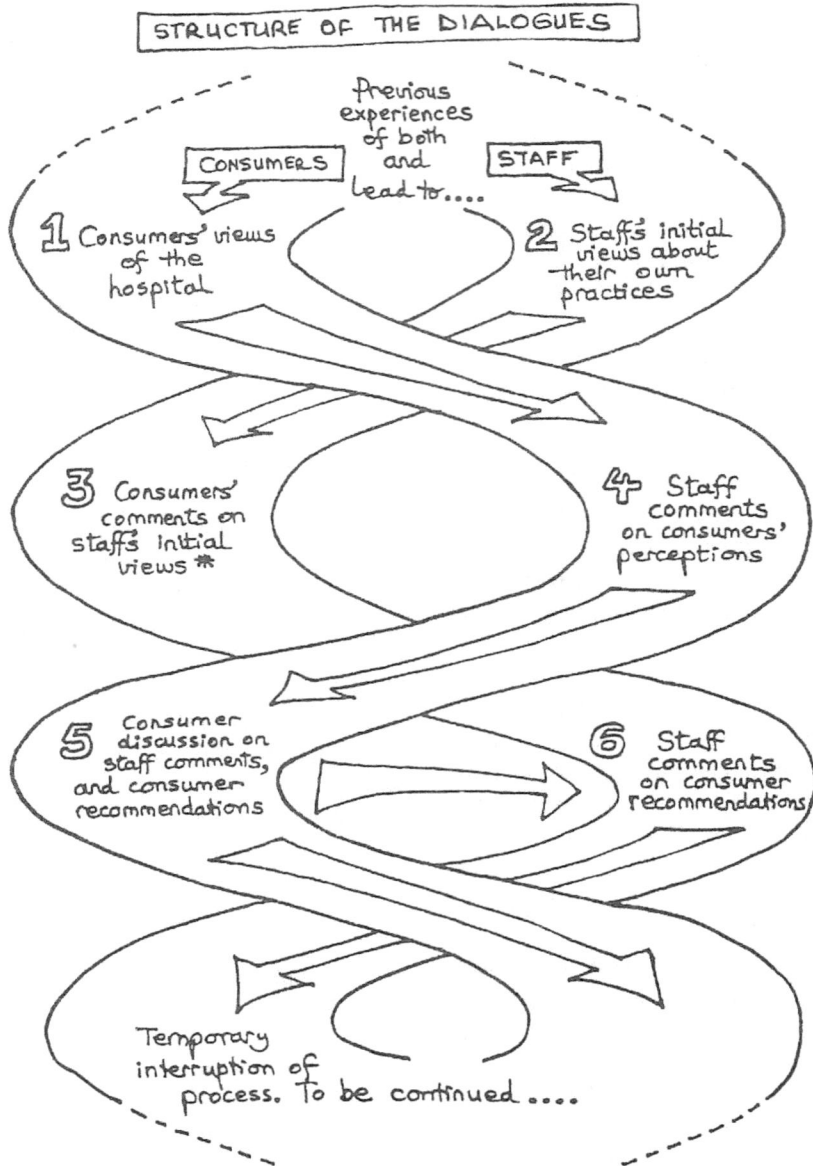

STRUCTURE OF THE DIALOGUES

1 Consumers' views of the hospital

Previous experiences of both and lead to....

CONSUMERS   STAFF

2 Staff's initial views about their own practices

3 Consumers' comments on staff's initial views *

4 Staff comments on consumers' perceptions

5 Consumer discussion on staff comments, and consumer recommendations

6 Staff comments on consumer recommendations

Temporary interruption of process. To be continued ....

* Time did not permit this material (at 3) to go to staff (at 6). Instead consumer discussion and recommendations (at 5) went to staff (at 6).

Figure 20. Cross-over 'snakes' dialogic research design in the U&I project

(Cited in Wadsworth with Epstein 2001:5)

relationships in one set of environmental circumstances as a resource for new trialling and further R&D in a new set of self-organising relationships in another environment with its own stakeowner participants and narrative history. However where the conditions are recognised as particularly alike, then resonance may more easily be achieved. For example you may not be establishing a consumer consultant office to house exactly four people with twenty drinking mugs and two mobile phones and computers—but you may note the transferability of the three principles of ensuring consumers can work together to get the mutual peer support they need, that they have the normal quality work resources essential to doing a professional job (so they are able to communicate, meet together with others, write reports and so on), and that they need maximum autopoesis to 'drive' their own enterprise.

A 'model' that compiles lessons learnt as a resource for others' future efforts

The U&I project set out 'to establish and refine processes by which staff and consumers in psychiatric wards could routinely collaborate to research and evaluate the experiences of consumers and make the consequent relevant and appropriate changes to hospital practices.' (Wadsworth 2001: 187) And in a sense the whole project was prefiguring: 'trying to build back into the system "time enough for understanding": time enough to come close enough to bridge the distances enough, to leave aside the second-guessing enough, to achieve understanding enough to dissipate the damaging fears and anxieties' (Wadsworth 2001 187).

It wasn't in the end seeking a 'new vision' or a 'breakthrough formula' which would leave distancing, 'othering', fears, anxieties and iatrogenesis as things of the past. In the end we saw how 'the system' mirrors and 'writes large' the nature of each human being and what we were seeking was to put in place something *equally systemic* to help discharge the forcefield of oppositional distancing by creating spaces and places for both professionals and end-beneficiaries to come 'side by side'—for staff to feel it was safe to come out of the nursing station, and for consumers to feel safe to tell staff what they were experiencing.

In order to tip the balance to the side of 'health, healing and recovery' rather than always or too quickly defaulting to 'fear, control and coercion', we identified the following kind of culture as necessary. Its key value was on constantly trying to bridge the distances between staff and consumers, both through staff members' fundamental desires to do a good and humanly responsive job and consumers' fundamental desires for their own wellbeing.

The twelve 'components' or characteristics of 'the model' that the U&I project had researched, developed, trialled prefiguratively and found necessary for 'whole systems change' (Wadsworth 2001: 134–161, 187–199) were:

1. A quality assurance/quality improvement framework
2. Not just one-way consumer feedback but also two-way staff–consumer communication and dialogue
3. Being comprehensive and systemic—not just 'adding on' a representative to a committee or producing a satisfaction survey, but using numerous methods, in many sites, with many elements of resourcing, involving many staff, across the whole organisational network and bureaucracy[15]
4. Being robust and built in—again, the components and characteristics were not onerous extras but integral to the way human service relationships (e.g. in case management and medical consultations) were routinely conducted
5. Achieving culture shift, supportive of culture carriers and building to critical mass
6. Drawing on not just a few but *multiple* consumer feedback and communication methods:
   - Sensitive interpersonal communication
   - Involvement in treatment plans
   - 'Spot' or ad hoc surveys, including quantitative studies
   - Exit/end-of-stay/satisfaction surveys
   - Case story narratives of service usage
   - Group discussions
   - Ward community meetings
   - Suggestion boxes
   - Complaints procedures
   - Individual advocacy
   - Consumer consultants
   - Committee membership
   - Consumers as educators, speakers, writers, researchers etc.
7. Including three sites for action, observation, feedback and deeper reflective communication:

decision-making sites, consumer-only sites, and staff–consumer dialogue sites. A 'missing 4th site' was also identified for staff peer support to help them persevere sympathetically and to match for staff the same support mechanisms as for consumers (see point 11 below), while involving staff–consumer consultants to ensure a consumer empathetic discourse prevailed

8. Taking place at all levels or scales of all relevant parts of the organisation/s that make up the mental health system (reaching right out into professional education systems, unions, the media and the wider community and economy)

9. Being centred on the 'hardest' spots (the acute unit and other high risk situations) and not focusing only on the 'easier' community-based areas

10. Employing consumers as staff to effectively eliminate some of the most damaging bifurcating boundaries and create a new interpersonal solidarity and unity of purpose[16]

11. Providing support resources infrastructure (personal peer supports, e.g. pair teaming, check ins and check outs, incident debriefing, paid locums, professional education, peer supervision/ mentoring, networking and membership of consumer-only support groups; supportive committees, and supportive managers, and in particular —discretionary funds for additional flexible and responsive ad hoc costs

12. Being both consumer-driven (initiated by consumers) *and* staff-collaborative (joined by staff.)

Working with complexity and paradox

The Essential U&I recognised the ongoing paradoxical nature of the mental health system, and the book ended with four 'endings' representing the various possibilities for culture change towards regular staff–consumer collaboration around seeking and acting together on evaluative feedback.

The first 'ending' was a pessimistic scenario in which the system defaults to business as usual. The second concluded with an optimistic scenario in which the system shifts to a healthier culture of inquiry. The third described the real ending at the time—involving a member of staff dropping off to the consumer research office a copy of the story *The Holy Man's Gift*. This was a tale about an ailing monastery and its Abbess who had sought the advice of a hermit living

in the forest. He had said he was unable to help but mentioned he knew that 'the Holy One was among them'. The Abbess returned to the monastery and recounted this curious observation to all who lived there, and then, under the impact of envisioning the possibility that each of them might be that Divine embodiment, they began treating themselves and each other as if they were so, and soon the monastery was thriving again. In a way this was a story of an ailing system that begins to act towards itself as if no part is unworthy and deserving to be hurt, diminished or mistreated, and instead all are worthy of respectful life-giving treatment.

A fourth ending was added as a post-script and this reported the way things had actually turned out, looking back from a much later point, by which time *both* the pessimistic and optimistic accounts had been partly realised—just as is seemingly the case for all human services and even for us as a species—both succeeding and still struggling to value primarily and consistently treating each other as sacred (from the Latin *sacre*, meaning 'whole') living parts of shared living systems. It seems the conditions for such wholeness may continue to 'patiently await' our species better and more fully knowing itself.

One U&I participant expressed this continuing paradox in the following poem which synthesised the constancy of the shadow of despair *and* the equally constant possibility of hope in the acute psychiatric stetting. Readers were invited to read the poem twice, firstly as if it was written from the standpoint of a staff member, and secondly as if it was written from the standpoint of a service beneficiary (Wadsworth 2001: 186), in this way recognising the shared mirroring of our deepest resonant (or cacophonic) systemicity:

In the cold of
the dark, I see
you stand before me
in a vision of
Rage; that neither
you nor I can
control. Weep for
You and me.
Strangers, never more.
Time and place for
you and I
  THEO PSATHAS[17]

TWO

Building in 'speaking action research as a second language' to a national youth homelessness prevention program[18]

Championed by national government

An even more successfully enduring whole-system use of action research in human services took place in the decade following the U&I project in the work of the national Reconnect program. This was the first nation-wide use of action research systematically throughout a whole human services program in Australia.

The Reconnect program, an early intervention program of the Commonwealth Department of Family and Community Services, focuses on engaging with young people who are homeless or at risk of homelessness. Locally based Reconnect workers assist young people make (and remake) the human connections in their lives—with family, schools, community and workplaces.

Reconnect has now used action research for over twelve years. Like the U&I project, the contexts in which Reconnect works with young people as well as a large number of other stakeholders are complex, changing and individual-specific. A standardised, evidence-based single 'best practice' approach was not seen as practically viable by the pilot Reconnect phase which then successfully used action research to develop its approach. The methodology has continued to drive its highly successful emergent character ever since (Crane 1998).

Systemic action research able to generate significant and lasting theory

One of the earliest outcomes of Reconnect's use of action research was the consolidation of a radically new way of doing youth work, an approach that has largely characterised the sector ever since. By closely observing *with* young people (and with their families, mostly parents, and organisations/services) what has happened over time in their lives, youth work shifted its logic of involvement from only being 'alongside the lone young person against the world', to understanding the factors that were excluding and driving the young person away from their primary sources of support, practical resourcing and nurture. From this came a

new stance—of being 'alongside the young person, seeing how they feel (e.g. up against the world) and then working with them to knit or re-knit their relationships' back to the people, groups and organisations they need, but this time with new mutual insight, understanding and respect, with responses that are more helpful, constructive and coherent for the young person.

To some extent this more relational practice had already begun to take shape. However, what the Reconnect pilot project did was use action research to clarify and distill the core principles of good practice and provide a clear and communicable framework for the new approach.

In a way this was an early capacity-building (autopoesis-strengthening) program in which action research was used continually to navigate service responses and build dialogue between 'critical inquirers'—the young people and their other stakeholder–collaborators. Here I will focus on the processes and structures that particularly resourced Reconnect's systemically sustained, effective use of action research—but see Crane 2006, listed at the end of the exemplar, for more detail about the development of Reconnect's use of action research per se.

Active support from policy makers and funders who saw the value of action research, and of a substantial published resource: an action research kit

One notable condition for the success of the program was the 'imprimatur' of the national elected government representative responsible for the policy and funding of the department that implemented Reconnect. Three years into the program, in the Foreword to a kit the department was releasing, the Minister commended the action research approach:

> The issues and challenges faced by Reconnect clients and service providers can be very complex.[19] Too often there's little time set aside to reflect on and improve existing activity and outcome for the client. Action Research provides a process that will enable you to systemically examine your current work practices and improve services.
>
> I believe Action Research will make a difference and lead to many benefits for services and clients alike. It will help you to identify what works, what doesn't work and, of course, what might work better. It will also help to build good practice models for others to

follow. Importantly, the research results will be used to guide and shape future Government policies that support young people at risk. (Crane and Richardson 2000: viii)

But much had had to happen to get to this point of executive support, and with hindsight its beginnings can be seen as having been far more modest and interpersonal—something critically important to its success.[20] However such typical beginnings, followed by a long and complex story of achievement (and challenge), are explored in other exemplars. What forms the focus of this account is the extensive fabric of built in methods and characteristics that have contributed to the acknowledged success and ongoing sustainability of the Reconnect program.

Well-documented inquiry and project reporting which mandates short, regular reports on two action research questions

An important component in Reconnect's use of action research has been its regular reporting on progress. In particular, a decision was made to require reporting after exploring two action research questions every three months (now annually) in response to service requests. In contrast to the reporting that is experienced in many human services at present as excessive, non-relevant and weighing down staff down, these reports:

- Are snappy and to the point, with brevity encouraged (less than a page each)
- Use a template that provides some guidance for services on what to report
- Allow services to choose what action research to include and not include
- May be in different presentation media (e.g. pictorials or DVDs)
- Are part of ordinary work practice and designed not to be onerous extra work (see 'The Day in the Life...' example that follows).

Reporting assists in answering one or more 'Questions of National Significance'

These are program-wide questions which relate to Reconnect's key objectives and to critical challenges identified in program-level evaluations. This systemically bridges between the use of micro action research projects with individuals and scaling up to program-wide use. Themes and insights are also identified from each year's reports, synthesised and fed back to services by a consultant for the department.

Peer pooling of action research knowledge: agency-based peer training of new workers, regional service network meetings and forums, national action research training conferences, and good practice forums

Insights are shared during local peer action research training which has been substantially further resourced by the holding of exceptionally successful national professional development conferences every two years. Prior to 2005 the national conferences followed a model of bringing together the approximately 200 Reconnect workers and local committee members with around twenty of the more experienced Reconnect workers to develop the conference process and run peer-conducted learning workshops. This was discontinued, much to the disappointment of the services, on budgetary grounds. However there are annual Good Practice Forums which services attend in regional clusters. Bringing together around seventy Reconnect workers in regional forums, these forums are a vehicle for sharing practice stories, consolidating corporate memory and identity, and gaining further training and support in action research.

Strong involvement by departmental officers, and invited contributions of external meta-consultants working as (train-the-trainer) facilitators

A strong feature of these national gatherings, and of the ordinary local and regionally based workplaces of the 100 Reconnect agencies around Australia, is the support of regional departmental officers. In addition, academic consultants have worked as facilitators and resource people, writers and publishers of resource material, web-managers and committee members for both the Good Practice forums and other aspects of the infrastructure.

A national Reconnect action research committee, action research in job descriptions and connected to training competencies: all supported by the funding department

The National Reconnect Action Research Committee has been a source of co-ordination and inspiration. Members have included experienced and keen local agency youth workers, and at times young people themselves, as well as committed government officers. It has had responsibility for monitoring, planning and constantly activating agency-based action research and providing both agency-specific and across-program synthesised reflections on the action research reports provided by services so that they can further improve their action research. Program-level insights generated are able to be considered by the department.

Local programs convey the action research philosophy to new Reconnect workers, and to assist this, an induction kit is currently being developed. Job descriptions are related to the three areas of action research training competency (see Crane and Richardson, *Reconnect Action Research Kit*: 5.13–5.21, 'Undertaking a Competency Audit').

A written compendium of the action research method, both in hard copy and online

A key resource that has helped Reconnect projects 'hold the story' as they continually remake their service responses using action research is the *Reconnect Action Research Kit* itself (Crane and Richardson 2000). It contains definitions, processes and examples, tools, challenges and trouble-shooting. It was initially published with a glossy cover in spiral-bound book form for a more professional look and maximum usability, as well as being publically available online:
http://www.fahcsia.gov.au/sa/housing/pubs/homelessyouth/reconnect_action_research_kit/Pages/default.aspx

Key internal and external experienced action research thinkers for deeper learnings

The authors of the kit, Phil Crane and Leanne Richardson, continued the initial work of the external consultant and facilitator Susi Quixley, and Phil in particular has also served on the national action research committee, contributed to conferences, run the 'ReconnectAR' intranet website and generally continued the three-way knowledge transfer partnership between local Reconnect people, the Social Work and Human Services program at the Queensland University of Technology, and the (now) Department of Families, Housing, Community Services and Indigenous Affairs branch responsible for the program. Key internal knowledgeables added more to the creative synergies, for example Dean Fraser, then of Anglicare Reconnect in the Northern

Territory, and Gabrielle Tidey-Passey, who established a specialist youth training consultancy.

State-based, regional and national action research conferences

Finding that other local human services such as schools and welfare agencies were intrigued with how Reconnect workers used action research and so easily moved into the guiding language of 'observe–reflect–plan–act' in their work, Dean Fraser ran a Darwin-based conference for sixty such interested people.[21] This mirrored the national conferences with around 120 Reconnect workers, agency committee members and regional and central departmental officers, and run by practitioners in collaboration with external consultants. Similar regional and local seminars were also held to further understanding of how action research worked in Reconnect.

Internal website

At such conferences and also in the past via the dedicated intranet website 'ReconnectAR', practitioners pooled their experiences and conclusions, exchanged examples and ideas for local action research systems and raised questions. Any of these kinds of resources work best when they are generated from the interest of practitioners as a self-organised answer to their own needs rather than as a 'prescribed instrument' that may have worked well elsewhere. The ReconnectAR website was discontinued in June 2006 and the department is reportedly looking at a number of options to meet this need. There is an action research page for Reconnects' Newly Arrived Youth Specialist Service (NAYSS) initiative which contains action research reports for Reconnect and NAYSS.
The address for this is: http://www.cmyi.net.au/NAYSS/ActionResearch.

Local action research systems as 'containers' to enable 'flow through', and aided by an iconic strategic question: 'What would it take?'

Local Reconnect action research 'systems' anchor the effort in the day to day and comprise: a cluster of activities that include access to all of the above, plus perhaps local reference groups, to help replicate action research processes, methods, activities and information systems; filing cabinets or a library of past examples, current active questions and data collections; and a suggestion box, notice board and whiteboard. Standing advice in the Kit was also to regularly destroy old data and retain only summary reports so as to keep the dynamic flowing. This dynamic is also achieved by regular, widespread use of the Reconnect iconic default question—'*What would it take…?*'—a question which helps propel movement from observation–reflection into planning–action.

A day in the life of a Reconnect worker in action research

A case example that helps bring to life the daily use of action research in Reconnect is 'Case example three' from the *Reconnect Action Research Kit* (Crane and Richardson 2000: 5.7) Danyelle Bodaghi of Darwin Connect took the time to create this valuable resource that illuminates:

- The way in which action research thinking is possible even in the immediacy of normal busy human services work—illustrating how time can be built in for action research
- The way in which Reconnect workers have learned to be alert, curious and questioning as 'the way we do things around here', more-or-less easily switching into the observe–reflect–plan–do mnemonic
- The continuous micro-interchanges between action and inquiry, and the ability to see accrued learning as 'best evidence so far' and to not overly congeal it in perpetuity
- How to keep collecting new insights and conclusions and find easy built in ways of storing them so they are accessible as advice offered to others (see the reference to the '12 to 15 file', Crane and Richardson 2000: 5.8)
- The constant driving of the processes by the lifeworlds of the young people and their families —not just so that workers 'get it right' for them, but also so the young people are resourced to 'get it right for themselves'
- The assumption that there will always be yet more resonance to be achieved (e.g. around grasp and usage of 'young people's language' rather than potentially alienating professionalised language, just as it was found that the term 'homelessness' itself was not wanted by young people (Crane and Richardson 2000: 2.6).

- The ingenuity and creativity sparked by sitting with the tension of a question that arises out of a discrepancy between an 'is' and an 'ought'
- The ease with which observations that might otherwise be rejected as 'just anecdotes' become instead an evidence base by being collected and recorded systematically (see the reference to use of the back of the day book, Crane and Richardson 2000: 5.9).
- How efforts are most assisted when practitioners feel confident either to point things out to each other (e.g. regarding discordant language they might be using) or to hear about discordance directly from the young people themselves when they are sufficiently 'alongside' in their relationships with them
- The scale of inquiry (e.g. where a macro question—'What would it take…?' [Crane and Richardson 2000: 5.9]—connects to a micro question that is explored in its own right by a small-scale school-based research study conducted by students and Reconnect workers [Crane and Richardson 2000: 3.17]).

Extract: Case example three. 'A "Day in the Life" of a Reconnect Worker using Action Research', by Danyelle Bodaghi, in P. Crane and L. Richardson, *Reconnect Action Research Kit*, Department of Family and Community Services, Commonwealth of Australia, Canberra, 5.7–5.10, including the example of a sub-project with a co-research group, from 3.17.

Postscript: National evidence base for efficacy
In 2008 an Australian government White Paper on Homelessness recognised as a guiding principle that the action research utilised in the Reconnect program was 'a legitimate source of insight for evidence-based policy and program design' (Australian Government 2008: 20). The data from the 2008 national census also attributed statistically a causal connection between the Reconnect program and the 20.8 per cent drop in homelessness among twelve to eighteen year olds (calculated using Supported Accommodation client collection data).

In 2010 the Reconnect program continues to see action research as key to its effectiveness in breaking the cycle of homelessness as well as its good practice principles of client driven holistic service delivery, working collaboratively, culturally and contextually

Case example three—a 'day in the life' of a Reconnect worker using Action Research
(Contributed by Connect, Darwin)

Being a Reconnect worker means that on any given day you can work across a huge spectrum of areas, using a number of interventions and with goals ranging from individual client change to long-term systemic change.

The use of Action Research in everyday work is imperative to the continued development of the Connect service in Darwin. With such a large emphasis put on the Action Research process in the pilot, Connect now has ingrained the use of Action Research questions and ways to develop/change how the program is run in response to client/community feedback, into every aspect of its service provision.

This is a typical (if you could call it that) day in a Connect worker's life...

8.30am–9.15am

Begin work, receive a message on the answering machine from Rita (Joanne's Mum who I provide case support to) requesting an immediate response. A phone call is made back to her after speaking with the other Connect worker, who supports the young person. Rita is asked for her preferred way of receiving support. The result was that the other Connect worker finds out Joanne would be OK about a meeting between them all.

Action Research Component

An ongoing Action Research question is 'whether it is more viable for the young person and their parents to have separate workers'. It was found in the pilot that this was often the case, but with the recognition that every client is different, this is a question that is asked of clients and ourselves every time we engage with a family.

10.00am–12.00am

Meeting with a youth detention centre social worker and othe key stakeholders regarding the development of a 'Community of Origin Visitors Scheme'. This meeting is to discuss the draft Background Paper created by a Connect worker and the creation of a time-line that allows for the optimum amount of consulation and contribution by relevant community members.

Action Research Component

Within the pilot, it was identified through client feedback and service assessment processes that there was a need for Aboriginal young people in detention to receive visits from other members of their communities with language, family or just community ties. This would be seen as a way to ease the feeling of dislocation and isolation from their communities and families, who are sometimes 2,000 km away. In response to this need and in partnership with the detention centre, Connect has drawn together a few key stakeholders in an effort to secure funding and put the beginnings of a model together, before further consultation is undertaken with members of the sector and the community.

1.00pm–2.30pm

Meeting with a young woman who is 14 years old. Went to shopping centre food court and discussed current issues. These included school truancy. self-harming behaviour and violent behaviour towards other people. On returning from meeting, a few observations regarding our meeting are placed in the 12 to 15 file.

Action Research Component

The key to making Action Research successful in terms of client work has been the ability to make it accessible on a daily basis. An example of this is creating a file titled *'what works with 12 to 15 year olds?'* This came about as a result of observations by workers and in dialogue with local agencies. This age group's support needs seemed to be different. The aim of this file is that when a worker has dealings with someone in this age group, they jot down what was effective, whether it be 'meeting for shorter times' or 'driving the whole time', and drop this in the file. This was a time-effective way of collecting information that was later collated. Then it was used at the service level and fed into an inter-agency process for improving access of under 15's. This helped to support services and improve their capacities to respond effectively.

2.45pm–3.00pm

Return from client visit and receive a message (amonst others) from the school counsellor at a local high school. Return her call to accept a referral for a 15 year old male requiring assistance with a mix of issues including extreme conflict with parents and the need to look at income support needs. Time make to meet with him and the school counsellor tomorrow.

Action Research Component

The school counsellors and Connect workers have jointly agreed to use Action Reseach to look at the best ways the service and school can work together to have the optimum result for the young person. This is at an early stage and tomorrow's meeting will be a good opportunity for observation and reflection on how collaborative early intervention. case work can happen. At a practical level, we are asking *'what would it take for the young person and their family to have more options for referral, advocacy and support?'.*

Example—young co-researchers help service planning

A co-research group of young people was set up to explore the question 'what would it take for young peoople to feel safe about accessing [the service] for support?' As part of a planning process. the young people coordinated their classmates' answers to questionnaires and interviews, and completed the observation and reflection phases.

The understandings about the issues of access and confidentiality and the service's profile provided rich and in-depth data that was used as the basis for further planning. The co-research group also produced a video for local schools that covered some of the issues raised in their inquiry processes (A Youth Homelessness Pilot sevice).

3.00pm–4.30pm

Pick up another client from school and take her to Centrelink in relation to a breach that has been imposed. Exceptional circumtances have come to light in our work with her. During this interview, it strikes me that Connect staff have been regularly providing additional information to Centrelink at the time of a breach and that a collaborative look at communication processes between the agencies might improve the information base for decision making. I make a note to follow this up with Centrelink.

Action Research Component

Anecdotal evidence indicated it was worth looking at this area. This insight led to communication with Centrelink and it was later decided we would look collaboratively at how the service and Centrelink could improve communication, particularly at the time of breaches. A page in the back of the service daybook (a book used between workers to communicate information during the day) was created to record client experiences and worker communications with Centrelink. This information was then able to go to the regular collaborative meeting we have with Centrelink staff as a basis for improving practice between the agencies and identifying any emerging issues. From the meetings, collective decisions could be made.

4.30pm–5.00pm

Message in the daybook from other Connect worker saying that Joanne says that she will meet with her Mum tomorrow night. Contacted Rita and told her that a meeting time has been made for tomorrow night after work at the office with her daughter. I help her prepare for the meeting and clarify with her the main issues she wishes to raise and discuss with her the potential impact on her daughter of speaking about these issues. The conversation ended with Rita being asked how she found phone contact as a way of getting support and indication that face-to-face was always an option. Rita says she was happy with phone support as the main way of communication, as it was very convenient for her.

Action Research Component

Another Action Research question constantly being explored by Connect is *'What is the most effective way to support families?'* One strategy for exploring this is for phone support to be actively offered to parents, as well as face-to-face meetings. There was some anecdotal evidence that parents often find phone contact a more viable and practical means of support. The worker records Rita's feedback on the Action Research observation sheet which has been set up to look at phone support, (a once a month focus). So far this is showing that phone support is a viable form of client work and not 'just a phone call'.

appropriate and accessible service delivery, ongoing review and evaluation and building sustainability:

> Action research is a key component of the Reconnect program. For Reconnect's early intervention methods to be effective, all services need to respond to their clients' needs using a reflective and improvement-oriented approach to service delivery. (Source: http://www.fahcsia.gov.au/sa/housing/progserv/hom elessness/reconnect/Pages/default.aspx)

References

Phil Crane, Evaluation Committee, Prime Ministerial Youth Homeless Taskforce, *Putting Families in the Picture: Supplementary Report*, Department of Family and Community Services, Canberra, 1998.

Phil Crane and Leanne Richardson, *Reconnect Action Research Kit*, Commonwealth Department of Family and Community Services, Youth and Students Branch, Canberra, 2000.

For an insider's detailed history and account of the characteristics of action research and Reconnect as an action research program, see: Phil Crane, 'Action Research in Social Programs', *Proceedings of the Action Learning, Action Research and Process Management Conversation*, Brisbane, 2006, pp. 1–16, available: http://eprints.qut.edu.au/archive/00005034/01/5034_1.pdf.

For a brief example from Reconnect in another setting, the Centre for Multicultural Youth Issues identifies three 'nested' action research cycles (arranged in a 'program logic hierarchy' from increasing frontline connectedness of young people, to improving knowledge in schools about refugee young people, to improving Reconnect services per se), available: http://www.cymi.net.au/policies/research.html.

For a definition and diagram, see Yoland Wadsworth and Chris Price, 'What is Action Research in Reconnect?', *Action Learning and Action Research Journal*, 7 (2): 64–69, available: http://www.alara.net.au/files/ALARV7No2.pdf.

THREE

Building in staff's 'caring to ask' for patients' and consumers' feedback in a general hospital[22]

A follow-up study to the Understanding and Involvement (U&I) project—entitled 'Understanding Staff' (US)—comprised a sequence of reflective practice action learning-style sessions among a senior staff group in a medium-sized, suburban general hospital auspiced by a religious order (Wadsworth and O'Brien 2002).[23] These sessions were intended to give 'time out' to identify the conditions for inviting consumer feedback and participation, including addressing the defences that kept staff and patients separated in the familiar 'forcefield of distancing' that was unwittingly block the desired capacity for deeper relationships of co-inquiry. To this end the flier featured the cartoon generated after the end of the U&I project (see Chapter 4 'We must hear from consumers…') which expressed the paradox of *wanting* to hear and *not* wanting to hear. The subsequent research sessions proved to be rich, honest and illuminative.

Not just one or two, but a wide range of methods for seeking input and discussing it

At the end of the previous chapter I explored the theoretical findings of the project about the conditions for 'care', but in this chapter I will focus on the conditions for building in the range of methods that emerged out of the research as viable and 'do-able'. As with the U&I project, there was at that time a growth of interest in consumer participation at the same time as the move occurred from *quality assurance* (QA) to *quality improvement* (QI), *total quality management* (TQM) and *learning organisations* (LOs). At a critical moment when we were very close to culture shift at the hospital level, this external impetus reached its zenith in a series of initiatives taken by the state Department of Human Services and the Commonwealth Department of Health and Aged Care for consumer participation in hospitals, primary care and community health.

The value of top-down requirement for consumer participation

Various government policy papers, plans, booklets, tools, kits, information resources, templates, and improvement strategies began to filter down and quality initiatives proliferated on the ground. One of the most comprehensive of all the many kits, manuals and resources produced over about ten years of this era from the late 1990s was the Consumer Focus Collaboration's *Improving Health Services through Consumer Participation: A Resource Guide* (2000).[24]

Yet all these efforts lived or died by the quality and strength of local interest, purposefulness and practical steps-identification, and these in turn depended on the strength of the complex human relationships between frontline staff, managers and their local end-beneficiary critical reference groups.

The necessity of strong bottom-up consumer interest, combined with a critical mass of interested staff

While top-down directives from central policy and funding agencies could help more fully encourage or mandate participation activities—and these requirements were critical to the pressure that problematised existing exclusion of consumers—none of them yielded real outcomes unless practice between professional service providers and service users at the service level was deeply altered. What was needed to deeply embed this were change processes at the micro level that did not ebb and flow with the pragmatic and utilitarian decision making of more distanced bureaucratic workers,[25] nor with the changing interests of their academic advisers or the good intentions of doctors, but instead continued as a locally embraced learning effort over many years, even decades. As well (and confirming the key ingredient in the success of the U&I project), the key missing ingredient in the US project was an active critical mass of consumers waiting to (or urging that they) be invited to 'come to the table' with staff. The initiative had instead come from an academic setting, and although received with polite interest and resulting in some significant engagement, including by the most senior influential staff, the forcefield simply proved too strong when both 'poles' were not 'at the table' and 'alongside' each other.

Sustained facilitation by an insider–outsider team who shared strong common purposes, and who could pursue the cycle of inquiry from action-observation to new theory.

Thus, although the Understanding Staff process was able to achieve only limited success with staff for a year or two, it did demonstrate how sustained facilitation at the outset can effectively commence the process of 'surfacing underdiscussibles' and understanding defensive routines, thus opening the door ready for the next stage. In this instance, in terms of new theory, we concluded that a deeper culture shift stemmed not from always second guessing answers, but instead from beginning with closely observing and asking questions. This was a move from what we called 'presumptive care' to 'responsive care'. While presumptive care relies primarily on applying previously acquired knowledge and set procedures based on the evidence and findings of earlier cycles of inquiry or research, responsive care can tic-tack back and forth between openness to new observations and reflections with patients and ideas or beliefs stemming from earlier inquiring, research, procedures and accrued practice wisdom—but potentially in innovative ways, since it is now responding to the particularity of *this* unique patient and their contextual circumstances.

In turn, the shift in the process of inquiry in the micro instance of an individual patient from presumptive to responsive was scaled up or 'writ large' in a shift from an organisational and institutional culture where to be a 'true professional' is to *already know*, to one where to be a 'true professional' is instead to know *how to find out*—particularly from the contextualised individual patient in question. This in turn rested on:

- 'Problematising' patients' silence and them not being asked for their input and feedback—by remembering the benefits of doing so and the risks of not
- Taking time out to re-connect with deeper care values and re-triggering memories of successfully having sought out and acted on patients' input in the past
- Having access to a repertoire of methods for regularly seeking input and receiving feedback
- Being supported by ongoing policy, funding and management encouragement of all of this
- Having high-quality training (or dialogue) about the practicalities of how these processes can work best from both patients' and staff members' perspectives (Wadsworth and O'Brien 2002: 31).

A critical mass of insiders able to take the ideas for action into actual practice

The repertoire of methods put forward by the senior staff group included some they had already begun to use, as well as many that overlapped with the full range listed during the U&I study. An important step in customising these for the general hospital environment involved arranging them to match each point along a patient's trajectory into, during, at and after discharge from the hospital (see Table 8), and in generating a sequence of questions with staff to which they wanted the answers (see Table 9).

Postscript 2008: For a short-term input of only months it is perhaps not surprising that eight years later there seemed little surviving culture change directly attributable to the work. There had been a near total change of personnel, with all participants having moved on or retired, with only one exception. Some had taken their learning to other places, with one confirming that 'it certainly changed my attitude to [one of recognising] the value of feedback and to finding ways of gaining such from consumers...it removed the fear of what might be said to more [one] of "us being in this together". Another consequence has been my preparedness to speak up and ask questions or make comments when I or a companion is a consumer'. Another reported 'I don't just plump up their pillows now—I ask if I can!'

TABLE 8. METHODS FROM THE PATIENT'S STANDPOINT ARRANGED ALONG A CONTINUUM-OF-CARE TRAJECTORY

Pre-admission: Interviews

At admission: Information booklet set out from the patient's perspective of arriving, finding their way around, being there for a procedure or admission, through to leaving; and including their rights to question, request etc.

Pre-, during and post-procedure: Sensitive observation and communication

During recovery: Face-to-face questions; access to advocacy, informal feedback; feedback cards at the bedside (See Figure 5: 'We want to know about your experience'); a 'lost persons' audit' to see how people found their way around the hospital; and suggestion boxes

At or just prior to discharge: End-of-stay questionnaires or discharge planning interviews and ad hoc Q&A surveys

Post-discharge: 'Day-after' routine follow-up courtesy phone calls; post-natal 'reunion days'; access to formal complaints systems; annual random sample satisfaction surveying; representation on committees (e.g. planning, review, management; consumer/patient forums or panels or advisory bodies); patient presentations at staff case conferences; self-advocacy or employment as consumer consultants; and an annual 'day in the life of the hospital' telephone survey of everyone who came to the hospital on a single day, with set questions addressing the continuum of care.

TABLE 9. DURING HOSPITALISATION BEDSIDE CARDS: 'WE WANT TO KNOW ABOUT YOUR EXPERIENCE'

What was your experience of the hospital on this occasion?

'On the whole it was..'

Can you give it a score out of 10? (Circle number)

0 1 2 3 4 5 6 7 8 9 10

Poor　　Not　　Good　　Very　　Excellent
　　very good　　　good

Is there anything you want to tell us?

....

Were there any particular things you wish hadn't happened? *Please describe*

....

Were there any things you particularly appreciated or admired? *Please describe*

....

Is there anything that would have made your stay better? *Please describe*

....

Please give us any other feedback you can

....

FOUR

'I don't see why not': effective leadership to build in client input to practice research in a child and family welfare organisation[26]

External ideas resonate with internal experience of a human services agency

After hearing a presentation at the 1997 Children Welfare Association conference about the U&I and US experiences, and in particular about the paradox of staff wanting consumer input but finding it immensely difficult, the then CEO of Glastonbury child and family welfare organisation, Vic Coull, asked me to meet with him and one of his senior social workers, Jenny Duffield.

There are two initial factors to be noted here—the existence of new ideas (in this case via an external consultant bringing insights from a previous, long period of engagement with another area of human services), and the existence of a leader whose own inquiry processes drove him to search out ideas that might help him better serve his social justice ends through genuine engagement with clients, co-inquiring with a colleague who also had a thirst for knowledge, and championing a path of such inquiry in his agency.

A three-year effort to build in a user-responsive practice research and evaluation culture

I will try and truncate this story into its key milestones to illuminate the sequence of events and activities that built a successful 'structure' that was dense enough to sustain significant inquiry practice with clients for a number of years.

Important precursor work, including a workshop on theory of action research

In the previous year Glastonbury had commenced a process of introducing 'practice research' with a one-off workshop by Dr Dorothy Scott, then a senior lecturer in social work at the University of Melbourne. She had stressed the importance of concepts like 'practice wisdom', and 'lived experience of clients'; the value of hunches and puzzles around practitioners' concerns and questions; the complexity and unique-

ness of practice contexts; the need for feedback loops between research and practice; and the need for such feedback to be feasible within the constraints of practice. The approach to the process was modelled on academic research: starting with a research question and the published literature, then defining participants and designs, drawing on documented data regarding client needs or characteristics, selecting observation tools and instruments, performing analysis and writing up. Staff were interested but had not proceeded very far with this after a year.

Crossing the Phase 1 threshold: the CEO authorises clients' involvement as research workshop consultants who are selected as 'critical friends'

To help staff start to operationalise the practice research concepts, I proposed 'practising what we were preaching' and asked Vic Coull and Jenny Duffield whether, if we had another workshop, clients might be asked to participate to assist in kick-starting the inquiry processes. There was a silent pause, and then Vic said quietly, 'I don't see why not'; and then confirmed he 'wanted as a matter of course, for practice research to be part of what we do'.

This was a significant liminal moment where a small, well-discerned decision meant crossing the threshold from 'how things had been' to beginning the process of 'how they could be instead'—a moment that could all too easily have defaulted to a more comfortable but more shallow inquiry effort, such as starting with only involving staff and remaining preliminary to ever meeting with clients. To give this new step of both risk and opportunity some practical shape, I drew on the U&I learnings and asked whether there might be at *least two clients* (principle of strengthening less empowered voices) who were *critical friends* of the organisation (principle of needing critical observations of discrepancy from an end-beneficiary standpoint, but within a sense of a 'we' with staff). I articulated this as 'people who love this agency but are very able to speak up and tell it where it's gone wrong!' (This is the matter of needing *critical intention* to improve something identified as discrepant but still being part of the living system.) There was another significant pause while Jenny mentally scanned her own experience and then confidently identified two such clients. Both subsequently came forward and took part.

A workshop to commence action research in practice

A briefing session was held early the next month to introduce the proposed inquiry process and plan the workshop with staff and the client consultants. This went well and later in the month the workshop was held.

The workshop had a tentative start as the new 'systems logic' of consumer presence kicked in and some other difficulties within the staff group were surfaced and dealt with (an important bifurcation between care staff and staff assisting clients' leave care). But by the end of the day twenty-two staff had developed ideas for going forward, with some palpable enthusiasm, and both staff and client consultants reported having had an excellent time together. In the course of the day a questionnaire was put together in the workshop to tap people's levels of interest, as well as their perceptions of their agency's interest. An initial whiteboard scan of reflective practice research already taking place was also collected, and a set of good questions staff wanted to ask clients was generated using the agency philosophy of building people's strengths.

Ideas shared in the workshop to ensure that efforts did not fizzle out included:
- The agency requirement that people report back on their practice research projects
- Rostering of project discussions for staff meetings
- Making initial efforts small and achievable, with projects to start immediately
- Establishing a consultative group of the (client) parents
- Establishing a small sub-committee to oversee sustaining the work
- Giving the projects titles to shape their identity
- Working out timelines for project completion and reporting progress.

Regular contact from external research consultant to assist building in practice research to the organisational systems

I was contracted for some continuing involvement and established a pattern of regularly telephoning the CEO, nominally for a progress report, but in practice more to act as a reflective sounding board and 'thinking partner', offering time to reflect on barriers to progress (such as major changes in the forms of government funding, having constantly to keep applying for program funds, much time-consuming

paperwork to meet various funder requirements, plus the usual budget cycle, annual general meeting, audit, and annual and financial reporting).

Despite the difficulties, in the following three months Vic Coull reported that:
- Each work program in the agency had been asked for at least one practice research proposal
- The client consultants had been involved in a media interview regarding a newly funded program that was using action research (the Commonwealth Department of Family and Community Services' Strengthening Families project)
- A position was being created for a Human Resources and Research Officer to provide the capacity to follow things through rather than the action research suffer from being a one-off, ad hoc project. This initiative in particular began taking the new ideas into agency cultural practice by providing a stabilising 'form' or container establishing patterns of expectations. See Table 10 for an extract from the 1998 job description.

Inquiry group forms and meets

A month later an inquiry group of four interested staff began to meet (including Jenny Duffield), and assembled a set of questions asking clients how staff members might best work with families (e.g. the process of engagement, turning points, needs, clients' preferences for one or two workers). They proposed to meet four times, to pay client consultants, provide child care, and have guidelines and consent/ethics forms.

Practice Research in all managers' job descriptions

A year later Jenny Duffield had been appointed the Human Resources and Research Officer and a decision had been made to include practice research as an area of responsibility in all managers' positions. All areas had put up practice research proposals but none had proceeded due to preoccupations with the new Strengthening Families program. The work of the inquiry group however had unfolded as a plan for collaborative dialogue with clients, and this took until early the following year to carry out in practice.

The CEO was also keen on a study to develop a non-positivist method for evaluation (to avoid the problem of premature evaluation that the Head Start program had suffered in the United States). He wanted

---

TABLE 10. EXTRACT: POSITION DESCRIPTION: HUMAN RESOURCE AND RESEARCH OFFICER

5. **Practice Research**

5.1 To act as a resource person to program teams to facilitate the implementation of practice research projects including assisting with program evaluation.

5.2 To facilitate the establishment and management of a practice research culture within the agency.

5.3 To assist, as required, in establishing practice research projects at a programmatic level.

5.4 To identify client trends, practice hypotheses and client comments, views and feedback about what works/doesn't work and propose practice research projects in collaboration with relevant staff, clients and other agencies.

6. **Client Consultants**

6.1 To assist, as appropriate, with the establishment and maintenance of client consultants for the agency's operation.

6.2 To develop a role proposal for client consultant within the agency in collaboration with agency staff and clients.

6.3 To assist and support client consultants, as appropriate, to perform their agreed role.

6.4 To identify and report on the contribution of client consultant to an open, responsive agency respect[ful] of client aspirations, issues and feedback.

---

this to go beyond a client satisfaction survey and involve a self-scorable set of questions that would touch on how parents and their children/families might see themselves as having more deeply changed (or not).

External consultancy network of other practice researchers

A further consolidating proposal was for the lone Human Resources and Research Officer to have links to an external support network of various disciplines.

Shifts in theory-of-practice resulting from professional reflective inquiry

Vic reported that social workers in a related development had begun noticing that one-to-one client support had established a baseline for very disadvantaged clients surviving, but they were no longer seeing gains. Subsequently they trialled a self-help group run by a group of the women clients (with staff backup support if the women determined they needed it). This had good results as the women self-organised a stronger mutual social support network. Vic also described the philosophy of the agency as beginning to shift from 'bringing clients to a service' to assisting 'clients be part of community and neighbourhood' (although he noted that service funding agreements were moving in the opposite direction).

Theorisation from practice influenced by ideas from elsewhere

When we spoke next Vic was searching for a way of conceptualising a more deeply collaborative and egalitarian relationship in which professional carers and service users could each be construed as 'citizens' to avoid the dangers of 'professionals as experts' and the impact which that typically had on diminishing client self-respect and capacity for self-determination.

Not without continuing paradox

Yet the impetus for professional social workers to protect women clients from demands (e.g. for feedback regarding observed change) and their trained preparedness to observe and assess (independent of the women's own judgement or input), seemed to operate as a 'default program', and slowly some of the determination to keep clients in the 'driving seat' slipped away.

In our last official meeting for our third year of journeying together, Vic and Jenny recounted their original anxiety about hearing input from clients and also observed the forcefield that remained which held in place a boundary between participation and professionals 'having' to make (forensic) judgements defensible in a court of law.

Nevertheless the agency had moved to open client files which staff and clients co-wrote. And Vic and Jenny's own self-sceptical approach continued.

A client consultants' panel in successful dialogue with staff

Dialogue with what was called the Client Consultants' Panel had also broken new ground for the agency. Four exchanges had taken place—one a week for four weeks, involving five staff and five client consultants (who were paid a modest honorarium on the basis that this was for staff development). The questions asked by staff of the clients were Appreciative Inquiry-style questions, as workers were searching for more precise positive directions from clients that they could follow in future. The questions were:

Engaging: 'What did the worker do that helped you engage [with the worker] at the start?'
Turning points: 'What did your worker do that made a difference to your life?'
Safety: 'What did your worker do that made you and members of your family feel safe?'
Closure: 'What did your worker do that helped you [towards being able to] finish up with Glastonbury?'

The process for the dialogue was seen as like that used elsewhere in the agency's social work practice ('safe family procedure'), and this established a familiar precedent within social work discourse. It involved the following:

Step 1 Staff and client consultants meet together over refreshments to discuss the process and pose the questions.

Step 2 Clients leave to discuss among themselves how they want to answer the questions (for forty minutes), taping the discussion (but turning off the tape-recorder when they wish).

Step 3 Client consultants rejoin staff to report on how they have answered the questions.

Step 4 Staff and clients then discuss together what has been said (for another thirty minutes).

As the client-only discussion was more spontaneous, their taped discussions contained more detail, and the client consultants gave the tape to staff to listen to and reflect on at their leisure. This had the effect of giving staff some more significant, unpressured reflection space.

In effect the protocol supplied the conditions for clients being able to speak freely *and* for staff to be able to hear. It was the kind of safe, quiet space the 'US' project staff reported they needed to be able to hear patients' upset complaints, and it represented the same kind of dialogue-across-a-safe-distance which

the 'Understanding, Anytime' project had constructed in its first year.

The CEO continues to draw on the outside research consultant as a 'thinking partner'

Less than a year later, Vic sent me a draft article he had written about the self-help group. It articulated in insightful ways his theorisation of the group's operation. His account described the women's lives and the agency's 'equal basis capability' (what Robyn Pound has called 'alongsideness' and I have described as 'shoulder to shoulder') that saw them as clients-as-citizens, exercising greater self-determination through an 'expanded polity' that could be empowering. Soon after, we had our final phone conversation about these ideas and I moved to a new university on the other side of the bay.

Postscript: Looking back from the vantage point of a 2004 Annual Report on the occasion of the CEO's retirement, the President of the Glastonbury Board (Kim Henderson) noted that Vic Coull had been a source of 'continuous and inspired leadership …largely responsible for Glastonbury's impressive achievements and the Agency's culture during the past decade'. Kim noted Vic's 'uncompromising commitment…insight, inspirational leadership, thoroughness, dedication and sheer hard work' and the resulting 'benefit of extremely high morale amongst staff… [reflected in] unusually high levels of staff stability'— indicators in themselves, perhaps, for an agency with a 'living systems culture'. The local member addressed the state parliament on the occasion, noting Vic's having been a 'true champion' of 'those in need', yet also able to attend to logistics in following through from values into actions (Tresize 2004: 610). Yet the same quiet tone in which Vic had said of client consultancy 'I don't see why not', was also characteristic of his genuine humility and ability to step away from a strong sense of hierarchy and yield to being open to 'not knowing'—critical to traversing both key *phase changes*. In interesting witness to this, one of the client consultants had been astounded to learn that the man at the roundtable (when we together planned the action research education) was actually 'the boss', as he'd approached the exercise quietly as an equal, alongside her, there to learn.

After ten years, however, Jenny Duffield had moved to another child and family welfare agency at which she was not carrying out internal evaluation and, tragically, Vic Coull had died of cancer early in 2008. The reflective practice work at Glastonbury had largely attenuated, and the Human Resources and Research position had morphed into being more about policy and organisational development interpreted as standards, compliance, Human Resources (personnel matters), risk management, health and safety and the like. As a general reflection on the sector, internal evaluation was still not seen to be as viable as external evaluation (particularly when undertaken by tertiary institutions), still frequently regarded as 'unbiased', and carrying greater weight with potential funding bodies.

However, the introduction of accreditation standards regarding consumer feedback and consumer participation across the sector was being seen by experienced welfare practitioners as leading to an increase in client participation in organisations and a new openness to building in a more rigorous culture of action research to facilitate this.

In a way the system had gone full cycle, with contemporary policy (the result of pioneering efforts like Vic Coull's at Glastonbury) now crystalising in the form of a new style of leadership which, despite an ongoing, systemic reluctance on the part of decision makers to engage in up-close-and-personal dialogue with professional staff and clients about clients' own experienced lifeworlds, is now seen as necessary to know *how* to plan to meet agencies' deepest valued purposes of effectively resourcing the lifeworlds of clients and consumers, and not get it wrong.

FIVE

Rocket science for a community: a neighbourhood house builds in social action research[27]

Community centres, or neighborhood houses, began to embrace efforts to build in research or evaluation processes in the late 1990s when the state government department for Adult, Community and Further Education (ACFE) ran a series of research methods seminars and a conference at the Australian Institute for Management. It supported this by also publishing a range of written resource material (e.g. Bradshaw and McRae 1996; McRae and Hazel 1997). These efforts gave legs to a policy of helping community houses incorporate regular, local data gathering about their communities and use of it to design their programs and activities in close response to changing community needs, in co-operation with local people. Topics for action research projects in houses across the state included addressing the special needs of women with young children, Indigenous people in the country, people with disabilities, retrenched men, older people, and culturally and linguistically diverse immigrant communities. Beyond discrete projects, however, the ACFE interest was in building in skills to carry out small-scale inquiry of this kind as a regular feature of how neighborhood houses would continuously go on responding to their communities.

Often research doesn't start where you think it will start

At the conference, the Coonara Community House reported on four years of working towards building its own culture of research (Wadsworth and Fitzgerald 1996, Wadsworth 1996), commencing with a question about how to respond to the recession that was, in the words of Jan Bourne, the then Co-ordinator: 'knocking our people around like skittles'.[28] Interestingly this social action research took a circuitous emergent route to address this, via a community study and a study of the house and its activities, while all the time learning research skills and conceptual knowledge. Later it emerged, as trust developed from members getting to know each other better, that many in the group were privately playing roles in their own recession dramas (including retrenchment, marriage stress, collapse of family incomes, having to shift house, and the endless saying of 'no' both to themselves and their children due to limited cash). Yet the research was not able to start here, nor even know this at the outset. Instead the group members were comfortable to begin by 'doing some research regarding others in the community'. Only later did the 'data collection' effortlessly move from 'research on' to 'research with', opening up the recession conversations *among* group members, eventually reaching some quite profound understandings.

Starting with the people's questions and pursuing their interests

Community houses live, survive and thrive around the learning interests, energies and passions of their users (teachers and learners), and the research effort to decipher these interests had to follow these same 'energy lodes' as a method too. So we 'started where people were at', and the group nominated that they:
- Wanted to know what activities people wanted the Community House to run
- Wondered whether there were people who might like to come to Coonara but who currently did not feel attracted
- Were curious about why some courses did well and others were short on numbers
- Wanted to know how to pick the right topics
- Wondered whether there were any local actions or campaigns that should be mounted
- Were querying how to retain people's interest in Coonara over a longer period of time.

'Modelling' facilitation

My tasks emerged to be meeting facilitator or catalyst, a source of information regarding technical research skills, reader/editor of the notes and a holder of the research narrative thread between meetings. All the notes were made during the meetings on large sheets of butcher's paper so 'what you said was what you saw we'd gathered'. There was minimal executive activity away from the meeting. In this way everyone shared in the full process of the inquiry, and all fieldwork which did take place away from the meetings was agreed at meetings then carried out by group members, with the results brought back to the group. A member of the group transcribed the meeting notes and later became research co-ordinator for Stage 3.

In facilitating the meetings, two key roles could be distinguished.

The 'catalyst' role comprised elements such as:
- Keeping things moving and ensuring the ground was being covered
- 'Channelling' the energies, interests and theoretical thinking of group participants
- Reflecting back a sense of group satisfaction and achievements
- Feeding back into the group the group's own questions, observations, reflections and thinking, in order for it to address or pursue these further
- Coming up with creative methods to free up the group's thinking and better express its intentions and ethos.

The 'compass holding' role involved:
- Reflecting between the group's meetings on the direction and logic of the group's deliberations in relation to its deeper aims
- Being a 'corporate' memory keeper
- 'Divining' the directions to keep moving in (revealed by people's energies and enthusiasm levels: leaning forward in chairs, keenness to talk, faces brightening, or a thoughtful hush, or disinterest, furrowed brows, head shaking, glazed eyes and confusion etc.)[29]
- Circulating material, articles and snippets to both express and contribute to the group's thinking
- Creative envisioning to contribute to the group's thinking, including 'channelling' people's deeper theorising and often unconscious making of connections that then proved valuable—even when it seemed people had 'got off the topic'.[30]

Emergent research design and built into people's busy lives to be do-able

It was a matter of building a research culture by 'doing it' rather than by commencing with any grand plan. In fact the three phases over five years emerged collectively as an enjoyable well-rounded activity that commenced with a shared lunch for the ten to fifteen people who met for half a day every month, constructing as they went the distinct cycles of inquiry, and eventually 'ending' (for the time being) with the publication of a book about people's experiences of confronting or overcoming the impact of the recession (Coonara Action Research Taskforce 1996).

Acquiring practical skills, concepts and a grasp of the 'living process'

In response to the initial questions, the group decided simultaneously to explore community needs and study what they were doing in the community house. The 'House Study' involved asking around seventy house users for their views about Coonara's activities; examining and analysing the lists of attenders; and the compiling of an inventory of what Coonara had to offer. One meeting we all went outside for an anthropological, observational 'ground round' to document what changes we could visualise. Field work indeed!

We circulated monthly bulletins containing meeting notes so all participants could keep track, and we also circulated the results of the first interviews and an article from *The Age* newspaper: 'Divorce on the Dole' which had resonated with members. People brought in more articles and other resources to supplement the 'data' throughout our years of meeting.

A list of all members was circulated to strengthen a sense of who was in the group and to avoid the new-member-feels-on-the-outside syndrome. At every meeting we also had cardboard name plates which we put in front of ourselves on the large table around which we met (as we realised that, although people had been introduced, at their next meeting they sometimes forgot each other's names, and were then reluctant to discomfort each other by revealing this.) We always met in a warm, friendly meeting room (with pinewood walls and handmade quilt on display), adjacent to the sounds from the kindergarten, and with views of the paddocks, playground, nearby school and house tops, and a glimpse of the hills. There were also milestone photos taken of the group. The group gelled as 'a group for itself' and this fabric of relationships was 'the field' in which effective inquiry became possible.

As a first contribution to the 'Community Study', Jan had spontaneously assembled a collage of photos and local media coverage. The 'Community Study' emerged as involving each member of the group going out and interviewing an opportunity sample of ten people (five friends, two neighbours, two total strangers and themselves) to ask:

• Why did they come to the area?
• What did they like and dislike about it?
• What were the effects of the recession for them?
• What would make living in their area more enjoyable?

As the taskforce found its own members came from most of the ten or so localities in the area served by the house, members asked people in their own local township areas as a way of making the task more do-able, both drawing on and further enhancing their own local 'ethnographic' knowledge. As well, people made an observational demographic study of each of the local areas that made up the Shire of Sherbrooke, as well as collecting formal Bureau of Statistics information from the municipal council.

Members of the group found all this both do-able and interesting. The scale of the inquiry effort matched the size and scale of the purposes, people's interests, and time, money and resources available. And, rather than being a 'too-small' or 'biased sample', what people experienced was the transforming and extending of 'ordinary talk' into more purposive small 'r' research. When the sixty sets of local views were compiled people had access to something far more substantial and comprehensive than would otherwise have ever been possible. The opportunity sample also roughly matched the area's key characteristics.

In the third phase, the 'Recession Study', the idea of collecting snippets or descriptions of hardship morphed into the collection of distinct narratives as respondents unexpectedly volunteered to write their own stories. Topic areas for the narratives were brainstormed by the group who had by then come to realise that they were part of the recession-experiencing community they were researching (in what was fast turning into a fully fledged community autoethnography). Procedures for collecting stories were refined and timelines settled. All the incoming stories were copied for all members so all were able to monitor the in-flow of material for quality, relevance and gaps. The voices of youth were found to be missing so two young people were promptly invited into the group.

The group also became engrossed in the business of learning about taping, transcribing and editing. When I facilitated the group's telling of its own stories, I had the tape commercially transcribed, and then edited it as a training illustration of the process for discussion at the next meeting. The process was in fact too elaborate for the scale of the work but conveyed messages about interpretation and respecting the speaker's own meanings that were very relevant. Another emergent aspect was the spontaneous offering of a photographic essay by a local woman who had attended one of the early meetings.

Strategic change-oriented theory emerges from purposeful inquiring

The studies not only described how people 'saw things now' but also enabled sharing of feelings and thoughts about them all the way through to making practical changes to the house, and eventually also saw the publishing of a book of insightful and inspiring stories about what people had done in response to the recession. There were conceptual insights; for example, the locality profiles confirmed the shared 'hills' environmental values as well as the idiosyncrasies that made each hamlet (or pockets within hamlets) distinctive. The environmental interest not only provided an important part of Coonara's 'corporate identity' and brought together many of those attracted to the house, but also contributed a valuable theoretical insight that distinguished 'Hills people's' handling of the 1980s–1990s recession differently from that of the 1930s depression generation. By positively valuing frugality (although more by 'sprouting potatoes' than by 'saving string'), this was not then a stigmatising practice to be discarded as soon as possible. Indeed, one of the early draft titles for the book expressed this: '*Not back to basics...forward to fundamentals*'.

Another theoretical crystallisation of understanding came from the very first story brought in when we were awaiting (with some trepidation) people returning from 'the field' on the first day. This literally first offering through the door turned out to be a poem with the title: *What if...?* This expressed exactly the ambivalence the group had detected as another key differentiating characteristic of this recession compared to the Great Depression—that of 'not knowing' what might happen, together with the possibility of *both* feared negative and unexpectedly positive, life-changing outcomes. The book by the Coonara Action Research Taskforce (1996) *What if...* was launched in great neighbourhood house style, with representatives of all major political parties in attendance, and the speech of the late, former senator Don Chipp who launched it, identified the results as constituting a legitimate 'impact statement for federal government economic policy'.

Ensuring there are a critical mass of 'culture-carriers'

The note-taker/transcriber of Phases 1 and 2 and facilitator of Phase 3 later became the Coonara Community House Co-ordinator and an important ongoing 'culture carrier' for the value and methodology of action research in her own right. A regular stream of community development, media and journalism students (often women who were house users themselves who'd gone on to higher education) also ensured that enough people learned the value of systematic inquiry efforts, and could explain why it should be done as well as provide enough confidence to 'do it', and remained in the organisation long enough to keep passing the baton. In a test of autopoesis, a 'Four Seasons of the House' project, a fourth phase, subsequently took place, facilitated by the Coonara Co-ordinator without need of assistance.

Postscript 2008: A strong test of the sustaining of a research culture is to return much later and see what if anything is surviving. In this instance I made contact with Coonara ten years later to find an active research group of young teenage women (concerned about their generation's self-image and nutrition issues) now mastering online surveys (!) and making use of an attractive website to communicate their work.[31]

However, it turned out there had been even more extensive, long-term effects. The Coonara co-ordinator who took part in the original Coonara Action Research Taskforce (CART) process, reported there had been a 'lasting legacy' well beyond the publication of a book of 'stories' about the recession in the local community, with ongoing, built in research now being 'the way we do things at Coonara'. She reported that:

> We use action research methodology really regularly. I am attending a meeting tomorrow at Melbourne University…regarding a research project that Coonara is currently involved with…[and realised] our CART project all those years ago instilled a culture of social action research into the culture of Coonara. [Factors in this included] mentoring and facilitation by Yoland Wadsworth and a significant grant from the Stegley Foundation. Coonara was then involved with the 'Speaking Back: Building a Research Culture for ACFE' project and conferences in 1996 and 1997, and in the late 1990s and early 2000s we used our action research skills to explore community needs in a small but effective manner. The information we gained led to a significant

growth in the range of programs at Coonara including the move into accredited vocational education for women in our community.

In 2003 Coonara was approached by Knox City Council to plan and facilitate a project aimed at increasing community awareness of [I]ndigenous reconciliation issues....We arranged a series of reflective community discussions to be held over lunch or dinner at each of the community houses in Knox. The discussions were deliberately kept informal but informative. [This] was very successful and attendances at all meetings were greater than expected. This project resulted in the formation of the Knox Indigenous Reconciliation Group that was still operating in 2006.

In 2004 Coonara received the first of four 'Reframing the Future' grants that focused on networking, reflective practice and action research, as lead agency with other community education organisations in our area.

In 2006 Coonara formed a Community Learning Partnership with Eastern Regional Libraries, Telstra, Ringwood North Community House and Healesville Living and Learning Centre to explore the ways in which our organisations [might]...meet the needs of our community, and particularly those with special needs, to become technologically literate. The partnership was funded by Adult Community and Further Education as well as in-kind by the member organisations. Over the year we conducted action research into our organisation's capacity as well as the community needs...In 2007 this partnership will continue without Telstra as the community-based organisations continue to explore this exciting and challenging new means of communication and information management.

In 2006 [I] participated in an ACFE funded research circle that explored issues that arose from the Melbourne University longitudinal research into ACE outcomes. [My] research project investigated the (non) participation of mothers using Coonara child care in adult education programs at the House. At the same time a tutor and e-learning champion participated in a research circle that focused on professional practice, [and she] successfully set up an online community of practice for Coonara tutors using a wiki site.

In 2007 Coonara staff acted as mentors for a group of 12–16 year old girls who established themselves as a group known as 'Girls Together'. Their aim was to improve self-esteem and positive body image in their peers. The girls obtained a grant from the Department of Youth for a series of activities, including a small action research project.

Leanne Fitzgerald,
Co-ordinator, Coonara Community House
(Personal communication, 26 February 2008)

SIX

Building in professional reflective staff development and student evaluation input in a tertiary education university department[32]

In an educational institution, the key 'human services relationships' are often more explicitly cast in the inquiry mode using the familiar language of teaching and learning. The schooling system, particularly in its primary and secondary forms, has tended to focus more on conveying a received propositional 'body of knowledge' (comprising the prior results of others' thinking and research in other settings), so that young people acquire the knowledge of 'how things are' (or seem to be, or should be) now (and in the past) in order to act in the world. However they begin also to learn how to take initiative to inquire independently, to pursue interest and curiosity, solve puzzles, learn to locate resources, data and people, and strengthen their information organising, sharing, analysing, theorising, conclusion-drawing and application skills.[33]

In the tertiary sector, this learner-directed adult education inquiry style becomes even more critical to success with teacher-alongside-student relationships to support it. This is not without its contradictions, just as in health, welfare and community services, where the impetus for the tertiary educator is currently also framed in industrial business terms as ensuring the achievement of well-measured 'outputs' of credentialled student 'performativity'.

In this paradoxical setting in which teachers are trying to resource students' self-directed, self-organising learning but are also being required to *guarantee* it takes place, in the late 1990s the

Psychology Department at Victoria University pursued two goals set at an annual staff planning day for the forthcoming year:

- To develop a program for staff development for quality teaching
- To promote collection of and utilisation of student evaluation and feedback regarding subjects/courses so that every subject is evaluated in some way every semester.

Student Evaluation and Feedback

Workshops canvas existing experience, identify issues and scope future action

A teaching staff member facilitated the professional development workshop topic and a new research fellow[34] facilitated a workshop on the second of the two topics at the departmental planning day. The student feedback/course evaluation workshop identified a range of efforts that staff were currently making, and it noted that the Centre for Professional Development was using a then new, quite lengthy questionnaire (based on a Course Experience Questionnaire [CEQ] developed in Queensland that eventually became widespread in Australian universities).

This was a time of some official enthusiasm for hearing 'customer feedback'—even as it struck all the same ambivalence, anxiety and defensiveness about 'performance' assessment that all one-way context-free feedback surveys encounter (comprising only the first step of a more two-way conversation between staff and students about meaning and consequences). Without such chances of real dialogue there remained a risk of CEQs not contributing to more student-responsive practice and continuing second guessing by staff about what the ratings meant and what to do about them. The workshop also identified that:

- There was no departmental policy on what was basic required practice
- Staff members did not know what other staff members were doing
- A standard generalised form only got at summary basics and needed more in-depth qualitative methods (such as documented informal conversation and focus group discussion) in which relational understanding could be built between teachers and students over the entire period of a

course, generating enough trust and safety for speaking more honestly, and time and space to hear, listen and work out how to respond, then try out and monitor change
- The Head of Department had not explicitly affirmed the value of a culture of 'hearing from students'
- The Centre for Professional Development's involvement was also potentially needed to discuss adapting and modifying the CEQ.

The workshop also covered a wide range of fears and desires but saw the risk of getting stuck on developing a 'fortress of procedures' rather than expanding a 'repertoire of responses' to students as co-enquirers. A pragmatic Head of Department decision that 'every subject needs to be evaluated at least once every course' led to a decision to start with a census of everything all thirty-three staff were already doing.

Census of students' evaluation and feedback methods used by staff, and circulation of this 'intelligence' among staff

This yielded a comprehensive range of methods from which the department later selected several as the minimal standard requirements. The more active involvement of students or student representatives in an advisory capacity did not eventuate. Nor did the departmental conversation continue towards getting richer responses, better response rates, deeper analyses or more innovative improvement. In fact a crucial loss of momentum at Phase change 2 occurred at the point when the twenty-page 'Resource Pack of Methods for Achieving Students Evaluative Feedback' was about to be circulated to all staff, and a practical minded, cost-and-paper-usage-conscious head of department decided that they needed only to be printed for staff who requested them. This may have unintentionally flagged the document as optional and the exercise as no longer considered an official ongoing priority beyond the two and a half years of the project.

Departmental policy on student feedback methods formalised with written guidelines

Nevertheless the census did form the basis for written departmental guidelines (Wadsworth 1999). The framework affirmed the department had a:

- Commitment to seeking new ideas and insights to inform teaching practice

- Interest in getting student feedback and committing time to reflecting on it, and regularly improving what was done as a result
- Reputation for being student-friendly
- Reliance on multiple methods: not just one-way standardised feedback but also talking individually and in groups
- Three baseline required methods:
    (i) Informal checking and inquiry before, during and/or after subject classes
    (ii) Formal end-of-course written feedback/assessment (administered in the week before the final, more poorly attended week)
    (iii) Occasional focus groups or discussion groups or/and student research project.

All new students and new staff informed of the department's expectations

In a further attempt to build in the new expectations to the departmental culture, the guidelines included a one-page 'Advice to Enrolling Students' which affirmed department policy that their input was welcome and advised how they could provide it, plus a two-page 'Advice to new staff' outlining the department's commitment to hearing from students and what was expected of staff.

Staff development for quality teaching

The second of the staff planning day's goals involved an attempt to move from isolated teaching to a more collective practice culture for quality teaching. An appendix to the 'Resource Pack' of student evaluation methods had been prepared by the Centre for Professional Development (CPD) and it linked the issue of student evaluative feedback with the issue of quality teaching. It addressed head-on teachers' defences that student ratings were 'just popularity contests for show ponies not serious teachers like me'; that 'students were fickle'; that good ratings were 'only given if they got good grades'; and that their lack of appreciation would 'mellow years later'. It made a strong case for the by then quite well-researched and documented value of student ratings as valid indicators of learning, with high inter-rater reliability for any particular course, and the lack of influence on rating teacher performance of grades, the 'easiness' of courses or even factors like gender or race.

However while it made a strong argument for student course evaluation/satisfaction questionnaires as necessary, it noted they were not able to deliver on two counts: not so much in terms of what they measured (observed), but of *how* they were *used* (reflection and planning) but that:

- They were inadequate as a summative evaluation of overall teaching quality (especially for teachers' job or job promotion applications)
- The minor differences between different teachers' numerical ratings were statistically meaningless, and cross-field comparison did not hold up (e.g. medical students give lower ratings than art students; small classes give higher ratings than large classes)
- They were inadequate as a guide to what to do differently, i.e. course improvement—because their generic nature factors out complexity and specificity and the questionnaires rarely seek qualitative data regarding the 'why' of dissatisfaction, or 'what to do instead'
- They may flag broad areas, but context was all-important, and ironically staff may resile from questionnaires when they fail to support them in improving their teaching.

Staff research colloquium to discuss student feedback and quality teaching

A follow-up seminar of staff about the CPD paper (addressed by senior CPD staff) kept the planning day agenda alive after the departmental course evaluation methods census had identified that enough staff were interested in commencing reflective practice group meetings on two campuses.

Staff self-organised critical reflection groups initiated by senior staff member

After the seminar, these reflective practice small group discussions were initiated with a written invitation from the Deputy Head of Department to every staff member to take part. He appended a twenty-seven-page chapter extracted from *Becoming a Critically Reflective Teacher* (Brookfield 1995). This addressed the need to critically reflect on one's own driving, unexamined assumptions if teachers were to be 'challenged and changed' (e.g. regarding the dynamics of power, teachers' presumptions of superiority, tendencies to downplay their knowledge, or opting for 'easy' rather than 'better'). I had an involvement in the start up of the campus-based groups, long enough to ensure each group had a convenor and had begun meeting.

Three different groups began meeting with some enthusiasm and continued for around three to five meetings each, over the course of around six months. They took the form of non-compulsory self-selected Wenger-style (1998) 'communities of practice' to maximise the chances of open and candid sharing of reflections and experiences. Groups evolved their own discussion formats, facilitation and organisation, and were free to morph, merge or wind up. Six of the thirty-three staff were key activators and encouragers of the various groups, in which just under two-thirds of the staff participated at least once.

Attempt to sustain culture by establishing a teaching and learning sub-committee

In the third year a standing committee was established to carry the work forward (e.g. the proposal to conduct a thorough evaluation of the perception of students on the Foundation Subject Review). Meanwhile the research fellow's contract was coming to an end.

In the fourth year the idea of a 'research culture' was taken up by a new professor to the department who proposed continuing with staff research groups. However the focus moved away from reflective practice towards how to intensify 'productivity' by increasing publication output and the number of research grants received in line with the university's new industrial business model.

Further resourcing of student feedback and staff reflective practice ended when a proposal for an ongoing, collaborative, teaching practice action research project involving staff and students was not awarded a CPD Teaching and Learning grant, ironically, on the grounds that that it was 'too much like a research proposal'.

Some time later staff held a seminar about why students were not attending classes. No one suggested asking or involving them.

With hindsight: the need for structuring reflective practice discussions

One key learning from this and other professional reflective practice and dialogue sessions is the need for a simple discussion structuring device that is easy enough to be remembered by participants (to be carried from meeting to meeting) but strategically powerful enough to focus the reflection, such as a simple form of the strategic questions outlined in Chapter 3:

- Observe—what is an issue (or issues) facing us at the moment?
- Reflect—what sense do we make of it (or them) so far? What would we prefer to see, do, or achieve instead?
- Plan—what would it take to get from here to there?
- Act—what is the first do-able step I or we could take? When, where, why and with whom?

Application in a schools area in contrast to a university

In contrast to the university experience, many resources and much published experience in reflective practice developed at this time in the schools education action research area.

An illuminating example (Burton 1995) from the former National Literacy and ESL Research Network of the National Languages and Literacy Institute of Australia (NLLIA) is a story of a school teacher, close to resigning from the pressures of demanding work, for whom even a Wednesday afternoon—theoretically devoted to course planning, writing teaching material and attending professional development sessions— was occupied with staff team meetings about mounting running costs and other non-teaching matters.

The availability of a reflective practice consultant

In this school example a reflective practice counsellor asked the teacher to write a 'Day in the Life' story observing her typical teaching day so they could reflect on it together.

The story is filled with unanswered questions as the teacher races from one class to preparing for another:

- Why did this activity hold their attention when another like it the previous week didn't?
- Is this video too hard for them? Or would it be better if there are two stages of instructions and then additional group work?
- Would it help raise learning interest in the Italian class if an Italian student spoke about her recent trip home? Or would it be distracting?

- Was the class—which was alive with discussion about an apparent side issue (phone calls from charity seeking donations)—in fact helpful to students in terms of the underlying course objective? Teacher training was against 'going off track'. But ten years of teaching experience had shown her that it can build richer relationships within the classroom, and can generate unexpected new thinking.

The use of a practice journal to aid reflective inquiry

The reflective practice counsellor then suggested the teacher underline the points in her 'Day in the Life' narrative where she felt she would have liked to stop, reflect further and work on. Interestingly it was not the negative issue of time and administrative pressure that the teacher underlined. Her real priorities were with two particular puzzles—why the class had liked a particular newspaper cutting activity and whether to see the 'sidetrack discussion' as successful or not.

Seeking students' feedback 'in-flight'

The teacher planned to extend (experiment with) the newspaper cuttings as a feature of future weeks—with each one featuring another country. By seeking informal student feedback immediately, she found their interest has been retained; in fact several promptly volunteered to collect other information about the countries the class planned to discuss. She later noticed that the students had also read their assigned article.

Making use of a written Q&A page in the classroom

She supplied a feedback sheet for the students to self-assess the value of the exercise in relation to the course's purposes (checking against interest in topic, speed of reading, value of note-taking, chance to discuss content, and ability to write a summary).

The teacher's confidence began to rise as she realised the value of regularly building in students' feedback and the consequent increased clarity she had about what she was doing and why. She met with the Reflective Practice Counsellor only four times but by then her initial misgivings about the processes of her reflection and students' feedback being overly time consuming had given way to mild exhilaration at realising that she had begun working her way through a range of questions she had long had, and to which

she now had some handy 'working answers'. She also now had some methods (e.g. practice journals) and a way of posing new questions (e.g. What kinds of activity encourage students to talk more? What kinds of class instructions are more effective?)

Availability of a wider peer network to continue supporting reflective practice

NLLIA had a network of 'research nodes': small groups of teachers who met regularly on a monthly basis for reflective practice sessions to share questions, actions and findings coming out of their micro-inquiry. The group itself had gelled into a strong community of practice that was also resourced with news of other classroom procedures.

Some form of recording of practice (observe) to aid and ground reflection

The research node used a standard method whereby each member shared a transcribed recording of one of their classes with a commentary or discussion in dot-point form. Eventually the group published a collection of their deliberations for use by other teachers.

The story concluded by the teacher observing of herself:

> [She]…no longer feels she lives from day to day in constant reaction to events over which she has no control. She still has days like this, of course. But, in the main, [she] enjoys the extra risks she is taking professionally, and is continually growing in confidence about what she is doing. (Burton 1995: 17–18)

Postscript: The university psychology department's and the NLLIA's reflective practice efforts were discontinued during the period when education went ever more heavily down the corporatised track and most local practices and cultures gave way to mainstreamed and centrally delivered directives and templates. In this particular tertiary example, SEU (Student Evaluation of Unit) forms are now compulsory; and SET (Student Evaluation of Teaching) forms are optional, but increasingly being looked at for staff assessment, promotion and so on. The style of performance identification rating items is as follows.

While often seen as valuable for their descriptive content, they leave practice only numerically rated and measured (*observed*) and do not enable *reflection* on *why* things are as they are, how things got to be good (or not), nor indicate how to change or create further *innovation* so things might be improved. Vital nuances may also be lost in the fixed choice of answers allowed.

Evaluation of units:

I do some of my best work in this subject.

I receive adequate help with areas I find difficult in this subject.

The feedback that I receive in this subject is helpful.

I understand most of the content of this subject.

I find this subject interesting.

The learning outcomes and expected standards of this subject are clear to me.

The workload in this subject is appropriate.

The assessment in this subject allows me to demonstrate what I have understood.

I can see the relevance of this subject to my degree.

Overall, how would you rate the quality of this subject?

Evaluation of teaching:

With this teacher, I usually have a clear idea of where I am going and what is expected of me.

This teacher motivates me to do my best work.

This teacher puts a lot of time into commenting on my work.

This teacher makes a real effort to understand difficulties I might be having with my work.

This teacher normally gives me helpful feedback on how I am going.

This teacher is extremely good at explaining things.

This teacher works hard to make the subject interesting.

This teacher really understands the content of this subject.

This teacher uses student ideas and comments to improve their teaching.

Overall, how would you rate the quality of teaching provided by this teacher in this subject?

VP very poor; P poor; S satisfactory; G good; VG very good; NA does not apply, no answer

SEVEN

Mid-winter reflection: building in the facilitation of continuing evaluation by a community health centre[35]

Like other super-sized regional human services, the Grampians Community Health Centre spans an enormous terrain extending out from its home-base, 7000-person town to encompass other regional towns, right across towards the South Australian border in one direction and halfway back to the state capital city in the other. With a surprising loss of community relationships that offered support and identity formation, combined with changing farming practices and other kinds of jobs, country people can find themselves pushed out of shape and deprived of many key properties of living systems—not unlike many city folk also faced with high rates of mobility, unemployment, drugs and alcohol, and low incomes in a high consumption world. Perhaps more than many other public institutions of the post-industrial human habitat, the small 'David' of community health services is charged with the near impossible task of resourcing the restoration to health of large numbers of 'person systems' made less viable, hale and hearty by the larger 'Goliath' of social, economic and political systems.

The core team in this network of community health services and programs has, since 2003, put in place an 'evaluation framework' both to respond to these challenges and to improve feedback to staff about their effectiveness in addressing them. Indeed it was not actually called an evaluation framework until some years later when it was realised that this was what had been achieved by the gradual process of moving to bring each of the centre's many activities to the relevant staff's conscious attention by incorporating regular checking and articulating of how they knew how well they were going in their constant encounters with their clients and the community.

What follows is a glimpse of that built in research and evaluation system that assists staff be better able to resource the life of their constituent local people.

An action research and evaluation framework, anchored in deep values

Perhaps the first component of this evaluation system was the encouragement of each new person employed in this service to become alive to the value and potential for the fuller life of all others: whether community members, clients, community groups or themselves and fellow staff. This begins in the employment process, is echoed in job descriptions and then in immersion in the culture of the centre. 'In this together', and 'better together' encapsulate the values based on an understanding in the country that 'what goes around, comes around'. It has been an intensely egalitarian 'alongside' philosophy that does not easily lose sight of those most in need of resourcing (given the stress of fire, drought, unemployment, ageing, low or precarious income, or any other resulting life-depleting and life-threatening states in the larger scheme of things).

A key value on interdependence and resourcing to empower each other to be self-reliant

A second underlying assumption of a living system widely adopted at Grampians Community Health is that of valuing maximising self-organising and self-determination through relationships with others. From clients to staff to Board to community and back again, the guiding belief has been that all rely on each other to resource each others' journey of change, growth and consolidation. The Department of Human Services 'Participation Policy' (2005) seems to sum this up: 'Nothing about us without us', or 'Doing it with us not for us'. This is manifested in the daily encounters between centre service providers and those with whom they are engaging, typically beginning with inquiring: observing, checking meaning, adjusting, 'feeding in' a response, possibly a proposition, followed by watching for new feedback, and so on, in a continuous conversational process that takes place within a fabric of local relationships and relevant 'people-systems'.

> *Never try to teach a pig to sing.*
> *(it wastes your time and annoys the pig)*
> DRINKING MUG (SOURCE UNKNOWN)
> GRAMPIANS COMMUNITY HEALTH CENTRE,
> 7 JULY 2005

Resourcing this staff–client and service–community co-inquiry is the key purpose of the annual program of research and evaluation, which every year culminates in an intensive mid-winter week of evaluation facilitation and consultancy.

An evaluation 'meta-consultant' to assist the centre's staff to self-evaluate

Hallie Preskill expresses nicely what is involved in the terrain of facilitating learning about inquiry as a built in, everyday organisational practice, particularly when we add the word 'research' to evaluation, and 'individual, group or community' to 'organisation':

> Over the last few years, interest in evaluation capacity building (ECB) has been increasing across organisational sectors around the world. While the means by which evaluators facilitate capacity building vary, their efforts typically involve helping organisation members:
> a. conceptualise, design and sustain ongoing evaluation practices
> b. link evaluation to the organisation's strategic mission and goals
> c. connect evaluation to other forms of organisational inquiry and decision-making
> d. develop evaluation knowledge and skills
> e. integrate evaluation practice with the organisation's systems, structures and culture
> f. facilitate the use of evaluation findings, and most importantly,
> g. think evaluatively. (Preskill 2007, workshop abstract)

Here I will try and bring to life the list of built in inquiry methods that together comprise quite a comprehensive research and evaluation system at the Grampians Community Health Centre by looking through the lens of the annual visit of the 'external internal' planning and evaluation research consultant. The consultant is one of the evaluation 'system components'—in this case a facilitatory resource, 'thinking partner' and 'meta-consultant' (consulting with the staff who in turn are providing their own consultancy to clients' inquiry).

This week-long meta-consultancy not only reflects fractally the same processes of inquiry and resourcing being undertaken by staff with their critical communities or clients, but also the same inquiry processes of their communities and clients in their lives, and with those to whom *they* relate.

Collective learning opportunities and individual consultancy

But like all the good practices developed in this service, the research and evaluation system started small—in this case, with an invitation in 2002 from the CEO to an external evaluation consultant to run a weekend-long evaluation residential retreat workshop. The consultant had seen from her own practice that 'one-offs' often had little lasting value and had been using (with various levels of government and non-government organisations for some years) a sequence of: 'start-up' workshop, followed by a program of individual project consultancy, followed by a further group plenary pooling of work and experiences. Two days of follow-up consultancy were thus planned to follow the centre's residential weekend workshop, at which initial work commenced on staff members' individual and group evaluation projects.

Set against a background culture of continuous organisational development

Not that this community health service was starting from scratch with the evaluation workshop.

Right from the 1970s, when it had commenced operations with a comprehensive needs study involving 400 local people and forty community groups and organisations, it had worked from a model of a community health service that should change as needs changed while still building and holding 'structures' that could contain and sustain 'best practice so far'.

Yet with the best will in the world to remain permeable to new input, and flexible enough to modify, discontinue or spawn new start-ups—success-ful formulae, once replicating, tend to perpetuate as busy, taken-for-granted action. Without assistance it can prove difficult for people to stop, look and reflect on what they are doing. Hence the annual winter reflection, evaluation and planning consultancy week.

Yet there was even more in the already established culture of 'how we do things round here' that made the centre especially able to get to where it had in extend-ing evaluative inquiry more deeply into the fabric of its work. These other contributing elements included:

- A 'green file' system for basic recording of activities, programs and services planning, descriptions, feedback sheets and evaluation (like a Quality Improvement Planning Programs system)
- A well-attended annual residential staff weekend for personal and professional development, morale building, feedback and insight, and getting to know one another

- A new staff induction system to equip newcomers with a manual that includes the philosophy and model of developmental evaluation used
- Occasional more in-depth research and evaluation studies commissioned of local consultants to provide more in-depth evidence (including statistical and demographic, but also the 'hard data' of closely observed trends in people's actually 'lived lives') and for evidence to underpin grants applications
- A general culture valuing what all staff, community Board and members and client groups see, feel and think, including ways of hearing these inputs, ideas and feedback; that does not punish people for mistakes or for trying new things and them not hitting the spot and which takes seriously the idea that all people can make life-giving changes and 'grow'
- A management approach that values and supports people coming up with their own initiatives, activities and programs in response to community trends, feedback and observation; and slowly trialling and building them over time
- And a standard annual three-year cycle of planning and reporting (including funding and service agreements) drawing on annual cycles of continuous improvement.[36]

An annual week-long period of action evaluation consultancy to all staff

The initial residential workshop regenerated a small amount of interest among some staff about how to look anew at their work. Then, as more staff became comfortable with evaluative inquiry as a built in process, the two days of follow-up consultancy expanded into an annual five days. In the early years of the consultancy being available, staff mostly worked on 'putting in the basics' such as after-the-event audit review-style questions that checked on objectives being met, combined with some open inquiry-style questions that gave some insights into what else might have been going on from the critical end-beneficiary's perspective.

Over the five years since this small start there has been an overall deepening of thought, combined with a greater 'corporate memory' being held by most staff of the basic 'mental architecture' of the R&D 'virtuous cycle' of action–observation–questioning–reflection–

new insights–and–planning. More are now able to identify the logic driving their work and the sources of their observations of the initial expressions of need, and revisit what they are doing.

The following account eavesdrops on a typical consultancy week for insight into where different kinds of programs and staff might be 'at' in their various evaluation efforts—and to illustrate how the winter evaluation reflection week works to encourage building in inquiry throughout practice. It:

- Illuminates the wide range of small-scale evaluative research activities that human services staff undertake to good effect as part of developing their own practice, activities, services and programs
- Shows the way this work operates in a more organic and iterative (emergent) way over years, continuously building on its own learnings
- Illustrates the effectiveness of drawing on specialised meta-evaluation consultancy to nurture this kind of activity rather than relying only on the occasional use of such experienced evaluation capacity for the more usual, often expensive, one off, after-the-event evaluations of a particular service or program
- Details the nature of this new kind of 'external in-house' evaluation consultancy.

The consultant starts early on the Monday morning by setting up the room. Here is her narrative...[37]

A place and space for reflection

'Setting up' the room means spreading out on a small non-intrusive table a notepad, pens and files from our previous meetings arranged in order of the day's meeting schedule, a folder of low-key resources (e.g. simple 'handy pages' about the action research/evaluation cycle, lists of audit review and open inquiry-style questions, copies of a sequence of action research strategic questions to ensure change), and a pile of feedback sheets for the sessions (one has to practise what is preached! –and they come in handy as an example of evaluation: see Figure 18).

Up on the wall I stick big laminated action research/evaluation cycle diagrams, and I hang a four-colour spiral mobile that helps to illustrate aspects of what we talk about (such as the intertwining of the four colour-coded moments of act–observe–reflect–

plan). Under the table goes a pile of research and evaluation books to distribute if needed, especially to new staff.

And that's as complex as it gets; since the key to success is the simplicity of the mental architecture that can help people locate whatever are the complex questions and puzzles they bring through the door.

This simple but increasingly familiar mental architecture works to 'scaffold' usage, and for it later to come to mind after people leave the room and go back to their busy work practice (when I'm not there). In fact, key to the success of the whole one-week-a-year endeavour is people picking up this ability to be able to self-navigate the dynamic and complex processes of:

Observation: looking, seeing, listening, hearing, feeling, noticing, questioning, and

Reflection: intuiting old and new meanings, making connections, having insights, and

Planning: thinking through the next action steps, and as many of the possible consequences and concrete details, and then

Action: while all the time trialling and observing for success, or not.

It's a great room. A cosy and tastefully colourful counselling room with pleasant suede sitting chairs and enough space for small teams, yet remaining intimate and restful enough with its windows onto an enclosed garden. A good 'space and place' that seems valued by busy staff for taking some time out to think. I can hear the music that is played both to ensure the centre feels welcoming and pleasant, and also adds a little more chance of privacy with thin walls.

In preparing, I realise that after five years I now have quite a level of familiarity with this group of people and their work, having accumulated detailed records of our talking about their many evaluation efforts over all that time. I have also helped them keep their own 'corporate memory' of the evaluations they've done over the years, and am also by now much more steeped in the 'local fabric' of what they do and how they work. I've become kind of an 'outsider-insider'; a 'critical and appreciative friend'. I know them better personally too, so my responses can hopefully be more closely attuned, although to be honest I never really quite know what will 'come through the door'. So it's pretty seat-of-the-pants 'thinking partners' work. With the emphasis on their thinking rather than mine, it really works best that I don't over prepare nor follow up afterwards. The value of what happens between us is thus in the crucible with and for *them*—I am their consultant on their work, and outcomes rest on what they make of it (in an analogue to their contributing to their clients and communities). It's a great sign when they start with the 'story so far' and can tell where they got to on what they planned last time we met. But equally, when they can't, I'm there to 'start where they are at' and work from there.

Day one begins

Evaluating an Indigenous men's group to assist their move to self-organising

Brett Baker[38] is first up this icy cold Monday morning and interested in talking about an Indigenous men's group he's been running in collaboration with the co-ordinator of a local Indigenous organisation. Initially it had been groundbreaking enough for local Indigenous men to meet at all, and Brett had hoped only that a small group might come at least once to 'yarn up' about 'relationships, respect and responsibilities'— topics that had emerged from previous reflection by him and with the Indigenous community leadership. So it had been rather startling that a steady group had gone on meeting weekly for nearly three months, and Brett is now wondering about sustainability. He's also got some insights into what has worked, and a bit of a 'formula' for running the meetings has emerged. But might the men continue it without him so he can go and start up another group elsewhere to meet other people's needs?

I ask about his hunches and how he could take them to the group, and he decides on a review of the past ten weeks, with four strategic questions to ask the men:

- Looking back at what the group has been doing— how has it been going?
- How strongly does the group feel about wanting it to continue?
- Can the group identify the 'formula'—are there parts of it they can see themselves playing to continue it?

Brett talked more about the deeper things going on in the group (in the context of the men's local community) and the living system metaphor proved helpful for thinking about how 'structure is being built

as you go along', and the need for flexible, permeable, transparent and more-or-less inclusive processes, at the same time as the men were treading a fine line between these open system processes and the safety and exclusiveness of boundaries needed to protect the development of their (albeit weakened by the colonisation process) propensity to self-heal.

Assembling an evaluation framework for a volunteers program

Sue Carmelham is next up, and at a different point in the cycle this year. While Brett was focusing on looking back and reflecting more deeply on his observations of Indigenous men's group life to derive new meanings and insights and planning a chance for reflective observation by the men themselves, Sue had by now a fairly settled volunteers 'Do Care' program and was 'bedding down' the Quality Assurance process on the 'other side of the cycle'. In particular she had a grant application which had triggered needing to map all the evaluation activities and methods she'd developed over previous years. Like others at the centre who have got to this point, it is often a nice surprise to realise what a lot of processes they have built in organically over the years, and which, in Sue's case, already added up to a quite robust 'evaluation framework'. For example, over the years we'd met, Sue and her team had developed:

- Detailed program descriptions
- Policies for their implementation expressing the various principles and governing purposes
- Operational work plans setting out intentions for the coming year
- A whiteboard that 'held' these visible for staff in the office
- Job descriptions that encapsulated coverage of the broad work task areas
- Training programs that conveyed accrued conclusions and assumptions to date
- Six-monthly telephone interview 'check-ins' to hear people's experiences, feedback, issues and ideas and monitor progress—involving all clients and all volunteers
- An office filing system and a Management Information System to keep all these records and the contact statistics accessible for reviews and reports
- Monthly and annual planning

- Three-yearly quality improvement (QICSA) accreditation reviews
- Use of the professional literature, networks and conferences to help pick up on new trends and changes impacting in communities' and clients' lives, new theories, concepts and ideas, and changes in government polices, language and goals; and to aid analysis and reflection for planning or generating adaptations, refinements or other changes
- An annual planning day (to which the above contributed).

Checking local and national evaluation systems for resonance with the critical reference group's needs

Once this locally grounded, practice-based framework had been mapped around the annual inquiry cycle and its elements checked against the act–observe–reflect–plan components for coverage and resonance, it also became possible for Sue to audit it all against the *National Standards Manual* chapter on continuous improvement and look for any gaps. This served (as well as being a form of grounded validation for the national standards approach and contents) to identify both in the national standards themselves and also in Sue's local framework a need for a more rigorous way to be able to identify new local community needs, and changes and trends emerging in relation to those not yet in touch with the service. Such a 'widened lens' suggested a need to ask how local workers could get to be in touch with the 'bigger picture' local environment of those they were not yet seeing. Sue also saw how the current local framework didn't pay as much attention as the national standards document did to formal auditing procedures and she realised she could easily formalise her collecting of statistics on retention and turnover. She planned to refine and add these areas to her local evaluation framework in the coming year. She also realised she would now be able to use the quite comprehensive local evaluation framework for similar grant seeking and accountability reporting in future.

Crisis planning in unfunded customised home care

Sue Palmer is a new staff member. She is facing a difficult situation in which there are plenty of community needs for special home care but a competitive market that favours cheap but less customised forms of appointments-based care, rather than the whenever-you-really-need-it special needs care that her '*care@home program*' has been offering at prices people can afford. An expensive and comprehensive external consultants' evaluation the previous year had decided it was viable, but this year staff and client numbers have halved and Sue is having to do it 'all very differently'. With the entry of other funded agencies providing for the more straightforward needs, the local niche market is proving economically unviable and unable to retain staff. A new area of need (for out-of-home activities) for the same special needs clients also does not yet come with funds (holders/providers), and grant applications are time and cost consuming to research and prepare. It looks like Sue may not have the 'luxury' of funded time to draw on past evidence and evaluation or undertake new research for the 'pointy end' of the business planning stage she now finds herself in. We don't get much further with thinking through the dilemmas she faces, and end up only reiterating the conclusions she'd drawn so far.

'In flight' evaluation learning

Next up are five members of the counselling team who squeeze into what is their 'home territory' family counselling room. New staff are a feature in their team this year too. Job mobility is common in human services and a challenge to 'culture holding' of the mental architecture of continuous action research and evaluation. I launch into 'What I the evaluation consultant do' and then we reconnoitre over the wide territory they cover—from observing the drawbacks of overly prescriptive funding 'buckets' that don't easily match local people's interconnected lives (e.g. a fire trauma turns out to have been triggered by a long-standing family issue, or a marital issue turns out to have been triggered by the stress of too many years of drought)—through to reflecting on the opportunities and constraints of currently favoured psychological treatment regimes and the importance of staying grounded in the truths and realities of local people's lives.

The feedback sheets I hand out at the end of each session (Figure 21) come back under the door and one provides instant feedback to me that the 'best thing' had been the 'What Yoland does' spiel which included a quick refresher on the four-phase action evaluative research cycle (based on the fold-out wall chart at the back of *Everyday Evaluation On The Run* (Wadsworth 1997b). Others said that now they knew better what I did, they would come more specifically prepared next time. CEO Jill Miller usually provides this briefing to staff but this year had been away. But I can see another systems process we can build in! And that night I draft up a spiel to accompany next year's 'Yoland is coming' appointments roster call (Figure 22. What the evaluation consultant does flier announcing visit).

Bridging the gap between local practice reporting and national policy accountability

At the end of the day Brett Baker ducks his head back in to see if he can ask about a national government funder's monthly 'narrative report' from another area of his work. The questions from Canberra don't seem to be coming from quite where the local Grampians area situation is 'at'—with which clients (and staff) have to deal in their daily reality on the ground. Together we translate them into 'first person' questions that might prompt a more illuminating way

of reporting on the situation to relate to where the Canberra people are 'at'. This is a story 'to be continued...' and we had resolved to revisit it the following year to see if it has 'worked' for the funders (and funded).

Postscript to Day One: taking time to learn the 'rocket science' of everyday evaluative thinking

There was an observation worth making about the process of people acquiring the action evaluation mental architecture. The plan–act–observe–reflect algorithm appears to be so simple that we often say rather apologetically, 'it isn't rocket science'. Yet Brett noted that while three years earlier when we'd first met it had *seemed* a terrific session he 'hadn't really got it' all! At the time we had worked through three of his projects (using the same algorithm) and he'd scored the session a '10'. He said he'd 'learnt heaps' and that it had been 'precisely what [he] wanted in order to submit a [particular] written evaluation...' He'd even said that what had been best was 'the creation of a

---

FEEDBACK PLEASE

(OK. Practising what is preached!)

Overall how did this session go for you? (Just in a word or two)

It was: ....

Want to try and convert that into a number? ...and rate it out of 10?!

    (On a scale from 0 = not of value to me, through to 10 = couldn't have been better for me) (Please circle)

         0   1   2   3   4   5   6   7   8   9   10

What was best about it?

....

What would you have liked to be different?

....

Would you say your confidence and grasp of evaluation has increased? (Tick box)

❏ Not really ❏ Not sure, possibly ❏ A little ❏ Quite a lot ❏ Very much so

Other comments you'd like to make about how the session should (or should not) be changed if it is run again next year?

....

Anything else you'd like, in terms of evaluation support, for the future?

....

Figure 21. An end-of-a-consultancy session quick feedback sheet

structured framework to fit my and our existing evaluations into that is useful for the development of the program and satisfies management'. Now, Brett revealed, it was only *this* year that he had *really* 'got it'; and he was 'over the moon' with his several times talking with me that day (he had come in as part of the counselling team too). While making a note to see if Brett still found the thinking to be accessible the following year, it occurs to me that, as with Coonara community house, this is rocket science for human services. It may actually be a way people *can* more consciously 'get airborne' or to where things can really 'take off'. It may be no less sophisticated in its application to the complex interactional social–emotional human world than rocket science is for the complex external physical–material world.

For three years Brett had been bringing very causally complex and sensitive human interaction projects to the table. Just this morning he had recounted an even more 'rich thick' narrative about the subtleties of Indigenous–white relationships (and

intra-Indigenous relationships), and how and why an Aboriginal leader had decided that Brett, a white European health worker, should be the one to facilitate the meetings. The story became ever more subtle as the leader's reflexivity about Brett's own analogic white community 'stolen generation' issues and forced relinquishment went into the mix (the new physics term 'systems entanglement' comes to mind here—a necessary condition for the permeability of sub-systemicities' boundaries: to enable new information or 'nourishment' to cross without 'trojan' threats crossing also). Furthermore Brett's close observations and insights had shaped his educational component on communication in the men's group. But now he was stuck at the point of needing to withdraw, facing multiple interactional issues, and needing to think through how to assist the men make the change. The action evaluation mental architecture became a bridge, a way of scaffolding the group and Brett taking the next logical steps, by suggesting what questions to ask next.

Simple and familiar, but also harder than it looks

We have few examples of how long it takes for people to see the theory of evaluation action research within their own thinking and be able to apply it consciously to small-scale activity in daily life. Even experienced researchers frequently lack a sense of this cycle, relying instead on only a familiar part of it, for example always either starting with a theoretical hypothesis leading to an experiment and deductive conclusion, without an easy way to take into account changing conditions, or inductively concluding from many instances, and then not abductively moving to interpretive meaning-making for a new theory to drive implementing a 'live' experiment. Grasping how these three 'moments'—of induction, abduction and deduction—might be seen as joined up and explicated in rich detail at any of the many 'moments' around the conceptual cycle took me eight years of PhD studies, reading 400 years of philosophy of science, and twenty-eight years of study and research! Many of us from the second generation of action researchers since the 1970s tell similar stories. Now that we are trying to show others what we know (so they can access it more quickly than it took us), it is perhaps no surprise that three years may be a minimum for grasping the basics. Yet we could start teaching the basics of this in kindergarten, given the accessibility of the algorithm.

What would you like to talk about this year with 'thinking partner' Yoland Wadsworth (author of *Do It Yourself Social Research, Everyday Evaluation on the Run and Building in Research* and *Evaluation for [truly] Living Human Systems)?*

Some puzzles, questions or concerns for which you still need answers?

Some observations you'd like to reflect on?

Some feelings you'd like to clarify?

Some reflections you'd like to take further?

Some plans you'd like to think through in terms of practice implications?

Some practice you'd like to systematise a little more without losing its quality and purpose?

Some project or program you'd like to evaluate retrospectively?

Some prospective evaluation of what you'd really like to do in future?

Grab a time space for you or/and your team by contacting Kerry Heinreich ASAP.

Figure 22. What the evaluation consultant does: flier announcing visit

Day Two

Reflecting on working 'backwards' around the cycle, from retrospective evaluation to prospective evaluation

Tuesday begins with us decamping to the larger main meeting room as the Community Care Options team is eight-people strong.

When we began five years earlier the team had just completed a client survey using a standard form and found it had not been as successful as it could have in terms of understanding people's experiences. They had decided to try building in more in-depth individual 'chats' as part of routine service package reviews. They had also wanted to do a service provider survey, basing it on what they'd learned from the client survey, and we'd talked about case study scenarios as a way of evaluating the team's operation. At that time we talked about what kind of questions 'went deeper' and could also come up with ideas for the future. We'd also talked about mapping a flow chart of referral assessments and handover procedures to be able to observe better how the logic of these was working and for clues as to how they could be improved. Plus we'd sketched a way of reviewing an information booklet. We talked especially about the need to STOP and take time out to achieve all these kinds of reflections.

By the following year, much of what had been planned had been carried out and our focus shifted to a planning day and the potential of staff narratives to report on how services had unfolded, or not. Alison Duxson, the team leader, especially reported liking being able to see 'a way to move forward and build on already existing structures'. The next year we met, Virginia Read reported that they'd used the action research evaluation planning tool (the sequence of strategic action research or 'living systems' questions) for a successful client counselling review and that they were also planning for their Commonwealth Aged Care Standards Review, which was linking into the community health QICSA agency accreditation. They mentioned another government departmental tool that unfortunately we were not free to improve (as it had become rigidly standardised and obligatory). We had quickly reviewed some other aspects of the service (ongoing new needs assessment, supervision etc.) as a way of reflecting on a bigger picture of 'where it was at' in its 'life cycle' of progressing the deeper purposes of the program.

Revisiting the issue of not having the time to STOP and think, the group decided that—in order to preserve a precious four hours (which they had identified all staff could simultaneously take each week) for thinking, reflecting, experimenting, analysing, reporting etc.—they would call it 'Practice Development' and mark it out in their weekly work plans. (Voila! Built in!)

The previous year when we'd met we'd had an interesting exchange about the upsides and downsides of formal satisfaction questionnaires versus informal, more interactively asked conversational questioning methods. The group had reflected on their last year's evaluation using three different methods—pen and paper surveys, focus group discussions and narrative—and had looked forward to planning how to improve consumer–community–client consultation and feedback. (The service did not yet have sufficiently active participation by service users in the design and evaluation of the service itself.) We talked through the different kinds of clients they were seeing (e.g. younger adults, parents with small children and older people), estimated the various demographic percentages of the seventy-seven clients on home-based care packages, and designed different methods to try with each.

This year we are looking at how these multi-methods had resulted in some good feedback, particularly from the group of young adults with disabilities who had felt confident enough to provide some more 'meaty criticism'. Unexpectedly for staff, they had also wanted to keep meeting together. In living systems' terms this created a possibility that the group could be asked if it would like to become an ongoing feedback reference panel of 'critical appreciative friends'. The use of 'internal–external' facilitators (community health centre staff, but not part of the Community Care Options program), was also reported as having worked well. However fewer people had attended the parents' forum. We explored ideas and insights about this and what next to try to experiment with (with the team deciding on lunch combined with a free children's activity). Finally, home-based interviews by the centre's community nurse were observed to have worked well for the frail aged group.

We also explore more deeply the issue of how to 'see anew' the otherwise tried and true; and how to tap the close observations of domestic care workers, often overlooked. Two methods are planned for the next service providers' survey—written questionnaires and quarterly small group meetings. There is some enthusiasm for also trying a 'What have we been learning?' item on fortnightly staff meeting agendas.

The other issue concerning the team this year resulted from the introduction of new intensive 'extended aged care in the home' packages. The need for better engagement with local general medical practitioners (GPs) has arisen from the conceptual insight that this work had made people's private homes 'the equivalent of nursing homes'. This helps reframe the purposes of such an engagement as 'a dialogue of mutual inquiry'—a kind of a 'study of GPs' by the community care workers, but inviting the GPs to 'study' the community care workers as well. A rough sketch is made of a series of questions each might ask of the other, possibly based on some real-life case vignettes to illuminate how things could go wrong (or well). We conceptualise it as a professional development session through the regional GPs Division to enhance the likelihood of GPs valuing attending.

The search for creative evaluation methods able to go deeper

Back to the family counselling room 'burrow' to meet with three workers who are twelve months into a three-year funded, multi-agency family violence program. They have just completed the first twelve-week program with men perpetrating violence or other abuse who are working on their own behaviour change. It has an associated partner program. Like many other comparable initiatives the challenge is to find more creative evaluation methods that might trigger the kinds of conversations and self-reflection that will help clients traverse the full evaluative research cycle for their own change processes. An experienced male worker is looking for a way of charting, even graphing, how far the men in the group are getting in this endeavour, including in relation to their partners' experience, over the course of the twelve weeks. Since the evaluation information is needed for both the course providers and the course takers themselves, and with workers paid sessionally to provide the course sessions only, the focus shifts to building in the necessary comparative data collection process to the actual content of the course itself.

Since the content of the course is attempting to build the men's internal strengths (by a cruel irony, most men report feeling most powerless precisely when they hit), the comparative evaluation that *they* need in order to know how they are going is the same kind of feedback that the course providers also need in order to know how *their* facilitation is going. Each is on a parallel research 'journey of discovery'—the men to crack the puzzle of how and why they are violent or abusive and what to do instead; and the workers to crack the puzzle of how and why the course does or doesn't resource the men not to be violent or abusive, and what to do more of or instead. In a way all are each others' 'critical and appreciative friends': accompanying each other into unexplored, scary territories through questioning, sharing of observations and interpretations, evaluating the forcefields that might be holding old patterns in place, envisioning and 'operationalising' preferred futures and celebrating the gains and mourning the setbacks.

Then I remember that the Bendigo-based St Lukes Innovative Resources people have produced tear-off graphical 'notice the difference' coloured pads using different images that clients can fill in to assist them 'see the change'. The graph, the pathway, the water tank, and the bomb-with-a-fuse come to mind as potentially useful—although the men can choose from many other images as well.[39] We discuss how the men might mark on the pads their own particular starting points ('I-was-here-then' and 'I-am-here-now') from week to week as a basis for telling their stories of what the changes to the marks from week to week mean for them (e.g. have they got further down the track on the roadway diagram? Or does a half an inch difference on the water tank being filled mean a lot or a little and why?) We also talk about how their partners might do the same (even trying using the same graphic their partner chose)—while remaining aware that it is the *meaning* of the marks they make on the scale that will be the crucial 'hard data', not the marks and the distance between them per se, nor even the same pad image. Thus while the sheets will not be strictly (literally) comparable, it may still be useful to see if the meanings of the marks might seem to be shared.

We then work on resonant language for the round robin check-in questions the facilitators might use to trigger the men's narratives around the graphical charts (e.g. 'How has your week been—can you say a bit about why you marked the chart pad as you did?';

'What do your two markings have to say about whether there have been changes in your ways of managing the anger? [or other negative feelings]; 'What can you say about any new insights you might have had during the week about why you get angry or violent or abusive in other ways?'; 'What else do you think is going on?'; 'Is it connected to anything else?'), and the check-out questions too (e.g. 'What are you taking away from tonight's session?', 'Was there a particular insight or new learning you can describe?'). By the end of the course the chart pad pages and associated verbal and written narratives might tell bigger stories of ups and downs, steps forward and steps back, insights gained and ground lost or re-lost, within a picture of more overall movement. We discuss parallel debriefings and note-keeping by the workers as a way of evaluatively charting their own parallel processes of observation, insight, learning and change (and even that they might be able to use the tear-off image pads themselves for their own practice).

And on throughout the week

The rest of the day and the remainder of the week pass in like fashion with staff working through their issues, questions, observations, ideas, theories and intentions and me acting as their 'external mind': an extension of their own thinking, helping surface feelings, bridging their observations and perceptions via their purposes to envisage next steps to take, and assessing the possible consequences of these, and identifying the best ways to ensure or notice what happens.

I want to highlight six other kinds of reflection encountered in a typical week of this kind of 'living inquiry systems' consultancy.

The non-conscious evaluation by the experienced (advanced) practitioner

As people deepen their reflections, achieve more powerful insights and plan new, more resonant actions for their activities, services, projects and programs over time, they are gradually 'expanding their neural networks' and practice repertoire to take in and make meaning of wider and wider ranges of practice experience. At some point they become 'advanced practitioners', increasingly unable to retrieve the complex webs of reasoning about experience that produces their unconscious virtuoso performance.

Bernadette Cossar is one such. Her 'Baby Think It Over' is a nice example of a program (involving teenagers in the care of a 'live', electronically monitored computer-programmed-for-a-reality experience replica human infant) that was initially imported already developed from elsewhere, but which in her skilled hands has 'taken' in this local environment. Bernadette has gone on expanding her community nursing repertoire in this instance both through practice as well as numerous short courses until these days little 'throws her'. There's an upside and a downside of this. On the downside she could become ever more speedily efficient in her work and not ever stop to ask any deeper questions. But on the upside, the greater her confidence, the greater her willingness to self-challenge when she encounters discrepancies in the worlds in which she moves. The more risks she takes, the more she learns; and that enables her to take even greater risks. She can increasingly comfortably sit with silences, probe delicately for repressed meanings, and think fast on her feet. Her own preparedness to discuss the undiscussibles encourages her clients and communities to also take risks and ask questions and surface long-held damage or other life-depleting experiences. Like other strongly intuitive, feeling people, she seems to have a built in 'life detector'.

The Board as evaluators

During the annual evaluation week there is always a night-time meeting between the CEO and the Board and their evaluation consultant. The focus of the meetings has varied from year to year—from how to conduct community-wide needs scans, to how to evaluate something specific like their 'buddy system' (Board members' direct and rotating involvement with a particular health centre program: attending a program staff meeting, accompanying staff into the community on their work etc.), right through to mapping a full evaluation framework for a three-year Board cycle and 'seeing whole' how much has been achieved. This is this year's focus. The evaluation consultant works with the Board (who are all local community members with a range of experiences from which to contribute) as 'meta-researchers and evalu-ators' themselves. While there is a contemporary risk of the community Board's role being reduced to merely that of a governance monitor of processes largely carried out by professional staff, at the Grampians Community Health Centre a strong insistence prevails that the community Board must have oversight of the mesh between the work of the health centre and the lifeworlds of their local communities.

In this way the Board is seen also as operating its own cycle of community needs assessment and service monitoring, observation, reflection, new insight, policy making, planning and follow-up monitoring of action implementation and working knowledge — whether in the course of a monthly meeting, annually or every three years, and whether it is in hearing a monthly highlighted program manager speak; performing buddying duties; commissioning their own 'community days'; attending Board Days to hear about new trends, concepts, comparative demographics, funders' demands or staff members' observations; reading client feedback survey results; or getting to know each other.

Ongoing in-service to keep up with new methodologies and techniques

This year the two-hour mini staff 'training' workshop on new and emerging evaluation methods (that is always part of the week's work) is mindful of nurturing staff's energies with new ideas for them, in turn to resource and nourish their clients' and communities' energies.

It is built in to follow a routine monthly staff meeting which itself illuminates many of the same strengths-building, self-organising, self-informing values and roundtable precepts that guide the work of the centre. It is chaired by a (rotating) member of staff, and the bulk of this month's time is spent in a round robin in which all staff who want to can share aspects of their month's work—a terrific input of 'system-augmenting feedback'.

After the staff meeting, thirty staff energetically pack into the main seminar meeting room and hear about two forms of narrative—Appreciative Inquiry (Cooperrider et al. 1987, 1999) and Memory Work (Haug 1987). Last year it was Program Logic and Program Theory.

I introduce the workshop by locating the 'turn' to narrative in the need to be able:

- To represent complex life/work 'whole'
- To explicate better the meaning of often quite abstract statistical reporting

- To go more deeply into what is of real value and meaning to people
- To achieve the shift—'the change in the story'—from 'what is' to 'what could be'.

I have chosen strengths-enhancing questions for the two exercises, both to show staff directly the way in which these methods can spark insights and also to raise their own spirits (and to show by extension how they could use the same exercise to achieve the same ends with clients). Evaluation rests on noticing a discrepancy so it technically doesn't matter if the focus is on the positively valued or the negatively unvalued (provided the latter remains somewhere in the picture and isn't denied). But if the negative threatens to blot out all other views and scenery in the picture then it's often best to start with the positive and come back to unhappy realities later when able. Plus the positive is often a fast track to seeing what might be better to try.

In the *Appreciative Inquiry* exercise (verbal narrative, in pairs) one person tells the other pair-partner about 'a time when they most felt they were operating as the…(e.g. the social worker, or counsellor, community nurse, youth worker etc.) they most want to be'. Then they swap. There is brief time to talk about the implications for new dreams and designs to try.

In the *Memory Work* exercise (written narratives, read out and reflected on in small groups of three to four), people are asked to write a half-page, first-person singular account of a memory of 'having found out something really important, or of making an important discovery in their work life'. Then as a small group, after everyone has read out their memory story, they talk about what they are hearing in it: themes, things that stand out, etc. There isn't time for rewriting and a second reading but I supply two-page summary handouts with definitions, the exercises and author references.

The methods are designed to 'show by doing' and trigger strongly energised exchanges of accounts between almost all staff. Nearly all staff stay throughout, with some not keen to leave even at the end. A number of staff indicate subsequently in our consultancy sessions that they would like to make use of the narrative methods/exercises in their own work to go more deeply with clients.

Sometimes a 'shallow spiral on a plateau'

After lunch, this year's meeting with the Tribal Youth Team is unexpectedly a little disjointed. It may be a sign of the impact of staff changes or some normal entropic inertia for a large successful program that has run a course over a long period and may be in need of 'a reviver'. It seems that previous, successfully developed evaluation methods, particularly some feedback sheets, have not 'jumped the gap' from initial to new staff. We spend the session revisiting them.

The institution of feedback sheets has waxed and waned in the wider business world as familiarity has bred complacency ('been there, done that, know what they say'). Yet change is constant and old solutions may subtly lose their sharp resonance. On the other hand old solutions may still be working well but need evidence of their continued relevance. All kinds of feedback systems may be helpful for the single new idea or fresh opinion that is foretelling a genuine need for remaining alert. In this case it may not be the quantity of feedback that is a key but rather the availability of the method for the new insight from even a single respondent who has sensed it like a canary in the mine. Perhaps the constant 'value adding' of new and more challenging questions or attractive techniques can keep feedback processes more alive, or better still they become part of the service or project's modus operandi rather than an optional add-on afterwards.

Feedback as part of the program content itself

Jillian's use of the creative arts in a family violence program aimed at strengthening women's resilience in the face of accrued abuse especially illuminates, for example, the discordance of ending a deeply creative and emotionally moving session with a tick-the-box pen-and-paper feedback sheet. In our discussion she designs an evaluation process as a series of questions built in to become part of the session itself to assist the women reify their own 'bio-feedback'. Thus the women are reflecting on whether and how *they* have experienced growth in their own sense of strength or resilience in relation to the content and interaction within the course session. She has also added a facilitators' debriefing meeting after each session using questions that mirror those for the women, plus questions that audit her facilitators' objectives and assumptions (program logic). Finally she plans an after course reflection to get further perspective on *all* the week-by-week experiences. Next time we meet we will see how this all went, and if there were elements that might be able to be 'bedded down' as replicable or sustainable enough (in their authentic form) over a longer period of time.

The tricky downside of programs that work well: the need to sound the bell!

Some 'systems' work fine for longer periods than others, and some parts may work longer than other parts that need more regular feedback and adaptive response. Yet the impetus to keep running from one action to the next without pause can also become habitual, especially when the 'pay off' is more immediately visible than the longer term impact of stopping for more thoughtful observation, reflection and fresh new insight.

One year Robyn Leslie, the energetic and compassionate Respite Care Program leader, flew past the door to say she couldn't stop for an evaluation session this time. 'Ah!' I said, 'sounds like just the time you should be able to!' and told her the story of Mother Theresa's rule (for which the famous Roman Catholic nun was also criticised on the grounds of hard heartedness) that her care-giving Indian nuns were to rise at the sound of a bell and retreat for prayers regardless of whatever were the immediate pressing care needs. In Robyn's attentiveness to the urgency of her programs' needs I sensed a fractal pattern repeating of 'good practice responsiveness' by the program's carers to clients' immediate and urgent situations—but how to slow things down and begin to apply brakes to those fast-turning wheels without leaving a trail of burnt rubber? How to sound her own bell not so softly as to be discounted, yet not so loudly as to induce too painful shock and the discarding of the bell, but just loudly enough to distract from the urgent current action? Fortunately Robyn laughed rather than insisting on her need to relinquish this single hour in a whole year; and thereafter 'sounding the bell' became shorthand for what it took to stop action in the moment in order to look at it.

But perhaps the most compelling reason why Robyn subsequently 'built in the bell' from that day on was what happened when she *did* stop to talk that day. I asked what were the discrepancies she was observing and instead of a mass of concerns continuing to wash around, she quickly named four nagging issues which she then talked through. Subsequently she swiftly took actions (e.g. regarding burgeoning referral numbers and lengthening waiting lists) that stood her and her program in good stead for many years to come.

Interestingly our four previous annual meetings together had followed the same pattern mentioned earlier of 'starting' at an 'end'—this time with an evaluation that urgently needed to be written up. The second year we met, she had 'stepped backwards round the cycle' to discuss the hierarchies of her program's logic and its objectives. Our third year retraced steps even further back to the need for dialogue methods to enhance understanding after the blow-out in numbers of clients had resulted in too much pressure on staff. And this year's meeting focused on how the new-style 'Team Day' that had come out of our talking the previous year was now working so well in helping forge strong team friendship relationships (using questions that staff volunteered they wanted to ask to find out more about each other) that it had freed Robyn to step back and think about something new altogether, in particular, what her distinctive management style's strengths and thin ice were.

An evaluation methodology for all staff

Finally, it is worth noting that the evaluation consultancy is available to all staff, including administrative, information technology and finance systems managers, as the same action-inquiry-new action mental architecture is seen as underlying *all* aspects of the health centre's service improvement, refinement, consolidation and change. Front office and administration manager Tania McKenzie, in the face of unworkably long hours and splits and cracks across the teams' work over multiple campuses, has adopted regular exercises in hearing from staff. She had seen how—by systematically and collaboratively altering practice, seeing how the changes went, reviewing them together, regularly using round robins and client and staff feedback sheets with good strategic questions—levels of mutual respect rose noticeably and a cohesive team formed and settled. Nick Monas, another staff systems manager, had wondered:

- How to be sure the staff supervision counselling service was staying fresh

- How the counsellors knew what their impacts were on staff and staff's outcomes
- Whether the staff residential weekend should be attracting every single last member of staff
- How to evaluate the IT consultancy provided to staff.

Slowly these surveys inched their way to the top of his 'To Do' list.

At the end of the week CEO Jill Miller and I always spend two or three hours reflecting on the lessons learned from the week's work. After returning to Melbourne I send a summary matrix of all the sessions along with the thirty or so feedback sheets from staff for use for QICSA evidence purposes. I also propose ideas for how we might incorporate the learnings and innovations we've discussed in the next year's winter evaluation reflection week (like deciding to continue the mini-workshop on evaluation methods; or introducing more formal mapping of people's 'program logic'; or something to revitalise more active consumer participation); and how to 'go deeper' to see if staff can move from overly quick surface explanations to more complex systemic reasoning, even about persistent or overwhelmingly painful issues that are starting to be seen more and more in country towns.

Postscript: In 2010 the annual winter evaluation reflection week was in its eighth year and in the twelve months before had modestly contributed to assisting staff inquire their way through a relatively seamlessly smooth change of building. The consultant's annual 'dance card' continues to fill rapidly, session evaluations continue to rate the consultancy on average at around eight out of ten, and the (albeit ever-briefer) mini training sessions continue to be received with enthusiastic ovations. The inquiry work continues.

EIGHT

'The story so far' of building in narrative evaluation action research workforce development for integrated health promotion[40]

For more than two decades the new area of health promotion has sought to address community health issues in a more developmental and preventive way: less through the lens of ill health and 'parts of bodies' (heart, liver, spine, lung) and more as it is lived by people in communities in complex lifeworlds (as articulated in the World Health Organisation's health promotion Alma Ata Declaration in 1978 and Ottawa Charter of 1986, and represented in state policy in support of Integrated Health Promotion).

Central departmental policy requires narrative to explicate annual statistical reporting, and narrative evaluation using an action research epistemology is identified as an integrated methodology to match the philosophy of Integrated Health Promotion

The NEAR project was a response by a large region of the then state Department of Human Services, North and West Region (DHS N&W) in Victoria to build a strengthened, integrated health promotion capability amongst local women's, youth, culturally and linguistically diverse (CALD) people and community health services for telling their stories: beginning with serving new health needs, reflecting on them, working with individuals and communities to develop and try new approaches, then monitoring and evaluating them in practice and making further changes as might be needed. Appendix 4 is an exercise that has become part of the NEAR process that assists workers reorient to health as experienced by the critical inquiring living 'organism', whether an individual or a community.

It has now operated for more than five years and trained or resourced more than sixty practitioners to inquire and think wholistically through telling the stories of their health promotion practice. It won the Australasian Evaluation Society national evaluation Policy and System Award in 2007 in recognition of its efforts to enhance systems-wide evaluation using this innovative methodology. In 2009-2010 the factors for its success are being formally identified as part of an

evaluation by its practitioner participants. I will summarise the conditions found so far to best ensure take up and self-organising continuation.

A train-the-trainer approach to teaching/learning about the methodology

Firstly, the NEAR process set out to ensure that learning about the methodology would not be 'just another one-off training event'. It wanted to ensure that not only did the use of narrative evaluative action research continue in the practice of health promotion officers' reporting afterwards, but also that some of these officers would help it snowball through replicating and extending the train-the-trainer approach within their agencies.

Linked to funding priorities and local workforce needs, with early identification of expertise to animate the capacity building

Community, youth, CALD and women's health services have organisational capacity building as a recognised funded priority (e.g. evaluation, information systems). After close observation of the health promotion field and its needs, a senior health promotion adviser with DHS N&W identified and engaged three practice research facilitators with extensive knowledge of action research, developmental evaluation and narrative, the community-based teaching of these, as well as the researching and development of case studies and other research resources for community health, women and youth participation in research.

A 'how to do it' manual developed by the participants themselves, and R&D framed as train-the-trainer peer education

There is a telling lesson in the first phase of NEAR with implications for building in all such inquiry efforts. While the later two phases incorporated ten and then thirteen agencies and a total of sixty practitioner participants, the first phase comprised only two agencies and only eight staff—ostensibly in order to develop the manual of resource material. Later phases were intended to benefit from the 'productivity gains' of having this manual available, and it has indeed proved valuable, particularly in Phase 3 when a hard-copy *QuickGuide* was produced to supplement the under-used web material. Yet in terms of the aims to 'up skill' health promotion workers in the use of the narrative evaluative action research methodology and the long-term replication of in-house NEAR training and support, it was the small number of initial practitioners from Phase 1 who proved the most notably and autopoetically effective. 'Making the road by walking', through that act of creating-the-learnings, appears to have galvanised them most to want to pass on the learnings *and* to know how to do so effectively.

One of the NEAR team of university collaborators had previously experienced the success of co-developing a manual with and by the first generation of consumer consultants in mental health services. Drawing on this experience, as well as contributing some potentially valuable ideas and exercises from other prior work with local community health practitioners (e.g. see Appendix 4), the university consultancy team, researched and developed the 'course content' 'live' with the Phase 1 participants. The participants' responsive evaluative commentary formed the basis of decision making about what material to use and in what ways. In effect the participants were not simply receiving a series of evidence-based best practice ideas as 'the way you can/will do it', but were thinking through (and being facilitated to think through) the experience for themselves and, in particular, evaluating the ideas and exercises from the standpoint of then teaching it themselves. In the process of doing this they became their own students. Subsequently they were able to produce their own in-house training programs, not so much by copying an external pattern that others had instructed them would work, but by generating their own internalised 'pattern' or format grounded in their own direct evaluative experience of the relevance and validity of the exercises and material.

The inclusion of strong peer support and backup external support, and a handy QuickGuide summarising the more detailed Manual of Guidelines, Resources and Case studies

The project team realised that the NEAR process, in particular the peer writing groups, were in some ways a systemic analog to what health promotion practitioners might be doing in turn with *their* communities, groups and individual clients: assisting people identify and articulate *their* story of:
• What they were doing in their lives and why
• What they wanted to do differently for their health
• What success they'd had so far (or not) and why

• What they wanted to do next.

The later *QuickGuide* synthesised a set of steps, a typical timeline and a format that had been found to work, but the depth and detail to which people were able to develop their narrative skill depended on further elements being built in—notably strong peer support writers' groups and additional backup for the opportunity for critical reflection from experienced peer, regional health promotion adviser or external consultancy, where needed.

Other conditions that assisted the building in of NEAR capacity

Before commencement
• People's own pre-existing interest and ability in story telling
• Their knowledge of action research and evaluation and their familiarity with them
• The availability of other published literature and case stories for ideas
• People's levels of interest and their own rationales for being committed to exploring their practice
• Time quarantined by strong and active management support
• Initial narrative guidelines generated by the department and strong regional departmental interest and support and long-term vision.

Phase One
• Preparatory, sensitising exercises within the on-site train-the-trainer workshop
• Invitation to/requirement of cross-agency contact and mutual support among practitioners and effective, supportive internal writing partnerships
• Development of a short, customized, annotated bibliography in response to request
• External experienced consultancy on-site and by phone, follow-up visits and email
• On-site follow-up group discussions to resolve deeper issues of voice and audience
• Production of other short written resources in response to demand (notably a 'Process Planner', see Appendix 4) and 'What makes a good narrative?', drawn from agencies' own criteria and generated from a training exercise combined with criteria drawn from relevant literature (such resources are re-generated with each new group of practitioners as their effectiveness derives from practitioners making conscious their existing,

unconsciously held criteria, which then become more consciously available)

- Allocated time/quarantined by management and participants.

Phase Two

- Compilation of the learning process guidelines, backup resource materials and six case stories into a manual, published on open access departmental website and as hard copy, made available to each participating agency
- A Transition Conference that reported findings back to regional health promotion workers, advisers and other interested departmental stakeholders for transparency, peer accountability and feedback; operated as a way of attracting interest from a new cohort of agency practitioners
- Regional and agency recruitment processes based on voluntary expressed interest and that stipulated management support for the time investment and required the narrative evaluation action research learning project work be built into work plans
- A cascading project design that started new cohorts of practitioners while continuing with the previous cohorts who were then acting as their agencies' trainers/motivators and inspirers
- Facilitation of the project matching this cascading design by providing direct facilitation and increasingly meta-facilitation as train-the-trainer work became support-the-trainer
- A trial of agencies' usage of the open access web materials without consultancy support in order to refine the web materials further.

Phase Three

- The addition of a handy and popular hard copy *QuickGuide* with the sequence of essential activities and exercises that comprised the process, the timeline and key resources from the manual (e.g. the Process Planner and 'What makes a good narrative?')
- The addition of another special written resource in the manual for the agencies to reproduce the learning process activities and timeline for train-the-trainer work themselves.

The value of long-term investment in action research resourcing

After five years of 'culture shift', and now that the project has gone long enough to be able to anticipate

that outcomes (differences in practice) are beginning to be observable and measurable, the NEAR project is undertaking a meta-evaluation to audit in more depth against the goal of enriching annual reporting to the DHS and for other uses. A more ambitious attempt is being considered to audit also against the greater goal of whether enriched reporting processes have improved integrated health promotion per se, and even whether an impact is identifiable in terms of improved community, group and individual health outcomes. However it may be too early for the latter, with reliance needed still on the 'front-end' theory that came out of previous research (that showed the drawbacks of non-narrative reporting, and inductively built the theory about the value of narrative in practice).

The project has proceeded from modest origins and slowly built its model of work in well-trialled practice at a local and regional level. It also developed the theory of action research evaluation as including the ideas of retrospective and prospective evaluation and published these in the Planner resource on the website. It has continually fed back its work into the greater health promotion system (primarily through conferences), attracting voluntary interest from more and more localities and regions, and is now poised on the threshold of 'critical mass' for take up by other regional and state levels of 'systemic organ-ising'. But to scale up will need central departmental support to integrate and co-ordinate the process within a statewide evaluation framework for integrated health promotion, and a way to take it to other regions.

Postscript: In 2010, subsequent to favourable assessment by the state government Auditor General's Office, the NEAR process is being examined by the department's central public health division for possible integration into a statewide health promotion evaluation framework. So, like all good stories, it is 'To be continued'.

References

The NEAR *Manual* is publicly available at: www.health.vic.gov.au/healthpromotion/hp_practice/eval_dissem.htm#near.

An example of a locally produced project resource ('Young Mums Rock!' by Joy Free, Research officer, Women's Health West) is available at: www. whwest.org.au/docs/ymr_ActionSheet3.pdf.

NINE

A non-government community support organisation builds in reflective practice to provide 'a hand up not a handout'

Yoland Wadsworth, Anne Pate and David Carlos[41]

Melbourne Citymission, a non-government community service organisation, is one of several which have worked deliberately over recent years to include a form of action research as a capacity-building approach throughout a large complex human service[42] and to support working towards a culture shift for greater empathetic resonance with clients and communities. Melbourne Citymission is one of only a couple of organisations which are unusual in the degree to which their research sections have worked in sustained and well-planned ways to build capacity over many years.

Start small from within a supportive Research and Social Policy Unit working closely with a Staff Learning and Development Unit, and in turn within a viable larger environment across the whole of the agency[43]

Like all successful building in of new culture, the effort started small—in this instance staff of the Research and Social Policy Unit and Staff Learning and Development Unit observed that a more strategic approach was needed to build in a new culture of reflection. Meanwhile the organisation was focused as a whole on how it could build inclusive communities —reflected in the way it was conceptualising its organisation at the time not so much as a static hierarchy of functions as a networked 'circle of circles' of staff and client communities of interest: diverse, but with a unity of purpose.

The agency also valued its then 150 years of history and long-standing cultural commitment to inclusiveness—evidenced in its 1855 slogan 'Need not Creed'—and continued to see itself as an innovative leader into the future with this philosophy. With staff working in welfare and health programs for people across the life cycle and all of life's transitions (children, youth, homelessness, adults and family, employment, education and training, disability, exiting prison, aged care and palliative care), Melbourne Citymission has prided itself on its ability to adapt to changing community life and emerging social issues.

Agency practices a philosophy of self-reliance and is strengths based: for example, 'homeless not helpless'

Melbourne Citymission also moved to a philosophy of building self-regard and self-reliance agency-wide that saw it embrace the collaborative and reflective style of its Reconnect program and look to extending use of this co-inquiry style in its organisation-wide policy of supporting reflective practice, 'agoras' of dialogue, debate and critical thinking. Explicitly wanting to go further than the traditional 'support model' and instead 'seek to empower people', the agency began expanding some of its traditional services into mini *oikos* of their own—such as an integrated family and community services centre; a participatory employment and small enterprise hub; and an early choices program for families with young children with a disability. All of this was consistent also with its interpersonal philosophy of being 'companions on the road...here to help each other'.

Supported by policy making, high-quality statistical data, and external consultancy

Comprehensive demographic analysis was undertaken through the CEO's office to underpin strategic and business planning. Elsewhere a sophisticated and innovative Snapshot Survey was carried out by the Research and Social Policy Unit for Client Profiling across (and involving) all service programs, supported by external consultants, including from universities. This provided baseline information about client characteristics that was invaluable for feeding back to staff and service users, and to inform marketing and fundraising staff and support advocacy.

Aided by postgraduate student research

The demographic data, coupled with the client profiling data provided by the Snapshot, informed organisational planning and the development of the research agenda and was intended to include a PhD scholarship established jointly with a partner university social work department (although this did not go ahead beyond the early stages).

Initial paper scoping the ideas

After the Research and Social Policy Unit had spent about a year exploring action research as a methodology that might sustain the work of the organisation and be consistent with the organisation's deeper values at the level of the service provide–service user interface, an 'Opportunities and Challenges' paper about action research in a large and diverse non-government organisation was prepared. This paper examined the current usage of research and evaluation in Melbourne Citymission.

Catalysts and champions' support from the 'middle', 'bottom' (frontline) and 'top' of the organisation, plus internal and external specialist consultancy, with external resources available (including a professional network, tertiary quality education and training, and written and online resources)

On the basis of this research and internal consultancy Melbourne Citymission assessed the existing situation against the criteria developed by the primary author as their external consultant[44] and found that, on the upside:

- The CEO saw action research as Melbourne Citymission's preferred model
- Both the Staff Learning and Development and Research Units had developed an appreciation of the methodology
- Several areas in the organisation were already experienced users (family, youth, Reconnect), there were external methodological support and resources available (a university action research program and a statewide systems and participatory inquiry, action research/learning peer support network)
- External funders increasingly required project and program evaluation to be built in from the outset.

Melbourne Citymission had a good record of sourcing needed funds for innovation to support such an initiative; internal and external education, training and workforce development capacity already existed; written action research material was available for further development; and an internal website was also thought to be a potential vehicle.

There were early signs of a high level of interest in forming an internal peer support community of practice of those using action research across the organisation, which might also help to guide the rolling out of a strategy. And finally there were more formal ways identified of building in the organisational commitment to action research in terms of annual business plans, monthly reporting against key indica-

tors, and a policy emphasis on the need for further user participation (e.g. a disability innovation grant).

Clarity regarding the challenges

On the other hand, given there is always tension between planning and reflection in 'the rush of emerging needs', there was as yet little reference to action research in organisational plans and strategic directions. Cross-organisational and standardised Quality Improvement work is more difficult in a dispersed, federated structure. Combined with often short-term project funding and task-focused job descriptions, it was still difficult to prioritise and quarantine time and space for deeper, 'bigger picture' longer term cultural change work and effective co-inquiry with service users.

Reflective practice located within the organisation's strategic directions 2006–2010, and Executive Team and CEO's endorsement

After a further period of time a discussion paper was prepared for the Melbourne Citymission executive that summarised a set of plans and co-ordinated actions to authorise and support 'Building a Culture of Reflection across Melbourne Citymission', taking into account a range of opportunities and challenges. The proposal cited the action research learning cycle as a way of conceptualising the vital role and substance of reflective practice, both for informal learning and more formal research, and to generate policy issues and identify needs for further research. The internal discussion paper noted that: 'MCM's diversity means that reflective practice will need to be "built in" in a variety of ways in particular program contexts'.

The subsequently executive-endorsed action plan included significant built in elements:

- Business plans to specify reflective practice
- The undertaking of a baseline staff survey
- Staff training
- A peer learning group (called the Catalyst Group)
- A communications plan
- A funding submission for resources
- Human Resources department to amend job descriptions
- Evaluation of the outcome of the work by the Research and Social Policy Unit and the Staff Learning and Development Unit, together with the general managers.

Not just a one-way staff survey regarding staff's needs but also a vehicle for drawing together an action research interest group (community of practice), and to be fully reported to the organisation

The follow-up survey of all staff (around 600 who received payslips, with 120 responding, or approximately twenty per cent of staff) became an 'interest-organiser' that fed into the planning of the train-the-trainer reflective practice workshops. These in turn led to commencing a register of all inquiry project questions that were being pursued by staff. The peer learning group was to meet face to face five to seven times over the following twenty months.

A thorough twenty-four page research report of the staff survey was prepared using SPSS and NVivo to analyse the results, and presented to the Catalyst Group.

Train-the-trainer reflective practice workshops, and follow-up consultancy

An initial one-day 'Professional Development Workshop—Reflective Practice Research for Strategic Change' was held as a 'Café of Possibilities' for fifteen strategically located staff, conducted by an experienced action research consultant from a university. This was followed by a day of consultancy to individual team projects and a later second whole-of-group workshop in which people reported progress on their inquiry projects. Eight of the fifteen who were peer committee members also attended an additional workshop session for facilitators of the group projects (the Catalyst Group). Table 11 describes the inquiry projects that resulted.

TABLE 11. MELBOURNE CITYMISSION STAFF'S REFLECTIVE PRACTICE RESEARCH TOPICS AND QUESTIONS

- When can you tell? Young homeless people's advice to workers about abuse disclosures
- Is private rental a realistic option for people from low income backgrounds?
- What is the best way to incorporate supports for non-verbal clients?
- What are effective ways to assist the staff (at a youth refuge) to learn about acquired brain injury?
- What are the expectations of the Continuous Quality Improvement system (at an aged care facility)?
- Understanding the experience of Middle Eastern populations
- Improving the success of a school holiday program by understanding why absenteeism has been a problem
- How beneficial are parent play groups?
- Is a play group an effective tool to link young mothers into the community?
- Exploring safety issues
- Caregivers' administration of medication: what are the predictors?
- How effective is secondment for the learning of a staff member?
- How can we build the culture of reflection across Melbourne Citymission?
- What makes an effective working group for informing research within a community organisation?
- What would it take to consolidate reflective practice within the family and youth team?
- Does the new case management model work?
- Getting the staff and client perspectives to resolve supervision problems
- How to improve information sharing across community services in the Western Region
- Committee of management participation
- How to align the perceptions of two groups of staff (management and 'subordinates') about issues of practice?
- Has the experience of the new induction process developed a greater sense of belonging to Melbourne Citymission?

An intranet web page for staff

An attractive internal web page was made for the participating staff that included:

- A colourful logo cartoon and a poetic inspiration
- The differently coloured café tablecloth 'teams'
- Photos of all participants
- Titles of their reflective practice research projects
- A chronology of the history of the reflective practice research project
- Supporting documents.

An executive briefing was provided on the Report of the Staff Survey on Reflection and Inquiry. The report was subsequently placed on the intranet and presented at other senior management meetings and forums.

Postscript: Internal consultancy and the continued meeting of the peer Catalyst Group (which joined with the action research training group) worked to further a reflective practice culture for another few years until 2007. The focus of the Research and Social Policy Unit (RSPU) then turned to the use of 'MORF', Melbourne Citymission's Measuring Outcomes and Results Framework, about which Anne Pate adds:

> MORF has been adapted from Mark Friedman's Results-Based Accountability. After trialing in four programs, each program is now supported by the RSPU to define client outcomes and identify and track performance measures. This process will further increase staff capacity for reflection on what they do, how they do it, how this can be improved, and the outcomes their programs achieve. The MORF will also greatly enhance Melbourne Citymission's ability to articulate its practice and how this intersects with policy objectives, providing an evidence base to inform our social policy and advocacy work.

By 2010 there was also a new CEO and a new head of the Research and Social Policy Unit.

TEN

An Indigenous art business narrative that builds in collective inquiring to 'reflect and shine'

Story narrator:
Kim Kruger for Shiny Shiny Blak Bling Collective[45]
Research commentary:
Yoland Wadsworth

Concluding this set of exemplars is a story from the world of small business to offer a glimpse of the relevance of the processes described in this book beyond human services to apply to *any* area of service, and beyond that to apply to social, political and economic life per se. The story not only describes modest participation in the economic production and exchange process, but may also be read as a narrative of a more 'wholly living inquiring economy'—a small *oikos*—or ethical home for the larger social 'we' (just as the household has been used in earlier chapters as a metaphor of the integral *oikos* for the individual self, group, organisation or community).

In this story we have the generation of living incomes from productive labour, but so much more than that. Instead of the processes of work and production being cut off from life (the all too familiar work/life split), work is integrated with the rest of life, embedded in and with family and community.[46]

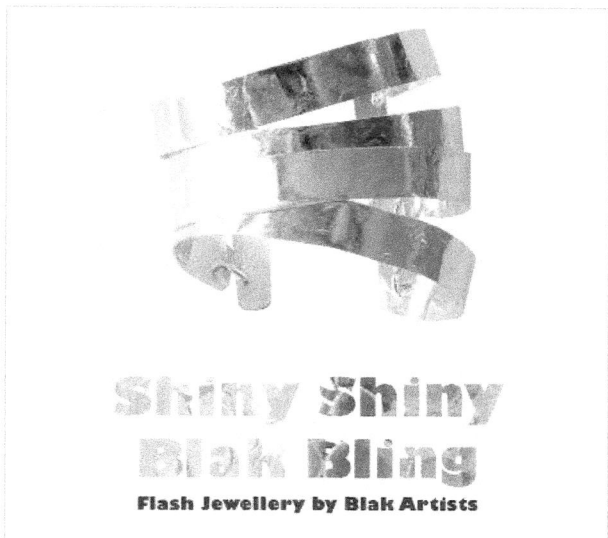

Shiny Shiny Blak Bling
Flash Jewellery by Blak Artists

The small publicity booklet for Shiny Shiny Blak Bling narrates the story of the commercial craft project's beginnings, its unfolding, and its conclusions to date about what might be seen as an energetic inquiry process bringing this small Indigenous art jewellery skills development and production collective to life. The commentary in the booklet effectively draws out the key conditions, properties and processes that animated and 'fed' this particular (more truly) living human system.

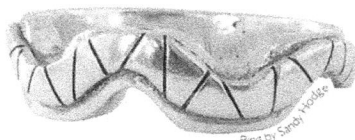

REFLECT and SHINE

The silver ring Shazzam, one of the first pieces of Shiny Shiny Blak Bling is now eternally with our dear tidda, friend, big cuzz, - Lisa Bellear. Community minded, welcoming, political, openminded, openhearted, compassionate, poetic, supportive, remembering the forgotten, protecting the weak, encouraging the strong and all those in between – Lisa was all these things. Things we took for everyday values, until we lost her. But with her in mind we can hold on to these values.

The story commenced with people's deepest heartfelt values

Its human, family, group and community values were embodied in the personhood of a loved tidda (sister), friend and cuzz (cousin).

In 2005 Donna Brown took a necklace by Siri Omberg to jeweller Peter Eccles to fix a broken link. Siri and Peter had worked together as jewellers and enjoyed competing for sales at Siri's renowned Emerald Hill Gallery in South Melbourne. While watching Peter work, Donna asked a million questions about jewellery making, and if he could show her how to work with silver. Donna started learning with Peter, they were soon making designs to involve other Blakfellas and Gail Harradine started learning too.

Then, looking back around the cycle, the narration *observes* closely how Shiny Shiny Blak Bling started. Where it came from. What happened. Who did what, when, where, how and why. The story began with a *discrepancy*. A broken necklace. But then there were 'a million' more questions, stemming from far deeper discrepancies of *interests, desires, unmet needs and the purposes they generated.*

After 6 months of parading around some deadly Bling, Donna and Gail approached other artists, applied for Skills Development funding from the Aboriginal & Torres Strait Islander Arts Board of the Australia Council for the Arts, and the Melbourne Blak Bling hand mill started rolling.

The learning processes *unfolded*; as and when *others observed and joined in*. Initial conclusions were drawn from going round the inquiry cycle for the first time. *Plans* made, and *action* taken to secure funding resources by beginning new human relationships into the wider world.

Peter open his workshop to six artists, an in-joke being some of us aren't artists at all. Coming from a long chain of jewellers, he was apprenticed at 15 to jewellery making. As he says now, he doesn't know how to do anything else. It's all he knows.

With tools and silver the group set up workshops in both Melbourne and country Victoria, with the equipment to continue to practice well into the future.

New meanings and identities were being made (or remade) together in close relation to another's doing-and-being—resonant with a vision of the desired long term.

Peter started with the hard task of making rings. No mucking around here. It seems tough, but Peter knew that all the skills the group would ever need for jewellery making, would be learnt in making a ring.

The new life of the 'second cycle' of the inquiry group is tested early for its strength of intention to traverse the difficult *Phase change 1* threshold from 'how things have been' to researching 'how things could instead be'. But artists are intent on emerging, and sensing-doing skills are acquired from an artisan who has a lifetime of practice wisdom drawn from mastering numerous hands-on learning cycles of his own.

> Peter's views on making jewellery filled the workshops like the rising silver dust. Pieces should be bold, chunky and visibly hand made. There's no point saving a couple of bucks on silver to end up with something tizzy and small. The pieces should be big and noticed. And no point making it look like it was stamped out at a factory. You can get that junk at any chain store. Seeing the hammer marks, the filing cuts, the hand sawn designs, shows it is hand-made by a real person who has spent time working on it, a one-off, unique piece that will never be made exactly the same again.
>
> *Ring by Kim Kruger*

The existing action-knowledge that the artists have asked to learn is coming from a received theory ('small is tizzy, but bold and visibly handmade are real'). And this offered theory of the 'bold, visible and culturally authentic' resonates with the real lifeworlds and contextual history of the group of nascent artists; and is adopted for new trial and error (or trial and success) by them.

> For some, first working with silver was filled with uncertainty. Silver is a precious metal. It's expensive. Why waste something so precious on Blakfellas? Silver is valuable. Blakfellas aren't.
>
> A lifetime of living in spite of, in opposition to, despite the prevailing racism of this country's culture, can make you not feel of value, uncertain, unconfident, hardened to interaction and life's harsh blows to protect what's at risk inside. A lot of effort goes into bolstering ourselves up, learning to value the important things in our culture, spending time with our mob and learning the family stories, history, achievements, cultural knowledge, and values. But no matter how much we are aware of our strengths, sometimes even this is not enough until it's translated into action.
>
> *Ring by Gail Harradine*

The existing life-depleting system's logic of excessive self-limiting are observed (sensed-felt), then more deeply *reflected* on and analysed (using intuitive-thinking) giving rise to a new theory—of the power of values-in-new-action.

> Working with silver does this. After working on a piece that is tarnished from soldering and lacklustre from acid, when the final process of polishing reveals the original design in shiny, shiny silver, it brings an enormous, immediate rush of achievement.

The new theory-in-action is checked (observed) through *reflection* on silver and its preciousness, and on Blakfellas moving from a lifetime of not being valued—and the desired metaphorical transformation, indicated by the autopoetic self-valuing that comes from deeply-felt value being *mirrored* back literally in the form of the external silver, is evidenced by the subsequent rush of energetic *inspired* achievement.

> Culture is expressed in another way, as old and new designs are forged. Working in groups artists come together to work, eat, baby-sit, gossip, fight and share the odd ring joke. Part of the process has been wearing other's Bling pieces to road test them, see how they're made, how they feel on the skin, how what we make suits other necks, hands, wrists, and have it shine in other circles. Another part has been supporting each other to work out the next stage in assembling a piece, making elements like chain, working out which bit to solder next, as well as mocking people to not get too big for their boots when they finish a really deadly piece.
>
> *Ring by Susan Liddle*

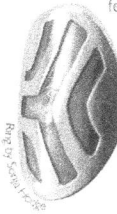

The group's co-existing social context for human co-regeneration and jewellery co-creation is described as comprising all of life—the whole *oikos*, including food, babies, care, conflict, gossip, celebration and humour—joined in the economic and collective evaluative research 'ring cycle', while self-confidently acknowledging both good work and (avoiding) 'big bootsism' on their own terms.

What has brought us together is the sharing of ideas, problem solving, determining our designs, translating family stories, reflecting on cultural symbols, and many other influences. We have been shaping our lives into silver and this has been quietly empowering.

We get to bash with hammers, blowtorch to the point of molten liquid, hand mill stubborn ingots into versatile wire, cure in acid to get rid of the tarnish, anneal with the torch again to relieve the tension, soften the metal, relax its molecular structure, madly file away the ragged edges and shape our own future. And still it is precious shiny silver. Just like it started. But shaped now with Blak thoughts, fears, hopes and designs.

And we are reminded again and reflect on the words of the poet Lisa Bellear:

> Keep on dreaming
> Keep on believing

Or to paraphrase
Shine On.

Kim Kruger May 2007

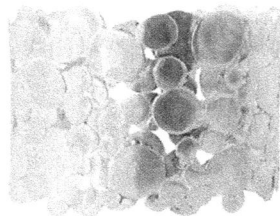

Cuff by Donna Brown

Finally, deeper *reflection* articulates the conditions and nature of the successful endeavour, succinctly defining the identity of the (intuitively felt and thought) nexus between 'silverwork' and 'Blakwork' as mutually shaping their 'shining on'.

The conditions[47] needed to build in[48] research and evaluation for living systems

...until it becomes 'How we do things around here'

The following draws out the key learnings from the forgoing exemplars (see Table 12 for a summary).

This is offered as something of an operational checklist to identify whether these conditions are being (or can be) instituted—remembering always that, while these come from an extensive and well-trialled evidence base, that practice base was itself situated and contextualised in times, places and relationships between real people, and these are always going to differ slightly (or a great deal) in any new setting. This section helps us avoid having to keep re-inventing the wheel, but at the same time we need to remember that not all of our human systems will have the 'staying power' and relevance of the wheel!

Beginning...

Encouragement of people's noticing and questioning

Organisational appreciation of anyone (clients, residents, other critical inquiry groups with professional or other staff,) pondering on their observations and queries, and actively encouraging them to share those observations and queries with several others, and then form (or work within existing) small but viable communities of practice inquiry (communities of 'practice science', communities of interest) to go forward and explore their issues, observations or reflections further. Change agency (and change agents), who are well connected to (i.e. grounded in) the field can help find the ways forward—essential to the continuing life of the organism.

For example: In the case of the U&I project this came initially in the form of the Deputy Director and then the Director of Nursing steadfastly supporting the contact and collaboration between the initiating social worker and the consumer organisation, and then all relevant researching parties for the next three years. In the case of Coonara it was the committee of management's support for the co-ordinator's idea of involving neighbourhood house members in social action research meetings facilitated by an external researcher, and later involving a member who was doing community development studies at university. At Glastonbury it was the CEO's initiative in contacting an experienced researcher who he'd heard articulate the paradox of staff wanting to hear from consumers and not wanting to hear from consumers, and then giving the go-ahead to involve clients. And at Melbourne Citymission the Research and Policy Unit began collaborating with the Teaching and Learning Unit about what staff had said about issues their clients were experiencing.

Continuing...

Core inquiry groups form and continue and are ongoing resourced

Organisational support is forthcoming for continuing and resourcing the small self-starting groups of questioning, curious, energetic 'driving interesteds' (approximately five to fifteen people) who become the inquiry 'culture carriers'; especially where including and privileging the critical inquirers or critical interest group's perspective as the 'compass' and source of driving interest for the inquiry, or where the critical inquirers have commenced the questioning themselves or have become strongly involved soon after inception. The core inquiry group works at first with those who see an issue and want change and actively want to inquire into it (rather than those who don't). Sceptical challenge is critical to research and evaluation, but not so early as to destroy it before it has had a chance to begin to clarify its desired form. This is a little like later in the cycle when any experiment needs firstly to be clear about what it is trialling or testing for, and then for the test to be adequately formed so it can indeed test the hypothesis.

As groups set out inductively to observe in more detail, begin to deepen their conversations with stakeholders or stakeowners to 'map and name the territory', form clarity out of the initial confusion, perhaps conduct a survey to gauge the extent of an issue or the interest in it, review existing 'data', sceptically challenge old assumptions, then reflect together on the 'data', analysing it, and drawing new conclusions with fresh implications for practice— ready for the deductive phase of trial and error (or

---

TABLE 12. SUMMARY OF CONDITIONS NEEDED TO BUILD IN RESEARCH AND EVALUATION FOR LIVING SYSTEMS

Beginning Encouragement of people's noticing and questioning

Continuing Core inquiry groups form and continue and are ongoingly resourced

For whom/for what? Critical inquirers-only groups may be needed

Who else? Wider collaborating networks of co-inquirers may grow and 'go to greater scale'

Scaling up and out Active interest from and ongoing working with people at all levels of the formal goals-objectives-aims-activities hierarchy, from micro to macro, and at all levels of the formal organisation, as well as throughout informal organisational networks

How? Drawing on a sequence of change-oriented (and consolidation-oriented) questions using a wide range of traditional and innovative research methods or techniques that can 'go full cycle'

Where and when? Embedded in, attached to, or carved out from existing meaningful organisational structures and processes

Facilitated by? Drawing on both internal and external resourcing, funding and supports, including:

- Meetings and networks
- Identified insiders (and outsiders) to act as facilitators
- Standing committees, working groups
- Job descriptions
- Registers of research and evaluation projects
- Individual work plans, service annual plans, program or organisational three-year plans
- Service agreements/contract reporting requirements
- Further education and consultancy
- Websites, chat rooms, e-list services and written and multi-media texts
- Budget and funds

success)—they may also need some funding and technical resourcing (e.g. time set aside in work plans, or other sources of living incomes for any who are non-salaried; plus office and meetings facilities, supporters and champions etc.)

This idea of iterative or recursive emergence is critical here, as the cycles of inquiry may most often start small, divert, diversify and so on, and may need to do so over some time, as:

> ...developing a theory is not so much an event as a process. As new data emerge, existing hypotheses may prove inadequate...the sense of what needs to be looked at and reported on may change, and explanations about what is going on may be supplanted by ones which seem to fit better. Such an approach is consonant with emergent design... (Massey 1998)

For example: Specific-purpose inquiry groups include research committees that have morphed into active inquiry groups in their own right—(as at Coonara or the mixed group of nurses who oversaw a nursing union study of fragmentation [Wadsworth, 1980]); or the core group of fifteen in the U&I study (Wadsworth 1998: 357). Or action learning style 'sets' such as the Lakewaters Hospital inquiry group, or staff–client panels such as at Glastonbury, or the Victoria University departmental staff reflection groups, the NEAR project's writers' groups, or Melbourne City-mission's café of possibilities 'table groups'.

For who/for what?

Critical inquirers-only groups may be needed

It is essential that organisations support the critical parties (end-beneficiaries) in both their inquiry, and their 'compass' and critical judgement, by having the chance to express their voice freely and safely. Early in any process this may most easily take place among others experiencing the same situation, thus providing the greatest chance of epistemic resonance and testimonial justice (Fricker 2007) and understanding (e.g. in a self-chosen self-help, mutual or peer support group, or possibly an offshoot, independently situated, or as the executive of the inquiry group). Support is needed for a similar process for any others who

experience relative powerlessness (who may not be the critical inquiry group). 'Critical friends' may be sought by critical inquirers, possibly from 'other' non-critical reference group/s if that is seen as desirable by them. (And most particularly, if the group experiencing less power are *not* the critical inquirers, but a secondary critical reference group, such as 'carers' or beleaguered staff, whose interests nevertheless are or need to be aligned with the critical inquirers they are wanting to be 'there for'.) This may need some funded and technical resourcing (e.g. fees for service, office and meetings facilities, and payment of mentor/supporters). Groups need to be enabled to emerge autopoetically rather than procedurally organised ('would you like to meet?' rather than 'you have now been allocated to a critical inquirers' group'!)

For example: A particularly successful critical inquiry group would be the Consumer Consultants Group that formed during the U&I study (Wadsworth 2001). As well as consulting to the U&I collaborative inquiry group and many other mental health services, it continued to emerge and ultimately incorporate as a community association and produce and publish its own literature (e.g. Melbourne Consumer Consultants' Group The Ultimate Exit Survey—Do You Mind...? 1997). The Glastonbury, Coonara and Shiny Shiny Blak Bling exemplars also illuminate the power of interested critical reference groups (clients or communities)taking the initiative, and being resourced and assisted by others.

Who else?

Wider collaborating networks of co-inquirers may grow and 'go to greater scale'

Organisations interested in system-wide inquiry need to find effective ways of nurturing the core inquiry group to extend or engage iteratively to involve additional and eventually all relevant stakeholders and stakeowners in collaborative or co-operative inquiry (including organisational decision makers and 'external' contributors as well as practitioners and end-beneficiary groups). In this way an identifiable network (of up to hundreds or more) may form and in turn become system-wide nodes of group or individual 'culture-carriers'. It may have less involvement per se than the core inquiry group but retains an interest in feedback and feed-in to the ongoing dialogic process, including dialogue within and between itself (not just network nodes to core inquiry group). It may comprise various participants in smaller inquiry nodes, dialogue groups or teams nested within a larger effort or isolated individuals; or other kinds of research, evaluation or peer learning groups. It represents and determines the system-wide reach and impact of the inquiry processes. In this way it operates as part of an ever larger feed-in and feedback living system (depending on the scope of the issue, topic or question). It may also need some funded and technical resourcing (e.g. new bulletins, a website, send-outs, chances to meet and communicate etc.) It may mostly be those who have come to learn from the inquiry experience, but may also include those who are resisting, defending, or otherwise.

Over time it may consolidate into a more formal collaboration or set of partnerships between groups, teams or co-operative communities of inquiry.

For example: Different examples of this would be the thirteen local geographic community area-based clusters of people associated with between three and six community-based early childhood services within a local government-wide services research and development project (Wadsworth 1976: 29–45); the twenty-two different kinds of professional paediatric hospital and community nursing groups across Victoria collaborating in a project about the impact of fragmentation on parents and children (Wadsworth 1980: 4–27); the thirty-five small action research projects across different wards, units and other organisational units that made up the U&I hospital-area-region-based consumer–staff collaborative evaluation project (Wadsworth 2001), or the four different service program 'table groups' from the initial Café of Possibilities workshop with which the Melbourne Citymission commenced its action research capacity-building process.

Scaling up and out

Active interest from, and ongoing working with, people at all levels of the goals-objectives-aims-activities hierarchy, from micro to macro, and throughout both the formal organisation and its informal networks

Policy makers, funders and management's active interest and involvement (not just support) is demonstrated in expressed permission and authorisation of inquiry and of taking risks (and expecting error), identification and reinforcement of rewards for engaging in inquiry that result in learning and in active involvement in the processes (including rewarding mistakes or false starts that become part of an inquiry process narrative)—and in the same active interest and involvement from all other relevant people in strategic locations all the way to the 'frontline'. These too may become involved in communicating with and meeting regularly (or as part of) the inquiry group. In some ways this serves as an indicator of system-wide inquiry—both as a goal and also as an audit criterion. Too top heavy or too middle heavy or only bottom up will mean the critical exclusion of necessary observations, experiences, insights, or expertise. This matter of achieving systemic scale relates to achieving 'critical mass'—the significant spread and volume of intention and action throughout an 'organism' that provides a tipping point difference between establishing a culture of inquiry and one that decays.

For example: The U&I project was a particular achiever on this count starting in one ward and extending up and out to the whole hospital, area, region and state, and eventually working with national and finally international policy making; as was the Knox Project for as long as it retained its research facilitation. Reconnect effectively tic-tacked between national, local and regional scales and NEAR between local and regional (and to a lesser extent) state levels. The Grampians Community Health Centre and Melbourne Citymission took it from the organisation-overview level to service and program specific to agency-wide (in the Grampians Community Health Centre case also including its executive Core Group and Board's participation). Coonara took it from being a special project to integration in its various education and children's programs as well as involving its Executive and Committee. Everyday Evaluation on the Run (1997b: Chapter 3) details examples at different scales, from individual personal reflection, to weekly reviews, special effort 'spot' surveys or built in routine observation, monthly collective problem-solving 'open inquiry' sessions, annual what-we-achieved and where-will-we-need to head next year workshops, and comprehensive program evaluations every three to ten years (resting on what is relevant at that scale, and not needing to drill down into full detail, this having been collected at a different scale of evaluation effort).

How?

Drawing on a sequence of change-oriented (and consolidation-oriented) questions using a wide range of traditional and innovative research methods or techniques to 'go full cycle'

Participants at all scales of inquiry become adept at using the mental architecture of an observe–reflect–plan–act–observe again full inquiry cycle. This means they can more consciously and effectively self-manage as continuously evolving adaptive-generative systems rather than as systems pre-'engineered' for predictability. This is not the same as 'always changing' and remaining in continuous implicate order (chaos), but always changing to sustain *enough* balance and replicating of ordering and *enough* change for adaptability or generativity, at whatever scale.

The art of progress is to preserve order amid change, and change amid order.
ALFRED NORTH WHITEHEAD,
ENGLISH PHILOSOPHER, 1929

To achieve this, a wide variety of detailed strategic questions, methods and techniques, drawing on all the key human capabilities (sensing, feeling, perceiving, experiencing, intuiting and thinking, judging, concluding, trial-enacting) help navigate the inquiry cycles, with innovative methods taking their place alongside more traditional methods. 'Mixed methods' is a currently popular expression of this, although its meaning here is less about triangulation to get 'the' truth, as to get all the different stakeholders' and stakeowners' truths, experiences, data and

perspectives, and to enable dialogue between participants about them, and about their bearing on future action. All methods and questions need to meet the challenge of achieving both (one-way) input and (two-way) communication (speaking and listening), dialogue and feedback about the input, data and experience in order for the inquirers or communities of inquirers to effectively form their judgements and analyses, derive insights, develop new theories and plan and take new actions.

For example: The U&I project drew on an extensive range of consumer participation methods and techniques (from formal complaints mechanisms, surveys and consumer-led discussion groups, right through to heightened awareness of 'normal conversation' between psychiatrist and patient as co-inquiry) in search of ways that could be built in to the fabric of mental health services to bridge the gaps between staff and consumers (Wadsworth 2001: 59–123). A strategic sequence of action research questions like those detailed in Chapter 3 were used in the U&I project, the hospital work, the Grampians Community Health Centre, Melbourne Citymission and NEAR workplace education.

Where and when?

Embedded in, attached to, or carved out from existing meaningful organisational structures and processes

All such inquiry processes need to find 'handholds' to become incorporated into the organism's (the individual's, group's, organisation's) 'fabric of lifeworld practices' and in recurring 'sites and moments' over substantial enough periods of time, for example a calendar of activity times, a 'mapping' of geographical places; linked to opportune structures such as OL (Organisational Learning), OD (Organisational Development), QA/QI (Quality Assurance or Quality Improvement), TQM (Total Quality Management), HR (Human Resources, Personnel or People Management), T&L (Teaching and Learning or Professional Development), CD (community development), CB (capacity building), strategic planning, other information and communications feedback systems or, in at least one documented instance, to the national constitution!

...plus in whatever will be the future linguistic, discourse, jargon or 'namings' of these kinds of practices. Language is thus one such 'site' and the different exemplars each reached for the best terminology within their own pre-existing cultures to try and express the new ideas. Important handholds have been where organisations have managed to retain or reintroduce a research office or evaluation unit (internal-externals), where the heads of research and evaluation units are part of management executive, co-ordinating or leadership groups, or have instituted arrangements with external-internal researchers or evaluators (in academe or private consultancy businesses) to develop a shared journey or history across several projects together. In most cases new 'spaces and places' must be carved out from existing structures and processes.

For example: Both Melbourne Citymission and Scope have their own research units. The U&I project found 'hooks' on which to hang the work in the hospital's then nascent Quality Assurance procedures (Wadsworth with Epstein 2001: 52–58), and were invited to take up on-site geographic location in the on-site nursing research institute, and later in the offices of the area mental health services. Other organisations have incorporated action research encouragement in their human resources, customer relations or quality improvement structures. In terms of language, Reconnect adopted the language of 'action research', which was more familiar in youth and education settings, while Scope, Glastonbury and Melbourne Citymission used the language of 'practice research' or 'reflective practice' as more familiar in social work discourse; and the Grampians Community Health Centre saw it as 'evaluation' given health's focus on outputs, outcomes, cost-benefits and improvement.

Facilitated by?

Drawing on both internal and external research and evaluation resourcing, funding and supports

To resource all of the above and prevent efforts from being one-off, short-term or discontinuous, or to strengthen and deepen to avoid only 'quick fixes' or overly shallow 'single loop' puzzle solving, the exemplars drew on:

Meetings and networks in which the inquiry group or extended networks can take time out from 'action' to move into 'reflection' and to 'come to the table' to share their experiences and raise questions (e.g. regularly scheduled special project meetings, planning and review meetings, seminars, learning conferences, forums and follow-up forums, ordinary regular staff meetings, professional association activities, peer groups, community meetings, residential retreats and in-depth dialogue opportunities—especially, for example for the development of shared language, or theoretical breakthroughs).

> Those who work in Stephen Hawking's lab…consider interaction and brainstorming so important that they structure it into their day. Twice a day everyone gathers in the Interaction Room for tea and theory. (Shepherd 1993: 167)

Or as Susan Blackmore the psychologist has put it:

> Neural…cells that fire together, wire together. (Blackmore 2000)[49]

Identified insiders (and outsiders) act as critical-appreciative facilitators: catalysts, consultants, educators, advocates, coaches and champions, who are experienced and confident enough about their grasp of 'whole cycle' inquiry, to be able to assist others journey from wherever they are to where they want to be, for example:

- To help people's emergent inquiry designs remain purposeful, focused, effective and do-able
- To help people think through any issues that might be arising, and flexible in response (or re-design in emergence); while remembering that 'flexible' derives from the Latin *flectere*, meaning 'to bend', and that too much bending can mean loss of the living organism's integral shape or form that may have its own valued purposes
- To ensure rigour, whether this means being sufficiently comprehensive, accurately evidenced, to avoid 'second guessing', comparative to observe change, sceptical, or logically exact in conjecture or experimentation, or orderly or organised (while remembering 'rigour' derives from the Latin *rigere*, meaning 'to be stiff'; so hold off on extremes of harshness, severity and restriction for the sake of the living organism)
- To assist identify any special conditions for

involving and hearing from critical reference groups or other stakeowners or stakeholders
- To advise on methods and techniques, both traditional and innovative
- To find and/or inject ideas from elsewhere that may help resource any stage
- To convey or help develop a shared conceptual 'second language' or mental architecture to be able to discuss where the inquiry has come from, is at, and might need to go next
- To assist those at *plan* to check they are well grounded in *observe* and *reflect* before moving to enact
- To assist those in *act* to check back to explain why, and move forward to *observe* and *reflect*
- To assist those in *observe* to move to *reflect* on action and move forward to envision new forms in terms of the purposes of the inquiry
- To assist those in *reflect* to go deeper, to re-examine the evidence, hear new perspectives in experience and see new patterns in the data of observation in the light of purposes, and to effectively ground new theory and practice while making connections that may not have been seen before
- To help weed out questions that do not assist the inquirer's purposes or lead nowhere, and identify sequences of questions that successfully achieve full cycle inquiry
- To do all of this at any scale[50]

Standing committees, working groups, job descriptions and work plans, registers of research and evaluation projects, annual and three-year plans, or service agreements/contract reporting requirements: Through positive support and sanction (e.g. requirements to continue to regularly report on new action research questions or projects; and to demonstrate adequate collaboration with critical inquiry groups and involvement of other stakeholders and stakeowners; to show that new problems and issues are replacing old ones that have been resolved or addressed etc.) people carve out the time to monitor and prioritise keeping inquiry going, overcoming the inevitable inertia that comes with having 'got things right' at 'the end' of a cycle of inquiry.

Further education and consultancy: To deepen understanding of the methodology and its use in practice and to continue the process of identifying new questions and scanning for emerging issues—provide facilitated peer teacher–learner opportunities using a train-the-trainer philosophy through introductory one-day workshops, short courses, practice-based training, workforce professional development, workplace- and community-based higher education, postgraduate study, 'mastery classes' and so on, supplemented with follow-up and ongoing consultancy for projects arising out of these.

Other communications media, websites, chat rooms, e-list services and written and multi- media texts: To 'feed' the inquiry with ideas, guidance, structure, tips, innovative methods and conceptual terminology and more, plus both internally produced write-ups and externally published articles, books, polices, protocols, pro-formas, procedures, facilitators' manuals, articles, papers, bibliographies, libraries, wall charts and posters, and tips and guidelines.

Budget and funds (including discretionary): To support all of the above as well as newly emerging activity, for example by start-up exploratory 'seeding' and 'seedling' grants; encouragement 'sapling' grants; consolidating full project 'tree' grants; followed by ongoing or regular iterative or recursive system-wide 'forest' funding. Such funding to be built into budgets to extend to *all* co-researching participants, including critical inquirers, critical inquiry groups, critical-appreciative consultants and sitting fees for stakeowners. In human services this is work for the purposes of service improvement and should be reimbursed as such. It is not volunteer work (for as long as staff's work for service improvement is also not voluntary). Discretionary funds for the critical inquiry or co-inquiring group are also an important component in support of emerging inquiry work.

ENDNOTES

1 I thank Marie Brennan and Lynton Brown for assisting with this short account which cannot do justice to what was a large, significant and internationally influential initiative in education in Australia.

2 A sign of this loss of human centredness might be, as previously mentioned, the consigning of human services (even the most highly sensitive such as disability, mental health and Indigenous) to the Tenders area of classified notices in public newspapers along side footpaths, public works and timber consignment. Or where consultants were to have no personal contact with the human systems in which they were to be co-inquiring in the name of national business 'competition policy'.

3 Although it is worth noting that, ten years later, some of these systems *have* decayed and feedback forms are not such an obvious feature of so many services any more. Workers may have come to feel they were either not learning anything new, or were powerless to change the quality of service, and customers may have become discouraged by not seeing much change as a result either. Appreciative inquiry as part of a burgeoning action research movement has offered an important circuit breaker for such loss of momentum.

4 I thank Bronwyn McDonald and Patricia Rogers for their responses and contributions to this account.

5 See its comparability to the sequence of action research questions in Chapter 3—or the TOP website for a diagrammatic depiction that illustrates the joined-up (cyclic) feedback version of Bennett and Rockwell's inverted 'hierarchy' (2008).

6 I thank Jon Kroschel and Merinda Epstein for their reading of this account and judgement that it sufficiently represented the U&I experience.

7 I was research design consultant to the auspicing consumer organisation on all phases of this work and co-facilitator with the U&I research officer Merinda Epstein. The work took place in Melbourne, Australia.
It is difficult to do justice to the size and complexity of the combined efforts of the more than 300 people who participated in these projects over nearly ten years. However the U&I work was extensively documented in published form in part because it was breaking such new ground, and in part—as Australia's first major health research grant awarded to a consumer organisation—because it was concerned to fully evidence its practice-based findings. There were four monographs and a manual: McGuiness and Wadsworth (1991), Epstein and Wadsworth (1994), Wadsworth and Epstein (1996a, 1996b, 1996c); a compendium: Wadsworth in association with Epstein (2001b); a book of policy advice published by the Melbourne Consumer Consultants Group (1997); a book chapter on its facilitation: Wadsworth (2001a); articles on

its use of dialogue: Wadsworth (1998), and its theory of the paradox and culture of acute psychiatric services: Wadsworth and Epstein (1998).

8 In Chapter 2 the U&I story was told in terms of us coming to see ourselves as inquiring within a large, complex, living breathing interconnected 'organism'—and of doing so systemically from a small beginning in a single ward, outwards and upwards throughout the whole hospital, to the mental health service regionally, to the central state department and eventually at the national government and finally the global consumer policy level. In Chapter 3 the U&I story was seen from the point of view of its operation as multiple inquiry processes and methods to build in consumer evaluation and staff–consumer collaboration on all the tasks of reflection, planning and trialling new actions. In Chapter 4 the U&I and sequel US studies were examined for what was learned about the ways in which the hospital as a complex living 'organism' protected itself from change—but, like an autoimmune response, how this also 'protected' itself from acting on its deepest values on assisting its end users to a fuller autopoetic life. Here in Chapter 5 the U&I project is described in terms of the 'structures' (or components) and conditions that it researched and developed to prefigure sustainable built in systems of inquiry-for-improvement in the long term.

9 These were: a contracted researcher's report—*Unlocking the System*; a collaborative pilot study with staff and consumers—*Understanding, Anytime*; the three-year main research study—the *U&I Project*, volumes 1, 2 and 3; an implementation study—the Royal Melbourne Hospital case trial and principles and practice *Manual for Consumer Consultants*; a volume of consumer consultants' advice on policy topics—*'Do you mind?' the Ultimate Exit Survey*; a consumer-conducted teaching and learning project—The Lemontree Project; and a Deep Dialogue project. A further ten years saw the continued independent researching of the ideas by consumer consultants in other hospitals, the University of Melbourne, a specialist 'Personality Disorders' service, take up in state departmental Consumer Participation Policy, and the statewide funding of consumer consultants (e.g. the work of Allan Pinches, Merinda Epstein, Jon Kroschel and Cath Roper).

10 Although the research and evaluation design consultant was me, I'll stick to telling this story in the third person so this exemplar can stand conceptually 'out there' in shared space and be analysed as the combined results of an 'achieved we' (Wadsworth 2001) rather than erroneously as the personal achievement of any one individual. I have written about the facilitation of this project through my own eyes elsewhere (in 'The Mirror, the Magnifying Glass, the Compass and the Map—Facilitating Participatory Action Research', in Reason and Bradbury 2001).

11 From the French *repertoire*, meaning 'again'; and the Latin *at*, 'before', and *portare*, 'carry'.

12 At the time, it was not conceptualised as a pilot but as a twelve-month study. However its success in making explicit the power of a dialogic design that did justice to both staff members' and consumers' voices provided the basis for emergence from small to large scale. It then attracted Australia's first major health research grant to a consumer organisation (from the Victorian Health Promotion Foundation) for three years for the main U&I action research study.

13 Keen readers may recognise this is *Phase change 1* in the inquiry cycle—at the threshold between observing how things had been on the hospital wards, and registering a 'strong enough' need and desire for change.

14 This is a model in the sense of describing a coherent set of factors working together to achieve an outcome in non-linear ways in this context and which others might recognise as valuable if their situations were comparable.

15 The systemic reach of the project was achieved over many years by the development of a core research work team of three consumer researchers and a research consultant; an 'inner inquiry group' (Collaborative Committee) of around a dozen (half staff and half consumers) which later became a Collaborative QA seminar of up to thirty people; a broader inquiry network which included the sixty staff and consumers who took part in the ward-based interviews, discussions and thirty-five small sub-projects, and later expanded to around 200 people strategically located throughout the state and national mental health system; plus a self-organised group of around twelve to fifteen consumers who were working as paid consultants in a range of different capacities (interviewers, librarians, committee members, policy commentators, speakers etc.) both within the project then increasingly called on by other services at area, regional and state government levels.

16 One of the key achievements and most long-lasting structural changes was the introduction of a new category of staff—that of consumer consultant—with a participatory research or quality improvement brief to aid the continuing dialogue between staff and fellow consumers. Not only is there now an enduring network (that has lasted over a decade) of consumer consultants throughout acute psychiatric, community mental health, rehabilitation and forensic mental health service settings in the state of Victoria, but the idea has spread to other human services, e.g. peer or community liaison, consumer or customer advocates or consultants within general hospitals, community health, culturally and linguistically diverse groups, local government, the utilities, private medical practice, legal centres, homelessness, drug and alcohol and Indigenous services. A key risk in these jobs (beside being isolated by single instead of the recommended team appointments, or subject to burn-out when too much was

expected), was to slip from *facilitating* dialogue and collaboration *between* staff and consumers to *substituting for* consumers and representing their views to staff without further joint collaboration by staff with consumers themselves on service improvement.

17 Published with the permission of the author. The poem was published on the cover of *The Essential U&I* (Wadsworth and Epstein 2001).

18 I thank Phil Crane, a long-time consultant to this program, for his valuable input into the draft of this exemplar.

19 There is further political complexity here, common to many efforts to introduce a change methodology like action research. In this case it had a bearing on the government's embracing of the Reconnect program, and thus action research. For example, this was a Minister who was a conventional political liberal with views about the rights of individuals to a better life (including taking a strong policy position against violence in the home, especially violence against women). However the then prime minister approved of Reconnect because of his own traditional conservative liberal belief that young people belonged in their families, something he insisted on enforcing behaviourally by removing income support for under eighteen year olds. The Taskforce, appreciating the potential for a narrow family re-unification approach to be seen as the goal of early into youth homelessness, carefully defined family reconciliation as having an emphasis on maximising ongoing family connection and relationship rather than prioritising where a young person lived (Prime Ministerial Youth Homeless Taskforce 1998). This approach to defining family reconciliation provided a robust basis for recognising the importance of family connection while also responding appropriately to the variety of living situations young people were experiencing (including family violence).

20 This more bottom-up and horizontal-across approach was in some contrast to another action research initiative by the same department which proceeded more top-down by awarding a contract to a large reputable government research institute (without experience of action research) to provide a national 'action research learning exchange' to resource small local communities that were part of the national 'Strengthening Families, Strengthening Communities' initiative. While this national SFLEX (Strengthening Families Learning Exchange) project appointed ten of Australia's most experienced and well-known participatory action research facilitators, and accomplished some outstanding work the initiative lacked a history of developing out of a densely supported local and regional presence and succumbed quickly to changed central political priorities in the context of a national election. The field soon lost much of this hard-won practice wisdom (including a high-quality manual—'Exploring Action Research in Your Project' by Katrina Bredhauer and Kelley Johnson—that was never published).

21 I worked with Dean Fraser on this as facilitator, as well as with other Reconnect workers, to produce some small written guides, a published journal article (Wadsworth 2002) and advanced workshops for potential trainers at one of the Reconnect national action research training conferences.

22 I thank Julie O'Brien for her input to checking this account for publication. Permission to publish the original monograph from which it is taken was provided by Mercy Aged Care & Health. I thank all members of the inquiry group for their editing and permissions on the original transcripts and report drafts.

23 Facilitated by myself (a university consultant) and a member of the Board who was a pastoral care educator in the larger auspicing body and who shared an interest in hearing from consumers and was also experienced in using a reflective practice methodology drawing on Paulo Freire's use of visual imagery as an inquiry technique. The action learning inquiry group comprised the two of us plus eleven senior staff members from all areas of the hospital—the CEO/director of nursing services, the business manager, the consulting suites manager, the medical director of emergency care, three nurse unit managers, two other experienced nurses, a social worker and the hospital chaplain. The group met six times in 1997 and while the work was formally completed a year later, some members continued to work on the 'problem of the paradox' (of wanting to hear from patients and not wanting to hear) until 2001.

24 This comprehensive resource to assist consumer participation in health was produced for the federally funded Consumer Focus Collaboration between the Department of Public Health, Flinders University and the South Australian Community Health Research Unit. The 148-page guide regrettably remained in the 'grey literature', though it is available for downloading from the *Participate in Health* website of the former National Consumer Participation in Health Centre, now managed by the Health Issues Centre in Victoria: http://www.participateinhealth. org.au/Clearing house/Docs/improvingguide.zip. The guide is 'for people working in health care organisations who want to increase consumer participation in the planning, management and evaluation of those organisations' and covers assessment and planning, some 'tools', managing the challenges, evaluation, frequently asked questions, and resources.

25 Indeed the local hospital efforts eased off when the department pulled back from requiring a comprehensive package of consumer participation methods instead opting pragmatically only for a single central patient satisfaction questionnaire and a community representative on hospital committees.

26 I thank Jenny Duffield for her input into editing this account as an accurate record of the work that had been done at Glastonbury.

27 I thank Leanne Fitzgerald for her input to editing this

account of the Taskforce's work at Coonara and for providing the additional postscript text.

28 Jan Bourne brought me in to work at Coonara at this point as a facilitator of a social action research project to address this issue.

29 Elsewhere I have described this as 'Navigating by Embodied Emotion' (unpublished paper to the 1997 Australian Sociology Association (TASA) conference, Wollongong, Australia)

30 I think this reflective-intuitive skill sometimes takes longer to nurture in groups—the ability to make connections between apparently disparate and distal observations to answer deeper questions, for example, 'What are we seeing here?' or 'Why is such and such occurring as it is?' or 'What have we learned that takes us beyond where we started?' or 'Where might the implications of this now lead us?'

31 Many online surveys unfortunately default to predetermined fixed choice answers, and Coonara's ageing research consultant then provided a list of strategic questions to better assist the young women not only collect data about 'how things were' for the girls they were questioning but also to gather their views *about* those situations, plus their ideas for 'what they could do instead'.

32 I thanks Heather Gridley for her reading of this account and assistance in ensuring it was an accurate representation of the work done.

33 An action research resource used widely at the secondary school level is the Student Action Team (SAT) process developed at the Youth Research Centre at the University of Melbourne by Roger Holdsworth. He notes that 'Student participation approaches, like Student Action Teams, are about supporting young people to question, construct and develop the sorts of multiple communities in which they live and wish to live' (Holdsworth 2006: 4) and, one could add, educational institutions in which they study, and future workplaces in which they will work (and in which they would want to study and work). In one example Student Action Teams were used to study student engagement. The students developed a sturdy database of factors and measurements regarding what engages students' interest and generated hypotheses and plans for testing them (Jackson and Smith 2007).

34 While at Victoria University in this capacity I researched the building in of research, evaluation and continuous inquiry to three settings—health, education and welfare. Glastonbury was the welfare case study. This, my own psychology department, was the education one. And the Lakewaters general hospital was the health case study.

35 I thank Jill Miller and Kerry Heinrich for overseeing the input to finalising this account as an accurate record of the work. Each of my narrative accounts of individual people's or group's practice has been carefully checked by those concerned and in some cases pennames have been chosen by them. I thank all members of staff for their permission to publish these accounts of our work together.

36 *Standard annual cycle*

Jan.–Feb.   Staff and programs commence the year on the basis of the previous year's assessment and planning

March   Staff weekend strengthens teams and collaboration for this year's action

April   The Board and the Core Group of senior program managers touch base with new community trends

May   Consumer input emerges after early months of work, plus formal needs identification

June   Annual 'mid-winter reflection' consultancy for staff evaluation of their practices/services

July   Core Group self-appraisals and commence strategic thinking

August   The Board, Core Group and all staff's annual planning week (includes QICSA report)

Sept.–Oct.   Individually and in teams, staff self-appraisals towards implementing agency plans for next year

Novvember   Staff hold 'Fish Day', a 'swap meet' to share ideas for detailed responses to emerging issues and for identifying staff and teams for new projects and continuing programs in the coming year

December   End of year celebrations and closure

37 I am the consultant.

38 Tragically, Brett Baker died in March 2008, after surgery. I continue to miss Brett's contribution and the depth and significance of his way of being-in-the-world that yielded such a thoughtful, reflexive and heartfelt professional working style. His capacity for receptivity reminds me of Lebanese philosopher Kahlil Gibran's observation that the more a cup is carved out, the more it can hold (1972, p. 36).

39 As noted in Chapter 4, St Lukes Innovative Resources have become internationally known for their strengths-based visual resources. The website discussing scaling kits and some of the uses made of them is available at http://innovativeresources.ezywiz.biz/default.asp?Initialcon tentID=21208. The scaling kit is also illustrated in Chapter 3 at the end of Question 1.

40 I thank the other members of the team involved in this work for their reading of and contributions to this exemplar: Karen Goltz from the auspicing region of the Department of Health, and Gai Wilson, McCaughey VicHealth Centre and Ani Wierenga, Youth Research Centre, both of the University of Melbourne.

41 This exemplar is co-authored by Yoland Wadsworth, consultant to Melbourne Citymission, Anne Pate, research officer, Research and Social Policy Unit Melbourne Citymission; David Carlos, manager, Staff Learning and Development, Melbourne Citymission. Permission for its publication has kindly been provided by Melbourne Citymission.

42 Others with whom I have worked similarly to build in reflective action research practice include Scope (formerly the Spastic Society of Victoria), a national government welfare income support agency in three states, and the seventeen community health centres participating in the NEAR project.

43 There are matters of scale that relate to success here. Several full-day workshops and consultancy sessions with a highly procedural pyramidal organisation of 26 000 staff and 6.25 million clients may expect less likelihood of persisting culture shift than the same input to an organisation like Melbourne Citymission with only 700 staff who see 4000 clients a week and have a strong practice and philosophy of responsiveness to build inclusive communities to support people.

44 These are the criteria I had derived from the U&I and US (Understanding Staff) projects and refined on the basis of my experience with all the other exemplars described—a summary of which appears at the conclusion of the exemplars in this chapter.

45 Shiny Shiny Blak Bling collective members in 2007 were: Donna Brown, Gail Harradine, Sandy Hodge, Sonja Hodge, Kim Kruger and Kye McGuire. I thank Kim Kruger for agreeing to work with me on this exemplar on behalf of the collective and for giving me editing advice and the collective's permission for the use of my research commentary.

46 At the same time, on the other side of the planet, the Danish home ware company Bodum® was finding the value of closing the work/life gap as well. In celebrating sixty years of successful business it explained how it had realised that its philosophy rested on its designers and staff being 'specialists in everyday life' which 'only just begins when we leave work'. In having dinner parties, eating breakfast or being particular about their kitchen knife, they noted they 'can't help but think' about bringing their 'work to home' and 'home to work' in continuous cycles of observation, invention and experiment (Bodum® store brochure, Copenhagen 2005).

47 'Strategies' is an alternative term to 'conditions' but is commonly used with rather militaristic connotations of 'cunning plans for deceiving enemies' which doesn't sit quite so well with the idea of open systemic inquiry! The term 'mechanisms' is also a commonly used alternative, but tends to reduce the ideas to being 'things' rather than, in practice, ways people relate to each other. The term 'component' could also be used here as it has a systems' meaning as 'a part of a greater whole', as does 'infrastructure' as the basic building blocks or structural foundations. However I think the term 'conditions' better gets at the circumstantial and dynamic provisionality (from the Latin *com*, 'together, jointly' and *dicare*, 'to agree') of what might otherwise risk being seen as a matter of 'adding on' separate elements in a rather mechanistic way. In practice at times it may seem a little like this, but it is worth

thinking about them also as more fluid, interdependent and taking place within complex 'real world', 'alive' human relationships over time.

48 The word 'incorporate' as a general verb and 'corporate' as a noun (from the Latin *corporare*, meaning 'form into a body') could also be used generically here for all the varying forms of living 'building in' or 'embodiment' that comprises the 'bounding' and density of 'energetic intention' of organisational culture. However the mainstream take up of the term 'corporate' as applying mostly to businesses in the current market economy and its reluctant take up in human services because of the sense of depersonalization accompanying it leads me to prefer 'organisation' to refer generically to all these forms of 'built embodiment'—individuals, groups, organisations, institutions, communities and networks.

49 But more widely attributed to Donald Hebb (1949) as the originator of this idea in neuroscience applied to organisational behaviour.

50 No wonder the names of many private research and evaluation consultancies resonate with the language of 'journeying', possibilities and change-making! Examples I have encountered include: Human Synergistics, Integrance Consulting, Learnsolutions, Potential Space, Initi8 Communications, InsideOut, Wavy Line People, EM-Power, Ahead of the Game, Thinkcoach, Thinking Partners, Aboutpeople, P.E.R.S.O.N.A.L, Breakthrough Consulting, ClearHorizon, PeopleChange, and my own living.systems. research. In Appendix 3 we see that the largest number of people in the human population may more often dwell in 'act' and 'observe', leaving a smaller number of people adept at this kind of 'reflect' and 'plan' activity. In living systems inquiry the demarcations based on preferences are not rigid as all have access to all capabilities associated with all parts of the full cycle, making it possible for all to assist each other co-inquire 'full cycle'.

Concluding words

The writing of this book has been driven by a need to understand the puzzles that have repeatedly presented themselves to many of us who work as researchers, evaluators and facilitators of inquiry. For some of us these puzzles seem unresolvable, perhaps inevitable, even part of the human condition. We are urged to adapt. Make compromises. Be realistic.

But for others of us the puzzles have themselves become the subject of research, evaluation and inquiry. Whether they were my experience (Wadsworth 2008d) of: a government committee drafting its report before receiving my commissioned research results, or services designed and implemented before local community needs were examined, or policy intentions (such as health development or community strengthening) 'reverting to type' and instead providing more tertiary medical treatment or individual casework, or efforts to refocus services on directly partnering with clients and consumers somehow becoming meetings between professionals without clients and consumers present, or the realisation that everyone is researching (service-users and professional staff alike), yet services resiling from building on this local knowledge and instead repeatedly preferring to trust distal experience in other settings, even overseas; or the non publication or under use of so many thorough and detailed research and evaluation reports.

Indeed all our experiences of the precedence of disempowerment, inequality and the exclusion of some by others in the headlong rush for more at others' expense—including the punishment and control of all those who might, whether articulately or inarticulately, protest this diminishment of life.

At a more generalised level are the persisting paradoxes and systemic issues for not just human services but perhaps our species as well, of:

- Changes that are wanted but don't happen
- Changes that happen that people *don't* want
- Decisions and 'politics' that seem unresponsive, insensitive or prematurely pragmatic
- Inaccurate presumptions, over generalisations, and an inability to see and hear what people are really saying
- Preoccupation with fixing things that are going wrong with little or no time spent stopping to make things go right in the first place, or
- The solutions becoming new problems when wonderful ideas lose their way, perhaps becoming overly complex or complicated; or people lose sight of the relationship between what they are doing and their deeper values and original purposes.

These have seemed to need a new way of thinking than that which brought them into being.

The transdisciplinary theory and practice developed in this book has brought to bear on these paradoxes and issues insights from:

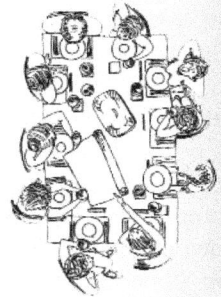

- The new systems thinking of physicists, biologists, human ecologists and other life science disciplines
- Epistemology, and in particular an integrated, recursive and reflexive meta epistemology that joins in a cyclic sequence: induction (descriptive generalisation), to theory building (abductive) and theory testing (hypothetico-deductive)
- Psychology as a way of understanding people's personal inquiry preferences and capabilities and
- Sociology as a way of seeing how these inquiry preferences and capabilities systemically develop distinctive social, political, organisational and institutional forms.

This integral theory yields a new way of seeing inquiry as the dynamic of all living systems, life as dynamic and systemic, and self-managing between the two, and power as resulting not only from certainty but also from uncertainty, not just from having answers but also from asking questions, from seeking as well as finding, from diversity that provides a complex morphogenic field as well as from the organ-ising and ordering that comes out of that hitherto chaos.

The full implications and applications of all of this are yet emergent and I look forward to the continuing conversation.

Drawing together the key intimations from the previous chapters

In conclusion let me draw out and summarise some of the key matters from all the previous chapters.

Chapter 1. *Some foundations*

Chapter 1 described a sequence of three somewhat chronologically distinct and sequential historical eras in which the emphasis shifted from research, to evaluation to continuous quality improvement. It concluded by considering whether the capabilities of each might be integrated into full cycles of inquiry in a new era of 'living systems'.

Taking from research: the benefits of more comprehensive and meaningful descriptive statistical and quantitative survey collection by contextualising them in in-depth observational qualitative study, using a range of both traditional and innovative research methods and techniques to identify values and purposes, and moving to include critical and sceptical reflection to reach new explanations, theories and conclusions, to inform plans and actions and to be experimentally trialled or tested in new practice.

Taking from evaluation: the benefits of retro-spective, after-the-event evaluation of what was of value, merit, worth or significance, by both auditing and reviewing against intended outcomes and openly inquiring into actual impacts and effects—and prospective evaluation of what would or could be of value, merit, worth or significance both in theory and in imagined goals and concrete practice in order to contribute logical indicators to test whether desired outcomes have been achieved.

Taking from continuous quality assurance/improve-ment: ways of combining the benefits of a whole systems change perspective with an action research cyclic model of inquiry, feedback and change to assist continuously inquiring-and-learning individuals within continuously inquiring-and-learning groups, organisations and larger social entities. Cultures of such whole cycle inquiring may offer to go well beyond 'single looping' between action, measurement and planning with the benefit of observation and reflection for deeper meaning and more effective change consistent with the deeper values and purposes of living systems.

Chapter 2. *Living systems*

In Chapter 2 a living system was identified as an auto-poetic, organically-complex *systemicity* of relational moving, forming and acting—and, through inquiring, to more-or-less know what to do (or not), with all parts 'doing their bit' (or not), all more-or-less following the plot (or not), all more-or-less 'appreciating' each other's contribution (or not); and relying on having times and places for:

- Remaining open to new feedback, input, ideas and beginnings; receptive to tentative, curious ques-tioning and bright new insights that form within relationships; making new connections, like little green tendrils from tiny spring seedlings needing the rich soils and waters of encouragement and protective shelters for them to incubate, be nurtured, take form and send down their roots sufficiently to see whether they may indeed be viable and fully alive
- Supporting young 'cellular' projects and clusters of encapsulated new ideas, activities, services and programs, where their boundaries have formed

around purposeful energies and values—while still being shaped, nourished and gradually exposed to the conditions of the normal terrain, enabling testing, assessment and adjustment, or gentle pruning and selectivity, until they grow stronger roots and thicker trunks and become better established. And, if they fail to 'take root', are lovingly returned to the great compost heap of new beginnings to become something else

- Sustaining and maintaining the by now more hardy and 'tried and trues', the perennials which do well given the soils and levels of rainfall and nourishment in the terrain, exposing them also to the late summer winds of change, heat and drought, dry and cold, testing their continuing capability, outputs, relevance and endurance, and retaining diversity and redunduncy

- Celebrating the harvest and the autumnal fruits of achievement and setting aside the seeds for new plantings, while mourning the losses, failed efforts and the deaths; and observing respectful ritual recycling of the still rich elements of previous life in mulch (carefully kept in the corporate memory for the next season's compost) to feed (and caution) possible new beginnings

- Keeping some fallow fields in which tired soils can recover, and in which the unseen micro-organisms and worms can do their job: chewing over the old experiences, reflecting quietly on the rich mix of still fragrant dried petals, mulling on the strength of the fibre of the stalks that held them up and the colour of the leaves that oxygenated them; mixing alchemically all the organic elements with the winter rain of tears and the spring air of new ideas to create a nice evolutionary 'soup' that can transform any toxic elements, until, in the gentle warmth of new intentions (borne of the friction between an 'is' and an 'ought' or an ought not), a glimpse of a bright new possibility is incarnated, appearing as a new green tendril above its solid earthy grounding.

Such a living human *oikos* may be 'built' at any scale—from a more hospitable self, household or home, to a service, community, organisation or global economy—from the accrued recursive actions of all those whose inquiring-and-relating comprise that *oikos*, including in relation to wider living systemicities of all beings. These processes of repeated energetic purposeful activity make patterns of practice dense enough to be 'as if' real and solid, with a presence that is certainly experienced as real and solid in consequence. Some of these may become dissonant or life-denying and we move to either adapt to or generatively change them. Others of them we find resonant and life-giving and we continue repeating, amplifying or extending them to new and differing situations over longer periods of time. Inquiring in order to go on acting under these conditions is a complex practice encountering ebbs and flows of movement, growth to critical mass, decay and dissipation and logics and purposes operating that give all these their characteristic patterns and forms—including sometimes the complex results of apparently simple and even single actions, contributing to unpredictability at the same time as being (more-or-less) reliably possibilistic.

Chapter 3. *Epistemology*

From Chapter 3 came an understanding of how to build in regular life-giving practice based inquiry throughout the 'body corporate'. A sequencing framework of questions, with their associated key capabilities and metaphorical locations to assist understanding the 'inquiry whole' was offered to help the traversing of full cycles of such inquiry: navigating through the various 'moments' and resting at the 'stations' (though not for too long or too little)—and all this taking place within more or less encouraging social relationships navigated by the critical inquiry group in collaboration with interested others. In these, 'data', information, 'existing results' and experiences are gathered, expressed, exchanged, worked with and reflected on. Conceptual distance and perspective is gained to identify new desired scenarios that can be articulated, theorised and enacted, championed by authoritative articulation, proceduralised (although not too much), encouraged and replicated (though not too perfectly) and grafted into and among the existing, then monitored, extended, revised or changed again using:

- *Questions for observing:* noticing and feeling the early signs of success or distress or of other differences between the patterns we were wanting (or not wanting) to form and their actual impact on those whose lives were to be enhanced—driven by an appreciative desire for a deeply valued (continuing or imagined) life-giving situation

- *Questions for reflecting:* capturing and 'congealing' accrued wisdom and conclusions from thorough and accurate observations and reflections, and for identifying the significance and meaning of these signs and experiences so as to gain new insights and ways of seeing and acting (including from dialogue between stakeowners or/and stakeholders) —driven by a desire for things to be different and better and fuelled by images or visions of such new states
- *Questions for planning:* implementation to try new ideas in practice guided by purposes, principles, theory and logic abstracted from the valued ways of being and doing
- *Questions for new monitoring:* and observing differences between the intended forms and patterns based on prior observation, reflection and planning and their enactment (e.g. from observation, management information systems, reporting on implementation, procedures documentation)—driven by attention to detail and logic to ensure alignment with the original deepest values and purposes that drove the original inquiry.

This sequence of strategic action research questioning showed how we could, in the context of communities of inquiry, move from 'how things are now' across *Phase change* 1 to consider 'how they might alternatively be', and then from 'how they could be' across *Phase change 2* to 'how they newly are'—from old dissonance (or valued resonance) to new (or repeated) resonance.

If the asking of all these clusters of questions, from their characteristic 'places and spaces', using relevant methods, techniques, capabilities and research styles is able to remain in healthy dialogue and avoid either losing touch and risking games of Chinese whispers or mistaking each other for the enemy and becoming Towers of Babel speaking at cross purposes, invoking reaction, demonisation and defence—then together, it was speculated, we might form very much more coherent life-giving worlds.

Significant indicators of healthy living human systems that have successfully built in these kinds of whole cycle inquiry processes may be:
- When all within any body corporate at whatever scale can describe and display the valuing of observation (i.e. show the value, presence and availability of this in practice and culture)—both literal, concrete sensing capabilities *and* associative, symbolic intuitive capabilities—that is, when seeing the truth of things in 'up close' detail is valued as much as seeing the truth of the 'bigger picture' from more of a distance
- When all can describe and display valuing of decision making—both cognitive, calculative, rational thinking capabilities *and* emotional, empathic, rational feeling capabilities—that is, when 'feeling things through' is as valued as 'thinking things through'
- When all can describe and display the valuing of both openings for and openness to feed in and feed back, and of constantly remaining permeable to new and life-giving possibilities (and detection of early signs if it is not life-giving, or and letting things flow through when not needed) *and* the valuing of boundaries and organ-ising, ordering, closure and of keeping the currently most life-giving forms, including guarding and valuing their keeping over time—that is, when the past, present and future forms and forming are *all* able to be valued for their contribution to the life of the whole
- When all can describe and display both the valuing of inner and inner-directed or systemic inquiry work: observing, reflecting, planning and acting in relation to that within the 'self' (at whatever scale), *and* the valuing of outer and outer-directed systemic inquiry work: observing, reflecting, planning and acting in relation to 'others' (at whatever scale)—that is, when the 'psychologically' ingoing and within, and 'sociologically' outgoing and between, are both valued for the parts they play in attending to the life of the whole.

In this way all may be more able to 'hold the story', having participated around the cycle sufficiently to *know* by having *seen* through the eyes of observation, *felt* through the empathic body, *intuited* the connections between observations and feelings, and *thought* through the articulation of these insights, conclusions and implications, all the way to successfully taking more effective new action.

And it is also in this way that the 'intelligent system' becomes one in which every organism (individual, group and at whatever organisational scale) is able to traverse their own cycles of inquiry *and* contribute to the traversing of larger collective cycles at greater scale. The hermeneutic nature of this means that each 'part' carries the 'mental DNA' for the whole cycle and can 'cover all bases', as each has sufficient grasp of the whole methodological process and its driving purpose, and of all the capabilities, moments or 'stations' around it. More ready, willing and able co-operators can cover for any absence of inquiry preference (whether acting-observing, reflecting, concluding or planning), as well as become maximally restored to autopoesis.

When this inquiry wisdom is robustly built in we may indeed become a species that has moved away from the unsustainable dangers of being either an overly prescribed behavioural monoculture or an endlessly quarrelling Tower of Babel where some scramble to the top on the backs of others who are misperceived as lacking inquiry capability, and are then rendered so. We may instead come to better know the value and truth of the rich diversity and mutual bonds of understanding and appreciation that are the source of our corporate species strength to live sustainably.

Chapter 4. *Human service*

Chapter 4 explored the implications of embodied full cycle co-inquiry by individual and collective systemicities for human services. The 'technology of wholistic inquiry' holds the possibility of human understanding and more collaborative action for the good of the 'whole'—whether the autopoetic individual, the autopoetic group, the autopoetic community, the autopoetic organisation or institution, or the autopoetic society, nation or global world.

'Nested resonant autopoesis' is a funny sounding way of saying we can all individually and collectively move more-or-less in concert for the energetic and full life of all *if* at each scale we exercise:

- Full cycles of inquiry that include all relevant stakeowners
- An appreciation of all of our inquiry 'gifts differing'
- A realisation that with our characteristic preferred capabilities inevitably comes characteristic unpreferred ones
- An understanding that for the good of the whole we are able to assist each other with our own most used inquiry preferences
- An understanding that we may be able to seek assistance with our own lesser used preferences
- An appreciation that others' lesser used preferences does not make them lesser people, just as
- Others not mistaking our lesser used preferences as

meaning we are less than the fully human beings either.

However from Chapter 4 it became clear that the favouring of certain inquiry preferences can result paradoxically both in ensuring the availability of expertise but also in the lack of it in terms of unfavoured inquiry preferences potentially resulting in defence, reaction and demonisation. This may typify not only inquiry efforts or even human services, but people and the human species per se. Here we saw the need to maintain our ability to span not only what people most favour, but also the lesser used inquiry preferences 'around the cycle'.

Thus if inquiring when 'in the grip' of unfamiliar responses can be quickly recognised as related to systemic stress and handled more rapidly with understanding and recognition, perspective and confidence, we may better accompany and resource each other towards greater mutual life—whether we do that with and for someone more directly or assist others inquire by reference to wider frames and scales that illuminate the contextual conditions for transformation. In this way human-created stress may remain healthy 'ginger' for life rather than becoming excessively dissonant and life-diminishing.

Chapter 5. *Exemplars*

Chapter 5 detailed ten exemplars of building in research, evaluation and continuous improvement in a comprehensive range of human service organisations. They showed, to varying extents, what organisations look like when they have begun to build in cultures of inquiry, and what they need to do to continue developing and sustaining such cultures by:

- Nurturing working in a co-inquiring responsive way with and for the people who are seeking support, assistance and resourcing
- Being continuously alert to the value of both life-giving procedural habits and processual change, and the value of constantly tic-tacking between these to maximise the chances of effectively organising, refining and replicating desired states of good practice, while remaining open to new input and feedback to revise, reinvent and create better practice
- Realising how small actions sometimes have large effects and how repeated actions are required to continuously commence, develop and consolidate new cultures of inquiry.

- Nurturing questioning and 'change-suggesting' in order to keep working towards achieving critical mass for wanted change, *and* honouring 'form-holding' and the rationales for keeping what is working in order to keep achieving critical mass for stability

In each of the ten exemplars people have found ways to inquire resonantly with (or as members of) their own critical inquiring groups, and to repeat or hold the forms or structures that best facilitate and sustain the living, embodied sequences of processes of

- Observation-while-in-action
- Reflection with a wider lens on those observations and the discrepancies that may be apparent
- Checking back against the initially planned 'holding patterns' and their original driving valued purposes and intentions
- Generating new insights and understandings from any revised valued purposes and intentions
- Driving change towards new and improved patterns of organ-isation to accomplish these valued purposes and intentions
- All the while learning from the defensive responses from current pattern holders, and keeping all stakeholders and stakeowners in the loops of dialogue
- Making and holding the new patterns of valued practice
- Then monitoring and observing them again…

Four key understandings

In explicitly setting out to build in research and evaluation into organisations, the exemplars also illuminated their practical embracing of the following four key understandings.

1. The need to enhance everyday inquiry capabilities
'Building it in' was seen to be much more than adding a management information system and statistical database, or specialist evaluations or pieces of traditional research—though these may well be part of the picture. Nor was it a matter of add-ons or add-ins, but more a matter of weaving or building in 'always actively inquiring' throughout organisations and communities. Not only a matter of having structures and procedures that organ-ise and systematise inquiry, but also that ensure the quality and strength of people's dynamic interrelationships—the capillaries, channels and connective tissue that bring the lifeblood and nutrients to feed inquiry and action.

Since the building blocks are people's ordinary inquiry capabilities and their stores of observations, reflections, working theories, knowledge and practice wisdom—already held by each and every person in any field of endeavour, 'assisted' and 'assisters' alike—then what we already know is a great resource (to the extent it resonates with the person or group with and for whom we are co-inquiring). Thus we always come, and inevitably, with pre-existing answers. But it is the strengthening of the questioning and listening capabilities (of all participants) that is primary so that there can be continual revision and expansion of our existing stock or repertoire. Hence inquiry for real understanding in *this* new situation always begins with new questions.

And every moment and every day begins with new inquiring.

© Judy Horacek www.horacek.com.au

2. The need to create concrete ways for 'person/people systems' to meet and inquire together with or as critical inquirers for their shared purposes and at whatever scale. In forming communities of inquiry the same rules apply as for any viable living organism—the grouping should be as much as possible self-initiated, self-chosen, united around their own shared purposes and of a scale that allows each to participate fully. Later as they grow from this core outwards, they may invite others to join or respond by encouraging new groups and communication channels. 'Cluster and con-nect' expresses the organic shape of systemic inquiry group formation. Groups may modify their purposes, but it is critical to success that they remain organ-ised around their own shared values and purposes: centring on the critical needs and interests of the ultimate beneficiaries of their inquiry, as it is those purposes that supply the critical driver and shape the boundaries to contain and 'hold' them throughout their duration. Others join as co-inquirers to the extent to which their inquiry purposes are bound up with, or the same as, or resonantly aligned with those of the critical inquirers. Sometimes an extended 'getting to know you' period may clarify just what are the shared purposes where these are initially less obvious, contested or unsettled.

3. The need to ensure ways to collect and share infor-mation, reflect on it and generate new knowledge
Provisional though the knowledge might be, every inquiry effort needs to have ways to gather and organise the responses to its questions, to be able to share this among participants and other relevant co-inquirers so the 'organism' at whatever scale can be maximally self-inquiring and autopoetic. A division of labour always presents a challenge in re-joining the inquiry information with those who are the inquirers to-be-informed. And the quality of facilitation that can enhance autopoesis also becomes so important. The exemplars illuminated the concrete specificity of what worked for each of them.

4. The need for ways to continue inquiring through action—and to facilitate learning about how to continue to inquire ever more deeply and widely
Because living systems research is a relatively new concept and field, there remains a tendency to default to the previously dominant pattern of seeing the in-quiry process and the operation of its logic as the special terrain of only those few people called researchers or evaluators. The specialised and qualified few may indeed have particularly developed their gifts for in-quiry or for parts of the cycle, and their contributions will be an essential component of an autopoetic inquiring system. But many are now turning their hand to assisting others build their own research and evaluation capacities in practice-based settings for more effective self- and organisational improvement as well.

Why the messages in this book may be more important than they seem

The community sector comprises 7% of GDP—twice the size of agriculture and mining, therefore making it one of the biggest industries in Australia.
RICHARD DENNISS, CRAWFORD SCHOOL OF ECONOMICS, AUSTRALIAN NATIONAL UNIVERSITY, 2008

In becoming a significant economic industry in its own right, it is sobering to consider that the human services sector has co-evolved as part of an economy which in turn has co-evolved as one of the most unequal societies in the world (Wilkinson 2006, Wilkinson and Pickett 2009). In continuing to replicate such unequal inclusion, there has also been an incapacity so far of political will to correct the catastrophic climate change also co-evolving with this economic mode of production and consumption. We appear to be witnessing a system-wide failure to inquire that is generating a kind of self-organisation no longer aligned with the survival of environments safe for human life (Spratt and Sutton 2008).

Indeed, viewed as a systemic co-creation, health, human and community services may be thought of as a kind of bifurcation with, and within, 'the economy' whereby the latter sets out ostensibly to meet human needs for food, shelter, comfort, culture, meaning and enjoyment of life (which it does spectacularly for some)—but paradoxically is driven by its own dominant rational logic to do this seemingly at great 'collateral' cost. We say resignedly and repeatedly, 'well it is business', and ironically in so doing it becomes systemically even more so. Having been permitted to 'have its head', economic relationships seem to have outsourced their 'heart' in a rather unholy pact struck to simultaneously generate a sector devoted to fixing, mending, healing, restoring, reconciling, educating and caring for all those hurt or excluded by (or to be grafted back into) this frequently damaging economic sphere. By a cruel trick of the outsourced heart, the helpers, in priding themselves on crafting their professional ability to care, also co-create the simultaneous 'lacks' and need for care as residing in the helped, rather than as a property of what the mainstream systemicity repeatedly rewards.

We contrast 'human values' with 'business values', as if business might actually not be fully human in its concentrated hard-headedness which seems to demonise and exclude (or alternatively sentimentally place on a pedestal) the soft-heartedness also necessary for human life and survival. Yet rational logical thinking performed at conceptual distance is as much 'being human' as rational embodied feeling performed at personal proximity.

The message offered by this book is that neither constitutes the whole of what it is to be human, and the socio-cultural and political-institutionalising of any one human propensity at the expense of another will generate the loss of inquiry capabilities essential to human life and ultimately survival. A clamour of ethnocentrism about any of the inquiry preferences over all others will not lead to anything much better than a Tower of Babel, so the answer would appear not to be to coerce one into being like another in a kind of colonising move. Nor does a division of inquiry preference labour get us full cycle as we morph into playing the inevitable games of Chinese whispers.

While arguably all need all, we have not yet learned how to retain dynamic balance by going full cycle through all inquiry preferences at every scale.

However if we are indeed a living biological species then we are a feedback-based organism. And if some inquiry preferences are being ignored, diminished, suppressed or rejected, then systemically

No longer riding for a fall?

we might anticipate a calling to resource the body corporate to sprout its own seeds for self-correction and self-healing. In this way we may begin to reinclude the visiting of all other parts of the inquiry process cycle. Just as the complex dynamic systemicities that have become what we see, did so by holding and copying ultimately endangering patterns, so also alternative complex dynamic systemicities can become what people would more deeply prefer by a critical mass holding and copying safer more integrating patterns for dynamic equilibrium. The attractors, as with all life, are there if we can detect their 'still small voice' in the general noisy din, such as when we recognise and rejoice when we encounter:

- deeply ethical business exchanges that give life
- instances of human service responsiveness restoring maximum autopoetic life participation
- individuals who appear well rounded people, within
- stable and lively families and communities
- healthy organisations
- compassionate and intelligent egalitarian societies and nation states
- global enterprises that act persistently to contribute to the life of all
- feeling better in ourselves and better together when we are united and harmonious enough
- being enough at peace with ourselves and each other, on
- a planet we see primarily as our home in
- a cosmos we are able to think of as our universe.

Is this the stuff only of abductive dreams and ideals born of reflection?

Or do we already have all the necessary inquiry-for-life capabilities that could enable us more routinely to move from the more life-threatening to the more life-giving?

How can we know? Only time and human inquiring will tell.

What is new is that the largest movement in human history has built itself without being masterminded from above. This is why I use the metaphor of this movement being humanity's immune response to political corruption, economic disease, and ecological degradation. The movement is not merely a network; it is a complex and self-organising system.

PAUL HAWKEN, 2007

Appendices

APPENDIX 1

How to Deliver Negative Evaluation Results Constructively

TEN TIPS FOR EVALUATORS

This summary has been compiled from a discussion on Evaltalk, the American Evaluation Association Discussion List, conducted June 2002.

It draws on assumptions that the primary purpose of evaluation is to understand the value, merit, worth or significance of programs or initiatives to guide action for improvement, and that people are more open to inquiring, learning and knowing what they should do to change things for the better when they are actively involved and can effectively process any feedback.

Details for each of the ten tips are available from the website (below).

1. Use a participatory approach from the start
2. Discuss possible negative results in the early stages
3. Inform clients immediately and often—'no surprises'
4. Build in time for course correction
5. Question the evaluation plan
6. Emphasise the positives
7. Tell the truth
8. Present results in terms of lessons learned
9. Provide suggestions for addressing deficiencies
10. Involve stakeholders in identifying obstacles and ways to overcome them

Contributors: Catherine Bingle, Barrie, Ontario CANADA; Bill Collins, Dartmouth, Nova Scotia CANADA; Susan Lilley, Dartmouth, Nova Scotia CANADA; Joyce Morris, Oklahoma City, USA; Burt Perrin, La Masque, Vissec FRANCE; Eileen Stryker, Kalamazoo, Michigan USA

Published by: Susan Lilley, Dartmouth, Nova Scotia CANADA

Source: www.chebucto.ns.ca/~lilleys/tips.html

APPENDIX 2

Key Drivers of Organisational Excellence

I identified a strong correspondence between a living systems epistemology (see keywords in square brackets) and the research described below—which identified fifteen significant factors or 'drivers' that differentiated 'excellent' workplaces from the 'generally good'. The authors noted that these key drivers were found to be present in varying mixes in all the workplaces considered excellent that were surveyed. The research concluded that quality working relationships represented the central pivot on which excellent workplaces were founded, underpinned by other key variables. These characteristics were seen as identifiable, quantifiable and able to be managed, leading the resear-Zchers to suggest that many more organisations could create such excellent workplaces. How much weight should be given to each of the 'performance drivers' was seen as a matter for further research—with no significance attached to the order in which they were listed.

Source: D. Hull and V. Read, 'Simply the Best Workplaces in Australia', ACIRRT working paper no. 88, University of Sydney, 2003, accessed 7 August 2008, http://www.acirrt.com/pubs/WP88.pdf

The quality of working relationships—people relating to each other as friends, colleagues, and co-workers. Supporting each other, and helping to get the job done. [*Action–Collaboration*]

Being safe—high levels of personal safety, both physical and psychological. Emotional stability and a feeling of being protected by the system. [*Stability, Reliable Boundaries, Connectedness*]

Having fun—a psychologically secure workplace in which people can relax with each other and enjoy social interaction. [*Action–Appreciative Evaluation*]

Getting feedback—always knowing what people think of each other, their contribution to the success of the place, and their individual performance over time. [*Observe–Reflect*]

Having a say—participating in decisions that affect the day-to-day business of the workplace. [*Action–Observation–Reflection–Planning*]

Clear values—the extent to which people could see and understand the overall purpose and individual behaviours expected in the place of work. [*Evaluative Observe–Reflect*]

Passion—the energy and commitment to workplaces, high levels of volunteering, excitement and a sense of well-being. Actually wanting to come to work. [*Meaning–Reflection*]

The built environment—a high standard of accommodation and fit out, with regard to the particular industry type. [*Resourcing Valued Action*]

Pay and conditions—a place in which the level of income and the basic physical working conditions (hours, access, travel and the like) are met to a reasonable standard. At least to a level that the people who work there see as reasonable. [*Resourcing Valued Action*]

Recruitment—getting the right people to work in the location is important, and their need to share the same values and approach to work as the rest of the group. [*Organisational Reflect–Identity*]

Autonomy [*Autopoesis*] **and uniqueness** [*Diversity*] —the capacity of the organisation to both tolerate and encourage the sense of difference that excellent workplaces develop. Their sense of being the best at what they do. [*Identity–Meaning*]

A sense of ownership and identity—being seen to be different and special through pride in the place of work, knowing the business and controlling the technology. [*Autopoetic–Plan–Act*]

Learning—being able to learn on the job, acquire skills and knowledge from everywhere, and develop a greater understanding of the whole workplace. [*Observe–Reflect–Conclude*]

Community connections—being part of the local community, feeling as though the workplace is a valuable element of local affairs. [*Observe–Reflect–Bigger Picture*]

Workplace leadership—how the immediate supervisor, team leader, manager or coordinator presented himself or herself. Their focus was leadership and energy, not management and administration. [*Inspire Autopoesis*]

APPENDIX 3

What's the Myers-Briggs® indicator[1] got to do with it?

Tucked away down here in the back of the book is a discussion of what has been a particularly valuable key—a kind of a Rosetta Stone—for my understanding of much of the detail of the human embodiment of the correspondences between the living systems cycle (Chapter 2), the research and evaluation epistemological cycle (Chapter 3) and the implications of these within human services (Chapter 4). It has been a valuable key that has yielded for me a deep understanding of how and why the best and worst is possible in human systemicities, including in human services and human social organisation more broadly (and indeed, the benefits *and* dangers of and within the valuable key itself). But why so relegated if it so powerfully illuminates understanding of the individual and social constitution of living human systems as inquiring?

The valuable key in question has been the Myers-Briggs Type Indicator® (MBTI®)[2]—or rather, the wider body of work of Carl Jung, Katharine Briggs and Isabel Myers and their successors and interpreters. However this work is not without controversy and people have had widely contrasting experiences of the Myers-Briggs® indicator.

On the one hand many people around the world have gained profound insights into themselves and others from the Jungian Myers Briggs formulation, including relief that they need not view themselves as 'abnormal' or 'wrong' because of their characteristic ways of being in the world—nor need they see other people's characteristic ways of being as better or as 'deviant' or inferior either. The value of these insights about *individual* people's characteristic ways of being and inquiring has for me been magnified by seeing the value of applications of this theory for understanding *social, political, organisational and community* characteristic ways of being and inquiring as well.

On the other hand many people (including myself) have experienced the inaccurate, unwanted and disempowering imposition of typifications attributed to the Myers-Briggs Type Indicator—particularly offensive where 'a type' is said to be 'assigned', or where people are 'given their type', 'slotted', 'sorted'

or 'weeded out'; or where the administration of the indicator results in people thinking they 'are a four-letter code'; or worse still, where stereotyping, typecasting, ostracism, shaming, exclusion or patronisation occurs (Murphy 2004); or when such stereotyping is used to promote further demonisation of otherwise healthy personality 'type' responses instead of seeing them, for example, as normal, contextually stressed responses (e.g. McGrath and Edwards 2000).

I hope to illuminate in what follows how these interpretations, experienced as *both* enlightening and liberating *and* constraining and damaging, can be understood using the theory itself. I hope to convey a way of thinking about the Myers Briggs formulation that may help illuminate the original, more integral or wholistic Jungian formulation consistent with its potential as a theory of inquiring human living systemicities, and which has proven so helpful to my thinking in this book.

Encountering the Myers-Briggs Type Indicator formulation in the social research workplace

For my own part, how I came to see the value of Jungian Myers Briggs theory for understanding dynamic complex living systems may serve as a way of introducing this new formulation.

Elsewhere I have told the story (Wadsworth 2006a) of first learning of the Jungian-inspired work of Katharine Briggs and Isabel Myers from two sociological colleagues, both of whom were working as consultants to practitioners within organisations that were trying to achieve social and cultural change. At first I thought it was just an interesting way of understanding some personal characteristics in order to work together more effectively as a research team. We found it did indeed save our particular research project from misery as we came to understand each others' differences and how those distinctive differences assisted us accomplish things differently. There was also a first inkling of how 'personality type' might be writ large as a sociological phenomenon when one activist consumer research group I was working with turned out to be modally very rational-feeling and intuitive (i.e. observing–evaluating–reflecting). Indeed half of the key people in the staff–consumer research team had the regular experience of feeling like 'canaries in the mind'[3] and the other half being the 'shot messengers'.[4]

I then began to see implications also for how we did evaluation research per se. Initially I thought it was just about different preferences for research methods and techniques but then I began to realise that what Carl Jung, Katharine Briggs and Isabel Myers were describing in human populations had implications for how *all* human populations—indeed all living beings—inquired to live per se.

Turning to psychology to understand the operation of emotion in organisational change

I and most of my sociological colleagues are typically apprehensive about psychology as an approach that locates behaviour in a rather pragmatic 'single loop' way, as originating *within the individual* rather than being a systemic property of the relationships *between people*—and thus factoring out (and then often rather uncritically serving) existing mainstream systems and power structures, often by 'slotting and sorting people into boxes'. But after spending some years in a psychology department to find out what I could learn from the organisational psychologists (who shared an interest in social and community systemic change and 'culture shift' and who were also having to come to terms with the importance of emotional defences for or against achieving cultural change)—and while I certainly found instances of coolly pragmatic and instrumental behaviourism—I also had a chance to explore the Jungian Myers Briggs body of knowledge. This seemed to hold much deeper promise as it was theoretically without the narrow and pathologising labelling of, for example, psychology's 'big five' personality type traits (of neuroticism, extroversion, openness, agreeableness and conscientiousness, Sternberg 1998: 585), or the non systemic nature of trait theory (which sees many separate and unrelated traits as 'adding up' to be a person's personality), or the 'learned dependency' that seems inherent in the omniscience of the Freudian 'external objective observer'.

Instead Jungian Myers Briggs thinking rests on noticing that people usually make a choice, if they have to, between four pairs of key mental processes and orientations that identify where people most focus their attention (inner or outer), how they take in information (discrete bits or as connections), process it (decide rationally on the basis of values or logic) and act on it (either seeking completion or remaining open). People sometimes want to stress they have 'a bit of each' (or access to each) which is experientially true and something I take to be epistemologically akin to being able to 'go full cycle'. However an important contribution of the Myers-Briggs indicator is that it focuses on identifying a *complex characteristic systemicity*, or characteristic set of connected choices made in action, particularly—and significantly—when a person is pressed for an urgent or immediate response to a situation or person in a crisis (and who only latter may further respond 'on second thoughts' etc.). Thus a critical difference between Jungian Myers Briggs theory and standard behavioural psychology is that the latter identifies separate variables or traits (one by one) in a concrete sensing, analytic kind of way, while the MBTI formulation sees how they *work together* (as systemic dynamic wholes) in a more complex, connecting, intuitive, perceiving way.[5]

These characterisations or typifications of *individual systemicity* seemed to me to be in turn also related to the characterisations or typifications of *social groupings* made by sociologists. Indeed after grasping the implications of the research statistics in the Myers-Briggs Type Indicator practitioners' accreditation training manual (1998), I began to realise they extended to applications in a wide range of traditional sociological areas of practice, concepts, typifications, theories and categories as well—including class, gender, socio-economic status, age and education, as well as processes like institutionalisation, socialisation, media and communications, criminalisation, social change and so on (Wadsworth 2005, 2008b).[6]

In addition I found that these individual human systemicities were theorised (on the basis of eight decades of observation of detailed practice) as co-generated with and by systemic 'gifts differing' (Myers and Myers 1980), or as how people experience themselves when they are 'most themselves', 'fully alive' in relationship with others, resonant 'with life' in the wider world of all beings[7] or in 'flow' (Csikszentmihalyi 1992). And also, when faced with stress: theorised as pushing people out of dynamic equilibrium, 'into the grip' (Quenk 2000), into one's inferior function (Myers and Briggs), shadow (Jung), or across 'thin ice' (to use my term below).

Here was a *systemic* understanding of how discrepancy is generated (or responded to) when a person's individual systemicity becomes perturbed, disturbed and potentially turbulent within their social collective systemicities. This was a systemic way of describing the use of energetic power that had two faces—push and yield—both necessary to life when oscillating sustainably (between order and chaos), but threatening life when too far into or too far from equilibrium (too much of one and thus too little of the other).

It became for me a way of describing power and its virtuous inquiry (full) cycles for both 'good' (towards fuller life) and vicious inquiry (incomplete) inquiry cycles for 'bad' (away from life) that seemed exactly in the territory of sociologists' historical interests in power and conflict, 'deviance', the breakdown of social order and its (re)institutionalisation (Wadsworth 2005). However a living systems approach also gave me new criteria for judging discrepant states without automatically demonising the action energy of 'power' (as focused, convergent, repeated certainty, or closing-ordering of the more fixed categorical and determinate form), or victimise as inevitably disempowering the yielding energy of generalised uncertainty (as decentred, divergent and receptive-opening to morphogenic chaos).

In not identifying actions which are 'in the grip' of stress as essentially pathological or individualised, but instead as systemic information or instructive feedback, then—just as appreciation of our 'best living systemicities' could assist replication of 'what works'—recognition of the specificities of our various 'worst living systemicities' could also provide 'advice' on what was needed to restore life. It was no longer a matter of avoiding (nor suppressing, projecting or outsourcing) one's defences of one's own 'thin ice', but rather of simply traversing it safely, using metaphoric planks to scaffold it from either side of the cycle from one's adjacent strengths (what I later describe as 'inquiry preference reach').

I began to see the two-phase change moments as more like a continuous dance between *yielding* to 'breathe in' for receptive observation, rest, reflection and regeneration, and pushing to 'breathe out' for purposeful action—*with each making the other possible.*

Using the Myers Briggs typology as a 'Rosetta Stone' key to the transdisciplinary correspondences

The connections I made between the Jungian Myers Briggs typology and living inquiring systems at all scales of systemicity (Wadsworth 2006a), and the correspondences between the four associated disciplines (systems, epistemology, psychology and sociology), have been explicated in the concept and characteristics of dynamic-stabilising systemicities in Chapter 2, the articulation of the inductive–abductive–deductive moments in full cycles of living systems inquiry in Chapter 3, and the characterisations of how these inquiry preferences might operate in any system of human service assistance in Chapter 4.[8] The illumination offered by a detailed grasp of the Myers-Briggs Type Indicator is not easily acquired (I myself have been an accredited user of it for over a decade), but it is also not necessary in order to grasp these basic correspondences.[9,10]

Table 13 below expresses the patterns of inquiry 'typifications' that may be identified 'from a distance' in all living systems, but which dissolve into infinite variability and indeterminate complex specificity in any particular instance when experienced 'up close and personal'.

The necessity (and dangers) of all theory

All of this, both the positive and the negative uses and experiences of Jungian Myers Briggs theory, reflects the pluses and minuses characteristic of *all* theories.

All theory, generalisations and conclusions have a capacity for illuminative explanation and endangering abstraction, error, omission or limitation, and ironically all the more so if they are particularly useful and comprehensive theories. That is, in 'sweeping in' many observations, extensive and deep reflection, and seeing broad patterns and repeating systemic forms and coming to very powerful new conclusions, a theory not only epistemically by definition includes things to the exclusion of others, but also acquires a driving logic that attracts inductively more observations of what it explains and potentially overlooks or discounts what it doesn't. In a way the whole of 'full cycle' social science is attempting to remedy these tendencies, indeed the capacity of the Myers-Briggs formulation

TABLE 13. SUMMARY OF CORRESPONDENCES BETWEEN INQUIRING LIVING SYSTEMS AND THE MBTI® FORMULATION

Properties of inquiring living systems	Corresponding aspects of the MBTI formulation
Relationality Purposeful activities taking place *within* an organism (intra-relationally), and *between* (inter-relationally) organisms, at different scales or levels of nested holarchic systemicities	*Source and direction of energies* Inner/Introversion (I) and Outer/Extraversion (E)[11] [See Figure 23][12]
Experience of information Particles, dots, parts, facts separated and Waves, lines, wholes, experiences connected	*Ways/forms of taking in information about the world* Seeing, hearing, smelling, touching, tasting 'things' (sensing—S), and 'Seeing' or 'sixth sense' of making connections 'between' (intuition—N) [See Figures 24 and 25][13]
Positive and negative valorising Embodied experience of felt discrepancy (at *Phase change 1*), and Calculating resolution 'fit' (at *Phase change 2*)	*Judging-deciding about it using* Ethics of embodied valuing (feeling—F) and Principles of logical reasoning (thinking—T) [See Figure 26][14]
Dynamic stability Fluidity, openness, releasing, dynamic, quickening, and Organ-ising, forming, containing, stabilising, slowing	*Ways of being in the world* Remaining open to new possibilities (perceiving—P), and Bringing to closure, concluding-deciding (judging—J) [See Figure 27][15]
Maintaining integrality *Dynamic oscillation between non-order (chaos) which is* negentropic, within a field of 'random', not-yet-connected possibilities, resources and inputs, and *Equilibrium-balancing (ordering) which is* entropic, identifying, forming, organ-ising, bounding-cohering, replicating as patterning	*Wholly living by* *Processual movement around cycles by* Sensing-perceiving (SP) and Intuition-perceiving (NP), and *Stabilising movement around cycles by* Intuition-judging (NJ) and Sensing-judging (SJ) [See Figure 28][16]

(of 'all types' round the cycle including deductive testing) to generate its own error detection and correction from within is key to its enabling a self-correcting autopoetic living system.

All generalisations are wrong. Even this one.
ALEXANDRE DUMAS

Every individual is an exception to the rule.
CARL JUNG

As we have seen throughout this book, the drive to live life, to respond to the uncertainty of discrepancies, and to seek new and better life forms, attracts inquiring human systemicities towards developing both retrospective explanatory theory and prospective provisional new theory. The relative certainty of the

latter takes us forward in confidence through the necessary moment of risk-taking into new concrete action and then detailed practice. 'Phew' we say. 'What a relief. Now we know *exactly* what to do and how to do it. Let's get going.'

But that 'knowing *exactly* what to do' is of course to risk being lulled into a false sense of security—when in practice, and partly depending on how closely grounded the prior inquiry has been, we may already be completely wrong! Indeed we may not even have a way of knowing at that point whether or how wrong we are. No wonder we get the ruler out so quickly to measure how things are going in the hope of seeing early results. Yet now that we have committed ourselves to a course of action we are tending to look for confirmatory news, and dangerously may not hear

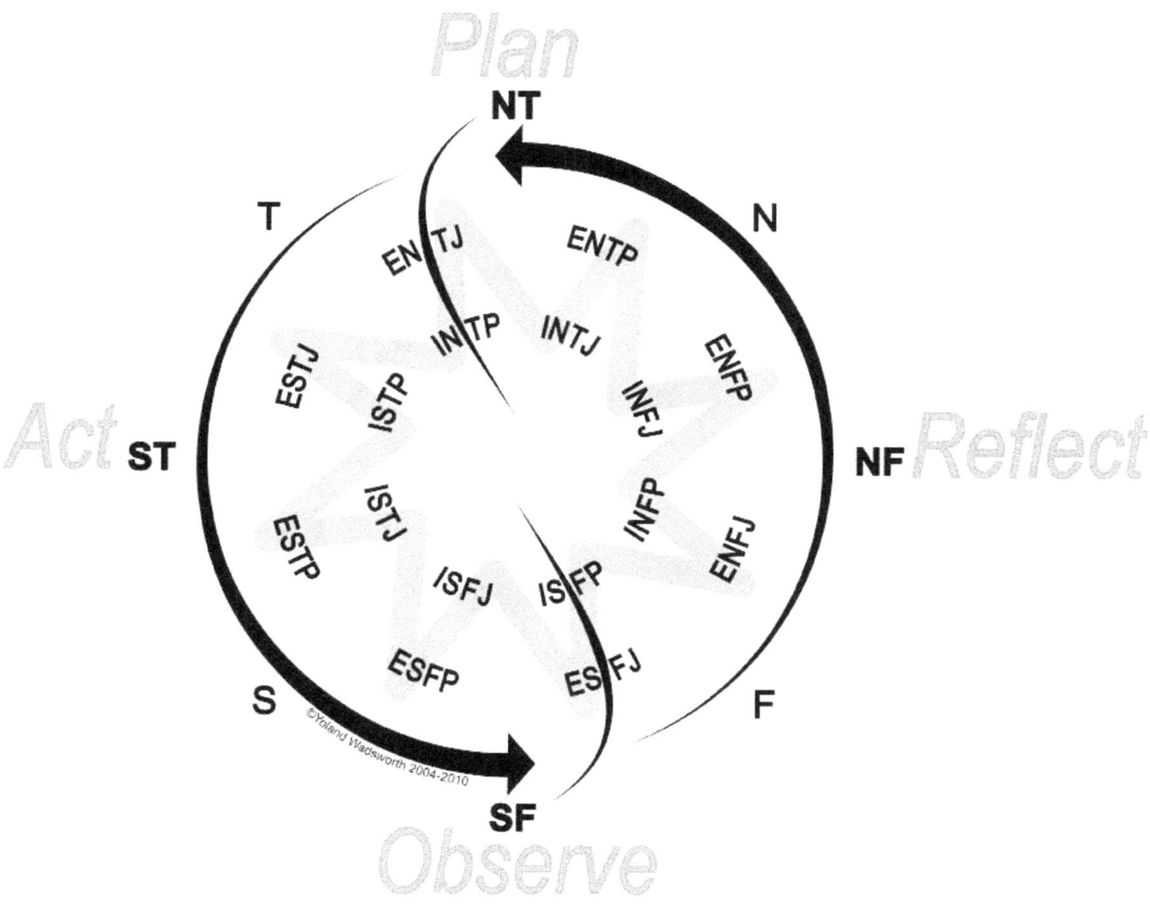

Figure 23. Source and direction of energies for relationality, moving within and between the inner (introversion–I) and outer (extraversion–E)

ISTJ	ISFJ	INFJ	INTJ
ISTP	ISFP	INFP	INTP
ESTP	ESFP	ENFP	ENTP
ESTJ	ESFJ	ENFJ	ENTJ

(Kroeger and Thuesen 1993: cover)

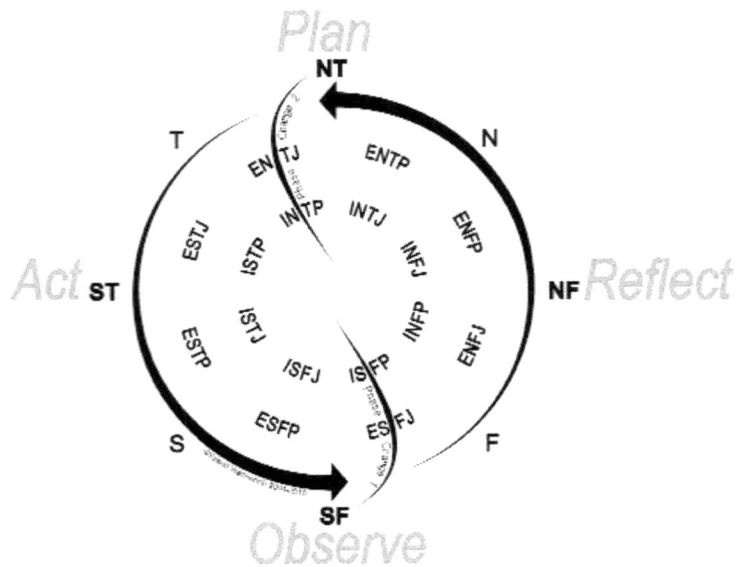

Figures 24. and 25. Two ways of processing the same information about the world: separately categorising (sensing–S) and connecting relationally (intuiting–N)

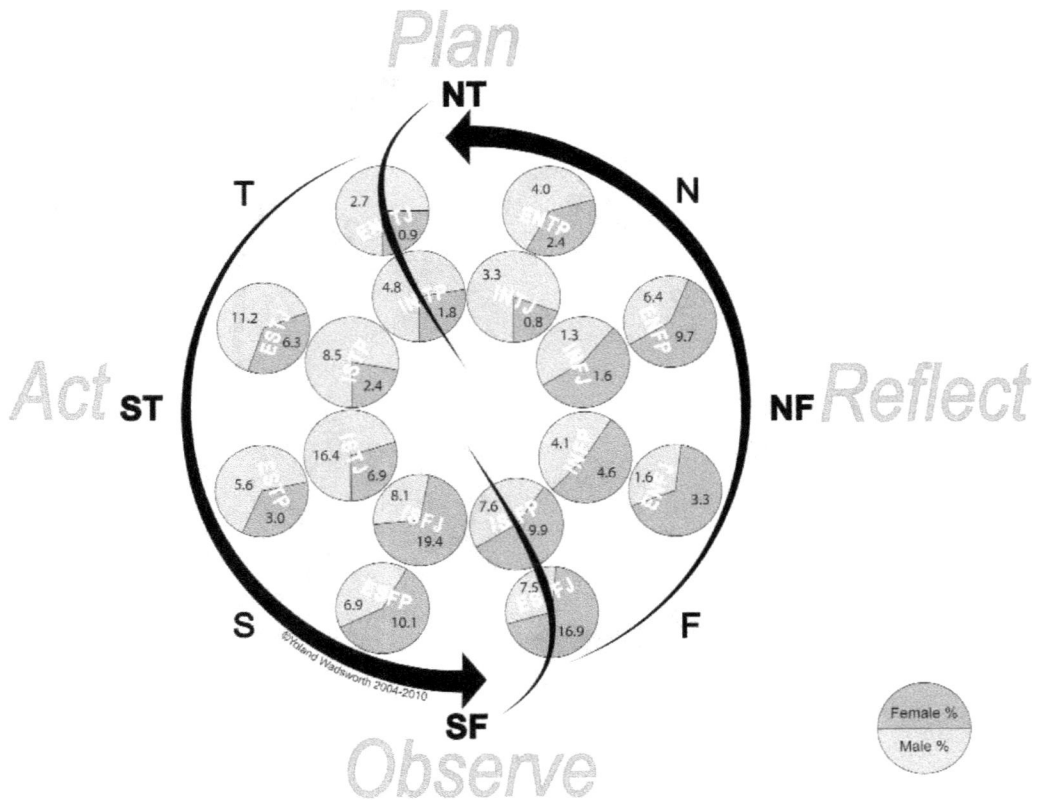

Figure 26. Different ways of judging/deciding about information and experience (rational feeling–F and rational thinking–T

(or even plug our ears to) voices expressing new observations of discrepancy or sceptical critique. *Presumption combined with wanting* to 'make things happen' and not talking about them any more can bring a swift end to anything that threatens to differ.

This tendency to presume in order to be able to act can, as we saw in the discussion of defences in Chapter 4, be like an immune response, protecting the organism, but also at times, if mistaken, more like an auto-immune response 'protecting'—from something that is needed for life-giving openness, critique and change (including valuable feedback that it is still OK to continue with the new or existing forms). Eventually excessive presumption may create an 'overly auth-orised' (even authoritarian) repetitive habitualism that does not allow the space of critique to flourish to do its work towards creating potentially more desirable life-giving forms.

Especially dangerous when the theory is about ourselves!

All of these matters apply with particularly sharp focus when the subjects of the theory (and strong theory) are the theorists themselves! Yet from infancy and throughout our lives we form all kinds of conclusions and generalisations on the basis of which we attribute this and that action, practice or culture to associated 'kinds of people'. We might put it down to gender, class, occupation, education, income, geographic location, parenting, life experiences, astrological sign, order of being born into a family, country of ancestry or any combination of these! In these ways we store up practice guidance for our next responses: building a repertoire of explanations, second guessing, presuming and assuming, to assist us calculate implications by which we navigate action in the here and now…even as we might sense that we may be wrong in the very next instance of actual practice.

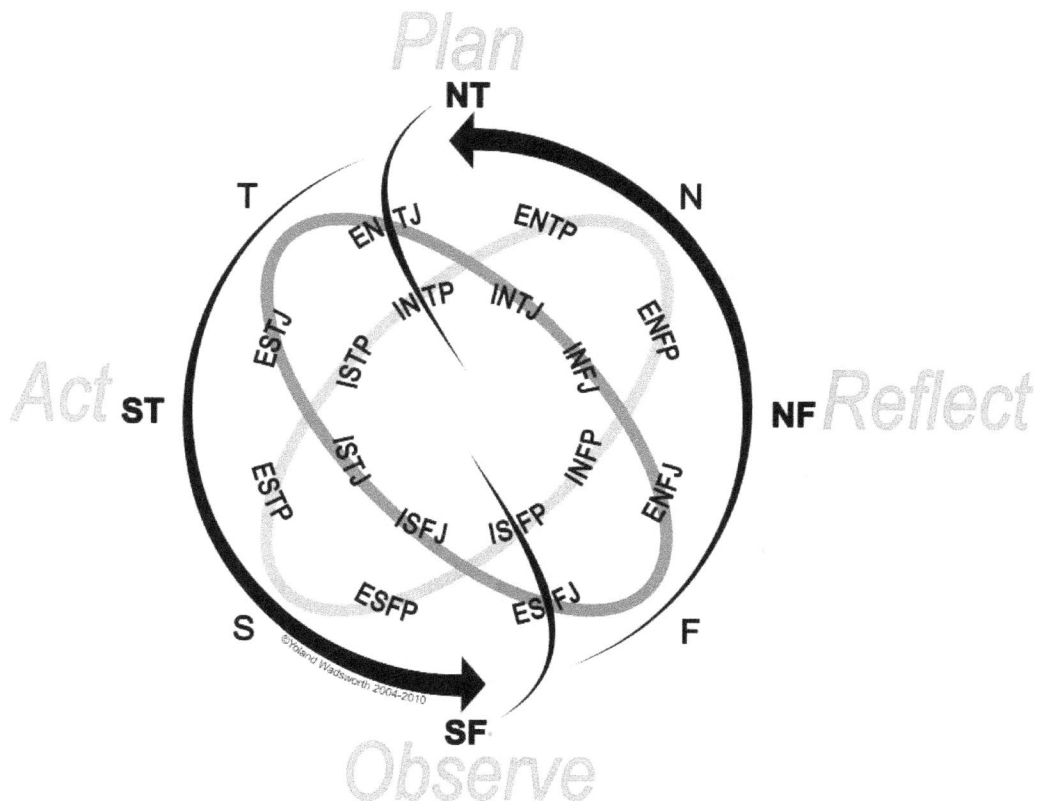

Figure 27. Processes for forming and transforming for dynamic stability: moving between openness (perceiving–P) and closure (judging–J)

Throughout human history and presumably pre-history people have observed patterns of similarity and difference in how we 'do life' reliably differently: how we communicate differently, receive information differently, make sense of it and act on it differently. Psychology, sociology and other disciplines and professions have just been modern attempts to systematise these, but philosophy, religion and astrology over millennia have all assembled schemas in and for their times and places. Our species has managed to live for far longer by getting these processes more or less right. Strangely it is in our own time that we seem to have swung rather dangerously out of kilter.

Building in ways to keep on observing, questioning and self-correcting

For sheer life's sake we cannot and do not re-invent every new item of knowledge in every new instance. In living systems inquiry our protection comes from remaining alert and as open as possible to that next instance being discrepant with our current theory-driven assumptions, and being able to inquire anew. This fluidity and permeability marks off real life from our modern reductionist and potentially overly neat theoretical and conceptual abstractions. No matter how helpful, they can only point towards 'realities' and can never fully represent them.

This is the essence of the deductive experimental phase ('How did it go?', 'Did it work for its intended

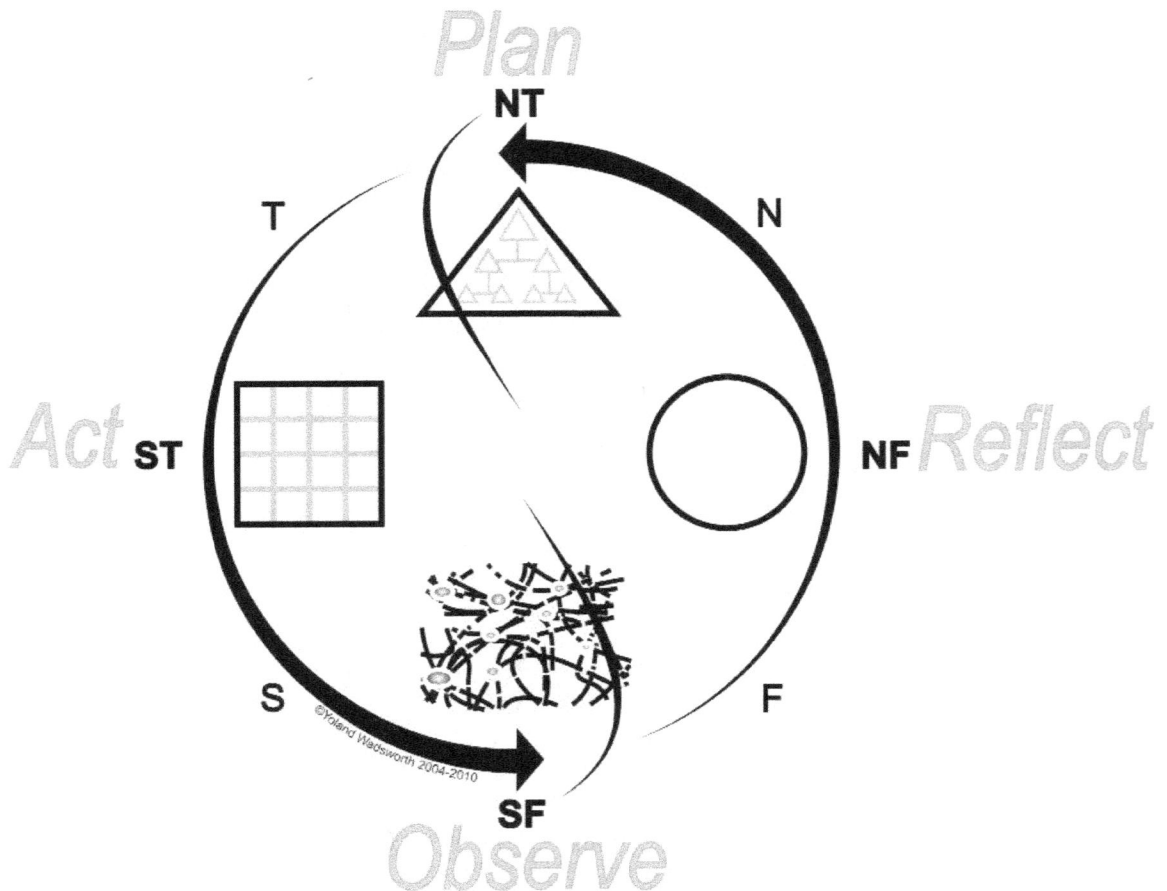

Figure 28. Imaging the processual and stabilising movement for integrality using all inquiry preference constellations through the four quadrants around the cycle

purposes?') and the new crossing of the *Phase change 1* threshold to inductively and abductively consider how else things may be seen and what might be better. It is also a compelling reason for numerous small-scale, real-world cycles to build towards larger scale practice with greater confidence.

Thus a theory only stands if we can imagine and be open to circumstances in which it could be wrong. If it can never be wrong it's not so much a theory as an essentialist (or eternal) belief or conclusion, and the inquiry-for-life process has ceased.

Perhaps the most reliable source of confidence of all, therefore, comes from *knowing how to continue to inquire*—rather than from knowing the essentially always provisional concrete findings, theories or categories from any *particular* inquiries.

Thus what any theory—particularly a Large Theory—needs for its own safety is a permanent inbuilt method to autopoetically assess, revise, confirm or dismiss it.

In this theory of living systems inquiry the iterative, recursive aspect of its inductive–abductive–deductive cyclic model provides for regular autopoetic revision of observations, findings, theories or categories from any *particular* inquiry in which it is used, and the theory of inquiry methodology (or epistemology) *itself* also remains a 'working theory', a 'best-we've-thought-of-so-far' theory: subject to revision using the same process of autopoesis.

In coming to see the close correspondences between the key elements of the Jungian Myers Briggs typology and the action research cycle, it seemed that the Jungian Myers Briggs theory could contain the internal capacity to self-seed its own autopoetic revision because it provides for 'types' or inquiring systemicities' preferences around a fully reflexive cycle.

Learn your theories well, but set them aside when you touch the miracle of a living person.

CARL JUNG

How can the Myers-Briggs Type Indicator 'get it wrong'?

Given the indeterminacy of all social theory, the detailed psychometrics for the Myers-Briggs type indicator explain a 7 to10 per cent rate of the indicator not working by a range of factors (Myers et al. 1998) included in the list below. I believe this indeterminacy may be even greater depending on three main factors. Firstly, the assisting external practitioner-observer's interpretations depending on their insight into the impact of their own preferences or lack of familiarity with or insight into those of others. Secondly, the many factors operating in the lives of those making use of the indicator for themselves. And thirdly those of any others who are observing, and guessing ('typewatching', Kroeger and Theusen 1993) about preferences operating. These include:

- Early environment and upbringing (e.g. offering or strongly modelling inquiry preferences that differ from or conflict with the child's)
- The impact on inquiry preferences of life influences, current environment or power relations in workplaces or families (e.g. where people are being encouraged to be more like other kinds of people or inquiry cultures than their own preferences)
- People having different degrees of insight into the typical operation of their own preferences (e.g. where they have grown up in a family culture or spent a long time in a work environment that has not understood theirs)
- People not having formed clear preferences or having complexity at Step 2®
- People being at different stages in their own inquiry preference development such as at different points through life (e.g. initially mastering main preferences; late in life experimenting with hitherto unpreferred ways)
- People may be under stress and find it difficult to identify their usual way of being
- The use of the indicator being imposed by others (e.g. incurring reactivity or resigned submission that mask genuine preferences)
- Lack of confidence or frank anxiety about how it will be used by others (e.g. resulting in second-guessing what are thought to be the 'right' answers or how someone thinks they 'should' be)
- A desire or type-specific ability to calculate how to

'throw' the findings and confound observers (e.g. a logical thinker deliberately ticks the boxes for preferring feeling)

- Answering as the person would like to be rather than as they would usually prefer (act)
- Mistaking particular behaviour or action as typical of a particular pattern (e.g. visionary risk taking or precipitous action when under stress, but usually realistic and practical)
- Assuming an organisational role will only be occupied by a certain 'type' without recognising that different inquiry preferences are associated with different approaches (e.g. to leadership, teaching, learning, helping etc.)
- The preferences of one person or organisation being judged through the eyes of another with different inquiry preferences (e.g. a creative development organisation full of ideas is assumed to be disorganised).

Table 14 examines how the 'full cyclic' formulation I have described in this book would see the typical difficulties and their systemic rebalancing in response.

> Comprehension, wonder and delight characterise unstressed observation of the operation of both one's own and others' preferred inquiry type systemicities—including understanding and acceptance of the contextually systemic operation of one's own 'thin ice' and that of others. Criticising others' thin ice is like criticising a brown-haired person for not having red hair—meaning that variation would not then be available to the individual, the group or the species. The integral operation of all preferences is how we can navigate around the cycles of inquiring in the direction of greater life.

This Appendix has focused on how Jungian and Jungian-derived theories may be thought of as concerned with how our processes of acting, observing, reflecting, planning and taking new action make each of us individually in some important sense inquiring 'nations of one', just as our collective systemicities—couples, threes, fours, groups, communities, organisations, institutions, all the way to global species and even cosmic scale—make us collective inquiring 'body corporates'. Economic organisations have had themselves, fractal-like, legally declared

TABLE 14. IMBALANCE IN USE OF TYPIFICATIONS

1. Categorical stereotyping and loss of unique individualism[17]

More often at the ACTION–OBSERVATION moments around the cycle

Rigidifying around a particular form/identity/MBTI code as a noun rather than a verb—typecasting, reifying, pigeon-holing—is perhaps the most criticised aspect of the MBTI approach and interestingly may have in part arisen because of the personal and socio-political contexts of its origins. Katharine Briggs' husband, Lyman Briggs, was a physicist who headed the National Bureau of Standards in the United States (responsible for establishing uniform rules of measurement) and Isabel Myers' husband, Chief Myers, was a lawyer. As with Jean Piaget's close observations of his own children, an important practical impetus for the women's theory came from Katharine and Isabel's interest in understanding the differences between themselves (both deeply reflective and feeling theorists) and their husbands. However their husbands' lines of work and own inquiry preferences (more cognitive and analytical), in an era of strong institutions of social control in the early post-Second World War era, also arguably shaped the familiar four-letter matrix of sixteen codes for which the indicator became both so popularly known and useful *and* was most subjected to critique.

Associated shapes: grids, squares, tables, matrixes

Systemic (balancing) response:

By stepping back to observe and reflect more deeply on the relationships between 'components', and see other bigger picture possibilities. Also by seeing 'categories' as socially-constructed, provisional, uncertain and fluid.

2. Risk of over-individualisation and loss of valuable typifications and unperceived commonalities

More often at the OBSERVATION–REFLECTION moments around the cycle

The MBTI formulation, particularly in its rigidified static form, can also invoke critical reactions along the lines that no patterns (or systemic inquiry preferences) exist, and that no assumptions at all can

AND SELF-CORRECTING SYSTEMIC RESPONSES TO RESTORE DYNAMIC EQUILIBRIUM

be made: 'He is a complete individual', 'She doesn't have a particular type', 'There is no such thing as a personal type', or 'I'm lucky, I have an equally balanced amount of every aspect'; 'I'm sure I change my type all the time'.

Associated shapes: Dots, wavy lines, 'outside the box'

Systemic (balancing) response:

Notice trends, themes, and repeated patterns and preferences ('we are all unique individuals—just like everyone else'). Consider the ways people come to agreed conclusions or otherwise have moments of certainty and clarity and galvanise for repeated action.

3. Risk of appreciative idealism to the exclusion of seeing negative realities

Most often at the OBSERVATION–REFLECTION moment around the cycle

While the Jungian Myers-Briggs formulation is a systemic understanding of people's 'naturally occurring differences' and thus 'there are no bad types', type preferences are seen as having a 'shadow side' which emerges systemically under stress to the living organism's capacity to pursue its purposes.

Associated shapes: Circle, and spiral

Systemic (balancing) response:

By seeing observation and analysis of negative discrepancies as vital to effectively inquiring living systems (to 'ground' both reflection and abduction to preferred ways of understanding or thinking that are not out of touch with reality) and to envision a preferred and currently non-existent state.

4. Risk of competitive supremacism and loss of appreciation of the value of all other 'types'

Most often at the PLANNING–ACTION moment

Energetic certainty from having 'seen it all' and worked out what is the best thing to do and why, and how one's own 'type' has made its vital contribution to the whole can lead to a sense that 'my type is the best type', or 'other/some other type/s are not as good'.

Associated shapes: Triangles, and pyramids (summits)

Systemic (balancing) response:

Restoration of observation of what all the other

inquiry preferences are contributing to the living systems inquiry cycle, and seeing how each rests on the others for its own successful performance making for interdependence. That is, at the next moment or standpoint the next type systemicity is 'the best' or most needed, and then the next, and so on. Fellow travellers journeying together around the inquiry cycle maintain some competence in all areas, even as some may feel unfamiliar or even queasy in their least favoured. Recognition that epistemologically we do not and cannot know everything about the lives and contributions of others, just as they cannot or do not know everything about us.

5. Risk of introjecting inferiorisation

The other side of the coin of 'type supremacism' is the view that 'there are no good types' or 'my type is not as good'. This introjected inferiority may develop systemically in co-dependent relation with an asserted superiority elsewhere, becoming a projection onto an idealised opposite typification seen as all-seeing and all-knowing, or alternatively a demonisation or derision of these qualities may take place (if they are taken by or yielded to others). In the absence of being able to take action, this may manifest as frustration or anger or manipulation, or a resigned sense of being at 'the bottom of the heap/hierarchy'.

Most often at the ACTION–OBSERVATION moment

Associated shapes: 'Lower reaches' of the pyramid

Systemic (balancing) response:

The insight that 'it takes all types' and that all human systemic preferences have an essential part to play in the whole (with all types of inquiry preferences being both capable of contributing—and capable of characteristic 'grip' reactions). The knowledge that everyone or every social organisation can go full cycle (more or less) in their own ways—seeing the other parts of the cycle through the lens of their own preferences.

'natural persons' in order to derive the powers of the individual for themselves—and the matching 'participatory democracy' or necessary whole cycle blood-flow feedback systems are yet to be developed to match and render them sustainable human systemicities.

Preferences and responses under stress

The inquiry differences 'around the cycle' may be thought of as operating to create within our species both a capability for dynamic rapid response (especially useful in a time of crisis or whenever we need to *move and change*) and a slower stabilising response capability (especially useful for longevity and whenever we need to '*hold our shape*' through more or less repeating effective forms). Both are equally crucial for sustainability, that is, the self-organising capacity to continue adapting and changing, generating new desired forms, and replicating desired old forms. However under crisis we tend towards a 'division of inquiring labour' that is systemically generated when we draw on our 'main suite'. When combined with scale, we see the Tower of Babel that potentially results from a state of perpetual crisis with, for example, those exercising maximum certainty (whether justified by the facts, experience and reflection on them or not) systemically accruing/ receiving more of the resources available, just as those who are yielding (whether desirable given the facts, experience and reflection or not) relinquish/have their share taken.

The more dynamically balancing autopoesis of 'all types' *together* is as important socially, politically and economically as it is within the *individual*. What we become together is an analogue to what we can become individually, and what we become individually reflects what we can become together. The life of each constitutes and is constituted by all others. We each are ourselves because of others—holding and being held in a web of life.

This reintroduces to the Myers Briggs formulation two critical aspects lost since the original Jungian formulation—firstly, the dynamic fluidity and uncertainty that means a higher level of indeterminacy than is usually obvious from the popular sixteen four-letter code 'boxes' and, secondly, a larger formulation that factors back in ways those sixteen differing systemicities might be perceived from *all* the perspectives around the cycle.

Complexity, fluidity and indeterminacy beyond 'sixteen little four-letter boxes'

Elsewhere I have noted:

> To fulfil its potential [the MBTI formulation] will need to leave the exclusivity of the 4 x 4 analysis (that…will continue to serve well in its organ-ising STJ aspect) and be presented in forms that illuminate its other more processual, intuitive, feeling and perceiving aspects—with literally more colour, sound, movement, poetry and 'rich thick description'… Somehow the 4x4 matrix (the square), must sit alongside with the wavy line, the circle, the cross and the triangle to make up a whole cycle, or eternal figure of 8, holograph, moving wheel or mandala— or whatever symbol of wholism is chosen to convey both change *and* stability, order/ organisation *and* chaos, dots *and* lines, action *and* non-action—the all.
>
> …[The MBTI formulation] 4-letter acronyms are thus always only going to be approximations to infinitely complex realities—like trying to neatly wrap in a newspaper package the fish and chips when they are also still living, moving, breathing animals and vegetables. The fish and chips can indeed be 'pinned down' and analysed/organ-ised as separate countable predictable entities from one perspective. *And* they may be seen as interconnected understandable living, moving, breathing infinitely changing organisms from another perspective. (Wadsworth 2006: 42)

This may indeed be why the MBTI formulation is both simultaneously so valued by those whose preferences lie in the parts of the cycle focused on change, and so elusive to the control sought by users of psychology to try to better serve the part of the cycle focused on existing replicated certainties (e.g. the status quo, existing 'structures of power').

The Jungian Myers Briggs' practitioner community considers 'type dynamics' (Myers 1999: 7, 35; Myers and Kirby 1999) to be particularly useful for thinking about how we access all key mental processes and orientations to achieve full life (e.g. Tufts Richardson 1998, Wadsworth 2006a)[18] as well as drawing on the more detailed Step 2® questions that yield levels of complexity and more 'customised' patternings of inquiring.

Building on this I have proposed in Chapter 3 the concept of 'reach' to represent more clearly and graphically how each individual may have differential access to much more—indeed in distinctive ways, to all of the inquiry cycle—than the four-letter code might otherwise indicate.

'Type dynamics' and the concept of inquiry preference 'reach'

For most people, depending on how the eight dimensions of the four two-fold pairs of preferences constellate their particular Myers-Briggs 'type' (or dynamic systemicity), there is a kind of order of favoured to less favoured mental processes and orientations to the world that not only take us well beyond the surface simplicity of the four-letter MBTI codes, but also give insight into how we might characteristically differently traverse the inquiry cycle. See Figure 29 for three of the sixteen constellations in graphic form. The order is thought to settle over the early decade or two of life as a person finds some approaches work better or feel easier than others, and a more-or-less typical response (particularly to an urgent need) is experienced as efficient to avoid a kind of 'jamming at the doorway' as all preferences might otherwise compete to 'offer their services first'. So, for example, in a car accident, one person may focus firstly on empathetically responding to the needs of victims crying in pain; while another will immediately telephone for an ambulance; another will firstly intuit that oncoming traffic is endangering everyone and then spring to direct the traffic; and a fourth quickly uses their mobile phone to photograph the scene. If there is only one person at the scene they may try and do all of these things, but again in their own characteristic order (or they may in fact act in an uncharacteristic order in the instance, possibly slightly less effectively or needing later debriefing).

The concept of 'reach' illuminates how the four-letter 'types' are thus 'mere keyhole codes' or indicators to understanding this fuller 'rich thick' living systemicity that lies behind the superficial appearance of narrow reach of any particular key-code. Figure 29 illustrates how we can use our own particular familiar systemicity to 'reach' around the inquiry cycle—including across the 'thin ice' of our least preferred inquiry processes—and in so doing connect with and understand others doing the same from theirs.

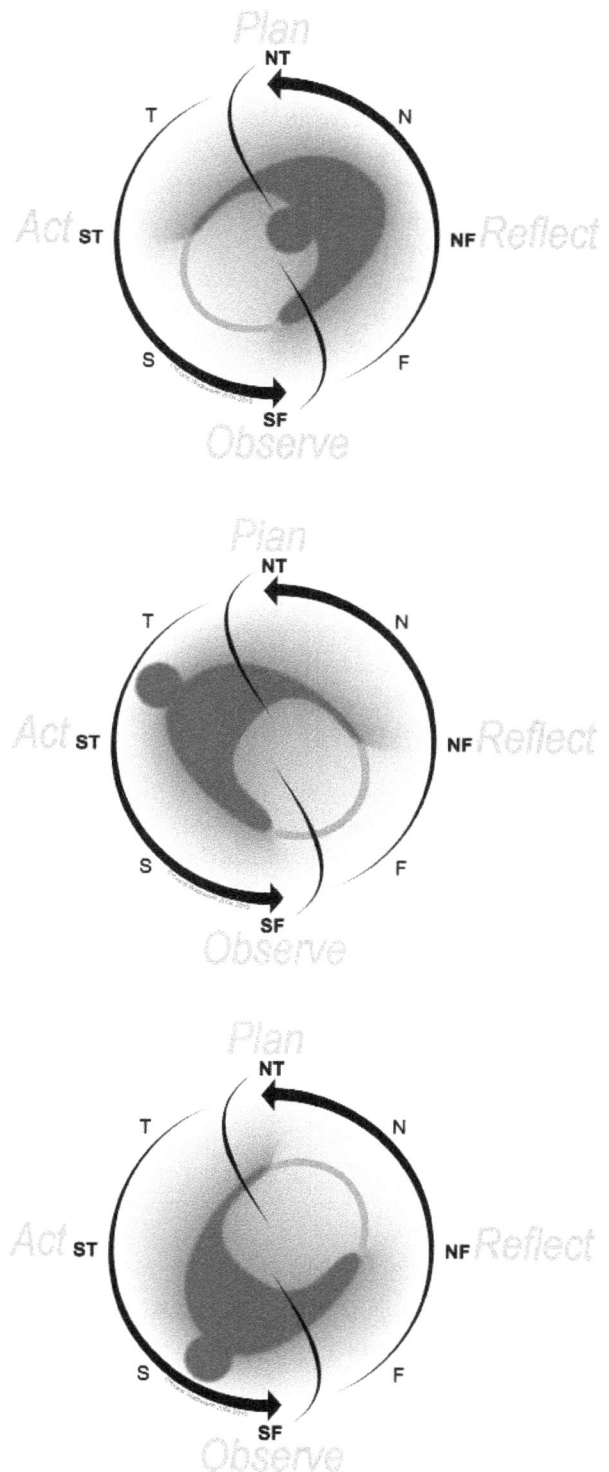

Figure 29. The concept of full cycle inquiry preferences 'reach'

In this way characteristic 'personality types' or mental processes and orientations we have for inquiring our way around living systems cycles are perhaps better thought of as less like 'little boxes', 'four-letters' or rigid algorithms and more like 'neural networks', clusters of overlapping and concentrated energy flows, or kaleidoscopes through which we see life in characteristic ways.

We are not one identity. We are not 'thinkers' *or* 'doers' *or* 'big picture people' *or* 'natural leaders' *or* any of the numerous other objectifying reductions that do not do justice to what else we are *also* as a result of complex social-biological-genetic processes and 'structures', social formations and enculturation. We may be all of these at different times and places, even as they may or may not be our preferences. Thus if we are to accept definitions that describe our own inquiry preferences or characteristic approaches these may most usefully be constructed by ourselves and together within our organisations or communities *autopoetically* to try and best capture our own ways of experiencing them and how they contribute to our own living systemic identity and those of others with whom we co-construct life.

'Knowing self and others (and all else)' becomes the way people become autopoetic at any scale. Thus we are all more or less able to get right round the full inductive–abductive–deductive inquiry cycle drawing on all our 'inner personality types' or living systems inquiry preferences, particularly at smaller scales of systemicity. And we get right round inquiry cycles at larger scales of living systemicity by contributing from our 'inquiry specialities' or 'type preferences' and receiving inputs from others' to make together integral deliberative 'communities of science'[19] of 'all types' in continuing close dialogue *together* to achieve individual and collective full cycle 'reach'. The alternative to this is where the parts have lost the hermeneutic ability to each 'hold the all' and instead dissolve into a plethora of homogenous personality 'type tribes', resorting to Chinese whispers, closed divisions of inquiring labour and Towers of Babel of competing voices, susceptible to repeated misunderstandings, conflicts, crises, threats, counter-threats, escalating risks and insecurities.

A new integral meta-conceptualisation of the Jungian Myers Briggs constructs

Here I summarise my depiction of how differing type systemicities might characteristically and differently be depicted around the inquiry cycle:

In this book I have depicted metaphorically how an integral inquiring 'human household'—a neo-*oikos*—might be thought of as a dynamic 'house of all types', of all four characteristic 'type systemicity shapes', matching the full act–observe–reflect–plan inquiry cycle.

In this way, as we traverse through all four 'quadrant shapes', we might think of ourselves as perpetually constructing and reconstructing such a metaphoric 'house of all shapes' (in contrast perhaps to only a pyramidal Tower of Babel!)

Here I return to the systems thinking of Chapter 2

TABLE 15. SUMMARY OF INQUIRY MODES, PRACTICES, SHAPES, CULTURES AND KEY MBTI INQUIRY PREFERENCES

Inquiry	Practice	Symbolic shape	Culture	MBTI inquiry preference
Act	Carrying culture	Square, grids, tables, matrixes	This is how it is done around here	ST-S
Observe Experience	Describing Evaluating	Outside the square/box, nets, weaves, dots, wavy lines, fragments	We're doing it well (or not so well)	SF-F
Reflect	Transforming Generating	Circles of connection, spirals	What we could do instead	NF-N
Plan	Mastering	Triangle, pyramid, summits	Now we know what to do next	NT-T

Figure 30. House of 'all types' and typifiying processes

and the way in which the human body may be thought of as the 'psychological home' for the individual, just as the domestic house may be seen as the individual self writ large, and human settlement as the 'body corporate' writ larger still in ever greater organic specialisation and capillary connectivity.

Figure 30 combines the four shapes that I detect are characteristic of the four quadrants of the inquiry cycle in a nice abstract symbolic mnemonic aide (in the light of Chapter 3).[20]

In the same way that we speak of 'a fully rounded person' who achieves joined-up 'reach' to traverse from 'how we do things now' across the phase change to creating and then instituting the new 'mainstream', we might also speak of a 'fully rounded partnership', or a fully rounded group, fully rounded community, organisation, institution, society or global community.

'Inquiring full cycle' means therefore that the mainstream must also include what is outside the mainstream. Only then will we have truly addressed exclusionary practices to re-integrate all. Only then will we have all inquiry preferences represented at the table—and integrated within an individual mind.

We know it when we see it—whether in a cohesive local neighbourhood where people 'know and are known'; or a cheerful, healthy and self-starting boys' gang on the train; an energetic, self-critical and welcoming community association that has been going for many years; a particularly vibrant but stable and ethical company with low staff turnover; a 'developing' society where people's families have lived and worked together productively for thousands of years; or a human service where people have a sense of humour, see themselves as continuously learning and where there is an absence of destructive tensions. Settings where 'all types' are in good relationship with each other—and not easily distinguishable as such because perpetual crises have been systemically abated and no longer repeatedly trigger people to be one-dimensional around their most preferred mental functions. Where people know who they are and the human life values they are there for, with none having to 'overdo their type' or 'under-do' it, exploiting or being exploited. Where people constantly stop, look, listen and talk things through…as do their larger social groupings, moving forward and changing to strengthen the good, while continuing faithfully the successful (but still well-examined) old forms, until they too are more or less joyfully superseded one day.

We have known these things for millennia and have been more or less passing on all the necessary inquiry preferences important for life—even as we ricochet in and out of seeing one as 'best' rather than holding the wisdom that all are needed at different process moments and under different conditions. We could be teaching more explicitly from kindergarten this kind of integrating knowledge about how to inquire. Like any body of knowledge it has its complexities and sophistication—and it also has its simpler entrée points and algorithms. The observe–reflect–plan–act cycle has introduced many to one such, as has the standard though more circumscribed business cycle of plan–do–check–act. Even the four seasons or a 24-hour clock-face can be the start of introducing this most basic of mental architectures from which to build more effectively inquiring life systems. In this book I have used the idea of the 'house of many rooms' as another device.

The urgency of the task is upon us. We can start steadily whenever or wherever or with whomever we are, commencing in any small patch or local field:

observing, listening, hearing, and sharing what we are seeing, feeling and thinking—including our desire that we and all others be taken note of, listened to, heard, and understood. Nothing could perhaps be more urgent than genuinely 'joining up' action with research with policy, and planning and evaluating new action.

Now we know just what to do—or rather, now we know just what to try out!

But why is it so hard to achieve dynamic change, and more easy to keep reproducing existing forms?

The final insight that can be derived from the Jungian Myers Briggs formulation concerns the question of movement for social change and movement for new social order and the difficulties of moving between the two: across *Phase change 1* without defaulting inevitably to the known and familiar, and across *Phase change 2*

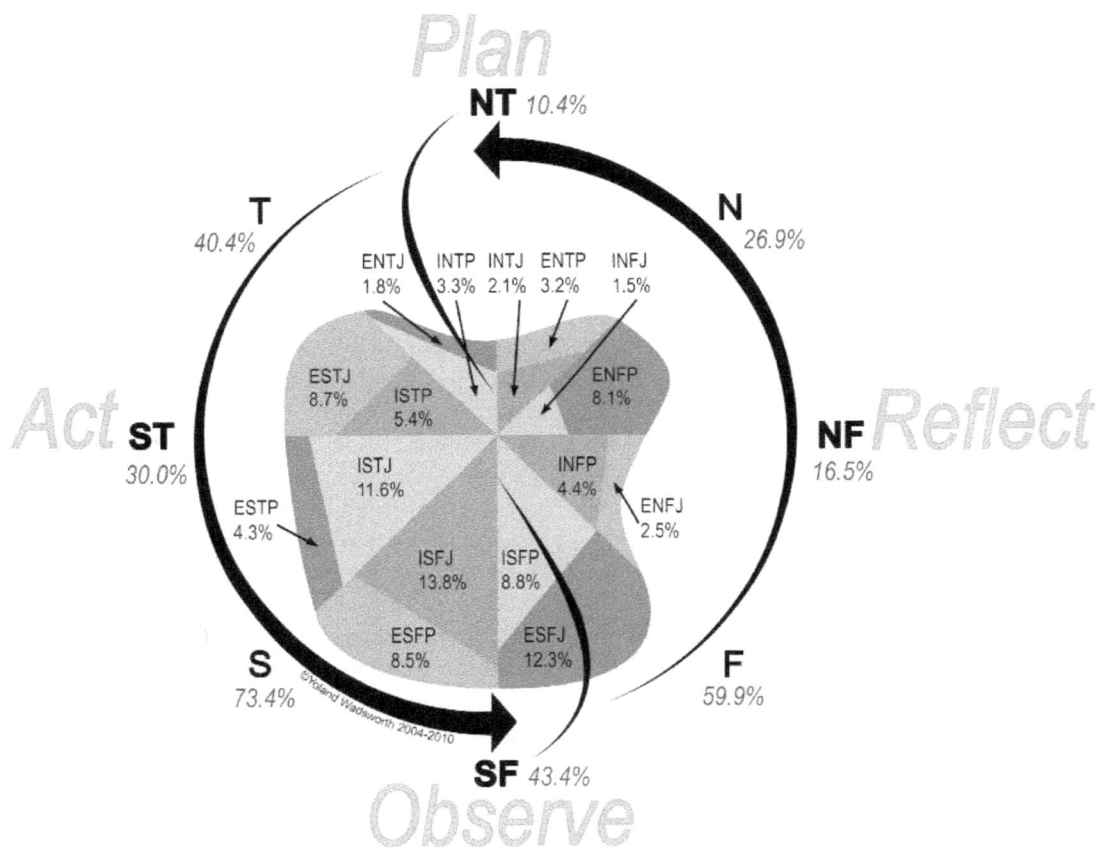

Figure 31. Approximate distribution of inquiry preferences around the cycle
(might *homo sapiens* have gone pear-shaped?)

Key to Figure 31.
Perimeter figures: Single letters (inquiry processes) are percentages of their opposite
Double letters (temperaments) are percentages of all four
Internal figures: Four-letter codes are percentages of all sixteen

without inevitably losing a new and better form and reverting to the logic of the prior iteration's form.

Drawing on the living systems theory of inquiry in this book, Figure 31 positions the statistical shape for each of the sixteen Myers-Briggs 'type' systemicities' dimensions proportionally around the cycle (Myers et al 1998, USA population distribution statistics, p. 298). It should be noted that while these are culturally western patterns, there appear to be strong cross-cultural similarities (which would not be surprising if they are describing the deeper inquiring capability of living systems). However the distribution and dominance of and within any varying pattern is inevitably socio-cultural in our species.

Thus, remembering that each person can reach around the cycle and this imaging is illuminating the 'density of focus' of these different inquiry preference constellations, the boundaries alert us nevertheless to the potential for social formations to confine people to exercising only their most familiar and best-used preferences. The upside in times of crisis (although only if people are in good enough relationship with each other and can 'act as one') mirrors a serious and endangering downside if people are not enabled to return to inquiring full cycle together—a downside of disconnectedness which precludes being able to develop the relationships of 'knowing and being known' to achieve the mutual understanding and respect that enables the acting as one in the first place.

The conclusions I draw tentatively from this conceptual imaging of the systemic generation and distribution of contemporary inquiry preference differences between people, given the speed and pressure demands in large-scale post industrial societies include:

- The majority of current human preoccupation is with *acting* in terms of existing received patterns, forms, knowledges and logics
- The majority of *observing* is checking that this is the case and then adapting with modified plans without necessarily moving to reflect more deeply on the existing logic
- Discrepancies that may initially be experienced in the form of embodied rational feeling may not be articulated, or are so only with encouragement, time and attentive receptive listening
- Time spent *reflecting* and in dialogue about such observations in order to make intuitive connections

to bigger wider pictures of contextual implication is significantly less, and the task of facilitating processes to move through *Phase change 1* and *Phase change 2* is metaphorically less like 'turning a wheel' and more like upending and turning over a 'whole pear'

- When there is time and space for all to observe and hear and share their observations and experiences, and contemplate how things might be connected and best explained, and work out the implications in theory and new practice—when all these inquiry tasks are accomplished more or less in concert—then well-discerned action can take place more or less effortlessly. When this is not the case, we see that the discrepancies, paradoxes, disconnects and stuck processes can remain, even with, and partly due to factors of high speed and large scale.

It may be possible also however to see why the human species can maintain its stability and resilience over long periods of time, but at the same time—in mass large-scale societies with divisions of labour built around inquiry preferences—slowly amass discrepancies like the apocryphal frog in the pot of water, getting hotter and hotter, yet still not 'seeing what is coming', or at least possibly not until the eleventh hour (or five minutes to midnight), even as we may indeed be 'going pear-shaped'.

It seems convincing evidence for involving all in autopoetically inquiring together 'around the cycle' at every scale, sometimes too slowly for some, sometimes too fast for others, but ultimately at the right speed if the looming alternatives to such thoughtful forms of deliberative participatory democratic inquiry are considered.

APPENDIX 4

An example of use of the sequence of 'whole cycle' research questions —in health promotion practice

[Revised] Extract from: Y. Wadsworth, A. Wierenga and G. Wilson, *Writing Narrative Action Evaluation Reports in Health Promotion—Guidelines, Resource Kit and Case Studies*, 2nd edn, 'Resource H', Victorian Department of Human Services and the University of Melbourne, Melbourne, 2007, www.health.vic.gov.au/healthpromotion/steps/evaluation.htm#narrative.

A planner/checklist of questions for writing narrative action evaluation reports.

Firstly, two design issues:

Who were our stakeholders?

Who are/were the interested people/stakeholders/or participants involved already? Who should have been? Who could or should also give their views as part of this story—or be here telling this story with us? Whose story is it?

What were the practicalities?

Together with our stakeholders/participants, where, when and how would be the best way to capture and share all our observations and experiences?

> *Retrospective evaluation*
> Firstly, looking back to see how things have gone so far…

What was being evaluated?

Name the area of activity, interest, issue, 'claim, concern or issue', practice or project…

What did we observe?

Looking at the whole [and]

Looking at the parts (e.g. a range of activities that make up the program, or different parts of a work area; or different aspects of a project), describe for each what we have, so far, seen, observed, noticed or heard about it.

Why were these things being done?

Why like this? Who identified the need? (Participants? Staff? The organisation?) What were all our hopes?

What was its value?— *'open inquiry evaluation'*

Evaluate value, merit, worth or significance so far. Overall, how is it going? Is it working well? (or not) What makes you say that? Describe what you've seen, observed, noticed, learned etc. (and what others have seen, learned etc. too). *Try answering using a three-column matrix format*: 1. Good or not so good? 2. I know because before (we observed)…3. Now it's changed in the following ways…

Did we achieve our objectives?— *'audit review evaluation'*

Did we set out to achieve certain goals or objectives in relation to this activity, interest, or project? What were they? What were our planned indicators and targets or signs of achieving them? Were they met or achieved do we think? What happened? What were the actual outputs and outcomes? *Try answering using a three-column matrix format:* 1. We set out to (describe goals etc.) …2. Were our indicators/targets achieved? 3. Not achieved? You might refer explicitly here to the statistical reporting accompanying the narrative report.

Why was it like this?—*analyse/think/reflect*

Stop and reflect on (and analyse) what we think we are seeing. Why do we think those signs or reasons actually made it good or not? What do we think was going on here if we saw that sign? What do we think was really going on? What is our reasoning or logic about this? How do we explain our successes or problems?

How did we feel about it?

Now stop and reflect on how we feel about it? What made us feel like that was a good (or bad) sign? Why did it seem like it was right (or wrong)? Good or bad?

A threshold or liminal question: did we want change or not to change?

Looking back, did we want to change or improve the activity, project etc.? Or did we decide we wanted to replicate it because it was going well? What did we learn?

> *Prospective evaluation*
> Now looking forward from 'what was then' to 'what could be'…

What was the vision?

Did we clarify our vision about what we had either hoped for next (and still hope for now) or, with hindsight, what would we do differently? Or what would be better? (Or even better?)

What needed to change?

What change or changes did we decide would be needed to bring the situation towards the desired/ideal/something better? What did we think it would take to make that happen? What actions, steps, pathways? Who else did we think needed to be involved?

What alternatives were there?

Were alternatives were considered? Even seemingly

'way out' ones or suggestions that seemed at first impracticable or unworkable at this creative 'out of the square' moment? Did we listen to soft voices, different-from-us voices, and community voices belonging to the least powerful or most stigmatised, and possibly ones we disagreed with at first?

What were the consequences that led to our choice/s?

What were the consequences of going down these different tracks we decided? What was the effect of taking up the idea? How did we feel about doing this? What were the responses to it by all the stakeholders? What were its strengths, weaknesses, opportunities, threats? Which had the most energy attached to it?

What actions came next?

When we settled on a course or courses of action, who was going to do what?

What support did you need?

What did we need in order to actually *do* it! What did it take—what support, assistance, information, resources, people etc. were needed?

Monitor…and…

What are we seeing now? Now that we are giving it a go? Did we monitor and observe, describe and evaluate the change we tried? What did we see changed as a result of what we did? And what have we already thought we might do next?!

Yes! It's an action evaluation research story!

An ongoing story…!

APPENDIX 5

Other integral theories of change

Chapter 3 presents an integral epistemology (a way of thinking about how we inquire-to-know through questioning) that drives both the essential dynamic of change *and* the stabilising organisation required by every living organism at whatever scale. It rests on a theory of living systems developed in Chapter 2. It has been explored further in Chapters 4 and 5 through the lens of human services (as an integral psychology of individual inquiry preferences) and of social groups (as an integral sociology of organisational research and evaluation culture).

There are many other such theories of the integral, also often using the heuristic of a central structural metaphor. I have analysed a large number of them of most relevance to the subject matter of this book in this Appendix according to four groupings:

1. **Circles/cycles/phases**
2. **Hierarchies/ladders**
3. **Analytic grids/matrices/categories/taxonomies**
4. **Images/colours/symbols/signs/logos**

Here I list and describe briefly the key, most relevant examples of each of these groups of theories. I then summarise my own in relation to them.

1. Circles/cycles/phases:

Kolb and Fry's (1975: 35–36) learning styles of 'concrete' experience (accommodate); observation-reflection (divergence); abstraction of concepts (assimilation); active experimentation (converge); see also Kolb (*infed* 2001) for learning style models.

Argyris and Schon's (1978) single loop (thinking) and double loop (thinking about thinking), drawing on *Bateson's* (1972) 1st and 2nd order learning.

Isaacs' (1993) triple loop learning (about how or why thinking should be accomplished).

Cooperrider and Srivastva's (1987) and *Ludema's et al.* (2001: 192) 4D appreciative inquiry's Discover–Dream–Design–Destiny/Deliver.

Zimmer's (2001) Open University action-learning systems approach: 1st, 2nd and 3rd order.

Stringer's (1996) Look–Think–Act.

Catholic Worker's Movement's (Jacques Boulet, personal communication 2008) To see, To judge, To act.

Shewart-Deming's (2008) PDCA business cycle: Plan–Do–Check–Act

Brown's (2002) P4D4 Decide/principles, Describe/(people)place, Design/potential, Do/practice.

Bell and Morse's (2005) citation of *Proclus'* fifth-century soft systems cyclic precepts of 'abiding, proceeding and returning'.

Sarkar's (cited in Inayatullah and Fitzgerald 1999: 16) social change cycle of five epistemologies (as part of a larger Progressive Utilisation Theory of history and political economy) comprising: Sense–Inference (science); Reason–Logic (philosophy); Authority (Religion); Intuition (mysticism); and Devotion/Love.

Tufts Richardson's (1996) circle of four spiritual journeys organising the four 'functions', temperaments and sixteen MBTI® typifications around a relational circle, and *Wadsworth's* (2006a) adaptation of this as a dynamic relational inquiry cycle comprising: the journeys of Works (ST-act and observe rational logic), Devotion (SF-act and observe with rational feeling), Harmony (NF-reflect and abduct new theory) and Unity (NT-plan experimental action).

Moore's (2002) cycle of rhythms: of flowing, staccato, chaos, lyric and stillness.

Tuckman's (1965) sequence of human groups' Forming, Storming, Norming, Performing, Adjourning/Mourning.

LaBonte's et al. (1999: 41) story-dialogue method of Describe, Explain, Synthesise, Act.

Holling's (1978) ∞ infinity symbol of ecosystem functioning fluctuating between chaos and re-grouping, and order and disintegration (see undated website for graphic).

Zuber-Skerrit's and design team colleagues' (2000) figure 8 process of design and management, joining Context with Practice via Vision.

Bell and Morse's (2005) sideways figure 8 from 'suggest & do', 'reflect & understand', 'connect & investigate', 'model & explore'.

Scharmer's (2003) U-shape process of seven-field structures of attention: Downloading, Seeing, Sensing,

Presencing, Crystallising, Prototyping, and Institution-alising.

Herrman's (1998) four-quadrants, cerebral and limbic 'whole brain' model is depicted as a mandala-shaped endless knot image in yellow (Experimental self—infers, imagines etc.), blue (rational self—analyses, quantifies etc.), green (safekeeping self—organises, plans etc.) and red (feeling self—sensitive, expressive etc.) overlapping roughly the categories of reflect, plan, act and observe.

The astrological signs and imputed cosmic order matching key stations around a cycle of life change (e.g. with Pisces sitting just past my cycle's *Phase change 1* or the MBTI INFP).

The Chinese Taoist eight-trigrams arranged around the yin–yang cycle of life and death.

Hindu mandalas: Wikipaedia's 'Mandala' entry also includes links to analogues in the North American eight archetypes medicine wheel and the circular journey labyrinth also found in Europe.

2. Hierarchies/ladders:

Wilber's (2005) AQAL (all levels, all lines, all states, all types) levels of consciousness arranged from red at the bottom through the colours of the rainbow to ultraviolet and clear light at the top.

Maslow's (1968) hierarchy of needs, from lower basic physiological and safety/security needs to higher self-esteem and self-actualisation needs.

Bennett's (1977) hierarchy of evaluating outcomes achievement (and Bennett and Rockwell 2008) from program development (feedback, conditions, practices, knowledge, attitudes, skills, aspirations, reactions, participation, activities and resources) to program performance (then the process goes 'forward' down through the preceding list in reverse order).

Arnstein's (1969) 'ladder of citizen participation', from least involved/least powerful at the bottom to most self-organising/in control at the top; see also *Wadsworth's* (1997b: 98) matching of Arnstein's ladder with a corresponding ladder of participation in evaluation.

Wadsworth and *Kneebone's* (1997b) cartoon of political-bureaucratic complex hierarchical process of hearing the voice of the critical reference group (Wadsworth: 35).

Rossi et al's (2003) Program Evaluation Hierarchy—need, design, process & implementation, cost & efficiency.

Sharp's (2005) Organisational Evaluation Capability Hierarchy—ad hoc, planned, integrated, meta-analytic, strategic.

Aristotle's hierarchy of questions—material (what is it made from?), formal (what is it meant to be?), efficient (what was it meant to be for?) and final (why was it made?), cited in Bell and Morse (2005).

Various Western and Asian philosophies that position the reptilian brain stem or emotional chakra at the bottom, moving or evolving up through the various other levels, chakras or organs, to the rational neocortex at the top/peak/apex of human developmental evolution/civilisation.

3. Analytic grids/matrices/categories/taxonomies

Wilber's (2005) four-quadrants or meta-map of Zone 1—'I' intentional; Zone 2—'It' behavioural; Zone 3—'We' cultural; Zone 4—'Its' social.

Flood's (1999) 'four windows' ideal-typical categorisation of process, structure, meaning, knowledge-power.

Heron et al.'s (Coghlan 2005) practical, experiential, presentational and propositional forms of knowing.

Eoyang's (2004) taxonomy of surface, deep and subtle structures cross-tabulated with act, describe, intervene/influence/ make visible, represent.

Herrman's (1995, 1996) four-quadrant whole brain learning: intellectual self/visionary; safe-keeping self/organiser; emotional self/communicator; experimental self/logician.

The Jungian Myers Briggs MBTI® (1999) 4 x 4 matrix of cross-tabulating Sensing, Intuiting and Feeling, Thinking with Extroverting, Introverting and Perceiving, Judging.

Ife's (1997: 46–47) 2-dimensional grid (top-down-hierarchic and bottom-up anarchic axis, intersected by positivist-humanist axis) resulting in four competing human services' discourses: managerialist, market, community and professional (corresponding to my living systems/Jungian Myers Briggs cycles of plan/act [NT], act/observe [ST], observe/reflect [SF/NF] and reflect/plan [NF/NT]).

Dean's (in Carney 2007: 17) Competitive, Authoritarian, Inclusive and Egalitarian classification.

Field et al's (1986) five epistemological categories: silence (mindless, voiceless, subject); received knowledge (from all-knowing external authorities); subjective knowledge (personal, private, subjectively/intuitively known); procedural knowledge (objective procedures for obtaining and communicating knowledge); constructed knowledge (contextual, created by selves, subjective and objective strategies) (also corresponding to the use of Jungian Myers Briggs 'personality preferences' as inquiry preferences in Chapter 3).

4. Images/colours/symbols/signs/logos

de Bono's (1999) six thinking hats to aid lateral thinking (seeing creativity as the behaviour of information in a self-organising information system): white—data; red—emotion/intuition; black—pessimism; yellow—optimism; green—creativity; blue—process overview/control.

Weil and *McGill's* (1989) four villages of experiential learning: village one—assess and accredit; two—experiential change to structures; three—experiential for group consciousness-raising; four—personal growth and self-awareness.

Sperry et al. (1969) and *Hellige* (2001) the left-brain and right-brain correspondences of left for the analytical, verbal, mathematical, logical, rational, definitional and structured; and the right for the lateral, intuitive, creative, visual, flexible, exploratory, global-synthesising and conceptual.

McMurray-Ryan's (McMurray 2000) 3D model of action research as an umbrella and six-colours boxes: black—entry; red—stop/inquire; yellow—analyse; blue—feedback; green—go/action; pearly white—clarify/evaluate.

Wadsworth's (2008a, 2008b) use of colour in the living systems corresponding cycle diagrams.

Plutchik's (1995) eight-colours Emotion Wheel-Cone.

The Enneagram non-hierarchic inverted U-shaped 'pathways' pentangle characterising nine personality types used in personal and organisational development (e.g. Palmer and Brown 1997) and spiritual development in mystical Islam and the Catholic Church

The Taoist yin–yang circular symbol, (path) way, and the use of the lotus in Asia (and the rose in Christian Europe).

There are countless others used in personal, careers, business and management development (e.g. all the differing constellations of learning styles, leadership styles, teamwork and management styles, such as the Singer-Loomis SD-TDI®); as well as all the numerous religious/spiritual, cultural/traditional and archetypal, and other holistic or integrative models of being and change.

Discussion in relation to my own theory, integrating all four systemic shapes

Patti Lather has identified these shapes as expressing in some as yet unknown ways key elements of how we understand the world. She notes the search for a way to 'diagram the becoming of history against the limits of our conceptual frameworks that are so much about what we have already ceased to be' (2006: 44 Table 3).

I have come to theorise these shapes as integrated by a helical *cycle metaphor* (or a double helix when 'scaffolded' by 'alongsided'/enabling inquiry facilitation [or inquiry impeding], see Chapter 4) as a unifying dynamic 'architecture' representing life as comprising always-changing *and* always-stabilising patterns of energetic flow. That is, at the same time as patterns of energy can be seen as indeterminate, they may also be seen as stabilising by becoming dense and repeated, appearing 'real and solid' (Chapter 2). I am using the *house* as an *'architectural' metaphor* to represent these energies as 'forming' and being organised in embodied 'space and place'.

In Chapter 3 and Appendix 3 I identified how this cycle of inquiring life morphs complexly between all four key shapes 'around the cycle' of :

• *Pyramidal triangular hierarchy* (at PLAN)—when peak certainty is reached with energy focusing around new knowledge conclusions (balanced by the always humbling knowledge that such knowing remains provisional)

- *Analytic square grid* (at ACT)—when energetic knowing settles into a more routinised phase of collectively organised 'business as usual', acting on and repeating (and defending) action on the basis of previous conclusions (balanced by knowing such action is always experimental and thus always needing to remain open to new questions)
- *Fragments and fluid wavy lines* (at OBSERVE)— when out of the dissipation and breakdown of the old, we move 'outside the square' to analyse and break down what is becoming discrepant/no longer whole, to begin the new synthesis of what is possible after reaching peak uncertainty, and yielding to readiness for change (balanced by the always augmenting knowing that this chaos of potential connection is pregnant with life-giving life-forming possibilities)
- *The circle* (at REFLECT)—when it 'all comes together' in inner or outer collective dialogue through making connections and generating new resonant understandings about the most *deeply valued* form/identity of the new (balanced by knowing that such abductive ideals need to strive to be tested and refined in implementable form), before the circle again soars high into 'a cone of certainty' around unity for planning new action.

I have concluded that any of these shapes dominating, or on its own, results in loss of the conditions for a fully living system. For example, a top-down *pyramid* has no movement without equally strong bottom-up and egalitarian and circular currents, risking a tyranny of 'the one and only'. A *square* matrix box is more egalitarian but again remains firmly squat in reproducing its own equilibrium structure, unable to be or do otherwise, or go 'anywhere different', risking inflexibility and rigidity with 'no way out' of 'the machine'. *Wavy lines and fragments* are full of rich and dynamic possibilities to feed the new form yet on their own can remain a chaos of movement 'all over the place' until form emerges to organ-ise specialised action to achieve valued purposes. And a *circle*, while the most democratically participatory of forms for the exchange of different perspectives, also risks 'going round in circles' unless it reaches conclusions and 'breaks out of itself' to move towards some form of organ-ised and energetic new action.

In opting for the larger metaphors of the structural *house* and a process *cycle*, I have noted that this is not always how we proceed in practice (although most do seem to follow this sequence as a matter of logic, sense, feeling or intuition when free to do so), but that it provides a way of illuminating a kind of 'reconstructed logic' (Kaplan 1964) that ensures ultimately that new inquiry is anchored in 'what is', energises change with what is most valued as life-enhancing (or least valorised as life-denying), and then 'visits' *every* part of the cycle (without suppressing, denying or skipping any).

At any one time in personal, group or human history there may be a preponderant positioning somewhere round the cycle (and not at others)—for example, currently, arguably dominant and favoured are the pyramid and square moments and repeatedly resisted are the yield-to-chaotic diversity and circle moments, with potentially near catastrophic systemic contemporary results for an economy dependent on its living environment, as well as for most women (not exclusively the bearers of powers of feeling-observation and intuitive-reflection but the majority gender that is). Thus one remedy available is to attend systemically to discrepancy and those able to notice and interpret most effortlessly—the human system's early warning system. In proceeding thus, and achieving a snowballing of participation together 'around the cycle' and the gathering in of *all* the key systemic inquiry capacities, we may ensure they are in more active collective service to what is 'for life' and the living.

This systemic approach to constantly *oscillating* between human capabilities while anchoring inquiry in the heart of deeply felt, embodied valuing, also offers a way out of the possibility of later unwanted or excessive idealism, premature pragmatism, unpopular destabilising utilitarianism, coercive mechanistic authoritarianism, meaningless duty for its own sake, mindless pleasure or unrelenting grief.

This heuristic mapping is inclusive—able to contain 'the all'—like Elisabet Sahtouris' insistence that her 'model of the cosmos must include all human experience' (2005a: 2). The dominance of one way of 'being, knowing and doing' can no longer be asserted without being aware of its relativity to both its opposite and to all others 'round the cycle'.

Like Jung, I think we are only at the dawn of this

new frontier of 'knowing self and others'. In history these understandings are not new, but they have hitherto been mostly esoteric, known only to an intellectual-political or religio-spiritual elite, with only scattered individual instances among the populace. In contemporary human life there is, with widespread educational systems, shared economic institutional life and distributed information systems via the internet, an historic possibility of more widespread insight. I remain in awe, however, of the many instances in which we do not yet appear to have an inkling of how each other's minds work: and how they work both radically differently and *reliably* differently, and indeed how they work systemically to the benefit of all *if free to do so*, while alternatively under excessive stress, they can work to the detriment of life. I have received a beginner's glimpse (on which this book draws) after thirty-eight years of using sociology to understand socio-political economy and epistemological 'typologies', and fifteen years of using the Myers-Briggs Type Indicator to understand healthy psychological epistemological preferences, and seventeen years of systemic-change practice informed by Taoism and an adult lifetime steeped in the ecological. I also know enough to not doubt that my current theory will already contain the seeds of its own revision!

Yet for possibly a long time to come, I detect the shape of a 'new big story' in this integral theory of inquiring living systems—one that might both shape and be shaped by a new age to come of greater self-knowledge and autopoesis. Not just the Greeks' 'know thyself'—but now also 'know thyself *and* know each other and all other beings' to assist our species avoid its regular acts of war and self-destruction, repeatedly mistaking separate aspects of its greater species being as 'alien other' and producing life-defeating swings in one direction or another, settling instead for building in a cultural wisdom of how to inquire to self-organise for healthy dynamic equilibrium.

ENDNOTES

1 The Myers-Briggs Type Indicator®, Myers-Briggs® and MBTI®, the words Step I® and Step II® and *Introduction to Type®* are trademarks or registered trade marks of the MBTI Trust Inc. in the USA and other countries.

2 Two American women, Katharine Briggs and her daughter Isabel Myers, were the prime movers in creating, during the mid-twentieth century, from the time of the Second World War, an inventory of questions yielding descriptions of a range of reliable patterns of human 'personality' or characteristic ways the mind both perceives (becomes 'aware of things, people, happenings or ideas') and judges (comes 'to conclusions about what has been perceived') (Myers et al. 1998: 3). From 1943 they based their research on the theory of psychological 'type' from the Swiss psychiatrist Carl Jung. The Myers-Briggs Type Indicator (MBTI®) has since become the most widely used such inventory in the world, an unchallenged claim by Consulting Psychologists Press, accessed 26 July 2010 www.cpp.com/products/mbti/index.aspx. It comprises two sets of questions that are seen as assisting the user to indicate (point towards, suggest) their own characteristic *patterns of preference* between four pairs of key mental processes and orientations to the world: introversion and extraversion, intuition and sensing, feeling and thinking, and perceiving and judging. The meanings of these are explained in this appendix, along with my 'take' on them as usefully describing the key inquiry characteristics of individual and socially systemic human life. The first set of questions (Step I®) yields sixteen possible main 'types' or patterns of systemicity, and the second set of questions (Step 2®) addresses a further five sub-dimensions of each of the eight key dimensions, yielding significant levels of additional complexity and variance within the main sixteen 'type systemicities'. The indicator is most often used in organisational development, workplace team formation, adult learning, relationships education and careers guidance.

3 'Canaries in the mind' was the name the project gave mental health activists who, like 'canaries in the mine' (who first gave a sign of deathly gases in coal mines), were first to experience the hurtful discrepancies between intentions and practice in mental health services and attempt to 'sound the alarm' to trigger felt observation and reflection, but could 'sing sweetly' enough to avoid defensive reaction at *Phase change one*.

4 'Shooting the messenger' was understood to be the fate of those who assembled the evidence, drew the conclusions, saw the implications and attempted to 'speak truth to power' thinking their messages would be (or should be) received and acted on at *Phase change two*.

5 Later I came to typify psychology's main approaches, using Jungian Myers Briggs and related temperament theory, to see *behaviourism* as tending to apply rule-based, concretely

observed, discrete linear cause and effect (ST-sensing thinking) in action (possibly losing sight of deeper values on autopoesis) and when in the grip of stress, possibly forcing a change in behaviour (e.g. by carrots or sticks respectively); *brief solution therapy* as tending to treat each person more personally as a unique individual who might select between different methods to try out something quickly and see if an effect is noticeable (SP—sensing perceiving); *narrative therapy* as assisting the person or group generate their own 'bigger picture story' of their past, present and future experience, encouraging personal observation and analysis of that experience and of their values to identify new conclusions or preferred ideas with implications for action (NF—intuitive feeling); and *cognitive behavioural therapy* (*CBT*) or *rational emotive therapy* (*RET*) as using the power of logical thought processes to 'think differently about one's thinking' to create a vision or an image of a desired future and do or become it by forming it in the mind, and then acting 'as if' it was now coming into being or already operating (NT—intuitive thinking).

I have concluded that these four approaches to psychological therapy (Gk therupeia, 'healing', making whole) can be thought of as 'mapping around the living systems cycle' from an orientation to restoring:

- *action* on the basis of existing conclusions, theory, rules, algorithms (e.g. *behaviourism*)
- *observation-action* in a quick and simple feedback loop (e.g. *brief solution therapy*)
- *reflection-on-observation* to construct a deeper new account or theory-story (e.g. *narrative therapy*)
- *planning and taking new action* by projective logical thinking, based on thinking about thinking/observing (e.g. *CBT and RET*).

While it may illuminate the value of one over the other (as an individual or group traverses 'full cycle'), and also whether any particular therapy resonates better with or supports the person's own preferences around the cycle, assisting 'scaffolding' across any 'thin ice' of unpreferred inquiry preferences, a risk lies in seeing any one as only or always the best approach for everyone. As with all of life, our particular inquiry preferences need special support and attention as we traverse the cycle in our characteristic preferred and unpreferred ways, in the end 'going full cycle' for fuller dynamic and balanced life.

6   *To take an example—that of gender.* In popular discourse as well as academic (including feminist) research and writing, there has been a critique of the hegemonic assertion that woman are 'naturally' nurturing, emotional, home-oriented and passive, while men are 'naturally' oriented to the outside world of things, action and rational thinking. Using the MBTI® one can assemble a detailed descriptive statistical picture of how many men and women have these characteristics in actual practice—and how many don't

(Myers et al. 1998: 157–158, 298. See Table 7 regarding gender). In a culture that has rigidified around the typified contents of these two categories, boys and men who behave in nurturing, emotional, inner and passive ways have been pressured to not be 'like women', and women who orient to the outside world of things and action and typically use rational thinking have also been (perhaps somewhat less mercilessly but nevertheless usually with punitive consequences) pressured to act not so much 'like a man' (or else pressured to indeed 'be like a man' to succeed in 'a man's world'). Indeed many in the women's movement often believed that women who entered powerful positions had been 'forced to act in masculine ways' (rather than, for example, at last being in their element of characteristic personal systemicity), while many men even in the men's movement felt the need to suppress impulses to express their 'inner housewife' and to try and be their 'masculine selves' before more-or-less coming to terms with their preferred 'feminine' or 'sensitive new age' systemicity. The voices that say that one can (or can't) be any or all these things continue to assert themselves, even after decades of showing that people can indeed be variously male and compassionate and yielding (or not), or female and powerful or thinking (or not), as well as in practice combining all differing aspects in far more systemicities than these two (e.g. Belenky et al. 1986, for differing types of women's ways of knowing that are comparable to those delineated by the MBTI®, and Connell 2005: 3–6, for differing constructions of 'masculinities'). Interestingly the derision of 'women's intuition' appeared to evaporate after many big picture thinking managers worked out their Myers-Briggs® preferences and realised that intuition was critical to their success! Ultimately however, while there are statistically more women with preferences for rational feeling and intuition than men, and statistically more men with preferences for rational thinking and sensing than women, the statistical distribution of these systemicities across men and women in the Myers Briggs' sixteen typifications is startlingly less than the cultural stereotypes suggest and affirming of people's internal experience of their own varied and complex gender preferences.

To take a second example—that of education. Comparable insights are possible regarding the organisation of education systems to create primary schools emphasis on 'received knowledge' about how things are already understood to work (to supply immediate practical knowledge for survival, safety and protection for the young of the species), secondary school for 'bigger picture' knowledge of how things are situated in larger worlds, and tertiary (higher education) needs for even bigger picture global knowledge and ideas. All the while, from kindergarten through to lifelong learning, there is a backdrop of resourcing the skills to autopoetically inquire to get answers to one's own questions, rather than only rely on 'being told'.

To take a third example—that of social change per se. The 'tracking round the cycle' by the institution of education may also be seen as an analogue to the past half-century of a corresponding movement from an ST/SJ post-war 'father knows best' 1950s (act on the basis of received knowledge), giving way to an SF/NF 'new age' of 1960s Aquarian love, harmony and change (feeling rationality to evaluate more life-giving possibilities); in turn yielding to the critique of the 1970s as the 'tyranny of structurelessness' and an NT/ST desire to do something to achieve goals (turn the reflections into new plans for action), followed by a 1980s explosion of replicative 'creative capitalism', the internet, expanding markets, inequalities and a new world order (when the new wholism succumbed to being pragmatically grafted into the existing capitalist mode of production). Now that order itself faces entropy, primarily through major environmental threat and overdoing the excessive productivity of the modal societal 'active works' (SP/NT) in the exhausting 24/7 fast thinking (NT) all-consuming (SF) lifestyle of the 1990s, and a range of (ST) fears and anxieties about risks and clashes, wars and boundary break-downs resulting from global dynamic conflict, inequality and imbalance. In many ways, in the 2000s we are perhaps seeking a 'new story'——of ecological sustainability, holism and harmonious peace (NF) even as we hurtle towards a high-surveillance authoritarian reaction coming out of stress. Embodied feeling, for so long in the societal (particularly the gendered business-political-economic) 'shadow', is demanding to be re-experienced and re-expressed as a source of a moral and ethical values 'compass' to chart a future course towards a more truly living human and all beings world. Slowly, these unaware ways of societies stumbling forward, ricocheting from one overly ordered extreme to an overly chaotic other, may give way to greater systemic self-awareness of what it takes to go full circle for a more balanced and dynamic culture of life. Or not (based on Wadsworth 2006: 44–45)

7 Neuroscientists are busy developing persuasive theories and electronic imaging of how this resonance might be taking place within human embodiment. The most recent imaging of correspondences between people observing an action and some kind of corresponding electronic activity in the frontal cortex is being theorised as a kind of inferential 'mapping' taking place in what are being termed 'mirror neurons' (Miller and Cohen 2001, Rizzolatti and Craighero 2004, Chklovski and Koulakov 2004, Insel and Russell 2004, Wallis 2007, Schutz-Bosbach et al. 2008). That is, an observed action triggers a correspondence in embodied brain neuronal action resulting in, for example, feelings being able to be inferred 'empathetically', or motor-tactile activity being visualised as a pattern that informs imitation or enables an inferred logic of another's intentions, beliefs or desires, and new action to be projectively imagined. These manifestations imputed to the brain (although the

human mind might be a better conceptualisation recognising the complexity of what might be taking place) might be seen as corresponding with the Jungian Myers Briggs terminology of sensing, feeling, intuition and thinking—which I am seeing as the ways by which we inquire our way around continual cycles of action, observation, reflection and planning. When combined with a theory of genetic adaptive response to environment (Ridley 2003, Yehuda and Seckl 2008), we may be constructing a new way of understanding the sociological embodiment of human inquiry 'gifts differing'. I speculate here from Ridley about the possibility that the biological human may in part be a socio-enviro-genetic manifestation in adaptive response to the pattern of existing preferences available in the emergent infant human's lifeworld. That is, that the human species not only 'takes all types' to inquire to sustain life, but also continually 'makes all types' where there is imbalance. This would require detailed observation of the familial generational patterns of 'type' inquiry preferences within social families. It may even one day seem less important to ask 'Is it a boy or a girl?' and more important to ask 'What inquiry preferences has your family called forth?' The little children may indeed turn out to be sacred (meaning whole-making) in ways we have not yet realised—albeit possibly hard work in tiny isolated nuclear families. Or on a larger scale, equally hard work if the Western species is trying to come back from eliminating millions of its sensing-intuitive-feeling women during the European witch hunts, as may be China after eliminating its Falun Gong spiritual practitioners.

8 Note this is correspondence between underlying conceptual processes and not in any straightforward concrete sense of 'correspondence' between the specific content of any particular human thought and action, or even in the specificities of cultural practice. In Chapter 3 I used the metaphor of computer hardware and software to try and draw this distinction between the 'software operating system' of any particular organism and its actual user-generated content. The type of pen and what is written. But knowing the software is a text document tells you something more about differences you might expect from that systemicity than if it were a graphics package, or a tabular matrix program, or a presentation projection program, or a sound media package. What the 'operator' of that characteristic systemicity does with it, how they traverse full inquiry cycles, or 'inscribe onto' their lives using their typical operating system, depends on a lifetime of complex detailed experience in lifeworlds that render it as infinitely rich and indeterminate as any complex living systemicity.

Thus, just as sociology sees its typifications, generalisations and theories as relating complexly to groupings, themes and patterns and only more-or-less reliably to particular individuals, so also the MBTI® sees that all people of each 'type' or kind of systemicity may simultaneously be in some ways like *all* others of that same systemicity, like *some* others (if specific content or experience is shared), and like *no* others of that same 'typification' (given the sheer complexity of differing content when you take into account the totality of a person's unique, detailed, unfolding complexity of experience and being compared to another's).

Both psychology and sociology (and indeed all people to a greater or lesser extent) go back and forth between this observing of unique 'up close and personal' experience, and making sense of its shared patterning and theorising, and systematising its shape, form, identity and action in its wider action field conditions. This theorising is part of life—of all inquiry cycles. Getting it wrong is 'simply' error needing feedback to make corrections.

9 I specially thank here my friend and thinking partner, Matt Smith, who grasped the relevant details of Jungian theory and understood these correspondences and then became accredited to use the MBTI indicator. I gratefully acknowledge his technical realisation of these new conceptualisations and the visual language contained in Figures 23 to 31 and thank him for our shared intellectual journey.

10 I also thank here Peter Tufts Richardson for his contribution of the circular arrangement of the sixteen 4-letter typification codes on which I build in Figures 23 to 28 to illustrate the living systemic nature of the Jungian Myers Briggs formulation (see Table 13). Elsewhere I have given an account of my painstakingly hand-calculating these associations with the epistemological cycle when I was referred to Peter's work. I am grateful for his generous agreement to my building on his work (originally published Wadsworth 2006a).

11 Myers and Briggs after Jung called this extraversion (not extroversion).

12 Figure 23 images the star-shaped pattern that comes from seeing how the dynamic of inquiring around a cycle moves back and forth between the inner (I) and outer (E) as the inquiring individual or group or larger social systemicity traverses through the inquiry preference clusters to reach right round the cycle. This would mean that as inquiry traverses full cycle there is a balancing oscillation between inner work and outer work—whether inner sensing, rational deciding on the basis of feeling, intuiting and rational deciding on the basis of logic, or sharing these in relationships with the outer world.

13 Figures 24 and 25 image how the Myers Briggs inquiring preference clusters might be seen through the lens of observing (S) and logically sorting (T) at the point of *action* (Figure 24) and through the lens of felt (F) connections (N) at the point of *reflection* (Figure 25). I speculate that the square shape and the circle shape are characteristic of each of these states of inquiry preferences, just as a top down pyramidal shape might accompany the logical calculation

(T) of a big picture (N), and a network, woven or wavy lines and dots image might accompany the detailed picture (S) of a felt (F) diversity of not yet organ-ised possibilities in a morphogenic field.

14 Figure 26 images the proportions of primary preference for either rational thinking (T) or for rational feeling (F) in traditional gender terms to illuminate how—while more men prefer the former as a first preference, and more women the latter as a first preference—significant numbers of men who prefer feeling (43.5%) do so as their primary preference and significant numbers of women who prefer thinking (24.5%) do so as their first preference in any immediate situation. As well, significant numbers each then 'on second thoughts' (or 'second feelings') switch to the alternative grounds for judgement as their second or third preference, and all also traverse full cycle to inquire for more or less effective living being. These Jungian insights, quantified by the MBTI® formulation for the USA population in this way, cast startling light on why the existing cultural reductionism to two dominant categories— male or female (with all the cultural typifications relating to thinking and feeling most frequently assigned to these binary constructions of gendered sex rather than to the more complex construct of humanness grouped into the sixteen epistemological 'whole cycle' systemicities by the Myers Briggs formulation)—may be part of what is culturally preventing the human species from realising the conditions for a more truly sustainable human ecology.

15 Figure 27 images a similar pattern of dynamic balancing as does Figure 23—but this time as overlapping 'atoms' regarding the opening/perceiving inquiry preference (P) in relation to the closing/judging preference (J). This would mean that as inquiry traverses full cycle there is a balancing oscillation between opening to new input, ideas, plans and actions and reaching closure about what has so far been observed, concluded, planned and enacted.

16 Figure 28 images the whole cycle in terms of its characteristic systemic organising shapes.

17 Stereotype—*n.*1a a person…that conforms to an unjustifiably fixed, usu. standardised, mental picture or thing, from the Greek stereos, 'solid', and *tupos*, 'strike' (impression).

18 Roger Pearman has also pointed out the parallels that Jung observed with the Navajo's traversing of the medicine wheel:

The Navajo believed that one became well by learning to walk the wheel and see life from the 16 points of view inherent in the soul. Their insight was that these sixteen points of view were impact[ed] by life experience such that one brother/sister of the Buffalo way (Thinking process) would not necessarily by exactly like another (although over time a sign of maturity was thought to be the acquired ability to see the world through others' preferred ways of seeing). Jung was deeply impressed by this view and it influenced his theory of type. (Personal communication, 10 August 2005, quoted with permission in Wadsworth 2006; see also Pearman and Albritton, 1997: 5–6.)

19 I draw on the term 'community of science' here to refer to whole communities of inquirers in the sense of *scientia* or 'knowing' (or 'whole cycle inquiry') in the same way as I use terms like 'inquiry group'; not in the narrow sense of a particular defined network or professional group of, for example, exclusively university educated people using particular preferred methodologies (such as deductive empiricism in controlled laboratory settings). The latter would comprise a sub-culture of my larger 'community of all humans and all beings' science', and need to remain in close co-relationship with all others to safeguard the life-giving whole.

20 Interestingly the Chinese have at the centre of their ancient Taoist earth religion an understanding that 'integral change holds form' or 'the circle contains the square'—or: 'Heaven contain earth'. Every Chinese monetary exchange traditionally conveyed this symbolic message in the form of a round coin with a central square hole.

References

Ackoff, R. (2004) Quoting Albert Einstein, EVAL-SYS listserv iimam@CAL-RESEARCH.ORG, accessed 10 June 2005.

Adams, P. (2005) *Late Night Live*, ABC Radio National, 14 August 2005.

Addams, J. (1910) *Twenty Years at Hull-House*, Macmillan Company, New York.

Alexander, C. (2004) *The Nature of Order—An Essay on the Art of Building and the Nature of the Universe* (four volumes 2003–2004): Part 1 'The Phenomenon of Life'; Part 2 'The Process of Creating Life'; Part 3 'A Vision of a Living World'; Part 4 'The Luminous Ground', Center for Environmental Structure, Berkeley.

Alexander, J. (1999) *The Spirit of the Home*, HarperCollins, London.

Applebaum, R.P. (1977) 'The Future Is Made, Not Predicted—Technocratic Planners vs. Public Interest', *Transaction/Society*, 14(4):49–53.

Archer, J. (1998) *Your Home—The Inside Story of the Australian House*, Lothian Books, Melbourne.

Argyris, C. (1993) *Knowledge for Action—A Guide to Overcoming Barriers to Organisational Change*, Jossey-Bass, San Francisco.

Argyris, C. and Schon, D. (1978) *Organizational Learning—A Theory of Action Perspective*, Addison-Wesley, Reading, Massachusetts.

Arnstein, S. (1969) 'A Ladder of Citizen Participation', *American Institute of Planners Journal*, 35(2):216–224.

Australian Government (2008) White Paper, *The Road Home: A National Approach to Reducing Homelessness*, Canberra.

Bachelard, G. (1938) *La formation de l'esprit scientifique*, Vrin, Paris.

Bamblett, M. (2008) 'Self-Determination not Invasion', *Noticeboard*, Victorian Council of Social Service, Melbourne.

Barbalet, J. (1998) *Emotion, Social Theory and Social Structure—A Macrosociological Approach*, Cambridge University Press, Cambridge.

Barrett, C. (1998) Review of J.M. Barbalet's *Emotion, Social Theory and Social Structure*, in the *Journal of Sociology*, 34(3):331–332.

Barton, J., Stephen, J. and Haslett, T. (2009) 'Action Research: Its Foundations in Open Systems Thinking and Relationship to the Scientific Method', *Systemic Practice and Action Research*, 22:475–488.

Bateson, G. (1972) *Steps to an Ecology of Mind*, Chandler Publishing Co., San Francisco.

Bateson, G. (1979) *Mind and Nature—A Necessary Unity*, Ballantine, New York.

Bates Smart architects (2000) quoted in 'The End of Work as We Know It', *The Age*, Part 1, December, p. 18.

Bawden, R. (2003) 'Transforming Engagement', unpublished keynote paper to the 6th World Congress of Action Learning, Action Research and Process Management, University of Pretoria, South Africa.

Bayley, S. (2006) 'Evidence Requirements for Evaluating Program Impacts', Victorian Auditor-General's Office, unpublished paper to the Australasian Evaluation Society, Victorian Branch seminar, 27 June.

Beer, S. (1972) *Brain of the Firm*, Allen Lane, Penguin, London.

Beer, S. (1979) *The Heart of the Enterprise*, John Wiley, London.

Beer, S. (2002) 'What is Cybernetics?', *Kybernetes*, MCB UP Ltd, 31(2):209–219.

Belenky, M.F., Clinchy, B., Goldberger, N. and Tarule, J. (1986) *Women's Ways of Knowing—The Development of Self, Voice and Mind*, Basic Books, New York.

Bell, S. and Morse, S. (2005) 'Holism and Understanding Sustainability', *Systemic Practice and Action Research*, 18(4):422–423.

Bennett, C.F. (1977) *Analysing Impacts of Extension Programs*, United States Department of Agriculture Extension Service, Washington, DC.

Bennett, C. and Rockwell, K. (2008) 'A Hierarchy for Targeting Outcomes and Evaluating Their Achievement', synopsis introducing TOP (Targeting Outcomes of Programs). See website for graphic, http://citnews.unl.edu/TOP/english/index.html, accessed 18 February 2008.

Betts, K., Hayward, D. and Garnham N. (2001) *Quantitative Analysis in the Social Sciences: An Introduction*, Tertiary Press, Eastern House, Croydon.

Blackmore, S. (2000) *The Meme Machine*, Oxford University Press, Oxford.

Blaikie, N. (2007) *Approaches to Social Inquiry*, Polity Press, Cambridge.

Bohm, D., Garrett, P. and Factor, D. (1991) 'Dialogue—A Proposal', www.david-bohm.net/dialogue/dialogue_proposal.html, accessed 24 November 2009.

Bohm, D. (2002), *Wholeness and the Implicate Order*, Routledge, London.

Bourdieu, P. (1984) *Distinction—A Social Critique of the Judgment of Taste*, trans. R. Nice, Harvard University Press, Boston.

Bradshaw, D. and McRae, H. (eds) (1996) *'Speaking Back'—Building a Research Culture for ACFE*, Adult, Community and Further Education, Melbourne.

Brennan, M. and Hoadley, R. (1984) *School Self-evaluation*, School Improvement Plan Secretariat, Education Department of Victoria, Melbourne.

Bridges, W. (2000) *The Character of Organisations—Using Personality Type in Organisational Development*, Davies-Black Publishing, Palo Alto.

Briggs Myers, I. (1998) *Introduction to Type®*, 6th edn, Consulting Psychologists Press, Palo Alto.

Briggs Myers, I. with Myers, P.B. (1995) *Gifts Differing—Understanding Personality Type*, Davie-Black Publishing, Mountain View, California.

Brinkerhoff, R.O. (2003) *The Success Case Method—Find Out Quickly What's Working and What's Not*, Berrett-Koehler Publishers, San Francisco.

Brown, L. (1988) Group *Self-Evaluation—Learning for Improvement*, Education Department of Victoria, Melbourne.

Brown, V. (2002) in Aslin, H. and Brown, V. A., *Terms of Engagement—A Toolkit for Community Engagement for the Murray-Darling Basin*, Bureau of Rural Sciences, Canberra, p. 15.

Buber, M. (1958) *I and Thou*, Charles Scribner's Sons, New York.

Burns, D. (2007) *Systemic Action Research*, Policy Press, University of Bristol, Bristol.

Burton, J. (1995) *The Art of Conversation or, How Usefully to Increase Teacher Talk*, Literacy and ESL Research Network, NNLIA, Melbourne.

Butler, C. (2002), 'Balance', *Challenge—Church and People Magazine*, 68, May, Johannesburg.

Caddick, M. and Moore, S. (1998) *Adding Value Using Customer Feedback*, RMIT Business Working Paper Series 98/5, School of Management, RMIT University, Melbourne.

Capra, F. (1996) *The Web of Life—A New Scientific Understanding of Living Systems,* Doubleday-Anchor, New York.

Carline, D. (2005) 'Know One Another', *The Australian Friend, Journal of the Religious Society of Friends (Quakers) in Australia*, 4:9–10.

Carney, T. (2007) 'Traveling the "Work-First" Road to Welfare Reform', *Just Policy*, 44: 12–20.

Cavendish, M. (1653) 'Of many worlds in this world', accessed 12 August 2008: www.firstscience.com/SITE/poems/cavendish.asp.

Chklovskii D.B. and. Koulakov, A.A. (2004) 'Maps In the Brain—What Can We Learn from Them?', *Annual Review of Neuroscience*, 27: 369–392.

Claiborne, S. (2006) *The Irresistible Revolution—Living as an Ordinary Radical*, Zondervan, Grand Rapids.

Clark, A. (2003) *Natural Born Cyborgs—Minds, Technologies and the Future of Human Intelligence*, Oxford University Press, New York.

Coghlan, D. (2005) 'Ignatian Spirituality as Transformational Social Science', *Action Research*, 3(1):89–107.

Cohen, L. (1992) 'The Anthem', *The Future* album, www.leonardcohenfiles.com/album10.html#78, accessed 8 August 2008.

Connell, R.W. (2005) *Masculinities*, 2nd edn, University of California Press, Berkeley.

Consumer Focus Collaboration (2000) *Improving Health Services through Consumer Participation: A Resource Guide*, Commonwealth of Australia, Canberra.

Coonara Action Research Taskforce (1996) *'What if...?'—Local People's Stories of the Recession late 1980s–mid 1990s*, Coonara Community House, Upper Ferntree Gully, Victoria.

Cooperrider, D.L. and Srivastva, S. (1987) 'Appreciative Inquiry in Organisational Life', in W.A. Passmore and R.W. Woodman (eds), *Research in Organizational Change and Development*, Vol. 1, JAI Press, Greenwich, Connecticut, pp. 129–69.

Cooperrider, D.L. and Whitney, D. (1999) 'Appreciative Inquiry—A Constructive Approach to Organization Development and Social Change', workshop, Corporation for Positive Change Taos, New Mexico.

Costello, T. (1998) *Streets of Hope—Finding God in St Kilda*, Allen & Unwin, St Leonards, Sydney.

Crane, P. (1998) *Putting Families in the Picture: Supplementary Report*, Evaluation Committee, Prime Ministerial Youth Homeless Taskforce, Department of Family and Community Services, Canberra.

Crane, P. (2006) 'Action Research in Social Programs', *Proceedings of the Action Learning, Action Research and Process Management Conversation*, University of Queensland, Brisbane, 2006, pp. 1–16.

Crane, P. and Richardson, L. (2000) *Reconnect Action Research Kit*, Commonwealth of Australia, Canberra.

Crawford, F., Kippax, S., Onyx, J., Galut, J. and Benton, P. (1992) *Emotion and Gender: Constructing Meaning from Memory*, Sage Publications, London.

Crotty, M. (1998) *The Foundations of Social Research–Meaning and Perspective in the Research Process*, Allen & Unwin, Crow's Nest, Sydney.

Csikszentmihalyi, M. (1992) *Flow—The Psychology of Happiness*, Random Century Group, London.

Dapin M. (2007) 'The Son also Rises', *The Age Good Weekend,* 4 August 2007:31–33.

Davies, R. and Dart, J. (2005) *The Most Significant Change (MSC) Technique—A Guide to Its Use*, self-published, www.clearhorizon.com, accessed 8 August 2008.

Deegan, P. (1996) 'Recovery and the Conspiracy of Hope', keynote paper, 6th Mental Health Services Conference, Brisbane.

De Bono, E. (1999) *Six Thinking Hats*, 2nd edn, Back Bay Books, Boston.

Denniss, R. (2008) Minutes, Annual General Meeting, Victorian Council of Social Service, Melbourne, 18 November, p. 6.

Denzin, N. (2002) *Interpretive Interactionism*, 2nd edn, Sage Publications, London.

Denzin, N. and Lincoln, Y. (2003) *Strategies of Qualitative Inquiry*, 2nd edn, Sage Publications, Thousand Oaks.

Department of Human Services (2005) *Doing it with Us not for Us*, Participation in Your Health Service 2006–2009, Melbourne.

Doidge, N. (2007) *The Brain That Changes Itself—Stories of Personal Triumph from the Frontiers of Brain Science*, Viking Press, New York.

Dumas, A., http://en.wikipedia.org/wiki/Faulty_generalization, accessed 8 August 2008.

Einfeld, Hon. Justice M. (2001) 'Rights under Threat, Obligations Forgotten', speech to the Queensland Advocacy Incorporated Annual Fund Appeal Breakfast, 17 November 2000, www.qai.org.au/documents/doc_89.doc, accessed 24 June 2008.

Emery, M. and Purser, R. (1996) *The Search Conference—A Powerful Method for Planned Organisational Change and Community Action*, Jossey Bass, San Francisco.

Eoyang, G. (2004) 'The Practitioner's Landscape', E:CO, 6(1–2):55–60.

Epstein, M. and Wadsworth, Y. (1994) *Understanding and Involvement (U&I)—Consumer Evaluation of Acute Psychiatric Hospital Practice*, Vol. 1: *A Project's Beginnings...*, Victorian Mental Illness Awareness Council, Melbourne.

Fineman, S. (1993) *Emotion in Organisations*, Sage Publications, London.

Fisher, D (1994) *A New Vision of Healing as Constructed by People with Psychiatric Disabilities Working as Mental Health Providers*, National Empowerment Centre, Massachusetts.

Fisher, F. (ed.) and F. Macdonald, (2006), *Response-ability—Environment, Health and Everyday Transcendence*, Vista Publications, Elsternwick, Victoria.

Flood, R.L. (1999) *Rethinking the Fifth Discipline—Learning within the Unknowable*, Routledge, London.

Fricker, M. (2007) *Epistemic Injustice—Power and the Ethics of Knowing*, Oxford University Press, Oxford.

Friedan, B. (1963) *The Feminine Mystique*, Dell Publishing, New York.

FWCC Friends World Committee for Consultation (2007) 'Golden Rule', *Asia–West Pacific Section Newsletter*, June: 74:1.

Galbally, R. (1994) 'Promoting a Healthy Health Care System', *Health Issues*, 40:16–19.

Geertz, C. (1973) 'Thick Description: Toward an Interpretive Theory of Culture', in C. Geertz, *The Interpretation of Cultures: Selected Essays*, New York, Basic Books, pp. 3–30.

Gergen, K. (2009) *Relational Being—Beyond Self and Community*, Oxford University Press, Oxford.

Geyer, P. (2004) 'Developing Models and Beliefs', *Australian Psychological Review*, 6(3):37.

Gibran, K. (1972) *The Prophet*, Heinemann, London.

Giddens, A. (1976) *New Rules of Sociological Method*, Hutchison, London.

Giddens, A. (1986) *Sociology—A Brief but Critical Introduction*, MacMillan, Basingstoke.

Greenfield, S. (2001) *The Deakin Lectures*, ABC Radio National, 7 May.

Guba, E. and Lincoln, Y. (1989) *Fourth Generation Evaluation*, Sage Publications, Newbury Park, California.

Gunderson, L. and Holling, C.S. (2002) *Panarchy—Understanding Transformations in Human and Natural Systems*, Island Press, Washington, DC.

Hamlin, J.K., Wynn, K. and Bloom, P. (2007) 'Social Evaluation by Preverbal Infants', *Nature*, 450:557–559.

Harris, D. (2007) 'Evaluation Governance and Reporting', unpublished seminar presentation, Victorian Branch of the Australasian Evaluation Society, VicHealth Melbourne, 21 June.

Haug, F. (1987) *Female Sexualisation—A Collective Work of Memory*, Verso, Brooklyn.

Hawken, P. (2007) *Blessed Unrest—How the Largest Social Movement in History Is Restoring Grace, Justice, and Beauty to the World*, Penguin, New York.

Hebb, D.O. (1949) *The Organization of Behaviour*, Wiley, New York.

Hellige, J.B. (2001) *Hemispheric Asymmetry—What's Right and What's Left?*, Harvard University Press, Cambridge, Massachusetts.

Henderson, S. (1997) 'Black Swans don't Fly Double Loops: The Limits of the Learning Organisation?', *The Learning Organization*, 4(3):99–105.

Heron, J. (1996) *Cooperative Inquiry—Research into the Human Condition*, Sage, London.

Herrmann, N. (1995) *The Creative Brain*, 2nd edn, Quebor Printing Book Group, Kingsport, Tennessee.

Herrmann, N. (1996) *The Whole Brain Business Book—Unlocking the Power of Whole Brain Thinking in Organisations and Individuals*, McGraw-Hill, New York.

Herrmann, N. (1998) 'The Theory behind HBDI and Whole Brain Technology', www.hbdi.com/Resources/Articles/ index.cfm, accessed 23 October 2009.

Hofstede, G. (1991) *Cultures and Organisations—Software of the Mind*, McGraw Hill, London.

Holdsworth R. (2006) Student Action Teams, Youth Research Centre, University of Melbourne, Victoria.

Holling, C.S. (undated) Figure 8 ecosystem animated visual tutorial, www.albaeco.com/english/htm/webbart/eco system.htm, accessed 15 February 2008.

Holling, C.S. (ed.) (1978) *Adaptive Environmental Assessment and Management*, John Wiley, New York.

Homans, G.C. (1975) *The Human Group*, Routledge & Kegan Paul, London.

Ife, J. (1997) *Rethinking Social Work—Towards Critical Practice*, Pearson, Melbourne.

infed (informal education and lifelong learning) (2001) entry on 'David A. Kolb on experiential learning', www.infed.org/biblio/b-explrn.htm, accessed 8 August 2008.

Inayatullah, S. and Fitzgerald, J. (eds) (1999) *Transcending Boundaries—Prahbat Rainjan Sarkar's Theories of Individual and Social Transformation*, Gurukula Press, Queensland.

Insel, T.R. and Russell D.F. (2004) 'How the Brain Processes Social Information: Searching for the Social Brain', *Annual Review of Neuroscience*, 27:697–722.

Isaacs, W.N. (1993) 'Taking flight: Dialogue, Collective Thinking, and Organizational Learning', *Organizational Dynamics*, 22(3):24–39.

Jackson, J. and Smith, M. (2007) 'Student Initiatives in School Engagement', *Connect*, 168:3–9.

Jantsch, E. (1980) *The Self-Organizing Universe*, Pergamon Press, London.

Jencks, C. and Heathcote, E. (2010) *The Architecture of Hope: Maggie's Cancer Caring Centres*, Frances Lincoln, London.

Jung, C.G. (1967) *Collected Works*, Vol. 13, Routledge & Kegan Paul, London, pp. 14–15.

Jung, C.G. (1983) *Memories, Dreams, Reflections*, Fontana Paperbacks, London.

Kaplan, A. (1964) *The Conduct of Inquiry—Methodology for the Behavioural Sciences*, Chandler, Pennsylvania.

Kauffman, S.A. (1993) *Origins of Order—Self-Organisation and Selection in Evolution*, Oxford University Press, New York.

Kauffman, S.A. (1995) *At Home in the Universe—The Search for the Laws of Self-Organisation and Complexity*, Oxford University Press, New York.

Kauffman, S.A. (2000) *Investigations*, Oxford University Press, New York.

Keirsey D. and Bates, M. (1984) *Please Understand Me—Character and Temperament Types*, Prometheus Nemesis Book Company, Del Mar, California.

Kilner, D. and Were, K. (2000) *Pursuing Customer Satisfaction in Human Services—An Organisational Handbook*, Social Options Australia, Stepney, South Australia.

Kiviat, B. (2007) 'It's What's on the Outside that Counts: Why Many Efforts at team-building Miss Half the Point', *Time*, 10 September, p. 50.

Kolb, D.A. and Fry, R. (1975) 'Toward an Applied Theory of Experiential Learning', in C. Cooper (ed.), *Theories of Group Process*, John Wiley, London.

Kretzmann, J.P. and McKnight, J.L. (1993) *Building Communities from the Inside Out: A Path Toward Finding and Mobilizing a Community's Assets*, Center for Urban Affairs and Policy Research, ACTA Publications, Skokie, Illinois.

Kroeger, O. and Thuesen, J.M. (1993) *Type Talk at Work*, Dell Publishing, New York.

Kübler-Ross, E. (1969) *On Death and Dying*, Tavistock Publications, London.

LaBonte, R. (1997) *Power, Participation and Partnerships for Health*, Victorian Health Promotion Foundation, Carlton South, Victoria.

LaBonte R., Feather, J. and Hills, M. (1999) 'A Story/Dialogue Method for Health Promotion Knowledge Development and Evaluation', *Health Education Research*, 14(1):39–50.

Lather P. (2006) Paradigm Proliferation as a Good Thing to Think With—Teaching Research in Education as a Wild Profusion', *International Journal of Qualitative Studies in Education*, 19, 1: 35–57.

Le Guin, U. trans. with J.P. Seaton (1997) *Lao Tzu Tao Te Ching—A Book about the Way and the Power of the Way*, Shambala, Boston and London.

Lau, D.C. (1963) *Tao Te Ching*, trans. D.C. Lau, Penguin, Harmondsworth.

Lewin, K. (1946) 'Action research and minority problems', *Journal of Social Issues*, 2:34–36

Listening Earth (2005) ABC Radio National, 24 March 2005.

London Edinburgh Weekend Return Group (1980) *In and Against the State*, Pluto Press, London.

Lovelock, J. (1999) 'Foreword' to E. Sahtouris, *Earthdance—Living Systems in Evolution*, www.ratical.org/LifeWeb/Erthdnce/foreword.html, accessed 8 August 2008.

Lovelock, J. (2002) *The Revenge of Gaia*, Penguin, Harmondsworth.

Lowe, I. (2009) Sustainability in our Suburbs website: www.sisuburbs.com.au, accessed 28 April 2009.

Ludema, J.D., Cooperrider, D.L. and Barrett, F.J. (2001) 'Appreciative Inquiry—The Power of the Unconditional Positive Question', in P. Reason and H. Bradbury (eds), *Handbook of Action Research*, Sage Publications, London, pp.189–199.

McDonald, B. Rogers, P.J., and Kefford, B. (2003) 'Teaching People to Fish? Building the Evaluation Capability of Public Sector Organizations', *Evaluation*, 9(1): 9–29.

McGrath, H. and Edwards, H. (2000) *Difficult Personalities—A Practical Guide to Managing the Hurtful Behaviour of Others*, CHOICE Australian Consumers Association, Marrickville.

McGuiness, M. and Wadsworth, Y. (1991) *Understanding, Anytime—A Consumer Evaluation of an Acute Psychiatric Hospital*, Victorian Mental Illness Awareness Council, Melbourne.

McMurray, A. (2000) 'The Use of Conceptual versus Physical Models in Teaching Action Research to Culturally Diverse Student Populations—A Preliminary Analysis', unpublished paper, World Congress of ALARPM, University of Ballarat, Victoria.

McRae, H. and Hazel, V. (eds) (1997) *'Speaking Back Again—Report of the 1997 ACFE Research Forum'*, Adult, Community and Further Education, Melbourne.

McTaggart, R. (1991) 'Principles of Participatory Action Research', *Adult Education Quarterly*, 41(3):168–187.

Macy, J. (1991) *Mutual Causality in Buddhism and General Systems Theory—The Dharma of Living Systems*, SUNY Press, New York.

Macy, J. (1998) *Coming Back to Life—Practices to Reconnect Our Lives, Our World*, New Society Publishers, Philadelphia.

Macy, J. (2008) 'Living Systems' tab on webpage, www.joannamacy.net/html/living.html, accessed May 2008.

Marmot M. and Wilkinson R. (eds) (1999) *Social Determinants of Health*, Oxford University Press, New York.

Marmot M., Davey Smith G., Stansfeld S., Patel C., North F., Head J., White I., Brunner E. and Feeney A. (1991) 'Health Inequalities among British Civil Servants: The Whitehall II Study', *Lancet*, 337:1387–1393.

Maslow, A. (1968) *Toward a Psychology of Being*, Van Nostrand Reinhold, New York.

Massey, A. (1998) 'The Way We Do Things Around Here': The Culture of Ethnography', paper to the Ethnography and Education Conference, Oxford University Department of Educational Studies, www.geocities.com/Tokyo/2961/waywedo.htm, accessed 8 August 2008.

Maturana, U. and Varela, F. (1980) 'Autopoiesis and Cognition—The Realization of the Living', in R.S. Cohen and M.W. Wartofsky (eds), *Boston Studies in the Philosophy of Science*, 42, Reidel Publishing Co., Dordrecht.

Meadows, D. (1997) 'Places to Intervene in a System', essay originally published in *The Whole Earth Magazine*, www.developerdotstar.com/mag/articles/places_intervene_system.html, accessed 6 May 2008.

Melbourne Consumer Consultants' Group (1997) and Wadsworth, Y. (ed.) *Do You Mind...The Ultimate Exit Survey—Survivors of Psychiatric Services Speak Out*, Richmond Fellowship, Melbourne.

Menzies, I. (1970) *The Structure of Social Systems as a Defence Against Anxiety*, Tavistock Institute of Human Relations, London.

Merton, R. and Bateman, J. (2008) 'Social Inclusion and Mental Health—Evidence and Practice', *New Paradigm*, Autumn: 12–17.

Miller, E.K. and Cohen, J.D. (2001) 'An Integrative Theory of Prefrontal Cortex Function', *Annual Review of Neuroscience*, 24:167–202.

Miller, J.G. (1978) *Living Systems*, McGraw-Hill, New York.

Mollison, B. (1999) 'Deep Ecology', *New Dimensions*, ABC Radio National, 6 January.

Moore, M. Alexander (2002) 'The Rhythms of Change', *OD Practitioner*, 34(2):24–28.

Morgan, A. (2000) *What is Narrative Therapy?*, Dulwich Centre Publications, Adelaide.

Murphy, A.P. (2004) *The Cult of Personality Testing*, Free Press, New York.

Myers, I. (1999) *Introduction to Type*, 6th edn, Consulting Psychologists Press, Palo Alto.

Myers, K. and Kirby, L. (1999) *Introduction to Type Dynamics and Development—Exploring the Next Level of Type*, 6th edn, Consulting Psychologists Press, Palo Alto.

Myers, I.B. and Myers, P.B. (1980) *Gifts Differing*, Consulting Psychologists Press, Palo Alto.

Myers, I., McCaulley, M., Quenk, N. and Hammer, A. (1998) *MBTI Manual—A Guide to the Development and Use of the Myers-Briggs Type Indicator®*, 3rd edn, Consulting Psychologists Press, Palo Alto.

Nader, L. (1972) 'Up the Anthropologist—Perspectives Gained from Studying Up', in D.H. Hymes (ed.) *Reinventing Anthropology*, Random House Pantheon Books, New York, pp. 284–311.

Noffke, S.E. and Brennan, M. (1991) 'Student Teachers Use Action Research', in K. Zeichner and R. Tabachnik (eds), *Issues and Practices in Inquiry-oriented Teacher Education*, Falmer Press, London and Philadelphia, pp. 186–201.

Nye, J.S. (2005) *Soft Power: The Means to Success in World Politics*, Public Affairs-Perseus Books, New York.

Otto, D. (1990) *Unlocking the System*, Victorian Mental Illness Awareness Council, Brunswick, Victoria.

Our Consumer Place (2010) *So You Have a 'Mental Illness'…What Now?*, Our Community Pty Ltd, Melbourne.

Owen, H. (2008) *Open Space Technology—A User's Guide,* (3rd edn), Berrett-Koehler, San Francisco.

Palmer, H. and Brown, P. (1997) *The Enneagram Advantage—Putting the Nine Personality Types to Work in the Office*, Three Rivers Press, New York.

Pascal, B. (1670) *Pensées*, trans. W.F. Trotter, http://oregonstate.edu/instruct/phl302/texts/pascal/penseescontents.html, accessed 8 August 2008.

Patton, M.Q. (1994) 'Developmental Evaluation', *Evaluation Practice*, 15(3):311–320.

Patton, M.Q. (2005) Introduction and speech by Alan Greenspan, 'Reflections on Central Banking', Federal Reserve Bank of Kansas City Symposium, Jackson Hole, Wyoming, 26 August 2005, accessed 29 August 2005 on EVAL-SYS listserv.

Patton, M.Q. (2006) 'Panarchy', in F. Westley, B. Zimmerman and M. Patton (eds), *Getting to Maybe—How the World is Changed*, Sage Publications, California, Chapter 2.

Pearman, R. (2004) 'Type Consilience—Unifying Knowledge on Type Development', www.qualifying.org, accessed 8 August 2008.

Pearman, R.R. and Albritton, S.C. (1997) *I'm not Crazy I'm just not You*, Davies-Black Publishing, Consulting Psychologists Press, Mountain View, California.

Peavey, F. (1994) *By Life's Grace*, New Society Publishers, Philadelphia.

Peavey, F. (2001) Strategic Questioning: An Experiment in Communication of the 2nd kind, www.thechangeagency.org/_dbase_upl/strat_questioning_man.pdf, accessed 8 August 2008.

Pedler, M. and Burgoyne, J. (2006) 'Distributed Leadership', *In View*, National Health Service Institute for Innovation and Improvement, 11:20–21.

Pedler, M., Burgoyne, J.G. and Brooks, C. (2005) 'What has Action Learning Learned to Become?' *Action Learning—Research and Practice*, 2(1):49–68.

Peirce, C. (1903) 'Pragmatism and Abduction', *Collected Papers of Charles Sanders Peirce*, Vol. 5, Harvard University, Boston, p. 189.

Pfeffer, J., (2007) 'Ten Questions', http://blog.guyKawasaki.com.2007/07/ten-questions-w.html, accessed 13 July 2007.

Pound, R. (2000) 'How Can I Make My Methodology Accessible within Health Care?' unpublished seminar paper, Department of Education, University of Bath, 23 October.

Preskill, H. (2007) 'Building Evaluation Capacity for Organisational Learning', workshop abstract, national Australasian Evaluation Society conference, September 2007, Melbourne.

Price, I. (2004) 'Complexity, Complicatedness and Complexity: A New Science behind Organisational Intervention?', *E:CO*, 6(1–2):40–48.

Quenk, N. (2000), *In the Grip—Understanding Type, Stress, and the Inferior Function,* 2nd edn, Consulting Psychologists Press, Palo Alto.

Quenk, N. (2002) *Was that Really Me?—How Everyday Stress Brings Out Our Hidden Personality*, Davies-Black Publishing, Consulting Psychologists Press, Mountain View, California.

Rabbin, R. (2001) 'Human Caring for Customers—Business with Spirit', *LivingNow*, Sydney.

Radcliffe, T. (2004) 'The Crisis of Truth-Telling in Our Society', the 19th Eric Symes Abbott Memorial Lecture, Westminster Abbey, ABC Radio National, 20 February 2005.

Ramos, J. (2002) 'Action Research as Foresight Methodology', *Journal of Futures Studies*, 7(1):15–28.

Reason, P. (ed.) (1988) *Human Inquiry in Action*, Sage Publications, London.

Reason, P. (ed.) (1994) *Participation in Human Inquiry*, Sage Publications, London.

Reason, P. and Bradbury, H. (2001) *Handbook of Action Research*, Sage Publications, London.

Reason, P. and Rowan, J. (1981) *Human Inquiry: A Sourcebook of New Paradigm Research*, Wiley, London.

Reason, P. and Torbert, W.R. (2001) 'The Action Turn—Toward a Transformational Social Science', *Concepts and Transformation*, 6(1):1–37.

Revans, R.W. (1980) *Action Learning—New Techniques for Management*, Blond and Briggs Ltd, London.

Ridley, M. (2003) *Nature via Nurture—Genes, Experience, and What Makes Us Human*, HarperCollins, UK.

Riessman, C.K. (2008) *Narrative Methods for the Human Sciences*, Sage Publications, Newbury Park.

Ring, J. (1991) 'The Pariah as Hero—Hannah Arendt's Political Actor', *Political Theory*, 19(3):433–452.

Rizzolatti, G. and Craighero, L. (2004) 'The Mirror-Neuron System', *Annual Review of Neuroscienc*, 27:169–192.

Roberts, A. (1979) *The Self-Managing Environment*, Allison & Busby, London.

Rosen, A. (1994) '100% Mabo—De-Colonising People with Mental Illness and their Families', *ANZJ Family Therapy*, 15(3):128–142.

Rosenbaum, E.E. (1988) *A Taste of My Own Medicine—When the Doctor Is the Patient*, Random House, New York.

Rossi, P.H., Lipsey, M.W. and Freeman, H.E. (2003) *Evaluation—A Systematic Approach*, 7th edn, Sage Publications, Thousand Oaks.

Rowan, J. and Reason, P. (1981) *Human Inquiry*, Wiley, Chichester.

Sahtouris, E. (1999) 'Less Than Perfect, More Than Machine', *Earthdance: Living Systems in Evolution*, www.ratical.org/LifeWeb/Erthdnce/, accessed 8 August 2008.

Sahtouris, E. (2005a) 'A Tentative Model for a Living Universe', Part One, http://via-visioninaction.org/html/sahtourispartone.html, accessed 8 August 2008.

Sahtouris, E. (2005b) 'The Biology of Business—New Laws of Nature Reveal a Better Way for Business', expanded version of article originally published in *VIA Journal*, 3(1), www.via-visioninaction.org/via-li/articles/Sahtouris_BiologyOfBusiness-full_version.pdf, accessed 8 August 2008.

Saunders A. (1999) Review of Waterson (1999) on *The Comfort Zone*, ABC Radio National, 4 December.

Saunders A. (2004) 'Cubbies: The Architecture of Childhood', *The Comfort Zone*, ABC Radio National, 3 July.

Scharmer, C.O. (2003) 'The Blind Spot of Leadership—Presencing as a Social Technology of Freedom', draft (only), www.dialogonleadership.org/TheBlindSpot2003.pdf, accessed 18 February 2008.

Schein, E.H. (1987) *Process Consultation—Lessons for Managers and Consultants*, Vol. 2, Addison-Wesley Publishing Company, Reading, Massachusetts.

Schein, E.H. (1988) *Process Consultation—Its Role in Organization Development*, Vol. 1, Addison-Wesley Publishing Company, Reading, Massachusetts.

Schön, D. (1983) *The Reflective Practitioner—How Professionals Think in Action*, Temple Smith, London.

Schön, D. (1987) 'Educating the Reflective Practitioner', Presentation to the 1987 meeting of the American Educational Research Association, Washington, DC, http://educ.queensu.ca/~ar/schon87.htm, accessed 8 August 2008.

Schorr, L. (2004) in Dees, G., Anderson, B.B., and Wei-skillern, J. 'Scaling Social Impact—Strategies for Spreading Social Innovations', *Stanford Social Innovation Review*, Spring: 24–32.

Schutz, A. (1976) *The Phenomenology of the Social World*, Heinemann, London.

Schütz-Bosbach S., Avenanti A., Aglioti S. and Haggard, P. (2008) 'Don't Do It! Cortical Inhibition and Self-attribution during Action Observation', *Journal of Cognitive Neuroscience*, early access reference: 080814062 822192–13.

Scriven, M. (1991) *Evaluation Thesaurus*, Sage Publications, Newbury Park, California.

Seed, J., Macy, J., Naess, A. and Fleming, P. (1988) *Thinking Like A Mountain—Towards A Council of All Beings*, New Society Publishers, Philadelphia.

Seed, J. (1988) 'Beyond Anthropocentrism', in J. Seed, J. Macy, A. Naess and P. Fleming, www.morning-earth.org/DE6103/Read%20DE/Beyond%20anthropo.seed.pdf, accessed 8 August 2008.

Seed, J. (1999) 'Deep Ecology', *New Dimensions*, ABC Radio National, 6 January 1999.

Senge, P.M. (1990) *The Fifth Discipline—The Art and Practice of the Learning Organisation*, Doubleday-Currency, New York.

Senge, P.M. (1994) *The Fifth Discipline Fieldbook*, Doubleday-Currency, New York.

Senge, P.M., Scharmer, C.O., Jaworski, J. and Flowers, B.S. (2004) *Presence—Human Purpose and the Field of the Future*, Society for Organizational Learning, Boston.

Sharp, C. (2005) 'An Organisational Evaluation Capability Hierarchy Model for Self-Diagnosis', *Evaluation Journal of Australia*, 4(1–2):27–33.

Shepherd, L. (1993) *Lifting the Veil—The Feminine Face of Science*, Shambhala Books, Boston.

Shewart-Deming PDCA cycle, summary and graphic, http://en.wikipedia.org/wiki/PDCA, accessed 18 February 2008.

Singer-Loomis Type Deployment Inventory (SL-TDI®), www.movingboundaries.com/index.html, accessed 19 February 2008.

Smith, D. (1987) *The Everyday World as Problematic—A Feminist Sociology*, Northeastern University Press, Boston.

Sperry, R.W., Gazzaniga, M.S. and Bogen, J.B. (1969) 'Interhemispheric Relationships—The Neocortical Commissures; Syndromes of Hemisphere Disconnection', in P.J. Vinken and G.W. Bruyn (eds), *Handbook Clinical Neurology*, 4:273–290.

Spratt, D. and Sutton, P. (2008) *Climate Code Red—The case for emergency action*, Scribe Publications, Carlton, Australia.

Stephens, J.R. and Haslett, T. (2005) 'From Cybernetics and VSD to Management and Action', *Systemic Practice and Action Research*, 18(4):395–407.

Sternberg, R.J. (1998) *In Search of the Human Mind*, 2nd edn, Harcourt Brace, Fort Worth.

Sting (2003) quoted in McCormick, N. 'What's Wrong with Being Pretentious?' *The Age Good Weekend*, 8 November; 30–31.

Stringer, E. (1996) *Action Research—A Handbook for Practitioners*, Sage, Thousand Oaks.

Stringer, E. (2004) *Action Research in Health*, Pearson, New Jersey.

Suzuki, D. (2004) 'The Nature of Things—Sacred Balance', SBS Television, Sydney, Australia, 15 January.

Swimme, B. and Berry, T. (1994) *The Universe Story—From the Primordial Flaring Forth to the Ecozoic Era: A Celebration of the Unfolding of the Cosmos*, HarperOne, New York.

Swimme, B. (2003) *What Is Enlightenment?*, www.enlightennext.org/magazine/j19/swimme.asp, accessed 26 November 2009.

Sykes, J.B. (ed.) (1976) *The Concise Oxford Dictionary*, 6th edn, Oxford University Press, Oxford.

Syme, L. (1997a) *Community Participation, Empowerment and Health—Development of a Wellness Guide for California*, California Wellness Foundation and the University of California, Santa Cruz.

Syme, L. (1997b) 'Individual versus Community Interventions in Public Health Practice—Some Thoughts about a New Approach', *Health Promotion Matters*, Issue 2, Victorian Health Promotion Foundation, July, pp. 2–9.

Syme, L. (2004) 'Social Determinants of Health—The Community as an Empowered Partner', *Preventing Chronic Disease*, 1(2):1–5.

Szirom, T. (2005) 'Evaluating Community Strengthening', SuccessWorks unpublished seminar presentation, to the Australasian Evaluation Society, 30 June.

Tagore, R. (1919) 'Batayaniker Patro', Kalantar, pp. 313–314.

Torbert, W.R., Fisher, D. and Rooke, D. (2001) *Personal and Organisational Transformations: Through Action Inquiry*, Edge/Work Press, Boston.

Townsend, P. and Black, D. (1992) *Inequalities in Health: the Black Report and the Health Divide*, 3rd edn, Penguin Books, Harmondsworth.

Tresize, N. (2004) *Hansard*, 5 October, Victorian Government, Melbourne.

Tuckman, B. (1965) 'Developmental Sequence in Small Groups', *Psychological Bulletin*, 63:384–399.

Tufts Richardson, P. (1996) *Four Spiritualities—Expressions of Self, Expressions of Spirit: A Psychology of Contemporary Spiritual Choice*, Davies-Black Publishing, Consulting Psychologists Press, Palo Alto.

Tufts Richardson, P. (1998) 'A Circle of Type', *Bulletin of Psychological Type*, 21(4):27–28.

Varela, F.J. (1984) 'The Creative Circle', originally in P. Watzalavick (ed.), *The Invented Reality*, Norton Publishing, New York, www.lifesnaturalsolutions.com.au/articles.php, accessed 24 November 2009.

VicHealth (2004) Australasian Evaluation Society seminar, VicHealth, Melbourne, 25 November.

Von Bertalanffy, L. (1968) *General System Theory—Foundations, Development, Applications*, George Braziller, New York.

Vygotsky, L. in Jaramillo, J. (1996) 'Vygotsky's Sociocultural Theory and Contributions to the Development of Constructivist Curricula', *Education*, 117(1):133–140.

Wadsworth, Y. (1976) *The Knox Project First Report*, Department of Health, Melbourne.

Wadsworth, Y. (1979) *The Final Knox Project Report*, National Council of Women Victoria, Melbourne.

Wadsworth, Y. (1980) *Let's Communicate!*, Royal Australian Nursing Federation, Melbourne.

Wadsworth, Y. (1982) 'The Politics of Social Research', *Australian Journal of Social Issues*, 17(3):232–246.

Wadsworth, Y. (1992) 'Getting it Right—Rethinking Community Needs Studies', keynote workshop paper, conference proceedings of the 2nd World Congress of Action Learning, Action Research and Process Management, University of Queensland, Brisbane.

Wadsworth, Y. (1996) '"We're doing some research…"—Building a Culture of Research', in D. Bradshaw and H. McRae (eds), *'Speaking Back': Building a Research Culture for ACFE*, Adult, Community and Further Education, Melbourne.

Wadsworth, Y. (1997a) *Do It Yourself Social Research*, 2nd edn, Allen & Unwin, St Leonards, Sydney.

Wadsworth, Y. (1997b) *Everyday Evaluation on The Run*, 2nd edn, Allen & Unwin, St Leonards, Sydney.

Wadsworth, Y. (1998) 'Coming to the Table'—Some Conditions for Achieving Consumer-focused Evaluation of Human Services by Service Providers and Service Users', *Evaluation Journal of Australia*, 10(1–2):11–29.

Wadsworth, Y. (1998b) 'What is Participatory Action Research? *Action Research International*, Paper 2. On-line: www.scu.edu.au/schools/gcm/ar/ari/p-ywadsworth 98.html.

Wadsworth, Y. (1999) '"Getting the Good Oil"—A Departmental Framework for Working with Students to Improve Teaching Practice', internal unpublished report, Department of Psychology, Victoria University of Technology.

Wadsworth, Y. (2001) 'The Mirror, the Magnifying Glass, the Compass and the Map—Facilitating Participatory Action Research', in P. Reason and H. Bradbury (eds), *Handbook of Action Research*, Sage Publications, London, pp. 420–432.

Wadsworth, Y. (2005) 'Gouldner's Child?—Some Reflections on Sociology and Participatory Action Research', *Journal of Sociology*, 41(3):267–284.

Wadsworth, Y. (2006a) 'What's a Nice Sociologist like Me Doing Using a Psychological Instrument?—Integrating the MBTI®'s Sixteen Energy Systems with Cyclic Models of Action Research', *Australian Psychological Type Review*, 8(2):35–45.

Wadsworth, Y. (2006b), 'How Can Professionals Help People to Inquire Using Their Own Action Research?', *Action Research Case Study*, No. 1, Action Learning Action Research Association, Australia, online www.alarpm.org.au/ files/ARCSNo1Wadsworth2005.pdf, accessed 8 August 2008.

Wadsworth, Y. (2005) 'Is it Safe to Talk about Systems Again Yet?—Self organ-ising Processes for Complex Living Systems and the Dynamics of Human Inquiry', Bob White Memorial Lecture, The Australian Sociological Association national conference, University of Tasmania, Hobart, 6 December.

Wadsworth Y. (2008a) 'Systemic Human Relations in Dynamic Equilibrium' *Systemic Practice and Action Research*, Springer, New York, 21(1):15–34.

Wadsworth, Y. (2008b) 'Is it Safe to Talk about Systems Again Yet?—Self organ-ising Processes for Complex Living Systems and the Dynamics of Human Inquiry' *Systemic Practice and Action Research*, Springer, New York, 21(2):153–170.

Wadsworth, Y. (2008c) 'Action Research for Living Human Systems', in B. Boog, J. Preece, M. Slagter and J. Zeelen (eds), *Toward Quality Improvement of Action Research: Developing Ethics and Standards*, Sense Publishers, Rotterdam, pp. 45–60.

Wadsworth, Y. (2008d) 'Living Systems, Epistemology and Human Relations in Dynamic Equilibrium', presentation to the McCaughey VicHealth Centre for the Promotion of Mental Health and Community Wellbeing and Australian Youth Research Centre, University of Melbourne, 28 October.

Wadsworth, Y. and Epstein, M. (1996a) *Understanding & Involvement—Consumer Evaluation of Acute Psychiatric Hospital Practice*, Vol. 2: A Project Unfolds..., Victorian Mental Illness Awareness Council, Melbourne.

Wadsworth, Y. and Epstein, M. (1996b) *Understanding & Involvement—Consumer Evaluation of Acute Psychiatric Hospital Practice*, Vol. 3: A Project Concludes..., Victorian Mental Illness Awareness Council, Melbourne.

Wadsworth, Y. and Epstein, M. (1996c) *Consumer Participation Program Orientation and Job Manual—Mental Health Staff–Consumer Consultants*, Understanding & Involvement, Consumer Evaluation of Acute Psychiatric Hospital Practice Project, Victorian Mental Illness Awareness Council, Melbourne.

Wadsworth, Y. and Epstein, M. (1998) '"Building in" Dialogue between Consumers and Staff in Acute Mental Health Services', *Systemic Practice and Action Research*, 11(4):353–379.

Wadsworth, Y. (ed.) in ongoing association with M. Epstein (2001) *The Essential U&I—A One Volume Presentation of the Findings of a Lengthy Grounded Study of Whole Systems Change towards Staff–Consumer Collaboration for Enhancing Mental Health Services*, VicHealth, Melbourne.

Wadsworth, Y. and Fitzgerald, L. (1996) 'CART—From the Horse's Mouth', *Community Quarterly*, 40:24–29.

Wadsworth, Y. and O'Brien, J. (2002) 'Caring to Ask—Some Deeper Staff Reflections on Seeking Consumer Feedback in a Hospital Setting', unpublished monograph, Victoria University of Technology and Mercy Hospital and Aged Care Services, Melbourne.

Wadsworth, Y. and Price, C. (2002) 'What is Action Research in Reconnect?', *Action Learning Action Research*, 7(2):64–69.

Wallis, J.D. (2007) 'Orbitofrontal Cortex and its Contribution to Decision-Making', *Annual Review of Neuroscience*, 30:31–56.

Walters, C. (2008) 'Brave New World', *Green Guide, The Age*, 20 November, pp. 24–25.

Waterson, R. (1999) *The Living House—An Anthropology of Architecture in South-East Asia*, Thames & Hudson, London, and as cited by A. Saunders, ABC Radio National, 4 December 1999.

Watson, J. (1968) *The Double Helix—A Personal Account of the Discovery of DNA*, Penguin Books, Harmondsworth.

Way, R. (1986) *The Garden of the Beloved*, Darley Anderson, London.

Weil, S. and McGill, I. (1989) *Making Sense of Experiential Learning*, Open University Press, Milton Keynes.

Weiss, H. (2005) 'From the Director's Desk', *The Evaluation Exchange*,11(2):1.

Wenger, E. (1998) *Communities of Practice—Learning, Meaning and Identity* (Learning in Doing: Social, Cognitive and Computational Perspectives), Cambridge University Press, New York.

Westley, F., Zimmerman, B. and Patton, M.Q. (2006) *Getting to Maybe—How the World Is Changed*, Random House, Canada.

Wheatley, M.J. and Kellner-Rogers, M. (1998) 'Bringing Life to Organizational Change', *Journal of Strategic Performance Measurement*, April/May:5–13.

Wheelhouse, G. in K.Cincotta (2010) 'Power to the People', *The Age Green Guide*, 1 April 2010.

White, M. (1997) *Narratives of Therapists' Lives*, Dulwich Centre Publications, Adelaide, South Australia

White, M. (2007) *Maps of Narrative Practice*, W.W. Norton, New York.

Wikipedia, 'Mandala', http://en.wikipedia.org/wiki/Mandala/, accessed 15 February 2008.

Wilber, K. (2005) 'What is Integral Spirituality?', Integral Spiritual Center, http://integralspiritualcenter.org/Integral%20Spirituality.pdf, accessed 15 February 2008.

Wilkinson, R. (2006) *The Impact of Inequality—How to Make Sick Societies Healthier*, New Press, UK.

Wilkinson, R. and Pickett, K. (2009) *The Spirit Level—Why More Equal Societies Almost Always Do Better*, Allen Lane, London.

Williams, B. (2008) 'Systems Concepts and Development: Bucking the System', *The Broker Online*, IDP publishers, Leiden, The Netherlands, accessed 10 December 2008, www.thebrokeronline.eu/en/Magazine/articles/Bucking-the-system.

Yehuda, R. and Seckl, J. (2008) *The Ghost in your Genes*, BBC documentary, www.bbc.co.uk/sn/tvradio/programmes/horizon/ghostgenes.shtml, accessed 8 August 2008.

Youl, R., Marriott, S. and Nabben, R. (2006) *Landcare in Australia—Founded on Local Action*, SILC and Rob Youl Consulting Pty Ltd, Australia, www.silc.com.au/BookletLandcareJVL.pdf, accessed 8 August 2008.

Zimmer, B. (2001) 'Practicing What We Teach in Teaching Systems Practice—The Action-Learning Cycle, *Systemic Practice and Action Research*, 14(6):697–713.

Zuber-Skerrit, O. (2000) 'A Generic Model for Action Learning and Action Research Programs within Organisations', *Action Learning Action Research*, 5(1):41–50.

Selected subjects index

New editions of other books by Yoland Wadsworth, available from Allen & Unwin in 2011:

Do It Yourself Social Research 3rd edition

*The bestselling user-friendly introduction to social research in the human services,
not-for-profit organisations and the community.*

'*Yoland Wadsworth's* Do it Yourself Social Research *is one of the most remarkable products
of Australian social science. Practical in its content, sophisticated in its ideas,
the book shows a passion for making social science a tool of democracy.
I know of nothing else that is half as good.*'

—R W CONNELL, PROFESSOR OF EDUCATION, UNIVERSITY OF SYDNEY

ISBN 9781742370637

Everyday Evaluation on the Run 3rd edition

*A widely-used introduction written for non-specialists in the human services who need
to do evaluation as part of a busy workload.*

'*Practical, useful counsel emanates throughout. Impressively grounded
in real world experiences.*'

—MICHAEL QUINN PATTON, AUTHOR OF 'UTILISATION-FOCUSED EVALUATION'

ISBN 9781742370439

For Product Safety Concerns and Information please contact our EU
representative GPSR@taylorandfrancis.com
Taylor & Francis Verlag GmbH, Kaufingerstraße 24, 80331 München, Germany